Waterloo
Making an Epic

Simon Lewis

FRONT COVER: *As a horse could be unsteady, Rod Steiger as Napoleon sits atop wooden boxes to ensure he is kept in focus.* © HEINZ FELDHAUS

BACK COVER: *Some of the 20,000 Russian soldiers dressed as French infantry march towards Wellington's army.* © RICHARD HEFFER

Waterloo — Making an Epic
© 2022 Simon Lewis. All Rights Reserved.

No part of this book may be reproduced in any form or by any means, electronic, mechanical, digital, photocopying or recording, except for the inclusion in a review, without permission in writing from the publisher.

Published in the USA by:
BearManor Media
4700 Millenia Blvd.
Suite 175 PMB 90497
Orlando, Florida 32839
www.bearmanormedia.com

Hardcover: ISBN 978-1-62933-833-0
Paperback: ISBN 978-1-62933-832-3

Printed in the United States of America.
Book design by Brian Pearce | Red Jacket Press.

Table of Contents

The Credits 9

Quotations 11

Introduction 13

Waterloo: *The Story* 19

A note about money. 21

Prelude 23

Chapter 1: *"Music And Banners…*
  Quite Beautiful." 33

Chapter 2: *The Real History* 45

Chapter 3: *"God! God's Got Nothing*
  To Do With It!" 71

Chapter 4: *Bondarchuk's* War and Peace. 99

Chapter 5: *"These Are The*
  Battle Orders, Sire." 121

Chapter 6: *"He Has Filled His Stage…"* 145

Chapter 7: *"We Ladies Just Have To*
  Follow The Drum." 181

Chapter 8: *"Let's Not Dramatise, Yet…" ....* 213

Chapter 9: *"And Above All…My Will!" ....* 223

Chapter 10: *"Nyetnam." ....* 235

Chapter 11: *"The Whole Of Bloody Hell Is Coming Up Out Of The Ground." ....* 255

Chapter 12: *"What Will Men Say Of Me…I Wonder?" ....* 287

Chapter 13: *"May I Have Your Permission To Try A Shot?" ....* 309

Chapter 14: *"Shoot At The Horses! Pile Up The Horses!" ....* 345

Chapter 15: *"It's A Bad Position, Wellington." ....* 361

Chapter 16: *"By God, It's Blowing Strong, Now" ....* 385

Chapter 17: *"Give Me Night Or Give Me Blucher." ....* 405

Chapter 18: *"This One's Going To Take Careful Timing…" ....* 429

Chapter 19: *"The Limits Of Glory…" ....* 457

Chapter 20: The Myth of a Longer Cut. 477

Chapter 21: Did Waterloo kill Napoleon? 491

Chapter 22: *"The Memory Of Your Greatness" ....* 503

Chapter 23: *"A field of glory is never a pretty sight."* The Conclusion. 521

Appendix: *Things They Got Right, Things They Got Wrong* by Stephen Dwan 534

Appendix: *The screenplay.* 547

Acknowledgments 571

Bibliography 575

Endnotes 585

About The Author 613

Index 615

Maps

Waterloo Campaign Area, 1815 53

Overview of battle, 18 June 1815 56

The *Waterloo* set, 1969 254

To Claire

And to Aslan, Igor, Mykola, Rashit, Tibor and thousands of their nameless mates in the then Soviet army, along with Bunchuk and his thousands of four-legged friends, who all toiled under the hot Ukrainian sun, without whom this film could not have been possible.

IN MEMORIAM

Philippe Forquet, Vicomte de Dorne
27 SEPTEMBER 1940 — 18 FEBRUARY 2020.
(la Bedoyere)

Christopher Plummer
13 DECEMBER 1929 — 5 FEBRUARY 2021
(Wellington)

Irina Skobtseva
22 AUGUST 1927 — 20 OCTOBER 2020
(Maria)

The Credits.

THE CAST: *Napoleon*, Rod Steiger; *Wellington*, Christopher Plummer; *Louis XVIII*, Orson Welles; *General Picton*, Jack Hawkins; *Duchess of Richmond*, Virginia McKenna; *Marshal Ney*, Dan O'Herlihy; *Sir William Ponsonby*, Michael Wilding; *Lord Uxbridge*, Terence Alexander; *Private O'Connor*, Donal Donnelly; *La Bedoyere,* Philippe Forquet; *Lord Gordon*, Rupert Davies; *Marshal Soult*, Ivo Garrani; *William De Lancey*, Ian Ogilvy; *Marshal Blucher*, Sergei Zakhariadze; *Lord Hay*, Peter Davies; *Grouchy*, Charles Millot; *Sauret*, Andrea Checchi; *Drouot*, Gianni Garko; *Cambronne*, Evgeni Samoilov; *Tomlinson*, Oleg Vidov; *Mulholland*, Charles Borromel; *Magdalene Hall*, Veronica De Laurentiis; *Gerard*, Vladimir Druzhnikov; *Ramsey*, Willoughby Gray; *Duncan*, Roger Green; *Officer*, Orso Maria Guerrini; *Mercer*, Richard Heffer; *Constant*, Orazio Orlando; *Muffling*, John Savident; *Colborne*, Jeffry Wickham; *Sarah*, Susan Wood; *Chactas*, Gennadi Yudin.

UNCREDITED: *Berthier*, Giorgio Sciolette; *Bertrand*, Boris Molchanov; *Captain Taylor*, Georgi Rybakov; *Caulincourt*, Rino Bellini; *Colson*, Vaclovas Bledis; *Corporal with Ney*, Ivan Milanov; *De Vitrolles*, Camillo Angelini-Rota; *Delessart*, Franco Fantasia; *Drum Major*, Valentins Skulme; *Drummer Boy*, Vladimir Levchenko; *Duke of Richmond*, Andrea Esterhazy; *Fainting Soldier*, Valery Guryev; *Fat Man*, Guidarino Guidi; *Flahaut*, Rostislav Yankovskiy; *General Baudin*, Attilio Severini; *Gneisenau*, Karl Lipanski; *Joseph Fouche*, Rodolfo Lodi; *Kellerman*, Lev Polyakov; *King Charles X*, Aldo Cecconi; *Lady of Louis's Court*, Andrea Dosne; *Lady Webster*, Isabella Albonico; *Lancer with Napoleon's hat*, Vladimir Udalov; *Larrey*, Yan Yanakiyev; *Legros*, Armando Bottin; *Macdonald*, Giuliano Raffaelli; *Macmahon*, Valentin Koval; *Maitland*, Vasili Plaksin; *Marbot*, Sergio Testori; *Maria*, Irina Skobtseva; *Massimo Della Torre*, Cambaceres; *Mckevitt*, Colin (Webster-Watson) Watson; *Normyle*, Pauls Butkēvičs;

Oudinot, Jean Louis; *Patsy,* Félix Eynas; *Percy,* Vasiliy Livanov; *Prince of Brunswick,* Fred Jackson; *Rumigus,* Pietro Ceccarelli; *Saint-Cyr,* Filippo Perego; *Somerset,* Viktor Murganov; *Wounded Officer,* Aleksandr Parkhomenko.

THE CREW: *Producer,* Dino De Laurentiis; *Director,* Sergei Bondarchuk; *Screenplay,* H.A.L. Craig, Sergei Bondarchuk and Vittorio Bonicelli; *Associate Producer,* Thomas Carlile; *Production Supervisors,* Alfredo De Laurentiis and Guy Luongo (Italy), Mark Riss (Russia); *Production Managers,* Mario Abussi and Guglielmo Ambrosi and; *Director of Photography,* Armando Nannuzzi; *Film Score, composed and conducted by* Nino Rota; *Music Consultant,* Wilfred Josephs; *Editorial Supervision,* Richard C. Meyer, A.C.E.; *Second Unit Director,* Anatoli Chemodurov; *Assistant Directors,* Vladimir Dostal and Allan Elledge; *Production Co-ordinator,* Anna Popova; *Production Designer,* Mario Garbuglia; *Art Director,* Ferdinando Giovannoni; *Camera Operators,* Giuseppe Berardini, J.N. Carpuchin, Nino Cristiani and Silvano Mancini; *Assistant Cameramen,* Daniele Nannuzzi and Federico del Zoppo; *Panavision Technician,* Heinz Feldhaus; *Set Decorators,* Emilio D'Andria and Kenneth Muggleston; *Costume Designers,* Maria De Matteis and Ugo Pericoli; *Wardrobe Mistress,* Nadezhda Buzina; *Make-up Artists,* Mikhail Chikiryov and Alberto De Rossi; *Hair Stylist,* Paolo Borzelli; *Special Effects,* V.A. Likhachov and Giulio Molinari; *Unit Publicity,* Grady Johnson; *Unit Photographers,* Alfonso Avincola, Peter Mitchell and Paul Ronald; *Dialogue Director,* William Slater; *Continuity,* Elvira D'Amico; *Film Editor,* Yelena Mikhajlova; *Sound Recording,* Gordon Everett and Muratori Primiano; *Sound Editors,* Alan Streeter and Les Wiggins; *Sound Post-Production,* Gordon "Mac" McCallum, Graham V. Hartstone, John Hayward and Stephen Pickard; *Military Consultants,* Willoughby Gray, General Nikolay Oslikovsky and General Alexander Luchinsky; *Co-produced* by Dino De Laurentiis Cinematografia S.p.A. and Mosfilm; Locations in Caserta (Italy) and Uzhgorod (U.S.S.R.); Interiors at Dino De Laurentiis Studios, Rome. Filmed in Panavision; Colour by Technicolor. Running time: 133 minutes.

Quotations.

SPIRIT SINISTER: *My argument is that War makes rattling good history; but Peace is poor reading. So I back Bonaparte for the reason that he will give pleasure to posterity.*

SPIRIT OF THE PITIES: *Gross hypocrite!*

Thomas Hardy, *The Dynasts*, Act. 2 Scene 5

The history of a battle is not unlike the history of a ball. Some individuals may recollect all the little events of which the great result is the battle won or lost, but no individual can recollect the order in which, or the exact moment at which, they occurred, which makes all the difference as to their value or importance.

1st Duke of Wellington[1]

The immense unacknowledged debt which we owe to the commercial cinema as an illumination of the story of mankind.

George Macdonald Fraser, *The Hollywood History of the World*

History is more or less bunk.

Henry Ford, industrialist[2]

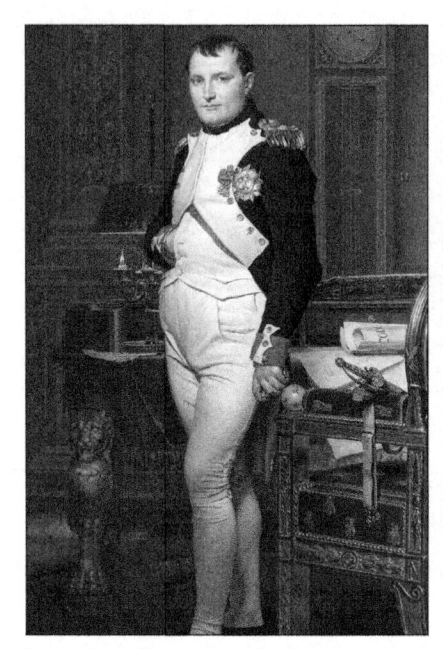

Napoleon Bonaparte by Jacques-Louis David / Rod Steiger.

The Duke of Wellington by Thomas Lawrence / Christopher Plummer.
AUTHOR'S COLLECTION

Introduction.

It was Christmas Day 1976. The cooked turkey and trimmings had filled the bellies of the Lewis family, who were now slumped like beached whales onto the orange Habitat sofa, they settled down to watch the TV highlight of the festive evening.

It was 8 p.m. and time for the ITV network's premiere offering. This coveted slot was usually reserved for a recent cinematic hot ticket making its small screen debut. Pressing one of six clunky switches on the two-year-old colour Philips TV, the picture flicked over to the nation's only commercial channel with its chorus of adverts. In the days before home video, a film would all but disappear after its initial cinema run. With a five-year delay for a TV showing imposed by the film distributors, a broadcast premiere was an eagerly awaited event. The rival BBC One channel was offering very stiff competition that evening with *The Morecambe & Wise Show*, which routinely drew in over twenty-million viewers with their mixture of sketches and star cameos; it was a heady mix. To win the ratings war that evening ITV had pinned their hopes on the first run of the 1964 British classic, *Zulu*. Owing to contentious political issues around South Africa's notorious Apartheid regime, it was considered too sensitive for the slot. The network had swapped it with their planned New Year's Eve offering:

Waterloo.

For the next three hours, a ten-year-old boy sat transfixed by the spectacle of war and drama, along with Rosie, the family whippet barking at the charging horses as they appeared to burst out of the telly. Periodically, he was forced to wait patiently as a seemingly endless stream of adverts for Boxing Day deals at Allied Carpets, package holidays on the Costa Blanca for Summer '77, would break the flow, until plunged back into the smoke and din. With the film over and the TV redirected to more festive fare, the boy's head buzzed with the visual carnival of combat he had just seen.

Almost immediately, he devoured books on the battle and the main protagonists, whilst building up a formidable army of 20mm plastic figures, courtesy of that staple of 1970s boyhood — Airfix. For years his initial interest was in the actual story, but scouring the local libraries, his avid perusal soon spilled over from the history section to film/TV in search of photos and information on the production. The shock of finding that this movie was *not* considered to be the *greatest* ever made, was the first of a series of life challenging moments!

Within three years, the boy, now a teenager, found himself a new, full-blown passion in the shape of cinema, turbo-charged by Kevin Brownlow's magisterial TV series, *Hollywood*, and a BBC Two season of Orson Welles' classics. Suitably inspired, he soon began making crude silent movies with a vintage 1950s clockwork 8mm camera. These tentative steps took him into a career in film and TV as an editor and director.

In 2012, the author realised an ambition to direct his own film, the polar opposite in scope and scale to the subject of this book.[3] This proved to be one of the most exhilarating and frustrating experiences of his life. It greatly increased the appreciation of the pressures and constraints that a filmmaker must prevail against. Riding the crest of the creative energy unleashed by a group of talented individuals is an extraordinary sensation, but one quickly realises the subtle dance required to collaborate effectively. This adventure was the culmination of a naïve dream to create epic movies, inspired by watching so many classics of the genre during his formative years.

Since the advent of laser disc, then DVD and later Blu-ray, it is finally possible to enjoy older films presented close to their original intention. This has been especially true of the great film epics, whose scope and scale have suffered most particularly on TV. Now, many been lovingly restored to the Hi-Def digital medium, capturing something of their roadshow heyday grandeur. This accessibility has also led to a greater appreciation by a fresh audience in how such extraordinary endeavours were put together. Few would doubt the artistic virtues and cultural significance of David Lean's masterpiece, *Lawrence of Arabia*, or *Ben-Hur* and *Cleopatra*. These have already been copiously written about and discussed, but there are still more stories to tell about this bygone era of giants.

The genesis for this book was in 2017. Perusing that shrine to movies of the 1960s and 70s — *Cinema Retro* magazine, and noticing that a certain film — *Waterloo* — had so far not featured, led to the offer of an article. With encouragement from its editor, Dave Worrall, work began making full use of research material that had been gathered over the years. There proved to be more than enough for the 5,000-word article. Once completed (it was published in 2020 to coincide with the fiftieth anniversary of the original release),[4] the creative juices flowed. This led to the flickering of a novel based around the concept of British actors in Soviet Russia, throwing in spies and the moon landing for good measure. Recognising the need for extra research quickly led to the most obvious of decisions — park the novel and tell the truth!

And now, let's celebrate one of the last great epics in the grand manner — *Waterloo*.

Who are you that is reading this book? First, I can surmise you are probably a fan, each with your own favourite scenes and quotable lines. But I suspect that many of you belong to one of two groups: epic movie fans and history buffs, with a liberal crossover between. Indeed, the ever-expanding interest in the battle, which still continues to spawn many books, in part because of the internet and flow of newly discovered sources, was for many sparked by the movie.

This is primarily a film book. But it is also a history book which encompasses not one but two, time frames. Firstly, the euphemistically named "Swinging Sixties," which arguably saw the most rapid and sometimes violent social change of any decade before or since, motivated in part by the chaos of the Vietnam War. The slow gestation of our subject meant it fell victim to these immense social and cultural shifts. But our story cannot be fully told without the context of the famous battle itself in 1815. To breathe life into sometimes dusty facts, a judicious use of contemporary accounts from memoirs has been employed, to remind us that this recreation of history involved humans who experienced: comradeship, exhilaration and hope but also fear, pain, gore and death.

It is often bemoaned why can't *they* just make a "totally accurate historical movie," I would suggest this is not only impossible but also undesirable. A filmmaker cannot serve two masters. The cold steel of facts and the subtle multi-hued mosaic of drama are rarely comfortable bedfellows. For the vast amount of historically set films, the facts have often been subordinated to a highly fictionised romance, in the often-mistaken belief that it is the only way of exciting an audience. Yet it is worth considering that the reason history is remembered is invariably because it is a good *story*. It is why artists, writers and filmmakers are drawn to retell these tales, inevitably through the contemporary lenses of their own time and culture. The filmmaker must ultimately follow the tenets and rules of cinema, diverge at the creator's risk, so facts must be subordinate to story. To what degree is a matter of taste and debate.

Boldly, the filmmakers, who you will meet in this book, chose to be "faithful" to the narrative of the battle, how far they achieved this goal is one of the themes of this book, and highlights the dilemma a filmmaker must grapple with when recreating a real event. With the input of several historians, the aim has been to present the facts as understood in the mid-1960s when the script was prepared, and then interpreted during the production. Historian Steven Dwan has compiled an exhaustive assessment in the appendix, which will give those with more of a history bent, plenty to chew on. As a fan himself, Steven suggests that the various "mistakes" do not ruin the enjoyment of the film.

Writing a book in 2021, it is difficult to be immune from the swirling culture wars that have engulfed much of the world. The battle, and its perceived place in the British psyche, has now found new relevance in the ongoing traumatic saga of Britain's tortured relationship with its nearest neighbours. Perhaps as a convenient short-hand, the script and the final film distil the battle into a straight English v. French fight, with some Prussians thrown in! With less than half of the Duke's force consisting of British redcoats, it is important to end the myth of the encounter being entirely a "*rostbif*" victory. The author will nail his colours to the mast and say all references to Wellington's forces will be referred to as the "Allied" army in deference to its true multi-European makeup.

In writing this book, I have tried to channel the starry-eyed passion of a ten-year-old-boy tempered with the critical head of a Fifty-something; it is a fine balancing act, for which you the reader must determine the success.

Let's all agree that *Waterloo* may *not* be a masterpiece by the precepts of cinematic art. It also holds the distinction of being one of the biggest flops in movie history. By rights it should be consigned to the bin and forgotten, but over the past half a century, it has spawned a steady army of fans. As has been so often proven, box office success does not always equate with either a good film or even a lasting one. The secret to longevity continues to be the holy grail for us all, and perhaps we are not meant to know. The fact remains that this "dead duck" is alive and well.

For all its faults, it is an honest attempt to retell a great historical event. As we will see, an almost unprecedented amount of time, money and effort went into this very laudable endeavour, where crucially everything you see was done for real, albeit with some sleight of hand. And it is this reality, that you can almost smell and touch, that gives the film its visceral power. Throughout the following pages, it will become apparent just the staggering sheer toil that was involved in capturing such scenes. If it is not considered by many critics as a "great film," I believe it can comfortably be described as a "great epic," and one of the most impressive of a much loved and often-maligned genre.

Our march to *Waterloo* will begin with a brisk canter through the evolution of the genre to the roadshow concept that had helped to sell these often hugely expensive productions. We will then see how audiences were transforming during the 1960s, and why by the end of the decade, assumptions about what was popular were dangerously out of date.

We will then meet our principal characters, both in front and behind the camera. First, the driven producer Dino De Laurentiis, who over a very long career made many fine films — and a few stinkers too! *Waterloo* was a watershed for him and drew to a close his term as one of Europe's foremost producers.

To set the project up required immense energy and tenacity, but its glorious ambition would not have been possible without the manpower of the Soviet state. Central to the deal was its star director Sergei Bondarchuk, whose previous film *War and Peace*, is widely deemed to be a masterpiece (a must watch for all fans of *Waterloo*). To follow it in what he considered an unofficial sequel, he hoped to reach those heights of excellence again. Being one of the first creative partnerships across the Iron Curtain it seemed to herald a welcome *détente*. Unfortunately, in 1968 the Cold War heated up with the crushing of The Prague Spring, and threatened to derail the project. We will look at the dangerous international tensions that swirled around the make-believe world of cinema.

Nothing exists in a vacuum and our story will touch on several characters and events, some infamous, and particularly to other film productions (many also personal favourites) of the era which for various reasons, primarily compare and contrast, have a bearing and give context to our subject.

Perusing Harry Craig's script, which wavers between the brilliant to the banal, allows us to see the envisioned scope of the story and perhaps identify some inherent flaws of the finished film already baked in. A précis of the screenplay is included in the appendix, which will allow fans to glimpse what was intended, and what never made it past the cutting-room.

Most of the book details the filming. From the ballroom sequence in Rome to the months of "battle" in Russia. We will hear many voices, both behind and before the camera, including some of the nameless 18,000 Russian soldiers who toiled beneath the Ukrainian sun.

The rediscovery of a fifty-year-old personal diary by one of the cast members will give us a unique, almost day-by-day, look at such an immense production. Helpfully, many of the entries included the scene description name: "Wellingtons Tree," "Ney's Charge," etc, which by checking against the screenplay has often helped with identification. While for other entries, to use the great Duke of Wellington's own words: "to find out what you don't know, by what you do,"[5] educated guesswork has been deployed. Being further down the playbill, the actor spent many lazy days away from the set, thus allowing us a peek behind the Iron Curtain. A world that, for good or ill, has gone forever.

The one black mark against the film is the controversy regarding the four-legged cast members, some of whom died during the production. We shall investigate the evidence.

As a working TV editor, the author will make no excuse for a detailed, and hopefully illuminating look at the editing process. This phase of film-making is so often merely glanced over by writers of cinema books. It is a cliche to say, but it is true, a movie *is* made in the cutting-room. The film's editor wrote a very detailed article about his work which will give a unique insight as never before, into the post-production of a movie in this era.

A film is not just the images, and we will look at the evolution of the soundtrack and the creation of the musical score. With the help of members of the sound team, we get a fascinating glimpse at the complexity of mixing an analogue stereo soundtrack. Again, much of this aspect of filmmaking has been ignored — until now.

Before we wrap up the editing, we will explore one of the persistent myths that has surrounded the film. Namely, the existence of a' much *longer* cut, in which some suggest lies a masterpiece — deep in a Russian vault.

When released to the world, we will look at how the film fared, and explore some reasons it was not the success hoped for.

For a few cineastes, the film is an object of hatred as, so another myth goes, it killed the "Greatest film never made;" namely Stanley Kubrick's *Napoleon*. We shall sift through the evidence to discover the truth behind the accusation: Did *Waterloo* kill *Napoleon?*

At the end, I hope we are left with a rich tapestry of all the blood, sweat and tears that went into making one of the last great epics. So, to steal a phrase from Rod Steiger in conversation with royalty, let us see: "…how they put the *bloody* thing together."[6]

Waterloo: *The Story*

(Columbia Pictures, publicity, 1970.)

Hard-pressed by the armies of a Europe allied against him, Napoleon finally signs the document announcing his abdication. The following morning, as enemy troops are watering their horses in the Seine, Napoleon bids an emotional goodbye to his Old Guard, the veterans of many campaigns, and leaves for his lonely exile in Elba.

Only months later, all France is electrified by news that Napoleon has escaped from Elba and has landed in the south, where a thousand of his men have gathered to greet his return. The corpulent King Louis XVIII calls his military advisors, Marshal Soult and Marshal Ney, and assigns them to the defence of the throne. Ney, once Napoleon's most trusted general, emotionally vows to the king that he will bring Napoleon back to Paris "in an iron cage."

Ney and his men confront Napoleon on the road leading to Grenoble. Round a bend in the road, Napoleon appears, marching at the head of his small army. Ney at once orders his men into battle formation and then gives the order to aim their muskets and fire. There is a dramatic silence as Napoleon halts, gazing steadily at the king's men, all of whom had fought under his command when he was Emperor. The men lower their muskets and burst into cheering as they rush forward to surround Napoleon: he has won his first battle on the road back. Ney throws his sword at Napoleon's feet, as a token of surrender, but Napoleon picks it up, hands it back and invites Ney to follow him once again.

Napoleon makes a triumphant entry into Paris, from which the king has fled.

But his enemies, England, Austria, Prussia and Russia are determined to destroy him once and for all and the armies gather. Napoleon is forced to mobilize as fast as possible to face Wellington and Blucher, who have moved their forces on to the plain of Belgium.

Wellington is attending a ball in Brussels given by the Duchess of Richmond, when word is brought that Napoleon has crossed the frontier.

Napoleon aims to divide Wellington's army from Blucher's, and after an initial victory over the Prussians, appears to have achieved his objective. But Blucher escapes and regroups his forces. Wellington withdraws his "motley army" of British, Dutch, Belgians and Germans to Waterloo, where he has arranged that he will be joined by Blucher and the Prussians. Napoleon waits until the rain-sodden ground dries out before he attacks. When Ney leads the first of many French attacks up the ridge, the British are well placed to defend their positions. Ailing and distracted by pain, Napoleon spends part of the battle out of touch with his army and, although close to a victory that could make him once again master of Europe, he is finally defeated by Wellington and the Prussian troops of Marshal Blucher.

A note about money.

According to the 2020 Official Data Foundation website:

$1 in 1960 is equivalent in purchasing power to about $8.79 in 2020
$1 in 1970 is equivalent in purchasing power to about $6.71 in 2020

£1 in 1960 is equivalent in purchasing power to about £23.18 in 2020
£1 in 1970 is equivalent in purchasing power to about £15 in 2020

In 1949, Italy devalued to US$1 = 625 lire. This rate was maintained until the end of the Bretton Woods System in the early 1970s.[7]

Sergei Bondarchuk during the filming of Waterloo. © RICHARD HEFFER

Prelude

It is 11:28 a.m. on Wednesday, 18 June 1969, one hundred and fifty-four years to the day since the cannons began their fearful cannonade over some fields south of Brussels in Belgium. The air is warm, humid, and bereft of any breeze; leaves hang limply on the scarce trees in the sweltering heat. Pops of colour dot the sandy brown landscape, provided by a smorgasbord of flowers now in full summer bloom.[8]

Sitting atop a fifteen-foot ladder is People's Artist, Sergei Fedorovich Bondarchuk; an imposing figure, exuding command "with abundant silver hair, penetrating dark eyes and a lyrical verb."[9] He clasps a pipe between his teeth whilst surveying the scene laid out before him. A few hundred soldiers of the Soviet Army stand in heavy blue costumes which depict Napoleon's famed Imperial Guard. Several dazzlingly dressed men, wearing twinkling gold braid, sit astride restless horses whose manes flick the still air.

Beyond this large group in the hazy distance, palls of dense black smoke curl high against the bright, cloudless sky. Just visible, from his vantage point, is the light pink cupola of Svyato-Pokrovs'kyy church, that just peeks above the dense sea of green foliage that covers the rolling hills. It is the highest man-made point in the vicinity and stands like a beacon over the village of Nizhny Solotvyn. This motley collection of simple, low slung wooden buildings, many adorned with pretty flower trellises, clustered around a dirt track along which trundled tethered horse and carts, scurrying chickens, and an imperious rooster. Thanks to the carefully placed smoke, this timeless, remote, rural speck of Western Ukraine, a part of the USSR, will be hidden from the cameras.

Born in this part of Russia during the very early days of the Revolution, for country-bred Sergei Fedorovich, it is no doubt pleasant to be back on familiar soil. For most of this year of '69, he has been in Rome, at the vast, ultra-modern studios of leading Italian producer Dino De Laurentiis, dubbed by all, with a warm nod to his pre-eminent position as a cinematic Caesar in the European film industry, as Dinocittà.

No one can deny that the lion's share of the credit for their joint venture, has been down to the tireless energy and determination of the diminutive Naples born "bundle of raw energy and volatile emotion."[10] Known industry-wide as Dino, he has spent half a decade setting up what would be one of the most expensive and expansive epics ever made. Now, thanks to the involvement of Mosfilm, that had brought the heft of the Soviet system, complete with an army to the table, both men had literally "moved mountains" to re-tell the story of Napoleon's famous defeat.

Sergei Fedorovich adjusts his wide straw hat, tilting it to shade from the glaring sun. He has promised his wife that he will not overtax himself, and instead makes full use of his lanky, energetic young assistant Vladimir Dostal, who sports an impressive drooping moustache that belies his tender age, to deliver his instructions over a megaphone. Whether consciously, the director appears to his Russian associates calm and mellower now as he edges towards fifty.

His previous work, a colossal rendition of *War and Peace*, consumed the best part of seven years, and tore every ounce of his creativity and energy to overcome a mountain of obstacles; from leaden Soviet bureaucracy to faulty film stock studded with crushed mosquitos. It also revealed a dark side of his personality; a tyrannical martinet.

"The director is Tsar," he once said in a candid moment. He drove many, particularly his actors, to almost their breaking point. But he paid a heavy — lethal — price. He must wonder, as his new immense behemoth ramps up a few gears: is cinema more important than life?

Now, on this day in June, Sergei Fedorovich with the tools to hand, his job is to wield the vast, cumbersome elephant of filmmaking with the delicacy of a painter. Despite being on home turf, he is surrounded by a babble of incomprehensible, machine-gun delivered Italian. Almost all the crew, supplied by the producer, have made the long journey behind the Iron Curtain, and were now duelling with bedbugs, and an intermittent water supply at Uzhgorod's premiere, in fact, only hotel, a few miles up the road. To the astonishment of the local communists, these Romans could be quite militant, and had downed tools in protest at the living conditions. Hailing from the well-spring of Grand Opera, their volatile passions can occasionally resemble the *Commedia dell'arte*, but with internationally acclaimed cameraman, the ever-smiling Armando Nannuzzi at their head, they make a highly professional team.

Although Sergei Fedorovich and Nannuzzi have locked creative horns, not helped by the occasional fog-of-war creep via translations, the two find common ground with the reproductions of nineteenth-century History paintings which they use as reference.

This day is no different. Having decided the next camera set-up, the director waits patiently on Nannuzzi and his team to complete their preparations. Cheerfully, Nannuzzi calmly supervises the placement of several other cameras to catch different angles and close-ups. He has up to five to play with. Periodically he peers through a blue glass monocle to judge the contrast values of the scene.

Lined up behind the crew are a row of imposing towers, upon which stand enormous lights, called Brutes, their beam and glare seemingly unnecessary as they bask under the relentless sun. In fact, they become vital for such bright days as they help to reduce harsh shadows and contrast on the actors' faces. Nannuzzi's job is to react to the fluctuations in sunlight and sculpt it for the lens.

Clustered around one camera, a series of rituals; an assistant pulls a tape measure a few steps from the lens, and a marker is affixed to the ground. A hand twists the focus ring and marks a spot on the dial with a pen. A man carrying a pot on a long pole moves gingerly back and forth, as a wispy trail of black smoke seeps from the holes in the metal pot.

Nearby, set at a discreet distance from the activity, stands a faded green cotton umbrella with white tassels which dance in the strangled air. Beneath, in the welcome shade, sits the intense, imposing figure of American actor, Rod Steiger, dressed in a heavy grey overcoat over his simple blue costume. He casually rolls his felt bicorn hat over his knees as he stares into the hazy middle distance, at once absent-minded and intense all at the same time. He is following The Method, an approach to acting that involves mining the depths of emotion. Almost no actor in the world, before or since, produces what is best summed up by his current director: "An explosion."[11]

Yet tensions must stir within this most ebullient and emotive of performers. Not only is his marriage on the rocks, his wife is out of reach, many thousands of miles away, but this avowed pacifist is playing one of history's most notable warriors. "I don't like Napoleon, but I admire him," he admits.[12] Slouched around are other members of the cast, some smoking, some dozing. A page in an open script with coloured notes flutters for a moment as it catches the merest hint of a breeze.

> Scene.160: NAPOLEON *looks towards the Prussians. His mood changes. He gives a violent cry…* "*But where is Grouchy? Godin-Heaven, where's Grouchy?*" NAPOLEON *suddenly grimaces with pain.*[13]

It is a pivotal point in the battle, and story, where the distant appearance of the Prussians on the edge of the Waterloo battlefield rather than the French detachment of Marshal Grouchy, while spelling deliverance for Wellington, means almost certain defeat for Napoleon. All morning they had been preparing this sequence to be shot; in total two pages of dialogue, long by comparison with many in the script. While the crew prepares, Steiger has been rehearsing with the sage-like Irish-American actor Dan O'Herlihy. Despite being temperamentally the polar opposite of his character, the impetuous and hot-headed Marshal Ney, O'Herlihy has learnt to "bite his tongue." The Brooklyn-raised "Emperor" routinely chops and changes dialogue and even suggests how to direct scenes; "we had a few arguments,"[14] he says candidly. Their spats are discrete, and not common knowledge amongst the crew. The director is aware of his star's "imperial" demeanour, but maintains: "Directing him, I felt every take was something new and powerful."[15]

Atop his lofty perch, Sergei Fedorovich lets the slight breeze cool his face. He cranes his neck from the immediate activity of the camera team and his brooding star. To his left are two simple, white-washed buildings, one larger than the other, which stand next to a dusty road lined with near-naked trees. He traces the road as it dips at a slow but sure curve down to a shallow valley which is studded with shoals of flowers amid small copses of trees. The track climbs up the opposite side and passes a rectangular farm complex of barns and a house tightly enclosed by a wall. His gaze travels up to the top of a long, flat ridge which curls with a slight decline away to the left. Midway, his eyes pause on a solitary elm tree standing like a lonely sentinel. The ridge finally slopes down to a much larger and grander chateau construction, which is flanked with a walled garden. Sergei Fedorovich has to shift on his precarious perch as his gaze moves back towards the ridge he is standing upon. Conspicuous is a white, squat windmill, its sails waiting patiently for the merest breath of wind.

The valley is almost a mile wide, the product of over a year's work. Today, except for the knot of people around the camera, it is almost empty; the ground, virgin and tidy. But for the next few months it will resound to the thunder of horses' hooves and the tramp of thousands of feet, kicking up dust and trampling the specially grown crops.

He is highly adept at orchestrating such large numbers for the camera. His previous work involved many gargantuan action sequences. To some, watching him work, god-like, was mesmerising: "And you see this mass become something — a line — a battalion…and all just with a voice."[16] Others, though, will not be so impressed, as they witnessed the many thousands sweating, waiting patiently for "The Voice": "They let them, I still feel it now, stay in the sun until they fainted."[17]

But for now, most of those men are camped in a huge tented complex some miles away. For weeks, they have been given training in nineteenth-century military manoeuvres; archaic cadence marching; swinging their left arm with weapons carried on their shoulders — tight and precise. They may not have to dodge real bullets but it won't be a picnic: "We filmed on rainy, hot days, during days and nights."[18] Many were in no doubt they were in the throes of "an obsessive madman."[19]

Situated a discrete distance, and hopefully downwind are stabled almost two thousand horses, the bulk being made up by members of a specially trained, and maintained cavalry regiment purely for Russian movies. Its very existence has amazed many: "In the age of rockets!"[20] Nearby, in a fenced-off area are a highly select group of 29 daredevils on horseback — all highly adept and fearless equine stuntmen: "The stuff they were doing was crazy, it was really nuts."[21] They will be required to "drop" a horse safely to the ground, but the controversy over the treatment of the four-legged cast members will mar the film's reputation.

If Sergei Fedorovich felt daunted by the task ahead, he does not show it; perhaps any anxiety he hides by playing with his pipe. He checks his watch — 11:30 a.m., with a slight nod he waves to Vladimir Dostal, who eagerly awaits his instructions. The younger man, after a quick stroke of his moustache, shouts through his megaphone for quiet and strict attention.

In a moment, all activity stops and eyes turn to the director, seated high upon his perch, the sun shimmering off his greying mane of hair. Hundreds of pairs of feet shuffle towards him as the swarm of international press hustle to get close; camera lenses, microphones and licked pencil points hover over note pads. There is a sense of expectation and heightened drama.

Sergei Fedorovich is handed a large Very flare pistol, which he quickly checks before looking up with an air of quiet command and confidence over the sea of faces below him. Satisfied he has everyone's attention; he speaks with a deep, low cadence — in Russian.

Some assembled journalists frown at one another: "What's he saying?" A female interpreter, Anna Popova, trying to keep up, broadly explains that the People's Artist is commemorating that fateful day of 1815. As the speech ends, Sergei Fedorovich raises the pistol high above his head and fires. With a sharp retort and a whizz, the flare arcs up into the still air and bursts against the blue sky. The crescendo is drowned out by the applause of the Soviet soldiers, and the more effusive Italian camera crew crying: *"Bravo! Bravo!"*

From the intense heat and dust of June, to bursts of torrential rain in autumn and beyond, to the threatening onset of a Russian winter, this valley sitting amid a vast plain deep in the Ukraine, would see a Herculean effort to capture history on film.

Steiger and the "French" scenes were scheduled to be shot first for what would take about a month. Although Russia's Mosfilm were co-producers, Dino's Hollywood partners were finding it hard to get permission for Western journalists to visit the set to feed the oxygen of publicity. The Russian authorities were keen to stress that the location was in a "restrictive military area." It will be a constant headache for the publicity department as the months of filming in Russia roll on.

Less than a year before, almost a quarter of a million Soviet soldiers had marched into nearby Czechoslovakia to crush the so-called Prague Spring. It was a tense moment in the Cold War, which had nearly derailed this and another fledgling experiment in East/West cultural collaboration. While just the merest Band-Aid had been applied over the rift, the area is a hotbed of possible dissent. At any point this "acting" army could be called upon to march away and fight for real.

As the throng of journalists melt back to a discreet distance, the painstaking process of cinema resumes. It takes many minutes for the background to be painted with the artistically correct amount of smoke. Finally, happy that the wafting clouds of oily black and grey puffs are dense enough, Sergei Fedorovich nods to Steiger.

The actor pulls himself out of his chair and leaves the coolness beneath the umbrella. He is sweltering, wearing a dove-white waistcoat, blue jacket with red trimmings and gold buttons, and adding to the discomfort — a long slate grey coat splashed in mud, specially produced by stamping and even rolling in the sod. Steiger smears his face with sprayed-on oil, so it glistens with a dirty, sweaty mask before clearing his mind ready for the word: "Action."

As film rolls at 24 frames per second through the camera, a Russian lady holds up a clapper-board which reads: *Scene 160. Take 1. Waterloo. De Laurentiis. Bondarchuk.*[22] She snaps it shut, holding it steady for a moment, before slinking away. Above on a platform, a grizzled Army commander in a civilian white cap barks some orders into his walkie-talkie. In moments, torrents of flame and smoke billow up in the background behind the line of blue costumed Old Guard Soldiers. Against this fiery backdrop, Sergei Fedorovich nods to his assistant Dostal, who finally yells: "Action!"

Steiger transforms into Napoleon. A violent man. Thumping his chest, he bellows: "Where is Grouchy?" He fists his hands to quell a rising rage and intense frustration. "Where in hell is Grouchy?" He screams at the top of his voice, making the nearby horses twitch and start. Steiger grimaces in pain, his face creased with tears. He places his hand on his belly. Doubles over in a painful spasm. He Stumbles. On cue, a ring of officers scurries forward, one catches him, just managing to steady the tottering volcano. He suffers an additional jolt, closes his eyes and cries. But this time, just a whimper: "Grouchy..." A portly Russian actor playing his trusted Doctor Larrey, mutters a plea for him to leave the battlefield in pidgin English: "Lie down for an hour?" Napoleon yelps with the invisible stabbing pain in his belly: "How can I go to bed...when men are dying with my name on their lips?" The officers lead him off.

"*Schtop*!" blares out from a huge speaker, and all freeze for a moment. Atop his perch, Sergei Fedorovich nods curtly — he is happy. There will be another take, but they must wait for the smoke to be suitably dense. Napoleon transfers back to Steiger, who slumps, drained. Then himself again, he comes over and modestly accepts congratulations. Taking a breather beneath the green umbrella, Steiger explains his fresh and nuanced conception of this most famous character, who has taken countless guises on film, but too often is mired in cliché or lampoon.

> I am playing him, especially during the battle, as a man unshaven, with eyes bloodshot, uniform rumpled, mud-stained and bone weary, suffering from cancer, haemorrhoids and other diseases, he was a walking dead man in constant pain. This is the man I want to show, in pain, trying to function with only half of his powers.[23]

This snapshot of acting intimacy at the start of filming in Russia would soon compete with the huge logistics of simulated warfare. But even as this immense work continued under the merciless Ukrainian sun, the world of the late 1960s was transforming. With nightly TV pictures of the Vietnam War spawning a revulsion against war in all its forms across the Western world, how would the public respond to a depiction in all its ghastly Technicolor glory of a hundred-and-fifty-year-old battle?

The often-maligned epic genre had been a mainstay of cinema since its beginning, helping to give respectability and garner critical appreciation for a burgeoning dynamic art form. It may have often been the antithesis of the "relevant and contemporary" — but the epic movie at its best, has sought to synthesise heroic archetypes and great deeds to stir the spirit, that tell us "the only true events occur within the human heart."[24]

With the Prussians now spotted at the edge of the battlefield, Ney played by Dan O'Herlihy and Rod Steiger as Napoleon discuss their diminishing options. AUTHOR'S COLLECTION

Napoleon cries out in frustration. The whereabouts of Grouchy's force could turn the battle back in his favour. AUTHOR'S COLLECTION

Theda Bara's Cleopatra *(1917) helped create the template for epic roadshow entertainment that was still in vogue in the 1960s.*
AUTHOR'S COLLECTION

CHAPTER 1

"Music And Banners... Quite Beautiful."

The infant "Flicks" that shimmered across makeshift hanging sheets at the very end of the nineteenth-century, did not emerge from a primordial cultural swamp. Gerald Mast, writing in 1976, observed that: "The wonder is that while the evolution of narrative fiction can be traced back to Homer, the movies have evolved such complex techniques in only eighty years."[25] The technology may have been primitive, but the speed with which early filmmakers invented a new international language was remarkable.

While the early comedies and melodramas pulled their inspiration from the stage, much of the evolving visual language came from nearly a millennium's worth of representative art. This rich seam of imagery was a boon for ambitious filmmakers, who sought to impress and amaze an enthusiastic nickelodeon audience with hitherto unimagined scope and scale.

Before the twentieth century, the highest genre of art was considered to be *Historia/* History painting. Originally these had overtly religious, allegorical and mythological themes, before giving way to more secular depictions of historical events, both past and present. Invariably, these paintings were romanticised, myth-making iconography intended to ignoble the depicted deed, and inspire the viewer with patriotic zeal and awe, in what was dubbed The Grand Manner.

During the nineteenth-century, the then recent Napoleonic Wars with their colourful splash and dash spectacle — with "tasteful" blood and guts — were embraced by many artists. Across Europe they all tried to outdo each other in the Grand Manner; Lady Butler's *Scotland Forever!* (1881) and Henri Félix Emmanuel Philippoteaux *The Battle of Waterloo: The British Squares Receiving the Charge of the French Cuirassiers* (1874), being two of the most iconic with their almost cinematic sense of motion and drama.

Serious money was to be made in the shop fronts of entrepreneurs, who would charge the public to come in their droves to view these giant spectacles. John Martin's apocalyptic visions with suitably dramatic titles: *The Seventh Plague of Egypt* (1823), *The Destruction of Sodom and Gomorrah* (1852), etc. drew tremendous crowds for special-effects extravaganzas of their time.

For the early pioneers groping towards what would be later dubbed the Seventh Art had nearly a thousand years' worth of storyboards from which to draw inspiration. Over a hundred years later, it is a well that continues to be eagerly drawn from.

It was the Italian film industry that kick-started the "epic" genre back in the early teens with super-productions like *Quo Vadis?* (1913), *The Last Days of Pompeii* (1913) and *Cabiria* (1914). The Italians, steeped in a rich cultural heritage from Ancient Rome, the Renaissance and Grand Opera, brought an impressive realism and accuracy to their ambitious productions. Visually, they owed an enormous debt to the Grand Manner paintings of the previous century, whose depictions of Ancient Rome have become the benchmark ever since. These fledgling efforts were the early blockbusters and helped to usher in the concept of the hour-plus "feature" film.

What is noticeable, even from these tentative beginnings, is the willingness to lavish colossal sums of money in the belief that bigger is better. Often this very extravagance would be a selling point in advertising. Despite the many piles of shattered dreams and ambition, this exuberance would be the genre's hallmark for over a century. Even before they ever reached an eager audience, epics would too often be drowned in their own excess. A combination of mismanagement, temperamental talent. nasty weather, or just downright poor luck, would often compound the demands of manipulating sizeable groups of people.

Just capturing such larger-than-life images on film was a colossal undertaking. Before the 1990s, most of what you saw had to be practically created; whether it was a model spaceship, a Roman amphitheatre or a pitch battle. Sets were often built full size, although trickery was employed, even from the early days, to expand the vista. These included glass paintings, false perspective and hanging miniatures, whether a castle, a ship or an army. As useful as these tricks often were, their limitations forced filmmakers to stage as much as possible — for real.

While Italy and other Europeans had briefly led the way with epic film production, the catastrophe of the Great War fatally curtailed much of this ambition. Half a world away, there was a new player in the game.

Hollywood was in its embryonic stage; small, ramshackle companies formed amid the orange groves bathed in Californian sunshine. This natural resource was the lifeblood of early film before practical outdoor lighting equipment. It was not long before the area built up a hub of talent drawn by the promise of almost constant sun. A director steeped in the culture of the Old Confederacy, who had moved his operation from the East Coast, was determined to rival the Italian super-productions who were celebrated as world leaders.

D.W. Griffith, a former actor, having seized many of the possibilities the new medium offered, had the confidence and ambition to tell complex stories with impressive scale. In 1915, it was his hugely controversial *Birth of a Nation* that finally gave the feature film prestige and popularity, albeit tinged with controversy. To modern eyes, this story of Southern families dealing with the aftermath of the Civil War, imbued with outrageous racism, is a challenging watch, but the ground-breaking cinematic techniques have anchored it as a film of great historical importance.

Intolerance, his follow up a year later, was an extraordinarily daring work. Weaving three historical and one contemporary story over three hours, it was envisaged as a plea for harmony in a world engulfed by war. The centre-piece was a recreation of Ancient Babylon with walls towering over 300-foot, complete with giant elephant statues, borrowing imagery, including semi-naked slave girls, from the Grand Manner of art. Griffith deployed an innovative camera move through the set, peopled with over 3,000 extras, which emphasised its three-dimensional aspect; still breathtaking even over a century later.

Despite the flurry of epics that wowed these early audiences, many of the pitfalls which would continue to dog the genre were already bothering critics. Writing in 1918 for *Photoplay*, Randolph Bartlett commented:

> *Cabiria* was a huge success, in spite of the absence of personal interest in the story, because in its day it was a novelty. *The Birth of a Nation* was a success, not because it was spectacular, but because its theme came right out of the heart of America's greatest crisis. *Intolerance* falls short of great success because it was too darned educational. *A Daughter of the Gods* despite its marvels of beauty, fell short, because the tale was purely artificial. *Joan the Woman*

related an epic fable, but fell just a little short of the intimate, human touch.[26]

Despite these critical sniffs of disapproval, audiences lapped up the ambition and excess. The short-lived Silent-Era would see increasingly more elaborate undertakings, none better representing the level of achievement than MGM's *Ben-Hur: A Tale of the Christ* (1925). The production ranged from Hollywood to Italy, where a spectacular sea battle was shot. A fierce fire aboard one of the full-size floating trireme constructions apparently killed several extras. Back in Hollywood, MGM enlisted 4,000 locals as extras and tethered hundreds of horses before forty cameramen in the iconic chariot race. Even if the result was exhilarating, it came at a terrible cost, with some reports of up to a hundred and fifty horses killed or maimed.

The coming of the Talkies in the late 1920s coupled with the Wall Street Crash fuelled a worldwide recession, curbing the ambition of filmmakers for some years. The notable exception was Cecil B. De Mille, who has become a byword for the epic genre.[27] For decades, he successfully married sex with religion in a series of stolid but entertaining productions: *King of Kings* (1927), *Sign of the Cross* (1933), *Samson and Delilah* (1949) and two versions of *The Ten Commandments* (1923) and (1956). De Mille knew what his audience wanted; simple melodramas with a veneer of respectability but laced with violence and sleaze, garishly wrapped up in the glitz and excess of a Christmas tree. It was a formula that worked, and the industry has continued to reference it ever since.

Hollywood in the early 1950s felt the tremors of a new threat: the tiny box in the living room — TV. At first, the studios tried to ignore it, but dwindling attendances could not continue unabated. Technology appeared to provide a solution. 3-D sparked an intense craze but was over almost before it had begun, not helped by the less than stellar product. It was realised what was needed were expansive and grand stories told on a scale that black-and-white TV could not match.

In 1951 MGM turned to a bestseller by Henryk Sienkiewicz of Christians in Nero's Rome — *Quo Vadis*, although written in 1895, it was still in print and had been translated into over fifty languages. MGM was determined to make the most awe-inspiring Technicolor entertainment that they could; basing production at Rome's Cinecittà studios. It was a canny move. As the Italian economy was struggling to rebuild after the privations of war, the studios offered giant sets and thousands of extras, all for a cut price bargain compared to America. The film became both a critical and financial success, and ignited a taste for the epic colossus for the next two decades.

3-D may not have been the elixir that Hollywood was seeking, but an event in September 1952 sparked a technological Big Bang. Cinerama, a complex system using three 35mm projectors to screen a magnificent, immersive experience replete with multi-directional sound, premiered with *This Is Cinerama*. For an audience used to black-and-white images on a square screen, Cinerama became an enormous success despite being shown in only a few cinemas world-wide as a roadshow or "hard-ticket".

The roadshow concept had been around since the Silent-Era with many variations. Then, those deemed (self) important films would tour major cities complete with a full orchestra in tow, playing in the most prestigious theatrical venues at higher-than-normal prices. Since the 1980s several significant Silent films have again been screened with a full orchestra that superbly recreates the Jazz Age roadshow experience. The author can attest to the sheer visceral thrill of experiencing *Ben-Hur: A Tale of the Christ* (1925) and *Napoléon* (1927), with the full weight of an orchestra enveloping the audience. The impressive 1917 Fox production of *Cleopatra*, starring "The Queen of the Vamps" Theda Bara, in some highly provocative costumes that would have made later screen portrayers of the Nile queen blush, played to packed theatres in this manner, even at the height of the deadly Spanish Influenza pandemic that claimed at least 50 million lives world-wide.[28] With the introduction of synchronised sound, the need for expensive touring ended but the concept of a high-end presentation, and its name, prevailed.

By the 1950s, roadshows were about creating the rarefied theatrical experience of exclusivity and quality. It would begin with bookable seats months in advance, albeit at higher-than-normal prices, sometimes when the film was still in production. Audiences were encouraged to dress up in their Sunday best, before taking their allocated seats in a vast auditorium. A few minutes of a suitable mood-setting overture would climax with the curtain uncovering the giant, curved screen before the movie itself would unfurl. An hour so later, the drapes would then close over an intermission with a musical ent'racte, offering the chance of a restroom visit before the movie resumed again. Another hour or so later, the show concluded with exit music as the audience, hopefully sated, filed out clutching a colourful souvenir brochure.

The intention was to give an experience that would be a talking-point for months. The strategy of the "hard-ticket" roadshow was to act as a showcase, playing a handful of prestige cinemas per territory (often just one per city) for extended periods. Then many months later, the film would be rolled out at "Popular Prices" to neighbourhood downtown "nabs," in often truncated versions without overtures and intermission.

Cinerama had kick-started the wide-screen gold rush, but its complex and expensive operation ensured that other systems broke out as more practical. CinemaScope was the most significant; using the standard 35mm film with a lens that squeezed a wide image which was then de-squeezed onto the screen. Cheap and convenient, it remained the *de facto* wide-screen projection system right up to the twenty-first century. Its big draw-back was the magnified grain on an enormous screen which often resulted in a rough and ugly image. The answer was using 70mm film, which yielded a beautiful velvet picture when projected. Several variants appeared during the 1950s and 60s, all designed to approach the expansiveness of Cinerama.

Films that merited the roadshow treatment varied enormously. When the heights of quality were achieved, audiences were whisked *Around the World in Eighty Days* (1955), feet tapped to an array of musicals including *Oklahoma!* (1955), *The King and I* (1956), and *South Pacific* (1958).

But it was the epic genre that really impressed with the big daddy of them all — the monumental *Ben-Hur* in 1959. MGM spared no expense to remake their 1924 classic, which starred who for many would embody the genre — Charlton Heston. The actor, speaking ten years later with a string of epics behind him, was well qualified to identify the pitfalls:

> I think the epic film is the most difficult genre in which to succeed creatively, or to put it another way; it's the easiest film to make lousy. It's terribly easy to let the whole thing just dissolve in kind of a seething minestrone of extras with torches, in which individual performers disappear completely.[29]

Despite a few scoffing critics, *Ben-Hur* is considered a superlative example of the genre. With its thrilling chariot race centre-piece, audiences embraced its sumptuous wide-screen excess, while the industry acknowledged it with the joint record for the most Academy Awards of eleven.[30] Its phenomenal box office led to a run of expensive productions, many filmed in Europe, all hoping to emulate its lustre.

The 1960s saw a colourful parade of costly, ambitious movies with historical themes: *Spartacus* (1960), *El Cid* (1961), *Mutiny on the Bounty* (1962) and *Lawrence of Arabia* (1962). But more often than not, success eluded many: *The Alamo* (1960), *55 Days at Peking* (1963), *The Fall of the Roman Empire* (1964) and *The Greatest Story Ever Told* (1965).

Perhaps the most notorious of the era was *Cleopatra* (1963). Produced over five years, the behind-the-scenes story is itself an epic too.[31] Shooting began in 1959 on giant sets of ancient Rome and Alexandria, constructed in the dank and drizzly British countryside of Pinewood Studios. The star, Elizabeth Taylor, fell seriously ill, which forced a shutdown. Eventually production resumed in Rome, with a new director and cast and rebuilding all the sets from scratch. Soon an avalanche of problems sent costs spiralling, topped off by the love affair between Taylor and her new co-star Richard Burton. Finally costing $44 million ($370 million in 2020)[32] it opened to huge excitement and success, but not enough to recoup the immense outlay.[33] *Cleopatra* was a watershed for the decade. It was becoming clear just how risky these monstrous productions had become, not helped by a growing apathy for such excess.

By 1965, after a string of heavy misfires, the cycle of Ancient World/Religious roadshow epics was petering out. It was said these films, particularly with a Biblical setting, were made for people who no longer went to the movies, this older audience preferring the cosy TV in the corner at home. In this new decade mere wide-screen spectacle was no longer enough to woo a more cynical, discerning and blasé patron. It was the magnificent *Lawrence of Arabia* (1962) which led the way, blending spectacle with intelligence. Widely regarded (certainly by the present author) as one of the greatest films ever made, it brilliantly illuminates one of the few truly mythical heroic characters of the industrial twentieth-century. While it perpetuates the legend of "Aurens" against the harsh, rugged desert vistas, it also subverts it with snapshots of Lawrence as just a man with feet of clay. Bravely for an epic is ensues the genre's *de rigour* of romance and instead gives prominence to the political and military milieu. By any standard, it is the Mount Everest of cinema due to the extemporary execution by the master David Lean leading a team of talent, all at the top of their game.

Its more grown-up view of history would become the genre's benchmark as producers sought to emulate its commercial and critical success with often lavishing large budgets on what could be described as "intelligent" historical epics. Columbia Pictures, keen to repeat their success with David Lean's Oscar-winning triumph, succeeded with the more modestly budgeted *A Man for All Seasons* (1965), but would later struggle to recoup the expensive *Cromwell* (1970).

Except for *Zulu* (1964), the marriage between epic action and a literary script was rocky at best. The two battle-themed subjects, *Khartoum* (1966) and *The Charge of the Light Brigade* (1968), despite being both handsome and well-written, sunk miserably at the box office.

More successful were Second World War stories, with their ready-made audience of veterans: *The Guns of Navarone* (1961), *The Longest Day* (1962) and *Battle of the Bulge* (1965). Also, James Bond producer Harry Saltzman's *Battle of Britain* (1969), which despite doing brisk business in the UK and Commonwealth countries, failed to excite Americans in such a key British event.

The decade had undergone a profound change across the world, and perhaps only with hindsight is it possible to detect how contemporary attitudes had morphed, and none more so than in relation to war and history.

The 1960s saw the counterculture emerge with a newly politicised youth across the Western world, galvanised by the widening, bloody war in Vietnam. Most of the major Hollywood studios had been slow to adapt to the changing times swirling around them. Their market was evolving rapidly as TV came to dominate popular culture. A 1967 survey by The Motion Picture Association of America (MPAA) soberly reported that more than half the US population *never* went to the movies. It was young adults aged between sixteen and twenty-four-years-old who made up the bulk of the audience. The studios, almost dismissively, offered cheaper and more modest product to this key revenue source, preferring instead to try and lure back the older crowd with big spending super-productions.

"They can be brought back through showmanship," said Richard Zanuck, as head of production at his father, Darryl's, studio of Twentieth Century-Fox.[34] The roadshow concept, despite some notable failures, was still considered profitable and worth the expense, with Stanley Kramer's hit comedy *It's A Mad, Mad, Mad, Mad World* (1964) leading to a string of epic comedies: *The Hallelujah Trail* and *The Great Race* (both 1965), that appealed to a very broad audience. The more serious, adult-themed subjects like David Lean's Russian epic love story *Doctor Zhivago* (1965) could have generational crossover; it was "acclaimed by teenage America as 'the most enjoyable movie of 1967'" in *Seventeen Magazine*[35] This helped it become one of the decade's biggest hits.

But it was the musical *The Sound of Music* (1965) that proved that family roadshow entertainment could still produce the mother lode. The Rogers and Hammerstein songs, coupled with Julie Andrews' almost angelic performance, would make it the top earner of the 1960s. To the ageing studio bosses, despite the seismic social changes swirling around their greying temples, it seemed their hunch was correct; audiences were craving the big and the brash, and the sentimental. Several mega-budget musicals were rushed before the cameras in the confident belief of huge profits. Yet, this spending spree could not have come at a worse time. The lid that had kept the counterculture at bay was about to blow.

In 1967, The Production Code that had been inaugurated in Depression-era doldrums of 1934 to "clean up" the screen was abandoned, with far-reaching consequences for the industry. It unleashed an avalanche of frank and adult-themed films; *Bonnie and Clyde* (1967), *The Graduate* (1967) and *Easy Rider* (1969), which found a ready and receptive younger audience who embraced stories of the "now" as: "hip," "groovy" and "far out." These mostly contemporary tales about everyday folk were filmed with a rough and ready, innovative, informal style. Provocatively, a world away from the old-fashioned high-end roadshow fare.

Perhaps only one film bridged this huge divide — Stanley Kubrick's *2001: A Space Odyssey* (1968). Its psychedelic light show effects were particularly stimulating when seen on the Cinerama screen, and resonated with a youth audience keen to "Turn on, tune in and drop out."

Not only were these new, youth-oriented films popular, they were often extremely cheap (*Easy Rider* cost $400,000[36] and made $60 million[37]). It led to a boom time — 177 films from the Hollywood Majors alone in 1968, with many budgets over the average of $4 million.

There was a looming crisis — the market was over-saturated, and without the audience to support it. The Bank of America had estimated that the *entire* US film industry was worth $2 billion, but once the hefty overheads of distribution were discounted, that left a "meagre" $240 million to *make* the films.[38] The absolute kicker was that total spend on production was around $400 million.[39]

Between 1968-70, twenty films, mostly those extravagant "sure-fire" musicals, cost over $10 million. Raising the stakes even higher, a few reached over $20 million; *Paint Your Wagon* (1969), *Hello Dolly!* (1969), *Darling Lili* (1970) and the Pearl Harbor reconstruction — *Tora! Tora! Tora!* (1970).[40] Each one of these roughly equating to a *tenth* of the total industry income. To make things even riskier, unlike today with home video and streaming services, there were almost no ancillary markets available to offset a stumble at the box office. Juicy TV sales were an option for already popular titles (*Cleopatra* had been sold to ABC in 1966 for a then record $5 million),[41] but if a film failed — it would be catastrophic.

Darryl F. Zanuck, whose Twentieth Century-Fox was so deeply mired in several musicals and "re-bombing" Pearl Harbor, summed it up with a dose of understatement: "You're never sure of a hit any goddamn time, but when you are talking $20 million, it's a bigger gamble."[42]

A reckoning was unavoidable, and the industry would endure a devastating "crash" in 1969. *Variety* commented a few years later that: "Hollywood got caught up in its own blockbuster fantasy which, combined with a national inflationary boom, saw fiscal discipline disintegrate."[43]

There would be another blockbuster chasing the elusive roadshow family audience, offering itself up as an "intelligent" epic to add to the list of $20 million-plus productions. An independent Italian producer marshalled $25 million ($170 million in 2020) from two Hollywood majors and Mosfilm in the USSR, to film one of history's most famous battles.

The giant, curved Cinerama screen at London Casino in the 1950s. This style of roadshow presentation was dying out by 1970. COURTESY OF DELFONT MACKINTOSH THEATRES.

Scotland Forever! by Lady Butler. AUTHOR'S COLLECTION

CHAPTER 2

The Real History

Napoleon Bonaparte, inspiring his own people with his military and political genius and his revolutionary fervor, became, within a few brief years, Emperor of the French and master of all Europe. In 1812, after 15 years of victory, he met with disaster in the Russian Campaign. By 1813, defeated by the combined forces of Austria, Russia, Prussia and England at Leipzig, Napoleon was driven to the very gates of Paris — there to await his destiny.

ROLLER TITLES AT THE BEGINNING OF FILM

The clash of armies on a June day in 1815 is one of the most dramatic finales that history has yet to offer. The ultimate defeat of Napoleon was a fitting end to an extraordinary career and epoch that had kick-started with the fall of the Bastille in 1789.[44]

Revolutionary France had unleashed violent forces with the cry: "Liberty, Brotherhood and Freedom," terrifying the crowned heads of Europe, who all sought to overthrow the fledgling Republic. It was out of the crucible of Revolution that a soldier born in Corsica, then recently annexed to France, rose through the ranks to become a general in his early twenties. In such volatile times there was scarce tolerance for failure — Madam Guillotine saw to that, but it was a perfect opportunity for young, thrusting and ambitious men to make their mark.

This era known as the Napoleonic Wars was almost the last time massed armies dressed to the nines and hit ten bells out of each other while standing toe to toe. Military uniforms had reached their zenith for style, panache, and an almost total lack of practicality. The annual Trooping the Colour in London is one of the last vestiges of this bygone age of war.

All armies used very similar formations to bring their men to bear. The limiting factor was the killing range of weaponry. The musket had gradually replaced the longbow of the Middle Ages. It was a crude, simple weapon that threw a small weighted ball down a smooth barrel. Barely evolved in over a hundred years, it was highly inaccurate, and required soldiers to stand shoulder to shoulder to deliver a volley at the enemy when they saw: "The whites of their eyes". The low velocity of the fired ball, and its shape which splattered on impact, caused horrible injuries to men and horses.

To attack, infantry usually moved in columns, which resembled an oblong; the short end forming the front rank. In this formation they would move quickly over rough ground. The principal weakness was that they could bring only a few weapons to bear in front. This was a major flaw as they often faced soldiers drawn into a long line, all able to fire their muskets at them. The bulk of infantry were known as Line or Foot, but there was another branch that would become the *de facto* formation for modern armies. The Light troops were elite men, they were deployed as Skirmishers working in small groups using natural cover to take pot shots at the enemy. Most Light troops still used the musket, but some fired the more accurate but slow to load — rifle. That ranker-*cum*-officer Richard Sharpe, the fictional Rifleman with the famous 95th Rifles, dressed in camouflage green, is a great illustration of the Light infantryman.[45] Their techniques of using ground and cover would become the basis for modern infantry tactics.

The key to ensuring a successful infantry advance was the cannon. With the carriage built of wood with a barrel of brass or iron, the cannon was the queen of the battlefield. Drawn by teams of horses, they were a very mobile and agile weapon, and were classed by the weight of the iron shot fired. The Twelve-Pounder was the heaviest to be used on the battlefield. The usual projectile was the Round Shot, a simple iron ball. It had no explosive charge, but was no less lethal. Fired horizontally, it would take out any and everything in its path; like the musket ball it was slow, so it was possible to see it coming straight at you. Its low velocity meant it was still deadly when it would appear to run out of steam like a cricket ball, and there were instances of novices trying to stop one with their foot, with unfortunate consequences.

At closer range, certain death was dished out with variants of exploding shells; often spewing a hail of musket balls which flew in all directions. The effect on tightly massed troops was fearsome; formations would break and rout to the rear. There were even rudimentary experiments with rockets in the British army, which could be just as deadly for friend and foe! Wellington reluctantly allowed Captain Whinyates to deploy his special Rocket Troop at Waterloo; where they acquitted themselves admirably.

At some point cavalry would charge in a great thundering torrent of man and horse. There were two key types: Light and Heavy. The Light Cavalry were like the Light infantry above, their job being to scout and harass by using smaller horses, like wasps annoying the enemy. For shock and punch, the Heavy Cavalry were deployed. Mounted on enormous horses and carrying hefty swords, they charged boot to boot in a great mass, almost like modern tanks. Many still wore body armour (front and back), a throwback to an earlier age. The cavalry charges of the Napoleonic wars were an awe-inspiring sight, but against infantry in squares they quickly lost formation.

If cavalry threatened, and there was time, the defensive measure was the square. Formed by sections of soldiers making the required side of four ranks. The front rank would kneel and hold their muskets topped with bayonets acting like spikes on a porcupine. If the formation held, it was virtually impregnable from cavalry. Only by using fast moving Horse Artillery to decimate the closely packed troops could these human castles be overpowered.

A Napoleonic battlefield was a maelstrom of violence and death, all dressed up as if on parade or in the drawing room. The predominant feature of these encounters was the immense clouds of smoke that eddied across the ghastly scene from the countless muskets and cannon fire. Confusion dominated. Commanders were right in the thick of it; keeping an overview was almost impossible. The purpose of a general on such a field was to not only command and communicate but inspire confidence by leading by example; he too was as open to a bloody wound as the lowliest private. It was a great leveller.

Something of the bravery, guts and absurdity of standing in full view of your enemy, can be seen in Artillery Captain Mercer's description of sitting high in the saddle as the advancing French moved towards him at Waterloo:

> This quieted my men; but the tall blue gentlemen, seeing me thus dare them, immediately made a target of me, and commenced a very deliberate practice, to show us what very bad shots they were and verify the old artillery proverb, "The nearer the target, the safer you are." One fellow certainly made me flinch, but it was a miss; so, I shook my finger at him, and called

him *coquin, &c.* The rogue grinned as he reloaded and again took aim. I certainly felt rather foolish at that moment, but was ashamed, after such bravado, to let him see it, and therefore continued my promenade.[46]

The aim of battles was not the annihilation of the enemy, but a rout — a disorderly retreat from the field which would hopefully produce a political settlement. That said, the slaughter could be terrible as these actions usually spanned only a few square miles. We should also not forget the rudimentary medical provision. Most wounds to limbs were treated with amputation by a rusty, blood encrusted saw — without anaesthetic. More serious ones were left for the gods to decide. What is extraordinary is how resilient these men were before the age of antibiotics. Most wounded soldiers would live to fight another day. They were hardier than their modern antecedents, as many came from the countryside where they would have become inured to nature's barbs. The other interesting point, considering the potentially awful wounds, was that few soldiers expressed the sentiments of revulsion and horror that their decedents, mired in the Flanders mud or the brutal Russian Eastern Front, would surely have done. Most accepted war and death as a part of life. Many believed the romance, the glory of war — and the gin — was a price worth paying.

One British officer summed up the prevailing attitude: "I should hate to fight out of personal malice or revenge, but have no objection to fight for *'fun and glory'*."[47]

It was upon this stage that Napoleon Bonaparte would strut for the best part of twenty years. Rising from a junior officer to general in a few short years, it was not long before he became a legend in his own lifetime. Appointed to command the Army of Italy in 1796 at the tender age of twenty-six, he quickly showed his extraordinary ability. Taking what was little more than a gang of impoverished ruffians, he routed the Austrians in a series of lightening battles, where determination and daring brought him victory. Conquering Italy and creating satellite States based upon the principles of the French Republic, he soon became a figure of suspicion by his political masters in Paris.

Feeding his growing sense of destiny and not insubstantial ego, his masters keen to side line him, approved his plan to invade Egypt to threaten British India. The campaign soon became mired in the sand, as first Lord Nelson's Royal Navy destroyed his fleet, and later his army was decimated by disease. As the political situation deteriorated in Paris, Napoleon jumped ship and left his army to die in the desert.

In Paris, attempts by politicians to use him as a "sword" backfired. A *coup d'état* made him consul and *de facto* ruler of France. Purporting to champion the ideals of the Revolution, he would subvert them completely by crowning himself emperor in 1804.

Over the next few years from the dawning of the nineteenth-century, France faced a series of coalitions of the continent's powers; the Austrian empire, Russia, Prussia — the leading German State, and all bankrolled by Britain. Her navy reigned supreme upon the world's oceans, negating the need or desire to field British troops. In a series of stunning victories, Napoleon smashed the combined continental armies at Austerlitz in 1805, Jena in 1806, and Friedland in 1807.

What did this man look like at the height of his powers? A contemporary gives us a snapshot amid a smoke-shrouded battlefield:

> There he sat on his little white Arab horse, in a rather careless posture, with a small hat on his head, and wearing the famous dust-grey cloak, white breeches and top boots, so insignificant-looking that no one would have recognised the personage as the mighty emperor — the victor of Austerlitz and Jena before whom even monarchs must bow — if they had not seen him represented so often in pictures. His pale face, cold features, and keen, serious gaze made an almost uncanny impression on my mind, while the glitter of the many uniforms which surrounded him heightened the contrast of his inconspicuous appearance.[48]

A shaky peace with Russia offered some stability as Napoleon's empire bestrode most of Europe. But the seeds of his downfall had already been sown. He involved himself in a dispute with his onetime ally and neighbour — Spain. Deposing the Royal family and installing his brother as king was the spark that lit the tinder box. Spain erupted into a maelstrom of violence, ushering in the word *guerrilla* as the population rose as one to eject the invader. Ignoring the rules of war, this insurgency sparked a level of barbarism not seen in Europe since the Thirty Years' War in the seventeenth-century.

Into this volatile situation, Britain sent an army to the Iberian Peninsula of Spain and Portugal. Despite a false start ending in a hasty retreat to Corunna in northern Spain, the British tried again. Led by Arthur Wellesley, a general who had fought a successful campaign in India as Britain flexed its muscles in the sub-continent, he quickly made his mark. Working with very able Portuguese and often unreliable Spanish troops, he ran rings around the French armies commanded by various marshals like Ney and Soult. Normally stalwart commanders under the direct control of their emperor, they floundered and bickered on their own with disastrous results.

Earning the soubriquet — The Iron Duke, this strict, taciturn disciplinarian inspired respect rather than love. He was a product of his class and background, born into minor Irish gentry he could be described as a "snob." Although he would often promote a man for outstanding service, he preferred to advance "gentlemen of class". That said, none of this should take away his extraordinary skill as a general — who never lost a battle, being not averse to ordering a retreat when it appeared the better part of valour.

He was not a cruel commander, but equally believed in discipline as the cornerstone of military cohesion. He issued draconian punishments on deserters and plunderers, including hanging. As his main two campaigns, the Iberian Peninsula and Belgium were territories of his allies, ruthless punishment for such behaviour was the only option to ensure the goodwill of the population. He also insisted that supplies were bought, rather than taken from the population, as was the French practice, all part of making friends and influencing people. That said, the appalling atrocities inflicted on the "liberated" towns of his allies, Ciudad Rodrigo and Badajoz by British troops went remarkably unpunished, although Wellington's anger at these events allegedly prompted him to describe his men as "Scum of the earth."[49]

Away from the battlefield, he was a hit with the ladies — witty and charming: "He is well made and knows it and is willing to set off to the best what nature has bestowed. In short, like every great man present or past, almost without exception, he is vain." Perhaps all must have at least one lesser attribute; his distinctive laugh, likened to a horse: "very loud and long."[50]

With a series of victories and tactical retreats, Wellesley was knighted Lord Wellington (becoming later a Duke), and made the best use of his small army as it criss-crossed the burning Iberian plain. High drama on the other side of the continent would start a train of events that would lead this taciturn Irishman and the ebullient Corsican to a field in Belgium.

Peace with Russia broke down in 1812. Napoleon invaded with an army of over half a million men, with the impressive name of *La Grande Armée*. The short, sharp campaign envisaged was denied as the Russian commander, Kutuzov, slyly refused battle. Instead, he drew the French ever deeper towards Moscow.

A terrible battle, the bloodiest of the century, saw both sides fight almost to a standstill at Borodino. The Russians retreated again and allowed Napoleon to take Moscow. Under the rules of war, this should have been the end of the campaign and resulted in a peace treaty. Much to Napoleon's chagrin, this didn't happen, yet he dallied. Meanwhile, the harsh Russian winter began to bite. A fire, started by the Russians themselves, largely destroyed the capital and made conditions even worse.

He then took the most fateful decision of his life — retreat, with winter closing in. The result was a catastrophe that has rarely been equalled, as his once proud army was utterly broken. While the embittered remnants of *La Grande Armée* staggered through the snowy Russian wastes, Marshal Ney, musket in hand, held the rear guard against ferocious sniping by Cossacks. What he lacked as a tactician, the red-headed marshal more than made up for it with courage and leadership, thus earning the soubriquet — "Bravest of the Brave." Reputably the very last man to leave Russia, Napoleon appreciated his quality, declaring: "I would have given everything rather than lose you."[51]

But the scale of the disaster was staggering; barely fifty-thousand men escaped with their lives. Even Napoleon's stepson, Eugène de Beauharnais, perhaps the most loyal of all his family and generals, was moved to write: "I don't look for glory now. The price is too high."[52]

Sensing blood in early 1813, the once subjugated European nations stood as one and marched. Napoleon, incredibly, formed a fresh army and almost manged to hold the onslaught at bay, before another shattering defeat at Leipzig. Later called the Battle of the Nations, it had involved over half a million men drawn from fourteen countries who slugged it out over just three days at a cost of 127,000 casualties, making it the costliest battle in all history before World War One.

In early 1814, the massed allied armies poured into France. Now with his back to the wall, in a few weeks Napoleon fought a series of short, sharp battles against huge odds. Notably the so called Six Days' Campaign during a chilly February, in which he gained four victories (Champaubert, Montmirail, Château-Thierry and Vauchamps) against Blucher's much bigger Prussian army. Yet, despite their defeats the allies with their immense combined strength took the upper hand and pushed inexorably towards Paris. Meanwhile, Wellington had routed the army of Napoleon's brother at Vitoria and pushed into southern France. The net was tightening.

Finally, the marshals, led by Ney, who had loyally followed their emperor, decided the time was up and forced him to abdicate. It was to be an honourable exile. The victorious allies chose the tiny island of Elba, off the coast of Italy, as his new kingdom. With characteristic zeal, the fallen emperor enacted a torrent of civic improvement projects in what he believed would be his home for life.

In Vienna, all the nations of Europe met to decide on a post-war settlement. Russia as the most powerful nation pushed its weight around. It didn't take long for all the nations' representatives to argue and scheme during the day, while dance and carouse through the night.

The surviving younger brother of the executed King Louis returned to his throne, and France quickly felt the dull, heavy hand of Reaction as the royalists attempted to erase twenty years of history. Within months, resentment and hatred resurfaced. Misty eyes looked towards the tiny island in the Mediterranean.

In March 1815, Napoleon returned. With his personal Guard of a thousand men, he slipped away from Elba and landed in southern France. He was greeted with great enthusiasm by veterans, but a more muted response from the people. Troops sent by King Louis to stop the usurper instead rallied to his colours. Most notably being Marshal Ney, who barely a year before had forced Napoleon to abdicate; he swapped sides and reluctantly threw his lot in with his former master. Without a shot being fired, the gout-ridden King Louis bowed to the inevitable, and fled. The emperor was back on his throne once more.

At first, Napoleon hoped to consolidate his position and placate his enemies by offering to be a constitutional monarch. It was obvious to all that conflict was unavoidable. The Congress in Vienna was temporarily united and declared war not on France, but on him — alone.

It would take some months for the full weight of the allies to march; until then, two armies in Belgium on the French border would find themselves in the theatre of war. The larger Prussian army was commanded by a seventy-two-year-old veteran with a deep hatred of Napoleon — Marshal Blucher. Wellington led the other which was a polyglot of British, Dutch and small German forces.

> We were, take us all in all, a very bad army. Our foreign auxiliaries, who constituted more than half our numerical strength, with some exceptions, were little better than a raw militia — a body without a soul, or like an inflated pillow, that gives touch

and resumes its shape again when all the pressure ceases — not to mention the many who went clear out of the field, and were only seen while plundering our baggage in their retreat.[53]

Wellington with his mongrel Anglo-Allied and Blucher's Prussians could only wait and see what the French would do, hoping the bigger Austrian and Russian armies would arrive in time.

In a few short weeks, Napoleon raised an army and planned a knock-out blow at Brussels to compel the allies to a negotiated peace. Moving his hastily assembled force of 124,000 men to the Belgium border in complete secrecy — he was poised to attack.

In the early hours of June 15, 1815, the French crossed the River Sambre at the junction between Wellington and Blucher's armies, catching them off balance. In an age when the horse was the fastest mode of transport, it took many hours for a full picture to emerge of the attack. As the Prussian outposts were pushed back, Wellington in Brussels was reluctant to issue orders until he was sure his "lines of communication" to the coast were not threatened. Ensuring a direct line to your base was the preoccupation of all commanders, and the severing of such was the aim in the game of manoeuvre. This delay almost proved fatal.

Quatre Bras. A crossroads on the road to Brussels also linked to the Prussian forces. Seizing them would give Napoleon the edge, as it would severely restrict co-operation between the allies. One of Wellington's Dutch commanders saw the threat, and without orders, reinforced the vital position with a holding force. It was in the nick of time as Marshal Ney, though not fully trusted by Napoleon, was given hasty command of a sizeable force to seize them.

As night fell on the 15th, Wellington and most of his officers were enjoying the thrill of a ball hosted by the Duchess of Richmond in Brussels. It was during that glittering evening Wellington learned the actual direction of the attack. His army was widely dispersed across the Belgium countryside, and would take many hours to concentrate. With the guests still waltzing in the candlelit ballroom, some units were alerted that a battle would soon take place — somewhere.

Next day, Napoleon faced Blucher and his Prussians over a series of villages around Ligny. Meanwhile, Ney prepared to attack and sweep the small defending force at Quatre Bras. It would take many hours for Wellington's men to arrive *en masse*.

The struggle at Ligny was brutal as two mortal enemies fought with no quarter given. Finally, Blucher, who had been trampled after a horse fall, withdrew his battered army to Wavre. This crucial decision would have significant ramifications. They were bruised — but not out.

At Quatre Bras, Wellington held the crossroads despite suffering a mauling. He too had narrowly escaped capture by French cavalry by jumping with his mount into a ditch for safety. Ney had almost captured the strategic position, but his reserve of d'Erlon's corps was summoned by Napoleon to the fight at Ligny. The inevitable confusion and countermanding of orders ensured these vital battle-winning men marched backwards and forwards, aiding neither commander.

As dawn broke on 17 June, the momentum was back with Napoleon — *if* he acted immediately. While convinced he had routed the Prussians, the direction of their retreat was unknown. He wasted some hours basking in his perceived victory, before detaching a sizeable force of 30,000 troops under Marshal Grouchy, to pursue the presumed full retreat of the

Prussians. As he set out on his quest, Grouchy opted to follow a formation which he mistook for the bulk of Blucher's force. His march would take his troops *farther* away from the main French army. Each step Grouchy's men took lengthened the odds for Napoleon.

Joining Ney at Quatre Bras, Napoleon was angry at his subordinate's failure to capture it, but refused to take responsibility for redirecting Ney's reserves. It was late afternoon, and Wellington had started his weary retreat towards a ridge line just south of a village called Waterloo.

By the time Napoleon ordered the pursuit, the heavens delivered a torrential downpour which turned the roads to mud. Artillery Captain Mercer was in the rear guard and memorably recounts seeing the emperor:

> Large isolated masses of thundercloud, of the deepest, almost inky black, their lower edges hard and strongly defined, lagging down, as if momentarily about to burst, hung suspended over us, involving our position and everything on it in deep and gloomy obscurity; whilst the distant hill lately occupied by the French army still lay bathed in brilliant sunshine. Lord Uxbridge was yet speaking, when a single horseman, immediately followed by several others, mounted the plateau I had left at a gallop, their dark figures thrown forward in strong relief from the illuminated distance, making them appear much nearer to us than they really were. For an instant they pulled up and regarded us, when several squadrons, coming rapidly on the plateau, Lord Uxbridge cried out, "Fire! Fire!" and, giving them a general discharge, we quickly limbered up to retire, as they dashed forward.[54]

As Mercer and the Cavalry retired in good order, they joined some 140,000 men and horses who did their best to sleep on the sodden ground across the four-mile field.

For the commanders, the night was spent anxiously waiting for confirmation of the Prussian whereabouts; the decisive key to the up-coming battle. Eventually, news came that Blucher had pulled back in parallel to the town of Wavre, and would march towards Waterloo at dawn. At this Wellington took heart, but knew it would be a race against time for him to hold on — if he could.

Sunday 18 June 1815, the sun shone, but the field was still a muddy churn. Napoleon, excited that Wellington had stood his ground, wanted to attack at nine, but the condition of the ground would not permit the smooth movement of cannon. Reviewing his army, he exuded supreme confidence, declaring: "I tell you that Wellington is a bad general, that the English are bad troops, and that this affair is only *un petit dejeuner*."[55]

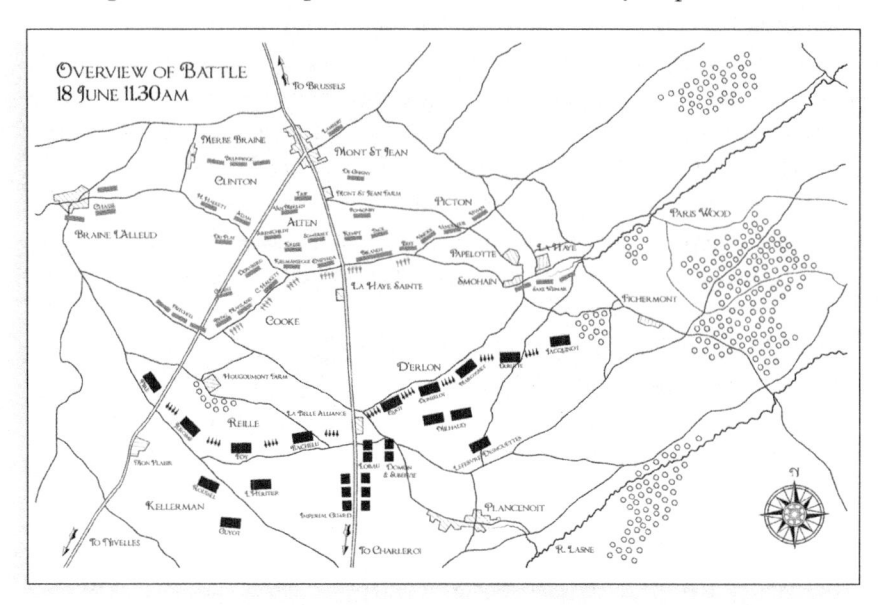

Overview of Battle 18 June 11.30am

The armies were matched, approximately 70,000 men each, but in every other way the French were superior. Most of them were veterans; experienced and motivated by a near fanatical devotion to their emperor. The army boasted more cannons, with the ability to out punch the enemy.

In Wellington's army, less than one-third had ever heard a shot fired in anger. He hoped to bolster his motley group of Belgian and Dutch troops, some who had fought previously for Napoleon, with British regiments, but most of his experienced Peninsula veterans were fighting the Americans. His plan was simply to hold and wait for the Prussians. It would be a defensive battle for which he was a master; judicious deployment of soldiers by maximising the lay of the land.

As the men cooked up breakfast and waited for the drama to begin, they would have cast an eye over the killing fields to come. The armies faced each other on two low ridges, dotted with copses and uneven ground. The allied army stood on a slightly higher ridge, which also had cuttings and hollow ways that would act as excellent defensive positions from cannon fire. The area was bisected by two roads, one being the main Brussels chaussée. Next to it on the French ridge was the inn, La Belle Alliance. The chaussée lowered into a valley before climbing up towards the opposite ridge, passing the farm of La Haye Sainte, which formed the fulcrum of Wellington's lines. It had been readied for defence by experienced soldiers of the King's German Legion.

Towards Wavre in the west, and the expected Prussian advance, Wellington had fortified several small farms, including Papelotte. But it was his right flank that most concerned him with the potential of being "turned" or out-flanked. In the way stood an extensive farm complex around a chateau called Hougoumont. Here were stationed two crack battalions of the 2nd Coldstream and 3rd Foot Guards under Colonel Macdonnell, plus Nassau and Hanoverians, who had been busy fortifying the walls with loopholes for firing.

It was here at 11:30 a.m. that the opening salvo was fired, which began a thunderous cannonade all along the line. Napoleon ordered a diversionary assault at Hougoumont as a holding action. This would be the first of many mistakes. The initial French attack drove through the covering infantry of Nassau and Hanoverians deployed in Hougoumont's orchard, and up to the walls. It quickly became a killing ground as over fifteen hundred French were killed and wounded in just the first hour.

The tactical goal was not clear to the commander of the assault — Jerome Bonaparte, younger brother to the emperor, once a king and now a middle-ranking general. Perhaps with something to prove, he pulled rank on his superiors, and demanded ever more troops into this most brutal if unnecessary encounter.

Three more times the French attacked. At one point a detachment broke in via the main gate and a desperate hand-to-hand fight ensued with Macdonnell, the garrison commander, helping to heave the heavy wooden gates shut. Private Clay was one red coated defender of Hougoumont:

> I saw the doors, or rather gates were riddled with shot-holes, and it was also very wet and dirty; in its entrance lay many dead bodies of the enemy; one I particularly noticed, which appeared to have been a French officer, but they were scarcely distinguishable, being to all appearance as though they had been very much trodden upon, and covered with mud; on gaining the interior I saw Lieutenant-Colonel MacDonnell carrying a large piece of wood or trunk of a tree in his arms (one of his cheeks marked with blood, his charger lay bleeding within a short distance), with which he was hastening to secure the gates against the renewed attack of the enemy, which was most vigorously repulsed.[56]

The fierce struggle would continue throughout the long, bloody day.

Seeing Wellington had not moved a man, Napoleon got the measure of his opponent. He next ordered what he considered being his main attack — a huge frontal advance at the allied centre, which included crack troops of General Picton. To prepare the way, some of his artillery was deployed to soften up the enemy, including his "Beautiful Daughters" — heavy Twelve-pound cannons. Thus, began a massive artillery barrage. Wellington instructed his men to lie down behind the crest of the ridge to minimise the damage from shot and shell.

Deployed in four dense columns of infantry totalling 16,000; d'Erlon's Corps advanced. As this imposing body of men marched across the valley and up the opposite slope towards Picton's division, they must have believed their sheer momentum would give them victory. As Bylandt's Netherlands brigade withdrew, the French moved towards the ridge line which now appeared almost empty of soldiers. Within thirty yards of their goal, two companies of British riflemen of the famed 95th, concealed in sandpits, opened fire on their left flank, which caused a momentary lack of cohesion.

At that moment, General Picton ordered his men to advance and deploy on the crest of the ridge studded with hedges. Comprising English and Highland regiments like the 92nd (The Gordons), the long red line moved rapidly to meet the assault. At twenty yards, Picton ordered a volley. The disciplined musketry did immense damage to the tightly packed French column. Ordering another volley and a bayonet charge, Picton's men were less than ten yards away from the enemy. A stray bullet struck the general in the head, felling him from his horse. Both sides grappled with each other in the hand-to-hand fighting.

Having stalled the attack, Lord Uxbridge, the cavalry commander, ordered his Heavy Cavalry to attack. While the Household brigade engaged French horsemen, the Union brigade commanded by Ponsonby, which included the Scots Greys, charged the mass of advancing infantry. For most of these mounted regiments, it was the first action they had seen since 1795; they had not been deployed in Wellington's Spanish campaigns.

What they lacked in experience, they made up for in courage. The shock of the hefty sword wielding cavalrymen on giant steeds was immediate and decisive. In the savage fighting that ensued, the French infantry were routed, leaving over seven thousand casualties and prisoners. Sergeant Ewart of the Scots Greys, amid the melee, famously captured a highly prized French Standard with its gold-plated regimental Eagle. The French cavalry who should have been in support had failed to protect the flanks.

The British cavalry, caught up in the blood-lust of slaughter, drove through the fleeing infantry, killing everyone in their path.

Amongst the sword-wielding charging Scots Greys was Corporal Dickson:

> We at once began a furious onslaught on this obstacle and soon made an impression; the battalions seemed to open up for us to pass through and so it happened that in five minutes we had cut our way through as many thousands of Frenchmen. We had now reached the bottom of the slope.[57]

One of those in the path of destruction was Lieutenant Jacques-François Martin:

> All bravery was useless…in vain our soldiers rose on their feet and stretched their arms out to try to stab with bayonets at the cavalry mounted on the tall, vigorous horses. Useless courage, their hands and arms fell together to the ground and left them defenceless against a persistent enemy who sabred without pity even the children who served as drummers and fifers in the regiment who asked in vain for mercy.[58]

On the opposing side was another eyewitness, Sergeant James Anton of the 42nd Foot:

> Horses' hooves sinking in men's breasts, breaking bones and pressing out their bowels. Riders' swords streaming in blood, waving over their heads and descending in deadly vengeance. Stroke follows stroke, like the turning of a flail in the hand of a dextrous thresher; the living stream gushes red from the ghastly wound, spouts in the victor's face, and stains him with brains and blood. There the piercing shrieks and dying groans; here the loud cheering of an exulting army, animating the slayers to deeds of signal vengeance upon a daring foe. Such is the music of the field![59]

As the wild charge continued, Napoleon, seeing the imminent danger, ordered a cavalry counter-attack which included Lancers. Reaching over ten feet, these almost antiquated weapons completely out-fought the sword wielding British Heavy Cavalry — some regiments lost over half of their strength. Their commander, Ponsonby, had been killed during the desperate action around the French cannon position. Belatedly, some Allied Hussar regiments charged to cover the shattered retreat of the Household and Union brigades.

Following their demoralising rout, the French opened a deafening new bombardment of the Allied ridge. This cannonade was so long and loud that it was audible across the channel in England. It also was heard some miles to the east by Marshal Grouchy, who had finally made contact with the Prussians at Wavre. "March to the sound of the guns," urged General Gerard, but Grouchy was adamant he must carry out the emperor's instructions to pursue. Unfortunately, the Prussians before him were the *rear-guard*! Meanwhile Blucher was urging the vanguard, comprising Bulow's Corps, who had not been blooded at Ligny, on towards Waterloo. Seeing the dust from these men and later confirmed by a Prussian prisoner — Napoleon knew the odds were lengthening.

At Hougoumont, Jerome had ordered up howitzers to rain down fire on the garrison, which duly became engulfed in flames. Yet as more troops were poured into the attack, the defenders steadfastly held on. Wellington, observing the fire, crisply instructed Macdonnell's men to station themselves wherever the flames had not reached. But neither withdrawal nor surrender was ever entertained. One of those ordered to defend the burning building was Private Clay:

> I being now told off with others under Lieut. Gough, of the Coldstream Guards, was posted in an upper room of the chateau, it being situated higher than the surrounding buildings; we annoyed the enemy's skirmishers from the window, which the enemy observing, threw their shells amongst us and set the building on fire we were defending; our officer placing himself at the entrance of the apartment would not permit anyone to quit his post, until our position became hopeless and too perilous to remain, fully expecting the floor to sink with us every moment, and in our escape several of us were more or less injured.[60]

The fearful French cannonade continued on to the Allied ridge, prompting Wellington to order a small withdrawal away from the shot and shell. To Marshal Ney, still rankling at the rout of d'Erlon's infantry attack earlier, it appeared the enemy was retreating. Left to his own devices on the battlefield, Ney's flaws came to the fore that day;

cool tactical thinking was quickly replaced by the thrill of the chase. Impetuously, he ordered several mounted regiments to follow him as he led the biggest cavalry charge of the battle — over 5,000 horsemen, who with sabres gleaming in the sun, advanced at a steady pace towards the seemingly deserted Allied ridge.

Wellington, watching this great mass of cavalry approaching, ordered his infantry into squares on the rear side of the slope, and left strict instructions to his artillery to keep firing before retiring to the squares. As Ney's forces rode nearer, the cannons loaded with canister shot blasted the French front ranks. Captain Mercer recalls the carnage his guns unleashed:

> I thus allowed them to advance unmolested until the head of the column might have been fifty or sixty yards from us, and then gave the word, "Fire!" The effect was terrible. Nearly the whole leading rank fell at once; and the round shot, penetrating the column, carried confusion throughout its extent.[61]

The artillery (except Mercer's battery)[62] fired one last round into Ney's cavalry at point-blank range, killing scores of men and animals, then made a dash for the safety of the squares.

As they crested the slope, French horsemen saw not a retreating army as they expected, but an array of twenty-seven squares with Allied infantrymen offering bristling, gleaming bayonets. Undaunted, the French spurred their horses into the face of the deadly musket fire. In one square was Ensign Gronow:

> The horses of the first rank of cuirassiers, despite all the efforts of their riders, came to a stand-still, shaking and covered in foam, at about twenty yards distance from our squares, and resisted all attempts to force them to charge the line of serried steel.[63]

As the squares held, the French cavalry quickly lost formation as they threaded past the immovable formations. They were counter-attacked by British Light cavalry led by Lord Uxbridge and were successfully driven back in disorder. Apparently without orders, several more French cavalry regiments joined the fray, including seven thousand Heavy Cavalry of the Imperial Guard. Between 4 and 6 p.m. about thirteen cavalry assaults were made upon the Allied squares. The foolhardy courage earning some grudging respect as Ensign Macready of the 30th Foot recalls: "Even our men saw this, and began to pity the useless perseverance of their assailants, and as they advanced would growl out 'Here they come these damned fools again!'"[64]

The slaughter on both sides was immense, with the balance remaining always in favour of the Allied foot soldiers in their unbroken squares. One proved to be a haven for Wellington as he was nearly taken by French cavalry: "Our Commander-in-Chief, as far as I could judge, appeared perfectly composed, but looked very thoughtful and pale."[65]

Marshal Ney, who continued to lead each futile attack, was unhorsed many times, and at one point was seen hammering a cannon with his sword in frustration. Although that day he lived up to his name: "The Bravest of the Brave," unfortunately what was needed was a cool-headed tactical understanding of how to win the battle. For whatever reason, he never considered supporting the futile charges with either infantry or horse artillery, which would have wreaked havoc on the tightly packed and immobile squares. Instead, the French cavalry, the pride of Napoleon's army, was cut to ribbons.

By now the Prussians under Bulow were approaching Napoleon's right flank, which was anchored on the village of Plancenoit. The trap was closing. To stem the tide, Napoleon deployed the Young Guard, part of his illustrious Imperial Guard. These troops clashed with the Prussians in a see-saw battle amid the narrow lanes of the village.

With the cavalry shattered, Ney, realising the mistake he had made, pleaded with Napoleon for infantry support. By the time the six regiments under Bachelu and Foy had arrived on the slope, Wellington had full use of his artillery on the ridge, which poured a murderous fire down on the attacking French.

During this disordered confusion, Ney received orders from Napoleon to take La Haye Sainte, the farmhouse stronghold less than three hundred yards from the Allied ridge. The German defenders struggled with a lack of ammunition and high casualties, but fought on bitterly before being forced to retreat from the position. At an enormous cost in lives, it became the first French victory of the day.

Ney ordered up artillery to pound Wellington's centre, which for the first time, was in danger of being over-run. One unit ordered to plug the gap was the Irish 27th (Inniskilling) Regiment of Foot, which found itself in the eye of the cannon storm and suffered nearly seventy percent casualties. One English soldier watching nearby vividly recalls the carnage that threatened to overwhelm him, and the army:

The banks on the roadside, the garden wall, the knoll and sand-pit swarmed with skirmishers, who seemed determined to keep down our fire in front; those behind the artificial bank seemed more intent upon destroying the 27th, who at this time, it may literally be said, were lying dead in square; their loss after La Haye Sainte had fallen was awful, without the satisfaction of having scarcely fired a shot, and many of our troops in rear of the ridge were similarly situated.[66]

Sensing victory, Ney sent word to Napoleon for the Guard to attack. This was the darkest hour of Waterloo. The field boiled in a seething, mindless maelstrom of bloodlust, without discipline or leadership, cloaked in thick black smoke so dense that soldiers could not see more than a few yards. Wellington's army was slowly being worn away by the steady pounding from the French artillery fire.

Behind the ridge was a stream of wounded and dying swamping dressing stations which were surrounded by grizzly mountains of amputated limbs. Thousands were fleeing up the road to Brussels. One regiment of gentleman volunteers, the Cumberland Hussars, fled as one in blind panic and terror, exclaiming that the battle was lost — they were later duly disgraced and disbanded. Brigades dwindled to regiments, regiments to mere companies. Everywhere were the dead, all mingled together on common ground.

At this stage, either side could have won Waterloo. Napoleon had hesitated to commit the Imperial Guard as the Prussians were making bloody headway in Plancenoit. Ordering a counter-attack into the village, two battalions of the elite Imperial Guard reserve stabilised the position. It was only a temporary reprieve as the tide was turning. More Prussian forces advanced through Papelotte and made contact with Wellington's left flank, which allowed him to deploy the remnants to his centre.

Shortly after 7 p.m., Napoleon played his last trump card — a desperate assault by the Imperial Guard. These moustachioed veterans, tall by contemporary standards at 5 foot 7 inches, intimidated all with their fearful presence and awesome reputation. He staked everything on an all-out attack. Buoyed up with "fake news" that Grouchy had arrived, the entire army advanced. Leading the way, and marching in two columns were the Guard — over 4,500 strong, all giants in their bearskin hats, with Ney at their head.

Wellington saw their approach — and brought his own last reserves into battle. Positioning his remaining artillery in the centre of the ridge, he moved up Maitland's Foot Guards and hid them in the tall grass. As the French came within easy musket range, Wellington shouted: "Now Maitland, now is your time." Maitland's men stood up and fired a series of volleys into the Imperial Guard, halting their advance. Without orders, Colonel Colborne, seizing the opportunity, ordered his crack 52nd Light Regiment to deploy obliquely on the Imperial Guard's left flank. Colborne's surprise appearance, pouring murderous fire, broke the elite French regiments who began retreating.

Wellington saw the French disarray, and judging the moment had arrived, waved his hat to advance. With a great cheer, the ragged Allied army assembled on the crest and, with fixed bayonets, began driving the mass of French survivors before them. Everywhere on the slope, the French line of battle collapsed with cries of: "*Sauve qui peut!*" (Save yourselves!), and began retreating in utter disorder.

By now the Prussians had taken Plancenoit, and had broken through Napoleon's reserves, driving the entire French right flank before their bayonets. The advancing Allied army joined them near La Belle Alliance. Napoleon tried to stop the rout by anchoring some squares of his remaining Old Guard directly in the road, but the shattered army streamed by them unheeded.

Marshal Ney stood with a broken sword, screaming: "Cowards, have you forgotten how to die!"[67] Only the last two battalions of the Old Guard rigidly held to their squares, a cocoon for Napoleon, who was raving like a madman. With his staff officers, he was bundled away with a cavalry escort to safety.

According to legend, the handful of Old Guard veterans still left standing defiantly, were called upon to surrender: "*Merde!*" came the rough, scatological reply from their commander Cambronne. Within a few moments, these stalwarts of innumerable battles were overrun and melted into the melee of the rout — and history. One of the last to leave the stricken field was Marshal Ney, blooded and covered in grime, on foot and helping a wounded soldier.

Exhausted by over ten hours of fighting, the Allied army were grateful for the vengeful Prussians to pursue the broken enemy. Wellington and Blucher met and exchanged pleasantries in their only common language — French. As Wellington returned to his HQ in Waterloo, the true cost of the day was clear, with almost all his staff officers either killed or wounded. Napoleon escaped into the night, suffering a mental collapse as he kept asking for Grouchy. His subordinate had followed orders to follow the

Prussians, but realising his mistake in not marching to the rumble of the guns, Grouchy retired in good order to France with his army intact.

The slaughter was staggering. Over thirty-thousand French were killed, wounded or captured. The Allied losses totalled over fifteen, and the Prussians lost nearly seven. Wellington's later mournful comment summed it up: "The next great misfortune to losing a battle is to gain such a victory as this."[68]

Napoleon dashed back to Paris, and after considering escape to America, surrendered to the Royal Navy. Taken to Plymouth, tens of thousands of his former enemies turned up to gawp, and even cheer the fallen emperor, whose appearance was described by a sailor:

> He is fat, rather what we call pot-bellied, and although his leg is well shaped, it is rather clumsy, and his walk appears rather affected, something between a waddle and a swagger — but probably not being used to the motion of a ship might have given him that appearance. He is very sallow, with light grey eyes, and rather thin, greasy-looking brown hair, and altogether a very nasty, priestlike-looking fellow...He never gave the smallest trouble to anyone, and every day was the same; he was very communicative and seemed fond of being asked questions; his manners are by no means good, and his voice very harsh and unpleasing.[69]

His desire to retire as an English gentleman was denied. Instead, with lessons learnt, he was sent to the oblivion of exile on Saint Helena, a tiny speck in the middle of the Atlantic Ocean. Whether it was cancer, the climate, poison, or just boredom, death took him aged just fifty-two in 1821.

In 1815, shortly after the defeat, Marshal Ney was sentenced to death by a vengeful French monarchy, his opponent Wellington, refusing to intercede. Standing before the firing squad, Ney declared: "'I have never betrayed my country. May my death render her happy. *Vive la France!*'" Then, turning to his executioners, he gave the word: 'Soldiers, fire!'"[70] Thus died "The Bravest of the Brave."

Wellington would enjoy the fruits of his victory. Although he would never fight another battle, he entered politics and became prime minister, a role for which he proved singularly ill-equipped. He would die in 1852, and be given a state funeral by a nation grateful for his service, and gracious of his faults.

The significance of Waterloo was immediate. From the stream of tourists and souvenir hunters who converged on the stricken killing ground, the bloody field became iconic. Almost all the artists, poets and writers of the day were inspired to immortalise those dramatic few days for an eager public.

Few battles have ever been so decisive and changed history. Marathon in 490 BC had seen the Greek City States halt the Persian Empire and thus allow for the development of democracy. Hastings in 1066: a management takeover of England which changed the direction of the country for five hundred years, kick-starting the building of an empire. Yorktown in 1781 led to the rapid expansion of the USA onto the world stage as a dominant player.

Waterloo marked the end not only of the Napoleonic Wars but brought, except for a few short conflicts, almost a century of peace to the continent. It was this stability on its back door which allowed Britain to look beyond its traditional arena and rapidly expand its empire. This disengagement, coupled with a sense of superiority, led to an unfortunate air of chauvinism that still mars Britain's relationship with its neighbours today. History often proves that victors rarely learn lessons from the past.

By the twentieth-century, the political repercussions of the battle were academic. The enduring fascination was with the high-stakes drama: A four-day campaign that ended one of history's most extraordinary careers in a nail-biting finale. It is the stuff of Shakespeare and legend.

To commemorate the one hundred and fifty-year anniversary, in June 1965, *Life* Magazine, the photo-journalist chronicler of the mid-twentieth-century, eschewed its usual contemporary photograph for its cover. Instead, they opted for a nineteenth-century painting showing stoical Redcoats repelling French cavalry.[71]

Buttressed between discussions of "The Law and the Homosexual Problem," and Kodak's new home movie system, Super-8, the magazine presented a spectacular full-colour spread of Grand Manner history paintings, to complement a detailed retelling of the campaign. In his editorial entitled "*Since Toy Soldier Days, a Waterloo Buff,*" George P. Hunt noted the enthusiasm of his article writer, which encapsulates the battle's continued fascination and relevance over the generations:

> Thomas Carmichael, my administrative assistant, has been a Waterloo buff since his toy soldier days. Not having been

around for the 100th anniversary, he was determined to celebrate the 150th…Tom had 4,500 toy soldiers by the time he was 10, got tangled up in his father's Napoleon books when he was 12, and that was that. He claims to have no great knowledge of the nuts-and-bolts detail of battles and campaigns. "What really interests me," he says, "is the character, personality and right-or-wrong decisions of the great commanders."[72]

It was only a matter of time before cinema woke up to the potential of this duel of military giants.

The nineteenth-century's Grand Manner history paintings have greatly influenced filmmakers. Charge of the French Cuirassiers at Waterloo by Henri Félix Emmanuel Philippoteaux (1874). AUTHOR'S COLLECTION

A scene from Waterloo *of French cavalry riding around the British squares.*
AUTHOR'S COLLECTION

Lord Hill invites the last remnants of the French Imperial Guard to surrender, painted by Robert Alexander Hillingford. AUTHOR'S COLLECTION

In the film, General Cambronne played by Evgeni Samoilov, shouts out an expletive in defiance. AUTHOR'S COLLECTION

Dino De Laurentiis winning the Best Foreign Language Film Oscar for Fellini's La Strada *in 1957.* AUTHOR'S COLLECTION

CHAPTER 3

"God! God's Got Nothing To Do With It!"

NAPOLEON: *"Cross the river and tomorrow we dry our boots in Brussels."*
NEY: *"God willing, sire."*
NAPOLEON: *"God! God's got nothing to do with it."*

For six years, it had been the dream of Italian Producer Dino De Laurentiis to bring the story of one of history's most famous battles to the screen. A voracious reader from classics to pulp and non-fiction, he had come upon the subject by chance; while "flipping through the encyclopaedia…my eyes happened to fall on the pages devoted to the Battle of Waterloo. I thought it over: epic scenes, Napoleon, Wellington…Yes, there was a film to be made."[73]

"He was royalty, he really was — they still talk about him,"[74] Veronica De Laurentiis speaking a decade after her father's death in 2010. Not an unbiased opinion, but few would argue that Dino De Laurentiis was one of the most tenacious, prolific, and successful independent film producers of the twentieth-century.

"An impeccably tailored bundle of raw energy and volatile emotion, he is not only a legend but also a character,"[75] recalled American director, Richard Fleischer, "a soft-spoken, unassuming Brooklynite,"[76] deftly describing the producer as:

> …short, dark, and with a high forehead, he has steely black eyes with bushy eyebrows that sweep up satanically at the ends. The word "gravelly" was invented to describe his voice, which he uses to bark out short, staccato, exclamatory sentences. His personality is the same as his speech: curt, abrupt, brusque.[77]

Veronica remembers the man who became known industry-wide as simply — Dino:

> He was a very driven kind of guy. In his business, he was very successful. He had his routine. He had his goals. He loved the movies. But he was a very tough kind of father because he wanted us to do what *he* said we should do. It had to be his way or no way. It was very hard.

Richard Fleischer, who worked and fought with him on several projects, added: "He can give you a smile with his lips only, the rest of his (face) immobile. It is like looking into the face of icy Death. I know."[78]

With a career spanning over half a century, this almost legendary figure was one of the last quintessential moguls. Dino was born in 1919 in Naples into a family that had pulled itself out of poverty. "He was a force of nature and he was indomitable, you know, he came from nothing," recalls his daughter Raffaella:

> He came from a little village under the Vesuvius. My grandmother's father died when she was twelve, and they were destitute. Her mother, whose name also was Raffaella, used to make pasta at home for the family — and my grandmother said to her: "Everybody likes your pasta so much, why don't we try to sell it?" And she started making it and they started selling it and it became incredibly successful. That's how they survived. When my grandmother was about 18, they had a pasta factory and employed many people. It was called *Pastificio Moderno*. My dad, as a little boy, he was selling the pasta. It was an amazing story. Characters like that don't exist anymore. Now it's a different world.[79]

These twin lessons of tenacity and entrepreneurship were ingrained early into the teenage Dino, but pasta soon lost its allure, as he became enchanted by cinema. Aged sixteen and keen to learn his chosen trade, he enrolled in Europe's oldest film school, Centro Sperimentale di Cinematografia in Rome. This being Mussolini's fascist Italy, Dino's studies were interrupted by the outbreak of war. With the threat of military call up, the young Dino was determined to master his chosen profession and took any job he could: actor, extra or prop-man. Aged just twenty-two and with the war in full swing, he produced his first film. On his second, he had to contend with not only a diva but also allied bombs threatening to stop production. Soon, he too was sucked into the war, with a spell of military service forcing a pause on his ambitions.

Just after the conflict ended with Italy ravaged and poor, he formed his own company and soon found success, both critically and commercially, with *Bitter Rice / Riz Amer* (1949). It was one of several Italian films dubbed collectively as Neo-Realist, which had a semi-documentary style that put the resurrected national cinema on the world stage — a source of pride after the trauma of war. He married the film's star, Silvana Mangano, and formed a short-lived but successful business partnership with fellow producer Carlo Ponti.

Perhaps their most significant collaboration was with the up-and-coming flamboyant darling of post-war cineastes — Federico Fellini, with Oscar-winning films such as *La Strada* (1954) and *Nights of Cabiria* (1957). He and Dino would fall out in the 1960s, although like many friendships, there were various attempts at working together again. At one point even *Waterloo* was mooted! The *Maestro* commented later about the offer, the proposed scale of the project and their respective characters: "I realised that between the two of us, the lunatic wasn't me; it was him. Compared to Dino, I have the good sense, the practicality, and the mental rigour of a civil servant."[80]

Despite the success of these small-scale films aimed principally at the Italian market, Dino yearned to become an international player. But as his biographers, Tullio Kezich and Alessandra Levantesi, have pointed out, he faced three principal obstacles. The proposed films must be in English and attract major Hollywood talent, both requiring a good grasp of the language which he did not at the time have. And finally, he would need large reserves of money, which as an independent, he did not possess.

He was lucky that the moment he wished to spread his wings came as Europe began the first steps towards closer union, with a series of treaties enabling links across industry and the arts. The Italian Film producers' association ANICA (Associazione Nazionale Industrie Cinematografiche & Affini), which included Dino, were successful in forging relationships across Western Europe, leading to co-productions which enabled bigger budgets and wider distribution.

> From the signing of the accord with France in October 1949, production companies benefitted from official collaborations, these enabled them to spread the risks and share markets with business partners from one or more foreign countries, pooling

financial, technical and artistic resources and take advantage of the benefits offered by the various national laws.[81]

By the early 1960s these fresh financing arrangements had doubled Italian film output to around 240, with over half pan-European, with Dino in the forefront. The ANICA was also keen to tap into the potential of the communist East, but until formal international treaties were negotiated, the area was off limits for the time being.

Looking far west to make lucrative deals with Hollywood was the great prize for European filmmakers. Despite Italy's growing reputation as a production hub, dubbed "Hollywood on the Tiber," co-production deals with Americans were rare, partly because of the lack of formal treaties. So, it was a coup for Dino to court Tinseltown royalty for a handsome rendering of Homer's immortal *Odyssey*, with an energetic Kirk Douglas as *Ulysses* (1954).

"What is this crap?"[82] was the initial response Dino received from the star's agent, Ray Stark, followed by a hefty salary demand. Upon meeting the actor, Dino found Douglas was "an intelligent man and maybe knew something about Homer." Deploying all his formidable Neapolitan charm and persuasion on the tough, sometimes difficult star, who described himself as a "son of a bitch,"[83] Douglas promptly accepted the role. Playing opposite him would be Mrs De Laurentiis, Silvana Mangano, in two roles; Penelope — literature's most long-suffering spouse, and the flip-side of the female psyche — the seductive sorceress, Circe.

Directed by Mario Camerini and filmed in 3-D,[84] the tautly budgeted production proceeded at Dino's small studio in the slums of Rome, where seafaring scenes were accomplished by "slapping together a contraption which would now look prehistoric, to rock ships back and forth as though they were on the waves." The hard work paid off. It proved to be an enormous success and has been credited with kick-starting the so-called Sword-and-sandal, also known as *peplum*, bargain-basement epics that kept the Italian film industry nicely ticking over for a decade.

It was Dino's next production that inaugurated his reputation for lavish epics. There can be few works to rival Homer, but one, written in the late nineteenth-century, has equalled the scope and power of the blind poet. With Italy doubling as Russia and clocking in at a bite-sized three-and-a-half-hours, *War and Peace* (1956) was a laudable attempt to capture something of the essence of Leo Tolstoy's monumental novel.

Dino had relished the challenges of adapting such a large work. "It would be a dream to film this," Dino said, although not blind to the potential pitfalls both artistic and logistical: "But if the greatest producers in the world haven't made it yet; *there* must be a reason."

The expansive scale of the narrative timeline had been a deterrent of a story spanning two decades with an army of characters. As the team of screenwriters began reducing Tolstoy's one million-plus words, Dino considered the key was to centre on the: "…love affairs. I said to myself, 'If I take this tack, I've got a popular story on my hands: you can never go wrong with a romance…I can fill in the background with the main parts of the plot, as many as I can fit into two or three-hour spectacular.'"[85]

While Dino had initially courted the young up-and-coming Richard Fleischer to helm his grand enterprise, the job went instead to an industry veteran whose career had begun in 1913. King Vidor was one of the leading Hollywood filmmakers of the 1920s with *The Big Parade* (1925) and *The Crowd* (1928) both considered American classics. With the coming of Sound, he continued to hit the mark critically, if not always commercially, with *Northwest Passage* (1940), *Duel in the Sun* (1946) and *The Fountainhead* (1949), but after forty years in the business his zest was fading, his final film was the epic miss fire *Solomon and Sheba* (1959).

Vidor, who was a Christian Scientist with a social conscience, was instinctively drawn to Pierre, the erstwhile hapless hero — overweight and short-sighted: "The strange thing about it is the character of Pierre is the same character I had been trying to put on the screen in many of my own films." He had tussled with Dino unsuccessfully to cast the brilliant Peter Ustinov, who had played a memorable Nero in *Quo Vadis* (1951), and was disappointed with the "star" casting of Henry Fonda for box office insurance. Acknowledging the actor's considerable talent, Vidor was frustrated at the obvious miscasting: "though a damn good actor…(Fonda) just did not understand what I was trying to say."[86]

For the female lead of Natasha, Vidor positively enthused over Dino's choice of the luminous Audrey Hepburn. Within the constraints of this adaptation of Tolstoy, Vidor felt the actress brilliantly personified the film's chosen theme in a way few of her contemporaries could have done: "If I were forced to reduce the whole story of *War and Peace* to some basically simple statement, I would say that it is a story of the maturing of Natasha. She represents, to me, the anima of the story and she hovers over it all like immortality…through the star we experience the passions of life. We stare in wonder, at the world with the star and at the star, and a magical interplay breaks out — best achieved with Natasha."[87] Not only was Hepburn a fine actress, she was also a hardy trouper having survived in war torn Arnhem during the Dutch famine of 1944.

This resilience was called upon during a shoot which threw up a torrent of headaches for the producer with his first taste of epic filmmaking. On hearing Hepburn was pregnant, something which would inevitably cause havoc with the best laid plans, Dino calmly rolled with the punches and rearranged. Tragedy struck when she suffered a miscarriage. Dino and his wife, Silvana, did whatever they could to help her through the emotional ordeal. Hepburn, ever the professional, returned the kindness by insisting she would stick to the original schedule.

"I would rather direct a battle scene with six thousand soldiers (than to) direct a love scene with two important stars."[88] said Vidor, of a sentiment that will strike a chord with any director who has ever tried to gently coax believable romantic intimacy between two actors. He was helped in both quarters by the eminent Italian director, Mario Soldati, who agreed to take a subordinate role as a favour to Dino to assist the ageing Vidor: "In the end, Soldati directed almost all of Napoleon's scenes (and battles)," said Dino, who it seems wanted to have some fun, "And I pitched in, too, directing a cavalry charge."

While the battles scenes are somewhat limp and anodyne, there is one shot which is worthy of King Vidor's best work. Henry Fonda as Pierre wearing an incongruous top hat, strays onto a hillside over-looking the battlefield of Borodino, and is transfixed by the panoply of war splayed across the opposite countryside. In one tracking shot we see lines of men and teams of horses dotted impressively over seemingly miles of fields and copses of trees, punctuated with white puffs of explosions. In the foreground is Fonda's (or his stand-in) hand meekly holding a yellow flower. After few moments struck by the horror before him, his grip loosens and it floats to the ground. This is not from Tolstoy's novel but is pure cinema, contrasting the puniness of the individual against the all-consuming juggernaut of war.

Praise must also go to British cinematographer Jack Cardiff, whose seminal work in Technicolor for Powell and Pressberger's *Black Narcissus* (1946) and *The Red Shoes* (1950), achieved some beautiful imagery for Dino's epic with the high-definition Vistavision format. One of the best examples of his work is a duel with pistols scene set in the snow. It is filmed on a soundstage with a sheet of glass in front of the camera painted snowy white to obscure the overhead lighting. Then for the sun, Cardiff bounced a single weak red light off the glass, the blurry smudge neatly suggesting the rise of early morning sun. While it took hours to prepare the glass much to Dino's frustration, he was so impressed by the final result that he showcased it in the promotional trailer.

"In sum, *War and Peace* was a typical example of cinematic stitching,"[89] he said later of all the chefs that had helped him stir the pot. For all its faults, like a miscast Henry Fonda, it remains one of the better epics of the 1950s, and does a reasonable stab at encompassing Tolstoy's vast canvas. Ten years later, this version would be eclipsed.

In 1961, Dino produced another epic: the spirited *Barabbas* with Anthony Quinn. It was expertly directed by Richard Fleischer, fresh off making the gutsy *The Vikings* (1958). The director, in his memoir, recalls a not isolated example of Dino's flair for showmanship — and manipulation. Respected French actress Jeanne Moreau was touted for an important role, so Dino brought her to Rome for tests, throwing open the doors to the enthusiastic press. The next day, the front pages on many papers were adorned with images of the iconic beauty, hailing Dino for his skill at landing one of Europe's top talents for his new super-production. A week later, Fleischer was nonplussed to hear Dino say: "We no use Moreau!... We use Silvana!" The director suspected that it had always been the plan to cast his wife in the role. Although he was happy with the choice, he rankled at being "played."

When casting the central role, the American director was made to be the fall guy when Yul Brynner, who had agreed to do it, was dropped for Quinn because Dino balked at his salary demand. "He *want* a fortune," grumbled Dino about the *King and I* star. "He *think* he really king of Siam."[90] A week later, Fleischer was stunned to receive a letter from Brynner, upset that he had been dropped simply because Fleischer *didn't like him!* He could never get to the bottom of what exactly happened, but the director had his suspicions.

The film opens with a depiction of the crucifixion, which has an extraordinary power to it, never equalled in all the countless versions of this iconic, if historically debatable, event. It was filmed on 15 February 1961 at Roccastrado, 120 miles north of Rome, and there would only be time for just *one* take, or wait — until 1979! The reason: a total eclipse of the sun. As the light drained from the sky that day, it is easy to imagine cameraman Aldo Tonti's nervous state as he prepared to shoot the scene with the wide-screen Technirama cameras. Many of the local villagers hired as extras were so awed by the spectacle of the three stark crosses illuminated by the glowering ring of the eclipse, that they dropped to their knees in prayer. This doing-it-for-real appealed to Dino's sense of showmanship and as a purveyor of spectacle.

Despite its Biblical origins, *Barabbas* escapes some flaws that drag down many devotional spectacles of the era, and deservedly became a major hit for Dino. "*Barabbas* proves my point that when you have a great story, you can produce an excellent piece of work with a skilled professional like Richard Fleischer...It was an enormous commercial success throughout the world."[91]

Dino's penchant for making ambitious films was very much an expression of a man who liked challenges, but there was method in these risky ventures. He was one of the early adopters of pre-sales. This was an example of the high art of The Sell, in which big budgets were paid for by distributors upfront by buying the rights to exhibit a film in a particular territory. It was all based on the package of top stars, a renowned director and a story that would have international appeal. The only thing the buyers didn't have to make their decision was the actual *film* itself! It was bold and required a talent to schmooze and persuade. Raffaella, who followed in her father's footsteps to become a successful producer herself, described how the onetime pasta-seller took on Hollywood:

> The few international movies in English that he had tried to make; he was always being screwed by these studios in Hollywood. Because they wanted to finance the whole thing, and just to give him a fee, and that's not what he used to do in Italy where he used to own the copyright. So, he came up with this system of pre-sales, which is still in existence. He divided the pie into each different country, and sold his movies to Spain, France, England, whatever. And then he went with these contracts to the banks, and they discounted the contracts up to 80 percent or whatever it was.

The autonomy that being outside the system provides also comes with a bigger risk. Before Dino could tout his pre-sales, he had to have some money in place. "If you're not being financed by a studio, you're called an independent. You must have your financing in place before you start," Raffaella explained of the complex, almost byzantine world of film finance:

> Then normally what you do is you go to the bank and discount those rights because you have to have a bond on a movie. You have to prove to the bank that's going to lend you the money before the distributors pay you in full, that you are going to be able to finish the movie. But that's standard today, it's the same thing, it hasn't changed. Back then, it had never been done before, and he kind of invented it.

Samuel Bronston, a "small-time"[92] American producer who set up shop in Franco's Spain, produced a series of colourful epics utilising pre-sales in a similar way to Dino. He also acted as a broker for the pariah state by trading in crude oil, and tapped into the Du Pont fortune by brandishing signed but blank completion bonds that permitted Bronston to borrow money, almost without limit. Although showered with success for *El Cid* (1961), his Madrid kingdom crashed and burned barely a few years later with *The Fall of The Roman Empire* (1964). The extraordinary story of Bronston's demise is a tale in its own right; a smooth-talking dreamer brought down by his inability to rein in the financial shenanigans of his lieutenants, which led to insanely bloated budgets and poor decisions.[93]

Dino ran a tighter ship but would spend money, often considerable amounts, even if he didn't have it to hand. He would aim to get what he wanted by offering a deal too juicy to refuse, the repercussions he would confidently confront later. It was joked that even as the ink was drying on a contract, that was merely the *start* of the proper negotiations. There was no doubting his business acumen, but he was not above some play-acting if it served him.

Richard Fleischer noted wryly that Dino's notoriously spoken English ("I no like" — "I like. We do", etc) could become quite incomprehensible if discussions, particularly around money, were not going his way; he would say: "'I no understand' and revert to hyper speed Italian." Business meetings could be a disconcerting display of histrionics, as the producer would work himself up into an apoplectic fit, as Fleischer recalls on occasion:

> He would yell and shout, pound the desk with his fists and elbows, jump to his feet and gesticulate accusingly at me. His voice filled with deep emotion. Shit, I would think, I've done it now. He thinks I'm an idiot. I'm fired for sure. Dino would drop back down into his chair, breathing heavily, and nod curtly to the translator, who would turn to me and say, "He loves it."[94]

After various aborted attempts to re-team after *Barabbas*, the two fell out and counter-sued with Dino pressing for an eye-watering $1 million for breach of contract. Fleischer had stared into "the face of icy Death." As we saw with Fellini, his creative relationships could be volatile, but the sheer, almost absurd size of the counter-sue suggests more of an extravagant gesture than a deadly cut-throat threat.

"There really wasn't a lawsuit," the director's son, Mark, himself a lawyer, explained:

I mean, it was a long, long relationship between the two, but knowing kind of Dino in the way he was…The impression is that this never really touched the two men. No, I mean, it is always totally serious and scary when you get involved in a lawsuit. I know that as a lawyer. But these were legal manoeuvres which didn't result in a lawsuit and an action, which had that actually happened, it probably would have been a very different ending in terms of their relationship.[95]

Eventually they would applicably drop their respective cases and resume their business partnership (including teaming up for the unfairly maligned and underrated *Mandingo* in 1975), but working for Dino could have its moments of "icy death."

The producer would have his fair share of flops and missteps, but stayed afloat during his seven-decade career with a mixture of determination and pragmatism, summed up by his motto — *Andare sempre avanti:* Ever onward.

There was a lot of money sloshing around in the early 1960s, it just required producers with the *chutzpah* to tap and channel it into ambitious projects. For him, it was simply a case of high-risk equal enormous returns: "The public, no matter how lazy or demanding it may be, will always go to see a film with an interesting subject, fancy production values, rich colours, and a cast of internationally famous actors. The more you spend, the more you earn."[96]

"He loved to do huge movies," remembers Veronica. "Not big movies — huge movies! The biggest movie you could do. He wanted to be the one to do it. He was one of the first producers in Italy to do huge movies. You've got to have the desire and the passion that burns so strong inside of you, that you would do anything to get it. And he did everything he could to get those movies going. He really did."

By the early 1960s, confident and successful, he embarked on a plan to build his own studio facilities in Rome to rival Cinecittà, the studio complex home for such epics as *Quo Vadis* (1951), his own *War and Peace* (1956), *Ben-Hur* (1959) and *Cleopatra* (1963). He took advantage of a government initiative which offered advantageous tax breaks, to rejuvenate the depressed regions of southern Italy, known as the Mezzogiorno. Buying hundreds of acres of wasteland just inside the designated area barely thirteen miles from Rome, he could have the best of both worlds. Despite the huge outlay, Dino believed it was a sound move: "The studio is an essential working tool…It's a way of containing costs, especially if you manage to keep general expenses down."[97]

At the ceremony to mark the first stone being laid in January 1962, a parchment proclamation was read out before the throng of state and film notables. It promised an exciting new dawn: "This vast complex, whose construction commences with this stone will benefit the entire Italian film industry, which…has contributed so much to Italy's image and prestige around the world."[98] With these heady words, work began apace under the supervision of his elder brother, Luigi, although eventually it would become a millstone around its *padrone's* neck.

His new facilities at Via Pontina, a stone's throw from the capital, cost $30 million, boasted five sound stages, 250 offices with central air-conditioning and a huge backlot. Officially it was named, with suitable modesty, the Dino De Laurentiis Studios, but was instantly dubbed by all as — Dinocittà. "It was modern," remembers Veronica, "it was beautiful, and he built everything in there, it was amazing." The *Maestro* Fellini was not so enamoured, calling it "a space station, an inaccessible outpost."[99]

Nether-the-less, it was a good time to invest because of the so-called Andreotti Law, enacted in 1949, which allowed generous tax breaks from the Italian government under the definition of a National film. The stipulation was that there must be an "Italian-language version" produced with an Italian on the writing team, and most of the crew and cast also nationals. Crucially, there were no restrictions on the director's nationality or whether the primary language was English.

Several other European countries operated similar schemes, including Britain, where the similar Eady Levy tax scheme encouraged Hollywood investment. This super-charged the production boom of the 1960s, most notably with the James Bond franchise.

Dinocittà quickly expanded, and soon strange shapes rose high above the skyline over Via Pontina, including a huge reconstruction of Noah's Ark.

Dino was embarking on the most ambitious and risky period of his career. Writing a few years later, Ralph Novak described how the Producer was seen by many:

> An industry veteran says, "People are surprised, but he's a gentleman…" Well, anyway, nobody walks around calling him a son of a bitch like they do with a lot of producers. His reputation as a tough, cynical and not hyper-scrupulous man to deal with

has been gentled. True, nobody seems sure how De Laurentiis finances his projects, using both "private investors" and intricate arrangements with studios. De Laurentiis himself says only, "Good stories are like real estate; if you have them, you can always get money."[100]

The Bible, regardless of any religious point of view, has an abundance of stories which, in their totality, convey the complexity and magnitude of the human condition. "There's enough material here for a hundred films," Dino said later; "this is one of those dreams I want to transform into reality."[101] So, a project to film the entire book would be both wildly ambitious but riding on the success of multi-Oscar-winning *Ben-Hur* — a sure-fire hit.

Dino raised a then staggering $17 million ($140 million in 2020) from a Swiss bank and struck a deal selling the US distribution rights to Twentieth Century-Fox, whose boss Darryl F. Zanuck, "Napoleonic, cigar-chomping, crusty old son-of-a-bitch"[102] was as canny and sharp an executive that Hollywood ever produced. So, it must have been a real meeting of minds and wills driving the hardest bargain as Dino screened the first cut: "Having seen *The Bible* and grasped its potential, Zanuck grabbed the film. Then I settled things with the Swiss bankers and pocketed an excellent bit of profit for myself."[103]

In the fall of 1965, with a year to go until *The Bible…In the Beginning* would be ready for release, the trade papers reported that Dino De Laurentiis had announced *Waterloo* as his next project. He promised that the famous battle would be "faithfully"[104] re-enacted, with *The Bible* director John Huston taking up the creative reins once more. "He was a wonderful guy," remembers Veronica. "I used to travel a lot with my dad — he took me to John Huston's house in Ireland. They shot (*The Bible*) a lot of it right there."

Huston was one of Hollywood's leading directors, something of a maverick, although considered highly professional and creative. Producer and founder of the American Film Institute, George Stevens, Jr., accorded him the best attributes of the industry with his "intellect, charm and physical grace," further adding, "he was the most charismatic of the directors I knew, speaking with a soothing, melodic voice that was often mimicked, but was unique to him."[105]

He had made his name as a writer-director with his debut *The Maltese Falcon* in 1941, starring Humphrey Bogart. He quickly established an impressive reputation with such instant classics as *Key Largo* (1948), *The*

Treasure of the Sierra Madre (1948), *The Asphalt Jungle* (1950), *The African Queen* (1951) and Marilyn Monroe's last film, the ill-fated *The Misfits* in 1961. Disgusted at the "witch-hunt" by the HUAC (House Un-American Activities Committee) in the early 1950s, he had renounced US citizenship and moved to Ireland, eventually becoming a citizen in 1964.[106]

He was almost the cliché of the traditional film director. "What I really like are horses, strong drink and women,"[107] he said of himself, but could have also included being a big game hunter, and an inveterate poker player. On some of his productions he had a stipend for gambling, as apparently, he usually lost heavily. To counter this almost boorish image, his deepest passion was reserved for painting; in short, a man of many talents, with a lust for life which he channelled into a laudable movie career, for which *The Bible* was his most ambitious.

Kick-starting the project in 1962, on the tailwind of *Barabbas*'s success, Dino had toiled away to bring this most famous of books to the screen. The original plan was to hire half a dozen of the world's most renowned directors assigned to different segments, but with a degree of pragmatism and practicality, this was honed down to just John Huston taking the reins.

Titled *The Bible…In the Beginning*, to give the option for an obvious franchise, the film concentrated on just the first 22 Chapters of Genesis — from the Creation to Abraham offering his only son in sacrifice to his God. A vast and impressive if dour work, which used the King James Version's archaic but poetic text as the basis for the dialogue written by Christopher Fry. Huston claimed no religious beliefs himself, although his daughter Anjelica was raised a Roman-Catholic, but he approached it "as a collection of myths and legends." When asked whether Dino agreed with his take, Huston replied that the producer "just wanted a very successful film. I don't think it was meant to be the word of God."[108]

The liveliest sequence was Noah's flood with Huston himself playing a comic turn as Noah, in a role originally offered to Charlie Chaplin. As the animals were assembled ready for filming at Dinocittà, Huston soon formed a bond with the ever-growing zoo as he toured the cages each morning. He later fondly related his special relationship with an elephant called Candy: "One time I started to walk away from her, and she reached out and took my wrist with her trunk and pulled me back to her side. It was a command: 'Don't stop!' I used it in the picture."[109] Realising such an affinity was essential for the character of Noah, Dino suggested Huston play the role himself — it was an inspired choice.

The ark itself comprised five individual sets, including a miniature, at a total cost of $1 million.[110] Veronica was barely into her teens when work began on filming: "I got an Arabian horse they had bought for that scene where all the animals were going in to Noah's Ark, and I used to ride him. I loved that horse, his name was *Ogar*." Shooting this sequence involving so many animals was a formidable challenge.

Unlike in the twenty-first century where CGI would be used, all the photographic effects tricks of the time were found wanting. Huston, with Dino's backing, realised it must be done for *real*. A circular track was constructed that led through the Ark's façade and back around behind the camera. Over this, the animal handlers trained their individual creatures to walk — two-by-two. Along either side of the approach to the Ark, deep trenches were dug. These were high enough to conceal the handlers walking along, out of sight of the camera, while leading their charges with long lines of nylon.

Not unsurprisingly, there were mishaps and close shaves. Huston himself as Noah taking the brunt; he was abruptly recast as Adam when his costume was inadvertently pulled off by Candy, the elephant, rooting around for peanuts, while another knocked him to the ground. A water buffalo charged up the gangplank and crashed through the Ark set, while an unsteady camel fell off the ramp into a tankful of water. This being just one of many headaches for Huston, not least keeping Adam and Eve's nudity suitably "U"-rated during the arduous shoot, and that elicited a quip: "I don't know how God managed. I'm having a terrible time."[111]

Released in late 1966 it appeared to be a box office smash, with a hefty gross of $35 million making it the top draw of the year, along with *The Hawaiians*, another period epic. Its success seemed to fly in the face of the view that epics were no longer popular, and should have ensured *The Bible* franchise. Yet this didn't happen.

According to Twentieth Century-Fox records, despite its healthy box office (routinely a large chunk of the gross is taken by the exhibitors), it failed to break even on its $27 million outlay of both production and distribution costs, with a $1.5 million shortfall, and thus there was no continuation after…*In the Beginning*.[112]

The problem was in trying to appeal to a wide enough audience, but ensuring not to offend any sensibilities, it fell between two stools. Huston's biographer noted the hub of the problem was: "The picture was not fundamentalist enough for the Bible Belt and not interesting enough for college students."[113] The juggling act when telling religious or historical stories to a mass audience continues to be a very fine line, as we will see, never more so than with *Waterloo*.

Inevitably,...*In the Beginning*, became a soft, easy and very large target for critics. Rex Reed of *The New York Times* noted rather brutally that: "At a time when religion needs all the help it can get, John Huston may have set its cause back a couple of thousand years."[114]

In the intervening half-century, the decision to use the archaic King James text and avoid an obvious religious point-of-view has given the film a timeless quality, and coupled with Huston's often breath-taking visuals in the luminous Dimension-150 70mm format, and avant-garde composer Toshiro Mayuzumi's mesmerising score, the film has kept a poetic majesty that deserves reappraisal.

Undaunted that he hadn't delivered a second *Ben-Hur*, Dino was not dissuaded from mounting another epic, or perhaps more to the point, his private investors were prepared to back him, on the basis he would secure lucrative distribution rights. Paramount, who had distributed *War and Peace*, came onboard early on, but with the understanding that top draw actors must be attracted. Several names were mooted: Richard Burton, Rex Harrison, Peter O'Toole and allegedly — Peter Sellers! With so many variables to decide, filming would be years away and too early to sign up any above-the-line talent.

By February 1966 *Daily Variety* announced that Irish writer, H.A.L. (Harry) Craig was already working on the screenplay with Huston, but no location sites had been set, as the decision depended on the availability of enough extras and horses.[115] Dino during this time was busy producing other projects: *Barbarella* (1968), *Danger: Diabolik* (1968) and *Anzio* (1968), ensuring Dinocittà was kept occupied during the slow gestation of his next super-production. The cutting-edge studio facilities were also hired out to other companies to help Dino pay the overheads. Most notably, was the construction of a full-sized replica of the Sistine Chapel, complete with the famous ceiling paintings, for Carol Reed's sumptuous *The Agony and the Ecstasy* (1965). This starred the solid Charlton Heston as Michelangelo executing the most ambitious interior decorating job in history: "I'm good with horses, wild animals, fire and flood, shot and shell, not so good with high places or spiders."[116]

Another production was *Doctor Faustus* (1967), starring cinematic royalty Elizabeth Taylor and Richard Burton. It was conceived as a permanent filmed record of Burton's stage production with the Oxford University Dramatic Society in 1966. Way down the cast list was a young aspiring British actor, Richard Heffer: "This was a momentous theatrical event for me, especially as I held the candlestick aloft that lit Elizabeth

Taylor's entrance as Helen of Troy — breath-taking!" This being the summer break after his first year at Oxford, he was excited to be in Rome making the movie version. He shared a number of scenes with Burton (who was also co-directing with Nevill Coghill), whom he described as a very generous actor, and supportive of the younger cast members, like himself.

The long, slow filming days allowed him ample time to amble around the sprawling studio complex.

> I took advantage of the situation to explore...driving an old Willis jeep to visit the abandoned epic sets rotting away...and the remains of a spaghetti western saloon (where Clint Eastwood had recently filmed) in a street of "fronts" was most entertaining. I never realised how tricky it was to enter the double swing doors being "cool". Unless one had practiced, the wretched doors swung back on one after entry and clobbered one from behind — *not* very cool!

He remembers finding the *Waterloo* production planning office:

> ...next to our stage, I discovered future films were being planned, and (as I spoke Italian) I enquired further — I then realised that a massive film of Waterloo was being prepared. I spoke to some of the planners (the nerve!), and wondered whether they needed English actors — they laughed, and said it was a long way off, but I got a photograph taken and registered.[117]

In a twist of fate, a few years later he would be back; suited and booted for *Waterloo*.

For now, the big problem was where to find a suitable number of trained horses and men to stage the planned complex action sequences. Italy would be the base for filming the interiors but was ruled out for the battle scene. This seems strange as the local industry had recently made a tonne of low budget *peplum*, so called Sword-and-sandal epics, which used casts of thousands, paid a few thousand lire a day plus a bowl of pasta. But these extras were rarely called upon to do much more than wave at emperors or run around in cluttered battle sequences. The complex manoeuvres of Napoleonic armies could only be achieved with professionally trained troops.

So, the net was cast over Turkey. Interestingly, Tony Richardson's *The Charge of the Light Brigade* (1968) filmed in 1967, found the required horses for the eponymous charge by using Turkey's Presidential Cavalry. Hungary, and Yugoslavia, whose army had been used for Abel Gance's Napoleonic film *Austerlitz* (1960), were also considered, but for various reasons rejected and the search continued.

During 1967, Dino was confident he could secure his dream casting with Peter O'Toole as Wellington and Richard Burton as Napoleon, although with no "running femmes roles" there was "No role for Liz (Taylor) — unless she'd accept a cameo."[118] But solving the logistical challenges meant everything was on shifting sands; O'Toole's involvement came with the caveat that production was based *away* from Italy, as he "won't work there."[119] These frustrations led to rumours that Dino was abandoning the project, but these were quickly denied. To reinforce the impression it was still happening, the trade papers reported that French writer Jean Anouilh was working with Craig on a final script.[120]

By September 1967, John Huston had backed out because of other commitments. According to his autobiography, a full year before he had worked on the script for what would be his next project, *Reflections in a Golden Eye* (1967); perhaps hedging his bets at the continual delays. Interestingly, he would shoot not only *Reflections*, which starred Marlon Brando and Elizabeth Taylor at Dinocittà, but also *The Kremlin Letter* (1970), which would have allowed him to keep abreast of progress.

Unfortunately, little information has survived on Huston's concept for the film. There is no doubt he would have delivered a very different creation from what emerged, perhaps it would have concentrated more on character than spectacle.

He was no stranger to combat himself, having served in the US Army Signal Corps, which was tasked with photographing the war. He produced several documentaries, including *The Battle of San Pietro* (1945), detailing US troops taking a small Italian town. With its shaky camerawork, it appeared to capture the realism of combat.[121] For a time, it was shelved, because of its apparent gritty realism by the top brass, before US Army Chief of Staff, George C. Marshall, intervened. Receiving a general release, it was also screened to army recruits as a snapshot of what to expect. Huston has been accused of faking much of it; the story goes that his unit only arrived just *after* the town's capture. That said, there is clearly very "real" footage in it, and considering the camera technology of the time, not captured without risk.

Whatever the truth, Huston and his team would no doubt have seen and been affected by the horrors of war. In his autobiography, he graphically described the aftermath of a failed tank attack, and confesses that he thought he had adjusted to the violence around him as a "proper soldier," only to awaken that night calling for his mother. "We don't know what goes on beneath the surface."[122] He followed this with another documentary about the deep psychological effects of combat on soldiers, which again was suppressed by the Army until the 1980s. This must have coloured the vision of his *Waterloo*.

Like so many what-ifs — we will never know. A photograph exists of Huston and Dino in the production office with an immense table covered with a battlefield map peppered by toy soldiers, over which Huston is directing with a stick, much to Dino's amusement. It is a publicity image, but it suggests the deep commitment to historical truth that would mark the project. Most directors' careers are pockmarked with unrealised projects; Huston's *Waterloo* is just one.

In late 1967, Gillo Pontecorvo, fresh from world-wide critical acclaim with *The Battle of Algiers* (1965) was in negotiations to direct. He would have brought a unique approach judging from his previous film; a brilliant piece of semi-documentary storytelling of the then very recent Algerian fight for independence from France. Filmed in stark monochrome and refusing to damn either side, it is still considered one of the finest films of all time. It would have been interesting how far he could have pushed the *Waterloo* material.

Dino's productions were very much a family affair. While his younger brother Alfredo would act as a line producer on different projects, his elder brother Luigi helped to set up deals, as Dino's youngest daughter Raffaella remembered. "He was the cultivated one who had studied in Bulgaria, in the Sofia University for years; he was the man of culture. My dad always looked up at him, and he spoke Bulgarian fluently." For years the De Laurentiis brothers had been eyeing up the Communist Bloc as a way of getting more bang-for-your-bucks for the large productions Dino wanted to make.

Luigi, with his intimate knowledge of Bulgaria, had made a deal with Bulgar Films for the all-important battle scenes. The communist government agreed to provide 10,000 men and 1,000 horses. But in the tense atmosphere of the Cold War, politics came into play as the troops were required for redeployment because of escalating tensions over Vietnam, and the Six-Day War in the Middle East.

Pontecorvo moved on and instead made a historical period film with Marlon Brando: *Burn!* (1969). It turned out to be a most disagreeable experience, as many productions with the egocentric Brando often were. How involved, and for how long in the *Waterloo* pre-production the director was attached, is unclear. Perhaps a hint at what may have happened can be gleaned from a passing comment about a later project, when Dino let slip: "With all your hesitations, you're worse than Gillo Pontecorvo."[123]

Meanwhile, by March 1968 Bulgaria was no longer an option but Luigi, who had continued to flirt behind the Iron Curtain, had secured a new, and potentially much better deal. Moscow now offered a solution as Soviet director Sergei Bondarchuk, who had recently finished a Soviet version of *War and Peace*, was available along with thousands of "celluloid-seasoned"[124] soldiers and trained cavalry complete with the Napoleonic uniforms and cannons used in that film. Speaking much later, Dino said that all he had to do was: "I'll put the idea to the Soviets; they can give me everything."[125] The truth is more prosaic.

The Italian producers' group — ANICA, for which Dino was a member, had spent much of the decade trying to break into this untapped territory. It was not until an inter-governmental Accord between Italy and the USSR was signed in January 1967 that the path was smoothed towards future co-productions.

> The huge economic capacity of Soviet State cinema was undermined by the limited scope of commercial activity and the poor returns achieved by film exports, characteristics that were the exact opposite of Italian cinema…Above all, Italian producers were attracted by the financial and material resources of the Soviet State system. In return, they were able to offer the Soviets a vast network of relations with western film markets.[126]

It is probable that hand-in-hand with the ANICA's lobbying was Luigi De Laurentiis working behind the scenes for Dino, as Raffaella explains:

> He could never do a deal with Russia. But at the prompting of his older brother, who he respected a lot, he decided: "Well what if we cannot make a deal with Russia, why don't we try to make a Russian film?" — And he has done many others.

The De Laurentiis brothers were not the first to make a deal with Russia. Fellow Italian producer Franco Cristaldi had been pushing to film the story of Umberto Nobile's disastrous scientific expedition to the Arctic in 1928. In the wake of the formal treaty, Cristaldi began protracted negotiations to make this as *The Red Tent*. Barbara Corsi, in a detailed article about the film, highlights the challenges that faced the producer, with clear parallels to Dino's own upcoming super-production:

> Cristaldi sought to reconcile three worlds and three modes of production, uniting the power of the Soviet state, the creativity of European art cinema and the reach of American distribution. The producer succeeded in his aim thanks to his ability to manage complex economic and diplomatic situations, but the final balance of the operation, while commercially positive, was disappointing relative to the energies deployed and future opportunities generated.[127]

With an international cast including Peter Finch, Sean Connery, Claudia Cardinale and Hardy Kruger, filming began under Mikhail Kalatozov's direction in February 1968. It would take a year thanks to many delays, not helped by the Soviet invasion of Czechoslovakia in August that year, which caused an East/West rift. Mosfilm's head, Vladimir Surin, did his best to smooth matters and get the film back on track. One gets the sense this co-production was a steep learning experience for both sides, as Barbara Corsi explains:

> The lack of urgency with which filmed material was sent from the USSR to Italy…was complicated by the long bureaucratic procedure which had to be undertaken every time people or things had to move from one country to the other. For the cold calculator Cristaldi, who was used to western economic criteria and bureaucracy, it was a torture to be subjected to Soviet-style disorganisation and failure to keep to time.[128]

The long shoot which included some scenes at Dinocittà in Rome, gave way to almost another year of post-production before *La Tenda Rossa* was released to little success in Italy in December 1969.

It is interesting that both projects had non-Russian stories, which suggest a genuine desire by the Soviets to embrace the perceived advantages of narratives with the widest possible reach. Also, perhaps they recognised that a Russian subject would be suspected of having a political agenda which might alienate a Western, and particularly an American audience.

On 17 May 1968, a formal agreement, brokered by elder brother Luigi, between Dino and Vladimir Surin of Mosfilm was signed. Specifying that the film would be shot in English with a maximum duration of 150-minutes, the document proclaimed that "the film will be of an exceptional artistic and spectacular level, such as to ensure a great international success."[129]

It was a sixty/forty split with Mosfilm as the senior financial partner, agreeing to stump up $8 million (later $10 million), and provide up to 16,000 soldiers of the Soviet Army, along with a full brigade of cavalry for the battle scenes to be shot in Russia. "You just couldn't afford to get that many people together in Hollywood or anywhere else," boasted director Sergei Bondarchuk.[130]

Bringing himself $6 million to the table, in simple terms, Dino handled the above-the-line costs of salaries for stars, script and director,[131] and the predominantly Italian crew and western actors, the principals' costumes, a team of stuntmen, and assorted props. He would also pay Mosfilm $1.3 million to cover additional expenses; the mighty greenback was emphasised, so keen were the Soviets to accrue foreign currency.

The Russians, in return, would supply the army, build the location set and make the bulk of the costumes, and recruit leading Soviet actors. In exchange for their investment, Mosfilm took the sole distribution rights for the Eastern European Communist Bloc.

It was estimated that the budget would have been treble had the film been made in the West. That said, according to the jointly signed agreement, it was $16 million: a hefty sum but not on the level of many of the overblown roadshow musicals then also inching towards the screen.

Mindful of the tax breaks and public subsidies available to squeeze every Lira for the budget, Dino successfully got a certificate of Italian "national status" for the film.[132] This must have required some wrangling. The sympathetic 1949 Andreotti Law, which had enabled him to enlist international talent, had been superseded by the so-called Corona Law in 1965. This put stringent limitations on Italian filmmakers by insisting almost all key collaborators were nationals. Fully aware that this law — number 1213 — would ultimately force a major change in his career, he was doubtless pleased to pull off the coup — perhaps for the last time. This "status" meant the film's distribution would be free of custom duties across the burgeoning EEC (European Economic Community).

Less successful, but showing some ingenuity, he wrote directly to a senior government figure, Matteo Matteotti, the Minister of Tourism and Entertainment, asking to have his battle story classed as a children's film.

This would allow access to public subsidies for the purpose of education. Various learned professors sat on a committee to examine the proposal:

> According to one member — Prof. Valentini — the film has a distinctly commercial character, with no particular characteristics of ethical principles that can benefit the education of young people. He also observed that anti-war phrases can't be understood by kids younger than 16 years, who rather tend to identify with the hero Napoleon.[133]

Finally, the chairman of the committee ruled that it would be contrary to the spirit of the law to declare the film a "product for children," adding that its unabashed commercial tone made it impossible to justify public support from an already "overburdened treasury."[134]

Undaunted, to cover his back end, Dino got a meaty $4.5 million credit line from the Italian Commercial Bank, on the basis he could cover it with the international rights he intended to sell.

The Hollywood major, Paramount Pictures, had been involved from the very beginning in 1965, but just as the Russians came onboard, there were wobbles at the company with its logo of a sturdy mountain.

The famed studio, founded in 1912, had recently become the plaything of a conglomerate in 1966. Gulf + Western, a onetime car bumper manufacturer from Grand Rapids had grown into a multi-million-dollar international organisation involving many subsidiaries. Its chief, Austrian born Charles Bluhdorn, dubbed "The Mad Austrian of Wall Street," had a genuine passion for the movies rather than as merely a profit generator, and devoted a quarter of his very busy day just to managing Paramount, to "put some zip and drive into it and to restore it to its old pride and glory."[135]

To help him, he enlisted a thirty-six-year-old ex-actor with matinee idol looks, Robert Evans. The industry was sceptical of this new breed of executive, but Evans was astute and understood the changing audience: "Today people go to see *a* movie; they no longer go to *the* movies. We can't depend on that habit anymore. We have to make 'I've got to see' pictures."[136]

With Bluhdorn's full support, Evans kick-started a twenty-year high of green-lit productions, including one of those "sure-fire" hit musicals — *Paint Your Wagon* (1969). The costs of this Clint Eastwood/Lee Marvin vehicle ballooned to $20 million thanks to endless problems and delays. Despite this mis-step, Paramount's stock tripled, and the company appeared to be riding high. There was no question Bluhdorn liked to spend a lot of money, even tussling with Joshua Logan, the director of *Paint Your Wagon*, who wanted to retreat from a difficult location site back to the studio backlot to help save costs, only to be overruled by the boss.

The Austrian was very keen on Dino's outsized project. "Charles Bluhdorn wanted *Waterloo* for the world,"[137] Evans said later of the original plan to put up two-thirds of the budget, in exchange for *all* distribution territories outside the Communist Bloc. With nightmares over *Paint Your Wagon*) still fresh, Evans was concerned at the high level of investment in just *one* film, however much of a "got to see picture" it might be. There appeared to be several reasons for this; primarily, Evans wanted to hedge his bets. His boss trusted his judgment, and "went along with my hesitation to limit our area of release to the Western Hemisphere (USA and Canada), France and a couple of smaller European nations." The reported investment was $7 million.[138]

This caution was no doubt influenced by the ballooning budgets threatening to overtake the studio's other projects: *Darling Lili* (1970) — $23 million, and $10 million apiece for *Catch 22* (1970), *On a Clear Day You Can See Forever* (1970) and *The Molly Maguires*(1970). This discreet step back by his main backer didn't seem to harm the strong personal relationship between Bluhdorn and Dino, who considered each other not just business partners, but friends too.

However, the timing of this decision must have put some strain on their relationship, as Dino was barely weeks from the start of principal photography. Conveniently, the producer had built up good relationships with other studios for his myriad of productions, and negotiations were quickly joined with Columbia Pictures with whom he had recently made the war film *Anzio* (1968), and the successful *Barabbas* in 1961.

It is not clear how much the studio invested, but they were keen to acquire a varied, and hopefully, lucrative spread of territories, including the UK and Commonwealth, less Canada, the Far East and almost all of Europe except France. Distribution rights to Italy alone were snapped up for $1 million by Euro International. A few months later, Robert Evans would have a moment of regret that he should have "nabbed" the "world" for *Waterloo*.

Despite such large amounts of money being lavished on this production, the actual figures are still very vague. Speaking to Hank Werba of *Variety* in January 1970, when the film was being slowly edited together, Dino said the *combined* Hollywood investment was just $7 million, although this figure was upped to $10 million from a "production source."

According to Hank Werba, this was "still cheap in De Laurentiis' mind for what he enthusiastically describes as 'one of the greatest pictures ever made.'"[139] Left somewhat dangling was that Dino "insists" the final tally was an eye-watering $40 million! Some sources suggest a figure of $28 million but if so, this might have been the accumulated distribution rights which Dino sold to cover his back end.

It stands to reason a canny entrepreneur will inflate the budget to justify the highest bid for distribution rights. Another comparable production of the time, *The Battle of Neretva* (1969), largely financed by Tito's Yugoslavia, had a widely publicised budget of $12 million. The director, Veljko Bulajić, said later that this was deliberately inflated to *up* the price of the rights — so it was a common practice. It is a safe bet Dino worked hard to cover his back-end and walk away with a hefty profit. Indeed, years later, he said the Russians absorbed most of the cost of actually making the film, leaving him sitting pretty.

Comparable films of scale at the time: *Cromwell* (1970), which also boasted extensive sets, thousands of costumes and battle scenes in Spain, cost a moderately high $9 million. A much bigger production was *Tora! Tora! Tora!* (1970), co-directed by Richard Fleischer, which cost virtually the same as *Waterloo* but in many ways was an even more logistical challenge. A conscious decision had been taken to use non-stars, so the bulk of the budget would be consumed by below-the-line costs. These involved full-sized landlocked plywood sets of a battleship and aircraft carrier, a large assortment of vintage aircraft to maintain and fly, extensive action filming at Pearl Harbor, with no free help from the US military — *everything* had to be paid for. On top of this there was a full Japanese unit, with *three* national directors (one of whom was the great Akira Kurosawa, who, before he was replaced, had spent over $1 million on material that was unusable). To supplement the "realness," a large special effects team worked with a fleet of miniatures, some up to forty feet long.

Richard Fleischer, in his fascinating memoir *Just Tell Me When To Cry*, described filming a hair-raising sequence with a full-sized battleship mock-up, stuffed with explosive special effects, launching too early as a squadron of real planes attempted to get in line, all before they arrive within camera range.

The scale of *Waterloo* was equally monumental, but the vast resources that came with Soviet involvement would have been an enormous saving for Dino, which the two above productions did not have. Whatever the actual budget was, this had been overtaken by the *combined* sold distribution rights ($25 million), which became the *cost* to recoup.

Still, in early 1969, a great deal of cinematic matériel had to be shipped behind the Iron Curtain. "I know that logistically it was incredibly difficult to do," Raffaella De Laurentiis, no stranger herself to mounting a huge movie project, surmised about the challenges her father faced:

> Everything had to be taken into Russia because there was nothing there. So, all the technical equipment, the cameras, the lights, the wardrobe (most of the costumes were probably made in Russia), the props, everything came from outside — the cast, the actors, the transportation. I mean, it was like going to war.

With the deal signed, Dino now had the resources to reconstruct the great battle. How to tell the story with the power of cinema was down to a Ukrainian-born country boy, Sergei Bondarchuk. Just shy of fifty-years-old, Bondarchuk was an impressive and imposing figure — tall with a head of abundant silver hair, penetrating dark eyes and impenetrable face. And Russian down to the very bone — passionate and mystical. He was at the apex of his career, having spent seven arduous years making what is still regarded as one of the greatest films of all time: *War and Peace / Voina I Mir* (1968). His almost superhuman effort had *literally* killed him — twice.

Henry Fonda, Audrey Hepburn and Mel Ferrer in costume for War and Peace *(1956).* AUTHOR'S COLLECTION

Herbert Lom as one of the best screen Napoleons. AUTHOR'S COLLECTION

John Huston as Noah in The Bible *(1965). He was originally signed to direct* Waterloo. AUTHOR'S COLLECTION

Noah leads the animals into the Ark, this was achieved by the trainers walking along side them in a trench. A splendid example of doing-it-for-real.
AUTHOR'S COLLECTION

Sergei Bondarchuk as a rising Soviet film star in the mid–1950s. JOAN BORSTEN VIDOV COLLECTION

CHAPTER 4

Bondarchuk's War and Peace.

The Cold War was at its height when the Soviet film industry mounted a cultural assault on the West. It was a period of tension and unease that culminated in the nearest humanity has yet come to doomsday — the Cuban Missile Crisis in 1962. Through the ebb and flow of Cold War politics, the Russians needed to assert themselves, and they saw cinema as a worthy battleground.

Russian cinema, having flourished in the 1920s with the seminal works of Sergei Eisenstein, Vsevolod Pudovkin and Alexander Dovzhenko, had stultified under the iron grip of Stalin, which resulted in only a handful of films produced per year. Adhering to the dull precepts of socialist realism, these were often heavy propaganda pieces with low entertainment or artistic merit. Stalin's death in 1953 allowed a partial thaw under the new leader Nikita Khrushchev. This led to the film industry being pumped with money and encouraged to expand national production with several semi-autonomous regional units. The biggest of these centred in the capital, and most prestigious, was Mosfilm.

In the late 1950s, this cultural thaw had seen a handful of foreign films reach Soviet cinemas with predictable results. Russian citizens lapped up the colourful, carefree escapism of Hollywood fare. One that became very popular was, rather unsurprisingly *War and Peace* courtesy of Dino De Laurentiis. Soviet cinema goers embraced the English Audrey Hepburn as the heroine Natasha. This provoked a powerful reaction from the intelligentsia, who wrote an open letter exhorting the regime to produce an All-Russian version of one of its greatest and most important works of literature.[140]

It was felt that the scope and scale of the story would be a terrific showcase for the skill and creativity of the rebooted Soviet film industry.

Mosfilm, with its size and influence, picked up the gauntlet. The immense challenge prompted the concept of multiple directors, and several prominent figures were approached. A consensus soon emerged that a single, bold vision was needed, and the brave decision was taken to entrust the entire project to a man with only one directing credit to his name.

Sergei Bondarchuk, a Ukrainian born in 1920, was a child of the Russian Revolution, growing up in tandem with the painful birth pangs of Soviet Communism. Influenced by an uncle, he had displayed an interest in the performing arts from a young age.

> As early as the first class, I performed a role in a play called *The Lost Children*. It was my first character role because I played the part of the father of these children. When I was very young, I played old men. I always had more success playing characters older than myself, and as far as appearances went, I remember that my hair used to be covered in tooth-powder...I wore a towel around my neck to suggest a beard.[141]

Aged seventeen, he declared to his family that he was "going to be an artist" but his "enraged" father instead demanded he become a "reliable" engineer.[142] The stubborn young Bondarchuk persisted and duly entered the Rostov Theatrical College in 1937. He became imbued with the Stanislavsky acting technique. This would be popularised a decade later in the American theatre as the Method; with such proponents as Marlon Brando, Eli Wallach, Eve Marie Saint and Rod Steiger. In simple terms, it advocated that the actor inhabits the mental world of the character. Perhaps the most famous quip regarding the technique was uttered by Sir Laurence Olivier while filming *Marathon Man* (1976). Bemused watching his Method trained co-star Dustin Hoffman, contorting himself mentally and physically to find the "moment," The great theatrical knight is reputed to have said: "Try acting, dear boy."[143] It captures the difference in approach and essence, which we will see will have a part to play in *Waterloo*.

In 1941, the Nazi invasion of Russia interrupted Bondarchuk's career, and he, like almost all his generation, would experience war at first hand. He served in the Red Army and saw active service in the Caucasus. As a release from the tension and carnage of war, he often entertained his comrades with renditions of Russian literature. Like many veterans of all armies and all wars, they rarely admitted the price that has to be paid to fight. Bondarchuk offered a hint of his own emotions in his treatise on acting, *Desire for a Miracle / Zhelanie chuda*: "I belong to the generation that the war found in the prime of life, which took part in it and repaid with their lives for the joy of a peaceful life. The war still leaves a wound in the soul."[144]

Following demob, he was determined to resume his theatrical career. After attending a lecture by leading film director Sergei Gerasimov, who had proposed "each actor should become the director of his role,"[145] Bondarchuk was inspired to become a film artist. Passing twelve exams in one week, his drive and determination were rewarded with a Stalin scholarship having graduated "excellent in all categories." In an early recognition of his talents, Gerasimov cast him in *The Young Guard* (1948), considered one of the most important Soviet films of the 1940s, in which "he gave strong and confident support to the main theme."

Although a tiny part, it brought him to the attention of another prominent director, Igor Savchenko, who was looking for the lead in his next film about a highly temperamental poet and revolutionary in 1840s Czarist Russia. The novice actor soon found himself in great demand. "At this time there were very few films being made...only eight films per annum, and I participated in nearly all of them. It was the most unpleasant time in our cinema...I had to choose whether to work with Savchenko or Pudovkin (the great Silent-Era director and equal of Eisenstein). I chose Savchenko."

It proved to be the right choice, as his role as the eponymous Russian poet in *Taras Shevchenko* (1951) put him on the map. His performance even drew personal praise from Comrade Stalin himself. Through his relationship with Savchenko, he learned the mechanics of film-making. "For me, he was an Academy. From him I learnt everything...editing, scripting...He involved me in all its aspects...So, I can call myself his disciple." A crucial skill Bondarchuk learnt from Savchenko was how to direct actors.

> He prepared the soil for actors and I as an actor worked freely and created freely in front of the camera. For example, if there was an emotional scene he would simply ask, "Are you ready?" and then it took place as a matter of improvisation. My technique as an actor and as a director is that of preparing the soil and allowing nature to create.

Over the next ten years would see Bondarchuk rise to become an actor of international renown, which was an impressive feat for a Soviet artist.

Still in his early thirties, with only a few credits to his name, he was awarded the extraordinary honour of becoming a People's Artist of the USSR. This gave recipients clout and prestige in a regime where such things mattered. Intriguingly, he avoided membership of the Communist Party, which most Soviet citizens considered almost a patriotic duty. Party membership was not a requirement for advancement in creative fields, unless one was angling for bureaucratic promotion. Instead, artists prided themselves on *avoiding* it as a badge of honour; personal success being a mark of one's own hard work and not a state leg-up. As he became an international celebrity, senior officials exerted pressure on him to join, which he later compared to the Hollywood anti-communist "witch-hunts" during the McCarthy era of the 1950s (which had also motivated *Waterloo*'s first director, John Huston to leave the USA for a time).

His portrayal of Othello in Sergei Yutkevich's 1955 film *Otello* also drew praise, with a full-bloodied performance complete with black make-up as he played opposite his future wife, Irina Skobtseva, as the doomed Desdemona. A role in *Escape by Night* (1960) filmed in Italy for Italian director Roberto Rossellini, brought Bondarchuk to a world-wide audience. Now firmly established as one of the country's leading actors, new creative opportunities opened up for him.

> As you remember, we had the "few films policy" — eight films per annum…and then they increased the quantity. It was a state decision. Therefore, when it was decided to shoot a hundred films, more film directors were needed, more film studios, more technicians, more equipment to implement the new plan. Many thought this leap forward could not be achieved in such a short time, but it was fulfilled.

This "leap forward" allowed Bondarchuk to take the inevitable step towards the director's chair.

> I wanted to direct films because as an actor I was only expressing myself…in one of the dimensions of the production. The influence of a director on a production is all-engulfing, and it was for this reason, more freedom for expression, that I became a director.

He made his debut with *Destiny of a Man* (1959), a personal and emotional story of a brutalised Russian POW rediscovering his humanity. Bondarchuk also played the hero, with a raw and truthful performance that cries out against the horror of war. Soviet culture historian John Lind observed that:

> After a decade of tractor-mad Stalin heroes in the USSR, Bondarchuk's *Destiny of a Man* offered us a hero who is visibly terrified, sweats, gets out of breath and cries — and damned well wants to live...Bondarchuk expresses on the screen the enthusiasm of one courting the language of cinema for the first time as a director, yet balancing successfully an explosive style with carefully timed restraint.

The film showcased a recurring motif in his work, that of the importance of nature; presented either lyrically or discordantly. "Life is a continual struggle between good and evil," Bondarchuk explained, "a disease against healthy organisms. Even when the presence of evil is limited, there will still be wars...wars of natural elements, hurricanes, earthquakes...planetary confusion...Einstein stated that absolute calm — is death."[146]

Riding this Soviet New Wave alongside the equally emotional and poetic *The Cranes are Flying* (1957), *Ballad of a Soldier* (1959) and Andrei Tarkovsky's debut *Ivan's Childhood* (1962), his film was immediately regarded as proof of a national cinema that was finding its feet after years of repression and stagnation.

Denise J. Youngblood, an emeritus professor of history at the University of Vermont, a specialist on Russian and Soviet cinema, who has written the only English-language book about Bondarchuk's *War and Peace* film,[147] said this creative bloom played into the West's preconceived ideas of the Soviet state:

> It's important to remember that the filmmakers that have attracted attention outside the Soviet Union are not the filmmakers that Soviet audiences loved. Not because their films weren't great. They were great. But because it suited cold warriors to point out how persecuted important artists were in the Soviet Union. And it's true, avant-garde artists did not adhere to the tenets of socialist realism. It was an anathema to them to make straight forward narrative realist movies. But the fact is that Soviet audiences did not like their movies, refused to see them. The canon outside Russia is defined by the films that nobody saw.

In the propaganda war that both sides of the Iron Curtain were waging, the warm capitalist West's embrace of these Russian exports would have been considered a win by the Soviet authorities. But despite the critical success showered on *Destiny of a Man*, Bondarchuk appeared to many industry veterans too inexperienced to helm *War and Peace*. Also, counting against him was that he was not liked by many of his peers, who widely considered him to be highly egotistical and arrogant. Perhaps an even greater, petty crime, in the ridged hierarchical Soviet state, was that it was felt he had risen too high too fast, without paying his dues. Professor Youngblood observed how he was further patronised by the cultured urban Soviet intelligentsia as little more than a "country bumpkin…but were dead wrong about him," as he was ideally suited for the task:

> He was extraordinarily intelligent, with a strong visual sense. He cared deeply about Tolstoy's novel, was determined that he was going to represent its spirit faithfully, that he was not going to do what he believed King Vidor had done, which is just take some aspects of the story, and throw them on the screen.[148]

Undaunted by the barbs, Bondarchuk was convinced of his own ability. His passion, confidence and determination are clear from one of his letters: "Why is it that this novel, the pride of Russian national character, was adapted in America and released in their cinema halls? And we ourselves cannot adapt it? It's a disgrace to the entire world!"[149]

In 1961, now having been entrusted with the job by Mosfilm, he was determined to erase that disgrace. It would consume the next seven years of his life — and literally kill him.

Leo Tolstoy's 1869 novel is one of the longest and most ambitious works ever written in any language. The plot covers the best part of twenty years of turbulent Russian history beginning in 1805, the year that saw Napoleon beat a coalition of Russia and Austria at the Battle of Austerlitz (see Chapter Two). It draws its primary characters from several Russian aristocratic families, who must navigate the travails of life, love, war and death, before being thrown into the crucible of the French invasion of 1812.

What is often forgotten with these great nineteenth-century tomes is that at the time they were not the preserve of the academic or the student, but the masses. As Professor Youngblood explained, it was warmly embraced by the Russian public as a rallying cry:

When the novel appeared in serialised form, it was like a popular serial would be today. Whether on television or streaming, it was the talk of all educated Russian society...Tolstoy's idea was that Russia had defeated Napoleon in 1812 through the Russian soul and the character of the Russian people, rather than through any military talent.[150]

Where the Dino De Laurentiis/King Vidor version concentrated almost exclusively on the principle civilian characters, Bondarchuk attempts to catch the immensity of the historical forces that threaten to consume Russia, with substantial attention given to many real characters like Napoleon, and the Russian commander Kutuzov. Perhaps only a system with little care for the financial bottom-line could make a movie on this scale.

The budget has been estimated at $100 million in the mid-1960s, although this is a gross exaggeration, perhaps from the pen of a publicist for its later US release; boasting the size of budgets was then seen as a marketable asset! What *is* certain, the Russian State poured many millions of roubles into its production, making it the most expensive ever made during the USSR years.[151] According to the publicity for its later US release, the statistics list construction of 170 outdoor sets such as the streets of Moscow, battlefields, and remote villages. Over 100 indoor sets at Mosfilm studios were created, including a ballroom as "large as the largest in the Winter Palace."[152] The contents of 40 museums across Russia were borrowed as props for the authenticity that Bondarchuk demanded.

Filming began in the fall of 1962 at the Novodevichy Convent in Moscow. The first sequence was of French troops executing "incendiaries" suspected of burning the city. Staged in a cabbage patch under the walls of the convent, it took a month to complete. The camera team supervised by husband and wife, Aleksander Shelenkov and Iolanda Chen, accused the director of acting like a dictator and refusing to act collectively — a serious accusation in a communist society. He blamed them for demanding excessive re-takes for "photographic reasons." What did not help was the substandard film stock they were using.

For such a prestige production, it had been decided to use 70mm, considered the gold standard for epics; a first for a Soviet movie.[153] The Russians had copied the American Todd-AO system during the recent cultural exchange visits, but the Russian manufactured film stock was marred by problems which would continue to plague the rest of the shoot. The cameramen complained it wasn't unusual to find squashed mosquitos embedded in the emulsion, or sprockets holes missing from the edge of the film. The resulting wastage of effort and time would have created inevitable tensions. Bondarchuk had wanted to use the superior and reliable American Kodak Eastmancolor, but was overruled for political and propaganda reasons — he would just have to lump it for the Motherland.

For the cast, Bondarchuk also stepped in front of the cameras to play Pierre, Tolstoy's bumbling hapless hero. Lyudmila Saveleva, an eighteen-year-old ballet dancer, with no previous acting experience, played the story's heroine, Natasha. She, like her character, ages through the course of the four-year production. Bondarchuk explained to John Lind (whose then girlfriend had also been shortlisted for "Natasha"), how he nurtured such an inexperienced actor:

> I did my best to let her nature work for her because Natasha was the symbol of life, everything living…I chose a girl who had never acted before because she had no stamp. No professional ways. She was like a clean white sheet of paper. But in herself she has this loveliness, this pulsating life, and one can look at her for a very long period and see this life in her. It was this human essence that I wanted to preserve and use as the basis for introducing the character Natasha…I played her Beethoven to awake in her some subconscious emotional sides. Even on location or on the set, I laid the ground for her as best I could, to find the right mood for the scenes.[154]

Bondarchuk resurrected careers of several actors who had been censored during the Stalin purges for some of the eighty speaking parts. Most notably Galina Kravchenko, and Anatoli Ktorov (who played Prince Andrei's aristocrat father), neither of whom had worked creatively for decades. He also cast the veteran stage actor/manager, Boris Zakhava, who had presided over Moscow's Vakhtangov Theatre for forty years, as the great Russian General Kutuzov.

Bondarchuk pulled extraordinary, if mannered performances, from all the actors, making them appear like people of the early nineteenth-century rather than of the mid-twentieth. "Psychological analysis is customarily employed to depict characters, but this is a false path." He explained his approach to visualising the book: "The cinema has made it possible to depict the rich spiritual world of Tolstoy's characters, the freshness and simplicity of their perceptions."[155]

To achieve this, "freshness and simplicity" did not come without cost. Vyacheslav Tikhonov, who played the brooding Prince Andrei, was already an established actor, often portraying salt-of-the-earth Soviet heroes. But this imposing six-footer was almost driven to a breakdown by Bondarchuk's unflinching determination to coax a convincing "aristocrat" performance from him. "I essentially had a duel with Tikhonov. I was forced to subordinate him to my will, vision and creative solutions. Maybe this is not good, but, unfortunately, it is the responsibility of directing."

Soon Bondarchuk earned a reputation as a tyrant, as he drove not just himself, but all those around him to the brink and beyond. As the production juggernaut continued, crew members came and went with Bondarchuk's ever demanding behaviour, often a major factor. It was not just Tikhonov who struggled; one actress was so intimidated she even lost her voice. Considered a workaholic who lived in the studio, some described him as a "dictator," while another admired his determination to preserve Russian culture.

Bondarchuk was unapologetic: "The director has studied all the material for the film; he alone knows everything. He is tsar and god."[156] This was ultimately too much for some. The tensions between him and the husband-and-wife camera team came to a head in May 1963, and the pair left after complaining it was impossible to work under such conditions.

After considering more experienced cameramen, the director reluctantly found a replacement in thirty-one-year-old Anatoli Petritsky, who, with little experience but bundles of youthful enthusiasm and self-confidence (plus a hefty dose of ego, he admitted later), stayed the course. Petritsky turned out to be an enormous asset, eventually earning the demanding director's trust and respect. One of his innovative contributions was to shoot the great ball sequence on roller-skates to capture smooth swirling moves. Such shots are now done effortlessly with the Steadicam which allows the camera to glide through space.

For all the finesse and attention paid to *Peace*: the love stories, balls, and a wolf hunt, it is *War* for which this production takes flight. The Soviet army provided around 13,500 troops and a brigade of cavalry, called the 11th Separate made up of 1500 horsemen, which were specially trained for work in films. They drilled the infantry to march at one hundred and twenty-five steps per minute as the French, and the slower seventy-five as their Russian forebears. Extraordinary attention to detail went into the costumes for both French and Russian armies, including the variations that were introduced during the historical time-frame. Sixty cannons were cast and designed to spurt puffs of smoke.

There were four major full-scale action sequences. The biggest was a reconstruction of the Battle of Borodino, which saw the French army grapple with the Russians on the road to Moscow (see Chapter Two). Unable to use the original battlefield, the unit moved to Dorogobuzh in Smolensk Oblast to recreate this epic encounter, which included building huge earthworks of the bloodily contested Raevsky redoubt. For six weeks, beginning in August 1963, the team toiled over the complex sequence which consumed 23 tons of gunpowder, 40,000 litres of kerosene and 10,000 smoke grenades, all artfully deployed by special effects supervisor Vladimir Likhachov.

The sprawling set was divided into zones, with a system of loudspeakers helping to coordinate the troops' movements. Proving himself an actual commander, Bondarchuk directed the armies with clear instructions, but often demanding multiple takes before he was satisfied. This soon exhausted the camera crew, actors and legions of extras, not helped by continual technical and organisational problems, even including a lack of film stock.

The souvenir book for the later USA release gives a flavour of the experience: "The re-creations of the battle scenes were done with such intensity that the luckiest performers were the ones playing the first to fall. As the battle continued to rage about them, they seized upon this opportunity to rest."[157]

The results are awe-inspiring even after half a century, as rows of marching men in meticulously researched uniforms move through plumes of smoke, which alternately cover and then reveal their almost balletic formations. To capture the energy and madness of war, the cameras were strapped onto horses, flown on high wires, and hung from helicopters; all creating an impressionistic maelstrom of carnage and horror.

Although Bondarchuk follows the historical record of the battle, it is Tolstoy who is his *real* guide. Often sequences are highly impressionistic; riderless horses careering madly around, flash cuts of flames, etc. It would be this "confusion" that would bother some critics, but this was central to Bondarchuk's view of war, as Professor Youngblood, explained:

> American critics when the film was released in the US in 1968 did not like the battle scenes. And felt they were too confusing, too chaotic. That was entirely Bondarchuk's point as it was Tolstoy's point. Bondarchuk was a World War II veteran…And it was very important to him, as it was to Tolstoy, to represent the war as horror, not some kind of neat game.[158]

One shot in particular ranks as one of the most awe-inspiring in cinema history. A long tracking shot that moves through a burning village with snatches of intimate vignettes; a soldier being bayoneted, another catching a chicken, all the while in the background thousands of men are fighting, before concluding with a cavalry charge — all perfectly choreographed. A behind-the-scenes film shows the careful precision and timing involved as the camera rolls along an endless stretch of tracks.[159]

There were no reported injuries to actors or soldiers during these scenes, although the same cannot to be said for the horses. Just one example, in the above sequence, we see some horses falling through a bridge onto burning straw. It is believed many horses were harmed or even killed during the shoot.[160]

The arduous weeks of filming left a mark upon the director:

> I recalled with horror the days of the shooting of the Battle of Borodino. Twelve thousand extras for two months are implanted in the mind. Every morning, soldiers dressed in those times were clothed and went on the attack, imitating the techniques of combat of our great-grandfathers. It was necessary to organise all this immense mass of people to avoid injury, which with such large battle scenes, where cavalry takes part, is rarely managed (fortunately, we did).

We should remember that he had to alternate with his other hat — acting.

> I had to transform from the director to "Pierre" and to think about what "Pierre" was doing and thinking at this time. Difficult when at the last minute, before I entered the frame, the news came that there were some scratches on the film, that it was under-exposed, and therefore we had to retake all the scenes shot five days ago.[161]

It was perhaps unsurprising that this Herculean workload would extract a high price. For Bondarchuk, it was a mortal blow. He suffered a massive heart attack and died — for three minutes he was clinically dead — before doctors battled for two hours to resuscitate him. On waking, he is reported to have said: "If I die, let Gerasimov finish it,"[162] (his former teacher and mentor). Rather than leave the production, he opted to rest and convinced the powers that they must allow him to continue. With propaganda over-riding all other considerations, against his wishes they ordered the first two feature-length instalments of the film to be readied for the 1965 Moscow International Film Festival — it would share the grand prize.[163]

With this first deadline reached, death grasped Bondarchuk once more. He suffered another heart attack during which he was again pronounced clinically dead — and survived. "He had two cardiac arrests, two clinical deaths." His daughter Natalya[164] remembers how, despite what would have forced many people to change their lifestyle, her father was not deterred: "He came to and set to work again. It was unbearable. Even for a man of such mighty health as my father was."[165] As a true artist, Bondarchuk would call upon these brushes with mortality to visualise Prince Andrei's death scene.

In the fall of 1965, Bondarchuk was back filming as the unit travelled to many locations across Russia, including: Mozhaysk, Kalinin and Zvenigorod. At one stop, gripped by a Russian winter, Bondarchuk, who was a keen wood carver, made a very impressive snow sculpture of Napoleon. Next day, much to the amusement of the unit, a cameraman had modelled a naked woman in a "frivolous pose." Before either could thaw, a Communist Party official ordered "such disgrace" to be destroyed.[166]

In October 1966, the last sequence was filmed — the Burning of Moscow in 1812. An enormous plywood set was constructed next to the Iosifo-Volokolamsk Monastery, just north of Moscow. Using six cameras with five fire engines standing by, the diesel-fuel soaked "Moscow" was set ablaze by Vladimir Likhachov's effects team. The director recalls special care had to be taken as "Russian extras tend to be lazy. Before this sequence, we had to send assistants round to wake up sleeping extras in dark corners of the set, otherwise they would have been burnt to death."[167]

Petrinsky laid a great length of camera rails that snaked around the set, over which the crew trucked through the flames. The efforts to capture this conflagration on film are death-defying. Behind-the-scenes footage shows a cameraman's bravery as he runs through the inferno with only the most basic of flame-resistant clothing.[168] It was reported that one of the operators was temporarily set on fire as he dollied his heavy 70mm camera through the flames, before being dampened down safely. This extraordinary sequence equals Borodino for sheer visual power; we are thrown by the scruff of the neck into the chaos and destruction, with cinders blowing through the frame as blackened faces scream and scurry about looking half mad. A true vision of hell on earth.

After four years of production, the cameras were finally stilled. It would take the best part of another year to complete post-production on the last two parts. Bondarchuk had chosen another very young key collaborator as his composer, Vyacheslav Ovchinnikov, just thirty-years-old. He had already worked twice with an emerging, visionary talent: Andrei Tarkovsky, on *Ivan's Childhood* (1962), and the mediaeval spiritual epic *Andrei Rublev* (1966). He had not been Bondarchuk's first choice, but Ovchinnikov fused classical and Russian folk music, to create a dynamic score suffused with a lyricism that won the director's approval. The prolific composer was also scoring a contemporary film, and he said that switching between two idioms stimulated him creatively.[169]

At the 1967 Cannes Film Festival it was standing room only, as the spectacular Part Three, *1812*, involving the almost hour-long Battle of Borodino sequence, was shown out of competition. When it hit Soviet screens three months later, the reaction was rather muted, and Russian audiences stayed away. The release of the final part, *Pierre Bezukhov* in November that year, saw a further decline in interest. It was a disappointing conclusion, as hopes had originally been high when the first two parts, *Andrei Bolkonsky* and *Natasha Rostova*, released the previous year, had been greeted with much enthusiasm and success.

As we saw earlier, Western audiences were losing interest in "epic" roadshow fare by the late 1960s, although there is not a direct correlation with the USSR. Professor Youngblood, though, believes the fall off owed a great deal to Soviet social and cultural changes that occurred during the film's protracted gestation:

> There was a real rise in television ownership at right about this time. And fewer Soviets were going to the movies. There was also a really pronounced move by the Soviet movie-going audience in favour of asinine comedies, really lightweight fair. And although Bondarchuk always had the audience in mind, it's a serious film. And by 1967, that time had passed for that among Soviet moviegoers.[170]

Aleksei Romanov of Goskino (Soviet film distributor) remarked: "49 million saw the first part in only five months…our film *War and Peace* did not have a single advertisement."[171] It is difficult to gauge how successful the film was, as some sources maintain that 135 million tickets had been sold in the USSR, suggesting that ultimately it was a success.[172] In an economy that was disinterested in profit, perhaps the question is irrelevant.

Strangely for such a prestige project, the Russian media paid little attention to it with barely a handful of reviews for part one, whereas thousands of articles were published abroad. Some suggest that Bondarchuk was unpopular with the Soviet intelligentsia, perhaps jealousy over the resources he had been given to play with.[173]

Overall, the critical reaction in Russia was mixed: "(the filmmakers)… chose the hardest but truest road. They *tried* to bring Tolstoy's thoughts to the screen…Directors don't like to bring ideas to the screen for fear of boring the viewer…Bondarchuk wasn't afraid of *boring the viewer*."[174]

The quartet of films would be screened in 117 countries around the world in a slightly shorter (409-minute) Export Version.[175] As a subtitled film was usually a hard sell in America, Walter Reade, Jr's Continental Distributors saw an opportunity to market the film as a special event as a limited roadshow release. Purchasing the US rights for $1.5 million, it was shortened and re-cut for American tastes, dubbed into English with narration by Norman Stone. This was known as the Kressel version, named after Lee Kressel of Titan Productions, who supervised the re-editing.

On 28 April 1968, it was premiered in New York, running six hours over two parts, and presented in 70mm. Lyudmila Saveleva and Bondarchuk's wife Irina Skobtseva attended the glittering event, with tickets at the astronomical price of $7.50 ($55 in 2020).

One of those in attendance that evening was critic Roger Ebert, who found his usual aversion to dubbing was quickly overcome: "The voices are so well dubbed into English that after 15 minutes you don't even look at the lips anymore." He was impressed, calling it a "magnificently unique film," heaping praise on the director in being "able to balance the spectacular, the human, and the intellectual…Bondarchuk is able to bring his epic events down to comprehensible scale without losing his sense of the spectacular. And always he returns to Tolstoy's theme of men in the grip of history." He also saw merit in Bondarchuk's performance as Pierre, equating it with "Rod Steiger and acts something like him, with bemused comments to himself and a quiet face concealing a furnace of emotion."[176] *Time Magazine*, though, was divided, finding that, "the movie is awesome in war and pusillanimous in peace."[177]

But most American critics were suitably impressed, with Judith Crist, writing for the *New York Magazine,* full of gushing superlatives: "The finest epic of our time, but also a great and noble translation of a literary masterpiece, surpassing our expectation and imagination." With a year to go before the titanic Cold War space race was due to climax, she believed that judging by their technical cinematic achievement, the winner seemed a foregone conclusion: "Those Russians…! And now, I bet they'll beat us to the moon!"[178]

The Kressel version would continue to be revived for special screenings around the world into the 1990s, in both 35mm and 70mm (unfortunately these later prints wore out because of their fragile magnetic soundtracks, long before the 35mm).[179]

In January 1969, the subtitled Soviet Export version opened in London. Submitted for certification by the BBFC (British Board of Film Classification), a clerical mistake mistimed the print suggesting a 507-minute running time, which has been repeated for many years. The mistake stems from the footage length of the submitted print, which was 70mm being counted as 35mm (there is a 20% frame height difference between the two formats).[180]

A brand-new DCP cinema quality restoration of the original Export Version by Mosfilm in 2019 has now made the Kressel version redundant.[181] Future generations will marvel at the best this film has looked in over fifty years.

It is difficult to do justice to *War and Peace* in words, as it is such an overwhelming cinematic experience. From its opening sequence: which begins with animation of atoms that coalesce and grow, before bursting through the earth onto a beautiful landscape; then the camera pans over a meadow and trees past a river, all overlaid with the gentle hum of nature. Over this, snatches of battle are heard: a gunshot, a cry. Cut to the title card superimposed over clouds, as the music grandly bursts forth with drama and poetry.

Throughout the film, Bondarchuk tries to visualise the psychological state of the characters through the abstract use of sound and idiosyncratic imagery. He uses his 70mm camera with the lightness of a painter's brush and is not afraid to deploy rough handheld camerawork at awkward angles to project the emotional state of the scene. The camera *is* us, the viewer; the sheer dynamic visual bravado cannot be overstated. At other times, he emphasises stillness and stasis by static, wide shots with daringly oblique chiaroscuro lightening.

Noted also is the contribution of the editor Tatiana Likhacheva, who created some often-startling rhythms and juxtapositions. Likhacheva and Bondarchuk experimented with many of the new techniques kick- started by the French *Nouvelle Vague*. These include jump cuts, and flash cuts with just a few frames of flames or shimmering crystal, which are deployed on an almost subliminal level. These compliment some in-camera effects, including fans being fluttered in front of the camera lens during the ballroom sequence. Perhaps some are a little self-conscious but the vast array of such tricks shows Bondarchuk's deep desire to not just illustrate the narrative, but the complex thematic ideas of Tolstoy.

Some critics complained that the film simplified the million-word original — and yes, it does. But unlike many later TV adaptations, notably the two BBC TV versions of 1972 and 2016 (the former with almost total fidelity, and the latter restoring the main characters conceived younger ages), Bondarchuk instead crystallises the *essence* of the book, often not following scenes through with conventional movie narrative progression. It helps to be familiar with the book, and doubtless Bondarchuk assumed a high degree of such familiarity by his Russian audience.

The depiction of Napoleon in the film leaves the viewer in no doubt that he is the cause of all the pain and suffering thus depicted. Vladislav Strzhelchik's performance is one- note and lacks any of the subtlety that almost all the Russian characters display. This seems a deliberate choice by the director rather than a shortcoming of the actor. Although there is great fidelity to the factual record, it is Tolstoy to whom Bondarchuk follows.

Tolstoy's Napoleon is a cypher, a mere channel for vast historical forces that are bigger than just one man. The writer presents the emperor as a pigmy, perhaps more morally bankrupt than evil. Bondarchuk quotes a lengthy passage from the book, to play as narration while Napoleon surveys the vast field of carnage of Borodino:

> And not only for that hour and day were the mind and conscience darkened in that man, on whom the burden of all that had happened lay more heavily than on others. Never, down to the end of his life, had he the least comprehension of good, of beauty, of truth, of the significance of his own acts, which were too far opposed to truth and goodness, too remote from everything human for him to be able to grasp their significance. He could not disavow his own acts, that were lauded by half the world, and so he was forced to disavow truth and goodness and everything human.[182]

These words paint a brilliant assessment of a character, perhaps even invite pity that such a person is incapable of appreciating the simple joys of life. This lack of empathy, that is so often a pre-requisite associated with tyrants, was also described by one of Hitler's secretaries, who said she never recalled the Führer discussing love, in anything other than the most abstract terms.[183]

For Tolstoy and Bondarchuk, it is this love and joy of the everyday trivial lives of their ordinary characters, and by that token, us, the audience, that *War and Peace* celebrates. This is best summed up by the film's closing thought, again taken from the book which ends seven hours of pure, exemplary cinema: "Since corrupt people unite among themselves to constitute a force, honest people must do the same. It is as simple as that."[184]

Nothing is perfect, but flaws aside, Sergei Bondarchuk's *War and Peace* is a towering work of art. As an adaptation, it remains faithful to the book, but where it shines is in capturing the poetic essence of Tolstoy, and in particular a sense of Russia: wild, cold, passionate and immense. It must rank as one of the finest cinematic achievements as an awe-inspiring epic.

Professor Youngblood is in no doubt to whom the accolades must be accorded:

> Nobody but Bondarchuk could have made this film, partly because of his creative instincts, his creative genius, his real understanding of film as a medium…But also because of his perfectionism, and his certainty that he alone knew how to make this film right…Bondarchuk was able to out Hollywood. And I think it was his authoritarian nature that made it possible for this film, actually to come to a conclusion.[185]

With Mosfilm's digital restoration released on Blu-ray in 2019 through The Criterion Collection, a new generation can re-evaluate it free of its Soviet connotations. Modern critics finding much to admire, with Keith Watson writing in *Slant Magazine* describing it as: "less a straightforward adaptation of Tolstoy's novel than a symphonic representation of its themes — its sense of drama, portent, and grandeur."[186]

Bondarchuk believed he had achieved his own goal with the project:

> The main and only task was to get as close to Tolstoy as possible, to convey his feelings, and through them his thoughts, his philosophy…I wanted to rise to Tolstoy and thereby try to rise to his genius, to introduce viewers to it. The task was incredibly difficult, which required tremendous effort, but at the same time inspiring.[187]

After seven years of toil on such a mammoth production, he yearned for a change of pace and artistic challenge: "I'm thinking more and more often about making a film without volleys of guns and human casualties. I am fascinated by Chekhov. So right after *War and Peace* I will shoot *The Steppe*."[188]

As so often happens, fate had other ideas.

In March 1969, Bondarchuk's magnum opus won the Academy Award for Best Foreign Language Film. He could not attend, and instead sent his young star, Lyudmila Saveleva, now blossomed into full womanhood, to accept the award from Jane Fonda at the podium.[189] He, meanwhile, was in Rome, already hard at work on *Waterloo*, shelving Chekhov for another day. "The proposal made by the Italian filmmaker Dino De Laurentiis seemed to me tempting. For any person living on earth, the question of war and peace remains one of the most pressing, exciting issues."[190]

Despite the similarity to his great work, Bondarchuk could not pass up the opportunity to further explore these themes:

> The shooting of Borodino had been most complicated. It was difficult first because of its scope. Secondly, these were not merely battle scenes but involved a particular theme: the problem of victory and defeat. I was convinced I would not touch such material again. But when the film was released, I was dissatisfied. The theme seemed unfinished.

He saw the new project as an unofficial sequel which picked up the story after the infamous retreat from Moscow.

> To follow Napoleon — A sick man — rotting inside; but who would not lie down, not while madly caught up in the force of his megalomania which led to Waterloo…(it) was more Napoleon's defeat than anyone's victory. There weren't any victors — 140 thousand troops — 52 thousand dead. For me, a film about War is a film against War.[191]

As he began work on *Waterloo*, he must have wondered if he could surpass his previous work within the constraints of commercial cinema, and achieve his noble aim.

Soviet-era postcards of the film star couple, Sergei Bondarchuk and his wife Irina Skobtseva, showing some of their popular acting roles. The two met during the making of Othello *(1955).* IVO BLOM & PAUL VAN YPEREN COLLECTION

Sergei Bondarchuk, dressed as Pierre, checking a piece of the troublesome 70mm film stock probably while shooting the immense battle sequences for War and Peace, *with Lyudmila Savelyeva as Natasha, out of costume.*
AUTHOR'S COLLECTION

Irina Skobtseva as the glamorous Helene (left) in a "Peace" scene. AUTHOR'S COLLECTION

Members of the 11th Separate Cavalry regiment splendidly dressed as Russian Hussars for War and Peace. © SHAHID SHANTYZ

The novelisation based on H.A.L Craig's 1968 draft screenplay. It includes scenes and dialogue not in the final film. AUTHOR'S COLLECTION

CHAPTER 5

"These Are The Battle Orders, Sire."

Since the dawn of cinema, three historical characters have been portrayed with the most regularity: Jesus Christ, America's 16th President, Abraham Lincoln and finally, Napoleon. The first recorded performance of the Corsican on celluloid was back in the last year of the nineteenth-century, in the film, *Amann* (1899), named after the then popular British impersonator, which also featured a "Duke of Wellington." Many films followed, often taking a tiny snap of history and layering on a sickly coating of romance.

In the immediate years before the First World War, European filmmakers had the ambition and the resources to mount larger productions, as we have seen with the Italians in Chapter One. A company with a name that projected the seemingly unassailable image of the most powerful empire in the world — The British and Colonial Kinematograph company — mounted what is considered Britain's first cinematic epic. Directed by an American, Charles Weston, at a cost of £1,800 (£210,000 in 2020), *The Battle of Waterloo* (1913) was filmed near Irthlingborough in Northamptonshire. Hundreds of residents were employed as extras, and there were so many volunteers that two shoe factories in the town had to close for lack of workers. It was reported some 2,000 "soldiers" and 1,000 horses with 50 cannons were used; although it should be noted, such hyperbole has always been deployed to sell epics. As the British army still had horsed cavalry regiments, a squadron of the 12th (Prince of Wales's) Royal Lancers was loaned to the production.

The regimental historian recorded:

> An accommodating American made the rounds of all the pubs at night to pay for drinks. The fact that Napoleon could not ride

and that a sergeant in the regiment appropriated Wellington's boots nearly prevented the film being made and "*C*" Sqn from taking part in the most exciting, best paid and least painful battle of the regiment's long history.[192]

As the art of filmmaking was still developing, it was photographed with simple, limited camera setups, which allowed this complex production to be wrapped in just five days.

Running a then still rare ninety minutes, the film was a huge success both in the UK and abroad. It received mixed critical reviews, echoing the same complaints epics still receive to this day. *Bioscope*, a British film journal, praised the action scenes: "from the point of view of an ordinary soldier in the thick of the battle,"[193] but found there was almost no dramatic or human interest. Thought lost like so many other Silent-Era films, some twenty minutes of *Battle of Waterloo* turned up in 2000, and the find gives a tiny glimpse of this early British attempt at an epic.

Comedian Fred Pimple saw an opportunity and spawned a parody, *Pimple's Battle of Waterloo* (1913), which featured Napoleon on a pantomime horse coupled with a bit of contemporary politics, as he is mobbed by a group of suffragettes! The "battle" begins after the toss of a coin for the first shot, and then followed by a charge by a troop of Boy Scouts.

It was France that produced what may be the most significant film about Napoleon to date. Abel Gance, a director with much in common with Napoleon, dreamed expansive visions. Inspired by his idol D. W. Griffith, Gance had already produced two very long films: *J'Accuse* (1919) and *La Roue* (1923). Resembling the nineteenth-century novels of Dickens and Victor Hugo, both these silent movies ran between four to nine hours, incorporating a mixture of melodrama and envelope-pushing cinematic storytelling techniques, with a particular emphasis on "rapid cutting," also known as "Russian cutting" — typified by Eisenstein's *Battleship Potemkin* (1926). Gance took the evolving art of editing to the next level creating dizzying montages sometimes involving cross-cutting between single frames.

Even as he started working on his *magnum opus*, the Silent-Era was drawing to a close; Sound with all its initial technical deficiencies would smother Gance's bravado style. Starring Albert Dieudonné in the titular role, *Napoléon vu par Abel Gance* (1927) consumed the energies of Gance and the finance of his backers. His planned multi-part film ended up being a five-hour tale of just the first steps of Napoleon on the road towards his destiny.

From a snowball fight, to Napoleon's invasion of Italy and intersecting the French Revolution, it is an extraordinary piece of cinema. The central hero is shamelessly romanticised; presented as a Man of Destiny, foretold to achieve glorious things untroubled by self-doubt or conscience. The hagiography slips into farce with a ludicrous subplot of a servant girl's unrequited love, complete with a flower-draped shrine dedicated to the diminutive general. But this aside, the film succeeds in conveying something of the magnetic appeal and power of the man and his turbulent times.

Gance was an avowed pacifist as projected so forcefully with *J'Accuse* (1919), and its strident disgust at the recent bloodshed of the Great War. To some critics, his biographical portrait perpetuated the Napoleon myth without any criticism or irony, with one denouncing it, in the era of Mussolini as: "a Bonaparte for apprentice fascists."[194] The fervent young nationalist Charles de Gaulle, future President of the Republic, was ecstatic when he attended its Paris premiere.

Gance countered the barbs by promising a more nuanced representation in the planned five later films. Seeing the moment that Bonaparte crowned himself Emperor thus turning to "the dark side" as the thematic and narrative pivot, he believed it was necessary to romanticise him as a young man so audiences would realise the difference. One wonders whether his artistic sensibility was too baroque and operatic to have pulled him back from the desire to create a visual deluge of high drama.

This is well represented in one sequence, which has the intensity of a Beethoven symphony. Gance inter-cuts the tumultuous energy and barely restrained violence of the revolutionary National Assembly dominated by Robespierre and Danton, with Napoleon struggling to sail a tiny rowing boat. The camera literally lurches back and forth to simulate both the natural and human storm.

Gance ends his work with an extraordinary visual effect, as the single square screen triples to create a panoramic image of the French army marching into Italy. His concept is described in the script in suitably grandiose terms:

> The broad panorama will now give way to separate action on each of the three screens, making possible extraordinary juxtapositions of images. Every symbol becomes palpable. The cinema enters a new era; from the melodic, it becomes the symphonic. The orchestration of the images on three screens will render

tangible the symphonic rhythm of the overture to this Iliad: the *Marseillaise* of the image.[195]

Dubbed *Polyvision*, it deployed three cameras and subsequently three projectors to show a super-wide image. Serving as the climax of the five-hour plus film, *Polyvision* was undeniably impressive, and the visual pyrotechnics Gance serves up in the final half hour of the film are truly mind-bending. The expansive panorama of *Polyvision* cascades into multiple images, flashing across the three panels in a light show that prefigured *2001*'s Stargate sequence, and the later visual cacophony of the digital age.

Yet for all the technical and narrative bravado, the film was a commercial failure, and only released in a highly truncated form, minus the *Polyvision* climax, in the USA. *Variety* summed up the nonplussed stateside response, then at the apex of the Jazz Age: (The film) "doesn't mean anything to the great horde of picture house goers over here…Nap wasn't good looking enough, and they didn't put in the right scenes for the flaps here."[196]

Its dynamic wide-screen concept would lie dormant for a quarter of a century until Cinerama (see Chapter One) adapted the visual concept but ignored the thematic possibilities. For decades the film would only exist in fragments before an obsessed English teenager, Kevin Brownlow, embarked on a lifelong quest to restore it. In his preface to his own book on the film, the renowned movie historian (whose contribution to film preservation is legendary), is in no doubt over Gance's place in the Seventh Art:

> If D.W. Griffith gave cinema the start, Gance grabbed the infant by the hand and gave it a breathless rush through life. Like a benevolent Mephistopheles, he showed it what its future might be. He took the cinema further, technically and aesthetically, than any of his contemporaries.[197]

In 1980, the first fruits of Brownlow's effort reached a new audience, including the present author, then but a callow teenager. Sitting in a packed auditorium at the Empire Leicester Square, and seeing it with a full orchestra conducted by Carl Davis, it was an absolutely extraordinary experience that kick-started a lifelong love of cinema — and led eventually to this book. As of 2021, Brownlow has resurrected five and half-hours, including most of the *Polyvision* sequences.[198]

The restoration is never finished. There's a scene to be dropped into the first reel, but whenever you make an alteration, you face the incredible cost of re-copying all the scores! So, you need a very good excuse. The French are restoring it again — and apparently, they have fresh material; Georges Mourrier is doing it at the Cinémathèque Française.[199]

As Hollywood wired for Sound, Europeans were making the last Silent films. One of these was a German production of *Waterloo* (1929), directed by Karl Grune, and starred a very effective Charles Vanel as Napoleon, in a story weighted towards the undeniably important Prussian contribution to the battle with Otto Gebuhr playing Blucher. While it boasted some spectacular scenes, the extras in the battles seem remarkably feeble and half-hearted, many of whom were no doubt exhausted veterans of the Great War. The film, at least in part, would enjoy decades of exposure as for many years it was shown every day at the Waterloo museum on the battlefield (the author saw it there in 1980). It was an impressive example of the skill and ambition of Weimer cinema, that had already produced such classics as *Faust* (1926) and *Metropolis* (1927) before the dark slide into Nazism.

The dying days of the Third Reich would produce another Napoleonic-themed film that was designed to galvanise the German *Volk*, and imbue them with a sense of sacrifice for the Führer. *Kolberg* (1945) was a semi-historical tale of the city's heroic defence against Napoleon's armies in 1806, following the Prussian defeat at Jena (see Chapter Two). It was directed by the regime's star talent, Veit Harlan, and starred the Aryan goddess, Kristina Söderbaum. The film was the baby of propaganda chief, Goebbels, who wistfully saw it as his, and the regime's apotheosis. With his clout, he could divert badly needed men and resources from the war to "fight" in the immense battle scenes,[200] all photographed in the rusty brown hues of Agfacolor. When the film was finally finished in early 1945, its intended audience was huddled in cellars and bunkers as the Red Army closed in on Hitler's Reich. Although it wears its propaganda theme brashly upon its sleeve, *Kolberg* remains an impressive and spectacular film despite serving one of history's most repulsive regimes.

Hollywood had periodically flirted with Napoleonic-themed films, but usually emphasising the romance. MGM's *Conquest* (1937) starred an affable and charming Charles Boyer as Napoleon, who woos the Polish countess Marie Walewska, played by a sultry Greta Garbo. It is a fine piece of Golden Age Hollywood romance with a first-class script, director, stellar performances and all with that unmistakable MGM glamour and glitz. *Variety* felt the lead had captured the essence of the historical figure: "Boyer plays the love scenes with brusque tenderness, and makes the character understood as a blazing individualist acting under reckless urges for power."[201]

British cinema, meanwhile, made a contribution that would make the most Philistine Hollywood producer blush with embarrassment. *The Iron Duke* (1935) starred a diminutive George Arliss at the titular player in a performance that seems to be more gargoyle than glorious hero. The veteran thespian had carved out a niche playing famous historical characters: Benjamin Disraeli, Cardinal Richelieu, Alexander Hamilton, Voltaire and the brothers Mayer and Nathan Rothschild. Many of these were charismatic tour de forces strongly influenced by the melodramatic Victorian stage of his youth; his aging Wellington was not his finest hour. At least some effort was afforded to the battle scenes thanks to the generous help of the War Office, even if the direction was poor:

> The film, surprisingly enough, is not at its best in its dramatisation of Waterloo, which has been so simplified that it seems a rather placid affair on the screen…Mr Arliss's Wellington, the authors have arranged numerous dialogic whimsies to illustrate the conqueror's benign and gentle humours.[202]

It appears the British public were unconcerned and eagerly lapped it up; *The Iron Duke* became the ninth most popular film at the box office that year.[203]

The war years would see Napoleon deployed as a surrogate Adolf Hitler in the fight against fascism. His unseen, nefarious presence lurks in the background of Winston Churchill's favourite film, *That Hamilton Woman* (1941). Laurence Olivier played a winged Lord Nelson who dallies with his real-life wife Vivian Leigh as the eponymous home wrecker, before sailing to his destiny in a spirited recreation of Trafalgar. His Corsican nemesis came out of the shadows to spar with Robert Donat as Britain's prime minister, *The Young Mr. Pitt* (1942), which detailed his efforts to build the Royal Navy in time for Nelson's decisive victory, with a clear parallel to equipping the Royal Air Force to do battle with Hitler's Luftwaffe.

Czech–English actor Herbert Lom essayed a brief but memorable Napoleon. His dark, brooding looks were perfectly suited for the role for which he would repeat for Dino's *War and Peace* (discussed in Chapter Three); full of pent-up energy and barely concealed aggression, he delivers one of the very best portrayals of the emperor on film. This most versatile actor would perhaps be best remembered as the long-suffering foil Chief Inspector Dreyfus, to Peter Sellers' inept Inspector Clouseau in the *Pink Panther* series.

In 1954, with the newly introduced CinemaScope process, Henry Koster would direct Marlon Brando as a brooding Napoleon in the full flush of the Method, wooing Jean Simmons in *Desirée* — another love story. It prompted *The Washington Post* to comment painfully: "a feast to the eyes and a torture to the ears, intelligence and sensibilities."[204]

The following year the French attempted to reclaim their hero in a three-hour colour epic — *Napoléon* (1955). It was directed by Sacha Guitry, a distinguished playwright and actor, who had stirred up controversy during the wartime occupation with accusations of collaboration with the Nazis. That he was considered a divisive figure is clear from his obituary: "his plays are composed with a carelessness which argues a very frail artistic conscience, while literary purists can prove that the language in which they are written is execrable French."[205]

Without seeing the rest of his *oeuvre*, it is difficult to see where *Napoléon* ranks; but it is a dismal affair. Guitry plays Napoleon's duplicitous courtier Talleyrand, who narrates a gallop through the emperor's life with Daniel Gélin and Raymond Pellegrin, sharing the titular role with reasonable credibility. Unfortunately, it plays like a *very* dull history lesson, devoid of drama and conflict — all tell, but little show.

The battle scenes, and there are many, merely comprise of extras running hither and thither all against the same rocky location background. An army of thespian talent troops past the camera with little to distinguish themselves: Yves Montand, Maria Schell, and even Erich von Stroheim and Orson Welles.

The production's sole saving grace is the use of real palaces in the shape of Malmaison and Fontainebleau, and the Palace of Versailles. It is a hagiographic work which again perpetuates the Napoleonic legend with much twisting and glossing over of facts. At one point, a character asks: *"What about Trafalgar?"* Guitry as Talleyrand waves the tedious question away as irrelevant: *"Leave that to the English."*

Again, to echo his obituary: "There is nothing nearer to idealism than an occasional pretty fancy in sentiment — a sentiment which was always entirely mundane and as entirely selfish as sentiment can well be." To a group of "Young Turks" — Jean-Luc Godard, François Truffaut, Alain Resnais and Agnès Varda etc, — about to unleash *La Nouvelle Vague*, the film stood firmly in the camp of conservative *Papa cinema* that they wished to shake up.

If Guitry failed to breathe life into this epic, perhaps Abel Gance could with a return to the subject thirty years after his own *Napoléon*, with an attempt to re-stage *Austerlitz* (1960), the emperor's greatest battle. The film is a pale shadow of the former work with a legion of cameos, again including Orson Welles, trying to breathe life into a creaking old-fashioned movie. The battle, when it finally arrives, is a weak mess of charging extras, inter-cut with studio interiors. Pierre Mondy gives a rich and charismatic turn as Napoleon, but cannot save a disappointing work by an ageing master sadly well past his prime.

Except for Bondarchuk's *War and Peace*, Napoleonic subjects were thin on the ground during the mid-1960s.[206] Dino must have hoped the time was right to revisit this colourful and dramatic era, as he hired for a considerable $121,000 (nudging towards a $1 million in 2020), Irish writer H.A.L. Craig to pen a screenplay for *Waterloo*.[207]

Known as Harry, Henry Armitage Llewellyn, H.A.L. Craig was born in County Cork, Ireland in 1921. Raised as a southern Protestant, he grew up in rural Limerick, where his father was the local vicar of the tiny parish of Kilkeedy. Literature was in Craig's blood from an early age, and soon after finishing school he published a collection of verse. After seven years at Trinity College in Dublin studying classics, he determined to be a professional writer. In 1962, he explained to *The Cork Examiner* that he had "always contrived to live by his writing, which has included verse, dramatic and film criticism, and books on subjects ranging from poker to Ben Jonson's *Discoveries*. He has avoided any form of regular employment on the grounds that, since writing is so painful to him, security would too easily persuade him to give it up."[208]

Growing up in the impoverished Irish countryside, Craig was deeply disturbed by the levels of poverty he saw. Often going hungry himself, he took to his bike to rally lowly paid farm labourers to the Workers' Union of Ireland. As a former member of the communist party, he was one of a number of far-left activists who infiltrated the Irish Labour Party and was considered a firebrand for his extremist views.

Craig was able to give voice to his criticism of the deeply conversative Ireland of the 1940s by joining the influential literary journal *The Bell*, under the editorship of Sean O'Faolain, "an outspoken liberal voice at a time of political and intellectual stagnation, fiercely critical of censorship, Gaelic revivalist ideology, clericalism, and general parochialism."[209]

In 1944, Craig criticised his fellow Protestants in Ulster for their anti-Catholic discrimination with economic factors rather than creed, being the primarily motivation, declaring it was an outrage that such things should be done in the name of "our religion."[210]

In 1948, a move to Britain with a job on the *Manchester Guardian* did not still his passion for politics. In 1956, during a BBC discussion programme, he raised heckles with his support for the IRA's border campaign, a foretaste of the violent thirty-years in Northern Ireland known as "The Troubles," which began a decade later. The national broadcaster was as ever caught in the crossfire of balance, bowed to establishment pressure to present the alternative Unionist case on television.

For this avowed communist and patriotic Irishman, it is interesting that he not only joined the BBC as a scriptwriter (allegedly, potential staff with left-wing views were vetted by a British Intelligence, MI5, with a representative lurking in a remote back room in Broadcasting House in London), but also penned Queen Elizabeth II's Christmas radio address to the Commonwealth in 1958. Much of Craig's output for the corporation had historical themes with an oblique political slant; like fellow left-wing and future screenwriter Robert Bolt, Craig wrote a radio script about Sir Thomas Moore called *Blame not the Bard*. Bolt famously retold the story of Henry VIII's doomed chancellor in *A Man for All Seasons*, before penning three of David Lean's great epics, beginning with *Lawrence of Arabia*. Also working on the BBC Overseas Service, Craig made several radio documentaries, including the Renaissance artist Benvenuto Cellini, and the last voyage of the Jacobean polar explorer Henry Hudson.

Although he married Peggy Anthony in 1955 and they had three children, it was rumoured he had more with other women. He was a notorious womaniser, with a reputation for "cutting a swathe" through female BBC employees. While acknowledging his charm, one of his "casual liaison's" Nuala O'Faolain believed he was incapable of a non-sexual female friendship with a woman, and had "complete moral empiricism"[211] which made him oblivious to the effect of his behaviour on others. His daughter, Siobhan S. Craig, though, believes this aspect of his personality is "somewhat exaggerated and sensationalised."

Craig was a man with huge appetites which were fuelled by chain-smoking and a fondness for the bottle. In this he found many like-minded male friendships which included fellow Irishman Peter O'Toole, along with Marlon Brando, and director John Huston. The two had worked on a script for a film about the Irish struggle against England in the early part of the century. Based on the novel *O'Houlihan's Jest* by Rohan O'Grady, this was apparently "expressionist" and according to Brando, the best he had ever read.

While this film was never made, it is easy to surmise that Huston asked Craig to write *Waterloo*. In 1968, three years into the assignment, Craig moved with his family to Rome, where he would live and work until his premature death ten years later. As well as *Waterloo*, he wrote two more historical war films: *Anzio* (1968) and *Fraulein Doktor* (1969), as well as another Napoleonic subject, albeit a comedy, *The Adventures of Gerard* (1970), based on Conan Doyle's breezy Napoleonic stories (this was penned in the early 1960s before he became involved in the Dino project).

Following *Waterloo*, he would write two more epics, with Arabic-themes, for director Moustafa Akkad: *The Message* (1977) and *Lion of the Desert* (1980), both starring Anthony Quinn, and the latter with a cameo by Rod Steiger as Mussolini.

Describing himself as a spiritual seeker, these collaborations with Akkad demonstrated Craig's abiding interest and affection for Islam, as his daughter, Siobhan Craig, a film history academic, explained:

> He was deeply engaged with both films, which were conceived by Moustapha as a way of fostering understanding of both Islam and colonialism in the west using Hollywood technology and techniques so that audiences would be drawn to them. Harry was very committed to this, both politically and spiritually...There was definitely some religious controversy surrounding the making of *The Message*. While he was writing the script, Harry lived for several months in Cairo, where he regularly consulted with the leaders of the four main sects of Islam.

In 1977, he wrote a novel, *Bilal*, a reverent retelling of the story of Mohammed. It emphasised the social justice elements over the religious in the Prophet's early preaching; an echo of Craig's early trade union and communist affiliations. Many wondered whether this Irish Protestant ever converted to the faith, particularly as his friends wryly noted his fondness for alcohol. According to his daughter, Siobhan: "He never converted, but found Islamic religion and history deeply moving. His novel, *Bilal*, reflects this."

In 1978, at the time of his death just six weeks after being diagnosed with terminal cancer, Craig was working on an epic script about Saladin, the legendary Islamic ruler who reconquered Jerusalem from the Crusaders.

While his talents ranged across many literary fields, some believed that his film work was probably his weakest. This is refuted by his daughter: "I disagree with the assessment that his film work didn't live up to his potential. His screenwriting career really only lasted about 12 years, and was cut off by his early death. He did make a lot of films in a rather short time. Financial considerations in the film industry, of course, greatly affected what films were made."[212]

A screenplay is a blueprint for the goals and intentions of the filmmakers. So far, two drafts for *Waterloo* have come to light. Unfortunately, the author has only seen the later one, dated 31 December 1968 written by H.A.L. Craig.

This draft runs to 135 pages. Formatting for screenplays had been formalised with the introduction of Sound in late 1920s Hollywood. In simple terms, all screenplays to this day work on a rule of thumb: one page equals one minute of screen time. It may appear arbitrary but as most scripts are dialogue led, over 120 pages it usually proves to be broadly correct. This standardisation allows producers to estimate the eventual budget based on the number of scenes set indoors or outdoors, etc. Although the scenes would ebb and flow, the final duration of the film would be 133-minutes.

The other draft, alluded to earlier, is labelled "revised final shooting script July 27, 1968," also penned by Harry Craig in collaboration with the renowned Frenchman Jean Anouilh. This distinguished dramatist, whose career spanned five decades, was an interesting choice. Though his work ranged from high drama to absurdist farce, he is best known for his 1944 play *Antigone,* an adaptation of Sophocles, which was seen as an attack on Marshal Pétain's Vichy government. One of France's most prolific writers, who often used historical themes to discuss philosophical ideas in what he dubbed *pièces costumées* (costume plays). These include *Becket* based on the murder of Thomas Becket, which was successfully filmed in 1964 with Richard Burton and Peter O'Toole (produced by Paramount, who were keen to repeat this star partnership for *Waterloo*). Anouilh believed his *pièces costumées* should centre around an "enlightened" character seeking "a moral path in a world of corruption and manipulation."[213]

How far these intellectual concepts made their way into the screenplay is unknown. Hiring two writers from the former combatant countries was probably a wise political decision, as Anouilh's name would have helped to pacify the all-important Gallic intellectuals. It is worth noting he was paid about $21,000,[214] less than a *sixth* of Craig's salary, whether this reflects his smaller contribution, or a less accomplished agent, is difficult to say.

The jointly named draft of July 1968 surfaced on an auction site in the mid-2000s. Despite much effort, the author could not locate it, but a couple of points can be made from the scant evidence available. Firstly, it was ready to go, hence "shooting script" but if the dates are correct, the eventual director Sergei Bondarchuk had only signed on in May 1968. He must still have been getting up to speed on the project, and therefore his contribution would have been limited. Also, it runs a colossal 224 pages, which equates to almost four hours, which suggests at one point a much longer roadshow film was planned.

By the time of the December '68 draft, Bondarchuk was immersed in the project, and the story he wanted to tell. Pointedly, Anouilh has gone from the title page, leaving Craig as the sole author, and the script is 90 pages shorter, which suggests a significant overhaul. Why Anouilh left the project is unclear, but his non-credit on the film, or in any other publicity, suggests it was not amicable.

There are three key elements to all screenplays — only two of which reach the audience. The first is the structure of the story which, barring some tweaks in post-production, will largely stay intact. This is true of the 1968 draft, which closely resembles the finished film; detailing the twists of fate that brought Napoleon and Wellington together to the fateful battlefield. See Appendix for a précis of the draft.

It fairly closely echoes the historical timeline but in the interests of drama conflates and compresses some events: notably cross-cutting Napoleon's invasion with the Duchess of Richmond's ball. In reality, his forces had crossed the border well over twelve hours before. The dramatic narrative advantages are too obvious to mention. Also, it would be a hard sell to a mid-twentieth-century audience to buy the fact that news of the momentous invasion would take over half-a-day to travel just thirty miles, even in the age of the horse. The film does correctly suggest that Wellington, was already "*aware Napoleon had crossed the border,*" thanks to rumour, when it is confirmed by the mud-splattered Prussian general Muffling, whose appearance shatters the party spirit in the ballroom.

Another compression is removing the general inactivity of 17 June 1815, when all sides paused for breath following the twin battles of Quatre Bras and Ligny. The script suggests these encounters are directly followed by a retreat in the pouring rain, ready for the big, final encounter the following day. Again, this change heightens the tension and maintains the story momentum. Finally, the Prussians are depicted arriving at Waterloo in just the nick-of-time, whereas in reality their forces were engaged in a slow battle of attrition on the French flank over many hours.

While most of the script deals with the four days of the campaign, the prologue is set a year earlier, as Napoleon has been forced back to Paris by overwhelming forces. From this opening scene in which Napoleon is forced to abdicate by his marshals, we encounter the biggest problem with the script, and the second principal element of a screenplay — its most apparent — the dialogue. While there are some real gems that capture character and nuance, much of it, to be polite, is idiosyncratic at best, and at worst — appalling.

The first line of dialogue has Napoleon saying: *"I will not consent to be a fallen statue."* It is a clunky line that may have sounded better in another language — there are many more. A little later, Napoleon fires back at the marshals: *"I despise ingratitude as the most foul defeat of the heart. Do you hear me, Ney? Pick up your scurrilous paper and go."* It sounds translated *into* English, probably a rewrite of the Craig screenplay.

One line, which must have caused a ripple of school-boy giggles amongst the British cast, has Napoleon, whilst surveying his enemy's dispositions, musing: *"I'll know the length of this English aristocrat in the first hour."* This double entendre around measurement, which wouldn't have been out of place in a Talbot Rothwell-penned *Carry On* comedy with Sid James, et all, was replaced by Steiger: *"…calibre of this English aristocrat…"* An obvious example of a blurred translation.

In contrast, much of the dialogue for the British characters is better: *"I don't know what they'll do to the enemy, but, by God, they frighten me,"* and mostly survives to the screen. One can surmise this was the work of Craig, while the "French" lines were penned by Anouilh amongst others, and then translated.

Perhaps the problem stems from these additional writers; with Bondarchuk and an Italian, Vittorio Bonicelli, sharing the final writing credits.[215] Bonicelli was a Dino regular having collaborated on *The Bible* (albeit uncredited), and written two TV series, including one based on Homer's *Odyssey*. He also wrote Vittorio De Sica's well-received, *The Garden of the Finzi-Continis* (1970).

Uncredited were three more writers, including veteran MGM producer Samuel Marx, who was responsible for the *Lassie* films amongst others during his 50-year career. Marx was in semi-retirement by the mid-1960s. His name as producer appears in a 1965 trade announcement with plans for a Waterloo film,[216] to be penned by novelist Elliott Arnold, best known for his 1947 novel *Blood Brother*, which was successfully adapted as the acclaimed 1950 western *Broken Arrow*. Arnold's screenwriting career was limited and unremarkable with the 1963 epic *Kings of the Sun*, a reputable highlight. While Richard Burton was mentioned to play Wellington; it appears the Marx/Arnold project was soon subsumed into Dino's, which was announced a few months later. Arnold's contribution was minimal and his name quickly disappears (he was not paid anything for his contribution by the Italian producer). Marx would stay briefly attached as an associate producer during John Huston's tenure on the project, while his scripting contribution is not clear, he received a hefty $30,000 for his trouble, second only to Craig.[217]

Renowned translator of classic literature (Camus and Gogol), Edward O. Marsh, was also hired at some point, presumably for his skills with Anouilh's French script, if so, we can say this was not his finest hour.[218]

On the page, Napoleon is a chancer and gambler: "*Elba? Of all places, why Elba? (he shrugs) I had better take what I can get.*" Little of the charisma that inspired armies is on display, although something of the cynical calculation, devoid of empathy, is successfully suggested with: "*A field of glory is never a pretty sight. But still...sixteen thousand Prussian corpses: Slap that news on the wall of Paris.*" Perhaps like many tyrants, a sneaking doubt as to posterity's verdict prays on the ego: "*I have made a mark in this world, haven't I, Drouot?*" And later, again: "*I feel there is something in these fields...in the clouds...in the air here...What will men say of me...I wonder?*" But there are many lines that attempt to portray the gravitas, but limply slip into verbiage: "*Surrender Soult? It is a gesture I have never made. I am not rehearsed in surrender.*" Finally, staring defeat in the face, he muses: "*Everything was won, then everything was lost. Twenty years gone in an afternoon.*"

There is almost no attempt to peek behind the mask, and at least suggest what motivates a man to order so many lives to fight for him, or fears that may prey on his mind. At one point, a clap of thunder motivates him to muse: "*We are in accord.*" Perhaps this suggests he sees himself as a god (of war), being so convinced he is above human concerns and weaknesses. It is an effective moment, but is left as no more than an "image" and never developed through the following pages.

The script attempts to pit Napoleon and Wellington in a mental tug of war, but neither is given very much meat. While the Duke appears to have even less to chew on, there are some nuggets. He is presented as a cool, aloof patrician with a healthy respect for his opponent: "*So I give him *'Fair Play'. I admire the enthusiasm he inspires. In a field of battle, his hat is worth fifty-thousand men...but he is not a gentleman."* He is foremost a professional soldier who reluctantly accepts the ghastly aspect of his trade: *"When you're in the presence of so many brave men, who are about to cut each other's throats, it is best not to be amused."* And later, as the guns fall silent: *"Sir, the French have fought me most honourably all day. I beg you to allow whoever's left to go home."*

One brief moment allows a brief peek behind the mask of command. It is during the disastrous charge of the Scots Greys, where driven by blood lust the cavalry loses all control, so Wellington orders a trumpeter to sound "recall." After a few fruitless moments where the shrill sound is producing nothing but annoyance: WELLINGTON *reaches out and pushes the* TRUMPET *from the* BOY's *lips. "Stop that useless noise (apologetically). You'll hurt yourself."* It nicely captures the mounting frustration of a general unable to maintain control of his troops, with the all-too-common irritations of loud sounds chiselling at one's patience. Unlike his opponent, the line suggests this great commander possesses concern and empathy for his men. It is good screenwriting; doing several things and it would survive to the screen.

It is Wellington's last line in the script, taken from the historical record, that plainly displays his humanity: *"I hope to God I've fought my last battle. I have lost some of my dearest friends today."* As we will see, both lead actors added and enhanced their dialogue to breathe some life into their characters.

Conventional wisdom holds that in drama the protagonist and antagonist must interact directly through conflict. Perhaps a modern interpretation would have the two commanders in some kind of man-to-man face/off. Luckily, the script and the film steer well away from this temptation. Much of the generated tension is through each commander trying to outthink the other. This is most effectively achieved by the cross-cutting between the two men during the storm-tossed night before the battle, as they each ponder their options.

While Wellington believes the mud *"will help us,"* he is acutely aware it also slows his saviour in the shape of *"Blucher and that could beat us."* Straight cut to Napoleon's headquarters, and a similar concern about the large detachment of the French army he ordered to follow Blucher. Despite an outward show of control: *"The roads are the same for everyone. Grouchy must walk* faster," there is a sense of doubt hovering at the back of Napoleon's mind regarding his opponent lined up across the opposite ridge: *"Why is he giving me his army? What do we not see?"* When one of his marshals suggest that Wellington is banking everything on the Prussians, the emperor erupts with disdain and bravado using some very vivid imagery to hide his doubts: *"Blucher is an old hussar and an abuse of nature — he has four legs. But Blucher cannot fly."* These effective cross-cut scenes would survive to the screen with only a few tweaks.

Around these titans, the script weaves into the historical facts a legion of characters, both real and fictional, fleshing out the top and bottom of the social order. The high preponderance of Irish "grunts" is clearly the influence of Craig. "Some of the colourful Irish soldiers in the movie were named after friends of Harry's,"[219] and possibly John Huston, who, also being of Irish extraction, spent some years on the Emerald Isle, and it is easy to see how both men were drawn to such creations.

> O'CONNOR *squelches through the mud. He carefully feels the skin on the* PIG's *back and shoulders.* "You'll give me a nice bit of crackling, won't you, darling?"

But for all the many introductions to so many minor characters, few are given any progression. Two stand outs are:

> STRETCHED *full length on the grass is the extraordinary figure of Commandant* RUMIGUS, *a veteran with one arm and many wounds.*
>
> *Captain* TAYLOR *walks at the side of the stretcher, carrying* PICTON's *top hat and sword.*

It appears all were cast, and the scenes presumably filmed. But none makes any further appearance in the script. Perhaps the gaping flaw that marks the screenplay, with its army of characters, is the lack of real emotional engagement, and so as the guns fall silent, there are few clues who survived, or not.

It is a shame that a newly published history book in 1968 didn't land on the planning desks at Dinocittà. British historian David Howarth wrote what is still one of the best primers for the battle: *A Near Run Thing: The Day of Waterloo*.[220] Delving through original correspondence and memoirs, he weaved the story of several survivors on both sides with the immediacy and excitement of a novel — or a screenplay. This book would have formed a terrific basis for the script, or at least imbued a rewrite.

Interestingly, there are several scenes in the film that are *not* in the script draft. Most notably, Napoleon bidding farewell to his Old Guard (see Chapter Nine): *"Goodbye, my children!"* Other extra scenes are markedly intimate and human, and for those familiar with the film, include: *"If I should fail tomorrow…"*; *"Who did you give your watch to, Hay?"*; *"In case anything should happen to you, what are your plans?"*; *"I have a son, no higher than your boot."* A script develops during the making of most films, but usually this involves rewrites of existing scenes or more often deletions, because of time or cost. It is probable these were later additions created during the filming, as we will see, to which the actors actively contributed.

What gives credence to these as much later additions, is that they are also absent from another work that should be mentioned at this point: the novelisation *Waterloo*, by British writer Frederick E. Smith, author of *633 Squadron* and filmed in 1964. Until the 1980s, this was a common marketing tool for tent-pole event movies, for which authors would work from a screenplay but be accorded a fair degree of creative freedom to make the work their own. Your author has a great deal of affection for Smith's book, as it was the only link between TV screenings of nearly five years.

A digression: His first copy was confiscated during a school maths lesson and lost for some time. A bereft teenager penned a letter to the author via the publisher which elicited an autographed replacement with a sweet note: "I hope this one makes up for the one you lost."

We must suppose that the December '68 draft was polished enough for Smith to base his work upon as he follows it closely, succeeding in expanding the characters and the history. He goes to some effort to explain what actually happened as he weaves his drama, with David Howarth's book listed as a source.

Curiously, he keeps swathes of the awkward dialogue almost verbatim, which seems strange for an English-speaking writer. He also includes those blink-and-you-miss-'em walk-ons above with similarly no progression. Smith's novel is not a work of great literature, nor does it intend to be, but it does a good job in bringing Craig's screenplay alive. It is well worth a read.[221] Smith, who served in the RAF during the war, continued to write several *633 Squadron* sequels, and a novel damning South Africa's repulsive Apartheid regime for which he received death threats. He died aged ninety-three in 2012.

To give it its due, where the script does shine is the third element — the "action," which describes what is *happening*. This is used by directors as a starting point for staging scenes as well as helping the various technical departments to prepare; pithy, but not too descriptive. In this, it is often superb:

The CAVALRY *scatter chaotically in front of the* SQUARES. *It is no longer a battle, but darkness, a whirlwind of souls and values, a storm of flashing bayonets.*

We will see more examples of these evocative "action" descriptions in later chapters; in particular, many scenes that were filmed but never made it into the final film. Their words will at least give us a small glimpse into these forever lost fragments.

With the involvement of the Russians, the filmmakers were at pains to maintain that the film would have "no political message."[222] According to Karl Marx: "The history of all hitherto existing society is the history of class struggles."[223] He believed it was economic forces rather than religion or ideology that were the driving forces in the flow of history. Was it possible to retell a historical story, with substantial investment by the Soviet State, with no political taint?

An early script draft was submitted to the Russian Cultural Ministry for approval. The story goes that an eminent Soviet professor returned a long and detailed Marxist analysis, the thrust of which criticised the depiction of Napoleon as a military adventurer rather than as a "proto-revolutionary." He suggested that the aristocratic Wellington should be portrayed as a "class enemy" — a pawn of a fascist ruling clique. This document was dubbed by the crew as "The Kremlin Letter," after the thriller sharing studio space at Dinocittà and directed by John Huston.

It is said that history is written by the winners, and *any* historical subject cannot fully avoid a political subtext. In subsequent interviews with the cast, there were light-hearted quips about Bondarchuk rooting for the Corsican, and "conniving" a way to rewrite history. The Soviet director admitted to journalist Ann Guerin that he was an "admirer of Napoleon and considered his defeat at Waterloo a tragedy because he says: 'From the Russian point of view, even though Napoleon was our enemy at one point, he was also the representative of revolutionary principles. Wellington was the representative of reactionary principles.'"[224]

How overt these ideas are in either the script or the film is moot, and highly debatable. From the commencement of the project, Dino, who was politically agnostic, stated his desire to "faithfully" retell the facts of the battle. As we saw with *The Red Tent,* Mosfilm sincerely wished to be a major player in the international commercial film industry by offering productions with wide appeal, which must, by definition, be free of any obvious agenda. As Dino found with the disappointing response to *The*

Bible, steering a middle-course ran the danger of a film becoming an orphan as it tried to be everything to all, but pleasing nobody.

Yet all artists must have a point of view, even if it is contradictory, and it will leak out regardless of any honourable stated intention to be even-handed. Despite the story being all about conflict, who to root for was a dilemma for the director, as he explained: "You cannot attribute greatness to a man who has killed so many, but our audience will have a human feeling of pity for Napoleon when they see this film." As we shall see, the Russian was often at a loss to understand the Anglo-Saxon mindset, describing Wellington's character rather nebulously: "He has emotion in him, but he has to cover it all up."[225]

And what of any hidden subtext from the one-time communist and life-long Irish nationalist, H.A.L. Craig? Having accepted a very large cheque to pen the screenplay, he no doubt accepted, to use Hollywood producer Sam Goldwyn's famous quote, that if you want to write a message: use Western Union![226] Perhaps, though, something of his politics can be gleaned as Wellington, in the ballroom scene, lambasts his men as *"scum"* and adds his opponent *"is not a gentleman."* The Duchess clips back: *"Arthur! What an Englishman you are!"* Like himself, Craig would have known that the Duke was Irish-born. "Being born in a stable does not make one a horse," was his reputed disparaging response.[227] But as a product of Eton College, sometimes dubbed "the nursery of England's gentlemen" he was completely imbued with the aristocracy of Albion's God given right to rule. Which for many outside the elite clique has often been seen as arrogance and insufferable snobbishness, characteristics the great Duke, despite his military prowess, certainly displayed. Was this the political point the Irish writer was hinting at, or more of gentle dig at his long-suffering countrymen's neighbours? Who knows, we each read what we want to read, but it is fair to say the writer endeavoured to tell the story as simply and powerfully as his talent allowed.

Perhaps the major handicap that is already clear on the page is the tension between history and drama. Inevitably, inaccuracies become embedded as the writers sought to weave a dramatic narrative for a mass audience. When Bondarchuk joined the project, he already had a deeper knowledge of the era than any other prospective director. Maybe this was more of a flaw than an asset, as he would have projected preconceived ideas and concepts onto the material.

In simple terms, was he too close to the subject to see it objectively? Or, as a non-commercial filmmaker, did he consider the requirements of a mass audience? During the production, he explained how he had squared the often-contradictory elements: "…pure historical truth doesn't interest me. There are three truths — Historical, artistic, and the truth of life. Historical facts are needed to confirm artistic truths. Every war is contrary to human reason."[228]

The Polyvision sequences from Napoléon vu par Abel Gance *(1927), arguably the best depiction of the Corsican on film.* KEVIN BROWNLOW

Albert Dieudonné in the title role. KEVIN BROWNLOW

Rare stills from Charles Weston's The Battle of Waterloo *(1913), regarded as Britain first epic.* IRTHLINGBOROUGH HISTORICAL SOCIETY

Shot in only four days, the battle scenes were rushed and chaotic. Below, the victor's Wellington and Blucher meet at the end of the battle. Note the Victorian gaslight in foreground. IRTHLINGBOROUGH HISTORICAL SOCIETY

Dino De Laurentiis (left) and Sergei Bondarchuk in Oriolo Romano which doubled for the French town of Grenoble, April 1969. AUTHOR'S COLLECTION

CHAPTER 6

"He Has Filled His Stage…"

By the spring of 1968, the money and logistics may have been in place — the cast was not. Richard Burton had by then dropped out, and it was announced in May, that Rod Steiger had been hired as Napoleon, with Peter O'Toole "practically set"[229] to play the Duke of Wellington. According to his wife Siân Phillips, the *Lawrence of Arabia* star ultimately passed on the role believing that the film would be a failure.[230] Losing this star was cited as one reason for Paramount's scaling back their investment in the project.

For Rod Steiger, Napoleon was a part he could have been born to play. Schooled in the Method, he would immerse himself in a role: "It encompasses anything that gets you involved personally in a part, so that you can communicate in human terms with the audience."[231] Born in 1925, this New York actor with a deep baritone voice was an imposing figure: stocky and tall, just shy of six foot, with large, round penetrating eyes. He almost cornered the market playing offbeat, often volatile, always intense, crazed characters. The son of a song-and-dance duo that split before his first birthday, he would never know his father. "My mother used to disappear for days at a time and things were pretty rough," he recalled of his tough, displaced childhood with an alcoholic mother: "We had shouting matches and struggles over bottles of liquor. There were unlit Christmas trees and cold houses and no dinner."[232]

During the Depression, aged just eight, the young Rodney would not only join the bread queues but also trawl the local bars to extract his drunken mother from her haunts. By the age of sixteen, he had run away from home, and was living precariously on the streets and relying on the generosity of strangers. Years later, he related a grim story to his biographer Tom Hutchinson, that while a teenager down on his luck, he was sexually assaulted by a priest, but denied that the experience had any long-term effect on his life.[233]

Active service in the US Navy had, he acknowledged, left an indelible imprint after he witnessed the wounded from the ferocious Pacific battle of Guadalcanal in 1942.

> I realised that they had killed their first human beings. Everything in their life, religion, society, parents had conditioned them not to kill. They were shocked that they had killed. To see this at first hand was shocking, but it was eventually useful for me as an actor, even though it was a very difficult experience. That look in the eye was unforgettable.[234]

He would later consider himself a pacifist, but he also acknowledged how many of these early, traumatic experiences he would channel into his chosen career:

> I used to pull my mother out of saloons, and I heard the neighbours' titter. I must have sworn to myself someday that I would do something good enough that they would respect the name of Steiger. I think that gave me a certain intensity. I made acting too much my life.[235]

In the 1950s, he was part of a crop of actors, most notably Marlon Brando, who burst forth and transformed the art of screen acting. They had studied at the famous Actors Studio in New York under Lee Strasberg. The emphasis was on using one's own life experience to create characters: "My generation of actors was taught to create different people," he later explained, "That's what an actor is supposed to do."[236] The results could be inspirational and super-charged with depth and energy, but also at times drowned in ego and self-absorption.

On the Waterfront (1954) was one of the first great cinematic showpieces for this new style. Directed by Elia Kazan, who was well versed in this new dynamic approach, it stared Brando, Eve Marie Saint, and Steiger in a tense tale of the strong-arm tactics of dockyard unions, in a brilliantly written screenplay by Budd Schulberg. Brando was probably never better on screen, and it is a tribute to not only his own talent but also the skill of the director to know when to rein in such visceral power. The same goes for Steiger, who gives a controlled and moving performance as Brando's brother. The two share one of the most intense scenes in almost all Hollywood cinema. Playing brothers, seated in the rear of a taxi, Brando castigates Steiger for making him throw a boxing match: *"I coulda been a contendah."*

The fission of emotion on screen probably had something to do with the tensions between these two very expansive, larger-than-life actors. Brando was dismissive and complained it took too long to shoot: "There were seven takes because Steiger couldn't stop crying. He's one of those actors who loves to cry. We kept doing it over and over. But I can't remember just when, how it crystallised itself for me."[237] Meanwhile, Steiger griped that when it came for his close-up, the great Brando upped and left, with the script girl standing in for his feed lines.

Brando's career took off, propelling him to become an A-lister, and allowing his ego to overreach his creative judgement. Meanwhile, Steiger carved out his own niche. Few actors on screen have conveyed such bubbling intensity, bordering on just the right side of madness as Steiger. He made a very distinctive heavy in the otherwise squeaky-clean musical adaptation of *Oklahoma!* (1955), an Indian in *Run of The Arrow* (1957), the infamous gangster *Al Capone* (1959), a corrupt millionaire attempting to flee to Mexico in *Across the Bridge* (1957) and with a lighter touch as camp "Joyboy" in the black comedy *The Loved One* (1965). His highly mannered performances, coupled with a reputation for being difficult, often rewriting his own lines, did not engender producers to hire him. In his defence, Steiger would say that acting was *his life*, and he took his craft seriously.

In 1964, Sidney Lumet, a New York-based filmmaker, was initially reluctant to engage him for *The Pawnbroker*, a harrowing tale of a holocaust concentration camp survivor dealing with his past. Under Lumet's direction, who had an intuitive understanding and respect for actors, Steiger gives one of his most impressive performances on screen; a masterpiece of quiet and stillness masking inward pain, in which the audience can feel the deep-seated angst buried within the character. He often cited this work as his best, and in particular the last scene where he — the pawnbroker — finds his employee and friend, dead in the street. Like a bursting dam, he finally allows emotion to surface and emits a heart wrenching silent scream.

A candid insight into Steiger's process of mining this level of performance, comes from an extraordinarily emotional and honest interview he gave to late-night TV host Bob Costas in 1992:

> When I did *The Pawnbroker*, I mean, my best moment of acting was when I came out the door. There's this boy who worked for me, who had become like a son to me, he's shot, he's bleeding on

the streets of Spanish Harlem. And I looked down on there, his blood and everything. And to help me get in the scene, I was thinking of my daughter. That's all I had to think about. *That's my daughter lying there dying.* And I can't do nothing. And I tried to use all of this into the acting — the props. It was chocolate syrup for the blood, right? But no, by now it's my daughter's blood. And I looked at my hands and there's my child's blood. And in the script, I'm supposed to put my head back and I'm supposed to scream in anguish and pain and rage at God, whoever you believe in. And when I did that, I thought of Picasso's painting of *Guernica* in the Museum of Modern Art. This is all going in infinitesimal seconds. Your mind goes — a second, 40 miles, as far as your brain's concerned. Right? And I remember he had these women's faces back with their mouth open and their tongues out. And obviously you couldn't hear a sound, because it's a painting, but it was the loudest scream I ever heard in my life. And my intellect and my instinct came together at the same time. Something in me said, don't make a sound, but look like you're screaming. That to me was the highest moment I ever had in acting.[238]

He would receive an Oscar nomination for his performance, but lost out to Lee Marvin in *Cat Ballou* (1965). It would be the role as a bigoted police sheriff from the Deep South, who crosses swords with a northern detective played by African-American actor, Sidney Poitier, while investigating a murder, that would bring him the coveted award. Norman Jewison directed *In the Heat of the Night* in 1967, which tapped into America's ongoing struggle with civil rights that had blighted the Union during the 1960s. Steiger brought all his power and presence, using a prop — 263 packs of chewing gum — to anchor the character:

I thought, "Wait a minute. I can let the audience know how I am feeling with this chewing gum." Bang! I'm out of the cliche. When this guy chews fast, you know he is upset. When he slows down, you know he is thinking. And when he stops chewing, you don't know what the hell he is going to do.

The director, Norman Jewison, realised he needed a firm hand with the actor: "I'd rather have someone overact and give me some choices than not be there at all. We would shout at each other…We had great respect and trust, and especially after he won the Academy Award, I was God."[239]

The leading film critic Richard Schickel praised Steiger's performance as "a wonderful piece of acting — humorous, shrewd and strong without being domineering or self-admiring."[240] While no one could deny the emotional power that Steiger brought to his roles, there was a consensus that, like Jewison, the actor needed, and welcomed a strong directorial hand. It would be the predominant theme echoed by critics throughout his career, deftly summed up by Brian Baxter when writing Steiger's obituary:

> He often over-emoted, and needed strong direction to channel his enormous energy and passion. Like the little girl with a curl in the middle of her forehead. When he was bad, he was very, very bad, but when he was good, well, Oscar came out to play.[241]

Despite winning the Academy Award, Steiger bemoaned that for a year the phone didn't ring. For an actor who lived only to work, it was a tough time as he battled with bouts of depression. His wife Claire Bloom related how her husband would wile away many hours, slouched on the sofa watching American football on TV. She described him as "near-catatonic" as he withdrew from his wife and daughter, Anna. He was only roused out of this by the offer of the leading role in *The Sergeant* (1968), a gay-themed story set in a peace-time army barracks. As Steiger's character descends into drink, depression and despair, this path roughly mirrored his own life.

Few of his contemporaries poured so much angst into their work. As his wife explained, he put his craft first before everything else in his life: "I couldn't understand how anyone could take himself so seriously." She noticed it was only when he was immersed in a role, he appeared to know who *he* was. She related a story that Peter Sellers, the great comic shape-shifter, told her when he once caught himself in a mirror kissing a lady, and thought his reflection seemed more real than himself. It was a good analogy for her husband, who completely believed in the roles he played; *becoming* that person.[242]

His next performance was perhaps one of the most unusual in a mainstream studio film. *The Illustrated Man* (1969), from a book by science-fiction writer Ray Bradbury, told a strange story of a man covered in tattoos. Steiger had to endure ten hours as make-up director Gordon Bau and a team of eight assistants applied the exquisite temporary tattoos to his body. Unfortunately, the film didn't succeed either critically or financially.

It was around this time that he was offered the part of one of history's most controversial generals — George Patton. A pearl-handled pistol carrying US commander who with a gruff hand, and a sharp tongue, proved to be one of the most aggressive and successful commanders of World War Two. Twentieth Century-Fox planned a lavish biopic that would be both critical and authentic. Steiger turned it down, although much to his regret when he saw George C. Scott win an Oscar for his trouble, remarking ruefully: "I got on my high horse. I thought I was a pacifist."[243]

Strangely, this avowed pacifist accepted the part of Napoleon, although with some reluctance:

> Epic films are not my forte, I like pictures like *The Pawnbroker*. I'm more at home in them. But I could not turn down the opportunity to be Napoleon. To play a historical figure is an adventure which I think one's life should be, and an education which I also think one's life should be. One also has the possibility for a few split seconds of existing somewhat near the level of those gentlemen, even though it's obviously on a fictitious plane.[244]

It was not until January 1969, barely two months before filming began, that Christopher Plummer was cast as the taciturn Duke of Wellington.

He was born in 1929, into what could be considered as Canadian aristocracy in Toronto, his great-grandfather had been a prime minister.[245] Despite being brought up solely by his mother in Montréal (his parents had divorced soon after his birth), he recalls having a happy, if formal "Edwardian" childhood. In the strict high-bound prejudice of the day, she was considered a social outcast by her upper-class peers, for the double sin of being divorced and having to work for a living. One can imagine the effect this "snobbishness" would have had on the young Christopher growing up.

As a boy, he studied to be a concert pianist, but was soon discouraged not only by the painstaking practice required, but its solitariness, too. It was the unlikely appearance, one day at a school assembly, of a monocled, elderly English actor named Bransby Williams, who rolled his Rs in the grandest manner of Victorian theatre as he hammed a variety of "Characters from Dickens," to the delight of all, that changed Plummer's life. Inspired by the fruity rendition of "Once more unto the breach" from *Henry V*, the young man eagerly committed it to memory, and next day, regaled his school mates with his own interpretation. Greeted with appreciative "war cries," recalled years later, he felt a "nudge" inside him that day. With his second cousin being the actor Nigel Bruce, most famous as Doctor Watson to Basil Rathbone's Sherlock Holmes, it appeared that the more gregarious art of acting flowed in the genes.[246]

When his family lost its money, he was unable to attend college, much to his later regret, but he was determined to make something of himself: "I decided to be bad and rough and find the streets rather than the gates."[247] With his eyes set on the stage, Plummer learned the ropes of his chosen craft by joining the Montréal Repertory Theatre, rubbing shoulders with the future Captain Kirk, William Shatner. His bourgeoning talent was soon spotted, and he found himself in a roadshow production of André Roussin's *Nina*; his part had originally been played by David Niven.

While his 1953 Broadway debut was a flash in the pan — his play closed the same night — he quickly found his feet. He played opposite Julie Harris in the later *Waterloo* co-writer Jean Anouilh's *The Lark*, and Henry II in the Frenchman's *Becket*, as well as Elia Kazan's successful *J.B.*, delivered in free verse. In 1955 he debuted in Britain for the Stratford Shakespeare Festival, in what would be the start of a series of well-received performances, on both sides of the Atlantic, of the bard's most iconic characters: *Hamlet, Othello, King Lear*, Mark Antony in *Julius Caesar, Richard III, Macbeth*, and emulating his teenage inspiration, as *Henry V*.

He would add to this gallery *Cyrano de Bergerac, Oedipus* and Henrik Ibsen's *A Doll's House*, all firmly establishing him as one of the most prominent classical actors of his generation: "highly talented and commanding performer, with good — if somewhat severe — looks, (and) a magnificent speaking voice."[248] The actor noted that directors often chose him for legions of patrician roles because he appeared to look as if he belonged to a previous century. He observed that many successful actors are fuelled by "a natural anger," but this was not innate thanks to his own "gentle" background, but he recognised that to play the great dramatic roles, "you have to learn how to blaze."[249]

Despite making his movie debut in Sidney Lumet's *Stage Struck* (1958), it took a while for the actor to establish himself on the big screen. In 1963, he played the crazed and insane Emperor Commodus in Samuel Bronston's colossal *The Fall of The Roman Empire* (1964). Directed by the able Anthony Mann, the film boasted a giant, full-sized set of Rome, a series of mass battles, a chariot race, and all dressed in sumptuous costumes. Plummer held his own against a gallery of heavyweight actors like Alec Guinness, Anthony Quayle and James Mason. Producer Bronston was no businessman but believed in quality and ended up spending a then enormous $19 million, which promptly crashed his cinematic empire. The huge failure of this film might have sunk the actor too, but the offer of a trip to Austria proved to be a turning point.

There, he would find international fame as the martinet Captain Von Trapp, who is tamed by a nun, in the phenomenally successful *The Sound of Music* (1965), a film he would come to loath, calling it "The Sound of Mucus." Later, he considered that his casting enabled director Robert Wise to steer away from "a sea of mawkishness," helped, he thought, with one "who was a shit — cynical, naughty."[250] Things had not started off well when he, a singing novice, was immediately thrown into recording the songs with Julie Andrews even before he had his first singing lesson.[251] He wanted out, and was only kept on board by the threat of a $2 million lawsuit. The young Julie Andrews, just 27, charmed him and the two became lifelong friends. A trace of this rapport made it into the film. During the romantic gazebo scene, the pair could not stop laughing as they attempted to kiss, thus ruining each take. Ever the pragmatist, the director Robert Wise had the inspired idea to film them in a silhouetted long shot; it would not only mask their giggles but create one of the most iconic shots in the film.

Over the years, perhaps like a good wine, the film and its reluctant star have mellowed gracefully together: "People were unnaturally sentimental about the film, so I always gave it a tough time." Some years later, he was at a party and had to watch the "damn thing…I was a prisoner! And then I thought, it's got everything — the lovely songs, the Nazis and the nuns and the kids. It's timeless and I'm grateful for it."[252]

But regardless of his distaste, it helped his career which began to garner a variety of roles. Offered a part in the spectacular *Battle of Britain* (1969), he insisted his RAF Squadron Leader character should be a Canadian as a tribute to his own countrymen's contribution to the battle. His uniform had an authentic Canadian RAF badge sewn onto it. He stepped back into another musical, this time a bawdy romp set in the eighteenth-century, *Lock Up Your Daughters* (1969), in which he played the foppish Lord Foppington, allowing a lighter side of his talent to shine along with such British comic scene-stealers as Glynis Johns, Fenella Fielding and Roy Kinnear. "I think," he said later of a part he enjoyed with relish, "that was a perfect example of being hammy, over the top, and yet getting away with it, because the character's so outrageous." While the film was not a success, it was particularly memorable for the actor as he met his future wife, Elaine Taylor, who had played his co-star Susannah York's maid: "And I fell for her, hook, line, and sinker."[253] They married in 1970, and for him, it was a case of third time lucky; the pair was still together half a century later.

In *Royal Hunt of the Sun* (1969) he played the Inca ruler, Atahualpa, based on a play by Peter (*Amadeus*) Shaffer, which he had also played on Broadway. In it he was required to use strange speech patterns to suggest the character's archaic language. As his character spent much of the movie bare-chested, Plummer improved his physique by swinging a spear for fifteen minutes each day. The film, which co-starred the powerful Robert Shaw, was not also not a success, and there were rumours that Plummer had become disillusioned at his choice of parts, and was considering retiring from the limelight to direct instead. As this did not turn out to be the case suggests it was not a serious thought, but may reflect a growing fear of being typecast in certain roles: kings, princes…and dukes.

By the late 1960s, he was an established movie star that could "open" a movie. Some, though, suggest he also had a talent — for making enemies; "Lots of them. And they all accuse him of being foul-tempered and stupendously arrogant."[254] The actor later admitted in his autobiography that at the time, because of his many starring theatre roles, he was "a pampered, arrogant, young bastard."[255] Whether unwittingly, he would channel some of this into his portrayal of the aloof patrician Wellington, brimming with supreme confidence in his own abilities.

Speaking many years later, the actor discussed his own process of getting into character, very different from his American co-star:

> There's no secret method about it, really. A method is only useful when you're in trouble, and your imagination fails you. Only then do you wonder: "What am I going to do with it now? I can't really figure it out!" Then what I'd do is personalize, to go back to my imagination and then come back with something new, halfway through what I'm doing. That's the only time I'm using a kind of method. *My* method…To me, what makes a great drama are the contradictions of characters, tonal shifts, the complexity of narratives.[256]

More than many actors, he would often be cast to play historical characters. He later described his pragmatic approach to doing research:

> When I do kings and stuff — the Duke of Wellington, for example — of course I read everything I possibly can. I don't overdo it, because if you overdo the reading, you begin to get

bored with a character. You have so many other opinions. You want to save something for yourself.[257]

With the two leads on board, the rest of the cast came together. The bulk comprised a mixture of veteran British actors of yesteryear, rubbing shoulders with the young up-and-coming. Jack Hawkins being the most well-known; a stalwart of British cinema, with an ultra-masculine voice but with a quiet, self-assured bearing, made him ideal for playing kindly patricians; *The Cruel Sea* (1953) and *Angels One Five* (1952). His Hollywood career was limited, but he continued to play powerful characters like the Pharaoh in Howard Hawks' spectacular pot-boiler *Land of the Pharaohs* (1955); and a drunken missionary in *Zulu* (1964) was a rare example of casting against type. Perhaps his major film roles were with British director David Lean, who expanded onto the world stage with the double Oscar-winners *The Bridge on the River Kwai* (1957) and in *Lawrence of Arabia* (1962). Hawkins played a memorable General Allenby as a perfect foil to the complex and troubled Lawrence played by Peter O'Toole.

Hawkins' most challenging role however was his battle with cancer, which resulted in the loss of his larynx that ruined the deep, commanding voice that had been his trademark. The only way he could speak was to belch out the words, but being the professional he was, he soldiered on. For all his subsequent films, including *Waterloo*, he was re-voiced by Robert Rietty, where again he would play a patrician — General Picton.

Michael Wilding, cast as General Ponsonby, had been a popular fixture on British screens during the post-war austerity years, and had found stardom by accident. This debonair, charming — gentle — man had been perfectly content playing second fiddle in Hollywood for years, before he was plucked from the chorus line: "Some fool of a producer came along and made me a movie star. Bastard. The most miserable day of my life." He was, by his own admission, quite a reluctant performer, and would happily give his lines to a fellow actor: "Dear boy, why don't you say all that for me?"[258] His urbane charm had been used to good effect when teamed with actress Anna Neagle, on a series of popular melodramas directed by her husband Herbert Wilcox: *Piccadilly Incident* (1946), *The Courtneys of Curzon Street* (1947) and *Spring in Park Lane* (1948) to cement his place as one of the most beloved British stars of the time. In Hollywood, he had appeared in two films for Alfred Hitchcock: *Under Capricorn* (1949) and *Stage Fright* (1950) and, like Hawkins, a Pharaoh in *The Egyptian* (1954).

Once married to Elizabeth Taylor, he had found quiet contentment with his next wife, actress Margaret Leighton, and both enjoyed semi-retirement from the screen. He, again like Jack Hawkins, was not in the best of health, having continued to suffer from illness related to his life-long epilepsy. Both men became good friends during the long and arduous *Waterloo* shoot, but it seems strange why they accepted these roles considering their respective health issues, which, as we will see, would become life threatening.

Although born in Liverpool in 1916, Rupert Davies, described as "bluff and burly…with an unruly mop of crinkly brown hair,"[259] was proud of his Welsh roots. He was a staple of British TV appearing in many popular and long-running series, including *Quatermass II, Ivanhoe, Emergency — Ward 10, Danger Man*. He was also the voice of Professor Ian "Mac" McClaine in the Gerry Anderson series, *Joe 90*. But it was as the pipe-smoking detective, *Maigret*, that he became a household name in 52 TV episodes from 1960.

As he joined the crew in Russia, it wouldn't be just his acting talents that he would call upon. Life in the dismal hotel in Ukraine would call upon skills he had learnt as a POW in Stalag Luft III camp, following his capture from the sea after his aircraft had been forced to ditch in 1940. He made three attempts to escape from the camp, all of which failed. The March 1944 mass breakout by 76 of his comrades was immortalised in the book, and later film *The Great Escape* (1963). Despite his Welsh heritage, he was cast as Colonel Gordon, commanding a Scottish Highland regiment.

Terence Alexander's casting as cavalry commander Lord Uxbridge reflected the actor's own wartime experience, as a lieutenant with the once mounted, but by then mechanised 27th Lancers. In 1944, during the Italian campaign, his armoured car was hit by German artillery fire, maiming Alexander, who carried a shard of shrapnel inside him for the rest of his life, and a permanent whistle because of a damaged eardrum. His war service had interrupted his ambition to be an actor, but after a brief meditation over becoming a priest, he would spend six full decades treading the boards.

He quickly established his brand; suave and well-mannered upper-class types in both drama and comedy, where he often played the straight foil for the likes of Norman Wisdom, Benny Hill, and the beloved double act, Morecambe & Wise. Despite some memorable films like Basil Dearden's *The League of Gentlemen* (1960), the Stage and TV would predominately occupy this prolific actor, including playing opposite Rupert Davies in

Maigret. For British TV audiences, his most famous and cherished role would be as Charlie Hungerford in the 1980s detective series *Bergerac*: "Over the years I've done a lot of rubbish, but I've kept working. And Charlie is the best part I have ever had."[260]

Leading the pack of dashing young blades was Ian Ogilvy, who had appeared in the highly regarded Vincent Price horror, *Witchfinder General* (1968), directed by rising talent Michael Reeves, and also co-starred Rupert Davies. A few years later Ogilvy would find fame as Simon Templar in the TV series *Return of the Saint*. But for now, he was still building his career step by step. He had already been flown over to Rome *twice* for auditions for different movies produced by Dino, including Franco Zeffirelli's *The Taming of the Shrew* (1967). He had got neither part, but with a need for British actors for his forthcoming spectacle, Dino felt he owed the young actor, and duly offered him the role of Wellington's 37-year-old right-hand-man, Sir William De Lancey.

Richard Heffer, who had hung out in the Dinocittà production office way back in 1966, received a call from his agent one Sunday afternoon in early 1969:

> I leapt on my old Harley-Davidson motorcycle and roared to London, arriving windswept in an ex-Swedish army greatcoat, with long hair, sideboards, and scarves around my neck. I dived into the hotel and strode into the interview room passing several suited actors awaiting their turn — Mr Bondarchuk took one look, stood up and raised his hands saying, "*Da!*" I had got it! Of course, this casting made every other English actor *furious*, as I was relatively unknown, and I endured endless remarks about how I had stolen "their part" (that of Captain Mercer, the legendary commander of G Troop, Royal Horse Artillery).[261]

The year augured well for an actor just beginning to build a career. He already had another feature film credit under his belt, with a role in Ken Russell's *Women in Love* (1969), during which he survived epic drinking bouts with the star bad boy, Oliver Reed. Television beckoned, when he landed "a leading part, surrounded by seasoned professionals" in a major BBC TV series *The Way We Live Now*, starring Colin Blakely.

Irish Donal Donnelly played an impish "grunt," Private O'Connor. An experienced theatre actor, including working with Lindsay Anderson at the Royal Court, Donnelly was pushing towards forty but still appeared to be in the full bloom of youth. "There was something mischievous, something larkish, about him…He twinkled."[262] He had made a memorable impression in Richard Lester's Modish *The Knack…and how to get it* (1965). A film that perfectly caught the spirit of youth and vitality in what would soon become dubbed "Swinging London." Donnelly played the eccentric flatmate who moves into Michael Crawford's house share. The two men push Rita Tushingham around upon an old bed across London in the film's most whimsical scene. Perhaps his casting in *Waterloo* was an attempt to bottle some of Donnelly's undeniable Irish charm.

Blue-eyed Russian actor Oleg Vidov was cast as a fellow "grunt," dubbed the Russian James Dean; with his classically handsome face he quickly became popular, particularly to younger female audiences. He had previously appeared in the large-scale Yugoslav epic *Battle of Neretva* (1969), which had also starred Bondarchuk, Orson Welles and Frenchman Charles Millot.

Probably the youngest male actor was seventeen-year-old Peter Davies, cast as Lord Hay. Davies, despite dropping out early from drama school, believed fame and fortune beckoned just around the corner. Appearing in a theatre production of *Richard II* staring Ian Mckellen, he was given just one line — specially created by the director. Peter rendered it with every ounce of his blossoming talent, prompting the director to remind him: "The sign, dear boy, of a *great* actor — is *restraint!*"[263]

But he was doing something right, as his agent rang him shortly afterwards with news of an audition in a huge, upcoming film.

> So, without thinking too much about it, I went to the BBC in Wembley. I had an appointment with a man called Bill (William) Slater; he was a director there. He was a super nice guy. I got filmed saying a few lines. He gave me a little bit of direction, saying try it this way, try it that way. A couple of weeks later, I was told I had the part, and the amazing thing was that I was going to be paid something like £900 (£15,000 in 2020)! It was a ton of money, especially for someone who never earned any, really.

The French characters would be played by mainly Italian, Russian and some French actors like Charles Millot, and handsome, aristocratic born Philippe Forquet. He, like Oleg Vidov, had become a hit with female filmgoers with his dark good looks and Gallic charm. In 1962, while still a student, he had been discovered by American director Robert Parrish, during the Paris filming for *In the French Style*.

To groom him as a new Alain Delon, he was lured by a contract with Twentieth Century-Fox to Hollywood. Here, he would fall in love with a beautiful up-and-coming talent. She had first been spotted by Richard Fleischer, while scouring the sea of extras to pick some suitable faces for a close-up during the spectacular arena scene for *Barabbas*: "one face truly stood out, that of an eighteen-year-old girl of stunning beauty. She was gorgeous. A knockout."[264]

Her name was Sharon Tate. She and Philippe would have a tempestuous relationship, perhaps not helped by predatory producers and agents, attempting to lure Sharon away with promises of fame and glory. Eventually demands of carving out a career in Hollywood became too great, as he explained: "Our careers just got in the way of everything…we drifted apart. There was so much pressure from everywhere."

After a year and a half, despite getting engaged, their relationship was over. Sharon would enjoy a meteoric rise, and find love again with director Roman Polanski, with whom she married in 1968. Heartbroken and disillusioned, Philippe retreated to New York and enrolled in the Actors Studio, studying the Method: "I hated it…I was lost, drifting…"[265]

Returning to Europe, Philippe's career soon revived with several meatier parts, and a new relationship with American model Linda Morand. In early 1969, the two were in Rome as he starred in *Camille 2000* (1969), directed by Radley Metzger. "My Agent had me meet Dino at his studios — a couple of weeks later, Dino introduced me to Sergei Bondarchuk, who thought I was perfect to play General La Bedoyere, Napoleon's aide-de-camp."[266]

The rest of the "French" were fleshed out by a variety of Italians like Ivo Garrani, Gianni Garko, and prolific TV actor Andrea Checchi, and Russians like Evgeni Samoilov and Vladimir Druzhnikov.

The sole exception was Marshal Ney, Napoleon's top commander, would be played by Irish-American Dan O'Herlihy. After graduating with a degree in architecture in 1944, he had quickly found the stage more alluring; his first part was actually the *lead* for foremost Irish dramatist Seán O'Casey in *Red Roses for Me*. There was markedly something special about the six-foot Irishman, as he was then cast by two major directors: Carol Reed in his IRA story *Odd Man Out* (1947) and the great surrealist Luis Buñuel for *Robinson Crusoe* (1954). He landed the role after the director screened the actor's first American film, *Macbeth* (1948), originally planning to use as its lead — Orson Welles, but considering him too big and too fat to convincingly play a castaway, O'Herlihy got the part.

Welles, the *Enfant terrible* of Hollywood, who took the cinematic world by storm with *Citizen Kane* (1941), agreed to do a cameo in *Waterloo* as King Louis, who flees upon Napoleon's approach. Welles had spent much of the past twenty years doing similar cameos in a host of European films, the paycheques he used to finance his own often rather haphazard projects, usually filmed around the continent. At this time, he was working on *The Deep*, along the rugged Croatian coast, which unfortunately he never finished. The story did finally reach the screen in the taut thriller *Dead Calm* (1989). Committing to Dino for just two days of work, it was rumoured Welles' salary was the third largest on the film, his going rate for a cameo which would capitalise on his name and fame.

In subsequent years, many Hollywood budgets have been skewered by often eye-watering star salaries. Was this the case with *Waterloo* to help account for its much quoted $25 million budget?

Christopher Plummer's stock had risen sharply by not actually doing anything. A few years before, Twentieth Century-Fox pulled out all the stops for what they hoped would top *The Sound of Music*, with *Doctor Dolittle*, to be directed by Richard Fleischer. Paying their star, Rex Harrison $650,000 was considered a hefty figure. Despite this cheque, keeping him on side proved to be a roller-coaster ride. Whether it was over the songs, or potential co-stars, the actor threw his weight around to the consternation of the exasperated studio.

At one point, Harrison, who fully lived up to his nickname Tyrannosaurs Rex, threw a strop and pulled out. A hasty search zoned in on Plummer, then in the middle of a successful run on Broadway with *Royal Hunt of the Sun*. Plummer had loathed playing Von Trapp even though it had made him into a star, and his acceptance of the role in another musical would only have been for a very fat cheque. He agreed to a fee of $250,000. Then the ever-contrary Harrison regretted his tantrum, and much to the studio's relief, put out feelers to be reinstated. Plummer was paid off with a handsome $300,000 for his trouble.

Using this as a base rate, his agent squeezed almost another $50,000 from Dino,[267] while Steiger was enticed with $385,000, the film's largest salary.[268] It should be remembered that they were second-tier stars in stark commercial terms. At the same time, Gregory Peck was paid $500,000 for *The Chairman* (1969),[269] while Robert Mitchum commanded nearly $900,000 for *Ryan's Daughter* (1970). Newcomer Christopher Jones, with very little experience, much to the chagrin of David Lean, was paid an astonishing half a million dollars to co-star in his Irish epic.[270] Lee Marvin and up-and-coming Clint Eastwood bagged $1 million/$750,000 a piece for *Paint Your Wagon* (1969).[271] All of these paled against the $2.5 million paid to husband-and-wife Burton and Taylor for the insanely bonkers flop, *Boom* (1968).[272] Dino had been keen to court Burton, and one must presume he would have been happy to stump up the Welsh actor's million-plus fee, although his marquee value was much reduced by the failure of *Boom*.

The film boasted an array of international actors as above, but although no one would doubt their respective talent and experience, few were of the expensive variety. Most of these actors worked in legions of medium-budget films in Europe, for which their salaries were relatively modest. The final total thespian roll call amounted to $1 million, and would have represented most of his above-the-line costs and therefore *not* a disproportionate expense for Dino. In fact, it represented a far smaller percentage of the budget than the four afore-mentioned productions which were approximately *half* as expensive as *Waterloo*.[273]

Perhaps more than most historical epics, a significant amount of money would be spent on "faithfully" recreating the world of 1815, from full-size sets down to the smallest coat button.

With March 1969 set as the start date, the primary job was to recreate the world of 1815 ready in time. Deep in the Soviet State of Ukraine, production designer Mario Garbuglia was leading a team of Italians and Russians to transform a stretch of potato fields on a collective farm southwest of the city of Uzhgorod. It was a daunting task, and worlds away from the bizarre and insane sets he had designed for *Barbarella* (1968), but after years of painstaking research it was time to prepare the battlefield.

Bondarchuk had filmed some battle scenes for *War and Peace* in the region which might have been the reason to shoot the new film here, but there may have been more political reasons for the choice of location.

From the mid-1960s, Czechoslovakia had been attempting to loosen the shackles which bound it to the USSR. Under First Secretary of the Communist Party of Czechoslovakia, Alexander Dubček, the state had experimented with liberalisation, which had culminated in a period known as The Prague Spring; a thaw — allowing greater personal expression and tolerating non-communist and social organisations. Inevitably, the thirst for freedom was not easily dampened, and the program of reform gained momentum.

This new openness was perhaps most visible to the outside world, with the extraordinary outpouring of cinematic creativity known as the Czech New Wave. This was potently signalled by Jiří Menzel's lyrical comedy

Closely Watched Trains / Ostre sledované vlaky (1966), which bagged the Academy Award for Best Foreign Film in 1968.

In a few brief years, Czech and Slovakian filmmakers had produced an impressive array of films with a large dose of surrealism, humour and sly political and social comment, notably the animation work of Jan Švankmajer. The sheer artistic ambition can best be seen in František Vláčil's three-hour medieval epic *Marketa Lazarova* (1967), which remains one of the hidden gems of world cinema, although barely shown in the West.[274]

In August 1968, this cultural explosion and relative freedom came to an abrupt halt, when Soviet President Brezhnev ordered forces of the Warsaw Pact to invade and crush the Prague Spring.

On the night of 21 August, Mario Garbuglia, the production designer who was supervising the preparation of the set, was staying in Uzhgorod, and remembers the sound of tanks rumbling through on their way to the Czech border.

In the town of Davle, just south of Prague, American actor Ben Gazzara recalled being awakened by "jet planes zooming overhead," and, opening his curtains, he saw Russian tanks, "lots of them — moving into position below us." The hotel receptionist was crying "Poor Czechoslovakia…It's the Russians. They've come like the Germans in 1939. They've come to kill our freedom."[275]

Code-named Operation Danube, a combined army of over 200,000 troops poured into the country. They were met with unarmed demonstrations and passive resistance, although in the resulting scuffles, eighty people were killed and many hundreds more were wounded. The photos of tanks menacing unarmed protesters flashed around the world, leading to condemnation and outrage. While key installations in Prague were captured by Soviet troops, legions of KGB officers systematically arrested Czech reformers in an effort to gag the government. Almost immediately the heavy hand of communist reaction thudded down upon Czech life, causing many to flee to the West.

Ben Gazzara was in Davle along the Vltava River, making a World War II film, *The Bridge at Remagen* (1969), which restaged the US Army's capture of the last intact bridge over the Rhine in 1945. The high-profile Hollywood presence complete with twenty-eight rented Austrian army armoured vehicles, made them a target. The invading Russians had been told they were liberating the town from the "American Army," but couldn't understand why "our people were giving them the finger. They were terribly nervous, the tension was palpable," recalled a Davle resident.[276] While the Russians were quickly placated, they confiscated the movie tanks and brought the production to a stand-still.

The unit, headed by British director John Guillermin, who five years later would helm Dino's *King Kong* (1976), was essentially trapped until producer David L. Wolper, who was in Vienna, could negotiate with the aid of the American embassy for their release.

With the real Russian tanks and machine guns being a forbidding threat, the producer secured a fleet of forty cars and taxis to take the eighty-strong unit (including a Czech defector) in a dramatic escape to Austria.[277] They left behind over $1 million worth of equipment, and forty reels (four filming days' worth) of unprocessed film, with the added sting of the insurance policy *not* including "war cover." The accumulated losses were "impossible to estimate."[278]

A few months earlier, the production had been accused by an East German newspaper, *Neues Deutschland*, of being "merely a cover-up for CIA and American intervention in Czech political affairs,"[279] even alleging that the film's Austrian army tanks were really there to support liberal Czech leader, Alexander Dubček. While the Czech authorities publicly backed the filmmakers, the police did launch an investigation into the newspaper's claims. Even after the company's swift departure, the producer, David L. Wolper, was still fending off hostile accusations, but strenuously denied involvement in any "subversive activities."[280] It was an ignominious end to a production that had been proudly touted as the first Hollywood film to be made in communist Czechoslovakia. Despite the efforts of cultural exchange, suspicion and mistrust hung like a shadow over working behind the Iron Curtain.

The invasion once again stoked up the Cold War and sowed distrust between East and West. This tension had caused work to stall on *The Red Tent*, the trail-blazing Italo/Russian co-production, until Mosfilm's head Vladimir Surin used his diplomatic skills to still the troubled waters. What effect the invasion had on *Waterloo's* preparation is unknown, but Dino often stated he was apolitical, and one can surmise Surin would have been equally keen to maintain momentum on their joint venture. With almost another year to go before filming was due to begin, perhaps a pragmatic decision was taken that the temperature would inevitably lower in the intervening months. Another consideration was that any delay would have repercussions further down the road, as the one thing that could not wait was — Mother Nature.

The chosen site for the battlefield and centrepiece of the film was ten miles from Uzhgorod, on a wide-open expanse near the village of

Nizhny Solotvyn. At the western end stand two hills which jut out above the almost flat plain, while at the opposite end bristle the motley vanguard foothills of the Carpathian Mountains that stretch far to the east. Garbuglia had designed the mile-wide set as a faithful scaled-down replica of the battlefield in Belgium.

The most prominent topological feature of the original was the two facing ridge lines across a valley, and to reproduce this Nature needed a little nudge. Soviet Army engineers were deployed to bulldoze two hills to create the gently sloping valley, before carving out four-miles of roads into the landscape.

Once the sod was turned, trees approximately 5,000 in number with many over 18-feet high, were transported on enormous trucks and lifted into place by cranes to create copses. One tree got to be a star, as it doubled for Wellington's historic elm under which he spent much of the battle. It stood like a lone sentinel on the Allied ridge.

To complete the landscape, the soil was sowed with wheat, barley and rye interspersed with a carpet of red and white flowers. Six miles of irrigation tubing was sunk to provide sustenance for the flora and movie rain and mud to order. When completed, it was given to the locals to irrigate their crops.

While the seeds were making their slow but sure journey to the surface, construction of the four standing sets for the various farms and even a windmill would begin in the early months of 1969. "Dino said he'd move mountains to make this picture," said Steiger later. "And he has — literally!"[281]

While Mother Nature slowly but surely pushed through the Ukraine soil, some 52 factories across Europe were busy making authentic costumes and props. These would have been the culmination of years of research by the art director Ferdinando Giovannoni and his team.

Italy with its unrivalled reputation for fashion was the hotbed of effort for the production, as several reputable companies put their shoulder to the wheel. Founded in 1932, E. Pompei — Rome, had been literally footing the Italian film industry and, in particular, many epics since the calling card of Mussolini's imperial ambitions, *Scipione l'africano* (1937). Thousands of extras had tramped before the cameras in their robust shoes made of the best local leather for *Ben-Hur*, *Cleopatra*, etc. Now they received one of their biggest orders from Dino.

With civilian jewellery and wigs made by Rome-based Nino Lembo and G. Rocchetti respectively, the firearms were the work of L. Daffini in Brescia. Formed after the war by the Daffini Brothers, the company quickly became well respected makers of shotguns. It was one of many small, almost cottage industry arms makers that are clustered in this area of Northern Italy, long famous over the centuries for gun making, with the skills being passed down through the generations. The quality of the local steel had been a byword since the days of armour in the Middle-Ages when Italian plate was considered the very best — and expensive.

How many authentic muskets they produced is not known, but it would have *only* been in the region of a few hundred, designed for use close to the camera. These were highly realistic, made of wood and the finest metal. Two different types of musket, the *de facto* weapon for infantry, were produced, which pay tribute to the meticulous attention to detail by the research team. The French Charleville had a small, brass fitting to its muzzle unlike the British Brown Bess musket; and it appears care was taken to distribute the correct props to their respective camps. As well as these authentic looking replicas, there was a far bigger order made for muskets made of cast-strengthened rubber.[282]

The extraordinary number of props, ranging from carriages to pocket watches, were made or acquired with the thoroughness of magpies by Rome-based E. Rancati. Founded in 1864, the company is still a treasure trove of theatrical props; their current website proudly proclaims ever-growing tallies of an endless array of props on their shelves.[283] In some close-ups in the final film, for instance, like on Napoleon's desk, it is possible to see maps, quills, letters, etc; all meticulously researched and placed and oozing authenticity. While researching this book, the company kindly delved into their archive and produced an assortment of drawings and plans that had sat gathering dust for half a century. These included one for an ornate and delicate iron wash basin. This item, which had been constructed, and no doubt used to decorate a scene, still lives on their warehouse shelves. Despite scouring the film, it has not been possible to detect this beautiful specimen of movie craftsmanship.

It was reported some 23,000 costumes were produced for the film, these varied in both detail and expense. The most exquisite being those required for close-up work with the Panavision lenses; including all those to be worn by the cast. It was in England that many of these pieces were made; at Bermans, the venerable London stage costumer founded in 1790. Richard Heffer remembers a tedious day before production waiting around at their fitting rooms, while a host of British, Italian and Russian actors took their turn. When he saw his outfit for Captain Mercer of the Royal Horse Artillery, he was impressed: "what a beautiful costume it's going to be!"[284] Although he was also concerned how he would fare, wearing the thick material and heavy helmet under the gruelling Ukrainian summer sun.

It was just one of thousands meticulously designed and researched by Ugo Pericoli, who was Professor of Costume Design at the University of Rome. Over five years, he and his team had culled information from European libraries and museums. Such was the level of detail gleaned that his work was later published as a book: *1815 — The Armies of Waterloo* by Seeley Service & Co in 1973. Judging from it, he had researched the correct uniforms for *all* the fighting units, but it is clear decisions were taken not to recreate some of these.

The most notable omission was the lack of Wellington's Dutch, Belgium and other German units that made up the bulk of his army. This would have probably been a creative choice more than anything else; instead, to aid the audience's understanding, you have simply red and blue opposite each other.

The French infantry were depicted in their blue uniforms with black shakos, many of these would have been made for *War and Peace*, along with the tall, bear-skin wearing Old Guard. The distinctive *Cuirassiers* with their metal breast plates formed the bulk of the cavalry, along with the white-coated *Carabineers* wearing their gold breastplates. The Light Cavalry were represented by the extravagantly dressed *Chasseurs à Cheval de la Garde Impériale* (pictured memorably in the famous History painting by Théodore Géricault as *The Charging Chasseur*, 1812), and the famed Polish Lancers with their lances and *Czapka* helmets. The Napoleonic French Line Artillery, dressed similarly to their infantry counterparts, were depicted manning their huge 12 pounder cannons.

For the red-coated British army, both the Line infantry and Highland Regiments were represented. The bear-skin helmeted Scots Greys are the highlighted cavalry regiment, as part of Wellington's Heavy Cavalry who all wore nearly identical uniforms. They are supplemented by the Life Guards with their Grecian gold-painted helmets and the Kings Dragoon Guards, their head gear being respectively similar to the French *Cuirassiers* and *Carabineers* (as above) and appear to have been shared. No Hussars or Light Cavalry were depicted, probably because they didn't wear red; the exception being Lord Uxbridge, played by Terence Alexander, who sports a magnificent blue hussar's uniform. A slight break with the "red" rule were the blue-coated British Foot and Horse Artillery, the first with their shakos, and the latter with their very impressive gold braid uniform complete with Tarleton helmet, which Richard Heffer as Captain Mercer, wore as described earlier.

The Prussians, who barely appear in the final film, were depicted with Line infantry and *Uhlan* Cavalry, their overall colour leaning towards dark blue and black. There are also several specialist uniforms that can be glimpsed for the staff officers in both armies, including individual Russian, Austria and Spanish foreign observers with Wellington's staff. All of which shows how much research and effort Ugo Pericoli and his team went to.

Where the needs of drama trump history, it is worth mentioning that almost all the uniforms depicted were what would have been Parade attire. On campaign, the bells-and-whistles of braid and brass would have been removed or covered up for obvious practical reasons. But if one is going to the expense of making so many costumes; make them as spectacular as possible (the same ethos applies to most wargaming figures). The historian may groan, but the filmmaker will defend this position on aesthetic grounds.

Before some grumble about Russians and Italians ignoring the facts of this famous battle, we should recall the approach of a British director on that rarest of beasts — an Anglo epic. Historian John Mollo spent years researching the correct uniforms for *The Charge of the Light Brigade* (1968), only to have the director Tony Richardson, insist the entire eponymous Light Brigade wear scarlet trousers, instead of just a single regiment. The Heavy Brigade, which also included The Scots Greys, were to exchange red for blue. Mollo's brother Andrew, also a military costume expert (they formed a company to advise on historical films, like *Doctor Zhivago* in 1965), considered that: "As it turned out the way the actual charge was filmed anybody on a horse was a Brit, so the whole issue of 'who were the good guys' was a bit pointless."

And in a mockery of immortal description of the "Thin Red Line" at the Balaclava battle, Richardson wanted the infantry too to be dressed in blue. "At first, he was worried about the scarlet tunics of the British foot soldiers, but John (Mollo) convinced him that rather than put them in blue or green, they should try various shades of red. Eventually they settled on a sort of crimson."[285] This had only come about after John Mollo fought a stiff rear-guard tussle, even suggesting brown as a compromise instead. The director only relented after falling into Mollo's trap upon seeing his mock-up sketches of the proposal; declaring the colour "awful."[286] It appears the British director was prepared to flout the historical record, and incur the wrath of historians to achieve a distinctive and evocative colour palette.

At heart, Richardson seemed to have identified a common problem with many period films; "Tony was terrified of what he called 'the vanity fair chocolate box look' of lots of people in bright coloured clothing — he wanted everything to be a bit subdued."[287] He was enthralled by the ideas of Lila De Nobili, the period and colour advisor, who worked closely with Mollo, the production designer, and the cameraman David Watkin, in a collective attempt to impose a "look" evoking nineteenth-century painters, like the Pre-Raphaelites. Watkin's use of vintage Victorian camera lenses on the front of his modern Panavision ones, being a laudable attempt at recreating an historic feel. While their desire for period authenticity, such as the actress' foregoing make up, and Richard Williams superb animation based on contemporary newspaper prints, all add up to a sumptuous snapshot of the Victorian high summer, it makes the tussle over the uniforms seem very odd.

In almost any colour film or TV programme, great care is taken to choose costumes suitable for not only the characters, but also to be tonally compatible with each other and the location. Today, creating a "look", thanks to digital technology in post-production, is standard practice but in the 1960s it was the exception. This example underpins the reality that movie-making aspires to be art — not documentary, and deftly illustrates the tensions between the artist and the historian. Who is right — is a continuing debate.

Andrew Mollo's creative film-making partner was Kevin Brownlow (*It Happened Here* in 1964), who was engaged as the film's editor — eventually. "I was determined to become a professional director, so turned down Tony's offer of editing *Charge*. Then I started seeing the rushes, and regretted my decision. I got a second chance; Tony didn't get on with his editors, and I agreed to take over so long as he didn't fire them." In 1968, during the later stage of the editing, he received two requests from Sergei Bondarchuk who was then in London casting his upcoming epic film.

> He wanted to see *Charge* and *Napoleon*. My restoration of Gance's film was some way off completion so he didn't get that — and in any case he should have seen the Triptychs, and no one was about to set up three projectors in interlock even for a man who had so many extras in *War And Peace*, he had to take to the air to encompass them all. He was rather bad tempered and very clearly contemptuous of *Charge*.[288]

While *Charge* depicts two much smaller battles (The Alma and Balaclava), the action is concise and very well handled, and uniforms apart, is commendably accurate. It is a very fine and intelligent film, beautifully shot with a regiment of top British thespians, Trevor Howard, Harry Andrews, David Hemmings, Vanessa Redgrave and John Gielgud. They all serve a superbly caustic and ironic script by Charles Wood which makes full use of Victorian language and idioms. Whether it *was Charge's* attack on the establishment and its hypocritical mores — unthinkable for a Soviet citizen, plain envy, or just a bad day; we will never know why Sergei Bondarchuk was "contemptuous."

In early 1969, with filming about to begin in Rome, a few months ahead of the battle sequence, Bermans in London had to prioritise costumes for the ballroom sequence. Twenty-two-year-old Ron Poulter had just recently joined the company. It was a heady time for Ron at the close of the "Swinging 60s," enjoying the illicit fruits of an office romance in between perusing dusty history books. The Italian researchers at Dinocittà were baffled by the peculiarities of Highland tartan and needed help.

> We only did the Highlanders, as they did not know what uniforms they wore; they sent over drawings of modern dress, I had to research the uniforms and draw and paint a few for Bermans. I know we did the Gordon's band as they had to be fitted for each bandsman, and some uniforms for the Gordon and Cameron Highlanders. Must have been about 200 of each and background uniforms.[289]

Bermans was the premiere company for costumes, and they had to handle several projects at the same time. "I was in the same little room as Nino Novarese, who was working on the costumes for *Cromwell*. We talked, and he showed me some of his books on uniforms he had published, I always remember how nice a man he was to me." *Cromwell* went into production a few months after *Waterloo*, beginning with staging some impressive battles with the help of the Spanish army.

Ron doesn't recall the total number of costumes the company produced for Dino (*The Longest Day* in 1962 was their record), he was too far down the pecking order to know, but his youthful muscles were deployed once they were completed. "They all went into a sealed lorry, valued at £25,000 (£420,000 in 2020) from Bermans Kingsway store in London; I helped load it. I was told the lorry would go straight to Russia, never to be opened until it got there. It was sealed by British Customs."

His time at Bermans was short: "I left and went to work at the British Museum Library for a lot more money!" But the skills he had developed during the research for *Waterloo* proved invaluable in later years, as he became an illustrator for the military history publisher Osprey, amongst others. "For Bermans, the film was just money or just another film. For me, it is a very great film, we will never see it's like again."

Quite by chance, a few years later on holiday with his girlfriend, he encountered the Russian director, proving an old adage:

> I went to Italy, Sorrento, with my lady friend. We were looking in a shop window and standing next to us was Bondarchuk and his wife. He was there for a Russian film Festival. As an artist, I have a good eye for faces; he was a very imposing and very striking-looking man. We saw him a few times in and around the town, and on the night of the film festival going into the cinema up the red carpet. No, we never talked to him. I wish I had now, but too shy in those days. Small world, is it not!

"It was a really great period of my life," remembers Veronica De Laurentiis. Back in Rome in early 1969, as preparations continued apace, she was itching to spread her wings and find her own path in life:

> I just turned 18, and my father wanted me to work in his office…(but) I realised I did not want to do that kind of work. I learned a lot from him, but he didn't give me the push I needed to find out what I wanted. I remember one day that my father was having a meeting with Bondarchuk…that afternoon my father came to me and said: "Do you want to play a part in *Waterloo*?" I looked at him and said: "Why not!" And then he took me to his office, and I spoke to Bondarchuk, who said: "You're beautiful, you have something special in your eyes, I want you to play this part, will you do it?" I said: "Yes, of course." But I was terrified because I had never done anything — and my mother was a big star! But I had the courage to say — let me try. It was a really fun experience.

Fun for some perhaps, but after so many years of slow and tortuous progress, hard graft now beckoned. Dino's most ambitious project was finally on the march.

Rod Steiger as Napoleon about to give the order to attack at Hougoumont.
AUTHOR'S COLLECTION

A scene that did not make the final cut, it may have been part of the battle of Ligny against the Prussians. AUTHOR'S COLLECTION

Christopher Plummer as Wellington in the inn set constructed on the Dinocittà backlot, note the beautiful lighting by cameraman, Armando Nannuzzi. AUTHOR'S COLLECTION

The Canadian star riding his faithful horse, Stok, on location in Russia. © RICHARD HEFFER

Michael Wilding as Ponsonby discussing the script with William Slater, the dialogue director. © HEINZ FELDHAUS

Rupert Davies as Gordon. © HEINZ FELDHAUS

Jack Hawkins as Picton. © HEINZ FELDHAUS

Christopher Plummer, Peter Davies and Terence Alexander as Lord Uxbridge. © HEINZ FELDHAUS

Left: Oleg Vidov with friend and mentor, Sergei Bondarchuk. Right: Oleg with journalist Joan Borsten during their whirlwind romance in Vienna after his dramatic defection from the East in 1985. © JOAN BORSTEN VIDOV

Philippe Forquet as La Bedoyere with Rod Steiger, the two became life-long friends during the making of the movie. AUTHOR'S COLLECTION

Dan O'Herlihy receives some last minute instructions from the director.
AUTHOR'S COLLECTION

Left: Charles Millot as Grouchy. Right: Bondarchuk with fellow Russian actor, Vladimir Druzhnikov as Gerard. AUTHOR'S COLLECTION, © MYKOLA KHOLODNYAK

One of Ugo Pericoli's research paintings depicting the British Line infantry.
© ANGELS COSTUME ARCHIVE

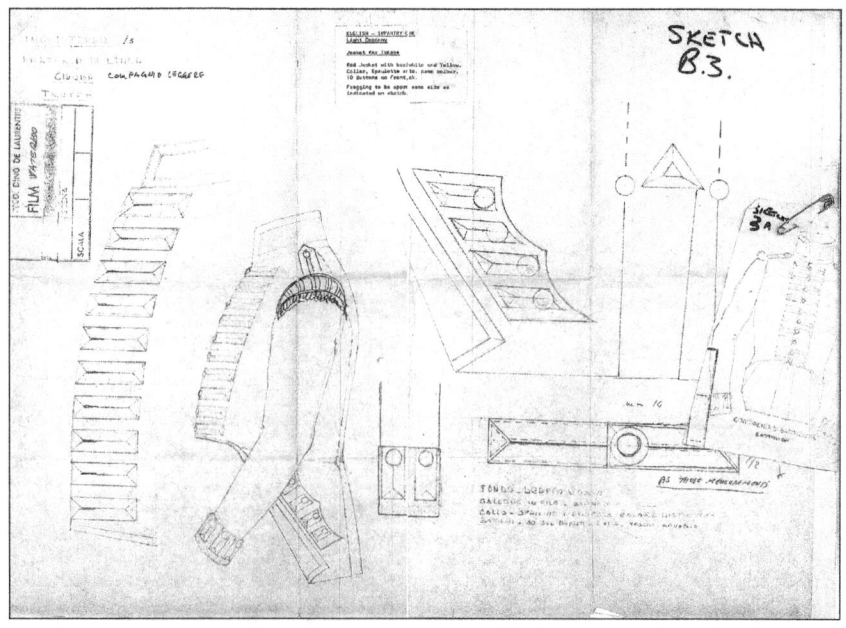

A pattern ready for the costume makers at Bermans. © ANGELS COSTUME ARCHIVE

Russian soldiers wear the finished pieces clustered around Wellington's Tree. These men would have been deployed close to the camera while those farther away would wear a simple painted tabard. Despite the authenticity of these costumes, historically they would have been only worn on parade with the 'bells and whistles' removed for the actual battle. © RICHARD HEFFER

Two teenagers: Veronica De Laurentiis in the Waterloo *planning office at her father's studio, Dinocittà, late 1960s.* AUTHOR'S COLLECTION

Ron Poulter strikes a pose in the basement of Bermans. © RON POULTER

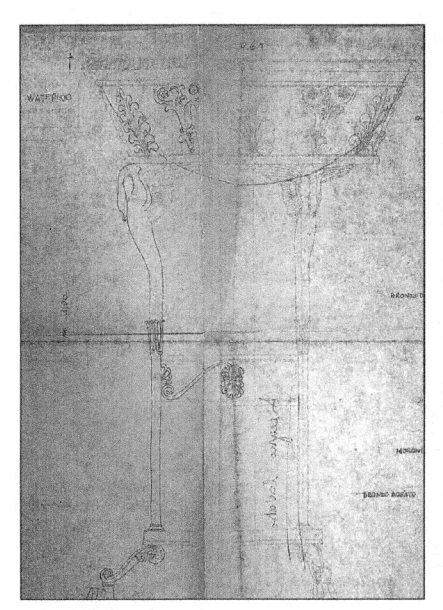

Design for a washbasin and the final item still on the shelves of the venerable Rome props company, E. Rancati. © E. RANCATI ARCHIVE

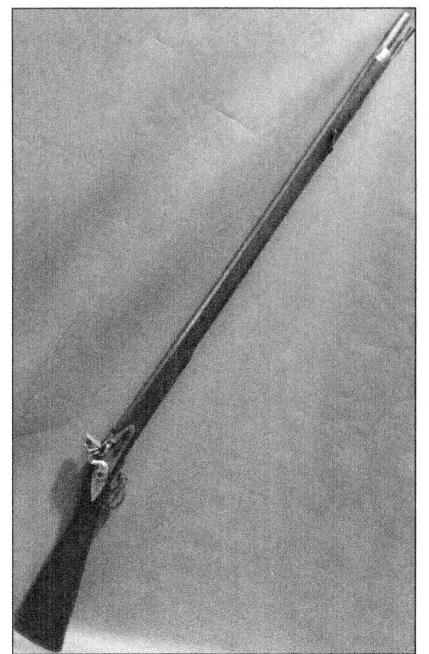

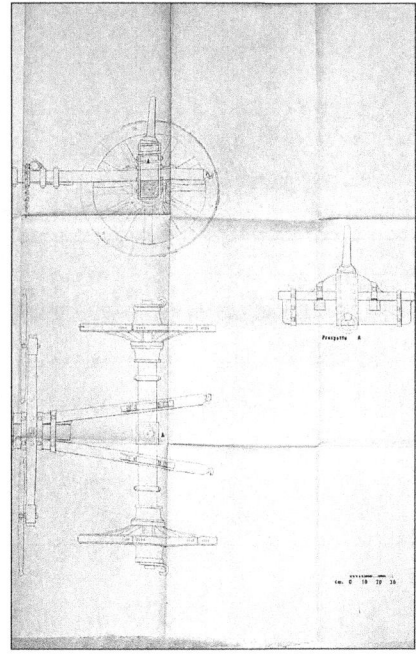

Left: One of the Daffini bros. made British 'Brown Bess' muskets, still available for hire. Right: Design for part of an artillery limber. © E. RANCATI ARCHIVE

Drum Major Grenville 'Nobby' Hall with his mace, which caused some problems during filming, leads members of the real Gordon Highlanders.
RONNIE BELL COLLECTION

CHAPTER 7

"We Ladies Just Have To Follow The Drum."

Scene.22: *The* BALLROOM *is a marvel of colour. The scarlet and gold of the Officers' Uniforms easily outshine the pastels of the ladies' dresses. But as we* COME CLOSER *we see that braids cannot compete with bosoms.*

Tuesday, 11 March 1969: A party is thrown to kick-start Dino's production at Dinocittà. Richard Heffer, the young actor who had touted for work at the planning office three years before, had returned to the studios: "just as I remembered them, but not looked so brand new!"[290] — he wrote in his diary. Despite all the years of planning, the start date had been abruptly moved forward; probably because of scheduling issues with the stars.

A few days earlier, Richard had just finished recording a BBC TV series in London followed by an energetic wrap party till the small hours, before just making his morning flight to Rome: "my adventure had begun!" Cast as Captain Mercer, this was his first day on set — and a long one, having left his hotel at at 5:15 a.m.:

> Did nothing all day but got dressed/make-up and sit — or stand in the studio. Left at 6 p.m. While a useless party was held to launch the "Mighty Project" — Rod Steiger turned up and Christopher Plummer. Jack Hawkins fumed at being kept waiting 13 hours for nothing.[291]

The first sequence to be filmed was the famous Duchess of Richmond's Ball. Historically, it had been staged in a carriage works in Brussels as described by the Duchess's daughter Lady Georgiana "Georgy" Lennox:

> My mother's now famous ball took place in a large room on the ground-floor on the left of the entrance, connected with the rest of the house by an ante-room. It had been used by the coach-builder, from whom the house was hired, to put carriages in, but it was papered before we came there; and I recollect the paper — a trellis pattern with roses…At the ball supper I sat next to the Duke of Wellington.[292]

This being a Dino epic — nothing less than lavish and sumptuous would do. The impressive set, complete with tall mirrors and wooden panelling, was far grander than the original, but it was intended to counterpoint the carnage to come.

It boasted over four thousand candles, which produced a very unpleasant smoky atmosphere. Igniting such a large number posed a technical problem. The solution: one workman climbed his ladder and sprayed the candles with lighter fluid; a second man followed close behind using a butane lighter. Snuffing out was equally tedious, requiring an old-fashioned, long-handled snuffer. The candles would become a hazard for all concerned in the hot ballroom set, as the wax soon melted and dripped down on unsuspecting heads of hair, costumes and naked shoulders.

It was an impressive space which inspired both awe and trepidation as teenager Peter Davies, cast as Wellington's ADC Lord Hay, recalled half a century later:

> The scale of the studio was unbelievable; it was a huge place, and that ballroom was absolutely massive, and they were real candles. It took forever to get things ready for a shot, and there were many people in there. It's hard to overstate the scale of this thing. The cameras were enormous. It's funny when you think about what they look like these days, but these things were giants — there were four or five of them.[293]

Unlike modern digital movie cameras today, which could easily capture the scene with so many candles, artificial lighting in the eaves of the studio was needed to achieve a workable exposure, because of the slow speed of film stock of the time (Eastman 5254, which had a 100T ASA rating). The cameraman was Armando Nannuzzi, whose affability made him popular with the crew.

Assisting him was his twenty-year-old son, Daniele, who had begun his apprenticeship following art school three years before. "My father was a huge personality, but a very easy, easy man. He was one of the most important directors of photography in Europe. He was very famous with the black and white in the beginning. Then came colour, and he won a lot of prizes."[294]

Armando had worked with many of the leading Italian filmmakers of the era, most recently with the great stylist Luchino Visconti on *The Damned* (1969), set during the rise of Nazism in 1930s Germany. Despite Nannuzzi's lack of formal training, he had a natural ability to adapt his talent:

> For him it was very easy to go inside one movie, the one story and then change and jump into another story with another kind of cinematography and other kinds of culture. He never studied; you know he had little culture, but after the war, it was so easy to work with the Luchino Visconti, and then jump onto a Pasolini, and then jump to a Fellini and then jump to another story, another culture. Every film is a masterpiece.

Post-war Italian cameramen — Aldo Tonti, Giuseppe Rotunno and Nannuzzi amongst others — had garnered an international reputation for creating a more naturalistic style than their Hollywood counterparts.

On *Waterloo*, Nannuzzi worked hard to replicate the subtlety of candlelight:

> We had thousands of real candles to light every morning. We worked under wax rain on the shoulders. I remember my father made an amazing lighting rig. The centre of the construction was open and there were sixteen Arcs — Brutes (very powerful lights) — sixteen in groups of four with a huge plastic screen. This defuses the light, making it very soft as if from the candles. Every angle was covered diagonally, not straight down from top; otherwise, you have the shadow on the eyes. And the light is amazing.

Using the reliable Eastmancolor film stock with cameras and lenses supplied by the Panavision company, most of the technical issues that had dogged *War and Peace* were avoided. "Filmed in Panavision" is identical to CinemaScope in yielding a super wide image, as described in Chapter One. At the time, the rental-only lenses from the Hollywood company were considered the industry standard for widescreen cinematography. Fifty years on in the digital age, the company still holds its own albeit with robust competition from the Germany's Arriflex. Early in the project's genesis, the plan was to shoot in one of the prestige 70mm formats of the day (Dimension-150, as used on *The Bible*). By the late sixties, the immense improvements in both film stock and lenses led to the belief that originating on the industry standard of 35mm nullified the advantages of the wider gauge.[295] The handful of 70mm prints required for the roadshow runs could be derived by "blowing up" from 35mm, and this would be the *de facto* standard until the introduction of digital stereo sound killed the practice in the early 1990s.

Perhaps the most dated aspect of the cinematography is the overuse of the zoom lens, which gives an artificial sense of movement while flattening the image. It had become a visual cliche by the late 1960s, and would disappear over the next decade as a stylistic device.[296] The frequent zooming sometimes distracts from the careful and often beautiful lighting and compositions that Nannuzzi and Bondarchuk achieved, echoing their studies of period paintings.

Costume Designer Maria De Matteis was tasked with designing the civilian costumes, meticulously researching the fashions of the time. The ballroom ladies are all clothed in the Empire style; a simple dress, white or cream, topped with a fitted bodice ending just below the bust, giving way to a long fitting skirt that skims the body. With its origins in ancient Greek and Roman culture, it had become popular in Europe during the Neoclassical era of the late eighteenth-century. It was Napoleon's first empress, Josephine, who popularised the "empire-style waist," and this "look" was enthusiastically embraced across the war-torn continent.

While women's fashion would become progressively more restrictive and buttoned-up in the Victorian age, the free-flowing Empire style would see a revival in the 1960s, reflecting the looser social mores of the era, that echoed the similar unconstricted 1920s "flapper." Two hundred years on, the dresses that swished across the Duchess of Richmond's ballroom would not look out of place in the swankiest nightclubs in modern-day Paris, London or New York.

A recent fashion website perfectly sums up the Empire style's enduring appeal:

> The style emphasizes one of the narrowest points on any woman's body and is great for shorter women because the raised waistline can create the appearance of added height. It's also a highly recommended style for women with wider lower bodies

since it draws the eye to the narrow upper body and can make the bust appear curvier.[297]

A common bug-bear of many 1960s films set in the recent past, particularly war films, was the anachronism of ladies sporting the decade's latest hair fashion. Thankfully, hair stylist Paolo Borzelli did his homework, and ensured that the cream of female society dancing in the Roman "Brussels" that evening was suitably coiffured in the height of 1815 fashion.

> Scene.21: The Duchess of Richmond confides to Cavalry General Ponsonby how she was invited to a parade of Highlanders: *"So I just rode up and down, in and out, and picked my fancy."* Her sixteen-year-old daughter Sarah approves; *"Mama, you chose such big ones."* Mother chides daughter *as the suggestion is slightly lewd.*

The ballroom was the only scene to feature the fairer sex. Virginia McKenna led the pack as the aristocratic Charlotte Lennox née Gordon — Duchess of Richmond, described as "one of the sourest, most ill-tempered personages I ever came across in my life…haughty and disagreeable."[298] In contrast, the actress was warmly described as being "delightful, beautiful and a very lovely person."[299]

She was a last-minute replacement for Olivia de Havilland, Errol Flynn's leading lady in many of his swashbuckling movies of the 1930s. During the 1950s Virginia McKenna had quietly blossomed into a leading lady of British cinema, notably playing opposite Peter Finch in the popular war time drama *A Town Like Alice* (1956), and with another Peter, this time the comic genius of Sellers, in *The Smallest Show on Earth* (1957). Perhaps her best starring performance was as wartime Resistance fighter Violette Szabo who was executed by the Nazis, and whose story was told in the very solid and powerful *Carve Her Name with Pride* (1959).

> So many things in my life which had started in fantasy, as it were, fiction, as an actress — although there have been a lot of real stories about real people, but nevertheless, I was just an actress interpreting these stories — have become part of my real life for various different reasons, and this particular film was one of those.

It was her 1966 film *Born Free*, in which she and her real-life husband, Bill Travers, played Joy and George Adamson, the animal conservators who had raised an orphaned lion cub, Elsa, to adulthood before releasing her into Kenyan wilderness, that truly changed Virginia's life.

> All on location, for the very first time, in Kenya...At the time, we didn't really think, "Oh, this is our life-changing experience," or anything like that. We were far too busy dealing with the various difficulties, challenges and events that each day brought. Some of them were very hard to deal with, some of them were just joyful, but it was a very intense and very demanding ten and a half months.

The arduous location shoot with real animals was well managed safely, but mishaps were sometimes unavoidable.

> I did have one accident, during the "getting to know you" period of two months before filming started, when one of the lions jumped on me and I broke my ankle. That was really nobody's fault...but it was one of those things which was just a chance thing that happened.[300]

The film, helped by John Barry's epic infectious score, became a huge international hit. The experience of making it in Africa, and its inspirational real-life characters, motivated the thespian couple to devote their energies to protecting the natural habitats and rights of wild animals. In 1984, following the premature death of an elephant in London Zoo, they set up Zoo Check. This would later be renamed the Born Free Foundation and describes itself as "an animal charity that's passionate about wild animal welfare and Compassionate Conservation...we work tirelessly to stop the exploitation and suffering of individual animals living in captivity or in the wild."

Virginia's personal passion, which would be recognised by an OBE (Order of the British Empire), is also eloquently expressed on the charity's website:

> Our love and concern for animals should go beyond those within our personal environment. We should see the world as a whole, see nature in its entirety and realise the importance of humans being part of the animal world and animals being part of theirs. It is only in this way that we can prevent the complete

destruction of our environment and perhaps, ultimately, of ourselves.[301]

By 1969, despite making two more films with her husband, both with strong animal conservation themes: *Ring of Bright Water* and *An Elephant Called Slowly*, both 1969, she considered herself semi-retired from her profession. "I was still plodding on with acting, really…I was enjoying it but a bit of my brain was already going sideways, I think! I was thinking about other things…" She no doubt accepted the few weeks of work in Rome, as a pleasant diversion and a welcome paycheque. She played the Duchess with her trademark understated "English Rose" of clipped delivery, poise, and elegance. "It was a tiny part but sensational to do, actually… quite an experience."[302] The Russian director felt that her Anglo blonde mature beauty exemplified an aristocratic lady of that period; dignified, chic and haughty.

Youngster Susan Wood, just sixteen, played the Duchess of Richmond's daughter, Lady Sarah, who is in love with Lord Hay (Peter Davies). "I'm pretty sure she had a ballet background. If you look at the way that she dances — she's got wonderful poise. I thought she was just brilliant."[303]

Garnering a speaking part in a multi-million-dollar movie was exciting, but when the moment arrived to walk before the cameras, Peter Davies was a bag of nerves:

> Until the filming started, the whole thing was a breeze. But when it came time to work, it was as terrifying as anything that had ever happened to me in my life. Suddenly I'm there for my first scene. I was meant to be looking across the ballroom and seeing Susan and just sort of smiling at her. It froze me stiff. And every time, just to do that little thing, all the candles had to be redone, and there are hundreds of people moving around. So, I quickly went into a state of absolute fear.

Stage-fright can afflict even the most experienced actors, and in such moments, some gentle encouraging words from the director are all a nervous actor craves, but this was not the case for young Peter:

> Bondarchuk, who was basically a very scary person as far as I was concerned; I think directors are (or tend to be), but he was particularly so, and that he didn't speak English as well so everything was through an interpreter — so it was scary. He was

impatient. There wasn't any effort to make me feel more comfortable. It was just like: *"This is someone who doesn't know what he's doing — why is he here?"* It was an absolutely miserable experience, and it got worse!

Help was at hand in the shape of the man who had auditioned Peter way back in London, now engaged as dialogue director. "Bill Slater saved the day. He suggested bringing Susan over and putting her right by one camera. He said: 'Just look at her and smile — Susan, smile at him.' And she gave me a lovely smile, and I just smiled back. That's where the shot came from!" Richard Heffer noted in his diary that the young actor: "was very nervous and stiff, but as it was his first moment on camera *ever*, it was hardly surprising."[304]

There is some historical truth to this shimmer of puppy love, as Lady Sarah was one of seven sisters *and* seven brothers.[305] But it was her sibling, "Georgy" Lennox, who did actually have a friendship with Lord Hay (the extent of which is unknown), whom she described as "dashing, merry youth, full of military ardour, who I knew very well." She noted with disappointment the young man's "delight at going into action; and of all the honours he was to gain."[306] A few days later following the fateful battle and its dreadful carnage, she wrote to a friend: "Poor Lord Hay that I regret the most — but there is no use entering upon such melancholy subjects."[307] Incidentally, Lady Sarah, a few months later married another soldier who was at the ball: Major General Peregrine Maitland of the 1st Foot Guards, who played a pivotal role at the climax of the battle.

Peter did not see his "love interest" socially: "I was out carousing with the lads and quite a collection of lads it was! So, I didn't see her outside of work, but I think she had a chaperone as she was young." Richard had noticed Susan was nervous working with so many experienced actors and had become "obviously miserable,"[308] under the watchful eye of her chaperone. He suggested inviting her for a night out with the younger members of the cast — a tonic which worked: "Susan appeared to enjoy herself which was the main object of the exercise and proved herself, a very charming and adult sixteen-year-old."[309]

Even though she was the boss's daughter, Veronica De Laurentiis, just nineteen, found being on the film set quite daunting: "I remember that I was kind of on my own. I was very shy, and I didn't know anybody. As I got to know them, I would talk to them."

Espying her across the crowded ballroom was one person whose face glowed the same colour as his scarlet costume. "I got absolutely gob smacked, like a puppy dog madly in love," recounted Peter Davies, fifty-years later about his teenage crush:

> When Veronica walked into the room — I'd never seen something so beautiful in my life. My heart still goes pitter-patter just thinking about her. I can just remember trying to be in the same room as her, as much as I could. I just remember her as being sweet and charming. She probably understood that I was fawning over her too, I suspect.

It appears the young Peter did *not* catch Veronica's eye. Her memory of who was who amid the swirl of the big scene is hazy. Unlike Peter's dealing with the director, she recalls Bondarchuk being attentive and sensitive towards her as a budding actress. "He was a very warm and nice man. I guess the fact that I got a part from him, that he realised that's what I wanted to do as an artist — he was really nice. He said the right things, and he made me feel at ease, so he was a good guy."

She does not recollect seeing instances of Bondarchuk's tyrannical directorial style as were on display during the arduous shoot for *War and Peace* (see Chapter Four). "Maybe he was, but not with me. Remember, I was the *producer's* daughter! You know how *that* goes! He was great. I liked him because he listened."

> Scene.21: CLOSE ON *the* CLAYMORE *of a* SCOTTISH SWORD DANCE. LIFT UP *to the legs of the* DANCERS, *to their kilts and bobbing* SPORRANS. LIFT TO *their faces. They are young tall* PRIVATES *of the* GORDON HIGHLANDERS, *chosen for their good legs and good looks.*

To add some authenticity, Dino had engaged some actual soldiers. Pipers and Drummers from the 1st Battalion, Gordon Highlanders Regiment, had been employed specifically for their unique Gaelic musical sound. Their forebears had fought in the 1815 battle as the 92nd Foot, which had been raised by the Duchess of Richmond's father in 1794. With her personal affinity for the regiment, the Duchess had requested a detachment to perform for her guests at the ball. As another daughter, Lady Louisa Lennox, recalls:

> I well remember the Gordon Highlanders dancing reels at the ball. My mother thought it would interest foreigners to see them,

which it did. I remember hearing that some of the poor men who danced in our house died at Waterloo. There was quite a crowd to look at the Scotch dancers.[310]

The march to the later Roman ballroom had begun when Nigel Oxley, then a captain in the regiment, had been approached while on holiday, in of all places — Elba — Napoleon's first place of exile. "The British Defence Attaché was staying in the same house as me on Elba. We got chatting one evening. He asked, would I like to help make the film by coming to Rome, and to Russia for three months." Whether it was the sun and sangria, the excited captain replied extravagantly: "Interested? — I should think so! We'll give you the whole Battalion! And the Scots Greys too!"[311]

Returning to the regiment's West German barracks at Minden, his CO Lieutenant-Colonel J. Neish was equally excited and fired the request up the chain of command. "When I contacted the MOD (Ministry of Defence) I was told I could take fifty men (including the Drums and Pipes) to Rome for two weeks and on NO account go to Russia…It sounded fun and different. I hoped the Scots Greys, who were also at Waterloo, would join in."[312]

Brokered by Oxley, a deal was struck with an agent from Dino at the regiment's West German barracks at Minden. Each soldier would be paid £7 (£118 in 2020) per day with a donation of about £2000 (£33,000 in 2020) given to the regimental charity fund. On top of this, the MOD levied a "hefty charge" for the use of Her Majesty's Highlanders.

The twenty-seven members of the Drums and Pipes Band, led by Pipe Major Joe Kerr, were seasoned travellers having completed engagements in Europe and many countries across Africa; they were joined by twenty-two dancers to perform the traditional Highland Reel.

All fifty-one, including their commander Captain Oxley and his wife, Easter, were housed in a sixty-bed hotel near The Vatican. The manager had been a POW in North Africa during the war, and had served as a waiter in the 8th Army Officers' Mess, so was well used to British army humour and antics.

Despite the pleasant surroundings, the serving soldiers still had to adhere to military protocol with Reveille at 04:00 a.m. followed by breakfast, before arriving at the studio at 06:00 a.m. for wardrobe and makeup. Oxley's men demonstrated The Argyll Broadsword Dance to Bondarchuk on the first day, "and he liked it." The dance, stemming from an ancient Celtic ritual, involves four performers flourishing their swords before laying them on the ground, points touching to form a St. George Cross. The dancers deftly move between the blades without touching them, all to the fast rhythm of the music.

But before filming could start, there was a delay when someone noticed a continuity issue on Drum Major "Nobby" Hall's mace, which was wielded at the front of the band. "The mace had, in bold silver letters round the top — WATERLOO," remembered Easter Oxley, "which was a battle honour given to the Gordons obviously *after* the event. Much shouting and everything stopped till a solution was found."[313]

With the error corrected, another problem arose when the five sets of four dancers marched into the ballroom and placed their heavy steel claymores in five crosses on the floor. Amongst the natives hailing from Aberdeenshire, Kincardineshire, Banffshire and the Shetlands was a 6'2" handsome New Zealander — dancing *not* being his forte!

Sheep farmer and ex-rugby player Roger Green was cast as Duncan, a Highlander. Considered something of an enigma, Green was a colourful character with a penchant for hard drinking and hell-raising. His involvement had come by chance when a friend, seeing an advert in the personal column of *The Times*, had secretly sent his picture to Bill Slater, who was casting the film in the UK. "To my surprise, one day the phone rang, and I was invited to the BBC studios for an audition. Now I was not, or had not been, a professional actor, nor could I dance and sing professionally. Of course, I could do all the above with a few drinks on board — I thought!" During the audition, he caught the eye of Bill Slater's male assistant: "Whilst he was telling us all about the forthcoming movie — he kept looking at me. My thoughts were *'Either I've got the part or he likes the look of my body,'* and I felt that it certainly wouldn't be the former. I thought, I'll just have my drink and get the hell out of here."[314]

He got the job at £150 per week after some haggling by his agent, and found himself in Rome surrounded by authentic Highlanders, who were skilled dancers. To the untrained Roger Green, trying to master movements honed over years, was a challenge. Captain Nigel Oxley remembered that, "he was sick" which did not help. "We tried to teach him to dance but failed."

Easter Oxley recalled the slow progress with staging the scene which was repeated 43 times:

> Nigel stopped the filming and refused to carry on the Broadswords reel, which is very tricky but not if you have done it dozens of times, like the soldiers — and unlike Roger Green.

He kept mucking things up, and the soldiers (up since and the soldiers (up since 4 a.m.) were well fed up. More shouting all round, and eventually a compromise was reached—they would only film him from the waist up.

It is *this* shot, with Green wielding the claymore, that marks his tiny moment in the film. He would travel to Russia and wait for months for just one more day of work. Richard Heffer noted it was a tough day: "Another gruelling session in the ballroom, with hours of total idleness wrapped up in gold lace and white starchy formal wear. Not the most comfortable way to spend a morning. Managed to take a minute's worth (screen-time) before lunch," he could see Captain Oxley's men working hard, "with the poor Gordon Highlanders quite exhausted!" The afternoon continued in much the same vein. "Again, manage to can (film) a little before 5:30 p.m., this is only the very opening sequence of a very long scene; we will be here *weeks* at this rate."[315]

> Scene.23: WELLINGTON *enters, tall, beaky, handsome, in a dark blue cloak lined with white. He politely depreciates the compliment of the music, at the same time making the company happy by acknowledging it. This was Wellington's way. His casualness was always deceptive; polite suggestions became absolute orders. He had the unique ability of combining good manners with the most abrupt command.*

Four days into production, and a delay to shooting Wellington's grand entrance into the ballroom brought tempers to a boiling point in the fetid atmosphere of the set. "There was a three hour wait for HRH Christopher *f**king* Plummer to deign to appear," an exasperated Richard Heffer wrote in his diary, adding that many of the cast had "all been very rude about him!"[316]

The young actor was still shaken, as he and fellow performer Jeffry Wickham had narrowly escaped injury that morning. Amid the notorious Roman traffic system, their car had been involved in a minor road accident on the way to the studio. When Plummer did finally arrive, he profusely apologised to all but maintained it was not his fault. The cause had been a standoff between Dino and Plummer's agency, CMA, who had advised him to sit tight in his hotel until a contractual issue was sorted.

Scene.23: (Wellington) *"In none of my campaigns have I had such a brilliant company, Duchess."* (Duchess) *"This season soldiers are the fashion. We ladies just have to follow the drum."*

Relationships improved as time went on. "Great break-through today," when Richard found himself sitting next to Christopher Plummer:

> ...who introduced himself — apologising for not doing so before! Nice gesture, so as we were left together during a break, I got onto riding and battles, and the usual film chat. If the truth were known — it was such a relief to be *able* to talk normally and not put on an "act of obeisance," that I was probably overzealous and "nattered on." However, I'm glad to have broken the ice with *everybody* in the picture.

To top it all that day, he had been offered a peppermint sweet by Bondarchuk, which was considered a "high distinction."[317]

Scene.28: (Duchess) *"Now I know how you won your battles — you danced the enemy to death."* (Wellington) *(amused) "I did, Duchess, I did. The whole secret of combat is in the legs. You stand fast or you run fast."*

As a counterpoint to the battle to come, the ballroom sequence centred around beautifully costumed couples waltzing the last night of peace before being interrupted by news of Napoleon's invasion. Some 200 extras, mostly trained dancers, toiled under the hot lights and smoky candles in the sprawling set day after day. Sword fighting and dancing are a fundamental part of most actors' training, so many like Richard, could learn the required moves quickly: "I did a dance that I learnt in ten-seconds as they had 'forgotten' that I had not been asked to any dance rehearsals."[318]

Some shots were accomplished with the aid of a carpet — as Daniele Nannuzzi explained:

> I was on the camera, which we put on one carpet and the grips slid it around, because we needed the scene from a low level — you see the dancers, and we go backwards. The floor was real parquet, very smooth. Usually, it was very easy to go with the camera dolly's rubber wheels for a move. But for this shot we need a camera very low.

The crew also needed to make themselves invisible as the walls of the set were completely covered with mirrors, so they were dressed as English officers. "But dressed like the actors, it was very easy to get confused with them in any reflections, as even the cameras were covered with red jackets."

Peter Davies, who admitted his dancing skills left much to be desired, found these scenes very difficult to do — with so much to get right, "and it got worse because dancing hasn't ever particularly been my forte. It was just a simple three-time waltz, and we practised it a lot. It's absolutely amazing how good it looks. It shows what you can do with a camera."

As any actor before a camera appreciates, the ability to know your lines and act is only part of the job. Whenever an actor moves in relation to the camera, the focus must be adjusted. This was then and still is accomplished by pre-arranged "marks" taped onto the floor at every change of position. Until the mid-1970s, most Studio movie cameras, like the venerable thirty-five-year-old Mitchell BNC used on this film, did *not* allow the operator to live monitor the focus through the viewfinder (at the time though Reflex viewfinders were standard in amateur 8mm and 16mm format cameras). They used a rackover system, which required the camera body to be shifted sideways by a lever to allow direct focus through a tube to be set. Then "marks" would be chalked/taped onto the floor and a corresponding mark made on the focus wheel. Once all set, the camera body would be racked back into position, ready for filming with the operator using a side viewfinder to judge the composition, but *not* the focus. Instead, it would be the focus puller's (like Daniele Nannuzzi) job to twist the dial at the appropriate moment, when both actor and camera hit their "marks." The results of all this pain-stacking work were only visible when the film was developed and screened, sometimes days later.

"I'd say to anyone — you try waltzing and landing on a taped spot!" remembered Peter, echoing the challenges that faced actors and extras alike. "It was absolutely terrifying working in that studio. Because with all those people — you make one mistake, or you don't stop waltzing on your tape mark, and the whole thing grinds to a halt. It was tough."

To fully capture the waltzing couples, an overhead shot was envisioned as Daniele explained: "They made, like in the Luna park, a basket on a wheel. The camera was exactly in the centre. And at the same time the basket was mounted on the round rail all around the ceiling. You see the floor with the people dancing around in the same point."

Back on the polished floor, bonds grew between erstwhile dancing couples. Richard was concerned when his "partner," Isabella Albonico, in a non-speaking role as intriguingly Lady Webster — Wellington's mistress, was not on-call because of an administrative error. "No one else knew — so I didn't dance (will spoil the continuity)…I don't know what will happen tomorrow."[319]

Next morning, Isabella turned up anyway, and the two danced: "…furiously for another gruelling thirteen and half-hour day, in camera perhaps — with one lovely tracking shot right across the ballroom to Christopher Plummer. However: an exhausting day, which ended with a cock-up, I'm surprised CP (Plummer) didn't walk off the set — I would have done."[320]

Although the "cock-up" has been lost to time, there were tensions over the under-written script from the very start. Christopher Plummer felt his famous character had been short-changed by the scripted dialogue, which gave no hint of the deep emotional aspect of the Iron Duke. In public, the stern patrician was calm and composed, but in private, his humanity would surface following the death of officers in battle. Sometimes, it was noted, he was tearful. The Canadian actor turned for help to the film's main historical advisor, Willoughby Gray, known as "Willo."

Tall, quiet and almost bookish with a shock of white hair, Willo was a breed of Englishman that has all but disappeared; an unconscious and unaffected eccentric. He often sported a monocle and habitually wore a kilt. He was ex-army with a distinguished career during the Second World War, commanding a reconnaissance unit with the British 11th Armoured Division as it fought its way from Normandy into the heart of Nazi Germany. For his gallant service reaching the rank of colonel, he was awarded an MBE (Member of the Order of the British Empire). The citation extolled his valour:

> He has shown great enterprise and complete disregard for his own personal safety on many occasions…The bearing of this officer under arduous conditions and his cheerfulness and willingness to do any work delegated to him unhesitatingly have been an example to those with whom he came in contact.[321]

But his war service had left a permanent mark. "Willo's dreadful liberation of the concentration camps — seven in ten days! He has had white hair for twenty-five years."[322] Following his demob from the army, Willo had pursued a career as an actor, predominantly on the stage (he had appeared in an Oxford University drama school production of *The Taming of the Shrew*, directed by one — Jack Hawkins in 1938) but had kept a strong interest in military history and in particular Waterloo. There was also a personal dimension as his great-great-grandfather had charged with the famous 2nd Dragoons, better known as The Scots Greys, and boasted of a personal acquaintanceship with the Duke of Wellington himself.

Willo knew "his stuff" and agreed to mine the Duke's recorded statements, even if they were out of context. "Let's give him back some of his wit,"[323] said Plummer. Both went to work with the blessing of Bondarchuk, as according to the actor in his autobiography, the writers had all left the show by then. One wonders if there were some "politics" going on, as the writer Harry Craig not only lived in Rome but according to his daughter Siobhan, he was on set, on at least one occasion. "He gave himself a very small cameo — he is one of the two soldiers who open the door for the departing generals when the Duchess' ball is interrupted."[324] For whatever reason it appears he did not join Plummer and Willo in their quest to "improve" the script; if he had done so, the erudite Irish *bon vivant* would surely have left an impression on the star's memory when writing his memoirs decades later.

Young Peter Davies does recall Harry Craig, who was "pretty garrulous," later visiting the set in Russia, "I remember him being with Willo." Craig's daughter, Siobhan, also recalls him relating tales to the family of hovering over the immense battle scenes, sitting side-by-side with the director in the army helicopter. Whether this was merely a social call or answering a cry for help, is unknown, but the evidence points to most of the additional dialogue being cooked up between the director, Willo and the lead actors.

These actions by the star caused some ructions: "C. Plummer is rewriting the script too — cutting out everyone else: so, all round he is not popular!"[325] This might have been the age-old tension between the "grunts" and the "top brass," as comparing with the script, only Wellington's dialogue was substantially changed. Many of these new lines enhance the drama and do much to humanise the Iron Duke.

How far Plummer cut other actors' lines is debatable, but Bondarchuk found the Anglo-Saxon mindset difficult to fathom and probably appreciated the enhancements. Plummer recalls an amusing story of a test session with the film's make-up artist, Alberto De Rossi, before production began. Bondarchuk arrived with his assistants and spent a few minutes scrutinising the actor from every angle. There was something clearly amiss to Bondarchuk's eyes as he pointed to the actor's mouth.

After a quick exchange of heated Russian via the interpreter, the question was posed that there was a problem with Wellington's mouth. Mystified glances between the actor and Alberto De Rossi, who merely shrugged, before another stream of Russian as Bondarchuk was adamant there was something amiss with the *upper* lip. De Rossi quickly understood the confusion, and with a mischievous twinkle in his eye, pointed at the offending area and asked in very thick Italian: "Do you mean — it is *stiff*?" The Russians enthusiastically nodded.[326]

It transpired that the source of the confusion was an Irishman, with his tongue firmly in his cheek, as a baffled Bondarchuk explained: "When I first talked to Peter O'Toole about the role, he told me Wellington was noted for having a stiff upper lip."[327]

The bigger a movie, the slower the pace and inevitable frustrations arise. The cast were often perplexed at the apparent disregard for continuity. "The schedule was confusing and the dance sequences most peculiar to my mind," remembered Richard Heffer. "We wanted to get the scenes right, but we were rapidly worn down by being on perpetual standby!"

The cast spent long hours in full make-up and costume, waiting in the small dressing rooms to be called. Teenager Peter Davies recalled the tedium it took to apply sideburns: "I wouldn't have been able to grow my own at the time."

Many of Richard's diary entries echo the daily slog: "Usual procedure — with a two-hour sleep after lunch, which resulted in a crick in the neck! Went to the girls' dressing room and chatted — Veronica managed to organise some tea! Then a quick background shot before breaking at 6:30 p.m."[328] And yet another entry details the monotony with just tiny moments in the limelight: "The usual procedure of waiting and eating, drinking coffee, chatting, sweating and coughing from the arc-lights and the candle soot. I danced in the scene — badly — but I danced, but that does not mean however that I was in the shot."[329]

The glamorous lure of Hollywood did not tempt Captain Oxley to accept an offer to appear on camera: "My main task was to ensure the soldiers were not taken advantage of." His wife, Easter, spent only one day in the world of film, but gives a vivid overview:

> It was fascinating to see how long the extras had to wait, and the jealous hierarchy they maintained among each other according to the importance or rank of their part in the film. So, the least important extras were made up starting at 6 a.m. moving along till all were done by about 10 a.m. Then the rehearsals started, extras took up positions and stand-ins took all the "stars" positions. Cameras and lighting took forever, and then it was lunch.

At about 2 p.m., the "stars" appeared from their quarters, each with a gang of personal make-up artists, runners and PR who drifted away when not needed. For morning rehearsals, the hundreds of real candles in the candelabras were not lit but then at 2 p.m. they all were, so any door opening caused a draught and candle wax would drip. If it hit a female extra in a low-cut ball gown—she made a face or yelped. Everything stopped—much shouting in Russian and Italian, and a make-up girl came rushing through to sort out the problem. Then a ladder appeared with a guy to pop up and trim the offending candle.

Scene.30: A mud-splattered guest arrives in the large shape of Prussian General MUFFLING; his dishevelled appearance causes a *mixture of courtesy and exasperation* across the Ballroom. *His fat personality makes him slightly comic. But he is too good a soldier to be a figure of fun.* "*That gentleman will spoil the dancing,*" remarks the Duchess. Wellington greets Muffling, who looks uneasily around, then blurts out: "*Napoleon has crossed the border with all his forces.*"

With news of Napoleon's invasion, the evening's frivolity came to an abrupt halt. Historically, a Lieutenant Henry Webster had arrived mud-splattered with a despatch for his direct commander, the Prince of Orange, who immediately handed it to the Duke. Reading it, without a flicker of emotion, he is reputed to have said: "Napoleon has humbugged me, by God; he has gained twenty-four hours' march on me."[330]

In the film, it is General Muffling, Wellington's Prussian liaison officer, who is the conduit for despatches from Blucher. He was played by a mud-splattered British actor, John Savident. Born in Guernsey in 1938, Savident had spent the war under the German occupation of the island. Such proximity may even have helped him with his character's Prussian accent. After serving as a police officer in Manchester, he turned to acting and built up a career as a character actor. Just prior, he had appeared in *Battle of Britain* (1969) and would work for Stanley Kubrick on *A Clockwork Orange* (1971), before becoming a household name to UK TV audiences playing the "bellicose but romantic butcher"[331] Fred Elliott in ITV's long-running soap opera *Coronation Street* for twelve years from 1994.

The casting of an actor with a big-boned gait may owe more to confusion between the historical Karl Freiherr von Muffling and a Prussian messenger whose huge, ungainly appearance prompted Wellington to describe as "the fattest soldier on the slowest horse in the Prussian army."[332]

Muffling was a general and the conduit between the two allies, and therefore his place would have been as close to Wellington as possible. Messages would have been delivered *to* him, not *by* him, but Savident's mud-splattered appearance in the glittering ballroom gets top marks for drama, even if it somewhat muddies the history.

Before shooting the scene, the actor had to undergo a last-minute make-up addition to replicate the storm blowing outside: "the weather that night (of the scene) was very wet. Before he came into the studio, he had to stand outside while an Italian prop-man popped up a ladder and poured a bucket of water over his head. He was not amused."

The effect of the startling news on the revellers that June night in 1815 was described in a letter:

> You may imagine the Electrical Shocks of such intelligence. Most of the Women in Floods of tears and all Military in an instant collected round their respective leaders, and in less than 20 minutes the room was cleared.[333]

Veronica De Laurentiis recalled this dramatic re-staging as being very impressive:

> I remember in the scene of the ballroom, even though there wasn't a lot of acting, Christopher Plummer had to do a lot there, when the door opened and they (John Savident as Muffling) come in and say that war had started and we had to all leave. It was a very beautiful, tough moment there. And it really worked. In the movie *and* on set.

Jane Lennox, another sister to Sarah and "Georgy" Lennox, was an eyewitness as men left for the war, and possibly death:

> I know I was in a state of wild delight; the scene itself was so stirring, and the company so brilliant…I was scanning over my tablets (dance-card), which were filled from top to bottom with the names of the partners to whom I was engaged; when, on raising my eyes, I became aware of a great preponderance of ladies in the room. White muslin and tarlatans abandoned; but the gallant uniforms had sensibly diminished.[334]

For Ian Ogilvy, playing Sir William De Lancey, Wellington's quartermaster-general, akin to a chief of staff, it was an undemanding part, with very few lines to learn, that only required him to "look concerned, but in an unruffled, English sort of a way."[335] He finished his dancing scenes with his "charming" wife Magdalene, played by Veronica, with a touching tiny vignette of parting as De Lancey marched off to war. It was a later addition to the screenplay.

> Insert scene: (Magdalene) *"May I go with the army? You can ask the Duke. He allowed ladies in Spain. We've had so little time together."* (De Lancey) *"Madeleine, a battle is no place…"* (Magdalene) *"I fear I may never see you again."*

"Then the day came that I had to do my lines." Fifty-years later, Veronica vividly recalled the atmosphere on set for her big moment:

> I was really scared because I said — Oh, what am I going to do? Then I saw that on the set they had put a platform up for us for the scene. It was a close-up of us talking and I remember that the whole studio, everyone, came to see Silvana Mangano's daughter say her first lines. And I'm like — Oh my god! But then they turned on the lights and Bondarchuk said: "Action!" — I wasn't scared anymore. In that moment, I said to myself, this is what I want to do, and so that was a cool, beautiful moment for me. But then life took me somewhere else, and I didn't pursue it until 25 years later.

Although her father was very supportive of her career ambitions, Silvana Mangano, her strong-willed film star mother, pressured Veronica to give up her dreams at the tender age of 19. Years later, after becoming a mother herself and a successful author, she would scratch that acting itch in middle-age.

When production moved to Russia, Veronica was asked to accompany her father as Bondarchuk planned to film another scene with her. It is pure speculation what he had in mind. Perhaps a clue might lie in one of the most moving accounts of the whole Waterloo campaign, which was written by her character, the young bride Magdalene Hall.

Hearing news of the battle and confused reports about the fate of her husband De Lancey, she rushed by carriage to the stricken field:

The horses screamed at the smell of corruption, which in many places was offensive…When we got to the village, Sir G. Scovell met the carriage, and opening the door, said, "Stop one moment." I said, "Is he alive?" "Yes, alive; and the surgeons are of opinion that he may recover. We are so grieved for what you have suffered." "Oh! never mind what I have suffered. Let me go to him now."

She found him lying critically wounded in a small cottage near the battlefield. For six long, sleepless days she nursed him as best she could. With no bandages to hand, she had to rip up her petticoat while applying the standard practice of leeches to the blooded wounds — but to no avail.

I stood near my husband, and he looked up at me and said, "Magdalene, my love, the spirits." I stooped down close to him and held the bottle of lavender to him: I also sprinkled some near him. He looked pleased. He gave a little gulp, as if something was in his throat. The doctor said, "Ah, poor De Lancey! He is gone." I pressed my lips to his and left the room.[336]

The scene, whatever it was — never happened.

Scene.23: (Wellington) *"They're scum, Charlotte…Gin is the spirit of their patriotism."*

Before we leave the ballroom, let us see what happened to two Irish reprobates at this swanky posh party: Mulholland and Mckevitt, *two rough looking* SENTRIES. Both creations of writer Harry Craig's Irish background, possibly, according to his daughter, based on real friends of his. The first was listed in *all* publicity, including on-screen, as played by Scottish actor Charles Borromel, who had carved out a notable career with supporting roles in a string of 1960s Italian *peplum* mini epics: *Pontius Pilate* (1961) as Caesar, *Messalina vs. the Son of Hercules* (1963) as Caligula, etc. One can suppose he was a resident in Rome and therefore freely available.

His sidekick Mckevitt, also played by a resident of the city, was quite a colourful real-life character. Listed as Colin Watson, his real name was Colin Webster-Watson, a New Zealand poet and sculptor. In a varied career, he had also been a dancer and comedian at London's notorious Windmill Theatre, as well as a radio sports commentator in Cardiff.

Described by Peter Davies as "A wandering upper-class bohemian socialite", the artist, as a fellow émigré in the city was a good friend of Craig's. His studio, "a wonderful, penthouse apartment, not hugely grand, but with terraces and lovely flowers, overlooking all those hills around Rome", was a popular stop for many celebrities including Gloria Swanson, Carroll Baker and Harold Robbins. His work, owing much to his appreciation of Picasso and reflecting his love of mythology and the sea, was described by a reviewer: "his sculptures are a marrying of movement and metal."[337]

One Sunday, during the shoot, some cast members, including Richard Heffer, accepted an invitation by Webster-Watson for lunch: "Colin showed us his bronzes, some of them most attractive."[338] With work gracing the collection of Jacqueline Kennedy and Aristotle Onassis, Peter Davies bought a pottery mask for the princely sum of £40!

The script, with some nice touches (MULHOLLAND *is feeling a rotten tooth with his tongue*), uses the pair as an example of Wellington's distain for his men: "Scum of the earth." In the film, there is a brief shot during Wellington and the duchess's exchange about the rough quality of two such soldierly "scum," who in the script are the two Irish characters. Comparing photos of the two performers, one would not want to place a bet on whether they are the *same* uniformed soldiers, staring ahead as the storm growls in the window behind them.

While Webster-Watson's involvement was perhaps no more than a cameo, he does appear on some of the publicity, but it's the invisibility of Borromel that is a complete mystery. There is no record or memory of him in either Rome or Russia, and so would not have been at the "battle." Despite many viewings, it is impossible to detect him *anywhere* in the film, and so his on-screen credit, in particular, is quite confounding.

In the script, the two are guarding the door to the anteroom which Wellington and his generals enter following news of the French attack. As is very clear to see in the film, a portly middle-aged Harry Craig himself, appears in a cameo as one of the sentries (on the left), while the other is not identifiable. It is also possible he may have had a chance to speak one of his own penned lines, playing *Mulholland, his eyes twinkling in his Caliban face, whispers across to Mckevitt: "Boney's the boy for bothering a ballroom."* The line, like many others, never reached the screen, nor, it seems, did his Irish *"beggars and scoundrels."*

Tucked away on the edge of the studio backlot were constructed a couple of structures for Napoleon and Wellington's respective Headquarters — the latter, a requisitioned inn. "It was actually set up in a corner of the studio," remembers Peter Davies, "which kind of illustrates how big the studio was, but this was like in a tent or something like that." It was the setting for several brief scenes designed to show the mounting tension of the commander as he desperately waited for news of the Prussians, via Muffling.

> Scene.67: Muffling plunges into Wellington's HQ with the vital news of Blucher's retreat to Wavre, with Grouchy's French following behind. Muffling assures him: *"You may fight your battle, Lord Duke."* Wellington, after checking his watch, politely asks Muffling to return to Blucher and beg him: *"to come to Waterloo by one o'clock."*

They developed this scene during the shooting, with Wellington asking Lord Hay for the time instead of glancing at his own watch. Awkward, Hay falters and De Lancey, played by Ian Ogilvy, crisply answers with the correct time. The shot is not only beautifully lit and composed, but also cinematic.

Echoing the Great Masters, director of photography Armando Nannuzzi conveys the effect of the single candle flickering over the faces of Wellington and his staff in the cramped room. As we discussed earlier, the candle would not have offered enough light without some clever extra lighting — testament to Nannuzzi's craft. In the scene, Lord Hay, played by Peter Davies, stands with his back to the lit table, plunging his face into shadow, foreshadowing if one is allowed the pun, his fate on the violent morrow.

In the script, the scene ends with the generals debating their chances of success, as Blucher and his Prussians need to trudge through the mud to get to Waterloo. In the final film, Wellington wraps up the conference and all leave, except Lord Hay, who he bids to stay a moment before asking; *"'Who did you give your watch to, Hay?'* He finds out that I have given my watch away because I think I'm going to die." There follows a short interchange between the two men about death, in which Plummer says mournfully: *"Having those thoughts sometimes makes them come true."* He stands facing the candle, its bright glow of flames dancing across his face; this is a character who understands death and war. It is a tiny vignette but offers a rare glimpse behind the mask of command, and it's beautifully played by Plummer who gives it great poignancy and delicately. At what point this was written, and by whom, we do not know, but it is inspired, and one wishes there had been more such scenes.

Peter found it very satisfying to play:

This was a very enjoyable scene for me because of the intimate dialogue with Christopher, without having to worry about dancing or controlling a horse! He was really nice, he really helped. He didn't exactly coach my dialogue, but he almost did. I also remember the scary Mr Bondarchuk being pleased with the scene and giving me a hug.

One suspects that the lack of huge logistical issues that dominated most scenes allowed the director and actors the creative space to explore and improvise. For Peter, there was a pleasant and surprising postscript: "my wife — when we were dating twenty-two years ago — she turned to me and said: 'Where's your watch, Hay?' She had checked it out somehow!"

> Scene.123: *Preceded by Bagpipers playing The Flowers of the Forest, Gordon's Highlanders take position on the crest of the ridge. They are noble — but in numbers, less than three hundred; they seem sacrificial.*

Out on the backlot, in the shadow of crumbling sets of Ancient Rome and the Wild West, the earth shuddered to the first salvos of the battle of *Waterloo*. It was here that the real Gordons, who had been forbidden to travel to Russia, would enact their counter-attack against the French on some rough ground, studded with pyrotechnics.

Captain Oxley was on hand beside the camera as the action was prepared: "There were a hundred soldiers — fifty real Scots (including our bus driver Mario) on the Left Half (I was just off set) and fifty Italian 'Scots' on the Right half." The hours ticked by as the cameras and effects were prepared, and the Jocks who had been up since the small hours were unhappy as lunch was delayed. Promised the next rehearsal would be a "take," they dutifully took their positions "stomachs rumbling in time with the drumbeat" but collectively they decided to make a point.

On "Action," the line of Highlanders "swept over the brow of the hill playing *Arrivaderci Roma*, a popular Italian song of the 1950s. 'Cut!' screamed the director, tearing at his hair. 'Okay wise guys, go get your lunch, and next time let's have a different tune!'"[339] Lunch may have mollified the Scots but the next problem was with the civilian extras as Oxley recalled:

> The two Dress Rehearsals were disasters — at the first explosion, the right half (Italian extras) fled back to the buses. I then suggested that the real Scots formed the Front Rank and the

Italians the Second Rank. Once again at the first bang, the Italians fled to the buses (including those carrying the Regimental Colours) and refused to take any further part. So, the real Scots did the Battle scenes on their own and loved the explosions. The Pipe Major and many others lost their make-up whiskers, but he played the Regimental march *The Cock of the North* with great Élan.

Before leaving Rome, the Pipers made a demonstration film for the Russian soldiers who would don kilts to play the Highlanders on the Ukrainian location. "It was a simple film showing how the band marched, counter-marched, the Drum Majors signals with the mace, fingers on the pipes, etc," Pipe Major Joe Kerr commented: "tae teach the MacIvans tae march."[340]

The month of filming allowed the cast and crew to enjoy the delights of Rome — The Eternal City. Captain Oxley's wife, Easter, only visited the set once: "I was quite happy not to go again and spent my time seeing Rome. But it was interesting and cured me forever of thinking it would be fun to be in a film."

Instead, she divided her time between nursing one poorly piper in hospital, as the staff was often on strike — and seeing the sights. Through the help of a friend, she and her husband attended an audience with Pope Paul VI in The Vatican; Nigel was honoured to "shake his hand."

A cultural tour of the Immortal City was arranged by the film company for the Gordons, but unsurprisingly the more salubrious attractions were a bigger draw. "The soldiers loved Rome, the bars, the cinemas, nightclubs and often hitch-hiked across the city." The regimental history gleefully relates two tales of the Scots abroad.

Late one night, Captain Oxley was woken from his slumber by the hotel manager at three in the morning. An altercation had developed between an irate taxi driver and a group of Jocks returning from their revelries; they had paid the fare with Embassy cigarette coupons. What, the manager asked frantically, was he going to do about it? "Just you pay it, and I'll sort it out in the morning," was the abrupt, sleepy reply.

One morning, perhaps the following one, the hotel restaurant offering of "a very appetising chicken dish, but one smothered in garlic" caused a mutiny to a man, as the "Jocks downed utensils and refused to eat 'this foreign muck'. Captain Oxley mollified the stricken manager, telling him:

'Steak, egg and chips. That's what to give them. I'll tell them that's on the menu tonight, and that'll keep them quiet.'"

That evening, after a hard day in the heat and melting wax of the ballroom, the Jocks filed into the dining room in high anticipation. Shock, horror and anger erupted as they were "confronted by thin strips of leathery meat, potato crisps and a boiled egg." Oxley, well aware of how bad the situation could become, politely but firmly advised the manager: "If you really don't want your hotel broken up, you should get the menu right. I can hold them for half an hour — after that you're on your own!" With some oaths and shouting from the kitchen, the riot was averted: "Within half an hour plates of succulent steak, with fried egg on top, and piles of chips were served to the starving Jocks."[341]

Originally quartered in a dull modern hotel on the outskirts of Rome, most of the cast gravitated towards the city centre with its echoes of *La Dolce Vita*. The plush Hotel de La Ville, at the top of the famous Spanish Steps, was a Mecca for artists and actors and became the favourite watering hole for the unit.

Peter Davies' agent, Jimmy Frazier, who was in town and working hard looking after his client's interests, dissuaded him from staying at the hotel. "'Oh no, it's expensive (he was a thrifty Scot). I am going to send you to the *Pensione Riviera* and you can get your *own* bottle of scotch, instead of wasting your money on expensive drinks here.' I was 17, and he was telling me to get my own scotch!"

The *Pensione Riviera*, which also housed Richard Heffer, was an excellent choice; an inexpensive and intimate Roman hotel tucked away, full of charm and character. "You had this little elevator that you had to put a coin into, that went up the outside of the building," Peter Davies warmly recalled his digs, "I had this lovely room and a balcony that you could hear the sounds of Rome coming up. The proprietor was a lady called Contessa Bimbi — she knew everyone in Rome, she would have cocktails in her little apartment there every evening. There would be all this gossip about Helmut Berger," and his mentor/lover, the flamboyant and brilliant Italian director, Luchino Visconti.

The hotel was popular with other visiting performers, including the British actor Jeremy Kemp, who was filming in Rome for a widely disliked director, and became a firm drinking buddy. "All he was talking about was — what a monster Michael Winner was," Peter Davies remembered. "I got a feeling that probably Jeremy Kemp was a bit of a monster too! He was perfectly nice — very *actor*-like. He was quite a star in his own right at the time."

No doubt due to the energy of his scotch drinking agent, Peter got invited for dinner at the home of one of Italy's top directors:

> I went to Zeffirelli's house when I was in Rome. Really lovely house, and Franco showed me his studio that was up above the garages; just all the designs from his operas. He was a very charming man, and he was recovering as he'd been almost killed in a car accident with Gina Lollobrigida…There was an executive from Paramount there, with his wife, and he actually said over the dinner table: "We saw your rushes…very good!"

Richard accepted a late-night invitation to a very different panoply of entertainment:

> Just as I expected — a regular dive; all queens (including one crew member!) — and we had the lot — a free drag show; one appeared naked at a glass-fronted door and knocked on it with his weapon whilst the drag queen pirouetted in fishnet and sequins…while I smoked and drank wine whilst talking high speed, colloquial Italian! But there was no danger for me, as it was funny — (thank heaven).[342]

Regardless of tastes, these "delights" would be in short supply when the cast reassembled a few months later in — Snake City.

Some of the 200 trained dancers filling the vast ballroom set at Dinocittà.
AUTHOR'S COLLECTION

Left to right: Ian Ogilvy as William De Lancey, Veronica De Laurentiis as Magdalene Hall, Peter Davies as Lord Hay and Susan Wood as Sarah.
AUTHOR'S COLLECTION

Serving soldiers with the Gordon Highlanders dancing in the ballroom. This was the first sequence to be shot. © RONNIE BELL

Left: Private Barry Williams in costume. © RONNIE BELL *Right: Major Nigel Oxley and his wife Easter in the late 1970s.* © MAJOR NIGEL OXLEY

Virginia McKenna as the Duchess of Richmond with Christopher Plummer, behind is Fred Jackson in a non-speaking role as the Prince of Brunswick.
AUTHOR'S COLLECTION

Sergei Bondarchuk issues last minute instructions for Veronica's big scene, with Ian Ogilvy looking on. AUTHOR'S COLLECTION

Filming the sequence meant many hours of waiting in the dressing room, Richard Heffer as Mercer and Jeffry Wickham as Colbourne, neither had any lines to say.

Left to right: Rome-based artist Colin Webster-Watson was given a cameo as Mckevitt (subsequently cut), John Savident as Muffling was not happy being doused with water for the scene. With them is Ian Ogilvy. Note the ladder in the background ready for a crew member to re-light the candles for another take. © RICHARD HEFFER

The Royal Palace at Caserta. Orson Welles as King Louis bids farewell to a lady of the court, played by Andrea Dosne, before leaving for exile.
AUTHOR'S COLLECTION

CHAPTER 8

"Let's Not Dramatise, Yet…"

> Scene.13: *The* CROWD *is in almost revolutionary fervor…* SER-
> GEANTS *are reading Napoleon's Proclamation. "It was the cry of
> injured honour that brought me back to France…"*

With filming at Dinocittà completed during April, the production moved out to locations around Italy. First stop — 25 miles northwest of Rome, along the ancient Via Clodia, to the small Renaissance settlement of Oriolo Romano. It would double for the French town of Grenoble, which Napoleon reached during his triumphant return from Elba.

In the film, Ney has just defected with a small army and is greeted by the locals with apparent enthusiasm for the returned emperor. In the centre of Oriolo Romano is the stunning Piazza Umberto I, dominated by the grand Palazzo Altieri, a popular location for many subsequent films, including John Madden's *Captain Corelli's Mandolin* in 2002. The palace, built in the late 16th century, is a fine example of Mannerist architecture applied to the fortified mansions owned by noble families of Rome. It is identifiable on screen by the small, thin clock tower standing aloft.

Across the square and situated past the Fontana delle Picche, is a balconied building which stood in for Grenoble's town hall, which, as of 2020, houses the Meridiana Caffe. Here Steiger, accompanied by Dan O'Herlihy, gave a spirited speech to the large array of suitably dressed locals.

> Scene.13: SHOW *the* CROWD: *wild, happy faces screaming their
> joy…Then, suddenly, they give Napoleon silence. He looks around in
> the silence. "I have come back…"*

Daniele Nannuzzi recalled the scene: "We used the square and the façade of the building where, from the balcony, Napoleon appears…the square was crowded…I remember that they carried an old soldier on a wooden stretcher who had lost his legs in battle. For the role, an extra was chosen, not an actor who had lost his legs in an accident."

The script describes a "Fat Man" also being held aloft by the crowd as a "pantomime" King Louis. The part is listed in the credits played by forty-year-old Guidarino Guidi, who Daniele remembers as "very fat," but doesn't survive the cut, although in the film the populace holds aloft a "Fat Man" effigy of the King and set fire to it.

> Scene.13: NAPOLEON *(to the crowd)* *"The Fat King in Paris has corrupted the honour of Frenchmen. He will be carried from his throne."*

Historically, Napoleon and his rapidly amassing army moved north to Paris. Bondarchuk and his army packed up and travelled south to Dino's home town of Naples, which would stand in for the lair of "The Fat King."

> Scene.8: *The* KING *glances significantly at* SOULT… KING *(calmly)* *"Let's not dramatize yet. General Bonaparte and his followers — a mere thousand men — are not very dangerous yet."*

It is reputably, one of the largest palaces in the world. And nothing Dino could take credit for. The Royal Palace of Caserta stands in the shadow of Mount Vesuvius in Naples. It was built by architect Luigi Vanvitelli in 1752 for Charles VII of Naples (Charles III of Spain), a Bourbon, related to the French dynasty that would soon lose its head in the Revolution of 1789. At the time, Naples was an independent Kingdom: reactionary and conservative, and seemingly impervious to the fermenting political shifts bubbling in nearby France. Caserta was the outward expression of a dynasty secure in power and designed to wow Europe with its opulence.

It would also play a minor part in the ebb and flow of the Napoleonic Wars. Firstly, Lord Nelson, following his significant victory at The Nile in 1798, arrived in Naples to be warmly welcomed by King Ferdinand and his court. Finding distraction with the beautiful Lady Emma Hamilton, he soon attempted to prop up the decadent regime. Later, he was forced to abandon the city when an insurrection deposed the terrified monarchs, before taking them to safety upon Royal Navy ships.

A few years later, Napoleon's most flamboyant Marshal Murat, a strutting peacock, puffed with arrogance and bravado, was given the throne of the newly acquired French satellite kingdom in 1808. When Napoleon made his mad dash from Elba, Murat attempted to support him before suffering a major defeat at the Battle of Tolentino at the hands of the Austrians in May 1815. This former King met his end with his back to the wall, facing a firing squad.

According to the 1996 UNESCO nomination for the World's Heritage list:

> The Royal Palace, the crowning achievement of Luigi Vanvitelli, anticipated the external appearance of 18th century buildings whilst at the same time representing the swan song of the spectacular art of the baroque, from which it adopted all the features needed to create the illusion of multidirectional space.[343]

The Royal Palace, measuring two and a half million square feet, has a symmetrical layout comprising four courtyards and three atriums. Spanning five floors it boasts 1200 rooms, 40 completely decorated with frescoes, and includes an extensive library and a theatre. The most impressive floor is reserved for the Royal Apartments. Long corridors with decorated terracotta faux marble floors, all lit by magnificent chandeliers encrusted with gilt bronze. They lead to the Throne Room, some over 130 feet long and lit by six windows; high above stretches the vaulted ceiling, which portrays "The laying of the foundation stone of the Palace. January 20th 1752" by the Neapolitan painter Gennaro Maldarelli. These spaces of the so called "Royal Floor" symbolise the absolute power of the then ruling House of Bourbon-Two Sicilies.

Under the direction of production designer Mario Garbuglia, set decorators Emilio D'Andria and Kenneth Muggleston, laid out a multitude of props around these glittering halls and apartments. These would double as Napoleon's palace of Fontainebleau, and the Palace de Tuileries (formally opposite the Louvre) in Paris, the ancestral residence of the House of Bourbon.

The gilt and bombast of Caserta was a suitable setting for Orson Welles as King Louis XVIII, who regains his throne following Napoleon's abdication, before being forced to flee upon his return less than a year later.

Welles would later say that his many star cameos were an attempt to bestow some "class" on mediocre films. His notable presence had graced a host of European films during the previous few decades, including two Napoleonic-themed ones. In Sacha Guitry's *Napoléon* (1955), he was the last cameo in the three-hour stilted cavalcade, with a very awkward performance as Napoleon's jailer on Saint Helena — Hudson Lowe. For Abel Gance's *Austerlitz* (1960), he played the American inventor John

Fulton, who tries to sell his invention of the submarine to the sceptical Corsican. Neither cameo play to Welles' strength, and one can see him rather bemused, calculating the Francs to Dollars conversion in his head.

Welles would have known Bondarchuk after they worked together on the Yugoslav epic *Battle of Neretva* (1969), but one suspects there was little persuasion required to appear in *Waterloo* — money talked. A few years previously, he had been approached by the Bond producers to play *Goldfinger*. If the story is to be believed, the offer was withdrawn as Welles demanded *too* much money. Considering the lucre available for the phenomenal Bond franchise — it must have been eye-watering!

Dino did not balk at spending money if he felt it enhanced his projects, but it appears Welles was a canny operator. So, after what should have been two brief scenes to shoot, the company found itself held to ransom by its illustrious star. "I have been told he was getting an enormous amount of salary per day," remembered French actor Philippe Forquet:

> By (his) contract, he demanded to do his make-up himself. He had to build and shape a Bourbon nose on his face with some sort of modelling clay every morning. It was supposed to take more or less two-and-a-half hours, but it took Orson Welles about four hours, and then he was not satisfied. He would get angry, hollering — "It isn't right…it looks terrible…I have to redo it" — and he'd tear it off his face! The Producer was about to faint. The production had planned on two days for Welles to complete his part, but with his wicked trick he worked eight days. I imagine his pay cheque was getting bigger, and it's exactly what he wanted. Of course, he didn't fool anyone, but what could the production do? One can't fire Orson Welles; they just had to put up with him.

There may be some exaggeration as to the number of days, as Bondarchuk said later he only had Welles for two days, but there is more than a kernel of truth to this story as Welles was notorious for playing the system. He would have seen such a large production as a cash cow, and no doubt played every trick in the book.

> Scene.8: NEY *(gritting his teeth)* *"I hate him now for the evil he is doing. I will bring Napoleon to Paris in an iron cage."*

With the make-up finally applied, the next barrier to overcome was one of language. Dan O'Herlihy as Marshal Ney enters and must show due reverence to his king; he was having trouble understanding the intentions of the director. Journalist Anthony Haden-Guest, watching from the side-lines, paints an amusing picture of lost-in-translation, international film production:

> Welles is — stunning. Every face muscle twitches, dragging its poundage of flesh, registering decibels of emotion, while his eyes float and cloud, ironic/affectionate/royal, while O'Herlihy clicks his heels, inclines his head, bows. But Bondarchuk hurries on, harangues O'Herlihy in Russian and executes the bow, heel clicks, inclination of the neck, at foxtrot tempo. O'Herlihy beams and swings into the routine again, Bondarchuk grimaces, bows again. The interpreter bows. The bemused O'Herlihy bows crisply back at them. The Russian assistant director bows briefly. For a golden moment they bow at each other, like the pecking chickens on the child' toy until they all stop, flushed, and O'Herlihy demands, "Do I have to fill the whole scene with bows?" O'Herlihy tried to fathom, "It's the translation problem. I always think he means the opposite of what he really means." Welles removes his gaze from Inner Space, swivels his eyes around. "He just means he wants no bows at all," he remarks imperturbably.[344]

> Scene.14: *The* KING *goes through a crowd of* ATTENDANTS *and* GUARDS IN WHITE *towards a large travelling coach…"Perhaps the people will let me go…just as they are letting him come…"*

In Welles's second and final scene filmed one evening, the overweight king, leaning on his cane, makes his way down the vast marble steps of his palace to a waiting carriage. The actor had been quietly watching the filming preparations from the side lines, and suggested a subtle change to Bondarchuk, who remembered:

> I prepared especially carefully for the second day — the shooting of the abdication episode placing the royal guards, confidants, and relatives. Welles arrived, made up his face (he does it himself), looked at the resulting stage set and said very delicately: "And what if the relatives stand by the carriage?" We rehearsed this scene again. Welles again asks: "Who is this left and right?" I said that this is the king's retinue. "And you cannot remove them?" he asked. "You can, I think, but where will all my splendour be?" And

we removed them. And I saw there is a lonely, useless person. All alone, going into the void. Only the sound of the cane is heard before the space absorbs it. Here you have a lesson of directing in its purest form.[345]

It is not a big detail, but perhaps is an excellent illustration of the stream of tiny contributions that happen on most film sets. A still shows the director's original staging with the infirm king followed by a trail of courtiers down the stairs. While one may harbour a nagging suspicion that the actor's vaunted ego may have played a part, without doubt, Welles' suggestion is an improvement, and neatly underlines the defeat of his regal character.

Most, even great and renowned directors will acknowledge the contributions from any member of their units. The author has some personal experience of this as a director on projects, in scale, a world away from the subject of this book. Fostering a collaborative environment on a set helps the creative process, but one must walk the tightrope between listening, and trusting your own vision. The key, in one's humble experience, is always to park the ego, and ask: does this suggestion, wherever it comes from, improve the scene for the good of the film?

From the outset, it seems Bondarchuk had discarded his martinet style of directing that had so intimidated his Russian actors on *War and Peace*, and embraced collaboration. Or perhaps, he felt at odds with the Anglo-Saxon language and was happy on this occasion to defer to the extraordinary talent that was Orson Welles.

Young British actor Peter Davies remembers meeting the living legend at the lavish party thrown at the beginning of production. With their shared passion for the Performing Arts, the callow youth felt sure it would be the start of a beautiful friendship:

> Orson Welles was there. I remember seeing him looking very serious about being photographed. And clueless youth that I was, I just kind of walked up to him and introduced myself. Fortunately, I do remember calling him Mr Welles — I'm glad I didn't say Orson! And I just remember him looking at me, thinking: *What is this person doing?* I said: "Mr Welles, I'm such an admirer of your work, I will never forget your face in *The Third Man.*" And he said nothing! He just looked at me like a Martian had stepped in to his space — and then sort of growled. What really makes it funny, is that I felt pretty sure Mr Welles would

say, *"Oh really! What are you doing for dinner tonight?"* I thought we would strike up a friendship. He may have shaken my hand and said thank you, but my expected outcome was a dinner invitation! I really thought I had enough interesting information about film-making that Orson Welles would want to have dinner with me. I thought it was assured!

Heinz Feldhaus, who had his hands full keeping the production Panavision cameras working, was less than impressed to be asked a favour by the visiting "King": "Orson Welles was there; a bastard, not very nice. He suddenly came up, or someone brought a camera to me to see if I could service it, and that camera had nothing to do with the film. And I said no."

Scene.8: (King) *"How those soldiers always exaggerate! In an iron cage. No one is asking that much."*

Although they shared no scenes for *Waterloo*, Christopher Plummer had got to know the great actor listening to his "outrageous" stories while they made *Oedipus the King* (1968). Plummer, in a warm tribute in his autobiography said: Welles was not just one person, but a crowd. A Renaissance man stuck in the modern world but who could belong in any period, except, he mused; "the Age of Reason."[346] Orson Welles was a living legend, although his time on *Waterloo* was very short — his presence was undeniably memorable, both on and off screen.

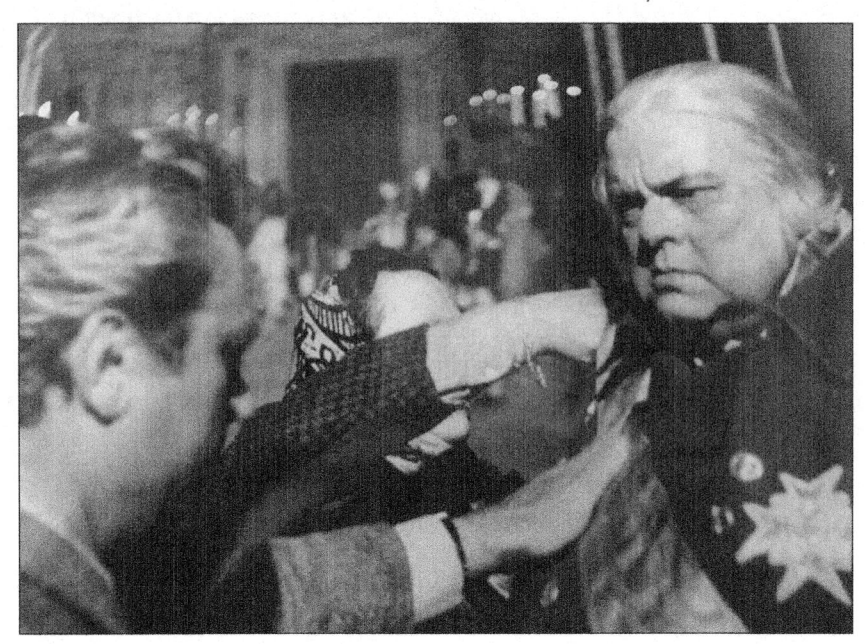

Sergei Bondarchuk has a last word with Orson Welles, as King Louis, before the cameras roll. © HEINZ FELDHAUS

The director's original staging for the scene of Louis's departure, before the actor suggested a subtle change. © HEINZ FELDHAUS

Left: Rod Steiger and Dan O'Herlihy on the balcony overlooking the square of Oriolo Romano. AUTHOR'S COLLECTION *Right: Cameraman Nino Cristiani.* © HEINZ FELDHAUS

The impressive square of the town. AUTHOR'S COLLECTION

Rod Steiger standing in the ornate Palace at Caserta for the opening scene as the marshals, led by Ney, demand his abdication. AUTHOR'S COLLECTION

CHAPTER 9

"And Above All...My Will!"

"'I'm very conscious of the hat,' said Steiger as he fingered his black bicorn hat, brooding up into it." The actor was musing to Anthony Haden-Guest, a journalist for *The Sunday Telegraph* who was visiting the Naples location in April 1969: "I'm not trying to think what Napoleon would have felt when he was saying farewell to his troops. I'm trying to think what I would feel."

They were preparing to shoot one of the "great tear-jerkers of all time" in the courtyard of the Royal Palace of Caserta; Napoleon's farewell to his Old Guard before going into exile. Having acknowledged defeat and signed the document of abdication, he takes leave of the bulk of his *Grognards* (he was permitted to only take a thousand men to Elba). The pathos and drama of this occasion quickly grew into myth, so it is surprising that it was not in the December '68 draft, but a later addition. It was the actor's biggest and most dramatic moment before stepping onto the field of battle.

> Steiger always refers to Napoleon as "he". "Anybody who identified with Napoleon would have to be a megalomaniac...Before this I read, oh, ten books about Napoleon." He shrugs, tilting the hat. "Then I stopped. It was getting contradictory. I am playing him," he says with relish, "as a very sick man."[347]

As we saw with his preparation for *The Pawnbroker*, Steiger worked hard to create the character he was to play, burrowing deep beneath the surface. Although historians question the extent of Napoleon's illness during his last campaign, there is no doubt he was past his prime. For an actor, this was an obvious starting point. Steiger contacted the American Medical Association in Chicago for a copy of Napoleon's autopsy:

> And they did!...which they sent to me, and ironically enough, they (British doctors in 1821) had cut him open on a billiard

table, you know, it's just incredible the Emperor of the world on a billiard table...And he was dying of cirrhosis of the liver or partially cirrhosis cancer of the stomach; incredible haemorrhoids, advanced gonorrhoea. He had a germ he picked up in Egypt that got into the lungs. So, the man, the last six years of his life, I played him at 45, was dying. And that gave me the basis of my conception, which was simply a man whose mind was so powerful.[348]

He was a dead man who wouldn't die. I'm trying to make him human and believable.[349]

Bondarchuk, a Russian and self-declared Tolstoian, and steeped in the Napoleonic era, saw Napoleon as a tragic hero who carried within him the seeds of his own destruction: "Tolstoy has a marvellous phrase. 'Napoleon was mortally wounded at Borodino.'" The bloody 1812 battle that had stunted the French advance on Moscow, which formed the centre-piece of *War and Peace*, was to Tolstoy the beginning of the end for the emperor's ambitions.

Bondarchuk acknowledged Steiger's starting point, but believed: "The illnesses were not the main thing that dragged Napoleon down. There was too much strength, and power concentrated in this one man. Such a man must always defeat himself."

Both being actors with an affinity for The Method, Steiger's approach chimed with Bondarchuk's philosophy about acting:

> It is necessary to create an entirely original character. Not just the clothes...because I think that the highest mission of the actor is transformation, to change the character into someone born anew. When I approach an actor, if I see certain features already in him, I try to pull them out, to make them brighter.[350]

Both were determined to avoid the usual caricature, as Steiger explained:

> All an actor has to do, to make you think Napoleon, is put on that hat and stick his hand into his shirt. That's why the point was not just to get all the details and Napoleonic lore correct. What Sergei and I tried to do was to cut through all the layers of myth and misconception which the history books have piled on top of the real man; we tried to discover Napoleon.[351]

Between them, they strove to present Napoleon as naturalistically as possible; clothing him in slippers and a dressing gown before disrobing him in a bath. As props help an actor, the two reasoned there was something that anyone in middle-age would have possessed. "Naturally, no one now knows exactly what the Emperor really was like," Bondarchuk remarked: "It is known, for example, that he used glasses…But the portraits showed nothing like that. He suffered from diseases. At times he was tormented by terrible pains — it was unlikely that the Emperor made 'portrait' poses. I did not want the film to be a Napoleon monument or symbol, but — Napoleon the man."[352]

While it is easy to create the external impression of power, Steiger grappled with how to convey the inevitable hidden pressures.

> When he walked in the room and everybody bows, they know that's the emperor: that takes care of the greatness…the problem for an actor is to try to create how he gets up, how he sits, the pain sometimes not to pass out when somebody is talking to you, little things like that, because greatness, you can't play…His ambition is to succeed and to win this last great battle to make the greatest exit in the world because he knows he's going to die within six years.[353]

According to his own research, the actor believed that the night before the battle, Napoleon, to keep his ailments and demons at bay, had "bombed himself out on laudanum."[354] Whatever the truth may be, Steiger used this detail to forge a very human foible-laden portrait. How far he could draw on personal experience of LSD et al., during the so called "Summer of Love" — is unknown.

During the early months of production in Italy, director and star met each night to act out ideas for the following day. Bondarchuk's wife Irina Skobtseva observed how they communicated with just body language: "from a half look, although they spoke different languages,"[355] along with the help of a translator and elaborate pantomime, the two developed a unique thespian language. As with Plummer, Steiger added and changed his dialogue with the full blessing of the director.

> Scene.02: *The* FRAME *showing Napoleon's Abdication remains frozen for a moment, then it comes alive.* NAPOLEON *is leaning over a table, (without raising his eyes)* "No. I will not consent to be a fallen statue."

In the opening scene where Napoleon is forced to abdicate, the script is very sparse and uninspiring. In the filmed version, Steiger erupts into a monologue when prompted to give up the throne by Marshal Ney. It not only brilliantly captures the vaunting megalomania of the character but also hints at the passions bubbling within the actor too.

> (Napoleon) *"Do you know what the throne is? It's an overdecorated piece of furniture. It's what's behind the throne that counts. My brains, my ambitions, my desires, my hope, my imagination. And above all… my will! I can't believe my ears. You stand before me waving a piece of paper crying: Abdicate, abdicate! — I will not! I will not!"*

It is a performance brimming with pyrotechnics which sets off the force and drive of the character in stark relief. As he pounds the air, trumpeting his words, "*I will not!*" Steiger's eyes bulge as every fibre of his being seems to glow with an inner will, torn from deep within the actor himself. It is a brave and raw artistic choice, which could be equally described as over-the-top, but how else, one wonders, do you convey the spirit and drive of a man who dominated continental Europe for a decade?

When co-star Plummer, wanting to size up his co-star, saw the rushes of these scenes, he was in a state of shock:

> It's the biggest bloody performance I've ever seen! He rips down the curtains, he chews up the carpets, he bellows, he screams, he cries — and to top it all, apparently Napoleon's got the most frightful indigestion, or the worst case of piles the world has ever seen! I can't compete with that![356]

Perhaps the power and rage that the actor exhibits came from his own political and philosophical beliefs that were in complete contrast to this character.

> I don't like Napoleon, but I admire him. I do not like him, because I am a pacifist and have a negative attitude to wars, fame and other attributes that are conquered by blood. But, naturally, I am not going to transfer my personal attitude to the role. I will try to play Napoleon for sure. Namely: I set a goal to show an already tired person who knows in his heart that he will lose this battle, but gives it, to give, as they say for history, in order to remain in

the eyes of humanity the Napoleon with whom he sought to be in life — a man of great ambition, exceptional abilities and energy.[357]

Bondarchuk was most effusive about his star:

> Steiger is a great actor, everything he does is surprising. Usually, the actor was shot for only four hours, but they were extremely fruitful, and his every take is unique. My task was to put him in the most favourable conditions for creativity. When he improvises, he improves the script. That is the difference between a performer and an artist. Directing him, I felt that every take was something new and powerful.[358]

Back in the inner courtyard of the palace, Haden-Guest looked on bemused as the tall, white-haired Willo Gray, the historical advisor, whips the few hundred local extras into a passable resemblance of Napoleon's elite Old Guard, with: "Smarten up there!" As he demonstrated "Present Arms," rigidly holding one of the Daffini Brothers replica Charleville muskets vertically in front of the body, to a louche extra whose last appearance was in an orgy scene for Fellini, as a eunuch.

Bondarchuk, described by an interpreter as a "Senior Intellectual," was setting up a high-angle shot from a top-story window overlooking the courtyard. Flicking through a book of storyboards he has drawn in pen and ink to help conceptualise the scene, Haden-Guest, watching nearby, described him as "broad, with a broad, sallow face, both amiable and petulant like a rather babyish lion…wearing a shapeless dark suit and a knitted tie (red) and a flat cap from which escapes dark/silvery hair, which is longish."

Once all is set, and the hired-for-the-day extras looking like tough veterans perfectly arrayed in ranks around the courtyard, Bondarchuk's assistant yells: "Action." There is a moment's pause before "Steiger congeals into Napoleon, (and) walks darkly forwards," out into the middle of the vast cobbled arena, ringed by the long, silent lines of the Old Guard. The morning sunlight catches the tiny streams of glycerine "tears" that trickle down the grizzled faces, including the ferocious looking Russian actor Evgeni Samoilov, who played the loyal commander of the Old Guard.

Steiger, in his great, stark black hat, steps up to a standard-bearer holding an embroidered Tricolour surmounted by a gold-painted eagle — considered a holy relic by the famed *Grande Armée*. Fingering the silk and braid in his hand, he kisses it, then a long pause before he begins to speak: "France has fallen," he bellows, allowing the echo to bounce around the ornate walls of the courtyard and animate some transfixed pigeons. He continues: "My Men! My Children!" The last line — an in-the-moment spark of inspiration: "I put that in myself, it seemed right."[359]

Reputably, Steiger performed this farewell speech almost ten times continuously, without interruption, and each time with a different reading and intonation. As he drew breath at last, the entire set warmly applauded the bravura performance.

In his biography on Steiger, Tom Hutchinson said that the star had a miserable time on the film, and rather grumpily complained that: "he (Bondarchuk) was limited to 'How are you?' and 'I come back soon'. In French, he could manage only 'Bonjour.'" The only anecdote that his experience warranted relating, was that during a scene, perhaps the one above, he had to deliver a long speech to camera; multiple cameras, a procedure that Bondarchuk often deployed:

> The scene was going well; Rod could feel the tingling sensation that signalled a moment of transcendence, one of those rare occasions when an actor surpasses himself. It was then that Bondarchuk shouted, "Cut!"

At least one camera had run out of film. Despite the expense of the production, the story goes that they were sometimes loaded with different lengths of film called short ends, rather than the full eleven minutes. These were the remainder of an exposed reel of film left at the end of a day's filming. Usually, they would be used for brief insert shots; for example, a close-up of a letter, but never for a dialogue or action scene.

Whatever the reason, Steiger complained that his performance suffered: "Rod burst into tears. 'You don't understand. This is not a job for me,' he cried. 'This is my life!'"[360] There is some dramatic license in this tale, as it is highly unlikely the use of short ends would have been a production policy. Perhaps the story is a mix of memories of technical glitches that are a feature of all film-making.

Daniele Nannuzzi, whose job this was to load the cameras with enough film for a scene, naturally dismissed the tale: "No, I think it's a legend, I mean sometimes it can happen if the scene goes on more than you decide, but normally — no." It *is* possible Steiger was referring to the farewell scene above, but if the story is true about repeating the scene multiple times, his performance would have exceeded the maximum eleven minutes that a film magazine could hold — thus requiring Bondarchuk to yell: "Cut!"

Working every day, Daniele recalled actor's intensity: "He was so inside Napoleon that he never stopped to be him for seven months. Also, after work, he was always walking with the hands behind his back, like Napoleon. He never stopped to be him. When he is playing, he is very intense, and you have to be quiet…he didn't want any disturbance. He was fantastic."

> Scene.18: NAPOLEON — *the freshest man in this feverish workroom prowls among the* SECRETARIES, *dictating several letters simultaneously.*

The script has an effective scene that shows Napoleon's mental prowess, and his preoccupations; from the mundane of boot supplies to high politics. It cleverly combines his agonising torment at being unable to see his son with concern at Wellington's forces on his border. All the while Steiger guzzles medicine, having changed the stage direction of *freshest man* to his conception of "a very sick man." One letter he dictates nicely encapsulates the justification for all dictators:

> Scene.18: NAPOLEON *(to No. 4) "To the Prince Alexis. You are wrong, Prince, I did not usurp the crown. It was lying in the gutter. I picked it up with my sword. The people put it on my head. Who saves his country violates no law. Signature."*

The monologue which survived with some minor tweaks to the screen, allowed Steiger to deliver all-guns-blazing, as he breaks the fourth wall to stare directly into the camera lens, his eyes wide with self-righteous arrogance and bravado. But shooting the scene bordered on low farce, as Daniele sensed some friction between director and star:

> He was very diffident with Bondarchuk — you know, when you *don't* trust. There is a famous scene when he is dictating letters to three different people. We shoot the wide shot first with three cameras as Napoleon moves from table to table saying something to this — something to that. Then we made the close-up. To be sure that he was in close-up — he takes off his pants! He played the scene in his *underpants* — with a jacket, but without pants. He wanted to be sure that they (cameras) were in close-up. But he

put his pants back on only when the camera took him full length. This is a real story!

It is easy to see Steiger's imploring cry has the ring of truth about it and expresses something of this most intense actor.

In 1969, the star's personal life was in high flux, as his ten-year marriage to British actress Claire Bloom was in serious trouble. There had been pressures and tensions from the beginning as both were very ambitious, driven with their careers. Steiger admitted later: "The excitement of doing a new part temporarily blinds you to the rest of the world. I'm the dullest of husbands when I fall in love with a role."[361]

In 1960, the birth of their daughter, Anna, did for a time bring them together. Claire, looking back on her relationship years later, commented that: "If our priorities were more need than passion, our relationship gave us many years of supportive family happiness."[362]

As Anna grew older, she resented her mother working away more than her father, which must have caused friction and growing bitterness.

Despite various attempts to do so, the pair had only worked together twice, on *The Illustrated Man* (1969), as discussed earlier, and *Three Into Two Won't Go* (1969) directed by experienced theatre director Peter Hall, who struggled with his first movie. The clash of acting technique between the predominantly British cast and Steiger's Method caused friction. One day, Claire was asked by Hall to persuade her husband to temper his approach — which cannot have been an easy conversation between husband and wife.

It is impossible and perhaps unseemly to speculate further on the breakdown of the marriage, but it appears Steiger left for the slow *Waterloo* shoot, hopeful he had a marriage to return to.

As a favour, he had asked a close friend of the couple, Broadway producer Hillard Elkins, to keep an eye on Claire in his absence. During the long weeks of separation, not helped by intermittent telephone systems and slow mail, it grew very clear that his wife and best friend had slipped over the line of friendship into an "intense" affair.

A tiny, affecting snapshot of his marriage can be glimpsed from young British actor Peter Davies. Seeing Steiger eating in the studio cafeteria, he, with the confidence of youth, sat himself beside the star. "Rod Steiger was absolutely at the top of my list of great actors, I remember sitting next to him having lunch. You know, I thought, this is cool, I'm sitting this close to Rod Steiger." When not in costume Steiger often wore black, which helped to show off a treasured present.

> He had this marvellous pendant around his neck with a sun on it. I remember asking him about that and he said it was a gift from Claire Bloom, his wife. He was very pleased to be asked about it, and I think other than that, my efforts of conversation were: "Yes, how are you? Would you like some salt?" I remember being taken with what a really nice guy he was; very straightforward and kind of sweet and amusing, not what you would imagine such a serious actor to be like.

"My family was destroyed by alcoholism,"[363] Steiger confided to critic Roger Ebert, who visited him on the faraway location of Uzhgorod in Ukraine. "I can't let up!" In his suite, room 340, the actor hung empty Chianti bottles and perused his collection of porn magazines, which he had successfully smuggled past the custom guards. Ebert noted how hard the actor's divorce from Claire Bloom had hit him. It had gone through on 10 June, about the time the actor arrived in Russia, which suggests a fast-tracked separation. "Something died on the way," he confided later to his biographer. "I'll take sixty per cent blame for the break."[364] His despondency was compounded by the speed of Claire's remarriage to their close friend Hillard Elkins. "Steiger had taken to calling him 'Ellery Hilkins,' and seemed to find some small pleasure in this practice."[365] As Steiger stared down a bottle of Chianti in his solitary moments, one wonders if it is not too fanciful to speculate that this "troubled" Napoleon was aware of how much Life-mirrored-Art.

After Napoleon's fall in 1814 and exile to Elba, his adversary Tsar Alexander paid court frequently to the only woman historians believe was the ex-emperor's only true love: the Empress Josephine. Theirs had been an unequal marriage from the beginning. He, a young man, brilliant at war but gauche in love, and she a widow with two children, allegedly pushed into it by her former lover, a senior politician. This marriage of convenience would lead to Josephine being crowned empress.

Political necessity demanded that Napoleon divorce her in 1809 and marry the daughter of the Emperor of Austria. This happy, if less demanding, union produced a son and heir. Upon his dramatic fall in 1814, he lost not only his throne, but his wife and son who had returned to his father-in-law — and enemy, in Vienna.

The film references this in the above dictation scene, which ends with Steiger sitting on the floor sifting through maps. During his formal protestation to Britain's Prince Regent about Wellington — his future nemesis — he abruptly pauses halfway through the name. In the heavy silence, with only a faint clock ticking in the background, the camera dollies into a tight close-up of Steiger, tears well up in his eyes, as he concludes his letter to his Austrian wife: *"My son is my future. And I would rather see him dead, than raised as a captive Austrian Prince."*

This dramatic, clever piece of counterpoint, nicely conflates Napoleon's concerns, both personal and political. It is much sharper focused on screen than in the script and suggests it resulted from that special synergy between director and star. Recalling Steiger's *The Pawnbroker* scene, one can imagine the mental torment he brewed up in his own mind about his daughter Anna, and his crumbling marriage, for one of the most effective, if often over-looked scenes in the whole film.

While we should not labour the analogy between Steiger and his character too far, both were dealing with emotional loss. One of the most poignant vignettes of Napoleon's turbulent hundred days, between his return from exile and total defeat, reveals the man.

Just before Napoleon left Paris for the Belgium frontier and Waterloo, there is a story that he went to the deserted Château de Malmaison, Josephine's home, and spent some hours in contemplation by her bed. She had died suddenly, a few weeks before his return to France.

"Napoleon was sick, tired and lonely," Steiger said later of his process of ripping emotion from deep within himself for his art, "I've been all those things so I can understand them. That was all I had to go on…"[366]

Both director and star were determined to create a very human Napoleon, here Bondarchuk tries on a pair of "granny" glasses which Steiger wears in the abdication scene. AUTHOR'S COLLECTION

Faced with a mutiny by his marshals, Napoleon ponders his options.
AUTHOR'S COLLECTION

In 1969, the Soviet Republic of Ukraine was still largely rural.
© RICHARD HEFFER

CHAPTER 10

"Nyetnam."

The Uzh River flows for almost eighty miles through the Tysa Lowland in Western Ukraine into Slovakia, its name derives from an ancient Slavic dialect word *už*, meaning Snake. One of the most prominent habitations along this waterway is the city of Uzhgorod, which roughly translates as Uzh City; or Snake City. For most of its history it was known by the Hungarian title of Ungvár, derived from the *Ung*, the Hungarian name for the Uzh and *Vár*, meaning castle or fort. Considering there are also Czech, Slovak, Polish and Romanian names for the city, one can understand that the area lies across a historical fault line.

Ungvár had been strategically important for millennia because of its position at the southern end of the Uzhok Pass over the Carpathian Mountains. It had been constantly ravaged by war, particularly during the apocalyptic Tartar invasions of the Middle Ages that had ransacked vast swathes of Eastern and Central Europe for centuries. In fact, for hundreds of years, Ungvár had been part of the Kingdom of Hungary and most of her people were ethnically Hungarian, linked politically with the vast central European polyglot Austrian Empire.

The Hungarian Revolt of 1848 was an attempt by the local aristocracy for more autonomy from the Austrian crown, but this was brutally suppressed, leading Ungvár and Hungary to be absorbed into the Austrian-Hungarian empire. The latter half of the nineteenth-century saw the city expand as an industrial and trading location, with a railway line linking to the important junction of Csap (Chop) opening in 1872. By the turn of the century, the population was predominantly of Hungarian and Slovak descent; with only one in five of Russian origin.

The First World War brought seismic changes as the Austro-Hungarian empire collapsed, having fought and lost alongside Germany. The city formed part of the newly created Republic of Czechoslovakia; becoming the administrative centre of the territory it enjoyed years of development as it grew into a modern metropolis. In 1938 it was once again reunited with the independent Kingdom of Hungary, which soon allied with Hitler's Germany. Like so many other cities in Eastern Europe, Ungvár was not spared the barbarism of the Nazi regime. In 1944, the entire Jewish population was transported to Auschwitz and murdered.

A few months later, as the German and Hungarian armies retreated from Russia, the city was captured by the Red Army. Renamed Uzhgorod, the Russians began a brutal programme of ethnic cleansing which decimated the Hungarian population; thousands were either killed, expelled or made to work in Soviet forced labour camps. In 1945 the Soviet Union annexed the area of Subcarpathian Ukraine, and the following year Uzhgorod became the centre of the newly formed Zakarpatska Oblast of Western Ukrainian SSR. During the next two decades, the region saw a massive increase in industrial production, particularly for the Soviet's ever important arms industry.

By the late 1960s, the fruits of this economic boom were not apparent in Uzhgorod, the area was still very rural with farming organised in huge, often inefficient collective farms. The leafy streets boasted few motor vehicles as life moved at the stately speed of a horse. Little had changed in hundreds of years. But with less than a quarter of a century under Russian influence, the area was a potential tinderbox. With a population of about 56,000 souls, there were simmering tensions between the various ethnic groups. It was hardly surprising that the 1968 invasion of Czechoslovakia would inflame passions. Many windows in the city displayed a simple candle as a silent mark of respect for their fellow Slavs.

As they congregated in Budapest, the western cast and crew of *Waterloo* would have been unaware of these tensions, as they prepared to cross into the Soviet Republic of Ukraine. Leaving the relatively friendly communist Hungary, some had enjoyed a meal of goulash and Riesling at a People's Cafe before boarding the Trans-Siberian Railway. All remember the journey as hellish.

What made up First-Class was a smelly and damp cabin with two makeshift wooden benches. Their fellow passengers often removed their boots, which added to the overwhelming stench, not helped by the locked windows. The endless hours watching the flat open plains of Hungary, "miles of flat land, peppered with horses and carts and simple wooden buildings,"[367] through the filthy windows was purgatory. The lavatory arrangements were spartan; a mere hole in the floor. One's business had to be done either standing up or squatting in full view; there being no door for privacy.

Five or six hours later, with the train chuffed into Chop, and then the fun began. "We got to the Soviet border, it was exactly what you would imagine in the Cold War," remembered actor Peter Davies, "I mean there were people with machine guns walking across the roof of the train, and dogs. It was scary."

The border guards at Chop were suspicious and officious, particularly to Westerners, making the passport/customs process slow and tedious. Ian Ogilvy, who had brought his wife Diane and two small children, was not spared the agonising pace as each one of six-year-old Emma's colouring books was scrutinised for anti-communist propaganda. But the guards soon lost interest in children's books upon opening Jack Hawkins suitcase. All eyes of officialdom were glued to pictures of naked American ladies colourfully displayed in various Adult magazines — the height of Western decadence. Examining each picture from every angle, the process became longer and longer. Unfortunately for Jack, his light reading matter was confiscated. When the actor politely asked for them back, he was greeted with a firm and final: *"Nyet!"*

This word came to symbolise life on the Soviet location, and would be bastardised into unit slang as: *"Nyetnam."* A reference to the escalating chaos and horror of America's Vietnam miss-adventure that dominated the late 1960s. There would, however, be some compensation for Jack's loss of reading matter. A month before, Rod Steiger had brought *his* collection through Customs unhindered, whereupon leaving, the American donated these well-thumbed pages to a grateful, freshly arrived cast.

After clearing Customs, the last leg of the journey was by car over bumpy and potholed roads north to Uzhgorod, where the unit expected comfortable and relaxing "digs." Hearts sunk as they showed up at the only hotel in town; built in the brutal, plain concrete Soviet style and painted in Bolshevik grey. A giant hammer and sickle sculpture dominated the town square which cast a stark shadow over the ground, parched brown from the beating summer sun. Jack Hawkins espied an "oasis" pointing at a solitary twig, leafless and dead; slamming his fist, he belched out: "Blaze of — gulp — fucking colour."[368]

Inside, they all had to leave their passports at the reception desk by orders of the police before being assured by the interpreter that, "It was a good hotel and the food was fine."[369] It was perhaps by Russian standards, but something of a shock for movie people used to the comforts of Hollywood-sized budgets. As part of the co-production deal, Dino had paid Intourist, the Soviet tourism organisation, the princely sum of $120,000 to pre-book 100 rooms for 134 days at the hotel who in return promised "upon payment in currency, to organize a night bar in the hotel, picnics and individual and collective excursions in the cities of Lvov, Kiev, Moscow, Leningrad and Zaporozhe."[370]

It appears Dino was short-changed as his crew quickly found out to their horror. The place was infested with cockroaches and bedbugs: "so dirty that we all got those animals in the mattress!" Shuddered Veronica at the memory fifty years later: "That was just terrible!"

Camera Assistant Daniele Nannuzzi, who was only twenty, blamed Dino — albeit with a chuckle: "It was very hard for us because he brought us Italians to Russia, and then abandoned us there for months! We were prisoners inside the hotel, like a military service for us. But the experience was fantastic because I was young, and I felt like a soldier."

The "Penthouse suite," which was the exclusive home of the above-the-title stars — Plummer moved in following Steiger's departure — was only two tiny cubicles, barely enough to breathe in, one quipped. The other chambers were even smaller and caused Ian Ogilvy to break down in tears, despairing how his family of four would manage for the next few months. While each had an allotted room, they were rudimentary with no plugs in the sinks, but to a recent student like Richard Heffer was "quite acceptable." although the older, more famous actors moaned and grumbled. Settling into his "suite," Christopher Plummer answered a knock on the door, to find a representative from Mosfilm who greeted him with a special gift from "Comrade Bondarchuk" — a jar of Caviar. As the actor, touched by the gesture, reached out to accept the offering, the visitor held on tightly and promptly demanded 2.50 American dollars. It was a taste of things to come.

For Peter Davies, the youngest member of the cast and possibly the entire unit, his tiny room brought almost visceral emotions. "I remember I was very homesick right away. I'm sure that's about one of the few times in my life. The first time being my first night at boarding school when I was 11…but I was absolutely hit by it there. It just seemed frightening and miserable, just wasn't what I expected, but still — quite excited about the whole thing."

Each corridor had its own concierge, often a lady "akin to women wrestlers, had hairy armpits and hairy legs."[371] They policed the comings and goings of the guests, although their stern and imposing demeanour blossomed into enormous smiles whenever six-year-old Emma Ogilvy would appear. She regularly had to run the gauntlet as they tried to grab her with their "powerful arms and crush her to their ample bosoms and pinch her cheeks and give her wet, smacking kisses and scream Russian endearments in her face."

There was a rumour among the unit they were KGB informers, with suspicions that the Soviet Secret Service were also monitoring phone calls. Roger Green believes he found evidence of this:

> The KGB bugged one of our hotel rooms, and the irony was it was the room of the great actor Jack Hawkins, who had lost his ability to speak properly due to a throat cancer operation earlier in the year. He was such a fine actor that the director was very keen to have him in the film. Jack used to speak in a very guttural way he had learnt without using his voice box. Nevertheless, KGB intelligence wasn't very good at choosing an appropriate actor's room to bug! Jack and the rest of us were highly amused by this finding.[372]

One suspects that the private lives of film people offered meagre pickings for the toppling of Capitalism.

Philippe Forquet remembered the rickety infrastructure of the hotel: "The elevator was out of order when we arrived and was not repaired when we left nearly two months later (we used the stairs!), in the evening the electricity went off for an hour or so." Considering the heat and dust of summer, a not unreasonable basic requirement was water for washing; unfortunately, the unit played a kind of Russian Roulette with the very intermittent supply. "One was taking a shower and all of a sudden no more hot water, so it meant a long 45 minutes to an hour wait, with your body covered with lather, before being able to rinse it off." More often than not, the tired and dirty actors were greeted with a bland "*Nyet*" — the water was off again.

Peter Davies remembered the culinary delights on offer. "When you went down on to the ground floor of the hotel, there was a dining room which was just for us, it was a very nondescript room." The food was definitely not as advertised. "You could starve to death in this restaurant," was Richard Heffer's verdict, with the cry: "No eggs *again!*" a constant refrain.[373] Edible meat was even rarer, with only meagre and uninspiring vegetables as compensation. "It was absolutely miserable," recalled Peter Davies, "It was shockingly awful — worse than school food! And it never changed. I wasn't a fussy eater — no one liked it."

The only item in abundance was borscht, a sour soup common in Eastern Europe often made with beetroots, which gives the dish a distinctive red colour. The endless days of this on the menu didn't help Steiger's frustration and depression:

> "*Borscht* again!" Steiger said, stirring the thick red soup, so the potatoes surfaced occasionally through the sour cream. "It's the goddamn stuff of life on this location. *Borscht* for lunch. *Borscht* for dinner. I'm afraid to come down for breakfast."[374]

Not everyone was afraid to venture into the dining room: "I never had trouble with the food," recalled the then sixteen-year-old Raffaella De Laurentiis, who would become a producer herself, notably *Dune* (1984) with its gruelling desert location in Mexico. "I've always been an adventurer, and maybe it's because of those days, you know. So, the more difficult a location; the *more* I like it!"

Even getting to the Russian location had been an adventure for Raffaella in its own right. She had set out with her father, uncle Luigi and brother Federico by plane to Budapest, but their hired car was nowhere to be found. Luigi, fluent in Bulgarian, could speak enough Hungarian to hire a taxi. All went well until a few miles from the Ukrainian border. The taxi driver could not proceed for security reasons and had to drop them. Thus, the four, complete with heavy luggage, were forced to trudge on foot. Dino, ever the problem-solving producer, hatched a cunning plan; using his teenage daughter as bait.

> I was sixteen; I remember what I was wearing. So, my dad said: "The three of us boys will hide with the luggage. You go into the middle of the street and hitchhike." So, eventually a tiny car stopped, and it was two Americans. So, you can imagine the scene, when this car stopped because they saw this young girl in the middle of the street.

The four of them then crammed into the tiny car. "I was in the front in the middle with them, but I had the gearstick between my legs," and set off along the pot-holed road towards the border. Forced to share two rooms in a wayside inn, the tortuous journey took 48 hours. Meanwhile, frantic phone calls were criss-crossing the continent trying to find the whereabouts of the missing De Laurentiis clan.

> We essentially disappeared from the face of the earth for like three days. Nobody could find us. Eventually we made it with

these two guys that were really kind and nice, and we made it to the border, eventually. I still remember my other uncle (Alfredo) waiting for us across this huge bridge…so, there was this incredible trip that I'll never forget, and sometimes even before he (Dino) passed away we were laughing about it.

It appears the car that had been sent to pick them up had been turned away by the police, because they didn't know what the cigarette lighter was. Perhaps also a story in its own right: the two Americans were on a mission to spring one of their friends from Russia; for which they succeeded.

Reading the various accounts of the unit's stay in communist Uzhgorod, the picture that emerges is not one of repression but just the drabness of life, as Raffaella's elder sister Veronica remembered: "What was fun was to go to Russia in that period, where it was very sad and very communist. Only people who were not Russian could go to the nice stores and restaurants. So, I saw a part of Russia that I had only read about. I have never forgotten that experience…really dirty and messy, but it was a lot of fun."

The undisputed heroes of 'Nyetnam" were the "camp followers" attached to this visiting "army" in the guise of Diana Ogilvy, Elaine Plummer, Claire Wickham, Elsie O'Herlihy and Miku Feldhaus, who brought a female ingenuity, order and emotional support. Becoming "Soviet housewives," every day they would stand in queues alongside the locals to buy whatever they could to rustle up nightly feasts.

Heinz Feldhaus recalled the special currency used on these foraging trips. "My wife, Miku, went to the butcher where we were to get some meat, and we only could get meat when we had foreign stamps. We exchanged any foreign stamps into meat and also paid for it, but the payment was next to nothing."

It appears the official currency of the rouble was of little value to not just the locals. "We got more German stamps because I got mail from Germany, and the funny thing was that I got a letter sent to my Munich address from the Bank of Italia for Mr Bondarchuk. As they say, everyone in Russia is the same — except!"

Following a work-to-rule Strike over "terrible" food, the predominantly Italian technical crew of about seventy-five were guaranteed a regular supply of pasta from Italy. Smoothing the waters was Alfredo De Laurentiis, Dino's brother, who served as one of the production supervisors. Addressed by all as "Alfredo," he wore a distinctive shark tooth around his neck, and did his best to keep up morale. "In the night on the (hotel) balcony, we organised our kitchen, making spaghetti with music, with a mandolin. Sometimes we just wanted to get away for an hour from our terrible inferno."[375]

A popular local watering hole was the Verkovina Restaurant in Uzhgorod; "cheap by our standards (9 roubles! — a soldier gets 3 roubles a month!)"[376] decked out with potted palms, and a silver ball on the ceiling which glittered as local singers crooned Russian versions of *Congratulations* and *Simon Says*. Alfredo would often preside over many raucous evenings which involved dancing, Roman-disco-style, which the locals tried to emulate with a Cossack shake. During one heady session, the police tried to break up the party but Alfredo, his shark tooth dangling from his neck, sent them away with a proverbial flea in the ear.

For all the discomforts the cast and crew had to endure at Uzhgorod's premiere hotel, they were considerably more comfortable than the thousands of men sleeping in a large military camp situated twelve miles to the south-east along a part cobbled road, near the village of Ruski Komarovtsi.[377]

Most of the men were young, like Igor Starchenko from the Odessa region. Having answered his compulsory call-up, he boarded a train which was buzzing with the rumour that he and his mates were going to be film stars. Arriving in the vast canvas encampment which was humid even at night, with nine to a tent, he joined scores of other raw recruits from the Carpathian Military District. They received their usual pay of around three roubles a month.

To portray Napoleon's veteran Old Guard, some 1,000 middle-aged reservists had also been called up. One of the units drafted to play "war" was the battle-hardened 128th Guards Motor Rifle Division. It had taken part in Operation Danube, the Soviet invasion of Czechoslovakia the previous year, and lost eleven soldiers killed.

Once this "movie" army was assembled, for three weeks during May 1969, they all had to learn Napoleonic drill and tactics, which involved hours of square-bashing in the heat, followed by a passing-out parade before the critical eyes of Sergei Bondarchuk himself. While the conditions were simple and spartan, most of the soldiers accepted they were in the military and took it all in their stride.

A distinctive tang to the air was supplied by the pungent smell of hundreds of horses that were stabled nearby on a collective farm between the villages of Volkove and Serednye. The Russian army was one of the very last to trade in horses for tanks, but just seven years before, in 1962, it had actually raised a *new* cavalry formation. The 11th Separate Cavalry Regiment, with 1500 horsemen, was a unit formed primarily for Soviet filmmaking, and paid for in part by Mosfilm studios, had first seen — or heard — "action" for *War and Peace*.

The regiment was primarily stocked with Russia's most renowned breed, the Orlov Trotter, noted for its great speed and stamina. Introduced in the late eighteenth-century by Count A.G. Orlov, the breed, notable for its fast-trotting gait, soon proved its mettle during the following century as a harness racing horse, where it consistently outperformed the best horses from Western Europe. Its sturdiness meant it was able to withstand not only the harsh Russian climate but also the country's almost medieval poor-quality roads. Standing between 15 and 17 hands high and weighing about 990 pounds, these large and muscular horses are often referred to as being 'gentle giants,' with an agreeable and intelligent temperament to match. While many other breeds have a fast trot, the great Russian Orlov Trotter combines this characteristic with exceptional stamina and strength, ideal for the demands of cinema.

To become a member of this prestigious unit obviously required not just a basic ability to ride a horse, but also the skill and confidence to jump ditches, hedges and other obstacles; also, to perform tricks with deft control, particularly to "drop" a horse safely to the ground. Naturally, those who had honed their skills in equestrian schools and particularly in the rough and tumble of horse racing were ideal.

One of these was Aslan Khablauk, an Adyghe Muslim from the Adyghe Republic in the North Caucasus region near the Black Sea. Living in this rugged mountainous area, this country boy had displayed a fearless streak from a young age by competing in horse races on the Kuban collective farm. He and the other junior riders had been taught by Gissa Khaneshevich Mezuzhok, considered one of the best horsemen in the region.

When a recruiting sergeant appeared in his village of Takhtamukai, despite his father's concern for his only son and heir, Aslan jumped at the chance to apply for the mounted regiment. When his son reappeared that evening, his father was angry because it seemed Aslan had been turned down for military service: "Get out of my yard so my eyes don't see you!" Such a rejection brought great shame on families and communities. Aslan's attempt to explain that it was only a temporary glitch fell on deaf ears until the return of the recruiter the next day.

Eventually, after a tearful reconciliation and then a hasty farewell, Aslan joined 660 hopefuls from his region alone and journeyed to the regimental HQ in the town of Alabino near Moscow, which was strewn with props of tanks and old aeroplanes, for the final selection. Following an intensive application process, just 16 remained, including Aslan.

The young man quickly bonded with the regiment's prized Orlov Trotters, a distinguishing feature of the breed being their devotion to a rider which could only be earned by a true animal lover. Conversely, the Orlov could make its displeasure known with its 900 pounds of horseflesh, muscle and bone, as Aslan recalled:

> There was a corporal Vorobyov, who served with me. He was particularly cruel — often beating his horse with a pitchfork. One day Colonel Edov caught him, and warned: "Son, this animal remembers an offense for seven years. Be careful!" And after some four to five months during our training, the horse threw off Vorobyov, and jumped onto his arms, broke all the tendons. After that, the corporal was invalided out of the army.[378]

Not all recruits were as comfortable and adept on a horse as Aslan. Luckily the gentle Orlov giants made them ideal for beginners. The closest twenty-one-year-old Ukrainian Mykola Kholodnyak had been to a quadruped was via grainy black-and-white images on TV. Drafted into the military in May 1969, he was not the only one who was surprised by his particular posting — the recruitment officer was equally incredulous: "Surely there couldn't be any cavalry regiments in this age of Yuri Gagarin in Space!"

On arriving at the regiment, he was assured it was an honour to be part of this specialist unit, before launching into two weeks of intensive training: "We were taught to sit on a horse and to ride. How to saddle it, put on the bridle, tighten the stirrups." He had his own horse named Bunchuk. "I was an ordinary cavalry soldier. Fed the horses, cleaned them, did a walk so they did not stagnate, and lived by the rules of the Soviet Army."

While riding skills were the priority, the recruits were still expected to master the military skills required for modern warfare: digging trenches and foxholes, firing machine guns and laying cables for radio communications equipment.

Training completed, Mykola found there was little movie glamour on offer as the elite horsemen settled into the location's tent city. Food was simple, although considered better than the usual army fare; while on holidays they would be spoilt with rice porridge, cocoa, a packet of cookies and two oranges. He spent his princely pay of 3 roubles and 80 kopeks a month on toothpaste, brush and cologne — there being few diversions in Western Ukraine.

His uniform as a French lancer included white trousers which were ordered to be kept spotless, and a hat like a bucket — made of cardboard and lined with fabric. "Since I had never been in a movie before the army, my attitude to the film was relaxed. But at the same time, it was interesting — *I am in a movie!*"

If there was a suspicion that it was all movie glamour, the young soldier would have described his life under canvas; baking hot in summer and freezing cold as the film shoot slipped towards another harsh Russian winter.

To lift morale, Dino hired the services of Italian singer Patty Pravo to travel to Russia and sing to the troops. The twenty-one-year-old had found success three years before with her first single, *Ragazzo triste*. It made history by becoming the first pop song ever to be played on Vatican Radio. But it was her 1968 hit that put her on the map with *La bambola* (The Doll), also awarded a gold disc, coupled with her debut album, which topped the Italian charts. Unfortunately, this rising star of Euro Pop found few new fans behind the Iron Curtain. "You know he had organised the things like that to entertain the army, but the army wasn't happy at all; they hated it."[379]

Camped in slightly more salubrious conditions were the Russian actors. But sleeping five to a room in a rundown local hostel soon engendered resentment at being treated as "second-class citizens." One of the senior Soviet actors pulled rank and demanded he be housed in the Uzhgorod hotel instead. People's Artist, Evgeni Samoilov, who was cast as Napoleon's Old Guard commander, General Cambronne, was outranked only by Bondarchuk and had the clout to insist. He was one of the few exceptions, as there was a strict protocol to keep communist and capitalist apart.

Near to the camp was a fenced-off area for the 29 stunt men: Italian, Russians and even Yugoslavian circus performers, who under the direction of the magnificently named Franco Fantasia, spent their time practicing horse-falls and other stunts.

Hand-to-hand sword fighting on horseback required specific training — with a dose of psychology. For practice bouts, the riders took off their tunics and fought bare-chested. The theory being that facing an armed opponent *without* a shirt motivates the instinct for self-preservation. This sharpens the reflexes, focusing totally on the actions of the opponent, forcing to defend oneself so as not to get the slightest scratch. Even wearing a shirt would result in potentially more wounds and cuts. When in full costume, the mentality was so ingrained as to ensure safety first combat — at least that was the intention. Aslan Khablauk earned an abrupt promotion stripe, a small scar to his chin accidentally nipped during a practice bout.

It would be the ability to "drop" a horse at a precise point for the cameras which would occupy this select group for the shoot. As we will see, the attitude to their four-legged partners was often ambivalent. These daredevils had the look and gait of brigands and sometimes even their bite, as Ian Ogilvy recalled one morning in the hotel dining-room as a stuntman, facing another rough and tumble day of horse falls, simply wanted an egg for his breakfast. *"Nyet!"* came the reply from a surly waiter. Everyone has a breaking point and hearing that word, yet again, was too much for this "brigand." He grabbed the startled waiter by the back of his jacket, "dangling him from one vast hand"[380] before shoving him into the kitchen with a loud thud. A few moments later, the door banged open as the triumphant stuntman emerged holding — an egg.

For the soldiers in the tented city, a typical morning began with Reveille before dawn, followed by a flurry of activity as the men pulled themselves out of bed, washed and assembled for chow. Then forming up into columns, they would be marched five kilometres to the location which stretched across the vast plain east of the sprawling village of Nizhny Solotvyn.

The area was studded with expansive vineyards, and friction soon flared up as fifteen thousand pairs of feet damaged crops to the anger of the local farmers, although they were placated with generous compensation payments. The carefully planted corn and flowers on the actual set were difficult to protect with such large groups of people (the miles of paths criss-crossing the set were an attempt to "keep off the grass"); eventually these too were trampled until there was only bare ground.

Arriving at a complex of wooded huts, the soldiers would be handed different military uniforms drawn from cardboard boxes. Although some of these were detailed costumes suitable for close-ups, the majority were simple coloured tabards, which were painted either red or blue by the soldiers themselves, and worn over their modern field dress, and on their feet, domestic tarpaulin boots.

There was not a great deal of enthusiasm at the prospect of film work, as Raffaella De Laurentiis graphically recalled: "They hated getting those suits on. A lot of them were shitting in the hats — it's the truth! It was their way of saying — they didn't like what they were being forced to do. It wasn't like they all showed up and loved every minute of it." This was particularly true of those appointed to play Wellington's crack Highlanders, they grumbled about wearing the tartan kilts which they considered mere "skirts."

Once dressed, the thousands of extras would trudge across to their allotted position, ready for the first shot of the day. This mass of moving humanity stretched as far as the eye could see and offered an extraordinary sight; marching in perfect step after weeks of training, deftly moving from column to line and square at the bark of command.

These men, whose ancestors hailed from the vast Steppes, and could have ridden with Genghis Khan's Mongol horde, now sported tartan kilts or bearskin helmets with an occasional cheeky wink of twentieth-century sunglasses and a whiff of cheap cigarettes.

Past the seemingly endless lines of infantry, squadrons of cavalry dripping with gold braid beneath snapping pennants, thundered past kicking up thick clouds of dust. The sharp, bright sunlight splashing coloured shadows on the ground of red or blue from the trim uniforms also bounced off the gleaming bayonets, creating bubbles of light that appeared to dance for miles. Less speedy but no less impressive were the teams of horses that dragged heavy wooden gun limbers and their drooping cannons. The mixture of metalled rims and horses' hooves pounding the parched earth almost drowned out the hubbub of voices and the brassy oompah of the military band, summoning the men to battle.

As this kaleidoscope of colour assembled on the sun-baked Ukrainian plain, they passed a large white sign that had two words painted in red: *Batepaoo — Waterloo*. With a typical dose of schoolboy humour, the British cast dubbed it: "Battypoo."

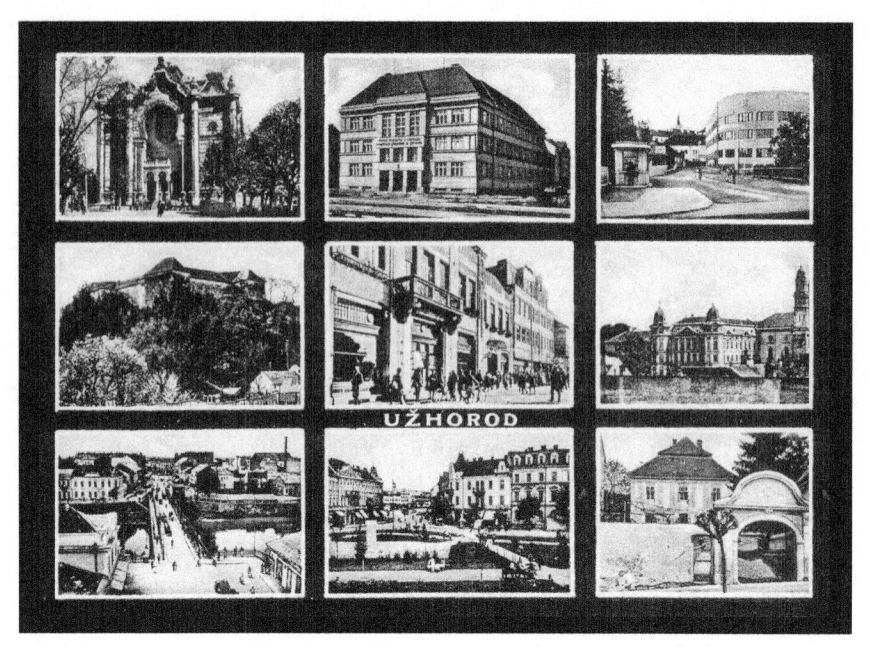

A pre-war postcard of Uzhgorod when it was part of Czechoslovakia.
AUTHOR'S COLLECTION

The city's largest hotel was home to the unit for six months.
© RICHARD HEFFER

Signpost to the film set from the main Uzhgorod road. © HEINZ FELDHAUS

Russian soldiers dressed as the French to be deployed in the background. They painted these simple tabards, either red or blue, themselves and the majority of the army was dressed this way. © HEINZ FELDHAUS

Members of the 11th Separate Cavalry Regiment. Aslan Khablauk flanked by the Dauchlezh brothers, all dressed as Prussian Hussars. © ASLAN KHABLAUK

Mykola Kholodnyak, dressed as a French lancer, with Bunchuk. © MYKOLA KHOLODNYAK

Dressed as French Cuirassiers, horsemen engage in some sword practice.
© ASLAN KHABLAUK

The French army prepare to march. © MYKOLA KHOLODNYAK

Russian soldiers splendidly dressed as Wellington's British infantry.
© RICHARD HEFFER

Some dressed as the French take a chance to cool off in the heat.
© HEINZ FELDHAUS

Mercer's G Troop RHA deployed on the left-hand side of the Allied ridge.
© RICHARD HEFFER

Dressed at Wellington's army, Russian soldiers take up position, note the neat column of cavalry in background. © RICHARD HEFFER

The WATERLOO Set
(approx and not to scale)

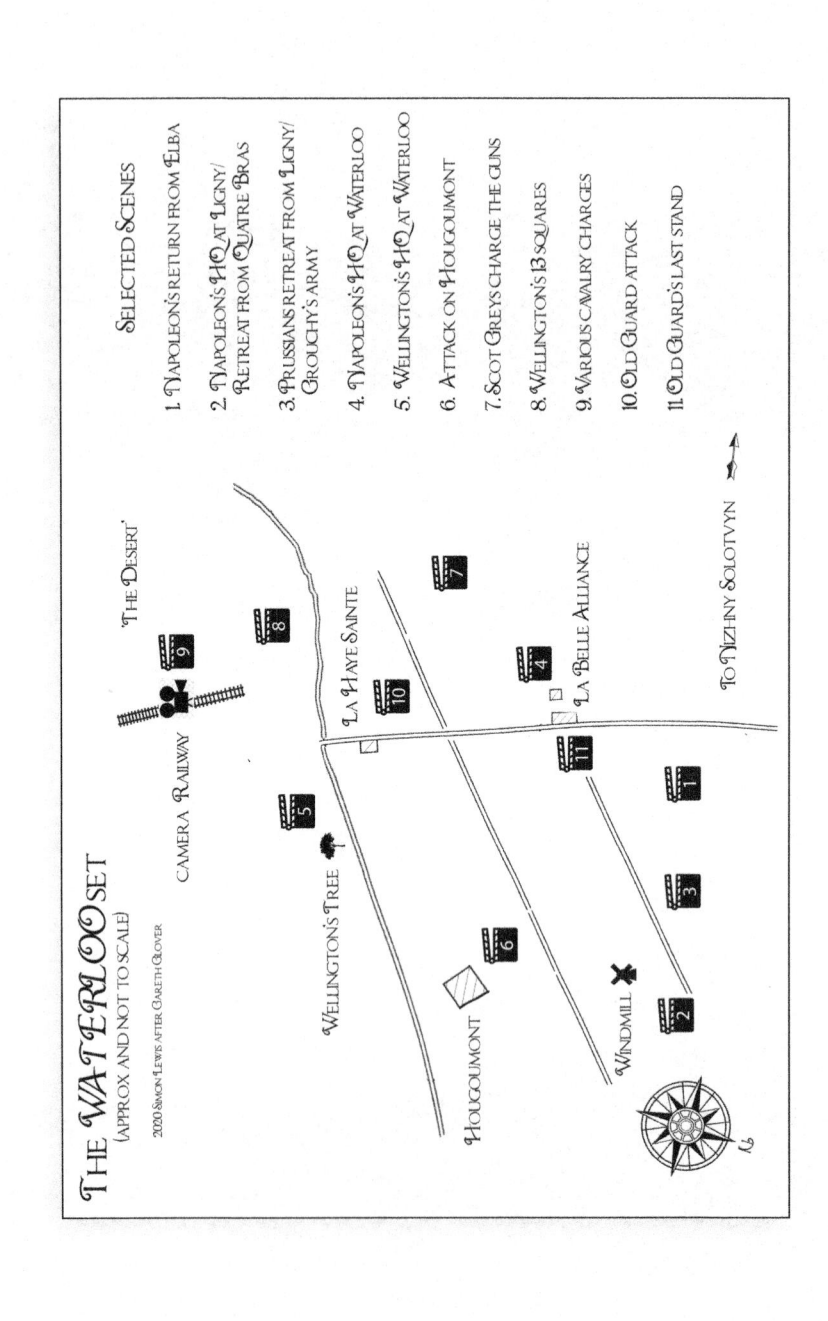

2020 Simon Lewis after Gareth Glover

'The Desert'

Camera Railway

Selected Scenes

1. Napoleon's return from Elba
2. Napoleon's HQ at Ligny/Retreat from Quatre Bras
3. Prussians retreat from Ligny/Grouchy's army
4. Napoleon's HQ at Waterloo
5. Wellington's HQ at Waterloo
6. Attack on Hougoumont
7. Scot Greys charge the guns
8. Wellington's 13 squares
9. Various Cavalry charges
10. Old Guard attack
11. Old Guard's last stand

La Haye Sainte
La Belle Alliance
Wellington's Tree
Hougoumont
Windmill
To Nizhny Solotvyn

CHAPTER 11

"The Whole Of Bloody Hell Is Coming Up Out Of The Ground."

It was one of the biggest sets ever constructed for a motion picture, a meticulous reconstruction of the Belgian original as described in Chapter Two. Amid the sown corn and flowers, and the copses of trees, were also several three-dimensional structures depicting some of the iconic conflict points. At the centre of the "French" ridge was a replica of the wayside inn and coach stop on the busy Brussels road named La Belle Alliance, which at the height of the battle became Napoleon's forward HQ. It consisted of two buildings with a small walled enclosure and stood next to a steeply inclined road, graced by a row of trees.

This led up to the tightly enclosed La Haye Sainte farmhouse, which stood just below the "Allied" ridge with its lone elm tree, which would be Wellington's impromptu HQ. The ridgeline gradually flattened out on the right, leading to the impressive construction of Hougoumont, complete with a walled garden and even a chapel tower peeking out. Both of these buildings had anchored Wellington's defence during the battle and had been hotly contested. In common with most film sets, they were designed to *look* the part, being only an empty shell constructed out of wood over a metal frame for stability. They were probably studded with the then "miracle" of asbestos to allow for repeated damage inflicted by the special effects department.

Willo Gray, the historical advisor, was perhaps always going to take issue with some creative decisions, but overall, he was satisfied: "'It's a mile long…scaled down almost exactly to half-size. Pretty good, considering,' says Gray. 'Of course,' he gestures airily, 'the French ridge curves the wrong way…but that hardly matters.'" He was concerned that the reduced size of the landscape would make it more difficult to choreograph realistic troop movements.

There was a structure built at the far end of the "French" ridge that did draw Willo's disapproval: "There was no windmill at Waterloo…There is no excuse for doing it wrong. Waterloo is one of the best documented battles in history. When I point out small inaccuracies, they plead dramatic license."[381] Actor Peter Davies recalled it was a continual issue for the historian: "I can remember Willo constantly moaning about the history side of it." Willo need not have fretted as thanks to careful framing by the cameramen, the offending windmill does not appear in the battle sequences. Serving instead as a generalised feature of the Belgian landscape, it was intended as a generic setting for several scenes away from the field of Waterloo.[382]

With the set prepared, the most important element was the army to "fight" over it, and the film had one of the largest contingents of extras in cinema history. Sources vary over the number of Soviet Army soldiers who appear in the film; 15,000 infantrymen, with 2,000 cavalry (roughly a *tenth* of those on the 1815 field), being the most probable.

Camping in their enormous tent city a mile or so from the battlefield, they would be roused from their beds long before dawn. Around 6 a.m. the assembled soldiers would file through huts to don their costumes, supervised by Pericoli and his team, which included wardrobe mistress Nadezhda Buzina, to ensure the correct period martial attire for each man.

Once fully clothed, designated foreground extras were often given glued-on moustaches and whiskers, while their faces were smeared with soot and fake blood. While a few clasped the Daffini musket replicas, most carried their regulation modern 1942 model rifles with bayonets attached, which fired blank cartridges. Fully dressed, (although the majority were clad in their painted red/blue tabards), they would march *en masse* to their allotted positions ready for the cameras by 8 a.m., although because of the slow machinations of cinema, it would often be many hours before the army was called upon to perform.

Despite the troops' allocation by the military, Bondarchuk complained that regiments would often be reassigned to other duties with little notice. One day, with cameras ready to roll, the entire army resplendent in their eye-popping nineteenth-century uniforms were ordered away, leaving the unit agape in bewilderment. It was believed they were deployed to the nearby volatile Czech border, still an area of high tension since the Soviet invasion the previous year.

Despite these irritations, having professional soldiers trained in 1815 tactics ensured they looked and behaved suitably martial. "This film could not have been made without those trained soldiers," Steiger remarked. "It would have taken assistant directors three days to put untrained men, mere extras, into position. When they broke for lunch, it would be another three days to arrange them again! These guys are superb."[383]

Superb or not, from some accounts it appears these men were treated as cinematic cannon fodder. Heinz Feldhaus, the quiet but efficient Panavision camera technician, remembers the soldiers who were culled from Russia's vast hinterland as uncomplicated fellows.

> They came, from the most part, far away from Siberia or somewhere. Oh my God, they were thankful if you gave them a plastic bag. They were looking at the bags, which we put each lens or whatever in. So, we gave it to them and that was basically their payment for the day. It was awful.

The heat, which often soared to 95 degrees, coupled with a lack of any shade across the vast set, was a major challenge for the heavily costumed soldiers. "We rehearsed for half a day," remembered Ivan Gleb, one of the thousands toiling under the sun, "after which we did several shots. When they were filming infantry attacks, everyone fell down — 'killed' — we were so tired in the sun in warm clothes. Eventually, the filmmakers appointed those who will be 'killed' while the rest who would advance."[384]

Hungarian draftee soldier Tibor Tompa recalled the discomfort of wearing his colourful Imperial Guard uniform made of thick cloth, and sitting beneath a hawthorn bush held up by two bayonet-capped rifles, to shelter from the blazing sun. With his home less than 40 kilometres away across the border to the south, he was promised a furlough only when it was due to rain for several days, and bring a welcome pause in filming. Although the rain did roll in during late August, for most of the shoot the sun beat down mercilessly. Tompa recalled the lunch breaks when the tired and sweating soldiers could enjoy a brief snatch of R & R, but still under the glare of the sun while "the crew were eating in the shade under the colourful parasol."

Occasionally there were welcome surprises: "One day some beautiful actresses arrived in an open red sports car. We bucks had our mouths open. But all of us bucks, depending on his personal temperament, either admired the car — or the actresses!" Such fleeting distractions apart, Tibor considered it a tough experience:

We had to deal with the large-scale battle scenes. These were sometimes recorded eight to ten times, sometimes even more. And we were available all day to the film's creators. It was also the case that we were filming sometimes at night and in the early hours of the morning. So, attending the set wasn't a dream.[385]

He and his mates considered that they were at the beck and call of "an obsessive madman," for whom they would have to march, "fight" and even "die."

Playing God — and Tsar — was Sergei Bondarchuk, who used a mixture of nineteenth and twentieth-century communication systems; walkie-talkies coupled with an army drummer by his side on an elevated perch or tower, to send orders to individual units. He later described the meticulous process of staging these immense sequences, a technique honed a few years before on *War and Peace*:

> I have a topographic map, a scenario, and I line up the troops according to them. First, I need to see the big picture. Then in this view I choose details. For example, in the foreground I have a group of soldiers. I work out the general behaviour, then of each soldier, and I fit all this into the scene. Then I take some other particular…So gradually, an organism of twenty-thousand soldiers is built up, which acquires a single energy, a common sense which contains believable details.[386]

"He was fantastic when he jumped up on the tower." Daniele Nannuzzi was often spellbound as he watched the director work:

> I always remember him — a big, beautiful man with white hair. We had in front 15,000 people — the French, the English, and the horses. You must be a general — a dictator! And then he gave orders with the voice, the Russian voice, like: "*Frantsuzskaya kavalerija v 100 metrakh nalevo.*" (French cavalry 100 metres to the left)…"*Vzvod soldat na 50 metrov napravo*" (Platoon of soldiers 50 metres to the right). And you see this mass become something — a line — a battalion. It's choreography — a painting — and all *just* with a voice.

These cinematic orders had to be conducted along the military chain of command using loudspeakers, which one stood next to at your peril, to echo instructions across the vast field from the Army commanders. "If you can imagine a big lorry and the whole of the back it was a loudspeaker," remembered actor Peter Davies, "The generals had these scaffolding towers that they sat on. They were a scary-looking bunch. We would sit across the commissary tent from them, and they looked like they were from Central-Casting Soviet generals. But they were probably perfectly nice."

These generals were the real deal, having fought with distinction during the war, with military records that humbled the very best of their counterpart, British and American commanders. General Alexander Luchinsky had been awarded the title of Hero of the Soviet Union, along with the Order of Lenin. He had joined the Red Army in 1919 at the very beginning of the Revolution and had progressed in his career despite Stalin's brutal purge of the Officer Corps in the late 1930s. He had seen action from the beginning of the Nazi invasion of Russia in 1941, fighting first in the Battle of the Caucasus in 1942. Quickly gaining promotion, he took command of the 28th Army for the gigantic Operation Bagration in 1944. One of the deadliest battles on the Eastern Front, where the mighty Red Army succeeded in punching through the German front line in Byelorussia, allowing the Soviets to retake the initiative and begin the bloody slog towards Berlin.

Joining him in the commissary tent was General Nikolay Oslikovsky, a decorated cavalry commander who had also fought in Operation Bagration. Unlike their western allies, the Red Army deployed ten cavalry corps during the Second World War. These horsemen were ideal to operate across the vast, empty Steppes, particularly when roads were so poor, and when the Springtime seas of deep mud often defeated tanks and motor vehicles. Operating independently, horse cavalry missions included large-scale raids, screening of troop movements, and hit-and-run attacks against the enemy flanks often deep behind their rear. Even as jets were flying across the European battlefield, these units, seemingly from another age, proved their worth on the Eastern Front.

On 04 May 1945, forward mounted elements of Oslikovsky's cavalry command made the historic linkup with US troops at Torgau, on the River Elbe, which marked the final encirclement of Hitler's crumbling Reich. In 1951, the general, now head of the cavalry academy tasked with training riders for the prestigious Red Square parades, earned the displeasure of Stalin for daring to maintain his friendships with Jews — he was lucky he only suffered a demotion.

Within a year Stalin was dead, and the old general was eventually back in favour and lent his considerable experience of all cavalry matters to the filming of *War and Peace*. These top generals, who had led tens of thousands of men into some of the bloodiest and most bitter fighting in all of human history, were as tough and no nonsense as they come, although they appeared to be tolerant of the demands of cinema.

Sometimes, though, the well-oiled military machine would be unable to carry out the diktats of the cinema Tsar. There was often conflict between the film director and General Oslikovsky. One day, Bondarchuk insisted on shooting a scene at two in the afternoon — hoping to catch the perfect light. The cavalry squadrons were organised by horse colour, the Orlov Trotter had black, grey, bay, and chestnut coats. Bondarchuk would then make a choice, depending on the lighting, which horses best suited the effect he required. Impatient to film, he and the general clashed — Oslikovsky insisting the horses were not ready; the forage to feed them was still *en route* to the set. Without a proper meal, he explained, they could not perform with the required energy. When an annoyed Bondarchuk insisted — Oslikovsky replied firmly: "I will order soldiers — but how do I order animals?"[387]

One of those cavalrymen who was no doubt waiting to feed their charge that day was Mykola Kholodnyak, who was not only an admirer of the director but also had a shared heritage. "S. Bondarchuk had my respect even before I joined the army. He was a famous actor and producer of Soviet cinema. By nationality, he is Ukrainian (like me). Prior to that, he starred in the role of Taras Shevchenko, the famous Ukrainian poet. I am grateful to him for that."

He enjoyed his time working on the film with plenty of opportunities to be on-camera: "I was mostly in the foreground, since I served in the 1st squadron, but was not filmed every day as I was a serving soldier in the army." Often required to play different units of the various nationalities, Mykola sometimes had to wield a lance, made of an aluminium tube with a silver-painted rubber tip. Most of the time though, he had to draw a sword; a crude affair made of tin — and safely blunt.

When he was first thrown into the fray doing fake criss-cross sword fighting, a question arose: "What do we cry? What should we shout when we are attacking?" In the Ukrainian or Soviet Army, the traditional Cossack war-cry was a guttural, bezerka blood-curdling yell that would have echoed across the bloodied Steppes during the centuries-long battles with the Tartars. What, Mykola and his comrades wondered, issued from the more genteel Frenchmen? "And they said: 'Just cry whatever you want, but just do not use bad words!'"

He, like Daniele Nannuzzi, was mesmerised by the director: "S. Bondarchuk is a master of cinema. However, during the shooting, he did not instruct by a megaphone. This was done by another, his assistant, V. Dostal. During the shooting of *War and Peace*, he got a heart attack, and therefore could not shout loudly. He wore a straw hat and quietly instructed V. Dostal."

He even "died" for the director who would pace before a group of soldiers, looking each one up and down before laying his hand lightly on a shoulder, saying quietly: "*You* — are to die!" It was an honour, and on that occasion Mykola was chuffed to pay the ultimate cinematic price. The work may have been tough at times, but he was in no doubt it was an exciting experience: "We filmed on rainy, hot days, during days and nights, but I do not regret it at all."

Not everyone shared Mykola's sentiments. Day after day, month after month, Heinz Feldhaus, the Panavision technician watching by the cameras, was distressed by what he saw of the teeming extras. "They were simple soldiers. Bondarchuk and his generals, they were the bastards. They let them, I still feel it now, stay in the sun until they fainted. That's why I have nothing nice to say about Mr Bondarchuk."

To direct an epic of this magnitude must require a certain type of personality; forceful and tough, qualities Bondarchuk was certainly endowed with. On top of the daily challenges of the shoot, the director would have had to deal with not only the commercial demands of the two Hollywood partners, Columbia and Paramount, who had representatives on set, but also political pressure.

Academic Denise J. Youngblood, an expert on the 1960s Soviet cultural landscape, believes Moscow would have had official "eyes" on their star director, adding to the pressure upon him: "Of course Bondarchuk had a political minder on the *Waterloo* shoot, undoubtedly more than one. Co-productions were a huge risk for the Soviet State; so many 'dangerous' ideas."[388]

Daniele Nannuzzi felt the Russian, who had grown up alongside the traumatic birth pangs of the embryonic Soviet State, was inevitably a product of his place and time: "He was really a very hard man, because he survived five dictators — from Lenin, Stalin to Gorbachev — all dictators. He survived. But he was a very sweet, sweet man. Except when he gave orders to the extras."

The director's "sweet" side had been more apparent earlier in the production, as Heinz acknowledged: "He was always the big Russian boss, which he was not really when we were in Italy. You could talk to him, and he was more caring. While in Russia, he had so many assistants, you couldn't really go near to him, and you didn't want to. He was not a team member, unlike the cameraman."

Heinz enjoyed working closely with the Italian camera crew led by the affable Armando Nannuzzi, for whom, in contrast to Bondarchuk, he had nothing but praise and respect: "A gentleman. He was a good daddy. But between him and the director, sometimes there were frictions because of language and also different habits."

Daniele recalled the team of translators milling around Bondarchuk for this most multi-lingual of projects, which lead to inevitable confusion and friction: "We had one Italian translator, Anna Popova, and another little man. But they always translated in a (formal) Russian way. Sometime there was a fight between Bondarchuk and my father. I remember just no communication at times, you know."

Rare behind-the-scenes footage gives a glimpse of the unit working together.[389] The director is constantly on his feet, bubbling with energy, his face creased in concentration. A lighter side is visible during an inter-crew football match, as he dribbles the ball uncertainly before kicking, with a sense of relief, towards more talented players.

What is apparent, even viewing mute material, is the quick-fire communication between the director, the cameraman and actors, with just tiny nods to the translators at their side. There is a great deal of gesticulation to convey ideas, to which Bondarchuk listens patiently before emoting in return. At one point, he grabs the hand of Italian Ivo Garrani, splendidly dressed as Marshal Soult, during a discussion around Napoleon's flimsy campaign table, whether out of reassurance or to illustrate a point, both men pause in their conversation and smile at each other.

Communication issues apart, most of the time Bondarchuk and his cameraman enjoyed a robust creative relationship as they discussed the best angles for the five cameras at their disposal. Once selected, it was Daniele Nannuzzi's job to get them set up and ready:

> I was the co-ordinator of the assistants. We had five cameras and three trucks full of equipment. I built wooden stretchers, like Sedan chairs, that could contain the camera and its equipment, which were very easily transported by the soldiers they had assigned to the camera department. And every morning I

had to place them. The set was so huge, so wide; I mean one was here, and another was one kilometre there. Once on the spot, we assistants mounted them, ready to shoot.

One of those soldiers drafted in as a "grip" was burly Rashit Sharafutdinov, a conscript soldier from Bashkiria, a Soviet province in Central Asia. He was well used to man-handling heavy equipment: "I served as an army sapper from 1967 to 1969. We were sent to the camera company. At the site, we set the scenery, set up towers, dragged equipment, laid rails for the movie camera."[390] This simple conscript from the Bashkir hinterland had little idea how many famous people he was rubbing shoulders with, but with the aid of his stills camera he documented the action up close.

When Rashit and his team had finished getting everything into place, Daniele could concentrate on his job as focus-puller. His workload had been compounded by one of the producer's money-saving decisions: "We were just three focus-pullers because Dino said: 'Ah, you go to Russia, they have good camera assistants there. They are very good.'" Arriving in Russia, Daniele was dismayed to find: "No, there were *no* assistants. Just soldiers." He and his team would just have to make do.

Luckily, Heinz Feldhaus could lend a hand: "Sometimes I even operated a camera when they needed a third or fourth one." His primary job was to ensure that equipment from the Hollywood Panavision company supplied via Samuelson Film Services in London, was properly maintained. "I kept the cameras rolling, and the lenses, and all clean." The workhorse was the heavy Mitchell BNC studio camera used for dialogue scenes: "Panavision lenses on a "blimped" (silenced) Mitchell, because Panavision didn't have its own camera then."[391] Meanwhile, the noisy (unsuitable for sound recording) but lightweight German built Arriflex 11b cameras were deployed for capturing the action. These had Reflex viewfinders, which allowed direct monitoring of focusing and zooming unlike the rackover system Mitchell BNC (see Chapter Seven).

Using these reliable units avoided many of the technical problems that had plagued the *War and Peace* shoot. Every evening, as Heinz cleaned the gear, Daniele handled the precious exposed reels, each holding eleven minutes of 35mm celluloid. "When they say: '*Schtop!*' I had to discharge fifteen magazines of film — every day. It was like a war for us — like an Italian soldier in Russia!"

To capture the action, Armando Nannuzzi had several vantage points to play with, including a military helicopter, a 100-foot tower, and an overhead trolley to whiz the camera into the maelstrom.

> Another fantastic shot is the point of view of a bomb coming. We made a huge tower, 25 meters, like a Tower of Babel. We put two iron wires on top of this. The camera was mounted upside down and slid on the wires, which goes into the heart of the battle. It's a very wide shot, and at the end of this wire there is a break made with rubber foam. The shot in the movie is a cannon — BANG! You see this cannon ball coming and then hit the ground in a big explosion.

These explosions were the province of *War and Peace* veteran Vladimir Likhachov and his Russian special effects team. Like a painter with a canvas, the background needed to be roughed in first, using trucks that could produce dense clouds of white, grey, black and brightly coloured smoke to order. This allowed them to not only enhance the action but also to mask twentieth-century intrusions: passing cars or Soviet-era buildings. Whatever concoction was brewed, which resembled the acrid stench of burning rubber tyres, environmental concerns were completely ignored.

Hungarian soldier Tibor Tompa was tasked with being Bondarchuk's liaison with Likhachov's far-flung units:

> Under the movable director's "opera" stand, we set up a small radio station, and from there I forwarded the director's instructions. As a radio operator, I worked for about three months in this position. Most of the time, I received instructions from Sergei Bondarchuk's assistant (Vladimir Dostal), who was standing above me, saying things like: "We need more yellow, and then reddish smoke on the left flank."[392]

Their orders received, the effects crew members, stationed upwards of two miles away, fanned the "filthy stuff" which because of the vagaries of the wind would often force the entire unit to wait many minutes in the burning heat.

Everybody ended each day smeared in oil and tar; a particular problem for veteran Jack Hawkins, who, because of cancer, had had his larynx removed. Every time he attempted to speak, he had to use his adopted, post-operative method of belching for each breath and inevitably gulped in the toxic air.

Likhachov's team were tasked with creating the effect of explosions near to the actors and extras that had to be both safe but still dramatic. Their heavy wooden bases would often be seen driven deep into the ground after exploding. The procedure involved a small charge, like a firework, lightly buried in the ground that would be detonated by a hidden wire, and designed to produce more puff than a kick. Flags or markers hidden from the camera would ensure no unwary foot got in the way.

Tibor Tompa, who was busy relaying instructions from the director, was well placed to see the explosions. He was impressed with the desire for realism: "There were a lot of plastic dummies in uniform around the impact. I saw with my own eyes that some one-legged, one-armed extras were also employed."

They also fired spectacular air bursts, which would have been shot via mortars with a timer charge to explode in a large, white puff. Lastly, anachronistic looking Napalm-like mushroom clouds of kerosene were belched skywards to add some colour and spectacle. For close-ups, a technician would deftly wield a pot with wafts of the "filthy stuff."

It was slow work, Daniele Nannuzzi remembered, even with the extras deployed and the cameras primed, all waited on Likhachov's artfully composed special effects. The result was often magnificent.

> He painted the sky like a painter. Fantastic. All morning was just for preparation with the wires for the explosions, and the military smoke machine — very greasy, very heavy. And he had like a piano with the contacts. When the shot starts, he was playing like a pianist — *Boom! Boom! Boom!* It was incredible. We had to shoot with five cameras, but very fast. And then we go closer, closer with the other effects. I mean, we spent months on these battle scenes.

With the heat, the noise and interminable preparation, attention would inevitably drift, and boredom set in. Army discipline across the wide field could be lax, with potentially dangerous consequences, as Igor Starchenko, another young soldier, discovered almost too late when he and some mates played "hooky."

After standing some hours in the scorching sun, he and his friends slipped away into one of the sown wheat fields. Hoping to stay hidden while they dozed in the heat, a film technician abruptly woke them up with an expletive — they were sprawled upon pyrotechnic charges; and if they hadn't been seen, would have been blown "the f**k up!" Spooked, the miscreants ran into the next field, and after catching their breath, watched the explosions — "It was intense."[393]

On a Napoleonic battlefield, explosions would have been rare, although the French did use howitzers, which created a lethal burst. Most of the ammunition that was fired comprised large iron balls, and so low was the speed it was possible to watch their progress. Soldiers could momentarily (for about two seconds) see a dot coming towards them, and then duck. For those unfortunates in the line-of-fire, the trail of destruction could be horrific. Just one iron ball could take off heads, go through chests, rip off arms, legs, before bouncing on the ground, rising and inflicting more of the same as it continued its lethal way. Even as it trickled out of steam, it could still have a bite, rookie soldiers sometimes lent out their foot to stop them, which usually ended with a footless man writhing in pain. One tiny saving grace for those fighting on the soggy Belgium battlefield that day was the balls tended not to bounce, because of the mud.

Pre-CGI it was very difficult — and censurable — to depict the effect of cannon shot safely and accurately, so the use of fiery explosions had become a cinematic short-hand for battle scenes long before *Waterloo*. Some more recent films like *Last of the Mohicans* (1992), *The Patriot* (2000) and *Master and Commander: The Far Side of the World* (2003) have displayed the hideous effect of non-explosive round shot successfully and accurately with lots of clouds of earth and wooden splinters.

One can surmise that Likhachov was a war veteran who had witnessed the ghastly spectacle of modern ordnance. It would be unsurprising if he did not emulate this for the sake of cinema rather than history. Instead, what he and his team did was to create an impressionistic sense of the lethality of the battlefield against a vast canvas.

> Scene.181: *The sky storms ceaselessly. The sounds of shots merge into a single thunder-clap. It is as though the sky split open. Everything disappears into darkness…*

Nature — rain and thunderstorms — played a pivotal part in both history and the reconstruction. Bondarchuk, attempting to bring some visual poetry, wanted nature to play a key role: "It was a difficult tussle with the producers. I introduced a hurricane into the battle, I wanted to show the importance to which Tolstoy credited the '*Rok*'"[394] This was a mystical concept broadly meaning destiny on an epic scale, unlike *"Sud'ba"* which refers to *individual* human fate. Bondarchuk wanted his Waterloo to echo Tolstoy's belief that the powerful savagery of Borodino in 1812 had influenced the course of history through a form of celestial energy.

> Scene.181: ...*A violent storm falls on the earth. Columns of black smoke rise high into the sky. They sweep the field and float back.*

Relics of the Great Patriotic War in the shape of wingless YAK fighters were used to create Bondarchuk's *"Rok"* — a hurricane that courses across the latter part of the battle scenes. These war birds that had once flown in dogfights with Messerschmitts over the skies of the Eastern Front, still packed a punch with their very powerful, un-silenced V12 Klimov engines. Securely anchored to the ground, they still appeared to be under air force control: "The funny thing was that the 'pilots' dressed as if they were to take off; helmet, goggles and aviator jacket."[395] The ear-blasting noise, coupled with a vicious punch of air that could blast a man off his feet, was a lethal combination that made all very wary. Dense clouds of acrid black smoke completed the hellish picture.

> Scene.92: NAPOLEON *rides onto the mound and dismounts. His feet sink into the mud.*

Less spectacular, but historically significant, was the mud. The torrential downpour the night before the great battle proved to be a decisive factor. The film neatly conceptualises this as Napoleon gets stuck in the ooze, and shouts to be retrieved. We hear Steiger's hushed narration: *"The only enemy I fear is nature."* To visually realise this slimy elemental force, part of the valley was flooded with the help of an irrigation system.

For one scene, fire engines spent two days pumping water into the soil and the finishing touch was supplied by the cavalry, who were ordered to trot back and forth to complete the churn. This major sequence detailed the mass attack by d'Erlon's French right wing with densely packed infantry columns, which the script describes as *"possess the ground like three creeping monsters."* To get to grips with Picton's red coats they first have to traverse the valley, but as the soldiers detailed to recreate this immense throng of armed humanity were soon so knee deep in mud, it quickly resembled Passchendaele.

Watching the thousands of foot-soldiers toil through the slime was cavalryman Mykola Kholodnyak who was himself under strict instruction not to soil his costume. He recalls that after four takes: "Everyone was black as Negroes, their uniforms were dirty, with a 'swamp' on their heads."[396] He recalls how difficult it was to keep clean amid the dust and mud; yet every evening their soiled costumes would be returned, and miraculously, a clean set appeared the next day. Who was responsible for the mass laundry of thousands of those garments is unknown, but these unsung heroes fully deserve respect.

Finally, with all the various elements ready, thousands of men and horses waited for one man atop his tower — Sergei Bondarchuk. Fifty years later, Daniele Nannuzzi could still recall the sheer visceral excitement as the cameras rolled:

> The emotion when he says: "Action!" And you can see the earth trembling — *frumm! frumm! frumm! frumm!* — with the step of the soldiers — *frumm! frumm! frumm! frumm!* — 18,000 people moving their feet — the noise! You can see them coming a kilometre away. The emotion when you see the bayonets coming over the hill — *frumm! frumm! frumm! frumm!* And you see this mass of people — I have goosebumps now! For us, it was like filming a *real* war. We had the same emotion.

The film catches something of Daniele's evocative memory in a scene that attempts to inject the naked fear of impending combat.

> Scene.132: Some of Picton's Irish redcoats of the 27th (Inniskilling) are lying down behind a hedge, supping "Dutch courage" in the guise of a ration of gin; they await the approaching enemy; *The* NOISE *of the* FRENCH ADVANCE *— a deep rumbling…is very loud*. Next to O'Connor is Macmahon who nervously fingers rosary beads: *"It's like…it's like the whole of bloody hell is coming up out of the ground."*

While many of the shots using helicopters and towers give a terrific sense of the scope and scale, this is one of the few moments that attempts to present a "grunts" eye view of battle. All we see, like them, is just a smoke-shrouded slope ahead, while the air rings with the menacing sound of marching feet. The fear and trepidation are well presented, as chirpy O'Connor played by Donal Donnelly, attempts to hide his own fear with gallows humour. Around him the others, as good Irish Catholics (played by Russians, including Oleg Vidov) are praying, causing him to quip: *"…nothing scares me more than standing next to a friend of the Almighty."*

Over the years, there have been suggestions that several visual effects techniques were employed to expand the vista of battle; glass matte paintings, and optical replication (as used by Kubrick for the attacking legions for the battle in *Spartacus*). There is no evidence, either in the film or from those on the crew, that any other forms of illusion were used — except one.

This was an ingenious, and very low-tech concession, to artifice — as two bleary-eyed cavalrymen discovered when they were awoken one morning at 3 a.m. for a very early filming call. While one, Mahmoud Dauchlezh, grumbled about Bondarchuk and the demands of cinema, his friend Aslan Khablauk pointed at the silhouettes of moving legions — black against the dawn light: "Don't swear, Dauchlezh. Look at those poor people who are up before us." His comrade was suitably mollified: "Wow! All those infantrymen woken at such an hour!"[397]

Suspecting something was amiss, they mounted their horses and rode over to investigate. To their surprise, the early risers were in fact rows of plastic mannequins being moved *en masse* by Bondarchuk's assistants ready for the first set-up.

Exploiting the physics of detail diminishing with distance from the camera, these 5,000 soldiers had been conjured up by the production designer in a moment of inspiration.

> Sometimes we had over 18,000 people, but with some huge, wide shots, there was not enough! And then Mario Garbuglia had a great idea. He made a model of a French soldier in blue, and English in red. Then with a plastic press, he printed bodies like the figures in the table soccer game connected by the rods (*Subbuteo*). Then he took a very long iron tube and put it behind the figures to fix them.

Each of these units comprised two real soldiers standing at either end of the eight plastic ones, held in place with a single wooden plank; this allowed the regiments to march forward. "They were just for very far away. But when you see that hill full of these 'battalions' moving — this was amazing. Remember — no special effects." There were also horse dummies, some standing with cavalrymen figures, with others playing "dead" splattered with red paint. The overall illusion of this *silent* army was helped by a few horsemen flitting backwards and forwards coupled with gusts of smoke — it was a very convincing deception.[398]

In the film they are deployed very effectively as Napoleon surveys the Allied lines just prior to hostilities. In one of Bondarchuk's trademark crane shots, the camera begins a very long pan across Wellington's army, studded with the lines of red dummies which are assembled along the entire opposite ridge. Meanwhile, we hear Steiger's voice: *"His main strength is beyond that hill. What he shows me is only a façade. He is clever. Clever."* Finally, the camera zooms back as the crane drops down to find Napoleon in foreground pointing at Hougoumont: *"We shall begin the attack there."*

Of all the principal three-dimensional sets constructed on the Ukrainian plain, the reconstruction of the château of Hougoumont, complete with outbuildings and even a chapel, was the most impressive. This sprawling complex enclosed with high, thick walls had been the right-hand anchor for Wellington's army. He had stuffed it with some of his crack troops who had immediately turned it into a formidable fortified stronghold. What was only intended as a diversionary attack would form the opening move of the battle, and figure as the first action sequence in the film; graphically described in the screenplay as the French try to wrestle for control of the vital position.

> Scene.107: *The* FRENCH…*break through the green wall. But a new horror rises up: The stone wall of Hougoumont. In the wall there are thirty-eight loopholes at different levels. The* ENGLISH *fire from behind the wall, from the terraces, from all the windows, from all the loopholes.*

Little information has surfaced about this complex sequence, but it is possible to surmise. As is does not feature any of the main cast, it is highly probable responsibility was handed to Anatoli Chemodurov, the Second Unit Director. On most movies with extended action, an ancillary team is formed with its own director, skilled with handling dangerous sequences. They are usually a semi-autonomous outfit, following general instructions from the principal director.

We know little about Chemodurov, who was apparently an actor who had appeared in Bondarchuk's debut feature: *Destiny of a Man*. He along with four others is credited as an Assistant Director on *War and Peace*, where he handled many of the battle scenes photographed by husband-and-wife camera team, Aleksander Shelenkov and Iolanda Chen. It is a fair assumption that the two men understood and trusted each other, and Bondarchuk was happy to delegate. They would collaborate on a further film together in 1975.[399]

Scene.107: FAVOUR LEGROS, *a huge sapper. As* LEGROS *runs, he swings a grappling hook underarm. Ten yards from the wall, he lets the hook go. He jerks the rope tight…Now there is fighting on the top of the wall. The living make use even of the dead: bodies are piled against the wall — a ladder of dead flesh.*

In the screenplay, the Hougoumont sequence offers tiny vignettes of characters to give a glimpse of desperate men fighting to the death. Legros was a legendary figure in the French army, renowned for his enormous height and strength. In the battle, he is remembered for breaking open the gates of the fortified complex with an axe, before attempting to storm the defences. After a brutal fight, with the garrison's commander Macdonnell helping to re-close the gates by sheer brute force, the attackers, including Legros, were either ejected or killed. In the oft-told story, only a young French drummer boy survived the carnage.[400] Wellington later acknowledged the vital role played by this short, sharp action: "the success of the battle turned upon the closing of the gates at Hougoumont."[401]

Armando Bottin, who is listed as playing Legros, had a similarly impressive physique. He had achieved success as a middle-weight boxing champion and competed successfully in bodybuilding tournaments. He had carved out a career in the cheap "epic" *peplum* genre of the early 1960s as a stuntman and "heavy." He would become a staple of the burgeoning Spaghetti Westerns, using such pseudonyms as Johnny Kissmuller, Jr., a reference to Johnny Weissmuller, the Olympic winning swimmer and later famous 1930s *Tarzan*. It is probable Bottin would have made a memorable cameo, before he became yet another of the legion of bit players who strutted their stuff under the fetid Ukrainian sun, only to end up as out-takes in a rusty film can.[402]

From what we can glimpse of this very impressive set in the film (and the trailer), it was a sturdy, three-dimensional structure constructed with great attention to detail. In one of the last shots where Wellington's entire army is advancing on the French, in the far background of the frame, it is possible (just) to see flames pouring out of the Hougoumont structure. Why this would have been done when it is barely discernible in the already busy frame — is a mystery.

What remained of the standing sets were burnt after the last scenes was completed. Mykola Kholodnyak one of the many extras, recalls waiting around in the pouring rain as they prepared to capture this final sequence. He got so soaked even his all-important military documents got damaged, in particular his identity card.

At some point the weather must have cleared before Daniele Nannuzzi joined his father in the army helicopter, as they endeavoured to get some final spectacular shots.

> We burned the chateau. It was a huge burning. And I remember my father was on the helicopter wearing short pants with his legs outside of the back door. The pilot crossed over the fire on top of the column of heat and flames — was terrible. My father was screaming: "Go up! Go up!" It was too close. Because he was wearing short pants, his legs were without any hair — completely burned!

Despite the immense effort to capture the battle on film, not everyone was impressed with the production. Heinz Feldhaus was scathing about the long, arduous and frustrating shoot:

> It was not a very great, organised thing. The special effects had to be all set up — the houses (sets) going up in flames. And then we do it again. And then there was the horse that didn't want to go. Or it was too hot, and some soldiers were fainting. It was just a monstrous shoot.

In his long career, he encountered some of the biggest talents in the industry. "I worked with many others, and my greatest hero is Stanley Kubrick." He considered there was a gulf of difference between him and Bondarchuk: "Stanley cared personally if the caterer is there in the morning, the mobile toilets are around, and if the first set is ready; so, he was a professional, very professional, much easier to work with."

The multitude of everyday considerations from toilets to catering, horses and a dog were the responsibility of the production manager. This role is perhaps one of the most important for any movie shoot, big or small. On *Waterloo* there were two — Mario Abussi and Guglielmo Ambrosi, who was known as "Memo."

He was fondly remembered by Peter Davies:

> Memo, just a fantastically, friendly, marvellous person who really was holding all that stuff together. He had a responsibility for getting us to the location, making sure that we knew what was going on. And so, we saw a lot of him. He was a key figure. Especially when we were in Uzhgorod because those were trying circumstances.

He would have to ensure all the crew, extras and equipment required on any given day were arranged and in the right place. The snail's pace of production inevitably meant he bore the brunt of the often-bored cast.

> I knew that there were a lot of frustrations; that you thought you were going to go to work and then you didn't and things like that. I just remember him being so kind and doing everything in his power to make us comfortable. He was always smiling, always friendly. I wouldn't have had any concept on the size of job he had. I would have just been an innocent youth.

Peter, who was still a teenager, was often confounded how the affable Italian could juggle an actor's "trivial" problems, while simultaneously dealing with the myriad of daily production headaches.

> I remember arriving at the set. On the road as far as you could see were soldiers marching to the location from their barracks with a military band playing. It was amazing. It would almost be like he was waving goodbye to you at the hotel, and then he would be there with the 15,000 soldiers.

The sight that would have greeted Peter was nicely captured in an evocative you-are-there description penned with suitable flourish by the publicity department:

> After a bumpy ride from Uzhgorod on a cobblestone road, running past 19th-century farmhouses with slate and tile roofs, one arrived at a vast open field, marked by a sign *Batepaoo — Waterloo*. Then up a muddy dirt road — Then a left turn up the muddy dirt road — past the raw pine temporary buildings housing the camera equipment, costumes and props for the film — to the crest of the hill, from which one could see the full sweep of the battlefield, dotted with thousands of moving men. A Red Army guard, armed with only a walkie-talkie, stops your car because a big scene is about to begin shooting in the centre of the battlefield. Moments later, the entire battlefield erupts in smoke and fiery explosions. Brass cannon, with a frightening noise, boom the length of the field. There is a direct hit on Napoleon's headquarters, La Belle Alliance. Smoke and flame pour from it. Closer to you, an explosion shatters the slate of La Haye Sainte, others hit

Hougoumont with the same effect, and it's hard to believe that these explosions are the wizardry of special effects experts and not real cannon ball explosions. Five cameras are turning on the inferno. Here and there, smoke and flame erupt directly at the feet of orderly columns of resplendent troops in reds, whites, blues and gold braid. Many fall, presumably dead. A cavalry company charges toward sonic cannon on your left through explosion after explosion. Horses, specially trained to fall by the unit's Italian and Yugoslavian stunt men, go down, their daring riders tumbling end over end, falling realistically, ritualistically into horrible ballets of death. You cannot hear yourself think. You cannot behold the frenzy, the fury, the stomach-churning, head-aching horror of it all. Then loud above the sound of the battle, a public address horn blares "*Schtop*," and something else in Russian. The scene ends. "Dead" men and horses rise up again and return, like so many sheep, to their starting positions. It is during the lull that the guard lets your car through. At the end of the road, firemen are putting out the last traces of the fire. Beyond it, on a mound, Rod Steiger, the most convincing Napoleon the screen will ever see, sits in a canvas chair under a blue umbrella conferring through an interpreter with Sergei Bondarchuk.[403]

Although generalised and impressionistic rather than a snapshot of straight reportage, it does neatly capture the changing priorities of the director. Much of his energy now being consumed by the complex action sequences, leaving his star feeling marooned amid the make-believe carnage.

The opening move of the battle saw an attack on Hougoumont. Wellington's army on the ridge behind prepare for the French assault. The set was a faithful replica of the original although there were no scenes filmed inside.
AUTHOR'S COLLECTION

276 WATERLOO — MAKING AN EPIC

La Haye Sainte farmhouse with Wellington's Tree behind. © RICHARD HEFFER

Artillery troop trot past La Haye Sainte (at right) with La Belle Alliance at the centre of the French ridge beyond. Note the rows of plastic dummies.
© RICHARD HEFFER

A rocking horse was fixed to a truck to allow close focus. Unknown rider but may have been stand-in for Christopher Plummer wearing hat in foreground. © RICHARD HEFFER

Jack Hawkins often sat on a box or stilts as he was unsteady on a horse.
© RICHARD HEFFER

Production designer Mario Garbuglia's clever idea to use these highly detailed plastic dummies to extend the army. FORTEPAN/ALEXANDER

Over 5000 were made, and proved popular with visitors. © HEINZ FELDHAUS

One of the young Russian soldiers detailed to be a grip for the camera team.
© HEINZ FELDHAUS

Umberto Torriero, the Key Grip helps with the Dyna Lens, invented to absorb vibrations, although not very successfully. It was used to do the telescope effect. © HEINZ FELDHAUS

Preparing to shoot the repulse of the Old Guard. © MYKOLA KHOLODNYAK

Rod Steiger with Lev Polyakov as Kellerman, note the smoke pot.
AUTHOR'S COLLECTION

Left: The 100-foot tower, note the cameraman half way up the rickety structure. © HEINZ FELDHAUS *Right: Diane Ogilvy looks at the director's opera stand used for issuing instructions.* © RICHARD HEFFER

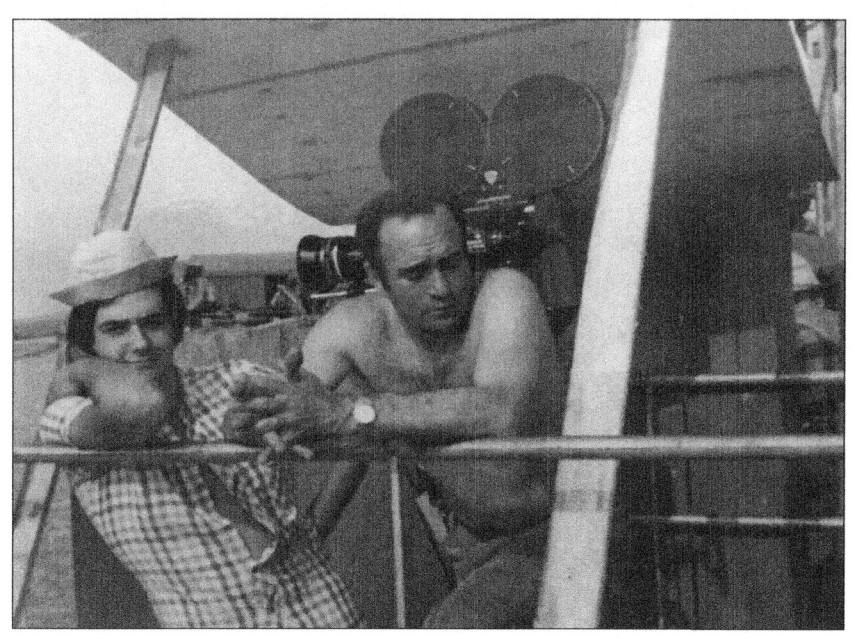

Daniele Nannuzzi and Nino Cristiani wait patiently for the next take.
© HEINZ FELDHAUS

282　　WATERLOO — MAKING AN EPIC

Unknown Russian lady displays the clapperboard for a scene involving French infantry. © HEINZ FELDHAUS

Bondarchuk with Armando Nannuzzi, preparing to film.
© HEINZ FELDHAUS

SIMON LEWIS 283

The camera team. From left: Nino Cristiani (Camera operator), Heinz Feldhaus (Panavision Manager), Daniele Nannuzzi (Focus Puller), Silvano Mancini (Camera operator), Giuseppe Berardini (Camera Operator), Federico Del Zoppo (Focus Puller), Paul Ronald (Still Photographer). © DANIELE NANNUZZI

Left: Continuity supervisor Elvira D'Amico with director of photography, Armando Nannuzzi. Right: Unknown make-up lady. © RICHARD HEFFER

The director confers with General Ivan Evgenievich Oslikovsky. © ASLAN KHABLAUK

The historical adviser, Willoughby Gray, known as Willo, leafs through a dog-eared script. © RICHARD HEFFER

Make-up artist Alberto De Rossi, holding what looks like his lunch, with Steiger. © HEINZ FELDHAUS

Bondarchuk's right-hand-man, assistant director Vladimir Dostal, who had also worked on War and Peace. *At right, Daniele Nannuzzi holding camera.* © HEINZ FELDHAUS

A rare moment of Steiger caught out of character, surreptitiously taken by one of the extras. © ASLAN KHABLAUK

CHAPTER 12

"*What Will Men Say Of Me…I Wonder?*"

"I'm even running out of sexual fantasies," Steiger lamented in July 1969. "That's how long I've been here."[404] By now, the star was becoming weary and depressed; reportedly nursing a bottle of whisky that had been smuggled in by one of the Italian crew members. Visiting critic Roger Ebert of the *Chicago Sun-Times*, described the scene in the hotel's "drab" dining room with only borscht on the menu as Steiger, Dan O'Herlihy and a newly arrived Christopher Plummer, shared a bottle of Scotch, and amused each other with long dirty stories. "Trying to bring my small measure of poetry into the world," said Steiger.

> So here was Steiger, staring into a bowl of borscht. "The role of Napoleon has always fascinated me," he said. "It is my hope that, when this picture is completed, the role of Napoleon will still fascinate me. But if Napoleon had to eat goddamn borscht every goddamn day, I wonder if Napoleon himself would have given a good goddamn."[405]

Modern historians play down Napoleon's illness during the campaign, but even the most cursory look at his lethargic behaviour, coupled with the fact he spent much of the battle a mile behind the lines, suggests here was a man not in tip-top condition. It has been thought the reason was an acute attack of haemorrhoids that prevented him from mounting his horse, which limited his customary practice of mobile supervision of the army.

Two days before the battle, it is said, his doctor lost the vital dose of leeches, which were a common practice relief for his "piles" (haemorrhoids) ailment. To fight the pain, the doctor accidentally overdosed him with laudanum. As we have seen, Steiger seized greedily on this historical titbit to form the basis of his characterisation. Bondarchuk creates a dramatic single shot that illustrates the potential implications of the emperor's below par performance; the lives of so many, dependent on just one lone human being. The setting was the windmill structure, whose existence Willo Gray, the historical advisor, had grumbled about.

In the finished film, on the morning of the battle, there is a vast and impressive single shot that shows the French army marching past the whitewashed windmill, as Napoleon sits hunched with his head in his hands. The script, which described him as *dozed off in a chair in front of the mill…not at all disturbed by the music and the cheers of the men marching past him*, was placed two days earlier in the story. Then his "doze" is interrupted by news that Blucher and his Prussians are assembled at Ligny; offering battle. The Ligny sequence was ultimately not only cut but rearranged, and will be discussed in more detail in Chapter Eighteen.

A peek at behind-the-scenes footage has a few moments from this sequence which suggest, in fact, that the scene's original placement may have already have been rearranged during the production.[406] The ground is very clearly muddy as it was on the morning of the main battle following the deluge the night before. The culprits: two fire engines sit near to the crew. Although the absence of Marshal Ney (Dan O'Herlihy), who historically was at Quatre Bras at the time of Ligny, could equally suggest that the scene was filmed with its *original* scripted intention.

In the film, the camera begins with a wide-open vista of the marching army before gradually zooming close into Napoleon's addled head. It appears thanks to the behind-the-scenes footage that the scene originally included a bit of extra "business" of Constant (Orazio Orlando), the emperor's valet, clad in a marvellous looking green livery costume, handing him a glass of white liquid, perhaps milk of magnesia. This rare footage also shows several other cameras being operated, gathering extra "coverage" for editing.

By the time the cameras rolled, the *regiment of infantry marching past the mill*, described by the script, had grown to the full contingent of 15,000 soldiers. As this brilliantly costumed army tramped behind the "Emperor," they also filed past the film's *real* emperors. Dino had brought over the family, including his daughter Veronica: "I remember my father just telling everybody — do this and do that. And then going over it with the director, as they had thousands of people there they'd gotten for that scene."

They were also entertaining the Hollywood moneymen, in particular the head of the vast Gulf + Western conglomerate. With Paramount

Pictures as one of its subsidiaries, Charles Bluhdorn had taken a very hands-on approach to his new acquisition, eagerly involving himself in the minutiae of film production. He had brought his wife and son with him to Russia, and was keen to boast to gathered journalists just how well his money was being spent: "'We have 15,000 troops down there,' he says ebulliently. 'Now, we just couldn't afford that in Hollywood… They gave this parade for us. I don't know how many generals.'" A journalist was curious if he had awarded himself a medal, after noticing something pinned to the lapel of his black suit. "'A decoration? No, it's not from here. I haven't finished the film yet.'"[407]

This enthusiasm was also echoed by his right hand-man, Robert Evans, who had spent days in a darkened screening room at Dinocittà enthralled by the hours of film material being shipped back. Giving his first interview abroad since assuming the vice-presidency for Paramount global productions, he did that rarest of things for a senior executive — admit to a mistake. Watching two hours of a rough edit plus an hour of rushes, Evans said he "flipped" when he saw the spectacular battle footage, and regretted advising his boss to pull back investment in the production. While his company kept the distribution rights to North America and France, the rest of Western Europe minus Italy had been snapped up by Columbia Pictures. He was convinced it was a blockbuster in the making: "Footage was so tremendous and Rod Steiger so staggering,"[408] he considered the actor's performance the best of his career.

Back amid the smoke, dust and heat, the star was becoming weary and despondent at the slow production schedule, and found little enthusiasm in the vast mass of humanity filing past him.

> "Don't you get a feeling of supreme power when you look around at all this?" asked a pudgy newspaperman from the Middle West. Steiger looks around at 'All This.' "No, I just get a feeling that I want to go home."[409]

A taste of Italian home comforts enlivened spirits during Dino's sojourn on the location, as his daughter remembers: "…lots of eating. My father used to organise all that. I remember lunches on a long table outside, during the weekend, maybe on a Sunday when there was no shooting. It was Italian cooking and Russian cuisine, both of them."

One can appreciate how welcome this was from Daniele Nannuzzi's memory of the first few weeks on location.

A truck arrived with Russian women looking like farmers, and they brought some wooden boxes full of straw for chickens. Our dishes were in the straw with the spoons, and everything inside these dirty and dusty boxes. The women then opened a milk tank and gave out soup. I don't know what was in it — pieces of greasy meat — it was terrible. The smell was amazing! And when you returned your dish, one of these women washed it inside another tank of water and put it back — without soap — nothing.

Standing in line for his lunch that day was Italian actor Andrea Checchi, cast as the Old Guardsmen Sauret, who had form as a rambunctious character, looking at the soup he considered:

…it was very thick and greasy and too heavy for him. He looked into the other tank, and saw it was very thin — because it was just water: "I want this!" And the woman says: "No, no, no." And he says: "This! — I want this!" So, she gives him it — just the greasy water for him.

The food was a constant problem for the unit: "In the night we prepared some sandwiches to eat for lunch time because otherwise it was impossible!" The contradictions of communism were not lost on young Daniele:

The crew ate under the sun — some tables and some chairs, but nothing much. The actors were in a different place — a tent with food. The mentality was very communist. Once Bondarchuk said to my father: "Armando, you don't have to eat this stuff. You come in my tent." And then one day I saw inside the tent. There was a table with a cloth, with silver spoons — like for a Tsar. And all the (army) officers were eating with him (Bondarchuk). Twenty years later, he was less communist. It was a terrible situation for us. But we go ahead in this way for months.

It is hardly surprising the unit kicked back when the opportunity arose. Mario Garbuglia, the production designer, remembers how work slowed to a crawl as the crew enjoyed the food and alcohol while Dino and his glamorous wife, Silvana, held court.

In the evenings, the generals would throw enormous banquets. Silvana, who was queen of these affairs, would perform Russian dances against a backdrop of songs, choruses and all the vodka you could drink.[410]

Veronica well recalled the copious amounts of spirits drunk:

> A *lot* of vodka drinking, I mean these Russians would drink vodka like you have no idea! Then they would go outside to feel like they were not drunk anymore because it was so cold. So, they would drink, go outside, return and drink again! It was fun.

As dawn broke, the party was often still in full swing as they set up Baccarat tables up which "Dino and Silvana, victorious as always, would cheerfully win back whatever we had been paid to make the film."[411]

Like a mirage, the glitz and glamour of Italian cinematic royalty soon disappeared as Dino took his family back to Rome, leaving his brother Alfredo to maintain morale. Steiger spent much of his spare time holed up in his "luxury" suite at Uzhgorod's premiere hotel. Most of the "French" cast of Italians and Russians had little command of English, and so the American found few people to converse with.

The exception was the young French aristocrat, Philippe Forquet, cast appropriately as Comte de La Bedoyere, Napoleon's aide and confident; he fondly remembers working with the star, and the two became lifelong pals.

> I particularly enjoyed evenings at the hotel restaurant, Rod Steiger and I were very good friends by then. We sat at the same table, sometime only the two of us, and other days with Willoughby Gray, the military advisor on the film. We talked, we joked, we drank quite a bit of vodka. When the meal was over, we'd all move up to Rod's place on the second-floor — one bedroom and one sitting room. The evenings involved kidding, joking, laughter, drinking, we'd also play cards; and lots of chattering about girlfriends, wives, affairs — all of these naughty things, of course! Just like a bunch of kids. I'm sure each one of us remembered these evenings for a long time.

This budding bond between the two men had gone hand-in-hand with creating small scenes designed to show Napoleon's humanity, all with the approval of the director. Perhaps due to the nearly twenty years between them, and at different places in their careers, it was a creative partnership shorn of ego and competitiveness. Interestingly, both had studied The Method at the Actors Studio in New York, although the Frenchman said he hated it: "I just couldn't relate."[412] Even so, both men seemed to find a synergy, once with amusing results, when they first began working together on the backlot at Dinocittà in Rome.

Two solid interior sets had been constructed; one for Wellington's HQ for night scenes before the battle (including Hay's watch scene, as described in Chapter Seven). While the other, comprising several rooms, was a faithful reconstruction of the Ferme du Caillou. Standing alongside the Brussels road, and now a museum, it was Napoleon's impromptu HQ the night before the battle. The set was studded with windows which allowed vistas of the Roman waste ground which effectively matched the rolling Ukrainian landscape.

The dining room, dressed with help from the props company E. Rancati with genuine period porcelain dishes, crystal glasses and silver cutlery, played host to the breakfast scene with the French high command — with an interruption.

> Scene.101: Napoleon joins his generals for breakfast. Announcing his intention to attack at 9 a.m., he is advised that the ground is still too muddy, and therefore useless for moving cannons. A distant church bell is heard from the village of Plancenoit; La Bedoyere says the priest won't give up his Sunday Mass. Napoleon, his mind wandering, muses: "*He won't have much of a congregation.*" All wait for his next words, before he *suddenly throws down his serviette and stands up.*

This scene, as filmed, ends with Steiger stomping from the room to the consternation of his commanders, with the consequences of the day of battle ahead preying heavily upon his soul. Philippe Forquet as La Bedoyere remembers the creation of an improvised fresh scene intended to extenuate the drama.

> Then the shooting moved to another room of that house, but only Steiger and I: Rod and the director wrote a scene that was meant to discover Napoleon's state-of-mind, but Rod wanted me to play that with him, and no one else. Since we first met, the two of us hit it off quite well. So, we started rehearsing a few times, and I learned the lines. Suddenly, while rehearsing, I don't know

what got in to us — we played it as if we were two raving queens! The entire crew burst into laughter — even Sergei Bondarchuck!

What was the eventual shape of the scene is unknown, as in both script and film the generals burst in on Napoleon and discuss their reservations for the upcoming battle. It may have been only a brief aside, but it shows the director's willingness to improvise and improve the written word. When Philippe finally saw the film in 1971, he confidently expected to see these specially created intimate moments, some of which he considered his best work with Steiger. To his disappointment, only one fragment survived the editing scissors.

Just before the cannons roar, the gulf between emperor and subject is bridged as they discuss fatherhood beside the La Belle Alliance inn on the Ukraine set, with La Bedoyere proudly describing his son: *"No taller than your boot."* Napoleon, while stroking a miniature of his own son, asks would he wish him to be here — at Waterloo — that day. Yes, La Bedoyere replies: *"So he could see you, Sire."* Napoleon, with the anguish of an absent father, replies: *"I'd give my heart, my life"* to see his child but not to *"witness this battle today."* It is a beautifully played duet which gives much needed warmth and humanity to the film, and suggests what the other lost vignettes of these Steiger/Forquet "business" may have looked like.

> Scene.161: NAPOLEON *is distraught. "After Austerlitz, I said I'd be good for six more years. Now it's ten years on and nine campaigns. A man has his day in war as in everything else…"*

One scene to make it through intact from the script was the film's opportunity to explain its theme and give voice to the lead character's soul. After Napoleon has his seizure, as described in the Prelude, and ushered off the field, he and La Bedoyere talk amid the ruins of the windmill, perhaps suggesting they are far from the battle. Napoleon ruminates on his declining facilities: *"Does age increase a man's wisdom — or just spoil his ability to gamble?"* The script projects his unadorned megalomania and ego, with a question about his legacy: *"What will men say of me…I wonder?"* It is La Bedoyere who suggests the rather nebulous and all too human desire for immortality: *"They will say you extended the limits of glory."* In the script, the Emperor seems resigned, grimly content with the thought, although accepting the almost certainty of defeat and his son's penury: *"…Even if he cannot count on forty-thousand francs a year."* The finished film is more succinct, with Napoleon posing a rhetorical question, that after all the bloodshed: *"Is that all I'll leave my son? The limits of glory?"*

Few, it seems, of the rest of the cast enjoyed the same rapport with Steiger that Philippe Forquet did. Aware that his role was competing with the roar of cannon and thunder of horses, the star had little room for manoeuvre, although one scene offered him an opportunity to "improve" on the screenplay, but not without some ructions.

> Scene.10: *Suddenly,* NAPOLEON *appears at the bend of the road. He advances slowly, followed by his* MEN, *their weapons at the ready…* PAN *the* ROYALIST SOLDIERS' FACES. CLOSE ON NAPOLEON.

Behind the "French" ridge on the set was another valley, and it was here that many of the large-scale scenes away from the battle were filmed. It was the setting for Napoleon's dramatic return from exile from Elba, where he and his small band of men find the road to Paris barred by an army sent from the King. In the film, this army is commanded by Ney, played by Dan O'Herlihy.

Ney was perhaps the most famous of Napoleon's top soldiers; as we saw in Chapter Two, he was dubbed "The Bravest of the Brave" for his command of the rear-guard out of Russia in 1812. He was the epitome of the born, simple soldier; the son of a barrel maker who had risen up through the ranks during the chaos of the revolution. An ardent Republican with no time for monarchy, he nevertheless fell under the spell of Napoleon and loyally served him across the battlefields of Europe.

His motives for leading a revolt of the marshals and forcing the end of Napoleon's rule in 1814 was almost certainly an honourable, if weary, desire to see an end to the fighting. By default, he served the reinstated King Louis, but it is not hard to imagine the turmoil this bluff soldier must have endured on being sent to confront his old master. His famous historical boast: *"I'll bring him back in an iron-cage,"* can be interpreted in many ways, and no doubt lit the creative fuse for actor Dan O'Herlihy as they prepared to shoot the dramatic showdown.

> Scene.10: The tension builds as Ney orders his men to aim — both sides are ready to fire at point blank range. Napoleon walks towards them: *"Soldiers of the Fifth. Do you not recognise me?"* An order wraps out: *"Fire!"* There is a terrible silence…

The night before shooting this scene, Steiger announced he had written some "improvements," and promptly presented the fresh pages to Dan O'Herlihy, who was *nonplussed* at his lack of lines:

> "That's the best part, Dan. You're gonna love it. You don't say anything! See how brilliant that is?" — "Me not saying anything is brilliant?" replied O'Herlihy. "Absolutely! The silence, you see? The tension! The drama! It's brilliant!"[413]

O'Herlihy had no doubt already memorised his lines for the next day's filming.

> Scene.10: NEY *has yet to make his move: pale and tense, like a statue…* "You should not have come back, Sire." *Then, Napoleon:* "France and I are the same. Did you think I could stay away from myself?"

The dramatic possibilities of the encounter were the selling point for O'Herlihy accepting the role in the first place. The actor grumbled that: "Steiger had the OK to direct, and rewrite scenes he appeared in." This understandably irked the Irishman, who admitted: "we had a few arguments."[414]

> Scene.10: *The tension snaps. There is an explosion of enthusiasm.* "Long Live the Emperor!" *They kiss his hands, embrace him; some fall onto their knee.*

Tensions aside, considering Ney's paucity of dialogue in both script and the finished production, there might be some exaggeration in the anecdote. Perhaps the scene grew and withered during the long, slow days in Russia, and Steiger's "improvements" were a step too far for his fellow actor. The drama takes some license with history, as the director himself acknowledged:

> In fact, Ney did not take part in the first meeting of Napoleon with the Royal troops. He switched sides later. However, in principle, it happened just like that: although resisting, Ney had to follow the general impulse of his soldiers. Such a liberty, which does not contradict the essence of history, is appropriate in a work of art that has its own laws.[415]

The film does very little with the dramatic potential of Marshal Ney's inner conflict, and his character is sadly underwritten. That said, O'Herlihy does his best to convey something of the hot-headed and impetuous soldier; particularly later as the battle is lost, he attempts to stem the rout while yelling like a berserker.

Reasons of ego and vanity are often levelled at stars for changing lines and even scenes in many movies. But the *Waterloo* leads, independently of each other, recognised the deficiencies in the screenplay and sought, with their power, to improve it for the sake of the film. Steiger took his work seriously and was often seen "in character" even after the cameras stopped rolling. To many, though, it appeared he had absorbed a little too much of his character's megalomania.

> One of the Italian crew summed him up. He framed his face with his fingers. "This is Rod Steiger's long shot." he said. Then he moved his fingers to frame only his eyes. "And this — this is Rod Steiger's close-up."[416]

As we have seen, the American actor was probably not in the best psychological state, but this highly emotional man was a professional performer, and used every *method* to do his job.

> I knew from my own ego, and it isn't much compared to Napoleon's, that when a man is driven and strong, he is also driven to loneliness and obsessed by being surrounded by weakness. It is very hard for a strong person to understand a weak one. He gets so that he says to hell with the rest, I'll do it myself. That's what happened to Napoleon.[417]

Bondarchuk described this force of nature the best: "One cannot direct an explosion, and Steiger is an explosion."[418] As work on the battle continued, Steiger's performance would compete with many more explosions.

> Scene.197: *The* IMPERIAL GUARD, *six thousand strong, are moving into* BATTLE FORMATION...NAPOLEON *is seen riding on his* WHITE HORSE... *"Let all who love me, follow me."* NAPOLEON *turns his horse dramatically and leads the* GUARD *forward.*

The scene is the climax of the battle as Napoleon throws in his last reserves — the famed Old Guard. This is the start of the sequence, with the Emperor leading his army in a final roll of the dice. The rest, as the Guard come to blows with Wellington's infantry, would not be filmed until the autumn. Steiger, along with many of the actors, had to take riding lessons, and did not enjoy the experience. In this dramatic advance, he had to ride *two* horses.

One was a white Arabian costing $4,000, specially trained to be gentle, but bolted when an aerial bomb exploded too close. Much to Steiger's relief, for the close-ups they put him on a rocking horse driven on a truck: "This is my idea of a horse."[419] This contraption was used for close-ups to maintain critical camera focus, and for less experienced mounted actors amid the potentially hazardous action.

> Scene.201: La Bedoyere and Ney swing their horses in front of Napoleon to shield him from the fire. Cambronne forces him to retire: *"Sire, if you stay exposed to this gunfire any longer, I shall order your own Guard to nail you up in a box."* With a laugh, he allows his horse to be turned: *"There is spirit in them still."*

Riding on a horse amid such noise and simulated chaos could be dangerous as Philippe Forquet, playing La Bedoyere, discovered during filming of this enormous sequence.

> A large part of Napoleon's Army was moving forward. At that moment we heard an extremely loud rolling of many drums. The horses got panic-stricken, uncontrollable, and ran in a state of frenzy every which way. Then I really got scared. My horse was running through tight ranks of soldiers carrying their rifles with bayonets pointed up — just about my height! Somehow, I recovered some control over my horse and I got out of there safely; luckily, I hadn't been skewered on one of these threateningly sharp bayonets.

Many of the cast and extras suffered the inevitable cuts and bruises; British actor John Savident was thrown from his horse and suffered some nasty bruises. While Italian Ivo Garrani, who played Marshal Soult, broke his ankle playing football and needed a leg cast. Luckily for the production, he had finished his last dialogue scene the day before the accident and could let his double finish his scenes.

As the Prussians ride into the flank of the faltering French army, like the proverbial cavalry-to-the-rescue for Wellington's beleaguered army, an officer rides up and informs Napoleon that Blucher is in the woods. Strangely, the location setting for this scene was the valley behind the primary set, described as a "ravine" in the script. It was Napoleon's pit stop after being persuaded to abandon leading the Old Guard in the above scene. Why this area was used, and not the main set, is unclear. In any case, the valley slopes are artfully strewn with the detritus of war by the art department.

Realising that the game is up, the film keeps one of Napoleon's most memorable lines from the script: *"I made one mistake in my life, I should have burned Berlin."* Although the outburst makes no historical, political or even strategic sense, the line is perfect logic for the character. It beautifully captures the psychology of a man who believes in his own illusion of power, with just a hint of nihilism. The more direct possibility of, say: "I should have hanged Blucher," would have sounded too personal, and strangely more brutal than torching a city! Contradictions and irony are so human, and it is a tribute to Harry Craig that some aspects of his writing do work very well, as they are so oft repeated by fans.

> Scene.233: THE MUSIC — BEETHOVEN — EXPLODES. *High flames leap up, lighting* NAPOLEON. INTERCUT *the rhythmic striking of the fire and B.C.U.'s of Napoleon's face. Sparks flash in his eyes; the smoke of the fire now reveals, now hides his face.*

As night falls on 18 June 1815, with the battle irrevocably lost, the beaten emperor suffers a mental collapse as Philippe Forquet relates, embedding himself alongside his character into the history:

> Napoleon was getting desperate. He'd been expecting Grouchy's troops as much needed reinforcements. But Grouchy never showed up; and Napoleon's army was losing the battle and withdrew. The Emperor wouldn't admit it, he didn't want to leave and was hollering and I (as La Bedoyere) told him something like: "Sire, if France has to have a future, you must leave now."

In the film's last scene, La Bedoyere utters the evocatively gruesome line: *"You must leave this place of dead flesh"* to Steiger's broken Napoleon who stands with rain coursing down his face looking like a lost child with his army gone — in total defeat. A still exists that appears to show Philippe Forquet and Steiger clinched in an embrace, perhaps another piece of "business" cooked up by the two actors. We see movie rain cascading down upon them as Steiger, his face creased and rent with angst, grips his trusted lieutenant's hand. "Then a few officers and I forced him into a carriage, which took him away. All that took place under pouring rain. It was the end of Napoleon's reign."

> Scene.233: (Ney) *"They will chain you like Prometheus to a rock, where the memory of your own greatness will gnaw you."*

When the "British" cast arrived in mid-July, Steiger was completing his last few scenes. The incoming actors found the American to be morose and reluctant to even shake hands. The delay to him leaving was partly down to Bondarchuk. He was waiting for the arrival from Moscow of a special lens; this was designed to capture the two adversaries in the same frame. But Heinz Feldhaus was not convinced about its value: "It's a lens with another in front. It was something very awful. In the end, I think it didn't work."

The director also wanted a visually potent image of Napoleon amid the carnage he had unleashed. He continued to experiment in vain while he waited for his special lens to arrive. While filming *War and Peace* he had tried to borrow an air force jet that could film some shots from the outer rim of the Earth. His motivation was more thematic rather than for mere spectacle. Unable to play with supersonic planes, he still had the free loan of another military craft to achieve his grandiose vision. "For me, helicopter panoramas give a feeling of a microcosm of the world — Tolstoyan view, if you like. But the cameraman does it — I don't like flying myself."[420] With Armando Nannuzzi taking to air with his camera trained on Steiger who "sat unhappily…in the middle of a vast field, while the Russians used aerial bombs and an enormous outside loudspeaker to give orders to the troops."[421] Whether the director ever succeeded in his "Tolstoyan view" is unknown, as no such shot appears in the film.

With the arrival of Plummer to resume work as Wellington, Feldhaus remembers there was some tension between the film's adversaries. "The actors had frictions. There were Steiger and Plummer that didn't like each other. One day, we could shoot easy with Steiger, and the other with Plummer because of each of them."

Quite what animosity there was is difficult to know as neither shared any scenes apart from the "special lens" — if it was ever shot. If we take Roger Ebert's memoir at face value, the two men were not averse to getting drunk together; the spartan hotel, terrible food, boredom and booze being a great leveller no doubt. Perhaps Steiger, who was itching to leave, might have been frustrated if he had to wait while work began with Plummer.

Towards the end of July, Steiger and the "French" scenes were in the can, and he was free to go. As he left the unit, he bequeathed his luxury suite to his on-screen adversary, and his not inconsiderable pornographic collection for the enjoyment and distraction of all. With him, it appears, went also much of the international press coverage of this major production.

Despite Soviet support for the film, the demands of commercial cinema soon clashed with Cold War paranoia. The Russians had emphasised that Uzhgorod was a military zone and therefore "off-limits" to journalists.[422] This was a bone of contention to the unit producer Tom Carlile and unit publicist Grady Johnson, who fought to allow press access during the shooting period. The issue was not just military, but also cultural.

When Carlile asked about sending a publicity executive to Uzhgorod, Bondarchuk is alleged to have snapped: "Why?"[423] Speaking to the head of Mosfilm, Vladimir Surin, the American producer was astonished to find that out of 5000 staff in all tiers of film production, the premiere Soviet film organisation was shy of one particular department. "Publicity? What's that?" retorted Surin to the bemused Carlile. "We are in the business to make pictures, and not worry how they are exploited abroad or at home." He explained that the choice of publicity stills was solely the director's prerogative, and they had little interest in the exploitation of a film.

While Dino and his elder brother Luigi endeavoured to smooth the wheels with the upper echelons of the Soviet government, there were signs of progress back on the "battlefield." Newton E. Meltzer, an American documentary producer from Visual Projects Ltd., with his crew of seven, got visas to shoot a 16mm promo film that Paramount aimed to screen later on TV. He "enjoyed almost total cooperation" from the director and the two Soviet generals Oslikovsky and Luchinsky, and was also given the use of the helicopter and pilot. One day, Meltzer's team found themselves in a sticky situation when they got stuck on a muddy battle slope, thankfully the speedy arrival of a Russian military carrier saved the day. For a month, they had to contend with downpours of rain, tropical heat and cloying damp, while communication was via French with "asides in pidgin Russian."[424] Despite the help from the production, Meltzer's main gripe was the crew's physical restriction to film in the local vicinity.[425]

Carlile and his press man Grady Johnson worked hard to satisfy the world's media interest in the project, but as the year anniversary of the Czechoslovakia invasion loomed, it was becoming more difficult. As a compromise, the Russians deployed their own cameramen and photographers, but great effort was spent to attract the best journalists to splash "ballyhoo" across the international stage.

With just twenty visas to play with, Grady and Carlile employed some impressive talent. These included: Anthony Haden-Guest for *The Telegraph* who had first visited the shoot in Italy, highly respected *Time* magazine writer/photographer team, Strobe Talbott and Harry Redell, along with leading photojournalist David Hurn for the prestigious *Magnum*, and British photojournalist Peter Mitchell would also join these "snappers" in the last weeks of filming.

It would be the Frenchman Paul Ronald and Italian Alfonso Avincola who would land the primary job as unit stills men for the shoot. New Yorker Simon Nathan was given a special four-week dispensation to capture photos in the ultra-high-definition 70mm format with his bulky, tailor-made camera that could take up to 11 frames-per-second.[426] Nathan, who had pioneered panoramic photography, had also lent his talent to the Bond franchise, and another epic, *Khartoum* (1966).

One of his images, taken from a high vantage tower, shows Highland Infantry advancing towards the French, and would grace the UK cover of Frederick E. Smith's novelisation. The image is so sharp it is possible to see some of Likhachov's special-effects team fanning smoke in the extreme background.

Johnson and Carlile tried to get visiting journalists attending the Moscow Film Festival to do a 750-mile detour via the film set, thus avoiding the need for extra visas. This request proved too much for the Soviet bureaucrats and was dismissed with a blunt "*Nyet.*" Instead, the publicists had to make do. It is interesting to note that most of the articles of the time written by journalists on the ground only cover Steiger's first few weeks in Russia.

Arriving in mid-July, Plummer and the British cast appear not to have been interviewed on location, at least from what the author has found; which gives credence to these reporting problems.

By September, after three months of filming on the "battlefield," the issue came to a head. Frustrated by the continued Soviet authority's intransigence, Grady Johnson filed a cable that whistle-blew on the hardships of getting access; he was duly expelled from the USSR, thus strangling further coverage.

Luckily for our narrative, one young man studiously wrote a diary entry every single day. Found after gathering dust in an attic for half a century; it allows us a unique glimpse behind-the-scenes, both on and off camera.

Richard Heffer had left the production at the end of March, now along with Donal Donnelly and Roger Green, he would be the last actors to re-join the cast in Russia. While he packed his bags in London ready for the long journey, he along with billions of others were looking skyward.

"Sunday 20 July 1969. Packed. Watched the Moon landing and walk on the surface." Thus Richard wrote later that evening in his diary, as he sat comfortably at a friend's house in complete awe. "Fabulous TV shots of astronauts on the surface — the whole experience, quite unbelievable — to see and hear the first people on the Moon *as it* happened, while sitting in London."[427]

Half-a-world-away in Uzhgorod at 4:56 a.m. local time, getting to share this historical moment had proved to be more of a challenge. The Russian media had refused to acknowledge this epoch-making event and had stuck some proverbial fingers in the ears; so, there was a complete news blackout. The communist Czech Republic broke ranks with their Big Brother and planned to relay the live TV transmission from the Kennedy Space Centre in Houston.

Determined not to miss it, a small TV was procured by Dan O'Herlihy and set up in Heinz Feldhaus's tiny room. "We had all the actors and their companions, their wives or girlfriends in our bedroom to watch the Americans go to the Moon on Czech TV." Luckily Jack Hawkins had a powerful long-ranged radio for the English audio, to catch that most famous utterance from Neil Armstrong. "We all did not speak any Czech, so we had a radio with *Voice of America*, and so that's how we were watching the Americans going to the Moon in our little room." As Neil Armstrong's foot touched down on the cratered surface, a mighty cheer went up in the small Russian hotel room that reverberated across the world.

Back in London, Richard, writing his diary as history was being made, echoed much of the world's sentiment as it held its collective breath: "The technical skill that gets them there, and hopefully back, is dumbfounding — let alone the endurance on the three men, especially the pilot of the command capsule, orbiting the moon." As dawn broke, with the drama still unfolding, he left his friend's house with them all glued to the TV, to begin his own lengthy journey.

He crossed paths in Budapest with Philippe Forquet, "who had just been sacked!" At least it was a better outcome for the French actor than his character La Bedoyere, who shortly after the battle was shoved against a wall by avenging Royalists, and summarily shot. Richard reached the railway station and "found the sleeper (train) and started jogging into

Russia; after some cognacs with the Hungarian locals, who hate the Russians, we finally arrived at the frontier. Waited for hours and finally got to Chop, where a car drove us to Uzhgorod and the hotel. I immediately fell asleep for twelve hours."[428]

While the American astronauts were successfully completing their historic mission, work continued apace on the story of one of the most significant events of the nineteenth-century. It was high summer now, and despite the departure of Napoleon in the guise of Steiger, the bulk of the action remained to be filmed. With yet more months to go, this "monstrous shoot" had — to steal a phrase — little more to offer than blood, sweat and tears.

The director (at left) with Rod Steiger (top) and Christopher Plummer (bottom). AUTHOR'S COLLECTION

Steiger sits astride a box to ensure he is kept in focus, Philippe Forquet is at extreme left. © HEINZ FELDHAUS

Steiger takes some last minute direction in an unidentified scene. © HEINZ FELDHAUS

A splendidly dressed Dan O'Herlihy as Ney with his wife Elsie, and son Lorcan, about to shoot the confrontation scene with Napoleon. © HEINZ FELDHAUS

Notice Ney's sword top left as he throws it at the feet of his old master. The scene was shot behind the main set, nestling behind the ridge in the right background is the village of Nizhny Solotvyn. © HEINZ FELDHAUS

Members of Wellington's staff officers, including some uniforms of the military advisors from allied countries. © RICHARD HEFFER

The unit filming with Armando Nannuzzi high up next to camera. Notice the huge 'Brutes' lights needed even on a sunny day. © MYKOLA KHOLODNYAK

Richard Heffer as Captain Mercer, RHA. © RICHARD HEFFER

CHAPTER 13

"May I Have Your Permission To Try A Shot?"

"Monday, 28 July 1969, Uzhgorod: Today I am twenty-three and waking up punch drunk at sunrise," so wrote a young Richard Heffer in his diary, full of high spirits as he celebrated his birthday; a milestone and a pause for reflection.

> I am a long way from the student of last year — I have earned my first money and acted for the first time professionally in films, television, radio and stage! — perhaps even to lay down a career. But all feel the same: especially the ambiguity of freedom — the need for company, and the desire for flight: the complexity of relationships.[429]

That morning he was weathering a hangover from a heavy binge the evening before. It had been a bizarre smorgasbord of entertainment in Soviet Russia: "...went to the local nightclub where Russians danced *The Twist* to *Auld Lang Syne* and decadent western hits! Lots of drinking and a bit of dancing. Celebrated the dawning of my 23rd birthday with Italians singing *Augurie a Te!*"[430] Eventually everyone staggered to their tiny hotel rooms safely, which was an improvement on a previous night when a semi-conscious Rupert Davies had to be carried back in a blanket.

Richard had now been in Russia a week but had yet to be on-call, although he had made the brief trip southeast of Uzhgorod to the location set. "A fantastic view as we arrived! 15,000 soldiers, hundreds of dummies, cannons, etc. — most impressive. Squadrons of cavalry galloping about in 19th century uniform!...Cuirassiers galloping over the ground and guns appearing through the smoke over the crest of the hills..."[431]

Since leaving the unit in Rome at the end of March, he had spent the intervening months reading the famous memoirs of his character, Cavalié Mercer: *Journal of the Waterloo Campaign*, published in 1870, which has gone down in posterity as one of the most vivid and evocative accounts of the war.[432]

Mercer had commanded G Troop RHA (Royal Horse Artillery) at the battle, and this versatile unit would have been an impressive sight on the move at full gallop. Six teams of eight harnessed horses each pulling their heavy, wooden limbers upon which sat the drivers, behind them the bronze, commonly called brass, cannon called a Nine-Pounder to differentiate from other calibres, on its carriage. The other crew members were all mounted, along with another sixty horses and riders needed to pull the various ammunition and equipment wagons to give the unit greater autonomy. This made it a very flexible and dynamic force on the battlefield. Two hundred years on, the British army still keep a detachment of Horse Artillery, which Mercer would recognise, as Her Majesty's Mounted Ceremonial Battery — the King's Troop Royal Horse Artillery, whose role includes the Royal Salutes to mark the grand occasions of State.

"My Grandfather was a keen 'point to point' rider and won many cups, so I was put to horse young." While he filled his head with research, Richard also brushed up on his equestrian skills to a military standard. "I was now in training, including visiting the London barracks of the Royal Horse Artillery as their guest and riding long hours in Trooper-style — I owned my saddle — to boost my confidence in what I knew might be arduous conditions in Russia. I was right!"

Arriving in Ukraine, all the "officer" cast members had to take lessons in military-style horsemanship, sometimes with firecrackers thrown at the horses' legs to practise control-under-fire. "Had a lesson with a bandy-legged colonel of the Russian army — he was pleased somehow! — I was very uncertain; although the saddle was military, I had to *rise* to the trot!"[433]

"The big stars had less experience on the whole," remembered Richard, "Christopher Plummer did very well to cope with his horse, as he was mounted throughout, with explosions all around him!" Due to his star status, he was promised the best! Named Stok — an ex-Police mount, the Canadian star became very fond of him. He felt honoured to have the finest mount in the Russian cavalry, until his groom confessed that his proud steed was actually thirty-years-old, and a veteran of cannon firing parades in Moscow, and consequently was stone deaf. Noting glumly that the Duke spent the entire battle in the saddle, he went riding with Stok every day to hone his skills. Michael Wilding, who amused the watching

Russians by donning white breeches and a Stetson which he had bought in California: "They seemed appropriate,"[434] he said as he joined the daily rides.

Teenage Peter Davies, although inexperienced, bonded with his mount: "I wouldn't describe myself as a horseman, but I've ridden a bit which really helped. I had a beautiful horse, and I had the same one the whole time, and the same groom. He was from the Soviet Cavalry; he was ever such a nice fellow."

Unlike most of the others, Richard was lucky being an experienced and confident rider, but a change of mount every few days would increasingly become a problem. "My horse was commandeered by a Russian — so I ended up with an old nag that was half dead — and got raw knees from driving it on the whole time."[435] Next day, he lost his "old nag" to Jack Hawkins, but at least he was working on healing his riding sores: "legs bad, but got some plaster…and soaked them in Friars Balsam — painful but effective I think."[436]

Like any green subaltern taking over a new command, it was quite a baptism of fire finding himself the *de facto* commander of this recreated G Troop RHA:

> I was the only English actor in my troop and spoke no Russian; the troopers were professional horsemen and tough as old boots — they were not lightly going to take orders from a foreign youngster…It was strange for me to live almost daily on horseback and ride distances with my troop across the plain; no-one else had that experience!

> Scene.91: *The French Army has now taken possession of the opposite heights…A metallic power of bayonets, swords, cuirasses, helmets and guns flash in the sun. All the eleven columns take up their battle positions.*

This being his first day on camera, Richard was determined to ignore his sore legs and head, even though his heavy costume was a challenge in the heat. For hours the entire contingent of over 15,000 troops, clad in French uniforms, had been painstakingly arranged along the opposite ridge, with a further 5,000 plastic dummies to increase the effect of Napoleon's great army readying for battle.

Clustered around the solitary elm tree that would famously take his name, Wellington and his large array of staff officers were positioned in the foreground surveying the enemy, "and so they put me into the scene too as an establishing shot of all actors in a group which I didn't object to."[437]

> Scene.78: LORD HAY *suddenly strikes his horse forward in great excitement, pointing towards the French Lines...*

The tree was also the setting for Peter Davies' first scene, as the excitable Lord Hay espies a significant figure on the opposite slope: "I remember being given a direction (I think it was Memo who was saying it). 'You ride your horse up there and you bring him around.' I had to say to Wellington: *'There he is, the monster on his great white horse.'*" The film beautifully retains one of the most elegant and pithy lines from the script for Wellington's response, which perfectly captures the aristocratic disdain for the parvenu Corsican.

> Scene.78: WELLINGTON *lifts and focuses his telescope; he smiles:* "So there is the great thief of Europe himself."[438]

Unfortunately, "elegant" could not be used to describe young Peter's performance in the first take:

> My horse got spooked and swung its back around and hit another on the hind legs, which set off a whole chain reaction. I didn't get into trouble that time, but it was two hours while they got ready to do it again. Basically, I had to learn to waltz on to a taped spot, and then having to ride a horse on to a taped spot!

These kinds of mishaps must have been routine on set with so many people and horses. The inevitable delays would have irritated the director who many found intimidating.

Watching him work every day was Daniele Nannuzzi, who that felt the energy required to orchestrate the moving legions in the background meant the director seemed to pay less attention to those closest to the lens: "Bondarchuk was, for me, was not a big director with the actors. He didn't care about the actors."

Communication was further hampered by the babble of translators and led to much frustration. There were three dialogue coaches speaking English, Italian, French and Russian who worked with the polyglot cast. "It was very necessary," explained the director. "You see, I don't speak anything but Russian — but I had to know everything would sound all right!"[439]

Amid this mix were Willo Gray fighting to defend the "facts" and William Slater, the BBC drama director, who had been engaged to audition the British cast and then retained as dialogue director. It appears his role was rather nebulous, ranging from helping with line readings, liaising with script and continuity supervisor, Elvira D'Amico, and a bit of basic "company cheer" to keep up morale. While he had coaxed a gentle smile from Peter Davies for his ballroom close-up back in Rome, it appears his suggestions were not always welcomed by Bondarchuk. "He had a rather mouldy time on set," recalled Richard, "always struggling to be heard and taken seriously. Willo Gray had similar problems, but was a much more *robust* character!" Unlike Peter Davies, Richard found the director who was, of course, a fellow actor, to be patient and willing to listen and discuss improvements. This is also borne out by the vignettes cooked up by the lead actors.

> Scene.78: *At* HAY'S *stirrup is a beautiful* DALMATIAN HOUND *that accompanies him everywhere.*

In the script, Lord Hay is accompanied by a faithful dog which can be briefly glimpsed in the film. "I just remember them turning up with it. It was a big dog, perhaps a Russian Borzoi. I think I had been expecting some nice kind of English dog, like a Golden Retriever. It featured more in the script. Perhaps it was too hard to control it or something." Whatever happened to this canine cast member is unknown as it did not feature in any more scenes.

> Scene.93: (Wellington) *"Now, gentlemen, before we go to work…a little sporting ritual."…A tray of* CHERRY BRANDY *in glasses is offered to the mounted officers.* WELLINGTON *takes the last glass. He raises it.* "Gentlemen — today's fox."

Richard' diary entry paints an evocative picture of the extras in full array standing in the late afternoon sun as they shot the stirrup-cup scene, a reference to the British aristocracy's love of fox hunting: "Background of some thousands of Napoleon's army — an entire hillside of cavalry and infantry, unbelievable sights and awe-inspiring. The beauty of cavalry galloping in formation, of lancers traversing a hillcrest in silhouette, banners flying!"

The heat bearing down on the open plain could be severe: "A light wind cooled the set (and sent the dust up) so it was not too unpleasant to work in, although with sword and fur coat and helmet and all, I find myself carrying a lot of weight around." The day ended with headache inducing local "champagne," but was considered a fitting end to "a fine birthday."[440]

Another interesting adjunct to this scene of toasting the enemy appears to have been filmed some weeks before. On-set stills show Napoleon's valet, Constant, played by Orazio Orlando, holding a small silver tray from which Steiger raises a glass of, presumably, brandy. It is probable this tiny vignette, though not in the script, was Bondarchuk's ongoing attempt to humanise his emperor and visually mirror the two commanders' state-of-mind. Steiger's intense stare at the reddish liquid was no doubt sparking the actor's creative juices, perhaps ruminating on all the blood his character would cause to be spilt.

The following day, filming continued around Wellington's Tree for more scenes of the very beginning of the battle. But judging by a heavily underlined word in Richard Heffer's diary, other intimate matters were of more concern. *Enterovioform* were anti-diarrhoea tablets, subsequently banned in the early 1970s, but there was a Ukraine strain of "Montezuma's Revenge" afflicting some newly arrived cast.

> Scene.102: *The sky is full of flying specks. The* CAMERA *is midway between both lines. We hear the cannon only at a distance. But for a moment, the day seems darkened by the terrible, almost slow-moving projectiles — the cannon balls of Waterloo.*

Richard left the set early, but stayed long enough to see "the fantastic sight of the opening artillery salvos from both sides — the slopes packed with troops and the smoke and noise and explosions."[441]

Mykola Kholodnyak one of the thousands of cavalrymen, had to turn his hand to the artillery one day. Joining a team of six, he remembered the cannons not only looked the part — but sounded it too.

> Those guns were fake, with large wooden wheels as high as a person, with a big metal tube. They used gunpowder packed in a plastic package and plastic cannon balls. To fire, they used a metal stick, which was hot at the end, and pushed into the gunpowder. It made a big *boom* — very loud — and sent the plastic ball flying toward the army.

To simulate the powerful recoil of a real gun, the wheel had a break which was yanked hard with a length of elastic. Watching the finished film closely, it is fun to see this effect being enacted where sometimes the recoil is a little too late!

> Scene.171: *The* CUIRASSIERS *ride crouched forward, as if they were riding into the wind. The* LANCERS *and* HUSSARS *sit on their horses with an open upright elegance.* MARSHAL NEY, *sword in hand, with his* TRUMPETER *beside him and the* CUIRASSIERS *looming behind, rides up the slope through a field of heavy grass.*

On 30 July 1969, work began on what would be one of the most impressive sequences in the film, and probably in cinema history — Ney's charge. This was the dramatic move ordered by Napoleon's leading marshal on his own volition, seeing what he believed was Wellington's army in retreat. Ney immediately ordered up thousands of French cavalry to break the Allied lines, but instead found not a rout but Wellington's infantry arrayed in a series of defensive squares. Resembling a hedgehog with bristling bayonets, it had been a highly effective defence against cavalry for hundreds of years.

The site chosen to stage this was on the left-hand side of the "Allied" ridge, on a wide-open part of the plain, dubbed "the desert" (see map). This was the opposite area to the historical placement, but was the only part of the landscape that would allow the thousands of cavalry to charge at full-pelt.

"Until lunch they arranged the soldiers — thirteen squares, with 400 men in a square in three ranks: laid out like a draught board (the ground being the white spaces)."[442] The Russian soldiers had been carefully trained to "fight" in this archaic formation, with those in the outer row kneeling on one knee with their rifle butts on the ground, tilting the barrel with an attached bayonet about 30 degrees. The second row stood with one leg forward and resting the rifle butt on the hip. Third row — fired the blanks, before handing it back to the fourth row, where it was reloaded.[443]

They presented a majestic sight with their red uniforms and silver bayonets glinting in the bright sunshine. For this master shot, none of the cast was required, but most came to watch anyway. Richard, who as a distant observer, missed the high drama exploding around the director's canvas chair.

A miniature battle had flared up between history and art; Bondarchuk was unhappy with the layout which had been meticulously arranged by historical advisor Willo Gray and Second Unit Director Anatoli Chemodurov, complete with the heavy heft that comes from two Russian military experts: the tough, high decorated war veterans Generals Oslikovsky and Luchinsky.

Amid a babble of interpreters with each side wielding historical maps and chiaroscuro storyboards to make their respective points, Bondarchuk insisted loudly that it may be accurate — but it doesn't make good cinema. Then Willo, calmly sticking to his guns, argued that he had followed the historical record, and absolutely refused to change his dispositions. Offering a solution, he patiently explained that if the helicopter camera was deployed correctly, it *would* be suitably cinematic. These two men became a focus for thousands of eyes as both refused to back down.

There was an eerie silence across the vast plain, with only the jingle of harnesses, an occasional horse snort and an embarrassed cough to break the tension, as a stalled Bondarchuk scowled in his director's chair. Then Willo, with total sangfroid, spoke calmly — that there was no point in him being there, if he would not be listened to. And with that, he turned on his feet and was off.

With the dignity that befitted a war hero and recipient of an MBE, with the sun bouncing off his monocle, and wind ruffling his tartan kilt and white hair, he strode past the cameramen, the stuntmen on their restless horses, and the entire cavalry glistening in their splendid uniforms.

Then, like a latter-day Moses, the sea of red-clad foot soldiers opened up to let him pass. Falling in line behind Willo, in a spirited token of respect and support, were the Russian military top brass along with Chemodurov. Willo was most touched by this show of solidarity and gladly accepted an offer of copious toasts of vodka by the Russian generals until all were "legless."

Perhaps a hearty lunch and many slugs of vodka helped to smooth things over, as by the afternoon, all was ready. As thousands gathered upon the baking hot plane that day, it was impossible for any camera lens to do justice to the sheer visceral reality which filled the entire field of view. The smoke and dust quickly enveloped the scene, bathing it in the yellow glow of the warm sun.

As relayed shouts of "Action" echoed across the field: Take 1 of Ney's charge began. At first, they were just flickering shapes — shimmering ghosts — too distant to discern through the haze. Then a low, deep roar shook the ground at the same time as a thick, pungent smell; a peculiar odour of man, beast and sheer, unfettered fear, reached across the field. Then through the veil of dust and smoke they appeared: "three thousand cavalry in full array galloped at the 'charge' right across the valley, over a hill and into our line of sight (silhouetted in their dust)…Very, very exciting to watch indeed."[444] Moments later, clearing the enveloping smoke, all riding hell for leather, thousands of breast-plated horsemen neared the foot of the hill.

Hovering high above in the military helicopter was Daniele Nannuzzi, assisting his father on camera. He vividly recalls this extraordinary shot from the unique vantage point:

> We were in the rear door. I was next to my father focusing the camera. There is a special — Tyler Mount from Panavision — which makes the camera float, so there is no vibration. And the zoom was on 250 mm — very close. The helicopter was stopped in the air, and the zoom was close on just Marshal Ney.

The brave marshal was played by Dan O'Herlihy, who as an actor, and not a stunt man, would have expected to sit back and just enjoy the spectacle. It appears, though, that right out in front of the wall of hooves and mountains of horseflesh was not an equine professional. Dan's Italian double had broken his back and was propped up in bed. The fall back of a Russian substitute didn't look convincing. So, instead, the actor stepped into the breach and saddled up to lead his torrent of cavalry forward himself. "I wasn't an expert horseman when that film started," recalled Dan, later with a laugh, "but I sure am now!"[445]

High above, the Nannuzzi father and son team kept the Panavision zoom lens tightly focused on the Irish actor, as he summoned up his courage to portray the fearless Ney:

> He takes his sword and goes forward…And then the zoom open, open, open up until you see — like a wave — white and blue coming in front of you. I was terrified with this ocean of horses coming — *brumm! brumm! brumm!* — the noise! There is a hill, and the camera goes down, and you see the cavalry come like a river of horses, and then it goes up and you discover thirteen English squares of red soldiers there, and the cavalry, like a river, going around them.[446]

Reaching the squares, the horsemen were greeted with the crackle of blanks being fired as they flowed around the indomitable red formations.

In the sheer, orchestrated chaos, many horses collided and tumbled into each other.

Igor Starchenko was one of the thousands of Russian soldiers playing the British infantry in the squares: "It was not scary, more like a game," as the 11th Separate Cavalry Regiment swirled around the tight red-clad formations, "they pounced and whacked the exposed bayonets with their tin swords." Starchenko noted many of the riders were, like him, just raw recruits, and rode their horses "unsurely," which inevitably meant some "horses had several bayonet stab wounds, which saved those who were standing in the square from being trampled."[447]

One of those recruits was rookie rider Mykola Kholodnyak, who had only received a few weeks of basic equine training before taking part in many charges. "I saw Marshal Ney (Dan O'Herlihy) himself during the shooting; however, I wasn't near the squares." He noted the rapidity of musketry from the infantry clustered together; the front rank would fire a blank — hand it to a man behind in exchange for a loaded rifle, and fire again: "Therefore the shooting was unstoppable. Like a machine gun."

As he and his mates cantered back and forth with their fake swords, he considered they "were in a winning situation in a fake fight, because the horses kicked up a lot of mud and it splattered those men in the squares. They were very dirty with all the mud splashing up on them…There were no major injuries during the movie shooting, except the moments when explosions showered me with soil and grass."

If trying to avoid bayonets and collisions was not enough, the riders also had to keep an eye out for carefully placed plastic bags half buried in the ground. These were packed with explosives with two wires leading off to a technician, often hiding in nearby bushes, who controlled the blast. This delivered more smoke and dust than a vicious kick, although anyone in the radius would invariably find their nose, ears and mouth full of Ukrainian soil.

> The explosions had that effect, that I was just wondering how they worked, and how it was done. The exact places of the pyrotechnics were marked with small red flags. If possible, we avoided them. Luckily, there were no explosions that resulted in injuries. The pyrotechnics were looked after very professionally.

While Mykola and his comrades waved their swords in the background, hogging the limelight closer to camera was usually reserved for spectacular horse falls. For just one shot, with the ground specially dug and slugged with straw, stuntmen trained their horses for three days to fall correctly. They suffered lots of cuts and bruises to hone their performance before the director was satisfied.

Reels of coloured tape were placed to demarcate the safety zone for the men in squares, but amid the smoke and dust, things could get dangerous. At one point, some soldiers panicked at the sudden appearance of horsemen out of a cloud of thick dust and smoke, and broke up their square. This is visible in the aerial shots taken from the helicopter in the final film. It is an extraordinary vision of chaos and drama and seems miraculous that there were no serious injuries.

Heinz Feldhaus recalled some friction with the military over the use of the 'copter, which may have contributed to the above panic:

> We sprayed the ground with water so that the dust didn't come up. But they were landing exactly over the dusty areas, and so we had dust in the camera, and the film couldn't be used. So, they had to do it all again. But the helicopter was under military instructions, and I spoke little Russian, so the director and his assistants had to sort that out.

Peter Davies just remembered there was, "nothing but clouds of dust and as it settled, there were ambulances there and people were getting up and brushing themselves down. I think a few horses had to be shot, sadly."

Perhaps the most poignant and shocking vignette of this awe-inspiring sequence, which brings home the brutal reality of restaging war, was witnessed by Christopher Plummer, watching from the side lines. As the dust cleared, the ghostly shapes of limping horses picked their way across the field in the waning afternoon light. Here and there, several were crumpled upon the ground. One caught the actor's eye as it pathetically tried to regain its footing. After a few pitiful attempts it stood up, but its head was clearly broken hanging at an awkward angle. The rider was nowhere to be seen, but from behind the safety barrier near to the spectators, a young soldier ran out towards the stricken animal. Ignoring the excited shouts of Russian assistants that he was ruining the shot, the youth, perhaps no more than seventeen, tried to calm the horse. His bereft face was clear for all to see, as the boy realised there was no hope. Reluctantly accepting the inevitable, he pulled out a knife and held the horse's head tenderly in his arms. With the cameras still rolling, the assistants shouting, and the spectators looking on impotently, the teenager deftly slit the horse's throat. As the poor animal slipped quietly to the ground, the entire field was stilled in a state of shock. Plummer shuddered at the heartfelt, pitiful sobbing of the teenager caressing his beloved companion as the only sound to be heard across the open plain.

The hot and dusty day's shooting was brought to a halt with the loud and determined intervention from a sudden thunderstorm. Perhaps not unwelcome because of the heat, which forced Richard and his fellow spectators to take cover beneath an army bivouac tent — that promptly collapsed.

This colossal sequence would be revisited many times over the next few weeks with each shot taking several hours to set up. Richard's diary gives a vignette of a typical day when there was not much else to do. He had been watching yet more charges of the thundering horses:

> …three takes in all, one of them looking very good indeed. Ian Ogilvy, his daughter Emma, Donal and I were a little party and played "eye-spy," etc, while waiting for the soldiers and generally it was a lovely day, warm and with a slight breeze to take the edge off the heat.[448]

> Scene.178: *Waves of smoke roll along the walls of the Squares. A line of French* LANCERS *gallop at great speed towards the 27th (Inniskilling) Square.* (Colonel Colborne): *"Shoot at the horses. Pile up the horses."*[449]

"Tuesday, 05 August. Same charge, another P.O.V. (Point-of-view)." With the impressive master shot complete, Ney's attack would be broken down into smaller scenes of different aspects of the French cavalry swirling around the indomitable Allied squares.

Richard's scene that day required him as Mercer and his Artillerymen to fire at the approaching French horsemen. Their cannon props were real and made of wood and cast iron: "My guns worked — made a hell of a noise!!!" On "Action" he shouted "Fire!" as his cannons belched out clouds of smoke.

> My horse, which again was a new one(!) was scared of the noise and bangs and reared up like a maniac (which might look impressive, but is difficult with four reins in one hand and a sword in the other!). However — all went well until the last take, when it bolted at the guns firing: nobody seemed to notice. Typical.

The next part of the sequence involved the artillerymen firing their last blank shot before bolting for sanctuary in the square commanded by Colborne (Jeffry Wickham).[450] Richard on "horseback, sword drawn, with Jeffry *inside* his square, giving orders to the gunners who were running towards me! God knows what the continuity will be like!"

He also had to struggle with his latest horse, who was clearly spooked by the noise:

> ...we set up the shot, and I was given the same jumpy horse — so I told them it didn't like the bangs! Did they listen? The first "take" it reared right into the camera and bolted, with me on it, sword in *right* hand, into the French cavalry. I was all right, and so was the horse, but it again was unnecessary to have to *prove* my point. So, they gave me another one, which was fine — only this time *Jeffry's* bolted, and with a groom hanging from the bridle! But apparently the shots were OK.

After lunch, which was, as usual, long and boozy, they set up a "panorama of the French sweeping into our guns, and up to the squares, with lots of stunts: I wondered if I ought to be commanding my gun, but was told 'no.' Again, continuity is berserk. Anyway, it looked impressive, whatever shot it was."

That evening, it took the sage advice of actor Donal Donnelly, helped along with some vodka and quince-juice cocktails, to calm him down: "He was very worldly wise and sensible, and I felt slightly ridiculous at being so anti the chaos."[451] Donal, playing a foot soldier, sometimes found his "zen" ruffled by his Russian comrades practicing their English on him with indecipherable Slavic jokes, which he wearily grumbled: "A joke you try to tell — in a language with which you are not fockin' familiar — is never, ever, fockin' funny."[452]

The big news that day was an X-ray confirming that veteran Michael Wilding as Ponsonby "had, in fact, fractured his skull" following a fall from his horse a few days before. His frail health was an enormous concern to the unit "so everyone is trying to pack him off to England."[453] Unfortunately for the actor, it would take another scare some weeks later before he could finally leave.

More often than not Richard would receive a call-sheet delivered to his hotel room in the evening detailing work for the next day and then arrive on set with nothing to do other than watch and take pictures.

Called again at 9 a.m. but in fact I didn't do anything — it was two scenes simultaneously; one with Wellington and Staff in a square and the other with Donal and Oleg doing their "conscientious objector" sequence with lots of cavalry, smoke and stunts. Spent all day setting it up, and shot it three times in the afternoon: looked very good — only I ran out of film at the beginning.[454]

In the scene, Oleg Vidov played Tomlinson, a British private who breaks under the pressure of the battle.

> Scene.180: *A large mass of* CUIRASSIERS *are walking their horses around the Square of the 27th...* DICK TOMLINSON, *a private with greying hair, is struggling with his comrades in the* THIRD RANK. *"Leave me alone, can't ye." He breaks out of the* SQUARE.

Conscientious objection had been recognised in Britain before the Napoleonic Wars due to the rise of the Quakers in the eighteenth-century, but uniquely her army was entirely made up of volunteers until 1916. Although the term "volunteer" was probably elastic when local magistrates had a wide range of sentencing options; miscreants facing Draconian punishment would often jump at the option to fight for one's country. Enlisted men would have been drawn from all walks of life, and rarely by *choice*.

Whether from deeply held religious beliefs or combat stress or even just plain cowardliness, there must have been many "Tomlinsons" on the field of Waterloo. The scene is in keeping with the changing attitudes to war that were becoming prevalent in the 1960s. One doubts it would have been included in another Russian film extolling the virtues of fighting for World Communism.

> Scene.180: *Standing amid the swirling cavalry,* TOMLINSON *ignores all pleas to return. He shakes his fist between both armies and shouts, "Why do men who have never seen each other do so much harm to each other?"*

Oleg Vidov, a young, rising Soviet star, was on the cusp of an international career. His widow, Joan Borsten Vidov, recalls how he was taken under Sergei Bondarchuk's wing:

> Sergei Fedorovich and Oleg met at the Cannes Film Festival in 1967. Oleg had just starred in a Danish movie (*Hagbard and*

Signe), the first Soviet actor the Soviets let play a western hero in a western movie (Sergei was the first to star in a foreign production but he played a Russian).[455] It was nominated for a Palme d'Or. Sergei was there, too — he was just finishing *War and Peace*. He liked Oleg, who was 23 years his junior. When Veljko Bulajić came to Moscow to cast the role of Nikola in *Battle of Neretva*, Sergei Fedorovich suggested Oleg. They got to know each other better during the long production.[456]

The Russians joined an international cast that included Yul Brynner, Curt Jürgens, Sylva Koscina, Hardy Kruger, Franco Nero and Orson Welles in Yugoslav President Tito's dream project. *Battle of Neretva* (1969) recreated his own epic battle, as leader of the Yugoslav Partisans, in the rugged mountains of Bosnia against an onslaught of Germans, Italians and Croats in 1943.

Its director, Veljko Bulajić had welcomed his fellow director's endorsement of Oleg during his casting foray in Moscow. "He was one of the rare (Soviet) actors who was allowed to travel freely, pick movies and directors because that was the time back then in Russia. Sergei Bondarchuk was behind him. He had recommended him. So, if Sergei could come, then Oleg Vidov could come too."[457] Initially, he been offered the film's main heroic lead, but Oleg saw more scope for his talent in another role:

> I fell deeply in love with the smaller, more unusual role of Nikola, the commissar of a partisan unit. Bulajić said, "Oleg, you're a fool, don't you understand that I can cut this small role out of the film but I can never cut out Ivan, he connects everything." I did not change my mind.[458]

Vidov gave a sensitive and moving performance as Nikola, a partisan soldier who is ravaged and crippled by typhus, which played against his handsome movie star persona. Largely financed by the Yugoslav state and using thousands of soldiers and locals, many of them veterans, this hugely impressive war movie would receive an Oscar nomination for Best Foreign Language Film. When seen it is original 3-hour version, it rightly stands as one of the most impressive examples of its spectacular genre during the 1960s.[459]

When casting the small but pivotal role of Tomlinson for *Waterloo*, Bondarchuk was keen to find an actor that could embody the film's larger themes about war that he wanted to express, as his wife Irina Skobtseva, explained:

> The scene turned out to be very memorable and powerful in its energy. Oleg is an actor of the Russian school, and therefore his soul trembled. He was volatile, very impulsive during work. That is why his scene in *Waterloo* was very memorable and powerful in its energy. Sergei needed a hero, someone who represented the whole planet, good-looking and well-built, everything Oleg had, and also the voice, temperament and significance, because you know what great actors were in the film. The episode was tiny — one soldier taking part in this battle, in this whirlpool, runs out screaming: "Stop it! Why are you killing each other?" This phrase was quintessential for the entire film, and a symbol of peace. Peace on the Earth. The Why, and what for are you killing each other? It really mattered to Sergei Fedorovich who would play this role — it had to be the triple-best actor, though in the shot he said only three phrases. He wanted it to be an actor with an "international" face — neither a Kazakh, nor a Ukrainian or Russian, but a symbol of a human being on this Earth. That's what Oleg was.[460]

Arriving on set, his blue eyes made him a hit with the bus loads of Russian tourists that visited the location, and one day, much to his amusement, he was mobbed by a group of starry-eyed teenage girls from Sverdlosk. With the encouragement of his mentor, the director, and enjoying a degree of approval from the Soviet authorities, Oleg was one of the few Russians allowed to fraternise with the Western cast.

Richard Heffer remembered the actor warmly: "it was very good to have a chum who was young and Russian and *fun!*" and even received a gift of a rare seventeenth-century faded icon from him. "Oleg was kept under wraps to start with, but although I had no Russian, he had a smattering of English — so we joked, and signed our meaning, and drank together when not working."

Drink-fuelled humour helped to cross cultural divides; Oleg, his hair dyed for the film "told lunatic endless tales of Russia, supposedly humorous, and laughed a lot — great waves of blonde hair everywhere with the dye just growing out! Unfortunately, the Russian joke is basic and rather grubby — but he is a lovely fellah despite."[461]

Recognising his talent, Dino had twice offered him a seven-year contract which would have almost guaranteed an international career "but the "committee" (Soviet Government) won't give him permission — so frustrating; one would have thought the Russians would welcome an international star of their own."[462]

Oleg commented bitterly years later:

> We were commanded by people who had nothing to do with creativity and common sense. The party bosses weren't acting out of purely ideological reasons, there was an element of envy of free, emancipated people…They can be talented onscreen but we can shove their faces in the mud…The psychology of boors. They kept us in slavery.

Rubbing shoulders with Western actors, who were free to travel, was a source of envy and frustration:

> Those foreign actors flew like birds, borders did not exist for them. And I could not do that. From that time, I literally became sick with the desire to live that way — to come and go without fear, relate to people freely, and not worry that "they" won't let me go out of the country.

Despite this lost opportunity for a truly international career, after *Waterloo* Vidov enjoyed success in the Soviet Union, helped perhaps by his marriage to Natalia Vasilievna Fedotova, a relative of Soviet President Leonid Brezhnev. Unfortunately, the marriage was soon on the rocks, with serious implications for the actor. Powerful forces moved to stifle his career; marrying into Soviet "royalty" could be a double-edged sword. Again, his mentor Sergei Bondarchuk stepped in to aid his prodigy. He introduced Oleg to a Yugoslavian actress being treated at a Moscow hospital. She then helped him arrange a marriage to another Yugoslavian which allowed him to leave the USSR legally.

Arriving in Tito's Yugoslavia, which had escaped the bounds of Soviet influence, he was warmly welcomed, and quickly settled in.

> Speaking from my heart, I felt at home in Yugoslavia. I purposely did not live in hotels but in private apartments so I could better hear the language and learn local customs. Yugoslavian

people host guests from everywhere with an open heart. Acting in their movies is one small way to say thank you.[463]

His happy sojourn was not to last. In July 1985, he was abruptly ordered to return to Russia within 72 hours, which prompted him to make a dramatic dash to Austria. Illegally crossing the Yugoslavian border, he was refused help by the US Embassy in Vienna. Luckily, the Austrian government gave him a travel document that allowed him to travel to Rome, where he could defect at the US Embassy.

While awaiting the slow cogs of bureaucracy, the actor stayed at a friend's house in the city: Richard Harrison, an ex-pat American star of local 1960s gladiator movies (including *Messalina vs. the Son of Hercules* (1963) with *Waterloo*'s MIA — Charles Borromel). "As the story goes, when Sergio Leone offered him the lead in *A Fistful of Dollars*, he said — give it to Clint. And the rest is history."[464]

The actor's pad was also a stopover port for a roving American journalist, Joan Borsten: "I would go off and do stories and then come back. And, I would end up at Richard and Francesca's house for pasta at midnight." Joan, the daughter of a Hollywood studio executive, worked for The *LA Times* and had interviewed many of the cinematic leading lights of Europe, including Fellini and Truffaut. Sharing the house, she and the mysterious Russian quickly hit it off:

> He kept following me around the house, and in his broken English telling me about his mother and his father and his aunt and his fans. And he left the Soviet Union and he couldn't go back…I did not fall in love at first sight, but he did somehow. A romance started pretty quickly.

And Oleg, in his autobiography:

> It took me forever to get across what I wanted to say in English, but she listened. She was kind, warm and open. In Joan, I saw a familiar soul. She wasn't after me for my looks…I felt like Joan was bringing cool water to a dying man and burning desert. I knew then that meeting her was my greatest potion.

In those first few heady days, she had no idea of how famous the handsome actor was until they bumped into a mutual friend:

And he said to me, "do you know who this man is?" And I said, "well, I understand he's a Soviet actor." And he said, "no, my dear, he's the Robert Redford of Russia." And I said, "Oh my God."[465]

Eventually, the paperwork was completed, and the USA welcomed its newest citizen. "He flew to Hollywood on 01 September 1985; I followed, we married and did many amazing things together."[466] While Oleg continued his acting career, including *Red Heat* (1988) and *Wild Orchid* (1990), the couple would build up a successful business distributing communist-era animation from the Soyuzmultfilm Studio. Following a long battle with cancer, Oleg Vidov died in 2017, aged 73. After his death, Joan completed his autobiography and produced a documentary about his colourful and eventful life, *Oleg* (2020).

> Scene.180: *There is a momentary pause, before* TOMLINSON *throws his gun away and disappears from sight among the horses — this odd, conscientious objector to the Battle of Waterloo.*

Given the free rein of the location and ready availability of the cast and extras, it is interesting to see how *out* of sequence so many of the scenes were during filming in Russia. This is the usual pragmatic filmmaking practice, but curious when all resources are to hand. So, it was after a week working on "Ney's charge" that attention shifted to the pre-battle shots, including ablutions at dawn.

Friday, 08 August, Richard had not received a call-sheet but was summoned from his lie-in for an afternoon start for what he thought would be only a brief insert scene. The script gave a sparse stage direction: MERCER *shaves and puts on a clean shirt*. "So, imagine my surprise to find that, in fact, Bondarchuk planned to show the whole beginning of the day of battle using my simple shaving with an open 'cut-throat' razor while a small mirror was propped on a cannon."[467]

Bondarchuk deployed the entire army, all dressed in British uniforms, to fill the background from La Haye Sainte farmhouse across the plain. In a movie cheat, the sequence was filmed at dusk to simulate dawn, and angled some 45 degrees from its historical position.

> So, there I was, in shirtsleeves, with a soapy face and an open razor for *hours*! All in delicious clean sunshine, thousands of troops were used in the background establishing panning shot — cavalry exercising, riflemen cleaning and firing guns (to clear

them), camp fires cooking breakfast, etc. It took a *very* long time to set up, as Bondarchuk also involved two other actors in the vignette — Oleg Vidov and Donal Donnelly; the crisscross of characters is typical of the director, interlinking the personalities for the audience.

Donal Donnelly played Private O'Connor, who had a memorable scene set the night before involving a pig — and a promotion. He wanders through the awakening army and passing Mercer's mirror, admires his newly awarded Corporal stripe; meanwhile a dazed and pensive Tomlinson played by Oleg Vidov saunters past. Bondarchuk encouraged the actors to work out the "business" between them, while he concentrated on orchestrating the thousands in the background.

> So, I chatted to Oleg and Donal for hours, and we worked out the little "stand-off" where I turn and stare at Donal (Officer to Corporal!), managed to inject a bit of light humour with Donal — he trying to peer over my shoulder into the shaving mirror, and me catching him at it, and turning around in aristocratic amazement, and he potters off grumbling.[468]

The handful of lines spoken involved Richard as Mercer greeting fellow Artillery Captain Ramsey, who was played by Willoughby Gray, the historical advisor in a blink-and-you-miss-him role.[469]

This single shot captured from a crane with a zoom lens took five takes before the director was satisfied. The take used in the film fleetingly shows the shadow of the camera before the sun dipped behind the horizon. It was not the only thing to disappear as Richard found out as he packed up to leave the set that evening: "disconcerted that a soldier had stolen my camera — being investigated." It was never recovered, although "I had luckily already had quite a few films processed."[470]

The next day was a Saturday, and the make-believe violence was stilled. Half-a-world away there was an event of such brutality that it has become singed into the iconography of that turbulent decade. It had a profound effect on one of the recently left cast members, Philippe Forquet: "I was vacationing in the south of France when I first learned of it."

In Los Angeles, members of Charles Manson's "family" had broken into a house at random and killed all the occupants — five people. The house was the temporary home of the film director Roman Polanski and his new wife, the up-and-coming actress Sharon Tate, who was also nine months pregnant. She and Philippe had been in a relationship some years before.

> A lawyer friend of mine thought he heard her name on the radio connected with these horrible murders in Southern California. I told him it's not possible. I imagined we would learn the following day that it just wasn't true…Later, when I heard about Sharon's death, I was sure it was a mistake. It had to be. I couldn't believe it, because I thought she was still in Europe.

Despite parting ways five years before, the two had remained friends and kept in touch. "I saw her a few times when I was in England and Italy; about one and a half months before she died. I saw her with Polanski in Rome, when I was with my current girlfriend, Linda (Morand)…I only talked to her alone for about 5 minutes that night."

Speaking in 1971 after he had "two really good roles" citing *Camille 2000* and *Waterloo,* he confided her death had deeply affected him: "I've been in love now, three times…but Sharon was the one I was most in love with. We were very much in love with each other…I know I will never marry. I wanted that with Sharon, but not anymore."[471]

His later marriage to his then girlfriend, Linda, didn't last. After another failed marriage, he would finally find happiness with Béatrice Manchon, twenty-five-years his junior; the two married in 1989 and would have a son.

Richard doesn't mention the ghastly event in his diary, but recalled that keeping up to date with the news was difficult in Russia. Philippe was a popular member of the cast, and the tragedy would no doubt have sent ripples through the isolated unit.

Ironically, her death would cause ructions on another film set at the outer rim of Europe. American actor Christopher Jones, who had been paid half a million dollars to appear in David Lean's *Ryan's Daughter* was filming in the west of Ireland. He had befriended Sharon a few months earlier while filming *Brief Season* (1969) for Dino in Italy. Despite being married, it was rumoured she and Jones had had an affair, and he lived in fear of her volatile husband Roman Polanski finding out. Regardless of the details, when Jones heard that weekend in August of Sharon's murder at 10050 Cielo Drive, Beverly Hills, a house owned by his manager Rudi Altobelli, he was plunged into a deep depression. Shortly after, he suffered a near-fatal car crash in his silver Ferrari (a $20,000 gift from Dino) over a cliff on Ireland's Dingle Peninsula. Jones said later: "I'd had a nervous breakdown over Sharon Tate's death."[472] Fifty years on, the terrible events inspired Quentin Tarantino's off-beat riff of the story in *Once Upon a Time…In Hollywood* (2019), with Margot Robbie attempting to capture something of the extraordinary, electrifying tragic allure of Sharon Tate.

On the following Tuesday, Richard was called again and eagerly arrived on set only to spend the entire day watching a rehearsal for the defeat of the Old Guard, presumably not filmed at the time. "Up Guards,' but it's all been muddled up — so we hung around all day watching the troop movements and left. Not very exciting."[473] He did note, though, the impressive "terrifying" black-clad Prussian cavalrymen that appeared in this climatic show down. It appears this giant sequence was attempted on and off over the next few months. Quite what was "muddled up" that day is not clear.

Historically, as the French Imperial Guard mounted the crest of the Allied ridge line, they saw before them a seeming empty field. Wellington had sprung a trap, and judging that the moment had arrived he shouted an order. The script echoed the popular version of…*His famous apocryphal line:* "Up, Guards, and at 'em." Whereupon a line of red-coated British troops sprang out of the trampled corn and let forth a few volleys that stopped Napoleon's hitherto undefeated elite in its tracks.

By the time this was filmed, the dialogue had been replaced by the now agreed version to the regimental commander: *"Now, Maitland, now is your time."* This was no doubt due to the intervention of Willo Gray, who continued to trim the script's periodic drift from the historical record. Richard's mention of the Prussians suggests that the rehearsal was for the final advance of Wellington's line against the French.

In the finished film, this is an incredible sequence which utilises every single soldier as the red-clad British converges across the valley, and up towards the breaking blue-clad French. *Not* very clear in the film, but visible from stills, are the Prussians streaming in from the left-hand side. It is unclear when this vast sequence was actually shot; the clue seems to lie in the fires that appear to engulf the inn of La Belle Alliance and the farm of La Haye Sainte. The latter was used there for several night scenes into September and appeared to be in good repair. It would have made much more practical sense to complete these big action scenes at the very end of shooting. It is possible that they were repeatedly repaired to a lesser or greater degree, surviving memories do not recall for what would have been the sole responsibility of the art department.

On screen, during the huge sequence thus discussed, we get one of the fleeting looks within the battle-scarred farmhouse of La Haye Sainte. Having lost the vital stronghold, British troops, with one sporting a flag, push into the courtyard and exchange a quick burst of fire with the French, before retaking the farm. At the edge of the shot over the farm walls, we see the entire "French" ridge engulfed in fighting with Wellington's army. This is very clearly filmed at the same time, probably under the local direction of Anatoli Chemodurov's second unit, and gives a breath-taking snapshot of the co-ordination and precision required with so many elements to juggle at the same time.

Daniele Nannuzzi recalls it was while shooting part of the Old Guard attack that sadly make-believe war became real. Richard, although not on set, noted the rumour around the campfire one evening: "…One old extra died, and some horses were killed."[474] It appears the man had suffered a heart attack, but not, it appears, directly related to the filming. As for the matter of the horses, this will be discussed in the following chapter.

A few days later, frustration and confusion appeared to be the order, as what should have been a 1 p.m. start was brought forward by some hours. Richard, along with several other actors, had to race to the set only to find the make-up department was "miles away." They made their way over to where the unit was filming:

> At last, we got there, only to wait until 3:15 p.m. doing nothing; then they have a two-hour lunch break! We were all so pissed off that with Willo and Melita, the interpreter, we had a bottle of white wine *each* and staggered back to see what, if anything, was happening.

It is not clear what scene was intended. Perhaps the director was acting on a whim of inspiration. No one appeared happy with the result:

> As the sun was setting, they eventually shot the scene in which Wellington and officers were supposed to end the shot by riding close to camera with the English charging in background — why, no one knows: and despite some rough words all round, we did two takes. What a waste of 10,000 troop and actors.[475]

A few days later, the disgruntled British actor found out his fellow Artillery officer character "Normyle has been called and *not me.*"[476] Referencing the Russian actor by his character's name in his diary,[477]

Richard would sometimes express mild irritation with his co-performer. "Normyle pestered me to go through (our) lines (he learnt them by sound, as no English Language skills)." The language was like an Iron Curtain between them as he confided in a later entry: "Normyle hovered as usual and we exchanged dubious pleasantries — he asked me to test him on his lines again today (all *m*ine of course) so I listened — being unable to tell him anything about the problem..."[478]

Strangely, the credits for Normyle list a British actor, Adrian Brine, but considering the closely knit cast, there is no reference to him in either Richard's diary or the collective memory. During the 1960s, Brine had appeared in a number of popular TV series: *Z Cars,* the critically acclaimed *An Age of Kings* (1960), and *Joe and the Gladiator* for the BBC in 1971. His *IMDB* entry includes a number of Dutch productions from 1969 onwards, and it suggests he had settled in Holland where he would not only act, but also direct a number of films for Dutch TV.

One can only speculate that the actor was engaged for the film but by the time of filming was forced to drop out. While he does not remember the details, Hans Kemna, his partner of fifty years, confirmed: "He did not appear in the film, he had other stage contracts in Brussels. He wanted very much to be in it!!"[479] Whatever the reason, a year or so later when the credits were compiled the records were clearly not updated, but even if he did not appear, we can consider him one of the many that got away, and worthy of mention. In 1990, he was at the top of the bill, alongside Tim Roth as Vincent Van Gogh and Paul Rhys in Robert Altman's *Vincent & Theo.* In 1999, he published *A Shakespearean Actor Prepares,* a book he co-wrote with his friend, the handsome leading man of the 1970s, Michael York. Adrian Brine died in Amsterdam in 2016, aged 80.

The author believes Normyle was played by Latvian actor, Pauls Butkēvičs, who is listed somewhat vaguely as "Officer with Wellington." Lumped together for scenes involving artillery, it is perhaps unsurprising that actors would be keen to garner what scarce pickings there were for acting opportunities. It is worth remembering Richard was the only non-Russian speaker in G Troop, which would not have helped matters as "neither of us has a word in common apart from 'cigarette'!" In the privacy of his diary, he probably derived a degree of perverse satisfaction, noting that Normyle "however has been killed off in the scene, so all was well."

That day he witnessed another "death" — not in the script, or the finished film — as the director had played God with the Irish "grunt" O'Connor.

Donal garnered himself a spectacular death — walking into the camera and pitching headlong into a puddle, showing his back lacerated and very bloody! As it was an evening shoot, he must have suffered: I was cold, despite standing by the Brutes (movie lights).[480]

Scene.88: EXCITEMENT *at the sight of* NAPOLEON *spreads along the Allied Line. There are several* AD LIBS *in a perverse admiration of* NAPOLEON…*like the English admiration of Rommel in the desert. Then the first verses of the good-natured satirical song…*(SINGERS) *"Boney was a warrior, o.i.o — Boney was a warrior, John François — Boney beat the Prus-sians, o.i.o. — Boney beat the Prus-sians, John François."*

It was more than a week later until Richard was summoned before the cameras and again back under Wellington's famous elm tree; for a musical interlude. With the troops lined up smartly, including a resurrected Corporal O'Connor, a few thousand Russians voices did their best to sing.

The song was a contemporary ballad to Waterloo, although the original lyrics suggest it was written *after* the battle as they reference the event itself! Being the pop music of their day, ballads and shanties often evolved and adapted as they were usually sung informally in taverns, ships and barracks, so it is highly probable lyrics were fluid.

This one has a link to the Breton maritime song *Jean-François de Nantes*, and brings to mind the cross-cultural fertilisation of the famous *Lili Marlene*, which was beloved by all sides in the Second World War, to appreciate the malleability of popular songs.

Scene.89: WELLINGTON *winks at* DE LANCEY. *"Quite brotherly business…(he turns his glass again toward Napoleon)…isn't it, De Lancey — killing?"*

This sequence brings to mind the "duelling choirs" in the iconic 1964 film *Zulu*, a fairly accurate reconstruction of the miniature epic struggle at Rorke's Drift in 1879. The two sides, Zulus and the small besieged British garrison, exhausted and bruised, exchange a choral chant across the stricken field. In both films, the singing is equally effective and moving; it is pure cinema, and all the better for it.

When men are facing potential death, hearty singing is surely one of the best ways of relieving stress and showing defiance to your enemy.

Military history is replete with many examples of armies going into battle with anything from hymns to bawdy songs on their lips, or a mixture for good measure. Historically, Wellington disapproved of cheering or any vocal outbursts, but who is to say somewhere along the two-mile-long Allied lines some soldiers did not sing out?

> Scene.89: Seeing the strategic value, Wellington replies, *"Anything that distracts or wastes time this morning we must indulge."* Overcoming his natural dislike of cheering, Wellington asks De Lancey to *"kindly announce me."* His subordinate obliges, and exhorts the army with *"Three cheers for the Duke!"* As his army dutifully obeys, Wellington rides past with *an amused gleam in his eyes.*

By the day of shooting, the rather uninspired *"Three cheers for the Duke!"* had been replaced by a chant that would not be out of place in a football stadium. Formed around the chorus of *"Our Atty"* — Napoleonic British soldiers' more acceptable public nick-name for a commander who although highly respected was not exactly loved; the verses have a touch of earthy British humour.

> *"Who gives salt to Marshal Soult? — Our Atty! — Who gave John François a jolt? — Our Atty! — Who's the beak that'll peck Boney's bum? — Our Atty! — Who makes the parlez-vous to run? — Our Atty! — Who's the boy with the hooky nose? — Our Atty! — Who's the lad who leathers the French? — Our Atty! — Who's the boy to kick Boney's arse? — Our Atty!"*

Shooting the scene was entertaining: "We shot three takes of Wellington being cheered by his troops — very amusing to watch soldiers trying to shout 'Our Atty' as the chorus! We recorded a basic sound-track, and they played it back to give the timing." In the finished film, as the men hold their muskets forward in the Present Arms position, very few of the thousands of mouths appear to be in sync except for Donal Donnelly as O'Connor, who gives the words suitable gusto.

As Wellington rides along the line, he is followed by his mounted entourage, many of whom were struggling with their mounts that day.

> Jack Hawkins' horse kept veering towards the right — so he gave up, after being led about on a rein! And Michael Wilding

nearly came off *his* and immediately got off to save his fractured skull, so not without difficulty we struggled through — especially as all the horses were ill with 'flu, and were coughing and in a shocking state.[481]

The animals were already a talking point for the Western unit and will be discussed in the next chapter.

After a very long lunch, they decamped along the ridge next to the La Haye Sainte set, which was to be the setting for an evening scene with the army taking up positions in the pouring rain. Picton, played by Jack Hawkins, expresses concern at the choice of battlefield. A potential misstep that Napoleon had also noticed as he surveyed the allied lines, given voice by Steiger with the immortal line: *"Never interrupt your enemy when he's making a mistake. That's bad manners."*

> Scene.49: (Picton) *"It's unsound, Wellington. It's no position."* He points up the military risk for the army with its back to the woods. Wellington assures him he saw this very ground a year before, *"I've kept it in my pocket for a day like tomorrow."*

Richard recalls the filming in his diary:

> We set up a *maniacal* shot of the retreat from Quatre Bras on the night before the main battle: Picton's scene with Wellington with all the Staff behind him on a hill. So, they plough up the hill, thus it turns into a bog and wonder why the horses can't stand up! Then they spray the *ill ones* with water because it was raining in the script — so no wonder they are dropping like flies! It must have been a good shot — files of infantry and cavalry moving past and some horse artillery manoeuvring in close camera and Jack in the middle with his brolly up, ticking off Wellington.

> Scene.49: Picton is concerned that the woods will turn into a death trap if they have to retreat. Wellington is adamant, *"There's no undergrowth in that wood. The entire army can slip through it, like rain through a grate."*

For Jack Hawkins, the wet ground was probably a welcome relief as Richard Heffer recalled: "Jack's main problem was the *dust*; he had a tracheotomy because of throat cancer and mimed his speeches, which were dubbed-in later…a charming man. But when the long days of horse and sun and wind-blown dust and smoke were at their height, it must have been very hard."

The preceding scene would have involved movie rain from hoses, but over the next few days the real variety caused havoc and slowed shooting to a crawl.

By the afternoon of 25 August, the sun was shining and Richard was on-call; the unit made good on the delay. "Much faster work today — done five scenes in all, including my riding forward and asking Wellington for permission to fire at Napoleon."[482]

> Scene.84: (Mercer) *"Napoleon has ridden within range, Your Grace. May I have permission to try a shot?"*

The scene is taken from an apocryphal story but this, along with the other vignettes involving Mercer, is not found in the historical Mercer's memoirs. Screenwriter Harry Craig was almost certainly familiar with the memoirs, and would have conjured up the scene from the Artilleryman's two encounters with the Emperor. The first, mentioned in Chapter Two; when Napoleon appears over the rise against a stormy sky as the Artilleryman covered Wellington's retreat from Quatre Bras. But he and his guns had another bite of the apple a few hours later, as he had his battery shivered in the rain as they took up position on the ridgeline south of Waterloo:

> Here for a second time, I saw Napoleon, though infinitely more distant than in the morning. Some of my non-commissioned officers pointed their guns at the numerous cortèges accompanying him as they stood near the road by La Belle Alliance; and one, pointed by old Quartermaster Hall, fell in the midst of them.[483]

Presumably, at the time Mercer did *not* ask *"permission to try a shot,"* but it gave Craig the inspiration for one of the film's many memorable moments.

Before cameras could roll and Richard play his line, he had to wait patiently as the star and director crossed swords over interpretation. Peter Davies remembered that Plummer would often grumble defiantly: "'Oh, that's how I'm going to say it, you know!' — and it was always for the better."

It seems Bondarchuk's synergy with Steiger was not repeated with the Canadian actor, with the sticking point often being the Anglo-Saxon mind set. "Chris (Plummer) played it very cool (to say the least) which was *not* what I expected, and he and Bondarchuk argued for ages — resulting in seven takes, although the scene roughly worked each time."[484]

> Scene.84: (Wellington) *"Certainly not. Commanders of armies have something better to do than shoot at each other."*

Whether there were any real tensions between the Canadian and the Russian is not clear, but one can detect a discreet distance between the two men. Perhaps Bondarchuk missed directing a Steiger "explosion," which was both challenging but creatively charged.

On 15 August 1969, the Russian sent a cable to his recently departed star, who was slowly decompressing from his character at his home in sunny Malibu. Both playful and touching, it was a heartfelt compliment for his performance: "Congratulations on your *200th* birthday!"[485] The date in 1769 saw the birth of Napoleon in Corsica.

With the scene "in-the-can," Richard finished early because of the "complete disregard for continuity," and instead read Mercer's memoirs. Lunch was in a new purpose-built structure in the unit camp area. He was disheartened to hear it was dubbed — "The Winter Restaurant — what a dreadful thought!"[486]

The summer was now over and still no end in sight as Richard wrote in his diary just past midnight on the last day of August: "September as I write! Could be another month — and the idea is horrific!"[487] With visions of a Russian winter and no doubt Napoleon's ill-fated retreat, a sense of gloom and despondency was sapping energy and morale.

338 WATERLOO — MAKING AN EPIC

Soldiers "take five" beneath the merciless sun. © RICHARD HEFFER

The cast at least had some shade, meanwhile a troop of cavalry trot past.
© RICHARD HEFFER

All the "officer" cast members had to learn to ride in "battlefield" conditions, with fire crackers thrown infront of the horses to teach control. © RICHARD HEFFER

From left: Rupert Davies, Ian and Diane Ogilvy, Elaine and Christopher Plummer, his PA, John Kirby and young Titus Ogilvy. © RICHARD HEFFER

British infantry stand in a square and wait for the French cavalry attack.
© RICHARD HEFFER

Armando Nannuzzi strapped into the military helicopter. © HEINZ FELDHAUS

The helicopter swoops over the Allied squares. Notice the radio operator in foreground, and the numbered signs in each square for quick identification.
© RICHARD HEFFER

French cavalry in a melee around the squares, taken by one of the riders.
© ASLAN KHABLAUK

Wellington and Uxbridge shelter in an infantry square as French cavalry mill around them. AUTHOR'S COLLECTION

Lord Hay (Peter Davies) about to meet his death as he exhorts his men to "Think of England!" AUTHOR'S COLLECTION

A detachment of tired horses being walked to their rest area near La Haye Sainte farmhouse. © RICHARD HEFFER

CHAPTER 14

"Shoot At The Horses! Pile Up The Horses!"

For all the colour and spectacle captured for the camera, it is laudable that almost no serious injuries, apart from some bruises and broken limbs, were sustained during the months of filming. But there is one aspect of *Waterloo* for which it has become notorious, and cannot be ignored.

Arriving in Russia, many of the Western cast and crew were shocked by what they saw of the four-legged cast members. "One morning we arrived at the area where the shooting would take place," remembered French actor Philippe Forquet:

> …we saw about 15 horses laying on the ground; they were dead, and had blood and big open wounds on their bodies, and some had guts hanging out of the belly. It was quite a shock. Technicians explained that dead horses on a battle scene would make it more realistic. These horses came from a Russian Army stud farm, and they had been killed a few hours before by Russian soldiers.

It was so unnerving for the newly arrived unit, having never seen horses treated thus for the sake of cinema before.

The movies were born in the last days of the nineteenth-century when despite the technological innovations of trains, motor cars and soon aeroplanes, for the vast majority of the world the prime form of transportation was still the horse. Perhaps because of centuries of interdependence between two and four-legged creatures, an affinity and mutual understanding had developed, which made the horse man's most reliable animal worker and companion.

In the very early days of Hollywood, before there were any established stunt men, riders were cowboys, often only a generation away from the hardy men who had opened up America's wilderness. These macho figures could perform many daredevil tricks and stunts with their steeds, all for a dollar a day. But it really was a case of "safety last" for both two and four-legged performers, with inevitable injury and sometimes death just a routine aspect of pioneer filmmaking.

As we saw in Chapter One, the filming of the chariot race in the Silent-Era version of *Ben-Hur* had resulted in a bloodbath of animals, although it did not spark any outrage or controversy at the time. Ten years later, it was a very different story, when another film resulted in equine carnage and finally brought about change.

In 1936, Warner Brothers were keen to capitalise on the popularity of their newest and hottest star talent. Tasmanian born hell-raiser Errol Flynn had shot to fame in *Captain Blood* in 1935, a modestly budgeted costume swashbuckler in which Flynn's charisma and star power were immediately clear.

Now, they planned an epic that would tap into the then current interest in Britain's Imperial past, and construct a story which would culminate in a terrific climax. Based more on Lord Tennyson's famous poem than the true history, *The Charge of the Light Brigade* was planned as a rip-roaring action film that would weave a fictional story from the simmering tensions of the Khyber Pass to the drama of the Crimea. Despite regarded as among the best Flynn movies, it has been branded one of the most infamous misuses of horses in Hollywood history.

David Niven, who co-starred with Flynn, titled his highly amusing autobiography — *Bring on The Empty Horses*, a quote attributed to Hungarian director Michael Curtiz, who was still coming to grips with his adopted language. He had a reputation for directing exciting and well-staged action sequences, with the aid of his riding crop for adding *emphasis*. According to bubbly 1930s Pre-Code star Joan Blondell, he was "a cruel man — sadistic, with animals and actors, and swung that whip around pretty good. But he was amusing and turned out some good pictures."[488]

He had made a Silent-Era epic, *Noah's Ark* (1927), which was praised for its incredible deluge sequence, involving some 600,000 gallons of water onto the set, in which it was reported three people drowned. Deep concerns were raised about safety for stunt work, and this led to tighter regulations being introduced the following year. Curtiz was an uncompromising filmmaker who strove for the best effect — regardless of cost.

For *Charge*, this highly romanticised and historically inaccurate account of the famed 1854 battle, a byword for incompetence and hopeless courage, Curtiz staged one of the most impressive action sequences to date. Filmed in California, hundreds of cowboys were hired, many of whom had worked on the multitude of westerns then being churned out, where safety was secondary to the seduction of a paycheque. All along Hollywood Canyon, which stood in for the Crimean Balaclava Valley for the climatic charge, was set with rows of tripwires designed to topple the galloping horses.

One of the most brutal techniques was the notorious "Running W," a lethal device designed to pull the legs of a horse mid-gallop. It had been developed by ex-rodeo rider and legendary stuntman, Yakima Canutt. When Curtiz yelled: "Action" — the charge was a free-for-all as the horsemen galloped at full tilt down this second "Valley of Death" — a sobriquet it earned as 125 horses were tripped causing horrendous injuries, with at least 25 animals being killed.

Errol Flynn, an accomplished horseman, was outraged not just by the animal cruelty but also by director Curtiz's indifference. The two men came to blows and had to be pulled apart. The charge sequence forced the US Congress to pass legislation to ensure the safety of animals in movies; The American Humane Society imposed very strict rules on the use of any animal in films. The ASPCA (American Society for the Prevention of Cruelty to Animals) followed suit and banned tripwires. Despite Flynn's popularity and the film's success, the black mark against *Charge* meant it was the only one of Flynn's movies not to be re-released by Warner Brothers before its TV premiere in the 1950s.

For the next thirty years, horses in "Hollywood" productions were well treated and would continue to play major if under-appreciated roles in countless movies. Recognising their huge contribution to the cinema and particularly the epic genre, Baird Searles in his glossy 1990 book, *Epic! : History on the Big Screen*, dedicates it to:

> ...All the four-footed actors (especially the horses)
> Some of whom suffered and even died
> In the making of these films
> Which would have been so much the less
> Without their beauty and grace.[489]

These eloquent words were never so apt and poignant than regarding *Waterloo*. As almost all Western countries fell into line behind Hollywood's lead, great effort was, and continues to be expended on safety and proper welfare. The East Communist Bloc did not have the same scruples. One can surmise a host of reasons for this apparent callousness. Perhaps the use of horses in everyday rural life was ubiquitous in what was then dubbed "The Second World," that a sense of pragmatism rather than obvious cruelty was the primary culprit. Whatever the reason, it is still difficult to condone any suffering for the sake of the movies.

Most sources state that the *Waterloo* production used almost 2000 horses, which had to be stabled and cared for during the long shoot. Most of these belonged to the special filmmaking unit of the Soviet army — the 11th Separate Cavalry Regiment — supplemented by the Moscow Militia, with their grey horses depicting the Scots Greys.

As we saw earlier, the health of many of the horses was poor because of an outbreak of highly contagious Equine influenza (horse flu). Like its human variant, it is spread through close contact by infected, coughing horses and contaminated buckets, brushes, tack and other stable equipment. Mildly affected horses can recover within a few weeks of quarantine and rest, while others can take up to six months. With these facts in mind, one wonders how this might have been accomplished with so many horses, and the frequent demands of the filming. This must have been true of one small, but vital group on the film.

A team of 29 mounted stunt men was assembled under the direction of Franco Fantasia, including Yugoslavian circus performers for their daredevil talents, expected to execute effective horse falls close to camera.

They were a colourful lot, as actor Peter Davies remembered; with their bandaged limbs testament to their precarious work:

> To me, as a very young man, they were heroic characters because they were so macho. The stuff they were doing was crazy, it was really nuts, and they were quite a few of them hobbling around with crutches and sticks and things like that. They were a jolly band of trovadores, those guys.

The cast suspected that they were spared seeing the worse of the injuries, with the big stunt scenes being filmed when "the sentimental English were not around."[490] But there were enough instances of daredevil riding to get a sense of what was happening: "They were very skilled — they could 'drop' a horse wherever the director wanted and appear to die in spectacular fashion."[491]

Ian Ogilvy remembers seeing contradictory attitudes from the stunt riders, who often had a *laissez-faire* attitude to equine casualties. Once, he saw a stricken horse which had collapsed out of sheer exhaustion, lying in the mud. Immediately, a dozen stuntman dismounted and clustered around the helpless animal. As one, they lifted it onto their shoulders before laying it gently on a dry patch of ground before trying to revive it. Ignoring the Russian assistants imploring them to return to their positions, like a group of mother hens, these "rough riders" patiently soothed and stroked the horse back to life.

Most of the cast found their mounts would change daily, which made it much harder for the amateur riders. The stunt team sometimes used Ian Ogilvy's horse when he wasn't working; one day, when given a new mount, he was told the previous one had died, and its corpse had been ignobly stuffed with straw and used as a prop. This fate was not an isolated case, as a shocked Philippe Forquet described earlier.

Not all the "dead" were real, as Russian soldier Igor Starchenko revealed when he and his fellow soldiers were arranged in different "corpse" poses in one scene of post carnage. Around them lay many "nags" from local collective farms who had been slugged with heavy doses — 200 grams of vodka "pumped into a vein," making them sleep for three-four hours. Unfortunately, the slow pace of filmmaking meant these equine "corpses" eventually stirred back into life, which required further doses with inevitable consequences; "after a few such injections, the horses were dying…very sad."[492]

The cumulative effect over time was unpleasant, as Daniele Nannuzzi recalls: "After ten days the liver of these animals was like a drunk — terrible. They ripped open the dead horses and you could see all the innards — outside. I mean, it was a war. Like a second military service — but harder."

When they were thrown into the movie melee, some scenes went far beyond make-believe. Perhaps the most notorious scene in the entire film is a sequence of horsemen careering over a crevasse some ten feet high.

It is based on an episode dramatised by the great French novelist Victor Hugo in his mammoth classic *Les Miserables;* it is worth quoting the passage as it served as a direct inspiration for the filmmakers. The setting is Ney's epic cavalry charge across the valley towards what he believes is the retreating Allied army. A brigade of French cavalry, sporting metal breastplates, carrying heavy swords atop enormous horses, make a wrong turn amid the smoke and chaos and happen upon a "hollow way."

> It was a terrible moment. The ravine was there, unexpected, yawning, directly under the horses' feet, two fathoms deep between its double slopes; the second file pushed the first into it, and the third pushed on the second; the horses reared and fell backward, landed on their haunches, slid down, all four feet in the air, crushing and overwhelming the riders; and there being no means of retreat — the whole column being no longer anything more than a projectile — the force which had been gained to crush the English crushed the French; the inexorable ravine could only yield when filled; horses and riders rolled there pell-mell, grinding each other, forming but one mass of flesh in this gulf: when this trench was full of living men, the rest marched over them and passed on. Almost a third of Dubois's brigade fell into that abyss.[493]

In the screenplay, Craig takes Hugo's words and fashioned a highly dramatic vista of death and glory.

> Scene.176: *The* FIRST RANK OF CUIRASSIERS, *the ground opening beneath them, drag desperately at the reins, tearing the mouths and jerking the necks of their horses. They thrust their legs full length forward in the stirrups. From the gallop, the front horses rear up to the terrible stand-still of their hind legs. But it is too late. The ranks behind act as projectiles against the ranks in front. Horses and riders are thrown on the road below; horse and riders fall upon them. More and more go in. Some horses keep their legs on the flesh beneath them.*

Little of this survives into the finished film. Instead, we merely see a group of horses appear to hurtle over a precipice. This is probably one of the least effective contributions by the art department. It is not clear what it is, other than a very well dug pit. There is no indication *why* the animals would throw themselves over. Just prior to this was the scene involving Mercer and Wellington, the filming of which is covered in a later chapter. The artilleryman says he has sighted his guns in a position to fire on the enemy forced to avoid the "hollow way." All of this is cut, and instead we see Mercer's Horse Artillery battery, with their guns poised to pour shot and shell into the melee.

> Scene.177: MERCER'S GUNNERS *swing their cannon around to add murder to accident in the* HOLLOW WAY. *The* GRAPE SHOT, *fired*

at almost point-blank range, creates now — *special effects* — havoc among the struggling horsemen.

On the page, it reads both dramatic — and brutal. Richard Heffer as Mercer vividly recounted the filming in his diary that evening:

> The cannons were lined up on the ridge. Me and Normyle (Russian actor) commanded two batteries from behind with drawn swords. They dug a pit in front of the guns, and the charging cavalry was supposed to crash into it in a spectacular heap. They did. But two horses were killed — one broke its neck, the other its legs — and the latter was a beautiful Palomino. Great shame.[494]

Even after many decades, the memory of the scene was still fresh for Daniele Nannuzzi who worked with the cameras:

> I remember the scene when the first line of cavalry fell down the hill. They made like a swimming pool of mud. And put blinkers to blind the horses because otherwise they would halt. And so, they galloped and the horses couldn't see, and they went down and broke their legs. The soldiers shot them.

Riding in the background was cavalryman, Mykola Kholodnyak who recalled how mannequins were strapped to some horses — being otherwise too dangerous for the stuntmen. With their eyes covered in blinkers, these animals were urged into a gallop: "And you can't stop horses at a race, they fell into that ditch — they broke their legs, got other injuries, then they were pulled out with a crane and cut."[495] Heinz Feldhaus, who also manned a camera, concurs: "Some soldiers and horses, they were over the cliff and fell down, and broken this and broken that. But *they* didn't care. Being in Russia — you keep your mouth shut."

Being a keen and experienced horseman himself, Richard Heffer watched the stunt work with dismay: "I think it was unnecessary; one can bring a horse down quite well *without* digging ditches."[496] He was right, there were much safer ways to pull a horse over.

For all the blood and broken bones, the scene has no basis in historical fact. Victor Hugo's account of Waterloo in *Les Misérables* has been the bane of historians for well over a century. For his research, Hugo visited the battlefield but preferred to draw upon existing stories and myths. We should remember he was writing a novel, and so was not honour bound by the facts. Thanks to his dramatic writing, the "hollow way" became part of the Waterloo myth during the nineteenth-century, when novels such as Hugo's caught the collective imagination in a way no dusty history book could. With the advent of cinema/TV, this myth-making has continued with *Waterloo* often being the basis of many currently believed "facts."

Fifty years later, the sequence has lost none of its shock value. "It's horrific!" was the response of a modern Horse-Master and Stunt Co-ordinator, Abbi Collins, who has worked on over a hundred films and TV productions, including *Poldark* (2015), *The Selfish Giant* (2013) and *Wuthering Heights* (2011). For this book, she kindly looked at the two big cavalry charges in the film: the Scots Greys and the French Cavalry attack, particularly the "hollow way," to assess how the horse stunts were deployed.

> I can see how there were so many deaths and lots would have broken their legs and/or necks and had to be shot. The part where a bunch of them were falling down the hillside into a ditch, look like real horses, I'm sure they didn't have horse dummies in those days. I'm certain many of the riders would have been injured too.

Abbi Collins, who is also writing her own book on the craft of stunt work, used her experienced eye to explain the different techniques that may have been used for the film.

> There were four types used. Trip wires, which would have taken an entire line of them out at once, and I didn't see that. The "Deadman" where a long length of rope or piano wire was tied to the horse's front leg at one end, and anchored to a solid object like a tree or a stake at the other end. It uncoiled as the horse galloped, then when it got to the end it wrenched the horse's leg from under it. I don't think that was used either as they all galloped in open spaces. The third was the "Running W" or "toe tapper," where the rider held a ring which had a rope shackled to the horse's leg, and when he pulled it up the horse tripped. It looks like this was what they used in the film, and you will see lots of horses going down on their knees because of this technique. The fourth is for the rider to pull the horse down by pulling its head around to one side as it is running, throwing it off balance

so it falls on its side. The rider puts his leg forward to avoid the horse landing on it. That is the only technique still used today. The horses are trained to fall using a soft sand arena, so that when the horse has its head pulled round sharply, it knows to fall down.[497]

It is clear from Abbi Collins's assessment that there was a very cavalier approach to stunts which used a combination of these techniques to facilitate the horse falls. It should also be noted that the last-mentioned modern technique was used for at *least* one stunt, as discussed in the last chapter which involved three days of preparation on straw-covered ground.

Mike Munn in his 1982 book *The Stories Behind The Scenes Of The Great Film Epics* reported that according to his research with "various members of Columbia (Pictures) publicity department, some 400 horses were killed while filming the Charge of The Scots Greys in *Waterloo* because trip wires were used."[498] This figure seems unlikely, as it would have been nearly a *quarter* of the production's horse establishment, but it recognises that there *were* injuries and deaths.

Richard Heffer, an experienced rider himself, has pointed out that to stage the vast cavalry charges, they needed all the horses they could get: "Inevitably with the *scale* of the battle scenes there were casualties, but I saw no cruelty or abuse of the horses — they were too important! Also, difficult to replace." Considering that the two primary units that supplied the horses were the greys of the Moscow Militia, and the specialist movie 11th Separate Regiment with their prized Orlov Trotters, common sense highlights the value of their steeds.

One of its members was Mykola Kholodnyak, who along with his comrades, took pride in the welfare of their mounts:

> The horses were treated fine. Three times a day they had 1.5 litres of soaked, salted oat. Hay was served all the time. It was forbidden for horses to graze on the grass (it would have made them sluggish). In addition, every day the horses were groomed and combed. In between shots, people ran up to them, giving them sugar and cookies. Luckily, the officers paid no attention to this.

We must also add the instance in a previous chapter of General Oslikovsky's refusal to allow the horses to be deployed before they had been properly fed, as an example of humane and pragmatic treatment. This cannot have been an isolated example.

But Daniele Nannuzzi, who was on set virtually every day, said: "I saw a lot of animals dead. They killed a lot of horses because they get them from an abattoir. And they were not beautiful ones." If most harmed horses were from this source, then that is another moral debate, far beyond the scope of this book.

Even the death or maiming of just one horse for cinema is hard to justify, and so the exact figure is perhaps academic. It is clear from the evidence that the four-legged members of the cast were not always accorded the same respect and care as the two-legged ones. Prior to its first American TV broadcast in 1972, the ABC Network bowed to pressure from The American Humane Society, and cut horse footage it considered "unacceptable." They had criticised the production for showing little concern for animal welfare and filming the horses without "proper" supervision.[499] It is a black mark for which the film can never fully escape.

Domenico Scala (on the right) was one of Italy's top stuntmen at the time.
AUTHOR'S COLLECTION

Left: Part of the 29 stuntmen pose for a picture. Right: A stuntman and horse attempt to clamber out of the notorious ditch. © MYKOLA KHOLODNYAK

A troop of French cavalry trot through the dust. © RICHARD HEFFER

Prussian Hussars, with their death head shako plates, prepare to charge.
© RICHARD HEFFER

Two French cuirassiers spar with each other in their training ground.
© ASLAN KHABLAUK

French hussars thunder past. © MYKOLA KHOLODNYAK

Amid the smoke of battle, British Heavy cavalry wait to charge.
© RICHARD HEFFER

This French rider came very close to the photographer during the mass attacks against the squares. © RICHARD HEFFER

The 'dead horses.' While some were real ones were drugged to make them sleep, most were stuffed props. © RICHARD HEFFER

Six-year-old Emma Ogilvy's painting of Uzhgorod in the back of Richard Heffer's diary. Painting lessons were just one of the pastimes indulged in away from the film set. © RICHARD HEFFER

CHAPTER 15

"It's A Bad Position, Wellington."

To survive one must adapt. And so it was for the cast and crew of *Waterloo*. After the initial shock of arriving in Uzhgorod: the poverty, the privations and the inverted logic that was Soviet Communism, it didn't take long for a siege mentality and humour to assert itself.

One actor reverted to old, well-worn habits. Rupert Davies, who had been a POW in the infamous Stalag Luft III during the war, had "built a whole interior for his hotel room from discarded pieces of set."[500] He also made a DIY toaster, and was often the go-to person for all those little extra luxuries. Like his iconic TV character Jules Maigret, which had made him a household name in 1964, he was always smoking his pipe, and during an era free of stigma and health concerns, had released a 45rpm single titled *Smoking My Pipe*.

Perhaps some of that POW spirit was also evident with poking fun at the system. "There was some kind of production flip chart and our names were on them, and our names would be in Russian," remembered Peter Davies — no relation. "My name looks like '*Retep*' in Russian. Rupert Davies (oh my God, he was a funny guy), I remember him getting endless enjoyment out of calling each other by our butchered Russian names." Roger Green often found himself being the Welsh actor's wingman: "Rupert used to 'employ' me to accompany him on visits into Uzhgorod: Not quite sure why, although I can imagine!"[501]

Although the area was a military zone with strict restrictions on movement, there was still much to enjoy in the area. In the hot balmy summer heat, a welcome distraction was bathing in the local river which presented a "very jolly Russian scene — beach balls, bikinis, fishing, air bed, tents, etc." Richard Heffer recalled after another lazy day, having also enjoyed a "hunk of Shish-Kebab and wine at a kiosk."[502]

Roger Green recalls the river as a place of refuge and privacy for the locals.

> We would swim out to a rock in the middle of the river and sit on it, and more than once people would swim out and talk to us about their problems with the *"Ruskiis."* They would do this because it was impossible to bug the rocks, apparently, and they would talk at great length about their problems.[503]

Away from the delights of the river, wandering about Uzhgorod was an eye-opener for Richard. "Explored the town properly for the first time and was not surprised with the result: lots of shops with no goods, or fifth-rate expensive ones — market (food), and the usual collection of cafes and beer shops…found the old church (converted to a museum) and the castle, as well as being able to buy a biro and some Lenin post-cards (big victory!)."[504]

Boredom and booze are close bedfellows, and this "vice" became a vital part of life. "Wine varied; sweet fizz harmless, red rough; beer very fresh — sometimes no tops to bottles as straight from the local brewery."[505] The unit considered the local beer undrinkable, but intermittent supplies of superior Czech lagers arrived in the town would create a miniature stampede. "The Russian beer was absolutely awful," remembered Peter Davies:

> I remember it made some people ill because it was not even sanitary — nasty stuff. Just about everyone got the runs at some point. But when you could get it, there was the Czechoslovakian beer that would come, and that was really good. So that was like the gold rush and somehow, we would manoeuvre to getting that. But then there was a place down in the town where the draught beer would be delivered, and then it would be drunk so you'd have to get there when there was still some left.

The locals were friendly, and curious to see these visitors from another world, as Richard found: "Peter (Davies) and I walked into town and had an ice cream (being 'looked at' the whole time as capitalist foreigners!)."[506] They soon learnt smatterings of the language to help with some awkward transactions. Ian Ogilvy attempted to make a purchase from a local shop and was refused; "Oleg (Vidov) got them as the old hag in the shop refused to serve capitalist foreigners." On another occasion, Richard almost stumbled into a fight: "Went for a walk along the riverbank, and saw some soldiers fighting, so came smartly back."[507]

Roger Green recalls the underlying tensions in this militarised region:

> They would say: "Me *Ukrainski nyet Ruski*" and spit on the ground. In fact, on one occasion we were in a bar in the town and some Russian military came in just — two of them. We were on the first floor when these two soldiers arrived on the same floor. They were manhandled forcefully down the stairs and out of the building by the locals — certainly a hotspot![508]

Ukrainian soldier Mykola Kholodnyak with just under four roubles burning a hole in his pocket, recalled that there were strict limits imposed on their R & R. They were allowed one day off every two months, or slightly more if they had been suitably obedient to their commanders. Once released at 10 a.m., they had the day to themselves. Being still required to wear their uniforms, it was difficult to relax as restaurants were off limits, but most frustrating was they could not buy any alcohol. Also, wearing their Soviet Army green garb would attract the attention of patrolling Military Police, often requesting to check their documents.

One such encounter resulted in a show of respect. The MP beckoned Mykola over and pointed to his unusual footwear: "What are those on your boots?" He duly explained he was in the cavalry, and was wearing his riding boots with small spurs attached at the back. At first, the MP did not believe him, saying: "We don't fight wars with horses anymore." When Mykola explained the work of his special regiment, the mood lightened as the policeman's tone became polite and genuinely interested. With a hearty slap on his back, Mykola was sent on his merry way. Apart from one special trip to Moscow, he and his comrades usually just sauntered around Uzhgorod, enjoying the cinema, the zoological museum and military-friendly shops.

To what extent there was trouble caused by so many soldiers in the vicinity is impossible to say. The stories recounted by the crew members reflect the fact that many of them were under-employed on the set and consequently spent a great deal of time around the town. By the law of averages, they would have experienced "trouble" at some point.

From Mykola's account, even off duty, they were expected to behave like soldiers and obey the military code, with infractions facing stiff punishment. It was a politically sensitive area and no doubt the patrols were an attempt to maintain a fragile peace in the locality. The vast majority of soldiers were probably very well behaved and just keen to enjoy a few hours away from a balling sergeant-major.

The world over, tensions often spring from strangers fraternising with the local womenfolk, as Richard found on another trip to a bar which was a potential flashpoint, but luckily help was on hand.

> Stopped off for wine and shashlik at a little "*kashtan*" bar on a roof. Saw a girl I'd met before…come over and asked for a cigarette — and stayed for some wine. Peter Davies and Oleg Vidov had turned up by then, and we chatted. Girl left, we left, but were stopped by some drunk Russian boys and accused (me) of picking up Russian girls! Oleg sorted it out, but they could have been nasty![509]

Richard found some local ladies *very* friendly when he took a walk in the square:

> …saw this Russian girl in a nightdress watching — she came out onto a balcony, and we played hide-and-seek all evening. Finally, she realised I was an actor at this hotel. We giggled a bit. The whole thing was very much like *Romeo and Juliet* in dumb language![510]

…and a week later:

> Went for my usual walk after dinner, and was hailed from the same balcony *again*: she came down to the street, and we smoked and chatted about "big-beat" — there is a student group in town, apparently. Her name of Natalie. But she was chased away to bed by her mother.[511]

The chance to savour some music and dancing was a splendid opportunity to experience Soviet youth culture.

> Found out the beat group of Uzhgorod was playing at 9 p.m. So, I found Natalie, and we all went off in a group, found the "Amphitheatre" of the town, and suddenly we were back in England! Lots of dolly birds in western "cool" gear (all homemade) and a proper group with amplifiers, etc. playing English pop songs! So, we danced until 11 p.m. in the open air.[512]

The town square, despite being dominated by a huge monolithic hammer and sickle, was a great place to make new friends as Richard found: "was picked up by a Hungarian girl asking me for a light! Nothing loath, I walked her home, and we agreed to go out on Saturday."[513]

The Uzh River was a popular trysting place when romance was in the air. "Lovely stretch of river with weeping willows, grass and lots of hills covered with forest sloping towards the water. Swam, ate and sunbathed: very pleasant — peaches in the sun with her wearing nothing but use of my shirts!"

Returning to the hotel that evening, Richard found another cast member had enjoyed success by the river: "Supper in the hotel with Willoughby Gray who had been fishing: so, we had his fish in a soup, which was delicious!"[514]

Willo's fresh fish was just one of the delicious meals that could be rustled up with ingenuity and creativity with a makeshift kitchen which served as a welcome diversion from the lacklustre hotel restaurant. "We were cooking in the so-called hotel on the balcony when we came home, as we all had one hot stove."[515] The camp followers had foraged in the local shops: "Diane (Ogilvy) had done a great job, with stew and wine and salad and yoghurt and coffee — all tasting 'proper' and very good indeed. Stayed until midnight drinking and telling each other ghost stories!"[516]

Dino's brother Alfredo was also a popular port of call, as he often served expansive meals in his small hotel room. "There were twelve of us in all, and Giovanni cooked Neapolitan spaghetti and roast chicken which was washed down with real Italian red wine and lots of grapes; was a meal to remember in Uzhgorod!"[517] Another fine meal well remembered was offered by the Plummers: "who had engaged the services of a chef," as Peter Davies recalled: "We were all invited to have dinner with Chris and his wife Elaine, who was such a nice person. They had a chef; it was nice food and nice wine and all of that."

Peter remembers Christopher Plummer was often aloof from the rest of the cast. "He was never in the dining room where we all hung out. He wasn't playing poker or anything like that. But he was always really nice on the set. But he was a serious person."

One day, he asked the young actor if he fancied a sporting tournament:

> I was such an idiot. I was such a kid. He wanted to play tennis, and I said: "Sure, I'll play tennis with you." So, we went down to this tennis court at the appointed hour. *Thwack! Thwack! Thwack!*

After about three minutes, he said: "Yeah, thanks. This isn't gonna work." He was practically a professional player!

Like POWs, indoor games become a perfect way to while away the hours, and Richard became something of a grand master. "Played poker for *kopeks* and eventually won two roubles (having to borrow two at one point!)…taught Donal and Peter Davies how to play Backgammon and discovered Jack Hawkins is a player."[518] Many evenings would echo with the roll of dice and a few drinks — or more! "Backgammon, supper, and a protracted poker school until the early hours — again not a good hand in the entire evening (played in Donal's room, and I lost a bottle of champagne there). Drinking with Plummer at dinner too much!"[519]

The long, tedious hours together encouraged camaraderie. Being the youngest, Peter Davies found himself adopted by several people. "Everyone kind of kept an eye on me; I didn't really know how to behave, and sometimes I got caught up in the negative side of things." Irish actor Donal Donnelly would often wrap on Peter's door first thing in the morning, summoning him up for an adventure. "He was always in total good humour, a lovely man. We would have these long, long walks."

Donal soon discovered Peter's Achilles heel and would pepper their walks with some gentle teasing. Just before arriving in Russia, Peter had appeared in a TV episode with the beautiful American actress Janice Rule.[520] She had played opposite Burt Lancaster in one of the decade's strangest Hollywood movies, *The Swimmer* (1968). The teenager had fallen madly in love with the 38-year-old actress, who was married to actor Ben Gazzara (he had escaped Russian tanks in Czechoslovakia in 1968, see Chapter Six). One evening during the shoot, blind love had given him some Dutch courage.

> I suddenly said; *I'm gonna do it!* And tapped on the door of her room, thinking that, you know, she might welcome me in. But she was very sweet about it. But she did *not* open her door. So, I was pining for Janice when I was in Uzhgorod, and Donal thought this was hysterical and would make up songs about Janice Rule!

The stark, empty hotel restaurant was the setting for bonding over a bottle of vodka:

> My unlikely friendship that I made was Michael Wilding. I used to sit with him for hours in that dining room. He was the

most wonderfully elegant, charming person. Typically, he would have a black shirt open at the neck and "W" embroidered on the cuffs. He would have a bottle of vodka; I can remember him offering it to me. I'm sure I didn't; certainly not at ten in the morning. He would sit there and say, "Let's have a drink, dear boy," and he would tell me all these stories about Elizabeth Taylor and their children, and then he would talk about his wife, Margaret Leighton. He was so un-movie-star-like in that respect and treating me like an adult, which you always like when you're 17. I think everyone did, but you know I made quite a bond with him. Hearing him and Jack Hawkins together, swapping movie-star stories — they were very funny. I can remember just sitting there and thinking: *I can't believe I'm sitting at this table!*

Richard formed a sweet bond with the Ogilvy's six-year-old daughter:

> …little Emma and I had a painting session in my room, she coming out best, I think![521]…Emma and I had another painting session, and then a walk, but rain caught us, and we had to shelter in some huge drain pipes by a path — very exciting for Emma because of the echo, etc. Then tea with the Ogilvy's and playing with their toys — a Russian space lorry and some cardboard bricks…A filthy day — but with hard thought and ingenuity it seemed to go reasonably quickly: only three weeks to go supposedly![522]

Emma, half a century later, had only hazy memories of her childhood interlude in Russia. She recalled the excitement of watching the moon landing as the unit huddled around a black-and-white TV; also, being taught to play poker and backgammon with the Italian stunt men.[523]

The wistful desire for home is peppered throughout Richard Heffer's diary, gathering urgency as the production continued its slow progress. Willoughby Gray hatched a plan that could be both diverting and utilise the abundance of under-employed actors, when he and:

Jeffry (Wickham) decided to cast Hamlet from the assembled — Jack was Ghost, C. P. Hamlet, me Laertes, Donal the gravedigger, Michael Wilding Polonius! It would have been an historic production.[524]

One wonders who was suggested for Ophelia! The idea didn't fire up the thespians, as only the following day Richard noted; "Luckily Willo has dropped his idea of Hamlet — great relief all round, I think!"[525]

Jeffry Wickham, who came from aristocratic stock, spoke fluent aristocratic Czarist Russian, a throwback to before the Revolution. To the absolute delight of the Soviet soldiers, he would often stand upon a table and recite in their language Shakespearean soliloquies and the heavyweights of Russian literature. During his National Service, the military had been particularly interested in Wickham's linguistic skills, and honed them for potential cloak-and-dagger Intelligence work. Whether the KGB were aware of the actor's background is unknown, but Jeffry assured his actor colleagues; he was not a spy!

Thursday 21 August 1969 was the first anniversary of an event that had turned up the heat in the Cold War. Despite concerns about possible unrest and trouble in Uzhgorod, for Richard, the day proved to be memorable in other ways.

> Anniversary of the Russian invasion of Czechoslovakia — but nothing going on in Uzhgorod…met Hungarian girl and arranged a picnic…down in the park…had a bottle of wine, etc., lay in the sun and the inevitable distinguished itself. But discovered that a nosy peasant urchin was hiding the whole time in the bushes! Shooed him away and sauntered back to the hotel. And its *crippling activity!*[526]

"Crippling" could have been the outcome a few days later as Richard again met up with his new lady friend.

> Foul weather still. As the rain was clearing, I ventured out, and we chatted for an hour or so by the river — then she bumped into her husband (!), and I had to make a run for it! — very difficult (he's a boxer or something dreadful). Back to savour the magazines of Rod Steiger — all filth, and rather amusing (anything to relieve the boredom).[527]

Luckily, Elaine Plummer could delve into imported Western cereal packets for a novel time-passer. "Memory of today will always be to see Jack Hawkins, Willo, Michael Wilding, Ian Ogilvy and me making model trains from kits enclosed in Kellogg's Corn Flakes packets — doled out by Elaine!"

The large supply was a direct consequence of an industrial dispute — the Italians had gone on strike because of a lack of *Fiocchi* (Italian version of British/American breakfast cereal). Alfredo De Laurentiis had mollified them with a large delivery of Corn Flakes, which Elaine then raided, "liberating" their enclosed little plastic trains. These "with great joy were assembled at the breakfast table, and Jack (Hawkins) cheered up and keenly pushed them around making *chuff! chuff!* noises from his damaged throat." Despite this "amusing breakfast" the rest of the day blurred into stultification: "…No work and a dull day; no post, so mainly reading and guitar and sleeping and eating — the usual frantic life in Uzhgorod."[528]

The weather turned to rain at the end of August. A temporary halt in filming made the actor desperate for any diversion.

> Going to the cinema! All in Russian, with lots of war documentaries to start with — very anti-German (World War II and Borodino — an odd mixture). Then a Mario Lanza film *Serenade to a Great Love* in Russian translation — great fun, and although the cinema was smelly and so were the Russians, it made a welcome change.[529]

With England's Football World Cup victory in 1966 still a fresh and inspiring memory, there was a high level of expectation as the qualifying games began for the following year tournament in 1970. On 10 September Donal dragged Richard along to the hotel's TV to watch his fellow countrymen from Northern Ireland square off against the Russians at Belfast's Windsor Park. Despite the star presence of a budding *Enfant terrible* of British Football, the game was a tremendous disappointment: "dreadful playing and a goalless draw! Even George Best wasn't doing anything; Donal was livid he had waited seven weeks for this match, and they can't even produce *one* goal!"

History relates how none of the countries of the Union got a sniff of the Cup Final — nor even for the next fifty years. The glory in 1970 went instead to the legendary Pelé's Brazil team, who won all their games including the final 4-1 clincher against Italy.

With the normally upbeat Donal gloomily downhearted, the evening ended like a damp squib, although Richard would have liked to have gotten wet: "Early to bed. No hot water again: God, what a country!"[530]

A cancelled call to the set one day allowed Richard to enjoy a lazy, almost halcyon day:

> How I longed to be in England! Then I sunbathed for a few hours, taking pencil, pen and paper — and composing *nothing!*

The mind is a complete blank here — ruined by the constant bombardment of trivia. Had a liquid "lunch" at 4.30pm with Rupert (five bottles of wine) and then Diana (Ogilvy) asked us for dinner-so tried to sober up for two hours (*very* difficult as everything spinning like mad!), walked to town and bought some white flowers for Diana (fresh air good for the system, etc!) and had a BATH!! — For some extraordinary reason the water was hot for the first time in weeks! Delicious — had a lovely *wallow*.

Suitably refreshed, the spaghetti dinner was "all very nice," and despite Donal and Ian "arguing about films," the evening went well. Willo impressed all by "showing his latest miniature — a perfect copy of Terry (Alexander) as Uxbridge — very clever and an exact likeness for the part." Willo was often seen with pad and paints, and was very adept at making tiny but exquisite miniature portraits of the cast in their costumes; these had been popular keepsakes before the age of photography. Richard noted ruefully that Willo was particularly proud of his rendition of the young man dressed as Mercer; so much so that he kept it! That evening, the fun eventually ended with a comatose Rupert Davies being carried back to his room.[531]

Exploring the Soviet Union beyond Uzhgorod was severely limited without travel permits. Peter Davies always regretted not accepting Mosfilm's open invitation to visit Moscow. Russian actor Oleg Vidov was very apologetic about his country, and like any proud citizen was keen to show a positive aspect. "Oleg was just a wonderful person," recalled Peter, "he kept apologising and saying, 'You're eating all this awful food, I'll have to take you to somewhere.' He kept trying to put this trip together for us on a day off, and you couldn't go anywhere without being in an official car because of it being in a military zone."

After a few failed attempts, Oleg made the trip happen with Richard, Peter, Donal and Heinz Feldhaus squeezing into a minibus before heading southeast past the film location site. "We went to this place called Mukachevo. It was like turning up in a Chekhov play — a little cottage with a fence around it."[532] Richard also described this little vignette of Old Russia in his diary:

> Three rooms, a dog, a porch, a garden, and lots of ornaments and hangings in the old style; wooden floors and very clean, lace curtains, curtain-pole and rings, and faded photographs — an

enamel stove (coal) with lots of room to keep things hot — a television, a radio; and the hostess, a charming middle-aged lady with a boss eye. We ate an *enormous* meal — soup with real chicken (killed today), vegetables. Shashlik in the garden that we cooked ourselves on a camp-fire, and lots of home-made wine; Oleg broke his no drink rule, and after a thimble-full was very bouncy and merry, getting his English all mixed up! Lots of laughs, with Donal and me swapping gags as fast as possible — but poor old Peter had a touch of 'flu, so he was quiet. Ate ourselves to a full stop!

Oleg then invited them to "tea and apples with a girlfriend of Oleg's (and her parents); the father was very chatty and communist, but delighted to see us and quite funny, his eyes lit up and twinkled when he talked about England, and described his ballroom dancing days!" Despite their full stomachs, the little band enjoyed a tour of Mukachevo town, which boasted an inhabited nunnery; Catholicism still being very strong with the local population. "With the sun sinking, and the trees in the graveyard turning, it was a very peaceful spot…it was really neat — it was a lovely day."[533]

"The pace is becoming unbearable."[534] The diary entries catalogue the attempts to stave off boredom, helped by copious alcohol. "Met Rupert Davies and drank two bottles of wine while getting the whole story of *Maigret*…went with Donal and met Memo…had Martinis! And Spaghetti! Unbelievable! Drank, chatted and joked. Jack Hawkins came up to complain about the noise! So, he joined in and drank some more."[535]

New Zealander Roger Green, waiting to do one small scene, was perhaps the least employed of them all, and not unsurprisingly he went a little stir crazy.

> Roger Green smashed up the hotel again last night apparently (seven weeks here and one day's work), and it seems he will likely be sent home: at any rate he blacked out, and afterwards lay into an assistant director and Oleg (who smashed a chair over his head!) So, the pace is hotting up![536]

It wasn't long before the recalcitrant was hauled over the coals, as Green recalled:

After a few weeks of these antics, the hotel director called me to his office and with Melita, the official hotel interpreter at his side, told me that there had been nothing but trouble since I had been staying with them. I responded with something like, "Yes, I have had a lot of trouble since I have been here," as if the locals, which was baloney, caused it. So, I was about to be asked to leave, but dear Jack Hawkins came to the rescue and said, in his halting way down deep voice, "Let…the…boy…stay." So, the 'boy' stayed and the behaviour probably stayed but tempered a little.[537]

Perhaps the most poignant passages in Richard Heffer's diary relate to a friendship that developed with a local photographer, Michael:

…who was marvellous, built like a Russian bear with flashing eyes and a shock of grizzled hair…he talked incessantly: about work, life, people, and we all got along very well, sharing fine bottles of wine and meeting his scientist friend who explored the Arctic, a nuclear physicist, and his wife and daughter. A very remarkable afternoon in the warm hospitality of a real Russian home.[538]

The film shoot was a big news story for the local paper, and so Michael got to spend many hours with his new foreign friends. As his time in the country drew to a close, Richard felt a sharp pang for the friend he was leaving behind.

He began talking, so we drank another bottle while he poured out his heart — and I inwardly screamed with pity: — how could he live here? I could go in a few days; Russia was an episode — was it fair that his small life-span should be devoted to one tiny lunatic country with no hope? Dreadful questions, and I collapsed with every fibre of my being — I, who had been complaining about a small delay in my return to England!…what a revelation from Michael, though! The urbane, fun, loving Russian bear with a beautiful wife and daughter trapped in this god-forsaken state! A nightmare come true, and I can hardly bear to think about it.

Jeffry Wickham and Willo Gray enjoying a relaxed liquid lunch.
© RICHARD HEFFER

Aslan Khablauk (left) and mate, enjoy some R+R at a local lake. Even off-duty they were expected to be dressed in their uniforms. © ASLAN KHABLAUK

Wellington reviews his army, while on the opposite ridge by La Belle Alliance, the French take up positions. RON POULTER COLLECTION

Dan O'Herlihy as Ney, steadies his horse, as he leads D'Erlon's massive infantry attack. © RICHARD HEFFER

As the French infantry prepare to get to grips with the enemy, a smoke pot is wielded in foreground. © RICHARD HEFFER

Mud-splattered British infantry prepare to receive the advancing French.
© MYKOLA KHOLODNYAK

Wellington rides up to take local command as his troops sit down to minimise the brutal effects of artillery fire. © RICHARD HEFFER

The real Gordon Highlanders advance on the Dinocittà backlot.

Months later, the sequence was completed in Ukraine. The Russian soldiers hated wearing the Highland "skirts." Notice the special effects unit supplying smoke in the extreme background. AUTHOR'S COLLECTION

Led by Dan O'Herlihy as Ney (at extreme right), the Old Guard advances for Napoleon's final role of the dice. AUTHOR'S COLLECTION

The Old Guard pass the burning La Haye Sainte farmhouse and get to grips with the Allied army. AUTHOR'S COLLECTION

With the battle lost, Napoleon attempts to rally his men by grabbing a flag before being escorted away by his generals. On horseback is the Old Guard commander, Cambronne (Evgeni Samoilov). AUTHOR'S COLLECTION

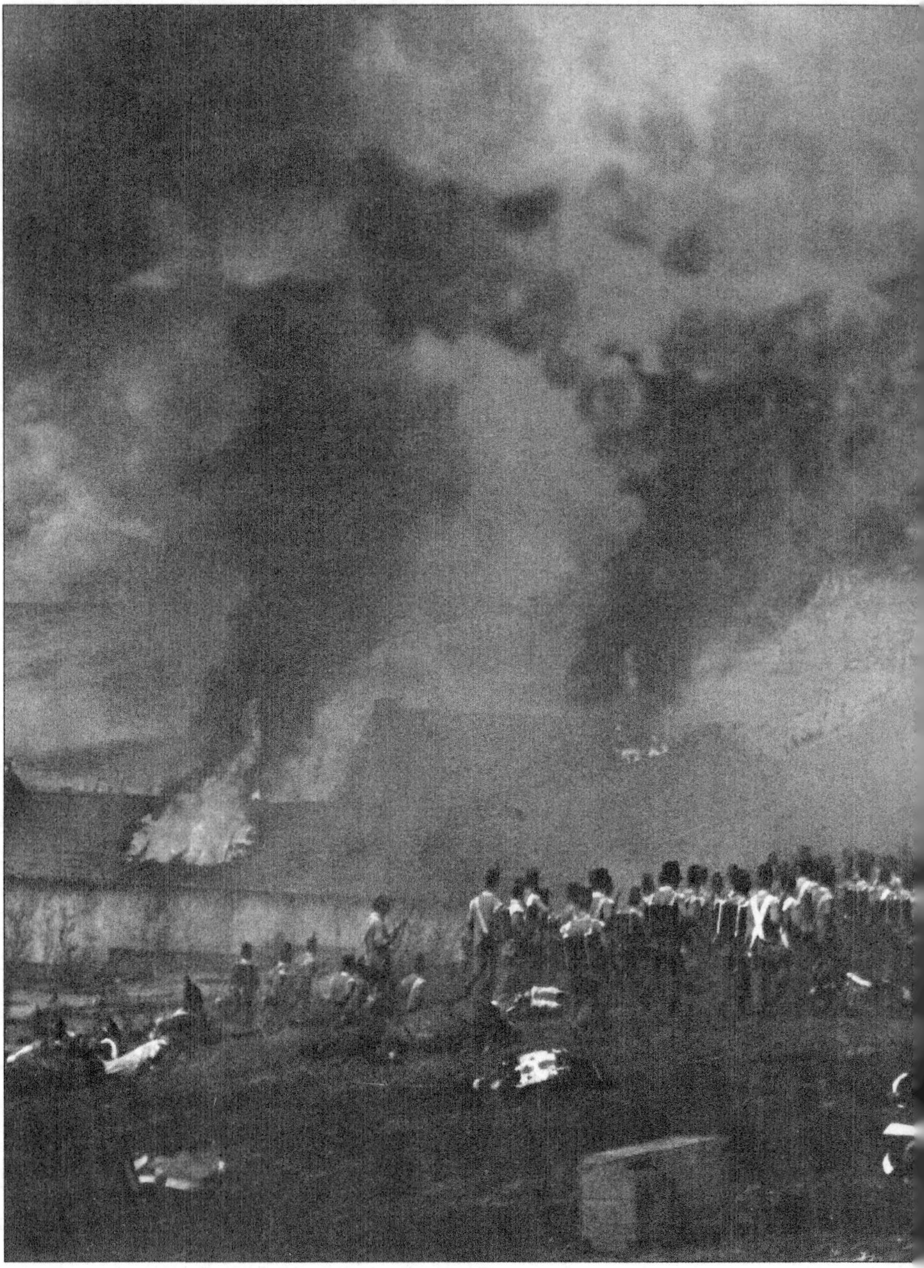

With the Old Guard repulsed, Wellington orders a general advance against the routed French. AUTHOR'S COLLECTION

British infantry wait in line as explosions break around them. © RICHARD HEFFER

CHAPTER 16

"By God, It's Blowing Strong, Now"

"All the trees are turning — yellow walnuts in the autumn of Uzhgorod — and it was spring in Rome when we *started!*"[539] As the summer ebbed away, there was a palpable sense of restlessness amongst the unit. "Great excitement today," Richard Heffer wrote in his diary during the first week of September, "because the fever of going home is in the air, everybody is counting down the days."[540] Christopher Plummer complained that the work rate had slowed to a crawl, grumbling that Bondarchuk would often disappear off to Moscow to receive indeterminate honours as befitted a People's Artist.

With Jack Hawkins struggling to breathe amid the acrid smoke-covered battlefield, there was genuine concern about the elderly members of the cast. Michael Wilding, a matinee idol of the 1940s, had long tired of the movies and was also not in the best of health. He had already suffered an injury a few weeks before, when he had fallen from his horse and fractured his skull. Then, one day upon returning to the hotel he announced, with a spot of British understatement, that he had just had an epileptic fit; something he was prone to.[541]

He was rushed into hospital, the conditions of which horrified the cast. From the waiting room to the wards, the hospital was filthy, with sprinklings of mice droppings on the floor amid seemingly countless discarded dilapidated army boots. This made Michael's appearance even more incongruous; smartly dressed as if he had been yachting at Cowes regatta; a blazer, scarf around his neck and sporting canvas and rope espadrilles shoes. His insouciance, though, could not hide his fear as he murmured that he was sure he would die there.

The cast were keen for him to leave and explained their concern to Bondarchuk. Their emotional appeal moved the director who readily agreed to bring forward Wilding's scenes, which included, with a touch of gallows humour — his death in the mud.

He was cast as Sir William Ponsonby, commander of The Scots Greys, who leads a half-crazed charge into the attacking French.

> Scene.137: *The* SCOTS GREYS *walk, then trot, then gallop up the interior Slope. Their black helmets with golden visors, their white plumes, the dazzles of their sabres, the step of their beautiful grey horses, give them a mythical grandeur.*

The 2nd (Royal North British) Dragoons, nicknamed "The Scots Greys"[542] because of the colour of their mounts, was one regiment of three — Royal Dragoons and the Inniskilling Dragoons — which formed part of the Union Brigade, commanded by Ponsonby. Curiously, the last two units were costumed and appear in some background shots but are not shown as part of this charge. It is left solely to The Greys to gallop towards the thousands of French infantry.

The visual reference is one of the most famous battle paintings of all time — *Scotland Forever* by the nineteenth-century British artist, Lady Butler. It is an almost cinematic image which shows The Scots Greys riding pell-mell towards the viewer. Viscerally, if heavily romanticised, it captures the speed and exhilaration that must have characterised a cavalry charge, and strongly influenced the script.

> Scene.137: *They come* STRAIGHT INTO CAMERA, *like centaurs in their magnificence — men with the chests of horses.*

Deploying 350 Arabian mounts of the Moscow Militia, Bondarchuk worked hard to recreate this famous painting, although not without cost to the horses. The master shots of this charge sequence were completed on another occasion upon the "desert" portion of the set (see map). This wide, flat area, which was also used for Ney's charge, allowed horses to gallop at full-tilt to elongate the action.

Daniele Nannuzzi was one of the camera team, as they captured the breakneck sequence travelling on a specially constructed railway with a diesel-powered locomotive.

> We put the five cameras in five different places on the train platform — one camera shooting on a wide (angle lens), one, almost wide — running parallel to the horses with the train

running very fast. There were hundreds of horses running. And then there is just one camera for just for one horse. This white horse had a special effect inside the iron bit in its mouth. And the zoom goes slowly onto this horse, and you then see the blood come from the mouth. And this starts the action for the slow-motion sequence.

The slow-motion moment is one of the most memorable in the film, and would have been achieved in camera by over-cranking at 100 frames per second, which slowed the action by a factor of four. "And this is the beginning of the effect of slow motion of the famous painting of Lady Butler, which is remade directly."[543] To achieve these front-on shots, a camera car was used, not without potential hazard when travelling at speeds of 30-miles per hour. "We used a camera car with a platform — very low, very close. And this is very dangerous because of the wall of horses so close to you. Each shot had meticulous care — *every* shot."

Inevitably some horses were injured, but Daniele reveals that there was a human casualty: "Yes, one stunt man died during the rail shot for The Scots Greys charge. I mean, he was dead because he is *playing* dead. He goes down and the horses all ran over on his body. One Russian soldier in Russia — the life of a one man was not so important at this time."

Potential death and injury were a serious concern when attempting another part of the famous Scots Greys charge.

> Scene.139: *The* CAVALRY *gallop across the face of the* GORDON HIGHLANDERS; *the* GORDONS *break ranks and, catching hold of the stirrups of the* SCOTS GREYS, *are propelled into Battle. Scotsman shouts with Scotsman as they go: "Scotland forever."*

Richard Heffer noted in his diary that the "Scotland Forever" action, with men hanging onto horses' stirrups, had been dropped during the shooting schedule. Historians doubt whether this actually even happened. The Gordon Highlanders Regimental History discusses the evidence and cited an attempt to shoot this scene for the film. It decided that it was on balance — highly unlikely. The Italian stuntmen, playing the 92nd (The Gordons), reputedly could not keep up running with the horsemen, and so the scene was abandoned.[544] One guesses the safety implications would have been overwhelming even for the gung-ho "safety last" stuntmen.

Back on this day in early September for what was intended as Michael Wilding's last day, Richard noted the frustration and delays after he had "decided to go to the set out of sheer boredom…Nothing had happened, but Michael Wilding had been there since 9 a.m. and was obviously livid." The intended shot was a close-up of Ponsonby leading the distinctive grey coloured horses galloping behind him. The delay appeared to be down to marshalling the 400 horsemen.

Luckily for the infirm actor, he could sit on the mechanical horse mounted on a truck carrying the camera. The charging Scots Greys thrown into confusion by attacking French Lancers was exciting to watch, despite a shortage of the correct coloured mounts: "lots of Scots Greys and some Browns — to Willo's annoyance; the horses should *all* have been Grey (hence name), charged everywhere through the smoke pursued by French cavalry." But one suspects weariness and a certain blasé was creeping in, as Richard noted: "I thought it looked splendid, but others demurred."

> Scene.155: *A group of seven* LANCERS *are pursuing* PONSONBY *and his* TRUMPETER.

Ponsonby's death had been prefigured in an earlier scene with Uxbridge, his cavalry commander, just before the charge. After offering a powerful pinch of snuff to his commander, Ponsonby relates how his own father was cut down by French lancers in a muddy bog. This is pure fiction as his father, a leading politician, had died peacefully in London nine years before, having never had a sniff of battle. William Ponsonby, though, *did* become bogged down in the mud during the fray but was captured. It is not clear *how* he died, although there is evidence that he was killed while being escorted as a prisoner to the rear.

It was already late in the day before the charge section had been completed, and preparations were under way for Ponsonby's death sequence in a bog.

> Scene.155: With the Lancers closing fast, Ponsonby hands his snuff-box and watch to the Trumpeter: *"Take them…for my son…"*

The scene ends with Ponsonby lying face up in a large puddle. "By the time they were ready to shoot, the sun had set, and it was practically dark, but in the end three takes were shot; the last by accident being perfect, with even the horse collapsing in a heap in the mud on cue!"

By sundown, Bondarchuk was still not satisfied, so "Michael has to do another day, though; pity, he wanted to go tomorrow."[545] Despite filthy weather, they finally completed his scene next day. With Michael Wilding free to return home to his wife, it was also decided to finish up his friend Jack Hawkins, too. Richard noted that Hawkins' last scenes as General Picton were finished quickly, and would have included his "death."

Picton was one of Wellington's most trusted generals who described him as "a rough, foul-mouthed devil as ever lived."[546] The script captures something of the gruff and tough general who had a brutal reputation, not helped by his notorious cruelty while governor of the slave colony of Trinidad.[547]

> Scene.149: PICTON *beats his horse, roaring with a voice of twenty trumpets:* "On, you drunken rascals. You whore's melts. At' em, you thieves. On you blackguards…" PICTON *never finishes his exhortations. He is struck by a musket ball in the forehead.*

Hawkins also had to sit astride the mechanical horse with hundreds of soldiers in the background, before a small charge would blow a bloody hole in his top hat. Picton's civilian costume is very conspicuous in the film, but it is never explained other than Wellington's cryptic comment following a sharp, disapproving glance at Picton, just before the cannons roared: *"I like my men well dressed for the enemy."* Historically, his had failed to arrive before the campaign began, and therefore he had to wear borrowed civilian clothes. According to rather lurid family folklore, Picton rode out in his nightshirt and top hat because he had overslept, and met his death with a shot in the back of his head, being so hated by his troops.

With a stuntman doubling for Picton's fall from his horse in the long shot, the venerable actor who liked to belch expletives out of frustration after losing his signature voice was free to travel home. "So, there's hope for all!" Richard lamented, while adding with a shudder that a fellow Russian actor "says I will be here until November — I hope he is wrong!"[548]

> Scene.169: *The branches of* WELLINGTON'S TREE *are ripped by shot.* WELLINGTON'S STAFF *are in a turmoil, their horses buck and bump.* (Wellington) *"By God, it's blowing strong, now."*

The lonely, single prop on the allied ridge line that stood in for Wellington's Tree was again the focus of attention in the second week of September. The poor arbour would feel the full force of fire and flames as the Likhachov's special effects department rigged up explosions for more scenes of the Allied ridge raked by French cannon fire. Richard was again an onlooker but agreed to film the spectacle with Ian Ogilvy's 16mm movie camera, which the actor had brought to make a visual diary. Richard and other cast members were instructed in the camera's mechanics and did their best, as he noted that evening: "shot some film on Ian's (camera) — Wellington's Tree under fire, lots of smoke and bombs — very little acting; unfortunately, Ian's built-in light meter has broken, but nevertheless I hoped for the best."[549]

None of this home movie material would ever see the light of day, as Ogilvy lamented:

> I took hours of 16mm film on location and cut it together — Columbia (Pictures) heard about my film and asked to see it — they incorporated my footage into a documentary of their own and then returned my stuff in pieces. I was too disheartened to put it back together again...I have no idea what happened to it all.[550]

Newton Meltzer's month-long documentary shoot in Russia had probably ended before Ogilvy arrived, and so it is possible that there were *two* behind-the-scenes films made of the Russian shoot. While we know that Meltzer's film, made for Paramount's publicity department, was screened on US TV, it has not been possible to find any evidence of any showing for the above Columbia-backed film, which would have been shown in the studio's release territory of the UK and most of Europe. It is possible though that Ogilvy's material made it into Meltzer's 13-minute film, whose whereabouts, as already noted, is still unknown.

> Scene.169: CANNON BALLS *sweep in like rain in the high wind.* (Wellington): *"Gentlemen, it is a general order. The army will retire a hundred paces."* WELLINGTON'S STAFF *go helter-skelter in all directions.* EXPLOSION *of ammunition boxes.* WELLINGTON *is left alone.*

Once the dialogue with the principal actors was completed, their places were taken by stand-ins as the dangerous explosives were readied for a "set-up where the tree was shattered by an exploding ammunition wagon! Fire and smoke everywhere! And the Italian (stand-in) who resembles Wellington more than Chris, reared his horse in confusion — looked very strange, but it might be 'great cinema' — who knows?"[551]

Scene.169: The Inniskillings trudge past the flaming tree. In their midst is O'Connor, who points out to his commander-in-chief: *"It's a bad policy, Sur, to stand under a tree in a thunderstorm. It attracts the bolts, Sur."* Wellington takes the *"impudent advice"* and rides away through shot and shell.

With his tree burning and the army withdrawing, Wellington makes a dash across the ridge while escaping several shell bursts. This time no stand-in, as Christopher Plummer had to ride his faithful Stok over a series of explosives set out over a few hundred yards. Assured that they would be only detonated *after* he had ridden past, he waited nervously for the signal. Hearing "Action" roar out over the din and noise — he and Stok cantered towards a line of planted red flags showing the explosives, which he expected would do their business harmlessly. Unfortunately, one of Likhachov's Effects team messed up the timing, so each one exploded with a generous puff of smoke and debris beneath Stok's belly.

The thirty-year-old steed, who had probably not achieved more than a trot in years, tore off at a spirited gallop. Along with Terence Alexander as Uxbridge, they careered far out of camera range with Plummer gripping not only the reins, but Stok's mane to keep in the saddle. Reaching open fields with no sign of the crew, they calmed their spooked steeds down, prompting Terence Alexander to quip that they must have galloped as far as distant Transylvania. It took a while to retrace exhausted hooves, only to find a cluster of empty chairs — the crew had broken for lunch.

Plummer was not a very keen equestrian, as Peter Davies recalled: "Chris did not enjoy being on a horse, and they got him the most docile horse that they could. There would always be someone right under the head holding it. He didn't want to be left without someone holding the horse. He was afraid it would run away with him."

Another day, under what was left of the tree, Plummer was relieved to play a scene on his two legs for a change. The action is set as the battle is reaching its climax.

Scene.198: Wellington stands in a field of beans watching the advance of the Old Guard towards his now meagre and mauled army. Gordon rides up and offers some beans to Wellington, who, trying to keep his cool, replies: *"If there is one thing in the world about which I know positively nothing, it is agriculture."*

Gordon shrugs and finishes munching his beans as the cannon fire intensifies.

Gordon played by Rupert Davies, costumed in Highland attire, rides up nonchalantly to his commander who is working hard to suppress his agitation. In the film, Davies commands the 92nd (The Gordon Highlanders) but his character Gordon was a construct of several historical commanders of Scottish regiments at the battle, created for the distinctive look of tartan and bonnet.

On set, the sun was beating down mercilessly on the open plain as Richard spent a lazy day which was "very hot — so sunbathed and watched the action alternatively…endless smoke and filth and explosions; very funny scene between Chris and Rupert — the latter munching beans and sporting a Scottish accent made in *Darjeeling*." The humour derived from Davies, whose heritage was Welsh, attempting a Hibernian "accent which left something to be desired (if a purist)!"[552]

The following day Richard was pleased to be on-call again for one of his handful of scenes. Arriving on set just in time to witness another gruesome death; "got there as Ian Ogilvy was being killed (marvellous effects — but *very* dangerous)."[553]

> Scene.189: Wellington confides his fear to De Lancey that if the farm-house is taken, *"my centre is broken."* DE LANCEY *turns to answer, but at that moment a cannon ball ricochets off the ground and hits him on the back.* DE LANCEY *is lifted several yards out over his horse's head. He falls down, bounces, and falls again.*

De Lancey was one of scores of Wellington's staff officers cut down by the lethal debris of battle that day — miraculously, the commander did not suffer a scratch. Later, the Duke graphically described what happened to his trusted quartermaster-general:

> De Lancey was with me, and speaking to me when he was struck. We were on a point of land that overlooked the plain. I had just been warned off by some soldiers (but as I saw well from it, and two divisions were engaging below, I said, "Never mind"), when a ball came bounding along *en ricochet*, as it is called, and, striking him on the back, sent him many yards over the head of his horse. He fell on his face and bounded upwards and fell again. All the staff dismounted and ran to him, and when I came up, he

said, "Pray tell them to leave me and let me die in peace." I had him conveyed to the rear.[554]

In the film, the effect of an exploding shell is well executed. Ian Ogilvy gives a credible performance as he is hit, staggers for a few moments before crumpling to the ground in agonising pain; his entire back ripped and shredded with very graphic make-up.

Badly wounded De Lancey was taken to a dressing station, but his condition was unknown for a few days. As we saw in Chapter Seven, he had just married the teenager Magdalene Hall, and it is possible Bondarchuk intended Veronica De Laurentiis playing the young bride, to scour the stricken battlefield looking for her dying husband.

His "death" over, the actor had a change of clothes and a brush up for Richard's scene, which was set as Ney's cavalry are unleashed from the opposite ridge and heading straight for the Allied line. Wellington and De Lancey happen upon Mercer and his guns and query their deployment. This scene set up the carnage of the "hollow way" which had already been filmed and discussed in Chapter Fourteen.

> Scene.172: Mercer and Normyle wait by their loaded cannons, *which are pointed at an angle of 30 degrees to the ridge.* Wellington and De Lancey ride up, and instruct them to hold their fire till the last minute before seeking shelter in the nearest square. De Lancey notices the *curious angle of Mercer's guns.* Mercer explains there is a *"bad hollow"* in front of them: *"worse than a pit. They must go around it."*

"My scene…was over very quickly really," Richard noted with a hint of disappointment, as Plummer had again altered the words, but at least he was pleased to get "some close-ups of orders, and chatting to Wellington (argument in retaliation for the earlier scene about permission to fire at Napoleon)."

Pleasure at an early end to the day's shooting was coupled with rumours: "great excitement today because the fever of going home is in the air, everybody is counting the days." The growing irritation and impatience are palpable in Richard's diary entry that day, with consternation at the news that Lord Uxbridge's scene where he loses his leg to shell fire had been cut. "Apparently the Russians cannot see the point of it — (as it is written, it's neither funny nor traumatic, they say) but *everyone* knows the famous lines and its *history!* However, as they've also cut 'Scotland forever!' I suppose they can do anything from now on."[555] As we have seen, there were probably good practical reasons for cutting the latter, but it suggests some friction between Bondarchuk and the chief-of-facts, Willoughby Gray.

> Scene.220: *Again the cannon balls sweep in around* WELLINGTON... *"Uxbridge, put the Cavalry against those guns." There is no reply. Then, in an almost normal voice* — (Uxbridge) *(O.S.) "I've lost my leg, by God."* WELLINGTON *leans over to see.* UXBRIDGE *is clutching his saddle. "By God, so you have." The situation is completely dead-pan.*

Of course, the famous leg scene *would* be filmed — perhaps at Willo's instance. But the cultural differences were still being argued over as Chris Plummer and Terence Alexander prepared to shoot it. On the page, the lines don't suggest an obvious interpretation, and Bondarchuk was at a complete loss at what to make of this legendary exchange.

Historians now dispute whether it ever even happened, although the apparent coolness between them may have had a basis in fact; the married Uxbridge had run off with Wellington's sister-in-law, causing a scandal in 1810. The two men did not meet again until just before the campaign, and on hearing news of Uxbridge's appointment to command his cavalry, Wellington commented dryly: "Lord Uxbridge has the reputation of running away with everybody he can, I'll take good care he don't run away with me."[556]

Whatever the truth, the phrase quickly entered into legend as a supreme example of British stoicism. Although by the 1960s the Stiff-upper-lip was already being lampooned by a younger generation, most notably by a group of Oxford-educated comedians, better known as *Monty Python*. The interplay would have been completely baffling to anyone not brought up in the orbit of British culture. The first reading of the lines did not resonate with the Russian director who instead mimed what he wished Christopher Plummer should do with his stricken comrade-in-arms.

In an almost poetic ballet, he was to dismount and carefully examine the bloodied leg, before gazing into Uxbridge's eyes with extreme concern. Then, cradling his subordinate, he was to carry him away — in the heat of battle. Both Plummer and Willo spent the morning schooling the director in the peculiarities of the British mindset. They explained that for a high-born Englishman any display of sentiment, even in such traumatic situations, was considered the height of bad manners. Instead, they suggested, such moments called for, at most, a restrained quip with the merest dash of irony. They got their way — eventually, but leaving Bondarchuk baffled by the Anglo-Saxon race.

Richard Heffer noted the Russians often could not square their perceived contradictions of his race that had helped the Soviets beat not just Napoleon but also Hitler, with the louche and insouciance of the British cast with their peculiar irony-laden humour. Plummer, with his upper-crust Canadian heritage tied to the old British Empire, was uniquely able to grasp it with the perceptive eye of a half-outsider, with one foot in the culture.

The creation of this scene must have been particularly poignant for actor Terence Alexander, as aged just 20, he was severely wounded during the Italian campaign. On 23 April 1943, his foot was half blown off by shrapnel when his command car was hit by shellfire. It was a year to the day since he had been called up, and he soon became a superstitious amateur numerologist with the number 23 assuming huge significance throughout his life.[557] The date of filming this scene is unknown, but one suspects it was not the afeared number — 23.

After the long, lazy days of inactivity, Richard was less than amused one morning to find that: "I should have been called, and that Willo and Normyle had done my work between them! A whole day's second unit shooting!" The scenes would have been supervised by Anatoli Chemodurov and were a variety of shots of cannons being loaded and fired amid clouds of smoke. Richard as Artillery Captain Mercer should have been part of these, and so his reaction was understandable: "I was livid, but it availed me *naught*; so, I watched the shooting during the afternoon and came home disgruntled." But the day had one more sting: "caught something too — feel very odd this evening and have returned early…no hot water all day again!"[558]

A good night's sleep subdued the "something" and next day was a chance to take centre stage with his Horse Artillery Troop; riding hell for leather in a complex shoot with the second unit. Richard, writing in his diary that night, captured the exhilaration of the day amid the heat and dust: "I had to gallop in charge of six guns, ambulance and field wagons — marvellous experience — and then review them as they rode past camera (meanwhile Wellington did a scene behind me)."

Fifty years later, and the memory had not dimmed for Richard, as he recalled the sheer thrill and excitement coupled with the danger:

It was amazing! Don't know how we did it! My dramatic move from first to second position on the ridge (Wellington's order) with the troop at full gallop. We assembled in the "desert" side of the massive set 2 x 1 miles! My troop had the right kit — lovely troop. With all communications via Russian army, I waited for a "Very" light (flare) signal from the camera position (as we were out of sight). Then on the signal, I led the whole Troop out at full gallop. So, in front, one very young English actor as officer commanding, behind six guns with full Russian horse teams; no common language, and if anything went wrong — instant death from being overrun by horses and guns. Remember, we were allocated horses daily — much to my horror — as one was unable to *bond* with one's mount; some horses were fine, others hopeless — pure luck! Anyway, the shot looked great and was like a black and white western! Dust, hooves, grime, the rumble of gun carriages and tingling of harness…It was probably the most exciting thing I have ever done on camera — and *no rehearsal*. Luckily, no men or horses died on that shoot. In real life, that was the Horse Artillery move that prompted Wellington to comment: "*That's the way I like to see guns move!*" It was a pretty hair-raising experience! But it was cut. I would have loved to have seen it!

Later that day, the unit decamped to the other side of the vast set for a large sequence of Wellington's army retreating from Quatre Bras towards Waterloo. The setting was the ubiquitous windmill construction that stood at the extreme end of the "French" ridge.

> Scene.44: *The* HIGHLANDERS, *led by* BAGPIPERS, *march past in a thrust of great exhilaration that completely kills the impression of retreat. To the tune of* MACPHERSON'S LAMENT, *the men sing. Amongst them is Duncan, one of the handsome dancers at the ball.*

Roger Green, the hell-raising Kiwi, who as Duncan had struggled to master The Argyll Broadsword Dance in Rome way back in March, finally had his moment. Roger, attired in a kilt as one of the Gordon Highlanders, joined the thousands of soldiers as they sloshed through the ever-deepening puddles under the merciless movie rain. While Donal Donnelly as the chirpy Irishman O'Connor, also slogging through the mud, had a few lines grumbling at the retreat, Roger had to exercise another skill that he did not possess.

> Scene.44: *As usual with the Celt, he sings the saddest song with most enjoyment: "Sae rantingly, sae vauntingly, Sae gallantly gaed he. He played a tune and danced it round. Beneath the gallows tree."*

It can be assumed that the singing was to a playback recording of the real Gordon Highlanders made whilst in Rome. Roger and his Russian co-players were still required to make it look convincing, although Richard, watching from the side lines, obviously winced: "Roger sang his song — appallingly! — which he has been waiting eight weeks to do." Roger, fifty-years-on, begged to differ at this assessment of his musical performance: "Let Richard Heffer speak for himself — I thought I sang this perfectly!"[559]

After Roger Green's last scene, he was free to leave. The job had entitled him to a British Equity Union card and a crack at an iconic role. With Australian George Lazenby not renewing his contract as James Bond, Eon Productions began a frantic search for a replacement. Returning from Russia, Green was spotted and invited to make a filmed audition as the next 007. Whether he was ever considered is unknown as Sean Connery agreed to return for *Diamonds Are Forever* (1971). Green's audition surfaced some forty years later on YouTube, thus allowing the world to consider if it had missed out on a Kiwi James Bond.[560] In a nod to his brush with cultural super-stardom, Green named his salty 2020 memoir *Shaken and Stirred,* which put some flesh on the bone of the hell-raising reputation of his youth. Speaking in 2021, "this hard drinking New Zealander who played Duncan is now 41 years sober, and is the founder of an alcohol rehab in New Zealand."[561]

That day had also seen another actor preparing for their exit; young Peter Davies remembers his "death" as being a curious mixture of the supremely expensive, and the downright cheap and cheerful.

> Scene.190: (Hay) *"Hold, boys, hold them! What will England say of us, Remember your wives, your homes and sweethearts."* LORD HAY *decides to do some soldiering: "Remember England, men…the sports of England…the grouse in August."*

"You are *not* having the boy say *that* line!"[562] roared Christopher Plummer after the read-through, leaving a bewildered Peter looking on, while a wrangle over the lines was conducted via gesticulating interpreters. Eventually a consensus was reached. Although the actor was disappointed to lose more of his paltry lines, it was time to create his bloody demise.

Filming that scene was scary, because I was in the square on a horse, surrounded by hundreds of horses, and yet the technology was so lacking compared to today. So, I was waving my sword around and shouting those lines. I had my "wound" underneath the hat, a string attached to the corner of it. I had to fall off the horse, pull the hat off and rip the collar off my jacket which has been *velcroed* on and that hid another "wound" under there, and then the camera panned down to me, isn't that amazing? The most expensive film ever made at the time, and I'm pulling a string on a hat and sliding off a horse!

They were approaching the homestretch as Richard noted in his diary: "Peter Davies finished his scene; so, everyone is heaving sighs of relief and seeing visions of England."[563] The exodus was well under way with both Davies', Ian Ogilvy, Terence Alexander joining Roger Green in the slow, frustrating process of leaving with confusions and complications over travel documents.

A few days later, and Richard and his artillery troop were back for another vignette that would never make the cut.

> Scene.142/3: A French HUSSAR MARBOT appears. *A corridor opens up in the chaos of the battle…* Marbot *gallops forward like a whirlwind.* Mercer and Normyle watch the rider come closer. Wellington and De Lancey speculate: *"A deserter? A traitor?"*

The historic Colonel Marcellin Marbot was one of the most colourful and dashing characters of his epoch. He fought in many of Napoleon's battles, and like a cat with nine lives, found himself in many scraps, with numerous wounds (13 in all) and scars to prove his courage. He almost changed the course of history when his hussar regiment just narrowly missed capturing not only the Tsar of Russia, but also the King of Prussia, at the Battle of Leipzig in 1813. At Waterloo, he commanded the 7th Hussars who were posted at the extreme right of the French lines, and tussled with the advancing Prussians. Surviving the battle, Marbot eventually penned his larger-than-life memoirs, which along with Mercer's, have become some of the most vivid portrayals of the Napoleonic Wars. They were the inspiration for Arthur Conan Doyle's splendid *The Exploits of Brigadier Gerard* stories, for which he paid a gushing tribute to, "the human, the gallant, the inimitable Marbot! His book is that which gives us the best picture by far of the Napoleonic soldiers."[564]

Screenwriter Craig was no doubt referencing both the real and fictional characters by this tiny vignette (he adapted some of Conan Doyle stories for his *The Adventures of Gerard* screenplay, currently filming at the same time).[565] It is based on a curious episode of a single French horseman who inexplicably galloped up to the Allied line; either a deserter, or perhaps a mad display of courage. It must have been one of those strange sights that all battles throw up, which exemplifies how the savagery of war twists the human psyche.

> Scene.145: *Marbot gallops angrily straight towards Wellington and shouts: "The Emperor!"* Then leaving a stunned Wellington, he turns around and gallops back towards the French lines.

The action, which must have involved an impressive exhibition of horsemanship by stuntman and actor Sergio Testori, was captured using multiple cameras, as Richard breezily wrote: "They did a scene with us seeing the French Hussar galloping through the line — two takes and a break for lunch."

This was followed by another bloody "death," not scripted but perhaps created with a wry smile by the director who often fenced History and Art with his monocled, tartan wearing historical advisor. "Ramsey's death scene with Willo's front exploding and bursting French letters (condoms) full of make-up blood — looked very good, but I think it was concocted to show his Waterloo flask."[566] This cherished prop, one might surmise, may have belonged to Willo's ancestor or another soldier upon that "blasted heath" in 1815.

While most wrapped for the day to return to the dubious comforts of the hotel, three actors assembled in the courtyard of the La Haye Sainte set for a night shoot for one of the most fondly remembered scenes in the film.

> Scene.59: Wellington notices something moving in O'Connor's knap-sack, and orders him to open it and revealing a pig, *"You know the punishment for plundering?"* O'Connor has to think fast, *"Stoppage of gin, Sir."* Wellington snaps back: *"Damn you, it is death."*

It is the night before the battle and Wellington along with De Lancey make a tour of the lines — just as O'Connor has liberated a pig. The strict commander enters La Haye Sainte farmhouse and finds his *"old friends — The Enniskillen."* This regiment of mainly rough-and-ready

Irishmen — 27th (Inniskilling) Regiment of Foot, is used to embody Wellington's famous remark of "The very scum of the earth," with Plummer's Wellington commenting wryly: "*I hang and flog more of them than I do the rest of the army.*" Wellington wasn't dubbed The Iron Duke for nothing, being very clear about plundering, or any crimes against the civil population: such infractions were punished with severe chastisement, including death.[567]

> Scene.59: Thinking quickly, O'Connor cooks up a story of how; "*This little pig has lost her way and I'm carrying her home to her relations.*" The absurdity moves his commander to laughter; "*He knows how to defend a hopeless position.*"

In the film, Wellington delivers a punch line: "*Raise him to Corporal!*" It is pure fiction, but as a piece of comedy-drama it is great cinema. Deftly played between Donal Donnelly, who exhibits far more fear facing his commander-in-chief than he does the French, and Christopher Plummer, making it one of the best vignettes in the film.

There is an extension to this scene, which touches on the stress and strain Wellington must have been under. As he and De Lancey leave the relieved O'Connor amid the laughter of his mates, Wellington pauses and says: "*If I fail tomorrow — I hope God will have mercy on me. For nobody else will.*" As the rain dribbles down his face, the mask of command slips and one gets a glimmer of the man beneath. It is a tiny and brief but highly effective later addition to a script that was often bereft of such intimacy. As they finished filming in the small hours of the morning, shivering in the cold and movie rain, the unit was about to get a colourful if brief boost to flagging energy and morale.

From left to right: Unknown, Richard Heffer, Oleg Vidov and Donal Donnelly. © RICHARD HEFFER

Left: Jeffry Wickham as Colbourne. Right: Elaine Plummer wearing Terence Alexander's Lord Uxbridge busby. © RICHARD HEFFER

402　　　　　　　　　WATERLOO — MAKING AN EPIC

Michael Wilding as Ponsonby leads the Scots Greys. He was sitting on the spring-loaded rocking horse on a truck. RON POULTER COLLECTION

The charging Scots Greys, the picture is probably taken from the camera railway wagon that travelled along side the horsemen. AUTHOR'S COLLECTION

The Scots Greys charge towards the French ridge. AUTHOR'S COLLECTION

Sergei Zakhariadze as Marshal Blucher leads his Prussian cavalry at the battle of Ligny. This scene would be used as part of the climax of Waterloo as his army rides to Wellington's rescue. CASPER RÖHRIG COLLECTION

CHAPTER 17

"Give Me Night Or Give Me Blucher."

Scene.34: *Prussian Cavalry charges,* MARSHAL BLUCHER, *a splendid old warrior of seventy-two, is charging, sabre in hand, at the head of the* PRUSSIAN CAVALRY...*he swings his sabre and shouts damnations: "Hell and sulphur to them! The gates of hell to them!"*

It was the third week of September, and the shoot livened up with the arrival of the "Prussians." Led by another People's Artist, in the impressive shape of Sergei Zakhariadze, a 60-year-old actor from the Soviet Republic of Georgia, as Marshal Blucher. He was a replacement for the venerable British actor Trevor Howard, who was in the frame for the role only a few months previously. Whatever the reasons for the new casting, it was an inspired choice for albeit a small role. Zakhariadze arrived with a contingent of fellow gregarious Georgians, who had a healthy disregard for communist rules and liked to enjoy the finer things of life — insisting on the best VIP standard. Overnight, the inedible grey hotel frugality blossomed with an impressive assortment of food and wines from their fecund native state.

In Russia, Zakhariadze was considered an actor of the stature of Laurence Olivier. He had been a leading light in the famed State Vakhtangov Theatre in Moscow, where he played all the great roles from Shakespeare to Pushkin. His *King Lear* was widely considered one of the greatest performed on *any* stage.[568]

Made up to play the 72-year-old Blucher, Zakhariadze was an impressive sight. "Looking magnificent!" as Richard Heffer noted in his diary, "Whiskers, moustache, and huge heavy features — blundering yet massively noble."[569] Nicknamed *Marschall Vorwärts* (Marshal Forwards) by his men for his aggressive approach in battle, Blucher was one of the most colourful characters in an epoch of many larger-than-life warriors. A cavalry commander of zest and energy, he had learnt his craft as a young man under Frederick the Great, Prussia's legendary king who dominated European battlefields during the late eighteenth-century. This Septuagenarian gruff old soldier was driven by an almost pathological hatred of Napoleon and the whole French race.

The crucible for such inveterate rage was the catastrophic defeat of Prussia by Napoleon in 1806. As the once fabled invincible Prussian army streamed in headlong rout following the twin defeats of Jena and Auerstadt, Blucher withdrew his thrashed forces to Lübeck on the Baltic coast. Faced with unavoidable defeat, he was the last Prussian commander to surrender. With Napoleon's reversal of fortunes in 1813, Marshal Forwards was in the forefront of battles that brought the allied armies to the gates of Paris in March 1814. With Napoleon's escape the following year, he was the obvious choice to command Prussian forces in Belgium.

He made no excuse for his lack of understanding of the science of war, as propagated by fellow Prussian Von Clausewitz in his military classic treatise — *On War*. His "head" was his glum Chief of Staff Von Gneisenau, who supervised the strategy and logistics which enabled Blucher to be the star. And star he was with his men and they loved him like a grandfather. From humble beginnings, Blucher had that rare common touch few commanders ever have. By 1815, the years of war had taken a toll on his mental state, which manifested itself by a belief that he was pregnant — with an elephant — as the result of a sexual assault by a French soldier!

This kind of back story is grist to the mill for any actor, and it is probable that Zakhariadze and Bondarchuk discussed this facet of the character. From the brief glimpses of the Georgian in the finished film, it is clear how well the great actor had captured the spirit of Marshal Forwards.

Richard was on set to catch some of it: "Great, open, bluff, heroic, *vast* acting, but somehow convincing! He sounded and looked just like a German and was marvellous to watch, 'full of sound and fury' certainly — but signifying *something*."[570] He snapped a photograph and was pleased when the "No.1 People's Artist of the USSR...gave me a special pose!"[571]

Zakhariadze as Blucher makes his first appearance at the battle of Ligny, leading his cavalry to stem the tide of the French advance. Their charge was very impressive as Richard recalled: "Blucher's Prussian cavalry are terrifying — all black uniforms with charcoal horses, lances, sabres and skull and crossbones on their helmets."[572]

Scene.34: *Suddenly* BLUCHER'S HORSE *is shot under him. He falls in a dizzy whirl. The* HORSE *rolls on him.* BLUCHER *is ridden over by his own Cavalry.*

Blucher's charge and the battle of Ligny would be cut from the film, although some of this action footage would be moved much later in the edit to beef-up the Prussians riding to Wellington's rescue like the proverbial Seventh Cavalry. In the final film, we see a bruised Blucher, recovering from his horse fall, being bandaged and gin applied to his chest as Gneisenau, played by German actor Karl Lipanski, discusses the momentous decision to retreat and combine forces with Wellington.

Scene.38: The thought of retreat enrages the old warrior: *"Have I come all this way to meet that runt of a Frenchman only to run from him?"* Gneisenau does not trust Wellington and wants to retreat to Prussia. Blucher, rubbing gin over his chest, says to desert his allies will bring dishonour. Grabbing his sword, he declares: *"I'm seventy-two and a soldier; this steel is my word. I am too old to break it."*

From the tiny snippets that made the final cut, it's likely the magnificent actor breathed life into the written lines. For once, the sometimes-awkward verbosity of Harry Craig's screenplay found a voice in Zakhariadze acting style.

Scene.38: (Blucher) *"I am the only man alive who can kiss his own head,"* before kissing Gneisenau's forehead, *"This is my head. You are the brains of the army."* (Gneisenau): *"You, Prince Blucher, are its heart."*

As he remounts his horse, Blucher praises Gneisenau, his dour Chief of Staff, and it is easy to imagine how the expansive Georgian would have played it; with all the emotion of a man born on the Steppes. Only a publicity still exists of this latter part of the scene, picturing Zakhariadze on his horse and sporting a bandaged leg. In the finished film, we next see Blucher back in the saddle as he endeavours to boost the morale of his battered army.

At dusk, Richard went to watch one of Bondarchuk's signature sequence shots of the Prussian army retreating after the drubbing by Napoleon at Ligny, (earlier that day they had filmed the Prussians filing out of the woods arriving at Waterloo). Their bruised spirits buoyed by a battered and bruised Blucher on his horse, showing defiance and determination. "The evening shooting with the Prussians was strangely stirring — flags, black uniforms, horses, a moon out, with overturned cannon and burnt tree as a backdrop, and the figure of Blucher smoking a pipe on horseback leading his men who stretch as far as the eye can see in columns of four."[573]

This was one of several sequence shots in the film where a scene is encompassed within a single camera move, in this case, a crane shot. The dawn sequence as described in a previous chapter featuring Mercer and O'Connor was another. While a further one being a similar crane shot of the French army crossing the River Sambre during the night of the ball.

This had been the very first sequence shot in Russia, and took an entire day to prepare around a specially built bridge over the Latoritsa River, near Mukachevo. For cavalryman Mykola Kholodnyak with only two weeks riding training, this had been his first taste of movie-making. Dressed as an Imperial Guard Lancer officer he had joined the entire contingent in costume to make the river crossing.

It was 15 kilometres from the tented city, and the trek across country caused much grumbling from the marching army. One of the foot-sloggers shouted out to Mykola: "Why are you on the horse? And we are walking?" And he replied, with a snooty grin: "Because I'm an *officer* and you are just regular soldiers." No doubt he pretended to ignore the swearing and cursing about "bloody officers" — and there was worse to come.

Camera assistant Daniele Nannuzzi vividly recalled the shot:

> It was almost night. There is an amazing sky — dark and you see a storm; it is raining. Then you see soldiers with cannons moving on the bridge, the crane goes down and you discover the army moving into the water in twilight. It took one day. I mean every shot, such a big scene was always one day of work because we had to prepare the cameras, erect the special effects, the lights because it was night. We have to wait till then. You cannot just arrive at six o'clock for a shoot at eight o'clock — No. You need a day of preparation for moving 18,000 people — it's not so easy.

Mykola was one of the many to get their feet wet as they were required to cross the river multiple times. He was relatively lucky being high on a horse: "But those poor soldiers had to go five, six times, all wet up to their necks through the river, holding their guns above their heads. It was not fun." One can imagine the miserable tramp back to camp with sodden clothes as night drew in.

These shots are time consuming to set up and arrange, but once executed prove to be effective and an economical method of shooting. Bondarchuk had created similar shots in his previous work and clearly liked the sense of immediacy and energy. With the invention of the Steadicam in the late 1970s, these types of shots have become even more dynamic and inventive; but even with their frequency, they still rarely fail to impress.

After ten days, Zakhariadze's star-turn was drawing to a close. With Napoleon's army routed, the exhausted victors meet to congratulate each other. This would be the last scene for both Zakhariadze and Plummer, and probably the Canadian reworked his final few dramatic, if somewhat stiff, lines.

> Scene.227: Blucher meets Wellington amid the ruins of La Belle Alliance to a chorus of cheers. They exchange simple compliments: *"It was hard bargaining, Blucher, all day. Without you it could not have been done."* — *"You have made history for your England today."* Wellington ponders the significance. *"I can't say how history will regard it — as a battle we won, or he lost."*

Historically, the two commanders merely exchanged a few, almost bland pleasantries, in the only language they both shared — French. Blucher's son wrote later to his mother: "Father Blucher embraced Wellington in so hearty a manner, that everyone present said it was the most touching scene that could be imagined."[574] In the script, having shaken hands, Blucher, his blood up, prepares to ride off into the night to chase the retreating French. Before he does, one of his men gives him a souvenir.

> Scene.228: *A party of* PRUSSIAN LANCERS *gallop back up to Blucher with a* TROPHY *on a* LANCE HEAD. *It is Napoleon's* HAT. *Blucher snatches it, "Where is the head?"*

Plummer looked on amused as his ebullient and creative co-star riffed a quite riveting improvisation. The black clad Prussian lancer played by a moustached Vladimir Udalov rides up breathlessly and eagerly jerks the prize towards his commander. Zakhariadze began by spearing the hat with his sword tip and waved it aloft before placing it on his head — back to front. Pulling it off, he rolled and shook it around a few turns. At that point, he ramped up the show by smelling it with a gutsy inhale before wincing at the imagined stench, then crunching it with his teeth. Gnawing it like a rabid wolf for a few moments, sated, he grimaced. To the excitement of the gathered extras, he concluded with a magnificent flourish as the battered hat sailed through the air into the watching ranks. German actor Karl Lipanski recalled the guttural roar that filled the air, as many hands attempted to catch the battered trophy.

When Bondarchuk yelled "*Schtop!*" the scene was over but the white-haired actor, one of the greatest Lear's, made a suitably extravagant curtain-call: "Zakhariadze gave a farewell speech to the soldiers — even as far as throwing flowers from his podium."[575]

Next day, Plummer and Jeffry Wickham left for home with a poignant parting, as Richard noted: "dreadful farewell — kissed on both cheeks by Chris P." With a dwindling cast — it was "a very gloomy evening."[576] Not helped by the police imposing a town arrest, reinforcing the sense of desolation for the dwindling garrison.

It was the last week of September, with autumn just around the corner. Dan O'Herlihy as Marshal Ney who had arrived way back in June, was getting to play his last scenes as the battle turns against the French. "Dan was being Ney all over the place — leading cavalry and infantry attacks — and with 800 horsemen it was a beautiful sight." Richard, armed with a Hasselblad camera, was drafted to help with taking some publicity pictures — it was hot work: "I nearly killed myself taking photos of the charging cavalry from in front, I only just managed to get out of the way!"[577]

A few days later, and work didn't get going until halfway through the day; "when the director condescended to appear! (Soldiers are up at 6 a.m.) Mad day — nothing done apart from cavalry and Ney going around in concentric circles surrounded by dense smoke and huge fire-balls; (no-one died!)" He ended the day's diary entry with "felt really fed up."[578]

On another day, his camera skills were put to further use when he agreed to assist Peter Mitchell, one of the newly arrived unit publicity photographers, who was determined to get the most dramatic pictures possible — they both got more than they bargained for.

> I busied myself by becoming Peter's assistant, and shot on the Nikon with electronic motor-wind during the charges; the first one, I got showered with mud, and the second nearly killed Peter and myself! — we were lying underneath a gun carriage while 900

horses charged at a full gallop towards us — but the dust from the first five waves of riders blinded the others, and some horses careered straight into our gun-carriage knocking us, and the carriage back six foot. Luckily, I had the presence of mind to drop the camera and grab an axle of the gun axle, while dust covered our equipment, and hooves missed us by millimetres! — Though Peter got hit on the knee! Shaken, we picked ourselves up and went back to the camera truck.

Later, his nerves settled once more gave Richard the chance to change sides, and play the star as he "was called up to feed Dan (O'Herlihy) some lines in a close-up of Ney — so I found myself playing Napoleon after all!" This extra shot is a good example of a "pickup," when during filming the script twists and turns and the need for small but vital extra shots becomes apparent. The author could not determine what this scene might have been, or even if it made the final cut. Richard's onset "feed" dialogue would have been replaced by Rod Steiger during "looping," which will be discussed in the following chapter.

Richard ends his entry with: "long day with evening shots of Ney…very dirty and tired."[579] These would probably have been part of the sequence depicting the repulse of the Old Guard with Ney, on foot, frantically attempting to stem the tide of the rout: *"Stand with me!…One more hour and we have them beaten!"*

The cameraman, Armando Nannuzzi, liked to film in the appropriate evening light, using a very large aperture to catch the last rays of the sun, which blurred the background into a surreal jumble of chaos. To extenuate the frenetic tumult, he opted to use a hand-held camera swirling around Dan O'Herlihy's Ney as he berates the fleeing troops: *"Don't you know me? I'm Ney, Marshal of France!"*

The following evening and a night shoot, with Richard keeping Donal as Private O'Connor company back on La Haye Sainte farmhouse set "armed with book, camera, backgammon and Mackintosh," for the action required rain and lots of it, making it cold and miserable. The scene, which takes place immediately before O'Connor's close shave with Wellington, involved the plundering Private losing his pig and bumping into a French sentry played by Italian actor Andrea Checchi amid no-man's-land.

Scene.57: O'Connor stumbles and loses his pig in the darkness, scrabbling after the runaway he comes face to face with — the French Old Guardsman Sauret — holding his plunder. The two face off before Sauret returns it and in exchange, O'Connor offers tobacco *with some by-play of exaggerated courtesy. Suddenly O'Connor runs at Sauret, who snaps into a position of defence.* The Irishman turns his face in profile and with a wink; "*So that tomorrow…if ye see me.*"

There was a sharp autumnal nip in the air that night, but at least the scenic dressed "fires everywhere kept the cold away." The animal co-star had its own interpretation of the action as "Donal chased his pig around for a few takes." This scene was another not to make the cut which seems a shame; although it's possible, albeit fleeting existence, is discussed in a later chapter. Even in the script, these two warriors were never destined to face off the following day in what should have been a narrative payoff. As we have seen, O'Connor met his fate by cannon fire, and Sauret is almost invisible in the final edit.

Considered something of a colourful character off screen, Andrea Checchi was also lost that long, chilly night: "after he played the scene, went inside a camper van, and he fell asleep." Recalled fellow Italian Daniele Nannuzzi of this popular figure: "The owner of the camper van closed the door and locked it, not knowing he was inside. And he woke up later, alone on the battlefield for the entire night while everyone was looking for him — always the same with Andrea Checchi." Meanwhile, a weary, cold crew arrived back at the hotel at 3 a.m. and found that "all the De Laurentiis horde had arrived."[580]

With the arrival of the "management" there was a tangible sense of impatience and desire to wrap up "The Mighty Project." There was frustration at the slower working speed of the Soviets, who appeared nonplussed with the financial demands of Western capitalist filmmaking. There is little anecdotal information as to the working relationship between director and producer, so one must conclude it was cordial and professional but lacking that extra creative synergy that was enjoyed with Fellini.

Once hired, Dino would leave his directors alone, and that seems true on this film too. In an interview, Bondarchuk acknowledged how he was given "complete freedom" by his producer (see Chapter Nineteen). It was said if he liked your face, whether an actor, writer or director, then you got the work. Film historian John Walsh, who has written a book about Dino's later *Flash Gordon* (1980), explained: "It's kind of an Italian superstition that you can kind of trust a man by his face. It wasn't about having a pretty face or anything, it was if he thought your face was sympathetic. Dino wouldn't get on an airplane if he looked at the pilot and didn't like their face."[581] One can assume he liked the Russian's face.

Whether out of a desire to crack the whip or to scratch a creative urge, Dino lent a hand by directing some scenes with the second unit: "I personally shot the most beautiful cavalry charge,"[582] he boasted later. In these last few weeks of filming, he must have reflected that this colossal production represented a watershed in his career. He confided to his production designer, Mario Garbuglia, that he was putting Dinocittà up for sale.

For the remaining cast and crew, at least they were all in the last stretch and itching to get home. The arrival of Irina Skobtseva, the director's glamorous wife for her small scenes, annoyed Richard as it delayed him going home: "Total gloom and despair — raved with Memo (Guglielmo Ambrosi, the production manager), because they are shooting Mrs Bondarchuk tomorrow and not me! And the reason is to finish Sauret (Andrea Checchi)!"[583]

The night before the battle, and the crowd of humanity try to keep themselves dry from the storm; Sauret, the Old Sweat, takes pity on some drummer boys.

> Scene.54: Like a father, Sauret watches over two DRUMMER BOYS sleeping beside their drums. One BOY wakes up shivering, and Sauret shows a veteran's trick for keeping warm: "*The old trick of Russia…The Cossack fires, they'd be all around…and us, we'd be icicles. Warm up, boy.*" *The boy warms his hands energetically.*

Amidst this sea of testosterone huddling in the rain-swept fields was a lone woman; Irina Skobtseva, playing the only female character on the movie battlefield. A striking blonde beauty with luminous blue eyes, Irina was one of the leading Soviet actresses of her day, memorably playing the doomed Desdemona to her future husband's brooding Othello in *Otello* (1955). With its director, Sergei Yutkevich, winning the Best Director award at the 1956 Cannes Film Festival, Irina captured the hearts of the prestigious French event by being named its "Miss Charm." While such an award may seem excruciatingly dated today, it reflects the strong impact she made in her cinematic debut.

She would consolidate her perception as a romantic heroine, with the film adaptation of Leonid Leonov's play *The Ordinary Man* (1956), playing Cyrus, followed by Klavdia Nikolaevna in *Unrepeatable Spring* (1957).

No doubt keen to display her versatility, she proved to be an equally adept comedic actress in Eldar Ryazanov's *Zigzag of Success* (1969).

Marrying Sergei in 1959, at the time of the *Waterloo* filming she was a full-time mum to Fedor, just two-years-old, and seven-year-old Elena (she would die aged just 47 of cancer in 2009). She had played another wife in a doomed, albeit divorce this time, on-screen marriage to Bondarchuk, as Helene in *War and Peace*. She would appear in every one of her husband's subsequent films, although her appearance in *Waterloo* is a moot point.

Cast as Maria, a *Cantiniere*, these were uniformed French camp followers carried out several duties from cooking to rudimentary nursing, some fifty years before Florence Nightingale and her "Angels" would administer similar care to the British Army. In an almost exclusively male environment, these ladies would often offer more *personal* charms!

> Scene.53: *Under a crude tent — two blankets held up by a musket and a knap-sack —* MARIA *is sleeping in the arms of the Grenadier,* CHACTAS...MARIA'S *hair is spread over* CHACTAS' *cheek. His breath stirs her hair.*

Gennadi Yudin, a Russian actor, played Chactas, another grizzled Old Guardsman; he, like Andrea Checchi, is reduced to fleeting glimpses. A publicity still shows Maria, slightly dishevelled, in the back of a cart with a drummer boy eating while talking to Yudin as Chactas. It is probable that the two previous scene extracts above were combined into a new one to show Maria's maternal nurturing instincts. Richard caught fleeting glimpses as he watched the filming: "only a couple of takes of the scenes — Drummer boys and Maria, the French positions at night, English fires, etc."[584]

In the screenplay, Maria makes one more brief appearance during the bloody attack on Hougoumont, where she and the drummer boys attend to the wounded. This may have echoed a similar, quite moving scene in John Wayne's magnum opus *The Alamo* (1960), where following a failed bloody assault on the defenders of the adobe mission, the field is littered with Mexican dead. Wayne eschews his often-overt conservative politics, allowing instead the sensitive artist to the surface. He shows shawl-covered women tending to the wounded, including a mournful shot of an old woman crossing herself that beautifully and cinematically underlines the futility and waste of war. What Bondarchuk did with this scene is sadly unknown as not only it, but his wife's entire contribution, never made it beyond the cutting-room. But not entirely.

Another rare still exists that suggests "Maria" may have had a tiny subplot throughout the film. It shows Irina in costume with her arms around her on-screen lover, Ghennady Yudin as Chactas, while a glum Andrea Checchi looks on, perhaps hoping to share the "bounty." In full Old Guard uniforms, they appear to all be standing in the Italian town of Oriolo Romano, which stood in for Grenoble for Napoleon's return from exile. In the film, the town square is packed with not only cheering townspeople but soldiers, too. Despite careful viewing, none of the three appear, but the above still suggests they were involved in the shoot that day. Two scenes later, we finally see Mrs Bondarchuk.

Following Orson Welles' moribund exit from the Palace de Tuileries, filmed at Caserta in Naples (see Chapter Eight), there is a sharp cut to the same staircase bulging with cheering crowds to welcome Napoleon. As his coach makes its way through the throng, sitting on top is a raven-haired lady in a rust red dress, waving her arms in delirium and exhorting the crowd. This is Irina Skobtseva as Maria. Moments later, as Steiger climbs out of his coach and is carried aloft up the stairs, there is a hand-held point-of-view shot of the enthusiastic crowd. Amongst them, and only for a few frames, is again, Maria.

Was there a tiny scene of the loyal camp follower reunited with her lover in Grenoble and then joining Napoleon's band as it entered Paris in triumph? There are no clues in the script, but as Irina accompanied her husband during his long stay in Italy preparing the film, perhaps he liked the idea of embedding his wife's character in the story long before the battle scene. Maria's deletion from the male top-heavy cast has always disappointed the author but at least we have a tiny glimpse of her.

Despite the existence of these two stills, we have no idea of what this feminine touch may have brought to the *Waterloo* battlefield. A tiny clue may be gleaned when her husband cast Irina again in a similar small role in his next film, *They Fought for Their Country / Oni srazhalis za rodinu* (1975). A war film set amid the carnage of the Eastern Front in 1942, where her glamorous blonde beauty, clad in battlefield nurse's outfit, looks incongruous against the grimy, dishevelled Red Army soldiers. Perhaps a forgivable foible: a husband desiring his wife to look her best.

Even in her nineties, Irina was still an impressive figure as Joan Borsten Vidov found when she interviewed the venerable actress for a documentary about her late husband, Oleg Vidov, at her dacha on the outskirts of Moscow in 2019. "She was one of those very special women produced by a now bygone era of film and theatre and the arts, that co-existed with a cruel system of government that did not value the individual. Russia doesn't make them like Irina Skobtseva anymore. I was happy to get the chance to meet her."[585]

Irina Skobtseva died aged 93 in 2020

Back on that cold autumnal night in 1969, Richard, returning to the hotel, was given the long hoped-for final call-sheet, and home: "I hope, I hope, I hope…"[586]

On the last day of September, Richard joined Willo Gray, costumed as fellow artillery Captain Ramsey for their concluding scenes; another night shoot starting at 7 p.m. With dusk drawing in, having spent the previous six hours just waiting, Bondarchuk scrapped a tiny insert shot of Mercer smoking a cigar, saying he "was only shooting the 'soup' one. So Willo and I re-wrote it."

The setting was the evening before the big battle as the heavens open and rain cascades down upon the poor benighted troops. Mercer and fellow artillery officers, Normyle and Ramsey, try to drink soup under a makeshift shelter, while they discuss their chances of surviving the violent morrow.

> Scene.60: Mercer estimates that: *"forty thousand of us are sure to die tomorrow." Normyle, testing the thickness — lifts out and pours back a spoon of soup.* An annoyed Ramsey tells him to eat up: *"it might well be your last supper."*

It is unlikely any officer not connected to the General Staff would have known the forces involved or even cared. The intention, perhaps too on-the-nose, was to make it clear the size of the armies involved and the obvious trepidation at the prospect of so much violence. Shooting the scene at night, the actors were doused with water that added to the discomfort. "It was *very* bad; I was soaked, and too busy thinking of home to concentrate properly! Besides, it will probably never appear."[587] He was right — it didn't. Although a variant of the dialogue, which was probably the actors' rewrite, can be heard over Mercer's spectacular dawn shaving scene as already described. The voices are the later re-recording artists in London, who supplied many noises-off ad-libs: "*We're 140,000 men. We're not the half of it. That's counting the French as well. 40,000 will be dead tomorrow. Eat your soup while you've got your belly.*"

As Bondarchuk called "*Schtop!*" Richard was free to go — if he could sort out his passport and ticket "couldn't believe it was happening — very shaky, tearful journey to the border."[588]

A day later, and he was back in London, but less than happy to find someone sleeping in his room: "Livid!" Taken in by friends, he was pleased to hear he had "lots of work in the offing, and good news of everybody." Decompressing, he "described Uzhgorod — and on the strength of which Adza (his agent) promptly took me off to a steak house and I gorged myself on steak and Brussels sprouts and wine!" Reacclimatising to home he found he "had stopped travelling mentally and physically for the first time in months."[589]

Back at "Batty-Poo," the last scenes to be shot were the final defeat and retreat of the French. The standing sets were set alight as the last remnants of Napoleon's Old Guard are huddled in a square surrounded by British guns and cavalry. It is filmed against the dying sun as it dips behind the distant hills.

> Scene.221: (Cambronne) *"Stand and form square. Form square."*
> *The* MEN, *including* SAURET *and* CHACTAS, *stop and face about. A* SQUARE *begins to take shape — resolute, silent and final.*

Igor Starchenko, one of the Old Guard extras, remembered a very steady hand. While pyrotechnics were exploding behind their backs, the camera was being pushed on tracks only a metre and a half in front of them. Starchenko and his fellow soldiers were firing their guns (with blanks) straight at the moving camera. The cameraman and his assistant both looked unnerved by the smoke and noise. The soldier remembered that the assistant, whose job was to control the lens for zooming and focusing, was visibly shaking. Yet his hand twisting the lens calmly "did what it needed to do."[590]

That hand was almost certainly young Daniele Nannuzzi, who was a focus-puller:

> I remember perfectly the scene of the Old Guard. They fired on us, of course, with fake bullets, but small splinters of material came on us. Only our eyes were protected with plastic glasses. Every scene was dangerous. When that mass went forward, between shootings, bombs and explosions, anything could happen. Ours was a dangerous job, but it had to be done.

> Scene.235: LONG SHOT *of the* LAST SQUARE. *A column of smoke collects in the sky above the Square. A red evening sun finds colours in the smoke.*

With the fighting over and the standing sets just burnt-out husks, the stricken field was strewn with most of the extras lying around playing "dead" by which the director sort to convey something of the slaughter.

> "But 52,000 men died at Waterloo," an enterprising journalist pointed out. "Would not that number give a more historically accurate picture of Waterloo's dead?" — "No, the camera cannot physically encompass that many bodies," Bondarchuk replied and then, with a twinkle in his eye, added, "But 18,000 still makes a greater spectacle than 2,000 or 3,000 which is all that Hollywood would have been able to afford if they had done this film."[591]

To extenuate the horrors of war, film extra Mykola Kholodnyak recalled how physically handicapped men, some without a leg, or an arm, were recruited from local villages. They were strewn across the field, dressed in ripped French uniforms with sleeves frayed and their faces smeared in red paint. Seeing these "wounded" soldiers crawling around and shouting in "agony" amid many horses covered in paint, sleeping off their slugs of vodka, appeared very real to Mykola: "it was scary to look at. And since these were night shootings, it intensified the eerie effect."[592]

There were three options available to film these scenes. First, to shoot during the day and use a dark blue filter to suggest night, known as "Day for Night" or more poetically "*La Nuit américaine*," was a widely used technique. Alternatively, to shoot at night would have been extremely impractical, as it would have required a huge number of lights to illuminate such a wide area.

Instead, Armando Nannuzzi opted for the most realistic but time-limited option — filming at twilight, as his son explained:

> At the end of the battle, when Wellington rides on his horse in the twilight, there are 20,000 dead bodies, horses, smoke, mud, blood with Wellington looking very sad. For me, this is a miracle of cinematography by my father. Can you imagine how to shoot it? Because the light is just five or six minutes. Over a few days we made just one shot at twilight. The light was only good for 10 minutes before there is night. We choose to shoot in twilight because it was impossible to light it. Also, its sadder — it is grey and blue.

With Plummer departed, Wellington would have been portrayed by his stand-in for the long shots.

Scene.230: CLOSE ON WELLINGTON. *He is shocked. As he moves, he looks down on the dead, as if he were paying them the honour of a review.*

Before we leave the battlefield, let us end with a vignette of the "dead" — Igor Starchenko as a fallen Old Guardsman. They were all covered with "blood" which he described as "a nasty brown liquid"[593] before being sprinkled with soot and ash. Then Wellington and his retinue rode slowly past, surveying the carnage in the moonlight. Perhaps nothing better sums up the movie make-believe than the stand-in moon.

This celestial object was, of course, on everyone's mind during the summer of 1969. Daniele Nannuzzi had been tasked with creating the mournful orb:

> There's a special silver paper for front projection — 3M — like shark skin. You put one light on it and it reflects it ten times brighter. I remember that we made the moon not round as it would look fake, but just one quarter less. And with blue ink, I made some spots as moon craters. And then we suspended the moon with a crane with one wire on top and two wires left and right, otherwise the moon would be moving. And then we put just one little projector light onto the moon. It was nice work.

To complete the illusion, smoke was fanned past it to simulate clouds floating across the darkened sky.

After 28 weeks, with autumn closing in and the threat of a Russian winter just around the corner, the production drew to a close. Heinz Feldhaus, who had been employed since the very beginning, wrapped in the middle of October.

> My last day was 14 October 1969. I think they did some close-ups or something, but basically the film was finished. When I drove back, they (border guards) took my car in bits and pieces, because they thought I was smuggling things out. They took all the sides of the car, everything out to look if anything is

hidden behind. It was a hard experience, but one I wouldn't like to have missed.

As the cast and crew departed, some soldiers stayed until the first week of December. Mykola Kholodnyak was one of those huddled nine to a tent, attempting to keep warm next to a small stove. The reason — another epic film was shooting in the vicinity: *The Flight / Beg* (1970), which incidentally starred *War and Peace* actress, Lyudmila Saveleva.

Eventually that too was completed, and the last remnants of the movie army up-sticks and marched away. By then the set had been handed back to the locals, complete with the irrigation system used to create mud. Soon the farmers reclaimed the land and tilled the soil for the next year's crop of potatoes.

Fifty years later, although the main highway from Uzhgorod has been widened and improved, there are still traces of a "field in Belgium" amid the Ukraine landscape. The tracks hewed out by Russian army bulldozers in 1968 are still visible, albeit smothered in undergrowth. Perhaps the most striking feature that still stands as a memorial to that summer of movie make-believe is the valley, man-made by Soviet Engineers, on the orders of an Italian who, without fear of hyperbole, had "moved mountains."[594]

Two cut scenes of the battle of Ligny. Above: While leading his charge, Blucher (Sergei Zakhariadze) is unhorsed, as his men gallop past him. Below: After he is saved from the battlefield, the film shows him issuing the vital order to withdraw to Wavre. This is the deleted conclusion of the scene. With his leg now bandaged, Blucher remounts his horse and exhorts his men to fight on. CASPER RÖHRIG COLLECTION

Left: Filmed in one shot at dusk, Sergei Bondarchuk (at left) and Armando Nannuzzi (at right) prepare to use the camera crane for the Prussians retreat from Ligny. Right: Prussian hussars. © RICHARD HEFFER

Sergei Zakhariadze as Marshal Blucher rides amid his army. © RICHARD HEFFER

Another cut scene: Blucher with his victorious Prussians amid the ruins of La Belle Alliance about to meet Wellington. CASPER RÖHRIG COLLECTION

A cavalryman (Vladimir Udalov) excitedly gives Blucher Napoleon's hat. Sergei Zakhariadze apparently riffed an extraordinary performance with the prop. CASPER RÖHRIG COLLECTION

Irina Skobtseva, the director's wife, is another casualty of the cutting room. Here she is dressed as Maria, flanked by her "lover" Gennadi Yudin as Chactas, and Andrea Checchi as Sauret. This was taken in Oriolo Romano and suggests there may have been a planned subplot between the characters. Neither of these three are visible in the final scene. MOSFILM STUDIO ARCHIVE/COURTESY OF FILMS BY JOVE

The night before the battle, Maria mothers a drummer boy (Vladimir Levchenko) whilst talking to Gennadi Yudin as Chactas. These three do not share a scene in the script, and this on-set still suggests it was reworked before filming — and later cut. CASPER RÖHRIG COLLECTION

Richard Heffer as Mercer (left), along with Willo Gray as Ramsey (in vest) discuss with Bondarchuk how to do their "soup" scene. Notice the fire engine hoses for the "movie rain." © RICHARD HEFFER

Deleted "soup" scene. Ramsey, Mercer and Normyle in the rain while discussing their chances of surviving the battle to come. © RICHARD HEFFER

De Lancey played by Ian Ogilvy is hit by an exploding shell. His gruesome makeup is one of the film's rare depictions of the "horrors of war." How much to show was just one of many discussions had during the editing stage. RON POULTER COLLECTION

CHAPTER 18

"This One's Going To Take Careful Timing..."

"The notion of directing a film is the invention of critics — the whole eloquence of cinema is achieved in the editing room."

WALTER MURCH, Editor; *Apocalypse Now!* (1979)

"Editing is where movies are made or broken. Many a film has been saved, and many a film has been ruined in the editing room."

JOE DANTE, Director; *Gremlins* (1984)

All the effort to "move mountains" was eventually coiled up tightly in hundreds of metal cans, stored in a deep vault beneath Rome's Technicolor laboratory. The uncut negative would have to wait many months before the final, unalterable decision would be taken to cut it into a movie. Firstly, the 35mm raw footage would be winnowed down and precisely honed after countless hours of trial and error, accepting or rejecting every frame of film.

Overseeing this task was an American editor, Richard C. Meyer. After his work was done, he wrote a very long and detailed article for *The Cinemeditor*, which gives a fascinating glimpse into the work-flow of a major feature-film of the time. It is also the most important document in the myth regarding a much longer cut.

Meyer had begun his career in the burgeoning US TV industry of the early 1950s, before gravitating towards B movies with such lurid titles as: *The Wild Party* (1956), *Undersea Girl* (1957), *Reform School Girl* (1957) and *Hot Rod Rumble* (1957). Amongst these, he edited two films for A-list director Anthony Mann: *God's Little Acre* and *Men in War*, both in 1957.

Much of the 1960s saw Meyer return to work on TV shows like *Iron Horse*, before resuming feature-film work with *Winning* (1968) and co-editing *Butch Cassidy and the Sundance Kid (1969)*, a commercial and critically successful western, for which he was awarded a BAFTA for Best Editing.[595]

Meyer, who by then had over forty credits to his name, had no idea who had suggested him to Dino for *Waterloo*. They had only met briefly in 1950, when the Italian was exploring working with more Hollywood-trained personnel. In September 1969, Meyer arrived at Dinocittà in Rome and prepared to start work on the most complex film of his career. The two men soon established an effective working partnership built on mutual respect; Meyer enthused about his employer:

> He is without a doubt the most fascinating individual I have ever met in this business; working and fighting with him was the most unforgettable experience of my life. It was exhausting, frustrating, extremely exhilarating, all at the same time…I was given complete freedom of expression, responsible only to Dino De Laurentiis. This kind of relationship makes working a pleasure to start with, especially on a picture as difficult and complicated.[596]

With the producer often busy on simultaneous projects, he came to rely heavily on Meyer, whose duties extended beyond supervising editor to becoming a surrogate producer. As a recognition of his trust and dedication, Meyer would be credited as Associate Executive Producer.

On most movies, the editor is engaged from the start of the shoot. This allows material to be assessed for either technical issues or structural questions. By the time Meyer started at Dinocittà, the last scenes were being shot in Russia. There had been a small Russian editing team (led by Yelena Mikhajlova) during the shoot, but it surprised him to find that only "part of it had been roughly assembled (approximately nine hours), but almost no real editing had been done when I started work." He was also amazed at the relatively small amount of footage that had been printed (usually just the "takes" the director is happy with) for editing, just three-hundred-thousand feet, which equated to about 55 hours. He had expected near a million feet, considering that most of the action scenes had been covered with five cameras, and often up to three for simpler dialogue ones.

In these digital days, it is easy to forget the issues that constrained analogue post-production. Today it is possible for anyone to make a feature film; shooting on an i-phone and editing on a laptop. At any point in the process a film can be rendered out complete with a reasonably polished soundtrack to complement images, carefully colour matched, with even an array of special effects. It is important to remember how different this was with analogue film post production. Until the camera negative was cut and a print made from it, combined with a soundtrack that emerged from a long and expensive incubation period, a viewable film didn't really exist on almost any practical level.

Before we dive into this vital part of moviemaking, it is worth giving an outline of the post-production process. Exposed camera footage would be sent to the laboratory for processing, but only the "takes" that the director deemed worthy would be printed to a positive copy known as "rushes/dailies." Vitally important for identifying any piece of film are the edge-numbers, every 16 frames, that are manufactured into the original negative and automatically printed onto the "rushes." During the cutting process, the work-print would become marked with scratches and dirt, but none of this damage mattered while the edge-numbers were readable. This would allow the camera negative to be conformed to match the work-print, which would then be used to make the release prints. Cutting the delicate and all-important negative was *only* done when the "final cut" had been signed off as "picture lock," as two frames were irrecoverably lost on each splice.

One of the first major decisions taken was to harmonise the work flow, as Meyer explained: "There was at one time an attempt at a Russian version alongside my so-called 'international' one, but this was soon discarded and a single version, much shorter than the usual long Russian film, was agreed upon." Nevertheless, a rumour has persisted regarding a longer cut, but the preceding lines must convincingly sink this theory. The myth that has grown up will be discussed in a following chapter.

As Meyer began work, he was concerned how to build a creative relationship with Bondarchuk as neither of them shared a language. Much as he had achieved with Steiger, the director used his thespian talent to "act out his ideas and to see almost exactly what he means to say, with only an occasional glance at the interpreter for clarification, and occasionally some literal translation." They were also helped by "an extremely intelligent Italian lady who translated not words but meanings and even emotions... This was especially valuable in our initial discussions about philosophy, music, literature and concepts of motion picture making."

But, as Meyer noted, the biggest barrier between them was ideological: "a completely different set of cinematographic values, which had to be reconciled to arrive at a picture." Bondarchuk would work with his small Russian editing crew, making a rough assembly of a scene before handing it over to Meyer to "do the styling." This unusual method, by Hollywood standards, created a "first cut of the picture was really a well-paced and styled cut, which was then the basis of discussion for subsequent lifts and changes."

Vital to keeping track of everything that had been filmed, particularly the dialogue changes and additional scenes, was Elvira D'Amico, who had been the location script and continuity supervisor.

> She literally remembered every camera of every take and the action and dialogue on each of them, even when there were different versions. After a few days of getting used to each other, I literally could trust her to the extent of not even looking at the film, which she said would not fit into the pattern of what I was trying to do. In addition, she was a marvellous sounding-board and also came up with countless brilliant and original ideas of her own, which were happily incorporated into the picture.

Although editing processes will vary from project to project, the usual procedure is first to do a "rough cut" of all the scenes shot faithfully following the screenplay, as this is usually done while the director is busy filming. These cuts are almost always very long and flabby, but few resemble *Waterloo*'s first epic pass through the cutting-room. "When I saw the five-hour first cut," recalled Meyer, "my guess was that the optimum length of the picture should be about two hours and ten minutes, which horrified everyone at the time because epics are supposed to be very long."

Quite what would have made the cut so long, Meyer does not discuss. It is likely that the immense battle sequences were assembled to run in real-time. This would have been to help the editing team get a sense of the material, and assess how best to cut it down. Looking through the 1968 script (see appendix), it is apparent how little *didn't* make the screen, and most of the deleted scenes are short, almost vignettes. We have seen through Richard Heffer's diary (and anecdotally from Philippe Forquet) that extra scenes, not in the original script, were added during filming, but on the evidence of the five that survived, they are tiny additions. It seems inconceivable that they would have substantially elongated the running time.

Meyer's assessment of the optimum length suggests there was a lot of narrative deadwood: "The creative dialogue on the editing of the picture was mostly theoretical and very general. The specific work was left to be done in a very modern and 'Western' fashion, a great tribute to the flexibility of the director."

Work progressed with several editors being assigned different scenes to work on, all co-ordinated by the First Assistant Editor Vanio Amici, whose job was to keep track of all changes. Their initial deadline was a screening for executives from Paramount and Columbia Pictures at the end of January 1970. It must have been a very busy, and short, Christmas holiday for the editing team as they strove to make the deadline. Dino, clearly proud of his big production, sent reams of festive cards to all and sundry; very large with a suitably appropriate holiday image of peace and love — a colourful still of one of the spectacular movie battle scenes!

In those early weeks of the New Year, it seems a prodigious amount of effort was spent into getting a version ready, complete with a temporary soundtrack. Movie audio has always been complex and time-consuming to create; balancing dialogue with a multitude of sound effects, and music — all mixed to create atmosphere and narrative clarity. In the analogue days, it required many sound editors to assemble the thousands of pieces of audio ready for the re-recording mixer.

This process is not usually begun until after a signed off "picture lock," which forms the anchor around which the entire sound work pivots to ensure everything remains synchronised. As the purpose of this special viewing would have been to reach a consensus for the "final cut," the presented version was far from finished, and most of the sound work would have to be repeated.

To compound the problem facing Meyer's editors:

> …was that much of the dialogue of the principal actors was unintelligible because of sound recording problems. Also, much of the English dialogue spoken by Russian and other foreign actors was unintelligible because of their lack of knowledge of the language…it became necessary to do a quick post-sync session, which I did with an enormously talented actor, Robert Rietty, who came from London to Rome for two days.

For any fans of this cinematic era, the voice of Robert Rietty is ubiquitous, and makes him one of the most prolific actors in film history. During the 1960s there was a boom in European films made for the international market, consequently hundreds of non-English speaking actors needed to be dubbed; Robert Rietty was often the solution.

Rietty, born to Italian parents who settled in England, was a child prodigy; treading the boards at nine-years-old, and later becoming a prolific playwright and translator of Italian work for the British stage. Discovering a particular talent for mimicry, Rietty found ready work dubbing other actor's voices. Amongst his most notable work: *Thunderball* (1965), replacing the heavy thick Italian accent of actor Adolfo Celi; Tetsurō Tamba in *You Only Live Twice* (1967), and Gregory Peck's handful of German lines in *Guns of Navarone* (1961).

Rietty described his work: "sometimes the director will be happy with the physical performance on the screen of an actor but not like his voice, in which case one has a great deal of license in changing everything." There was one job, he recalled many years later, that stood out as a supreme faith in his abilities: "sometimes directors get carried away with themselves, and it reaches an exaggerated state where in, for example, *Waterloo*, I ended up there in 98 different voices."[597]

Meyer says the figure was eighty-five, including a few lines of the principal actors, but regardless of the exact figure, there is no denying the enormity of Rietty's job. The process was known as "looping" and involved two hundred separate "loops" of about 30 seconds of noisy on-set audio. Each one would roll continuously (with the corresponding film section as a guide) through a tape player while the recorder ran an identical loop of virgin magnetic stock. This painstaking process was the "stage" upon which Rietty would perform, trying to mimic the voice intonation while matching the lips. Meyer was in awe of this *tour de force*: "…with Robert changing voices in mid-loop at times, at other times recording one loop six or seven times to get in voices of all actors. It was the most remarkable session of its kind I have ever experienced."

One actor that needed to be re-voiced was Jack Hawkins, who, as we have seen, had lost his larynx because of cancer. For several years, Robert Rietty leant his voice to help the great actor maintain his career.

> As long as he mimed a sentence and merely used his lips without any sound at all, he could sustain a whole line…But to do that he had to gulp air, swallow and then burp it from the stomach, and in that burp formulate two or three words. But he couldn't sustain more than that before closing his lips and going through this action again, and it meant that after every three or four words there was this movement of the shoulders and closing his lips…it was very tough to disguise that or add little sounds to link words.

Rietty remembers one recording session when the veteran actor came in to watch his "voice": "It was nerve-racking for me and when I'd finished, they said, 'Well Jack, what do you think?' And very charmingly he said: 'Well (gulp) I'm (gulp) speechless.'"[598]

With all the dialogue re-recorded, Meyer and his team prepared their "preview" version. This would require making a "Temp Dub," a rough sound mix, which as a film editing contemporary, Alan Jones, recalled "was always a headache as the cutting copy had normally been re-ordered several times!"[599] Something of the hectic rush involved is evident from Meyer's account of his crew's feverish activity:

> We had to do another quick mix, preserving as much as possible of the — by now — very chopped up temporary music and effects sections, plus some original dialogue by the principal actors, plus all those many loops we had recorded temporarily, in order to try to come up with a sound that would impart the feeling of the mood of the picture. It was done, often without rehearsals, in one day, with one single English mixer in an Italian dubbing studio. It was very good. We had now arrived at what would officially be called the first cut which was shown to the distributors.

Meyer recalls being slightly disconcerted by the executives' response: "Strangely enough, the comments were much more concerned with historical accuracy than with the impact of the picture on audiences and their reaction." He noted there were discussions about the causal link between Napoleon's defeat and the rise of Prussia, to the final catastrophe of Hitler: "There were even several comments and suggestions how this could be shown symbolically at the end." It appears the screening resembled more of a university common room than a Hollywood executives suite, as Meyer was "amazed" how many people "of balanced judgement" were still "hung up" about the battle and its significance. "All this carried us a little bit beyond what we tried to do and would stir even more controversy than the film will undoubtedly do already." Meyer was concerned that many of these issues beyond the film, would not equally preoccupy the critics upon release.

Meyer does not mention the running-time, and his article is confusing over the description of the "first cut," which he uses to describe that early five-hour assembly, *and* this preview version. It seems inconceivable that Dino would have invited the distributors to view anything much longer than three hours. Films with long running times have always been tougher to exhibit, as they limit the number of screenings per day.

Academic historical questions aside, this preview would have resulted in a consensus and allowed Meyer and his team to work towards a final version. "In many ways our 'first cut' was far better than many things that were tried in the intermediate stages before we arrived at a final cut." Again, it is not clear to which "first cut" he refers, but one must assume he means the executive's cut as above.

> The "first cut" was essentially the work of one point of view, whereas subsequent changes were results of suggestions by many people to which all of us maintained an open mind and many of which we tried. In the final stages of the editing, I felt we had gone astray, too far away from our original point of view.

Comparing a script draft with the final film, most of the deleted scenes are tiny, involving characters far down the playbill. Often, the dialogue has been retained as off-screen (O.S.) voices. Even the director's wife Irina Skobtseva, although in some publicity credited as Maria, except for a few frames, doesn't survive in the finished film. Several others listed on the credits barely appear: historical advisor Willo Gray as Ramsey has one brief line ("*Morning Cav*") and is gone. Roger Green merits a single close-up as Duncan in the ballroom, but Scottish actor Charles Borromel, despite his on-screen credit, is completely off-screen! There can be few films for which the majority of the cast emblazoned with on-screen credits barely even appear in the final product.

One major sequence was almost entirely cut and rearranged. After Napoleon crosses the border, he must face the Prussian forces at Ligny; his generals rouse him from his sleep as he slumbers before the windmill. The shooting of this scene was discussed in Chapter Twelve, with the camera having framed 15,000 men, slowly zooms into a tight close-up of Steiger with his head in his hands, a simple and elegant portrait of the stress of command. It would be moved to the beginning of the main battle sequence, making a dramatic cut from Napoleon's irritation at the slow start to hostilities: *"In his favour!"*

It is probable that the decision to move the scene was taken during filming as it ends with a "match cut" close-up of Wellington dozing under a tree. This simple visual juxtaposition effectively shows the two commanders' state of mind. Wellington is asked by Uxbridge: *"What are your plans?"* Flippantly, Wellington replies: *"To beat the French."* This tiny scene does not exist in the script, but one wonders whether Bondarchuk, having shot the windmill scene, had a moment of inspiration. That said, as discussed earlier, the rearranging the scene may have been taken *before* it was shot. A good director will spend the shooting of a film constantly editing it in their head, and one suspects having pondered the original scripted conception of this spectacular shot, he may have felt it worked much better later on, with a thematic cut to the cool-as-a-cucumber Wellington.

In the script, Blucher leads a cavalry charge at Ligny, during which he is unhorsed. Rescued, he agrees to his subordinate's plan to withdraw to Wavre. Meyer moved this charge scene to the climax of Waterloo as the Prussians make their in-the-nick-of-time appearance. The shots appear to have been "flopped," so the cavalry charge from screen left to right (all the horsemen now hold their swords in their *left* hand; on average, most people are right-handed for what would be considered the sword carrying hand), this is in keeping with the allied attack which is depicted with the same thrust of direction.

Confusing screen direction is known as "crossing the line." For example, in most films, two characters talking will be filmed and edited to be facing each other. There are myriad variations of this, but maintaining screen direction is scrupulously adhered to as it helps the audience to follow the story, albeit on a subliminal level. This is very important in action sequences, as they can often be frenetic and confusing, but maintaining screen direction ensures comprehension, momentum and power.

Strangely, the decision to empower the Prussian arrival led to a decision to cut the denouement as Blucher and Wellington meet as the guns fall silent. As we saw in the previous chapter, the scene which involved Sergei Zakhariadze's creative ad-lib with Napoleon's hat *was* filmed. Why this scene did not make the final cut is a mystery, as both historically and narratively it would have brought the victors neatly together. One wonders if the euphoric tone of victory might have seemed out-of-place amid the slow, mournful coda; the ghastly aftermath of battle.

As Meyer and the team began to re-arrange and rework sequences, frustration arose:

> It was a nightmare trying to reconstitute some of the work previously done and subsequently altered without records being kept, which was my error. I was caught off-base by the suddenness and extent of the "trial and error" changes after the "first cut" and had, therefore, not had time to make a "reference dupe."

Making a "reference dupe," also known as a "slash dupe," was a copy made from the edited "work print" using reversal film in either colour or black and white, either way the image would be ugly and crude, complete with scratches from handling. Film editor Alan Jones recalled that before the era of videotape, they were the workhorse of the film cutting-room.

> Slash Dupes were used for everything and as they had fewer joins, they handled projection better than a poorly joined cutting copy when some editors were rotten join makers. They were used for track laying, looping, pre mixing, etc. The most useful thing for sound editors was that the Moy (Rubber) numbers showed through which enabled original sync to be found.[600]

Their main *raison d'être* was the all-important edge numbers, as discussed earlier, to maintain the link with the camera negative. These copies would never have been considered of any archival value, before being junked at the end of the job. They did, however, have some financial value, as Alan Jones explained: "We pinched them after a production to be sold onto the next production as spacing for track laying to generate 'cutting-room lunch money.'"

With the consent of both director and producer, Meyer "proceeded to re-establish the previous point of view with the same type of stylisation we had in our first cut." Meyer described the editorial approach he imposed on the material:

> The style that more or less subconsciously emerged…the idea of presenting a very intimate conflict between Wellington and Napoleon…unwittingly, what this style meant in practical terms that this picture is a picture of close-ups and long shots. There are very few medium shots in the picture and this gives it a style of its own.

He realised that a film which comprised enormous action sequences could become tedious.

> The biggest problem in achieving a unity was to be sure not to make the battle too long and the various pieces of battle as completely unrepetitive as possible. There are, in a battle for instance, interludes of cannonades with the big guns which were — strategically very important…To use these cannonades as interludes

and transitions, at the same time not overdo them and bring them in too often, was just one of the many problems.

The depiction of war has always presented one major challenge: how to show the savagery of combat. Released in 1969, *The Wild Bunch* had ignited the debate about film violence; Sam Peckinpah's slow-motion death scenes caused great controversy and had pushed hard against the boundaries of taste and censorship. From Richard Heffer's diary it appears several characters met gruesome and spectacular deaths, which suggests there had been an honest attempt to visualise the reality of battlefield casualties at Waterloo. We can also see this from the description of the "horrors of war" that had been shot using local legless/armless Ukrainian locals, which were ultimately excised.

The most gruesome death in the film De Lancey's (Ian Ogilvy) demise, which shows his back eviscerated by an exploding shell. The make-up is extraordinary, and leaves nothing to the imagination, and is far more realistic than anything shown in *The Wild Bunch*. It is a shame the film, and indeed the script, makes no other reference to the obvious gruesome carnage wrought by such visible violence. Bondarchuk did not shy away from showing the horror of war in *War and Peace* battle sequences, with limbs being blown off, bloodied and bruised soldiers and the gruesome dressing stations.

Whether there were concerns about the certification which would have limited the audience, or an aesthetic choice, the editing team debated the issue at length.

> We had decided to use very little blood and gore, even very little hand-to-hand fighting during the battle. At many times during the decision-making process in the final stages of the editing, we switched sides in our attitudes toward that problem. One of us would always think we desperately needed it, with the rest of us saying, "No, it no longer needs it, it is unnecessary because it is a different kind of picture."

As the editing process drew to a close, the focus was on nuance and simplicity of storytelling.

> During these final weeks of editing practically around the clock, with a marvellously co-operative crew of twelve Italian, American and English editors, we also eliminated all previous

attempts at getting "fancy" and "tricky," which was completely unnecessary in a picture as beautifully photographed as *Waterloo*.

The late 1960s saw a brief surge of split-screen effects; different bits of action on the screen at the same time. Notable uses of this technique were *Grand Prix* (1966) and *The Boston Strangler* (1967). In both films the concept is well used and enhances the drama of motor-racing, and serial-killing, respectively. Even at the time, opinions were mixed about their effectiveness, and it is probable that by 1970 it was considered a fad that had passed,[601] as Meyer explained:

> I had a difficult time throughout, warding off all the fantastic multiple-screens, superimpositions and other complicated opticals. In its final version there are four partial fades made in the camera, and not one single dissolve or other optically made effect except for the very simple titles.

After months of work and endless discussions, a single version was agreed.

> Almost imperceptibly the picture got shorter without anybody really trying for any specific length and the final cut, to everyone's satisfaction, turned out to be exactly two hours and fourteen minutes. It is, in my opinion, the shortest and therefore probably most effective epic on record.

Finally, with "picture lock" signed off by producer, director and editor, work began in earnest to build the soundtrack. Meanwhile, the next question: what kind of musical score could compete with the roar of cannons, explosions and the thunder of horses?

"I was asked to do the music to *Waterloo* at a moment's notice," remembers British composer Wilfred Josephs, best known for his extensive TV work including the haunting theme for one of the greatest documentary series ever: the twenty-four part *The Great War* (1964). He was invited over to Dinocittà for two weeks in March 1969, as filming began on the ballroom set.

> I was supposed to write the pre-shooting stuff on the spot, such as the waltz for the ballroom scene. They said they wanted

a *Bridge on the River Kwai* effect, so I wrote the music and had to record it with about ten Italian players using music stands pinched from the ballroom set while they were re-lighting it between scenes.[602]

The *Kwai* effect (the Colonel Bogey March) requested was in the shape of a two-hundred-year-old song that had become a favourite of soldiers marching away to war: *The Girl I Left Behind Me*.

I'm lonesome since I cross'd the hills,
And o'er the moor that's sedgy;
With heavy thoughts my mind is fill'd,
Since I parted with my Naggy
When e'er I return to view the place,
The tears doth fall and blind me,
When I think on the charming grace
Of the girl I left behind me.[603]

With Bondarchuk "delighted" with all his "pre-shooting stuff," Josephs flew home expecting to be called back months later to finish the job. Instead, it would be *years* before he found out why the call-back never came from Rome.

I discovered that I had been used as the whipping boy; Bondarchuk had wanted the Russian composer Vyacheslav Ovchinnikov (*War and Peace*), and De Laurentiis had really wanted Nino Rota all along. Rota, however — whom I've never met — meticulously put down every bit of my music on the cue sheets (which means I still get the odd few pounds of royalties), with the result that about 12 minutes of it survives in the finished picture, the ballroom scene, and my use of *The Girl I Left Behind Me* (which dates from that period) as a descant (counterpoint) against my main theme (part of the *Kwai* idea). *Waterloo* was very much the big break, which wasn't a big break at all.[604]

Josephs was obviously chosen for his Englishness and appreciation of traditional folk music. Those "12 minutes" probably included arranging the various authentic songs and tunes that are heard throughout the film amongst the British troops. As a recognition of his work, he is billed as Musical Consultant on the credits beneath Nino Rota.

Rota had finished working on one of Fellini's most dazzling works, *Satyricon* (1969), a kaleidoscopic journey through an imagined Ancient Rome, "probably the most unusual film score that Rota ever penned; its weird and whacky compositions being far removed from anything that cinema goers might associate with Imperial Rome."[605]

Nino Rota was born in 1911 as Giovanni Rota; considered a child prodigy, he earned the nickname of "Nino," that would become his name for life. While still a teenager, he caught the ear of the renowned conductor Arturo Toscanini, who encouraged him to study composition. Winning a scholarship to the Curtis Institute of Philadelphia brought him to America, where he became immersed in the country's musical culture, particularly folk and the "pop" music of George Gershwin, Cole Porter and Irving Berlin.

Rota soon became a hugely respected and popular composer collaborating with all the notable post-war Italian filmmakers, including Vittorio De Sica on *Boccacio 70* (1962) and *The Condemned of Altona* (1962), Luchino Visconti on *Rocco and His Brothers* (1960) and *The Leopard* (1963), Franco Zeffirelli on *The Taming of the Shrew* (1967) and *Romeo and Juliet* (1968).

His most famous, being his long and fruitful relationship with the *Maestro* — Federico Fellini. Their collaboration spanned 70 films over twenty-seven years, and was the perfect synergy of their respective talents, as music critic Craig Lysy explained:

> Due to Fellini's often-disjointed imagery and fragmentary narrative style, Rota's was always tasked to write a score which provided continuity. Remarkably, it was Rota's melodious, stanzaic music, which provided essential gravity, a cohesive unifying force, which held the films together.[606]

Some of their more renowned works include *I Vitelloni* (1953), *La Strada* (1954) and *Nights of Cabiria* (1957). The sixties would see Rota create his most distinctive scores with *La Dolce Vita* (1960), and what is widely regarded as Fellini's masterpiece: *8½* (1963), a dizzying semi-autobiographical fantasy which Rota pulls together with a jaunty circus march, creating a unifying main theme.

"Rota's film music style is characterised by a certain good-humoured energy verging on satire," commented Jim Paterson, who is a prolific composer for video games, and runs the website, *Mfiles*, dedicated to classical and film music.

His style was like a blend between the theatrical irony of Prokofiev and the impish wit of Francis Poulenc. He sometimes used a light jazz idiom, and could be compared with Mancini in some ways. He avoided the overly sentimental by seemingly coming at the subject obliquely, with a slight sense of the absurd.[607]

Rota's jaunty jazzing style would seem a world away from an epic historical drama, but in 1956 he had scored Dino's *War and Peace*. Marshalling a full orchestra, he produced a moving and dynamic score. The juxtaposition of the title is beautifully realised with the powerful main theme that transmutes it into a tender lullaby. When Natasha, played by Audrey Hepburn, dances at her first ball, Rota composed a hypnotic piece that became iconic — "Natasha's Waltz." When the smitten Prince Andrei, played by Mel Ferrer, the actress's real-life husband, watches Natasha dance with another man, determines that if she smiles at him on the next turn, they will marry. This is underscored with an entrancing waltz which fourteen years later would be redeployed to the Duchess of Richmond's ballroom for *Waterloo*.[608]

While Rota's score for *Waterloo* might not be considered amongst his best, he worked hard to create a sonic "epic" sound that was both moving and haunting, subverting the bombast. John Mansell, an avid film music collector and critic, discussed the score in his review of the subsequent soundtrack release on CD:

> Rota's music was a crucial and also an important component of the movie. The opening is dramatic with brass and strings, giving it an urgent and imposing feel, setting the scene for much of what is to follow. Rota's score is effective within the battle scenes; it underlines and heightens the tension and gives support to the aggressive action that is taking place on screen. The score accompanying the somewhat jolly and ram-shackle British, Scottish and Irish is less than regal or dramatic, but Rota gives a greater sense of pomp and ceremony to the French forces. His score also purveys a sense of futility, and highlights the senseless killing of hundreds of men to gain a few feet of ground. This music seems to ask: "Why do wars and battles such as this have to be fought?"
>
> The music that Rota composed to accompany the Scots Greys as they charge headlong towards the French lines is masterful. It conjures up the adrenaline rush that the troopers must have felt

as they hurtle towards an unknown fate, but then as the film goes into a slow motion, Rota too slows the music and underlines the impressive sequence with an almost celestial and romantic piece performed on organ and strings, that momentarily create a mood that is calm and serene.

The composer utilises brass and percussion, aided by strings to create a highly agitated atmosphere as we see the British unleashing hails of bullets against a cavalry. As the scene comes to its conclusion, Rota returns to an arrangement of the central theme that is performed on a melancholy sounding solo violin depicting again the waste and the senseless act of war and the madness and carnage of battle.[609]

While Rota worked on the score in Rome, at Pinewood Studios, just north of London, a team of sound editors led by Les Wiggins began "laying" thousands of sound effects of cannons, guns and footsteps that would be eventually mixed into a single track. It is probably an open secret that most of what one hears in a film, apart from the dialogue, is often specially re-recorded using a variety of unusual and disconcerting objects, artfully manipulated to maximize their audio properties. Originally called "Footies" until an American editor attached his name to it — Foley, when done well, perversely, should not be consciously noticed. Also known as "Sync Fx", it is still standard practice to recorded them for *every* film and TV Drama as recording good, clean dialogue takes priority over other sounds. When a film is sold to a foreign territory a separate music and Fx track, "M&E" is part of the delivery to allow any dubbed foreign dialogue to be mixed with it. Graham V. Hartstone, then twenty-five-years-old, was part of the Pinewood sound crew, and explains the Foley recording process:

> Foley Artists, often with a dancing background, brought not only their particular skills at assimilating and repeating the footsteps required but also suitcases filled with a variety of shoes. After viewing each "loop" (see above), the Foley artists decided who would perform the footsteps for each character on screen, select their shoes and the appropriate surfaces, plus a piece of cloth to make the movement sounds of clothes. The Boom Operator followed the action, adjusting the distance to introduce perspective. "Streamers" or "Wipes" were applied to the picture. Diagonal lines drawn along the film, which when

projected travelled across the screen at a consistent speed. When the line reached the edge of frames, it was a start cue for a particular piece of action.[610]

Waterloo opens with Napoleon's marshals led by Ney striding down the palace hallway to confront their emperor. The drama is emphasised by the loud, crisp echo of boots, all marching in unison. One of Graham's colleagues was Stephen Pickard, also in his early twenties, who helped record these sounds which were performed by the foley artists.

> I do remember recording those footsteps very clearly! The reverb or echo, was achieved using an echo chamber. It was a small square enclosure made of brick. It had a doorway big enough for someone to get into. There was a large speaker and a microphone on a stand. You would either move the mike closer or further away depending on how far the characters were from the camera. It was trial and error.

While Stephen, Graham and their colleagues worked long hours, including night shifts at Pinewood, to create footsteps, horse noises, and all the audio maelstrom of battle, it still left the dialogue to be delt with. Most of the location audio was considered unusable, not helped by the blast of those Klimov engines for the hurricane effect.

In March 1970, a mammoth three weeks of "looping" took place at Pinewood supervised by Robert Rietty. This involved replacing the dialogue of eighty-five characters, plus every line by the principal actors while, according to Meyer, "the picture was still in a state of flux." In between fetching cigarettes for Christopher Plummer, Stephen Pickard, recalled his role in the process.

> My job entailed sitting at a desk at the rear of the theater close to the mixing booth. I had the job of switching the audio of the guide track from the stage speaker to the headphone which the actor wore, and signalled to the mixer when he was ready to record. I would switch the audio from the speaker to the headphone, and adjust the level if the actor required it. Once the recorded line was approved, I had to identify it by speaking into a microphone placed on my desk. I also had a list of all the loops in front of me so I could identify them correctly.

Most of Rietty's sterling work of "looping" a few months previously would have been redone, although his distinctive, mellow voice is still evident in the finished film — for instance, as Charles Millot's Marshal Grouchy. "Robert Rietty was always great to work with," remembered Stephen, who would work on many subsequent projects with him, and his female counterpart, voice artist Nikki Van Der Zyl, "I was lucky to work with, and know them both. At the end of the *Waterloo* sessions, he gave me a gift of Monsieur Lanvin aftershave lotion. I still have the container somewhere.[611]

One of the principles to return for "looping" was Dan O'Herlihy who had crossed swords with Rod Steiger during the shoot. It appears the months of separation had healed some friction between them: "We are getting along fine — we are not working together now," O'Herlihy told *Variety*. He was excited about what he saw on the screen, and intriguingly noted that the movie was two-and-a-*half* hours long at this stage; "now that the long, Russian pauses have been cut."[612] His work done, he retreated to his Irish bolt-hole in Killarney for his first break in nearly a year.

Young Peter Davies was another actor brought back to "loop" his lines. He remembers little of the process as he could only see the thirty-second clips he had to replace, although he noted all his filmed scenes were intact: "They just showed you little bits. The most exciting thing for me was getting a ride back in Christopher Plummer's Rolls-Royce; I thought that was so cool." It had been a gift in lieu of payment from producer Sam Spiegel for Plummer's cameo as General Erwin Rommel in *The Night of the Generals* (1966).

By May 1970, Meyer was supervising sixteen sound editors working "long, nervous hours of many seven-day weeks" in both London and Rome. With the pressure of the schedule, they split the workload. While Nino Rota composed and recorded the score for the second half at Dinocittà, the first half soundtrack was "mixed" at Pinewood.

The famous British studios were considered at the time to have the best stereo mixing facilities and crew in Europe. The chief sound mixer was Gordon McCallum, "the most sensitive and intelligent sound man I have ever worked with in Europe." He would work on over 300 films during his forty-year career, with 1970 being the high point. He would gain an Academy Award for *Fiddler on the Roof* (1971), and nominations for *Ryan's Daughter* (1970), *Diamonds Are Forever* (1971) and later *Superman: The*

Movie (1978). Speaking years later, McCallum described his approach to the sound mixing craft:

> I think perhaps I'm lucky that — it's the quality I think I had — was to understand, even before they said it, from the film, what the director had been trying to do, what was demanded of the track to support the film. I mean, I always regarded the soundtrack as being just one ingredient in the overall thing of trying to create the right dramatic or comic or whatever effect you wanted to achieve.[613]

Known simply as "Mac," McCallum had an imposing reputation as John Hayward remembers when, at the tender age of twenty-four, he got promoted:

> Cyril Crowhurst was the boss, and had given me the chance of a lifetime to work on the "dubbing desk," not because, as I thought, I was "really good" but because there was nobody left in the sound department that would work with Gordon K. McCallum. He was a complete tyrant, probably because of his relentless passion for perfection. He actually was a very nice guy and probably the best mixer in the world at the time. *Waterloo* in 1970 was only my third film.[614]

Although Mac and his crew's work on *Waterloo* would not be recognised for awards, it stands as one of the most impressive stereo mixes of its era.

Unlike today, stereo soundtracks were still the exception in 1970, mainly restricted for musicals and some epics. Stereo sound had been introduced with Cinerama in the early 1950s,[615] which offered five tracks/speakers behind the enormous screen, and enveloping surround sound via a ring of speakers in the auditorium. With the introduction of 70mm systems, which carried 6-track stereo, the configuration became known as Todd-AO Discreet, and was the standard for 70mm releases until the 1980s. One of the most noticeable aspects of these audio presentations was the directional dialogue, where the voice would match the character's position on screen.

When producer Samuel Bronston was completing *El Cid*, his third epic produced in Spain, the sound was entrusted to McCallum and his team at Pinewood. "That was our first stereo, and really for me the horizons opened up as we came to stereo — so much more opportunity."[616] He was immediately excited about the new technology and its possibilities:

> With a monaural track you can enjoy a film very well, but you're not as involved in it as much as you are with a stereo track. If you've got a good stereo track, and particularly when you think of a big screen, you need to be involved in it, and that opportunity was presented by 4-track stereo which we started doing then, and later 6-track and so on. All those Bronston pictures were a big test and very good, very enjoyable.

To prepare for working on *Waterloo*, John Hayward was requested to pull out of the vaults a reel from another Bronston epic. For the young man at the beginning of his career, it was a revelatory experience:

> Mac sent me to the vaults to fish out the reel he had mixed in 1963 of the horse and sword fight in *55 Days at Peking*. We set it up as carefully as we could on the old wooden Westrex desk and played the reel to check out the theatre. The soundtrack truly amazed me, 6-track magnetic sound in all its vast, loud, Hi-Fi glory! I'd never heard anything like it in my life. It fashioned how I was to regard sound for the rest of my life.

During the rest of the decade, Mac and his team would mix many of the big European epics, as well as the Bond films. "Then we started the Bonds, and they were monaural for a long, long time and they earned so much money, everybody said why ever go to stereo?" These iconic action-adventure epics would not be mixed in stereo until *Moonraker* (1979) by McCallum and his crew.

Fellow Dubbing Mixer Graham V. Hartstone described the complex and time-consuming process of mixing stereo:

> The crew comprised three Re-Recording Mixers. All the dialogue was meticulously pre-mixed by the lead mixer Gordon McCallum, then he, and one of the others, combined the prepared Sound FX tracks into pre-mixes: Foleys (footsteps etc), atmospheres, explosions, guns, horses, crowds, etc. Each clip was panned with "pan pots" by the third mixer on the front desk. Surround sounds were achieved by sending the track to the rear speakers with a delay of about 2 frames. Each sound was levelled,

panned, equalised and balanced as we thought suitable. Once the pre-mixing was complete, we embarked on the final mix. The lead mixer on the main console handled the dialogue pre-mix, the music, and any last-minute additional tracks. The other two mixers on the front desk played the pre-mixes on the multi-track faders, and panned any additional mono tracks. Reverb was achieved using our physical echo chamber, with a tape delay if required. As there was no automation, we rehearsed each ten-minute reel, noting down levels and equalisation settings on cue sheets. Once we thought we were competent, we put the recorder on the line and "went for a take!" The director was obviously present to approve…Sometimes we would have maybe three or four takes in which some sequences were better in one take than another, so the sections with the best mixes would be cut together to make the final Print Master. We also mixed down a Mono track for 35mm release.

Stephen Pickard was able to spend time sitting in the main mixing theatre, and watched Mac at work.

> Mac was a wonderful person. A brilliant mixer and he was always nice to me. When I could I would sit in on sessions. Often, he was working on his own, hard at work on the dialog tracks. He would often spend hours cleaning them up. Today's dialog recording to me has intelligibility issues, and I don't think Mac would have approved. He was old school, a perfectionist.

A few years later, "rock and roll" machines were introduced which allowed mixers, like Mac, to start/stop and pick up at any point in a reel. Until then, as described above, a reel had to be mixed in one run, tense for all concerned.

> During stereo sessions, Mac would be controlling levels on dialog, while in front of him on the console below, mixer Colin Le Mesurier or "Mesh", would handle all the "pan pots" (for stereo panning), and Mac would often yell at him if he made a mistake. He had infinite patience with Mac, and never answered back! Mac often got frustrated, and when it reached a peak, which often happened, he would go out to the restroom to wash his face and return if nothing had happened.

As we can see, creating stereo soundtracks was very time-consuming, expensive and stressful to produce, which made *Waterloo* a tough assignment for McCallum's Pinewood crew, "that was a hard stint," he said later. The process was not helped by the three principal people responsible, the director, composer and editor, would rarely all be where they were needed at the same time to make decisions. "This resulted in considerable confusion, wasted motion and personal frustration," admitted Meyer. For several months during this hectic year of post-production, Bondarchuk was back in Russia acting in Andrey Konchalovskiy's adaptation of Chekhov's *Uncle Vanya* (1970). This also featured Innokentiy Smoktunovskiy and Vladimir Udalov, who had presented Blucher with Napoleon's hat for his impromptu scene in *Waterloo*.

In the Pinewood dubbing studios, John Hayward recalls his initial recollections of the Russian director:

> Sergei was a brooding, surly man at first, grumpy one might say. He was tall, rotund and very impressive, a real presence. When we got to know Sergei better and he understood that Mac and his team knew what they were doing, we learnt that Russian Vodka as we know it was not "firewater," but a smooth and rather pleasant drink.

McCallum, speaking years later, recalled having a pleasant working relationship with the director who, despite his lack of English, made up for it with acute emotional intelligence.

> He knew when he was being taken for a ride! And if somebody said something in English, which he picked up in no uncertain manner, he put him in his place! But no, we got on very well. And he wanted me to go over to Russia to do the Russian version. It never transpired in the end, for one reason or another — it would have been fun.

John Hayward was one of the mixers, sitting for long hours in the darkened dubbing theatre as the soundtrack slowly took shape:

> An outstanding memory of mixing the actual battle was that it started with a single cannon shot firing at a distance of probably a mile away. Les Wiggins, a great track layer and lovely man, was the supervising Sound Editor. He had quite rightly treated

this very scientifically. He knew the distance; he knew the speed of sound, so he laid the cannon explosion accordingly. Well! The sound took forever to arrive, and my memory was of a thunderous Sergei Bondarchuk leaping up from the front seats of the theatre, hurling Russian expletives to all and sundry. What this meant was that Les went away and laid loads of explosions with masses of different timings. It took a day and a half to get just this one thing right. I don't remember for sure, but I think the timing ended up quite close to the visual of the cannon being fired.

The heavy workload meant the team who were working long hours, seven days a week, was then compounded by the producer, as Mac recalled: "And after we'd been working for quite a long time and done all the pre-dubs. We'd been working for, oh I should think about six weeks on it — and he re-cut the entire thing!"

Meyer, in his article, does not mention this, but it is clear from the above that there were a great deal of changes made. Nino Rota subsequently grumbled that much of his music was re-cut and reordered, which would have been the consequence of this re-editing.

Dino would comment later that he was unhappy with some editing decisions: "Unfortunately, Bondarchuk cut many of Steiger's best bits, because he thought he was overacting. On the other hand, Bondarchuk didn't speak a word of English and wasn't capable of reading the screenplay." As he made this comment, many years later when the film's reception was a fact, one feels he is being disingenuous. If Dino felt the "best bits" were being lost, it seems implausible he would have not fought to keep them. He said that: "to keep the situation under control, I went to work with an American editor, but in order to simplify things, we were forced to chop out all sorts of great stuff." [617]

If we take these words at face value, we can detect tensions between the key players. Young John Hayward, watching from the side lines, sensed simmering conflict between the director and the editor: "I never knew what the politics were, but Sergei Bondarchuk did not like Richard C. Meyer one little bit." Hayward didn't realise at the time that the American was also wearing a management hat as an Associate Producer, which may have been the source of the director's frustration and irritation with movieland politics. John Lind, who interviewed the director during this time (see Chapter Four), recalled that: "He was somewhat fraught because of his dealings with the American studio executives. His first assistant director (Vladimir Dostal), who was in the hotel room with us, described them as 'gangsters' and 'mafia.' Otherwise, he was generous with his time and surprisingly mystical."[618]

Perhaps we should not try to read too much into these "tensions." Meyer's account presents a more harmonious and consensual view of the creative process (indiscretion not a wise move when writing in a trade paper), but with time always knocking on the filmmaking door, tempers inevitably fray.

However, the decision, for whatever reason, to re-cut after "picture lock" is unusual as it creates immense problems for the sound crew. McCallum remembers the knock-on pressure: "And the date was not moved, as you can imagine, so we had to start all over again, terrific hours. And we just finished about the day before David (Lean) arrived with *Ryan's Daughter*, another long, big stereo epic."

Not surprisingly, McCallum became ill after six months of intense hard work, but as a true professional he was soon back at his controls: "I went to the doctor when we'd finished the job, I didn't hold the picture up, naturally!"

Meyer would pay tribute to the professionalism of both units in Rome and Pinewood, who successfully completed the English and Italian versions almost simultaneously, "Quite a feat under the circumstances." He relates how some of his own creative ideas about the soundtrack were not pursued: "I did not get my way entirely because my ideas on sound were obviously too abstract and unusual for the powers that were. Technically and artistically, within the limits set, it is the best piece of stereophonic mixing I have ever heard."

In his article he does not elaborate on his concepts but did explain the process that was adopted: "Eighty percent of all dialogue is recorded mono, or quasi-mono, with no extreme "swings" ever, and the "surround" speakers are used only sparingly for carefully integrated special effects or ambience." What is curious about his words are they seem at odds with the evidence. The UK home DVD release of the film in 2000 boasted a 4.0 Dolby Digital, which appears to be a straight port from the 4-track stereo master soundtrack. It boasts widely spaced directional dialogue (swings) and a lively surround track sound. During the battle scenes it comes alive with cannons, cheers, thunder of horses and even cannon balls that seem to fly from to and from the surround channel; very apparent when Lord Uxbridge loses his leg!

Within the technical limits of the time, it is impressive. And a credit to Gordon McCallum, who was at the top of his game. He summed up the finished film as "good in parts — curate's egg. A big spectacle…Anyway, that was very hard work." It should be stressed that along with all films until the introduction of Dolby Stereo in the late seventies, it would only play a mono track in the vast majority of cinemas.

By the autumn of 1970, the post-production work was finally completed at Technicolor in London. The negative was cut, "without a mistake despite the many problems and the great rush." Then the production of hundreds of prints began (via Technicolor's three-strip matrix Imbibition process), as well as the handful of bespoke 70mm "blow-ups" which boasted the stereo soundtrack for the high-profile premieres and road-show runs. The British Board of Film Classification viewed and passed the finished 132-minutes and 33 seconds for a "U" (Universal — Suitable for all) certificate.[619]

Waterloo "was now in the lap of the gods, history and the public."

Napoleon is wracked by pain as the army marches past him, this cuts to Wellington in gentle repose beneath his tree. This juxtaposition of scenes does not appear in the script, but may have evolved during filming. In many places, the editing directly contrasts the two commanders state of mind. RON POULTER COLLECTION

Deleted Scenes. Left: Napoleon raises a glass of brandy, probably an on set inspiration. Right: A Wounded Officer, Aleksandr Parkhomenko, dies at Napoleon's feet. AUTHOR'S COLLECTION

As Ney's cavalry charge, Wellington questions the deployment of Mercer's cannons. He has sited them opposite a deep ravine. AUTHOR'S COLLECTION

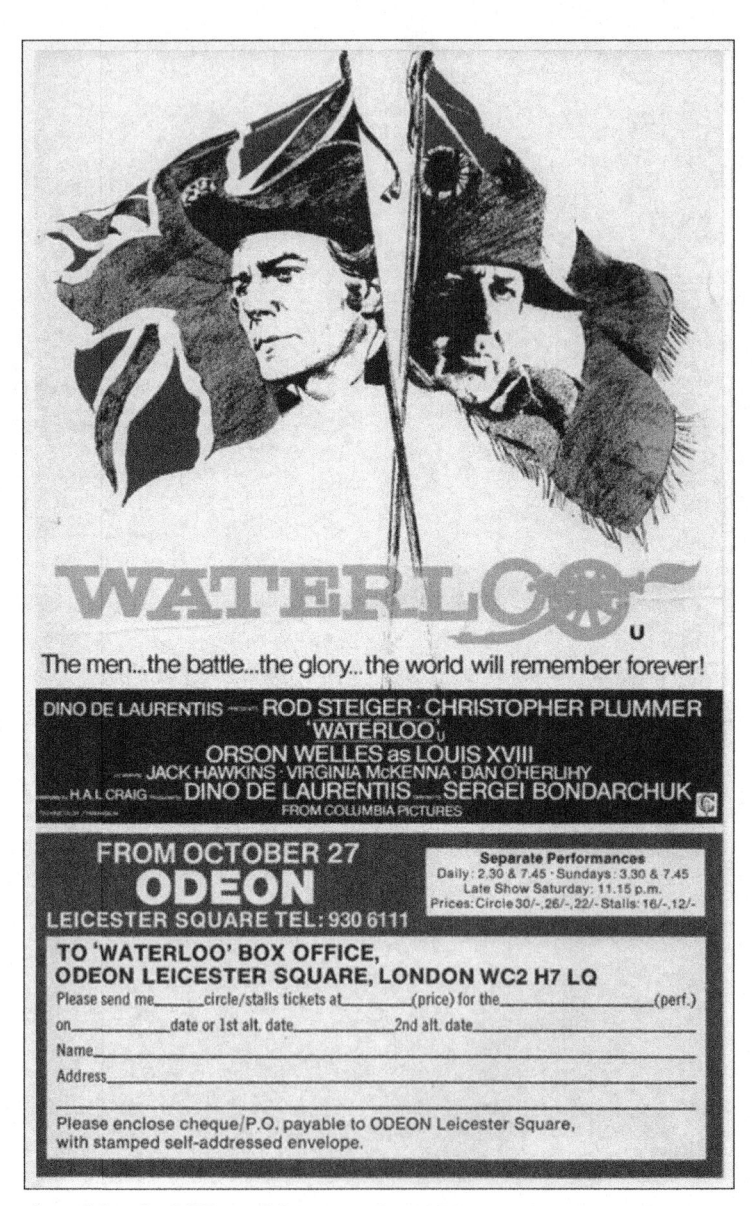

An ad for the UK roadshow run in 1970. AUTHOR'S COLLECTION

CHAPTER 19

"*The Limits Of Glory...*"

"*The Men... The Battle... The Glory, The World Will Remember Forever!*"

Monday, 26 October 1970 saw the world premiere take place at London's Odeon Leicester Square in the presence of Queen Elizabeth II and Prince Philip. It was a charity event in aid of The Soldiers', Sailors' and Airmen's Families Association, with added ceremony and martial pomp in the shape of the Bagpipers from the Gordon Highlanders, who had also appeared in the film. Sergei Bondarchuk had flown in from Russia with his wife Irina, who ensured she could curtsy to a Queen.

Dino was excited to bring his family to the grand event. "It was amazing!" Veronica remembers how excited her father was:

> ...and so honoured, I remember him saying: "You all have to come, you will have new gowns and you will meet the Queen." He was very proud of the fact that he could bring his family to meet the Queen. I will never forget that moment. For me, too, it was so amazing that I had a part in this big movie and I met the Queen! We just shook hands. It was amazing just to be in her presence.

There was one person who suffered a bout of stage fright as they patiently waited in line to press the royal flesh. Suddenly a voice chimed above the gentle murmur of anticipation: "She's coming, she's arrived, she's HERE!" That moment, Her Majesty took Rod Steiger's hand, "clasping as though she would never let go and talking the small talk that is expected on such a walkabout. 'What a vast movie!' she chimed. 'A huge epic!'" The talented actor found himself tongue-tied and spluttered the first thing that came into his mouth: "'I don't know how they put the *bloody* thing together.' It was the word 'bloody' that did it... Her aide shot Steiger a reproachful glance at putting the Queen through such a grievous experience."[620] With a touch of Eliza Doolittle's *faux pas* in *My Fair Lady*, luckily Steiger staved off a one-way trip to the Tower of London.

At least young Peter Davies did not have to navigate the etiquette minefield, and instead took his seat in the audience with his family.

> It was amazing, and I wasn't on the receiving line, but I got within a nose of the Queen, which is pretty impressive you know. My parents had come up to London for the occasion. My mum thought it was a bit bloodthirsty! Seeing it for the first time and not knowing what it was going to be like…seeing it on the big screen and the Queen being there and all that, it was heady stuff. I was convinced I was on my way to being a major actor; it didn't quite work out that way.

As the burgundy red curtain closed over the screen to the fading strains of Nino Rota's score, Her Majesty rose to her feet and joined in the standing ovation — the evening was considered a triumph.

Perhaps it was always going to be an easier sell in Britain, but next day the leading protagonists decamped to Paris — for a very different reaction. "I remember the outcome as if it were yesterday," said Dino with a shudder years later; "the one in London was a great success, and the one in Paris was a fiasco."[621]

It seems the presence of the same Gordon Highlanders in the shadow of Napoleon's tomb in Les Invalides opened old wounds and raised the hackles of the Parisians.

> They did us the honour of coming to commemorate in Paris the defeat of Waterloo, and that at the invitation of an American production company which ensures the launch of the film produced by a director…Russian.[622]

This affront to national honour was too much for the writer, who suggested:

> It remains to us to imagine the day when the Japanese will produce a film devoted to the French disaster of June 1940, they will gather some heirs of the panzers of the Second World War to make them parade on the Champs-Élysées.

These scathing words were echoed throughout much of the French press, often with a chauvinistic tone to it; Russian Bondarchuk's Marxist credentials being eyed with suspicion. Some, like Jean de Baroncelli, in an even-handed review, was initially impressed with Steiger's appearance. "Familiar silhouette. Little corporal's outfit. Suddenly, he turns around. Surprise: he is unshaven, he wears glasses, he looks old, tired, almost haggard." But by the next scene, Steiger's "cabotage marathon" performance had repelled him, with his: "Sweating, blowing, screaming, whining, rolling bulging eyes." He noted that although the actor eschewed the familiar Napoleonic pose of hand in waistcoat, he had replaced it with "a series of exhilarating effects that Bondarchuk's staging emphasises at will." But with the battle scenes, he lauded the director for surpassing his earlier *War and Peace*. "This Waterloo should earn him his marshal's staff…a fantastic spectacle of a magnitude, a majesty, often even of a surprising plastic beauty." Ultimately, de Baroncelli was disappointed that it perpetuated the popular conception of the Napoleonic myth, noting ironically that: "it is a Soviet director who, this time, rekindles the flame."[623]

While in Paris, Bondarchuk was interviewed by Patrick Sery. He described the director with "the romantic, energetic and impenetrable face of the Russian man, this fifty-year-old Ukrainian…is perhaps the most international of Soviet directors." In a pithy exchange, there is a slight sense of defensiveness on the part of the director, perhaps in the wake of the premiere "fiasco."

Having made two Napoleonic themed films, Sery wondered if it signified a particular Soviet taste for "unusual characters." Perhaps mindful of his current location, Bondarchuk attested, "Napoleon was the greatest statesman and the greatest hero of France."

> *A great exterminator too?*
> Of course, he spent most of his time getting people killed. But the dimension of the character, imposed by time, remains.
>
> *How do you represent Napoleon in decline?*
> I humanised and de-mystified him. I wanted to forget his "hand in the waistcoat" side and show the image of a complex man with his qualities and his problems like anyone. We must not forget that at forty-six-years-old the Emperor was then aging and sick.
>
> *Why did you not choose a Soviet actor to interpret him?*
> Rod Steiger seemed to me the ideal actor. His great talent does not need words to imply the character's depth. It is a force that

comes from within and knows how to express the secret of a human being with a remarkable economy of means.

Your agreement with Dino De Laurentiis, capitalist producer par excellence?
I am very happy with our cooperation. His thinking is solid, his funds too. He left me complete freedom.

How much did Waterloo *cost?*
I don't know, that doesn't interest me.

Doesn't your film seem to proceed from a very Marxist vision of history?
Does not matter to me. I did it as I felt after consulting tons of records. Historical truth is, I believe, reproduced…I only shoot the films that interest me…I will never do anything against my people…I work for art, which must glorify humanity, give rise to faith and improvement in man.

What influences you?
Only one really important: that of life.[624]

On both sides of the Channel, caustic opinions echoed each other. *Le Monde* grouped the British reaction under the banner: "The English love Napoleon more than *Waterloo*."[625] Before the opening salvo of: "'Merde!' I would be tempted to echo Cambronne's word,"[626] yelled Patrick Gibbs in *The Daily Telegraph*. Despite some good notices for the acting, the involvement of the Red Army was a bone of contention: "This will please the Czechs,"[627] joked *The Times* ironically. With condemnation at the crushing of the Prague Spring in 1968 still raw, *The Evening Standard* believed that the British cast should have refused their contracts in solidarity with the Czechs.

But the overall critics' ire was aimed at the script which "has caught the Russian habit of rewriting history" wrote Gibbs, accusing the writer H.A.L. Craig of collecting all Wellington's known phrases, and probably "to have invented a few more." One wonders how Mr. Gibbs would have found some of the original dialogue *before* Plummer and Willo teamed up to improve it!

Le Monde concluded that: "it is obvious that the sympathies of the authors go to the Emperor," as Wellington had been diminished by "grossly simplifying the character to present him in his most *British* aspect," this contrasted with Napoleon, presented as "a tragic and human hero… gives him the beautiful role with an audience, inclined to prefer the great defeated adversary."[628]

The more specialised cinema magazines were often kinder, but the major gripe was Rod Steiger. While *Variety* praised his "Method performance, with his sudden blazes of rage highlighting his moody introspection,"[629] *The Monthly Film Bulletin* was irritated by "The alternation of choked Method whisper and deadpan peremptoriness, presumably meant to differentiate the private and public Napoleons, soon grows remarkably wearisome. Only Christopher Plummer's Wellington, suave, witty and improbably Byronic, provides the equilibrium so sorely needed."[630]

Rich writing for *Variety* was a lone voice of approval: "Despite the fact that the battle is the focal point, and a striking din-laden affair it is, the film is raised from being just another historical war epic by the performances of Rod Steiger and Christopher Plummer."[631]

Almost all praised the technical effort of the battle scenes. "The real strength of the film, however, lies in the way the Panavision camera has been used to give breath-taking, panoramic power to the magnificently staged battle scenes, which teem with fighting men, cannon, horses and smoke. No one can fail to be captured and excited."[632] But this was problematic for Marjorie Bilbow in *Today's Cinema*: "To re-create the sights and sounds of a famous battle so accurately is a remarkable achievement, but it is a hollow victory if your audience longs to sue for peace."

Despite listing its shortcomings, some like Marjorie Bilbow predicted box office gold, helped by its "U" certificate allowing children to see it, and therefore widening its potential audience: "Should go well initially as a hard-ticket attraction, selling on the star names and the glamour of the pitched battle to which distance lends enchantment."[633] Graham Clarke was convinced that it "surely cannot fail to draw huge audiences."[634]

Few box office figures are available, but it was ranked fifth in the list of UKs hard-ticket/roadshow releases for 1971.[635] Following the premiere at the Odeon Leicester Square, it established a house-record take in its first week with just 16 performances of £22,719.[636] Transferring to the Metropole in 70mm, it enjoyed a successful run for six months, including breaking their house-record before playing in two further major West End venues until October 1971, completing a year of continuous exhibition.[637]

It is curious how little marketing was deployed for such a tent-pole release. Since the birth of eBay at the turn of the century, the author has maintained a continual search for any items related to the film. In the best part of two decades, many posters and lobby cards have turned up, but little else. Apart from the previously mentioned novelisation by Frederick E. Smith, there was also a very thin illustrated book, titled *The Field of Waterloo* by Paul Davies, published by Pan Books, which, other than two stills from the film, is a straight history book.

In 2021, during the final stages of writing this book, a very rare item did finally appear on the selling website; a circular jigsaw made by the British Waddingtons boardgame company. Once purchased, Claire, the author's wife, patiently put the five-hundred pieces together to recreate a very colourful and tasteful design, adorned with a number of stills (some not seen before) from the film. Appearing in 1970, the jigsaw was obviously an attempt to "cash in" on the UK release of the film, but the paucity of other objects suggests there was no concerted campaign of "spin offs."

At the time, it was mainly the big budget musicals (and Disney) that spawned any merchandise (although the bulging warehouses of unwanted tie-ins for *Doctor Dolittle* (1967) severely dulled the corporate appetite until *Star Wars* ten years later), but it is worth considering the UK release of *Battle of Britain* in 1969, which sparked a plethora of books and models. This being the era that saw an enormous popularity in plastic modelling kits, particularly from the Airfix company, it seems a missed opportunity not to have tapped into a very keen generation of children.

Yet, Dino was obviously aware of the rich vein of eager young minds when he tried unsuccessfully to have the film classed as "for children" under the guise of education, albeit for tax purposes (see Chapter Three). The deletion of most of the "blood and guts" during the editing to ensure its "U" certificate, shows there was a genuine desire to appeal to this demographic.

Attracting that young audience was helped by some free publicity thanks to an iconic TV programme that will resonate with British readers of a certain age. *Blue Peter* was broadcast twice weekly at tea-time; in an era of just three TV channels, it was *the* show for generations of children, and perfectly embodied the BBC's ethos to "inform, educate and entertain."[638]

On the 7 January 1971 episode, flamboyantly-dressed presenter Peter Purvis introduced a lengthy clip from the film full of fire and fury, then followed it with a demonstration of Wellington's very own cavalry sabre he wore during the battle. The film would again be referenced on the show twice more during the next few months, including part of a feature on stage costume and make-up. It was fronted by that intrepid, always "game" presenter John Noakes. Sporting a Napoleonic red coat, shako and side burns, with his trademark chirpy humour in a broad Yorkshire accent, he did a little ditty about "Why the battle of Waterloo started late,"[639] though minus his faithful sheepdog sidekick, Shep! With their incredibly successful money-raising drives (often collecting milk bottle tops) for a variety of needy causes, it is hard to overestimate the huge cultural pull of this programme in the 1970s. It is safe to say millions of, perhaps, mainly boys, would have pleaded with their parents to take them to "the pictures" to see *Waterloo*.[640]

Ironically, the film would enjoy probably its largest ever audience five years later on Christmas Day 1976. The ITV network had originally earmarked either *Zulu* (1964) or *Patton* (1970) for their 8 p.m. headline slot. For various reasons, the IBA (Governing TV body) ruled them out, with *Zulu* rather unfairly falling foul of the politics surrounding South Africa's brutal Apartheid policy.[641] As the nation flopped in front of the "telly" on the festive Day evening, the popular choice was of just two main channels. The BBC estimated their scheduled offering of *The Morecambe & Wise Show* garnered 27 million viewers (one of the biggest audiences in UK TV history); this was then followed by *Airport* (1970), which dropped by 5.5 million as it went head-to-head with *Waterloo*. Stats for ITV are not available, although they appeared to have garnered just a *third* of the audience share for the overall day. But even with a rough estimate of five million watching *Waterloo* that evening, it was probably its most glorious moment in the sun.[642]

The Academy Awards ignored the film in 1971, but in the UK, BAFTA recognised the huge technical and craft effort; Best Costume Design (Maria De Matteis and Ugo Pericoli) and Best Art Direction (Mario Garbuglia), with a nomination for Best Cinematography (Armando Nannuzzi). It shared Best Film in the David di Donatello Awards 1971 with *The Garden of the Finzi-Continis* (1970) and *The Conformist* (1970). This prestigious Italian award recognised the immense skill and artistry of the local industry, nurtured by leading figures like Dino De Laurentiis.

The Italians were some of the most enthusiastic cinema goers before the full lure of TV took hold, and consequently the film enjoyed reasonable success at the local box office, with a take of ITL1,020 billion ($1.6 million). The local distributor Euro International had paid Dino $1 million for the Italian rights, a hefty sum for which they clawed back. Expectations were high that this take, in just one European territory, would be dwarfed when the film crossed the Atlantic.

In April 1971, it went on general release in North America with a "G" rating (General audiences — All ages admitted); shorn of ten minutes, which involved trimming rather than removing scenes.

Roger Greenspun's review for *The New York Times* set the tone for most of the States-side reaction: "the particular dullness of Bondarchuk's attempt to translate history into cinema makes *Waterloo* a very bad movie."[643]

Steiger's performance once again drew the lion's share of approbation; "disaster," said *The Washington Post's* Michael Kernan, adding his "soft and pudgy face under the famous Napoleon hat dangerously resembles Lou Costello."[644] Paul Zimmerman of *Newsweek* didn't mince his words either, declaring, "Steiger is just plain awful as Napoleon."[645] Roger Greenspun adding another fictional resemblance as: "Steiger plays a peace-loving Napoleon, crafty, tired, much weighted with the destiny he seems never to get off his mind. Like a Willy Loman, not wholly aware that he has lost his territory."[646] John C. Mahoney for the *Los Angeles Free Press* took a caustic swipe at the actor's professed pacifism: "that peace medallion he always wears…to identify himself with the people's movement…presumably to hail his limo…Surely he could find no better anti-war statement than revelling in two hours of military battle logistics."

Mahoney continues with a rapier-like assessment:

> International stars drop in at their appointed hours and character, delivering still-life aphorisms, and disappear before they can be identified…Rod Steiger's Napoleon grimaces from the pain of advanced cancer, VD or some exotic malady which is never diagnosed…Periodically, he shuffles off to his room, returning, without explanation, bright and glassy eyed, like some imperial nineteenth-century junkie.[647]

The critic had perceptively picked up on one of Steiger's creative acting choices, to depict the Corsican "bombed out on laudanum."

Christopher Plummer fared only slightly better, his performance earning a soubriquet "as invented by Noel Coward"[648] from Charles Champlin in the *Los Angeles Times*, perhaps a step up from Lou Costello! Tony Mastroianni for *Cleveland Press* felt that: "Plummer's Wellington is sometimes effete and the entire British side of the story is told through the eyes of gentlemen officers who look upon war as a sporting event."[649] Andy Israel for *The Stanford Daily* assessment was inadvertently a highly accurate description of the real Duke, when he described Plummer's essay: "as a man driven by his own self-love, supremely self-confident of both his personal magnetism and his military abilities."[650] While the *Los Angeles Free Press* adding that he: "constantly bathes and primps between epigrams."[651]

The film's sheer expense riled many, including renowned critic Roger Ebert, who three years before had heaped such praise on *War and Peace*, but considered that this time: "Bondarchuk is so overwhelmed by his $25 million budget, and by his obsession for aerial photography, that his leading characters turn out scarcely more human than his extras."[652] *The New York Times* was equally unenamoured: "In movies, the look of quality is almost always a crushing bore. And Bondarchuk especially applies his delicate palette with the subdued refinement of a sledgehammer."[653]

The Stanford Daily prophetically noted: "I think this will be one of the last few epic pictures. Rising production costs have already driven the studios out of the United States when filming large cast pictures, and the trend toward the low budget or medium budget films like *Easy Rider* could make *Waterloo* and films of its genre as rare as *Ben-Hur*."[654] John J. Mahoney, sticking the boot in, added brutally that: 'Twenty-five million dollars could revive a sensibly run film industry, or salve the sores of a diseased society which promotes waste as it ignores poverty."[655]

The "crash" that we saw threatening in Chapter One had finally rolled over Hollywood. It was a series of hugely expensive Musicals, originally seen as a panacea, that almost washed the industry away. One after the other — *Doctor Dolittle* (1967), *Paint Your Wagon* (1969), *Star!* (1968) and *Hello Dolly!* (1969) — failed spectacularly.[656] All the major Hollywood companies reported colossal losses as the over-production and shrinking audiences (weekly attendances had dropped off by 40% from 1965)[657] created a perfect storm.

"The Mad Austrian of Wall Street," Charles Bluhdorn, who had reviewed the *Waterloo* troops in Russia almost two years before, was hoping his pet subsidiary Paramount Pictures could recoup its outlay of approximately $12 million. Despite pulling back their investment on the advice of production chief Robert Evans in early 1969, a few weeks before its London opening in October 1970, the studio had acquired additional rights for South America, Spain and Portugal to join their French and all important North American territories.

Paramount needed to not only recoup their original investment, but also the additional prints and advertising costs.[658] The release would need to gross roughly $15 million to break even — it was a tall order. With the recent heavy losses most notably with *Paint Your Wagon* (1969), *Darling Lili* (1970), *Catch 22* (1970), On a *Clear Day You Can See Forever* (1970) and *The Molly Maguires* (1970), the studio was "probably holding its breath, hoping its picture sells... The failure of this film could mean the epic has met its Waterloo."[659]

"*Waterloo* was a disaster,"[660] was the verdict of Robert Evans, the then head of production at Paramount. It appeared his original hunch had been correct when he advised his boss Charles Bluhdorn to *not* "nab" the "world" for *Waterloo*. Unfortunately, their "nabbed" territories were where the film fared worst.

While it opened on a roadshow basis at The Criterion, New York's premiere 1,766 seat theater, this was the exception. This prestige form of gradual release may have benefited the film, but as we have seen most studios preferred the now ubiquitous smash n' grab of an all points, national roll out. *Waterloo* would not be the first, or the last, to live and die *very* quickly.

To get an idea, let us look through the entertainment pages of a randomly chosen newspaper — *The Deseret News* — the longest-running in Utah serving the good people of Salt Lake City, which is also the world headquarters of The Church of Jesus Christ of Latter-day Saints. On 31 March 1971, an ad announced an "Exclusive Salt Lake City engagement" of *Waterloo* at the 21 Century Theater. This 985-seater prime roadshow venue had only been built in 1967; with a futuristic 155-feet high-domed design similar to the famed Cinerama Dome in Los Angeles, it boasted an 80-foot-wide curved screen (the second-largest in Utah). Across the road was her sister venue, the 22 Century, which had bedded in David Lean's *Ryan's Daughter* (1970) for a successful roadshow run.

Playing just two performances of *Waterloo* a day, within two weeks the newspaper ad had been amended to offering a "Big Second Feature" with the John Wayne western, *True Grit* (1970). This was an attempt to shore-up the lacklustre footfall with an already proven sure-fire hit.

Perusing the other cinematic offerings on show locally in Salt Lake City — *Love Story* (1970) now in its "4th Big Month," was cleaning up. Fellow epics like *Patton* (1970), that year's big seven Oscar win was "held over!" and *Tora! Tora! Tora!* (1970) — "Now at Popular Prices" after its roadshow run was basking in a "4th Record Month."

Also playing at three local venues, including one in its "5th Big Week" was another British historical drama — *Cromwell* (1970), a $9 million Columbia Pictures release. Whether this tale of religious strife chimed a particular chord with the descendants of Brigham Young's Mormon followers, to skewer its local popularity, is hard to say; *Cromwell* was considered a flop in the US. But it cannot be denied it fared better than its sister epic, which after three weeks was replaced at the 21 Century with a re-release of *Lawrence of Arabia* (1962).[661]

The film's poor performance was largely echoed across North America.[662] According to the National Association of Theatre Owners, its country-wide take after some six weeks of release was: "good-fair in the east, poor in the southeast, fair-poor in other territories."[663] In a final tally, it grossed slightly over $3 million and came fifty-first in the yearly box office take.[664] It was marginally ahead of the notorious sex-change comedy *Myra Breckinridge* (1970) with the magnificent Raquel Welch, George Lucas's debut *THX-1138* (1971), Michelangelo Antonioni's hippy hymn *Zabriskie Point* (1970), and the handsome but sombre *The Last Valley* (1971).

All the above cost considerably less than *Waterloo*, which magnifies the total loss to gargantuan proportions. According to David Pirie in his 1984 book *Anatomy of the Movies,* it topped the list of "All Time Flops" at the North American box office, before being elbowed away by *Heaven's Gate* in 1980, with rentals (the actual amount returned to the studio) of just $1.4 million.[665] This is slightly misleading, as it listed the loss against the full $25 million of worldwide rights, not Paramount's actual investment. So, it can be denied this dubious distinction as it slithers ever so slightly down the "flops" poll, bumping the studio's other money pit *Darling Lili* (1970) to the top position instead (it lost around $20 million).

Luckily for Bluhdorn and Evans's Paramount, the enormous success of the tearjerker *Love Story* (1970) kept the company in the black. Meanwhile, a certain young Francis Ford Coppola was in production on *The Godfather* (1972), which would prove a box office goldmine the following year.

The film's release in 1971 came at the end of a spate of war films, which included: *The Bridge at Remagen* (1969), *Catch 22* (1970), *M*A*S*H* (1970) and *Kelly's Heroes* (1970); many of these had a cynical and dark take on conflict, even the so-called "just" war against fascism. As we saw above in the pages of *The Deseret News*, there were two other major war epics pulling in the bucks.

The most significant being *Patton* (1970) with its "warts and all" portrait of the controversial US general, appealing to both hawks and doves, which was richly rewarded — both critically and financially. The other was the $25 million reconstruction of the Pearl Harbor attack in 1941 — *Tora!*

Tora! Tora! (1970). It had a comparable budget to *Waterloo*, and attempted to show both sides fairly and honestly, before concluding with a terrific and spectacular action climax. Produced to follow up the success of *The Longest Day* (1962), it was considered a flop on its original release, suggesting that audiences were no longer enamoured by historical epics. In fact, it *would* make a modest profit, which chimes with the ballyhoo of "4th Record Month" blaring out from *The Deseret News*.[666] It may not have enjoyed the blockbuster success envisioned, but this dramatisation of a traumatic American defeat resonated with a country that was examining its conscience amid uncertain times. All these films, in some form, were influenced by the one defining saga of the decade: the Vietnam War.

A glance past Andy Israel's *Waterloo* review quoted above from the 02 April 1971 issue of *The Stanford Daily*, the Californian University's student-run paper, reveals the trauma of the ongoing war in South-East Asia. It reported a meeting attended by 250 people to hear former UN ambassador George Ball speak some home truths: "We have stayed too long and spent too much in blood and treasure. We shouldn't have gotten in the first place. So, let's write this unhappy chapter off." He also referenced the ongoing trials of US soldiers implicated in the notorious Mỹ Lai massacre of over 500 Vietnam civilians in March 1968, as "a time for an examination of conscience for the American people."[667] This single event had graphically illustrated to the American public, and the world, the horror and futility of not just the Vietnam agony, but war in general.

Even with the wars of the last fifty years, Iraq notwithstanding, Vietnam seared a generation. The reasons and causes are far beyond the concerns of this book, but an appreciation of its effects may help us see the world of 1971. Perhaps more than anything else was the almost uncensored TV pictures, in garish colour, which entered the living rooms of the entire world. This slow drip-drip of blood and gore was unprecedented. Ever since, military establishments have carefully restricted press access to war zones, which have only been challenged in recent years with the distribution of unsanctioned body-cam footage. The mass family TV audiences were seeing material that only war veterans would have experienced, and gradually learnt a coping mechanism.

Looking again at our 1971 snapshot of *The Stanford Daily* is a cartoon which looks at part of a series, entitled "*When the Hippies take over!*" It is like finding a hieroglyph in an ancient tomb; the sense and purpose of the image being lost in time. Showing a "Hippy" dressed as a "Cop" with a "cool it" badge and firing a "tranquilizer gun — in case the villain gets nervous,"[668] it encapsulates that 1960s phenomenon of counterculture.

Youth rebellion against staid Western mores and energised by the Vietnam War, it represented a utopian vision of a new society which scared the establishment to its foundations.

In 1969, Stanford University was just one of thousands of institutions across America that had seen a series of sit-ins by up to 8,000 students over several contentious political and social issues, with the war being the major one. TV pictures of police firing tear-gas into the crowds of unarmed demonstrators helped to polarise society, which suggested, at least for a time, that a profound change to materialist Western civilisation was just around the corner.

Calling for "Peace and Love" — the so-called "Hippy" youth generation of the 1960s baby-boomers is perhaps best appreciated by what could be loosely described as a counterculture epic. With a cast that dwarfed *Waterloo*, nearly half a million people congregated on rolling fields in upstate New York in August 1969. Michael Wadleigh's enthralling landmark concert Oscar-winning documentary, *Woodstock* (1970), perhaps more than any other, captures the counterculture *zeitgeist* with its undercurrent of defiant opposition to the Vietnam War.

Nothing better encapsulated this than when Country Joe McDonald began strumming what would become one of the most iconic anthems of the era, *I-Feel-Like-I'm-Fixin'-To-Die Rag* AKA *The F-U-C-K Cheer*, and the entire crowd got to their feet and joined in:

And it's one, two, three,
What are we fighting for?
Don't ask me, I don't give a damn,
Next stop is Vietnam.
And it's five, six, seven,
Open up the pearly gates,
Well, there ain't no time to wonder why,
Whoopee! we're all gonna die.[669]

Featuring over seventeen artists from an incendiary The Who, to the haunting sonority of Joan Baez, and the mesmerising, almost apocalyptic rasping chords of Jimi Hendrix, McDonald's protest Rag was the only song to have its lyrics displayed on-screen as a sing-a-long. With a three-hour-plus running time, dynamic split-screen imagery blown up to 35mm CinemaScope from 120-hours of 16mm,[670] and presented complete with an "inter*fucking*mission," this roadshow-*esque* entertainment was greeted by a hungry, enthusiastic baby-boomer audience; grossing over $30 million in the US alone.[671]

The director, Michael Wadleigh, speaking years later, succinctly summed up the film's cultural impact on a generation:

> Woodstock is pretty timeless. The general human condition — war, peace, the generation gap, human rights, our relationship with the Earth — can all be looked at within a kind of metaphorical construct called Woodstock. I think more and more people are describing the film Woodstock as epic. You know, as the sort of left-wing version of (Nazi film) *Triumph of the Will*.[672]

Woodstock was emblematic of the changes that were sweeping through American cinema from the late 1960s as young, fresh talent super-charged the staid and decaying industry. This burst of creative talent for the first time told stories about contemporary life with a veracity and explicitness never seen before, epitomised by *Easy Rider* (1969). To a predominately young audience, this New Wave addressed to *their* times, hopes and fears.

The majority of the population in both America and the other Western democracies looked on aghast at the left-leaning counterculture as personified in *Woodstock*. This silent mass was the status quo and had little desire to overturn it. Many, particularly in the States, were supportive of their government's policy in Southeast Asia. That said, there was little of the flag-waving propaganda and gung-ho spirit that typified the 1940s war effort, and instead just a heartfelt desire to support the "boys" in Vietnam, and get them back home safely. By 1971, a Gallup Poll found that 60% of the American population considered the war to be a "mistake;" society was gripped in a war-weary malaise.[673]

Against this cultural, social and political upheaval, which played out in different hues and tones across the western world, *Waterloo* was offered to the public. It is perhaps hardly surprising that contemplating a trip to the cinema to watch a film detailing a hundred-fifty-year-old non-American event, depicting war on a grand and colourful scale, would be a tricky sell. Regardless of its failings, one wonders if there ever was a big enough audience for the subject. In 1968, Stanley Kubrick announced plans for his own *Napoleon* film to be produced by MGM, but fear of the eventual cost and concern at its commerciality killed the project (see Chapter Twenty-One).

Hollywood entered the doldrums of recession, and was forced to do some soul-searching, as dwindling audiences and rising costs made big budget films too risky. Although the next decade would see a handful of expensive historical-set productions: *Nicholas and Alexandra* (1971), *Young Winston* (1972), *Ludwig* (1973), *Barry Lyndon* (1975), *The Wind and the Lion* (1975), *1900* (1976) and *A Bridge Too Far* (1977), almost all lost money, and heavily; thus, temporarily ending this type of film. For the best part of a decade, Hollywood would shy away from such big enterprises, until *Star Wars* (1977), *Close Encounters of the Third Kind* (1977) and *Superman: The Movie* (1978) spawned the era of visual effects-laden extravaganzas that now dominate popular cinema well into the twenty-first century.

The dawn of the new century saw a brief revival of the epic in the wake of the enormous success of Ridley Scott's *Gladiator* (2000). In the hands of visionary directors like Peter Weir, *Master and Commander: The Far Side of the World* (2003), Wolfgang Petersen, *Troy* (2004) and Scott again, *Kingdom of Heaven* (2005), the results, with a hybrid of real and pixel, were not only very impressive with a strong sense of period, but often intelligently told too. While this new breed of a long-thought dead genre utilised the very best CGI technology, their budgets were often as astronomically high as the days when thousands of real extras rather than pixels were deployed. But too often the age-old problems with the genre of everything dissolving into "a kind of minestrone," where spectacle swamped the story leading to audience apathy, has seen this latest cycle too fade into history.

Despite its UK appearance in the early days of DVD, the film has been largely ignored on home video for many years. This 2000 release, while boasting a good rendition of the stereo audio, with the picture in its full Panavision ratio, was marred by an inferior video encode which offered a weak image. Like the previous VHS release, the BBFC (British Board of Film Classification) demanded approximately 30 seconds of cuts; the horse falls as discussed in Chapter Fourteen.

In 2021, the author was approached by Oscar Beuselinck of Mediumrare Entertainment to help with a planned special edition Blu-ray for the UK. This was an exciting opportunity to use some of the audio from interviews conducted for this very book, the youthful exuberance of these men and women, now in their autumnal years, added immensely to the emotional timbre of *The Making of Waterloo* documentary. Joined by Waterloo expert, Robert Pocock, the author also contributed an audio commentary which discussed both the historical and cinematic points-of-interest. While the release had to conform to the BBFC's cuts, the extras that were able to be assembled allowed the story of the film to be told for the first time. Its long overdue appearance in the high-definition format may owe more to the studio's apparent disinterest in all but its most iconic titles than concerns over animal welfare in the film. For over a decade the BBC have regularly broadcast a HD version offering the impressive stereo sound, albeit with the BBFC dictated cuts.

Despite appearing on VHS in the early 1990s, the author is unaware of any plans for a digital video US release; perhaps memories of its disastrous 1971 distribution still run deep. In 2019, a German release of the full European cut surfaced on Blu-ray, and a year later the Australian video label, Imprint, also offered a release for the Hi-Def market. This disc boasted a very informative featurette by leading film historian, Sheldon Hall (who generously referenced the present author.) These welcome releases finally give fans all over the world a chance to enjoy this classic in the best available home format on the on the largest screen that pockets allow.

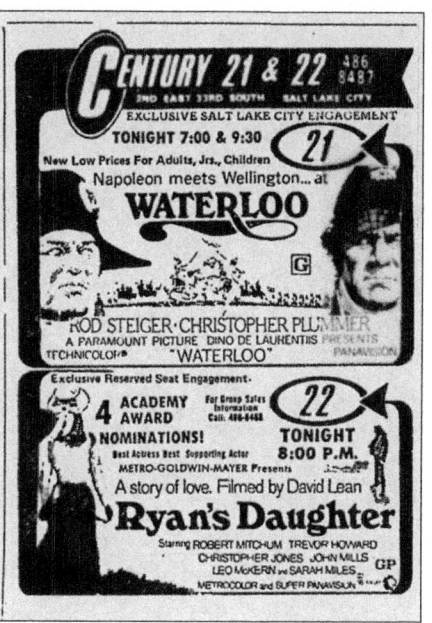

An ad in The Deseret News *at the start of the disastrous North American run in April 1971.* AUTHOR'S COLLECTION

In the UK that summer, the film was still playing in provincial cinemas long after it had disappeared in America. As of 2021, The Royal, St. Ives, is still in business. AUTHOR'S COLLECTION

A selection of international posters. Clockwise from top left: Russia, Poland, Italy and Czechoslovakia. Notice they only feature Napoleon, often with striking symbolism. AUTHOR'S COLLECTION

The Waddingtons board game company issued this jigsaw puzzle, a rare example of a tie-in to the film's UK 1970 release. © SIMON LEWIS

An impression of a deleted scene where two British and French soldiers meet and haggle over some plunder in no-mans-land before the battle. Painted by artist Ron Poulter, who had worked on the costumes for the film. © 2021 RON POULTER

CHAPTER 20
The Myth of a Longer Cut.

Philippe Forquet, who played La Bedoyere, was disappointed not to see what he considered some of his best work in the finished film. He suspected much of it had been lost on the cutting-room floor. He heard later that a considerably longer version was shown in Russia, as was the Soviet practice.

> I found out a movie released in Occidental countries had to be at the most two and a half to three hours long; but in the Communist East, such as Russia, a movie was eight to nine hours; so, spectators went to the theater two evenings in a row. There were four intermissions, and people brought their food (usually fat lard, bread, and they did not forget vodka).

While this is fanciful, for years a myth has sprung up of a much longer version of *Waterloo*.
And some people swear they have seen it.

> I remember having the pleasure of seeing the "Russian" cut of the movie in a theater in Chicago…parts like Blucher being pulled from under his horse after some of the fighting scenes at Ligny…It was the best four hours…I had ever spent in a movie theater![674]

Even one of the many extras, cavalryman Mykola Kholodnyak speaking half-a-century later, recalled his only visible appearance in the above scene:

> Yes, I saw myself in a shot, just in the episode where Napoleon's cavalry rode to attack the Prussian gunners. I was in the uniform

of a Prussian gunner. The French cavalry started the attack. We fired off the fake guns — seven shots — and ran away as if in a panic. To recognise myself later in the movie, I ran away in a zig-zag fashion.

This scene was probably part of a sequence depicting the battle of Ligny, which saw the Prussians defeated, and described evocatively in the script.

> Scene.35: *A regiment of* FRENCH LANCERS *is pursuing the fleeing enemy. They gallop into a* TILTED CAMERA *— a sudden, toppling wave…a black Paolo Uccello forest of lances.*

He described seeing it at the Mosfilm studios in the capital, where he and his regimental comrades were invited for a special screening in January 1970.

> All us soldiers were sitting in a special cinema, and it was the *English* version of the movie. They had a few translators in the cinema, who were translating the words into the Russian language. At the premiere of *Waterloo* at Mosfilm, I saw myself. But then this shot was cut out.

His memory is fascinating. As we saw in Richard Meyer's article, the editing work began in mid-October 1969, but the only other date he mentions is May 1970 as the *start* of the sound mixing process. Mykola is adamant that the date of the Mosfilm screening is correct. The question is; what was presented to the Russian soldiers that day?

That the soundtrack was in English means we can discount any *Russian* version, which accords with Meyer noting the intention to create a single International one. We know a cut was prepared with a simple soundtrack (all re-voiced by Robert Rietty) to screen to the Hollywood executives — in January 1970. This was not considered a finished version, as the intention was to gauge reaction from the backers. The most plausible answer is that Mosfilm, being partners in the production, may have been sent a copy of this work-in-progress edit as a courtesy. Perhaps Mosfilm were so rightly proud of their contribution that the screening was simply an opportunity for the participants to see themselves. As already noted, Mykola's fleeting moment of fame was subsequently cut from the released version.

More intriguingly, at least three people recall one particular scene in the original 1970 UK release, which subsequently disappeared. Firstly Steve Dwan, who has a lifelong interest in the Napoleonic era and contributed to this book (see Appendix): "I distinctly remember the scene with Donal Donnelly's character and the Guardsman the night before the battle — where a plundered pig is exchanged for tobacco." The shooting of this scene was discussed in Chapter Seventeen.

> That was in the cinema release I saw back in 1970, and I can still picture it now: O'Connor drops the struggling pig and chases it across the fields toward the French lines. Sauret suddenly appears with the pig in his arms. O'Connor is seen approaching cautiously at a slightly left orientated camera angle, looking left and right as he comes on. The two face off and the Frenchman (also looking left and right) exchanges the animal for some of O'Connor's tobacco. O'Connor then points at his face, so Sauret will know him if they chance upon each other again on the following day. I have a vague recollection of the *cantiniere* Maria and drummer boys collecting wounded around Hougoumont — but not as clear as Donnelly's scene. My visual memory of it is quite strong, even 50 years later.[675]

To this, the author adds the memory from an old friend and former colleague, Paul Stevens, who saw it at Birmingham's roadshow venue — The Scala Superama in 1970:

> It was pouring with rain, the sound of a pig — cut to close-up of pig, then tilt up to O'Connor crouching and letting the pig suckle on his finger, saying something like: "Come on me darling, come to daddy." He grabs the pig and jumps up out of the bushes into a clearing where he's confronted with an Old Guardsman also foraging. Neither of them moves — just look at each other, then O'Connor says words to the effect: "No need for any unpleasantness now, I reckon we'll be busy enough tomorrow." Then it cuts to the scene that's in the film.[676]

The similarities are striking. The author also distinctly remembers Paul demonstrating the end of the scene by jabbing his finger to his face, which perfectly echoes what Steven Dwan described. It is obvious both saw the same piece of film — somewhere.

Finally, we have actor Richard Heffer, who was actually on set for that night's filming keeping Donal Donnelly company, who also remembers seeing it: "Yup, there was a scene with pig — don't know what happened to it." The controversy that surrounded the treatment of the horses resulted in some censorship cuts; perhaps the pig could also have been "harmed," prompting an excision? He was adamant: "No cruelty; was funny and pig very jolly!"

It is difficult to account for these memories. The author has read through the continuity script which detailed the final edited film — shot by shot — completed a few weeks before the October premiere, and could not see any anomalies. It measured in line with the listed duration of 133 minutes, as noted in contemporary reviews and advertising. This is confirmed by the memoir of Ron Poulter, who had worked at the costumer Bermans in London, researching the correct uniforms for the Highlanders Pipes and Drums. He along with other members of staff would be the very first people to see the finished article outside the post-production crew, for a special press screening on the morning of the world premiere. Sitting in the Odeon Marble Arch at 10.30 a.m. that day, Ron remembers the "demarcated" auditorium: "a few actors were one side and workers, like me, on the other."

Becoming an instant fan of the film that morning, he soon became very familiar with it during its year-long roadshow run in the capital: "I have seen the film many times in London at many cinemas and only seen the *one* version." He became so *au fait* with it that he could identify cut sequences while leafing through stills of the film that a friend at Columbia Pictures showed him. Ron said "he brought out 2 or 3 big boxes of stills for me to pick out a few. The boxes had hundreds of stills in them, many with scenes from the film I have never seen on screen."

Ron has never seen O'Connor momentarily losing his plunder on that rainy night. So how are we to reconcile these contradictions? Was the version Ron saw that morning a different print from the one that would unfurl before Her Majesty later that evening, across town at the Odeon Leicester Square?

A few years previously, when roadshows were more common, there were several instances of films opening at one length, usually in 70mm in just a handful of venues, before being cut down for their later general release in 35mm. Significant examples include: *The Alamo* (1960), *Lawrence of Arabia* (1962), *The Blue Max* (1965) and *2001: A Space Odyssey* (1968). For the last named, after the premiere Kubrick decided to shorten his film. While waiting for the negative to be re-conformed for making new prints, he ordered the handful of 70mm prints then showing, to be recut as per his updated vision.

We know a handful of high-end 70mm prints were struck for the initial run of *Waterloo*.[677] These would have been produced via a different bespoke work-flow from the general release 35mm prints (see below) — and earlier, to be available for the premiere run in October 1970. Could this explain the contradiction?

It cannot be stressed enough that alternative versions of films (during an initial release) in commercial Hollywood is almost unknown before the digital age. The subsequent release of *longer* versions started to become a rare treat in the 1990s: a four-hour *Dances with Wolves: The Special Edition* in 1991 being one of a handful of examples. This would never have happened without the break-out success that greeted Kevin Costner's directorial debut with his three-hour version the previous year.

Back in the 1970s, there were a few instances of very *successful* films balloon for their initial US TV showings. Extended running-time meant extra advertising revenue; a three-hour version of *Superman: The Movie* (1978), which aired on ABC in 1982, being a prime example.[678] By contrast, *Waterloo* limped onto TV in 1972 — no anecdotal evidence has surfaced to suggest this version was any different from its shorter US theatrical running-time.

In the digital age, cinemas receive films via streaming or hard drives, and it is therefore possible for studios — in theory — to update *during* a release; *Cats* (2019) being a notorious example.[679] In 1970, this was not an option.

The 35mm release prints of *Waterloo* were made in "Color by Technicolor" courtesy of their UK lab. Known as "dye transfer," this was a very complex system that involved three strips of film (matrices) copied from the negative; each were then doused in a dye of a primary colour before being embossed onto a blank film, followed by a fourth strip carrying the soundtrack. It is not difficult to see that making another version would have had a very high cost attached and therefore been unfeasible. That said, for the US release with its reduced running time, a new set of matrices were created and shipped to Technicolor's Los Angeles lab for making the mass run of prints — standard practice for international releases.

So, what did Ron Poulter see at the press screening, and was it different from what played for Her Majesty? The answer is a very definitive — NO. Four days later, Ron went to see it again at the Odeon Leicester Square: "I had tickets for the first Saturday's evening performance, as I did not know

I was going to get a press ticket." He is adamant that the 70mm print he saw, which had played at the premiere, was *exactly* the same version. There is every reason to accept Ron's memory as it accords with the published running times, etc. While Ron's testimony (along with most other fans) confirms all the evidence, the author cannot offer a convincing explanation for the fleeting glimpse of a scurrying pig in the no-man's-land of Waterloo.

But what of the unnamed audience member who enjoyed his "best four hours" of *Waterloo* in a Chicago theater?

For most fans of the film, there is a movie Holy Grail, steeped in almost as much myth and legend as the illusive prize of King Arthur's knights. "At the time," Ron Poulter recalled, "we heard that Russia had a 4-hour version like *War and Peace*, but who knows?"

Let us look at the evidence of a much longer "Russian" film.

The joint agreement between Mosfilm and Dino specified a final version no longer than 150-minutes (see Chapter Three). As Richard Meyer stated: "There was at one time an attempt at a Russian version alongside" his cut. While the original agreement only mentioned one film, it appears perhaps with Mosfilm's increased investment, that there grew the intention for a second, presumably longer version, exclusively for the Communist East. If we run with this thought, the question is, what would have made up this longer film?

The English language screenplay was, as we have seen, written as a two-hour plus entertainment. Actor Richard Heffer remembers seeing a stack of scripts on location in *seven* different languages; these were probably just translations of the master draft version, but they could have contained additional material. Richard periodically grumbled in his diary that a fellow actor would "steal my lines." Latvian actor Pauls Butkēvičs was cast as fellow artilleryman Normyle; "my Russian *Double*!" He would dutifully echo Richard's lines much to his irritation. "He always wanted to ask if he was saying the words right!! I assumed he was filming the Russian version of the script (that we were told about, but never saw enacted)…When not trailing after me he was used as an extra!" The two men were never able to get much beyond: "cigarette?" So, rather than "stealing" Richard's lines, the Latvian may have been just trying to brush up on his English.

The intention may have been to create the additional Russian version with Eastern European actors doubling for the English-speakers and Italians. Quite to what extent this was accomplished is difficult to ascertain. It wasn't, though, unprecedented in cinema history.

With the introduction of Sound in the late 1920s, the still evolving primitive technology did not allow any way to "dub" soundtracks into a foreign language. To solve this problem, in both Europe and Hollywood, producers hired duplicate French, Spanish, etc. casts and filmed on the same sets overnight after the primary speaking actors had gone home. A notable example is Tod Browning's *Dracula* (1930) — whose Spanish language alternative is widely regarded as superior to the well-known Bela Lugosi classic. And proving that comedy is truly universal, Laurel and Hardy re-filmed some of their classic slapstick shorts in phonetic Spanish — with often hilarious results.

So, it is quite plausible that a Russian duplicate version was shot. But it has to be said that no one mentions any examples of this, as it would have made practical sense to shoot such scenes directly after the English rendition. There is another possibility that the "longer" version would have involved new scenes for just the Russian actors. Intriguingly, we do have some evidence for this.

A tiny glimpse of what could have made up a longer Russian running time comes from Aslan Khablauk, another member of the 11th Separate Cavalry Regiment, an Adyghe from the North Caucasus region, near to the Turkish border. Many years later he spoke to a local writer, Saida Jaste, who had come across his connection to the film by chance. Aslan described how he spent much of his time dressed as a "French cuirassier" before being given "the role of marauder or vagabond who stole horses and robbed travellers." He went on to describe to Saida Jaste a particular scene he played with a fellow horseman:

> Aslan with a laugh told that once, when they were filming a scene of a robbery, they, shouting and hooting, galloped at full speed through the forest, where cuts of beautiful fabrics were scattered. At full gallop they grabbed these cuts from the ground, and since S. Bondarchuk allowed them to speak to each other in any language, Aslan shouted in Adyghe: "Mahmud! Grab this silk!" But another soldier grabbed this cut, Aslan's horse got entangled, and he shouted at his comrade in anger, and cut the fabric with a sword. The guys got into their roles so much in this episode it entered the film without change.[680]

No such scene exists in the film, or even in the screenplay, so quite what this was is difficult to determine. The writer says she dutifully wrote Aslan's words but as she was not familiar with the film, understandably she did not probe further. The only direct link to *Waterloo* is the mention of the director's name, but could Aslan have misremembered? The famous Bondarchuk would undoubtably have stuck in the memory, more than say; Aleksandr Alov Martin or Vladimir Naumov. Who? I hear you ask.

These two co-directed the other film for which Aslan recalled more anecdotes for Saida Jaste. Set a hundred years later during the Russian Civil War, *The Flight / Beg* (1970), was also being filmed near Uzhgorod at the same time. A perusal of this three-hour- plus epic shows several spectacular charges in battles, fully using the 11th Separate Regiment (including a dangerous stunt of a rider picking up a Soviet red flag from the ground while galloping at top speed), and several sections involving horsemen in snow-covered forests — but nothing that closely matches the above description.

As we have seen, members of the movie cavalry regiment were invited to see an early cut of *Waterloo*; perhaps they also saw *The Flight*, at a similar stage of editing. It is possible that Aslan *did* see himself on screen during one of these special presentations.

Mykola Kholodnyak, as a fellow cavalryman, took part in the filming for both, and it was the reason he was still shivering in the tent city at the beginning of December 1969. He doesn't remember the scene described above, either in real life, or on screen.

On balance, it is much more believable that Aslan's blink of fame was in a later film, and that he misremembered which director was wielding the megaphone as he galloped wildly through the forest. We should not discount the remote possibility that it *was* Bondarchuk. The film not only starred his *War and Peace* actress Lyudmila Saveleva, but the director team had helmed *Taras Shevchenko* (1951), Bondarchuk's breakout as an actor. So, he may have done it as a favour. But to bastardise one of Wellington's pithy lines: directors of films have better things to do than to film for one another…

Even if we accept that there may have been additional "Russian" scenes shot for *Waterloo*, the question is moot. As the film entered post-production in Rome, the work quickly focused on a single English language edit, as described by Richard Meyer in Chapter Eighteen. It was reported that the aim was for a three-hour movie, with an intermission for roadshow presentations in Western Europe and America,[681] while a similar figure of 200-minutes being mentioned by two trade papers in 1971 (after the editing had been completed).[682]

As we have seen, the roadshow concept was dying, and many studios, including the film's co-financiers, Columbia Pictures, were shying away from lengthy movies. Their UK based *Cromwell*, in post-production during 1970, was also intended to be a three-hour roadshow (director Ken Hughes' original final cut was 195-minutes),[683] but it too was shaved back to just under two-and-a-half hours as a standard release. It was this policy change that may have been the driver behind the final two-hour plus running time for *Waterloo*.

But the question remains, where did the myth of a longer version originate? An intriguing clue comes from Ann Guerin's interview with Rod Steiger for *Show magazine* shortly before the US opening, where she states: "The original version of the movie ran for five hours and it will be shown in Russia at that length. But it has been cut to 129 minutes for the Western world."[684] While the second figure, although out by only a few minutes, is still incorrect for both the European or American releases, and suggests who ever quoted it was doing it from either memory or hearsay.

Where these figures originated from is unclear, but as she appeared to have only interviewed the actor, it is probable *he* was the source. The mentioned "five hours" tallies neatly with Meyer's "first cut," which was only ever a first pass through the material. Perhaps when Steiger returned to the production to re-voice his lines, a casual conversation may have thrown up reference to this very long first cut, and the onetime intention for dual versions, and then repeated to the journalist. On balance it is most probable that this is what she is referring to, via inadvertent misinformation. This has fed into the legend of a hidden four or even five-hour version, for which, as we have seen, there is no actual evidence.

A final, tantalising snippet comes from Pinewood Studios sound mixer Gordon McCallum, who mentioned that Bondarchuk asked if he would be interested in travelling to Moscow to mix the "Russian" cut. Did he mean the Russian language soundtrack or an alternative version? If we are to accept Richard Meyer's timeline, the ancillary version was abandoned early in the editing process. McCallum and his sound department would not have got involved and met Bondarchuk until many months later. Was Bondarchuk still hoping to do another edit? Possibly. But the call from Moscow never came.

For twenty years, the myth continued to grow because of the shroud of the Iron Curtain. Information was hard to verify, and so the idea persisted that deep in the Mosfilm vault was the hidden gem of a longer cut in all its Russian glory.

With the collapse of the USSR and a momentary thaw between East and West, it was possible to seek answers. In 1993, the author contacted the Head of Mosfilm Studios, Vladimir Dostal, who had been Bondarchuk's young assistant on both *Waterloo* and *War and Peace*. What did the studio have in their vaults?

> As for the film *Waterloo*, it was shot in only one version. Mosfilm does not have any cuts or fragments not included in the film. The "more lengthy" Russian version, which you mention in your letter, does not exist.[685]

Upon a more recent enquiry while researching this book, Mosfilm stated that in their vaults was: "Our version — approx. 133 min."[686] This conforms to the well-known International English-language release. During the 2010s, the studio embarked on an ambitious programme of restoring and digitising much of their Soviet-era output, with much of it available for free on their YouTube channel. Amongst these offerings appears to be the original Communist Bloc 1971 cinema release.[687]

Entitled *Ватерлоо*. It conforms to Philippe Forquet's noted Russian preference for movie intermissions; Part Two begins with Wellington's army waking at dawn on the battlefield. Combined, it runs 131 minutes (on the website it runs a few minutes shorter as it plays at the higher Russian TV rate of 25 frames-per-second). It runs slightly shorter than the International version, with tiny nibbles from some scenes.

It does, however, have one *extra* shot!

As Ney and the marshals march down the vast, ornate corridor at Caserta to demand Napoleon's abdication, there is a wide shot that runs almost thirty seconds of this determined group pacing towards the camera. Quite what the purpose of this single addition, which breaks the staccato editing rhythm at the beginning of the film, is yet *another* mystery.

Also, this version retains the English soundtrack but uses a very cheap alternative of a single Russian commentator "para-dubbing" — translating all the dialogue. This was a usual technique in Soviet films for foreign languages, and Bondarchuk used it for all non-Russian characters in *War and Peace*.

Sadly, as fans of this film, we must accept that the longest existing version is — the International 133-minute — that we all know.

In 1982 a tantalising unseen snippet of *Waterloo* appeared in a TV mini-series, *The Charterhouse of Parma*: for its brief reconstruction of the battle, some outtakes from the film were used. From a very hazy memory:

some Scots Greys canter from left to right, close to camera before swooping down into the valley and towards the French ridge in the background. While this angle of Ponsonby's charge does not appear in the final film, some stills do show that it was staged, and presumably filmed, from a very similar point-of-view.

The author, then a teenager, well remembers these fleeting moments, and despite the lack of a VCR, was convinced these were *unused* clips from the actual movie — subsequently backed up by other people.

Directed by Mauro Bolognini, with costumes designed by Ugo Pericoli, no doubt making use of his *Waterloo* research, it is easy to surmise how the Italian producers would have accessed this material. It should, though, be remembered that Dino had long since closed his Rome facility, but this suggests that at least in the 1980s some film cans still existed in a vault, probably somewhere in Italy.

With the sporadic reappearance of a variety of hidden cinematic gems, who knows what time will throw up. The spectacular air combat outtakes from the 1969 film *Battle of Britain* eventually emerged from a UK vault and spruced up several TV history documentaries in the 2000s.[688] It is hoped that one day the long-forgotten *Waterloo* material may yet see the light of day and find a new lease of life.

Two unidentified scenes: A camera crane runs on tracks through a wood to film either French or Prussian infantry. © ASLAN KHABLAUK

A mass attack filmed at the extreme right of French ridge. The British redcoat in the foreground suggests it could be part of Picton's repulse of the French advance. One wonders were they taken for a longer cut. © ASLAN KHABLAUK

Stanley Kubrick on the set of A Clockwork Orange *(1971).* AUTHOR'S COLLECTION.

CHAPTER 21

Did Waterloo kill Napoleon?

The story of *Waterloo* is not complete without discussing — "The Greatest Film Never Made." Over the years, cineastes have trained their fire on the former as the reason the latter never saw the light of day: "My hatred for this film halting Kubrick's *Napoleon* is immeasurable."[689] As usual, the truth is more complex. But the two films have always been intertwined.

In April 1968, Stanley Kubrick's *2001: A Space Odyssey* was unleashed on an unsuspecting world. With a hefty budget of $10 million and designed as a prestige roadshow, the film stands as one of the greatest achievements in cinema history. Science-fiction had until then been the preserve of poverty row productions, and was not considered worthy of A-Picture Hollywood treatment. Over four years, Kubrick had laboured to create innovative special effects that would stand scrutiny when seen in 70mm Cinerama to tell a story of Man's cosmic destiny. It hit the counterculture zeitgeist with its elliptical narrative and mind-bending visuals enhanced, for some, by Marijuana and LSD.

In the autumn of 1968, a French newspaper announced: "This week, several hundred books on Napoleon were shipped from Paris to the London office of Stanley Kubrick."[690] While he continued to shepherd his Space saga through its general release, he had already plunged into his next project, which he described as "an epic poem of action." To him, Napoleon was "one of those rare men who move history and mould the destiny of their own times and of generations to come."[691]

Perhaps more than any other filmmaker, Kubrick loved to research to the nth degree. Before committing to what would be a very expensive and ambitious project, MGM agreed to forward development funds to enable him to prepare his epic. As he had with Arthur C. Clarke on *2001*, the director needed an expert to anchor his research. He not only bought the rights to Oxford University professor Felix Markham's acclaimed biography of Napoleon, but engaged him and several of his brightest students. Another recruit was the renowned military historian, David G. Chandler, who had recently completed a magisterial account of the emperor's campaigns.[692] Kubrick's widow, Christiane, recalled he was drawn to the blood and thunder of the battles: "it was very much a boy thing."[693]

Markham's students immediately set to work on analysing and cataloguing the vast amount of research data from approximately five hundred books. "You really earned your nickel working for Stanley,"[694] declared his long-term assistant Tony Fetwin. Some fifty key characters in Napoleon's story were identified, and a system of index cards was devised to cross-reference based on significant events. In the pre-PC Age, it was the most efficient way for Kubrick and his collaborators to retrieve the required information at any point, without the wasting of time and energy that had been so frustrating during the making of *2001*.

The level of detail was extraordinary. It has been suggested that there was a card for almost every day of the Corsican's life, noting not just the activities of the key characters but the weather and other minutiae. Around 18,000 images were collected of contemporary prints, paintings, maps and uniforms. From historical research, the work moved on to the practicalities of filmmaking; scouting locations across Europe would yield 15,000 photos taken by assistants. Even samples of soil from the Waterloo battlefield were collected to allow a match of the colour and dirt to be recreated on another location.

Kubrick's brother-in-law, and later producer Jan Harlan, recalled the filmmaker's most satisfying part of the movie process: "He loved research and study…Pre-production and editing were his joy — filming itself a necessity."[695] Harlan had originally joined the "family firm" as one of the army of researchers for the film, and being a German speaker, he had helped Kubrick during his pan-European negotiations.

MGM had agreed to finance the film, which was budgeted at a modest $3-6 million (a quarter of *Waterloo*). Despite spending so many years in the UK's MGM Studios at Borehamwood shooting *2001*, Kubrick much preferred the authenticity of location filming. He planned to shoot across France and Italy for most of the interiors, confidently expecting this could be completed within two or three months. He envisaged a tiny documentary-size crew filming in the plush palaces, which would already be dressed with period furniture and artefacts. The Front Projection special effects system that had been used effectively for *2001*'s opening "Dawn of Man" sequence was also to be employed as a cost cutter.

It was the many battles scenes which would soak up the vast majority of the time and budget. Initially, Tito's communist Yugoslavia had been chosen; a popular venue for many large-scale productions of the 1960s. Kubrick was adamant that to do them convincingly would require no less than 40,000 infantrymen and 10,000 cavalrymen. "I wouldn't want to fake it with fewer troops because Napoleonic battles were out in the open," he explained in 1968: "...like vast lethal ballets, that it's worth making every effort to explain the configuration of forces to the audience."[696]

Although the Yugoslavs could provide the required locations — they could not field enough troops to realise the sheer scope of the director's vision. Bizarrely, their communist neighbours in Romania agreed to supply the battalions of troops at $2 per man per day, and then march them to "fight" in Tito's neighbouring Yugoslavia. This idea inevitably soon fell through, but was soon modified by deploying those Romanian soldiers on their home turf — with 5,000 cavalry thrown into the deal. The potential health risks with so many people working closely together, which will strike a chord in a post-Covid-19 world, were considered by ordering 'flu vaccines in bulk. These troops needed to be costumed, and a figure of $40 per unit was offered. But Kubrick was convinced there was a cheaper alternative. He found a New York company that produced both a drip-dry and fireproof paper fabric. Tens of thousands could be manufactured for less than $4 each, onto which could be printed the different uniforms and paraphernalia of buttons and stripes, etc. As with *Waterloo*, the foreground extras would be clothed in cloth while the paper-wearing troops stood in the background. Kubrick conducted many photographic tests to find the precise, minimal distance from the camera to deploy his drip-dry army.

Since he had padded the New York streets as a photographer in his teens, Kubrick was driven to push the cinematographic envelope. He planned to make use of natural light as much as possible with faster lenses to allow longer shooting days. For interiors, experiments were conducted using candles, which as we have seen was extremely difficult with contemporary film stock and lenses, particularly given the chosen 70mm format.

Determined to spend most of the budget on his armies, he planned to avoid employing major stars and their hefty salaries. He noted a recent report in *Variety* that showed that four major films (not named, *Paint Your Wagon* would have been one!) with top stars all failed to recover even their high salaries. For the leading role, he was looking for someone who could portray the extraordinary combination of "restless energy, the ruthlessness and the inflexible will" coupled with a "tremendous charm,"[697] which all who met the Corsican remarked upon. Several "Napoleons" were considered; from Jack Nicholson, the Oscar-nominee for *Easy Rider* (1969) to some British actors — David Hemmings or Ian Holm.[698] For other roles, a host of talent was mooted: Peter O'Toole, Alec Guinness, Jean-Paul Belmondo, Laurence Olivier and Charlotte Rampling.

For the pivotal role of the empress Josephine, semi-retired Audrey Hepburn was approached. Christiane Kubrick noted her husband found the bawdy no less interesting than the battles. Apparently, Josephine enjoyed wearing wet muslin dresses to parties to stress her natural curves; "Stanley was fascinated by that." Costume designer David Walker dutifully produced sketches for some "provocative" dresses. Whether Hepburn was aware of the semi-nude acting requirement is unknown, but she politely declined the role.

Christiane Kubrick said that it was the disastrous Russian campaign of 1812, and the volatile relationship between Napoleon and Josephine, which would form the dominant themes of the film: "Over time, however, Stanley became as obsessed with the man's failures as much as his achievements. He wanted to explore how someone who did everything so carefully and correctly was also capable of messing so much up."[699]

For many years, this extraordinary project lay in the wilderness of myth, before a copy of the screenplay surfaced on the web in the early 2000s. Dated September 1969, it runs to 148 pages, which would equate to a 2½ to 3-hour final movie. Jan Harlan described it as a "reader," and observed that Kubrick's scripts rarely resembled the finished film, as is borne out by reading the few that have appeared on the internet. They are almost completely shorn of the descriptive "Action" that we saw in Harry Craig's *Waterloo* draft. Unlike, for instance, David Lean or Alfred Hitchcock, who liked to perfect their screenplays with every detail pre-planned, Kubrick, the so-called control-freak, preferred instead to riff and explore beyond the written word, through intense and prolonged rehearsals to find the emotional core of a scene, before deciding how best to shoot it. Both approaches have their merits and ultimately depend on the personality and methods of individual directors — and patient backers.

Harlan, speaking years later, seemed to be apologetic over the quality of the 1969 script, maintaining: "Stanley was not a great writer...He had no false pride in this area and hired writers to help him."[700] The script opens with an echo of the "Rosebud" sledge in *Citizen Kane* (1941) as the infant Napoleon clutches a teddy bear (an anachronism — they were not introduced until 1902), and sucks his thumb while listening to his mother tell him a bedtime story. The narrative unfolds at a fast pace as it gallops through the half a century of war, politics, love and sex from birth to death; mainly told with copious amounts of voice-over. This was a preferred technique of the director who used it on several films; the tone was often ironic and designed to counterpoint the action. "Reading the screenplay, it is impossible to tell whether Kubrick likes Napoleon or loathes him,"[701] was the assessment of Jean Tulard, one of France's leading Napoleonic historians. That kind of ambivalence was part of Kubrick's creative makeup and is apparent in much of his work. His method of honing scenes through exhaustive rehearsals and subsequent multiple takes was often his way of trying to answer such questions, which ultimately made him a great filmmaker.

Allied to his preparation, Kubrick wanted to gauge the competition, as he had done with viewing almost all science-fiction films to date for *2001*. Screening every available Napoleonic-themed movie that he could, he declared there had "never been a great historical film" or even one which could be described as "good or accurate." Principally, he turned his fire on Abel Gance's *Napoléon* discussed in Chapter Five), which "I found it to be really terrible. As far as story and performance goes, it's a very crude picture."[702] In fairness to the Gance film, Kubrick is very unlikely to have viewed anything more than butchered fragments. Film historian Kevin Brownlow's painstaking restoration did not begin in earnest until the 1970s and was not screened until 1979, as we have seen Bondarchuk had been keen to see it during his casting sessions in England.

Kubrick apparently found much to admire in Bondarchuk's *War and Peace*. By hook or by crook, he obtained a copy of the John Huston period *Waterloo* screenplay. He was satisfied it was a very different film than the one he planned. He no doubt kept a close eye on the progress of Dino's epic via the trade papers — and his own sources. And then another competitor appeared throwing their hat into the ring.

British director Bryan Forbes, after three years of preparation, planned to make *Napoleon and Josephine* in late 1969. He was one of the country's leading filmmakers of the 1960s, having made a number of well-received films produced by, and sometimes starring Richard Attenborough: The Angry Silence (1960), *Whistle Down the Wind* (1961), *The L-Shaped Room* (1962), *Séance on a Wet Afternoon* (1964) and *The Whisperers* (1967). Owing much to his background as an actor, his quintessential understated British sensibility led to work that was sensitive and character-driven, often specialising in exquisitely-made, intensely intimate chamber pieces.

Unlike the American, Forbes conceived a more compact and modest affair for his biopic: "Stanley, I think, is much more interested in spectacle and he would probably show four or five battles...I'm much more interested in the human emotions, relations and depth of the characters and I think my past films bear this out."[703]

His wife, actress Nanette Newman, said he was "obsessed" with the love story, which would have been the narrative focus, having visited Josephine's charming residence, Château de Malmaison outside Paris, many times during his detailed research.[704] "I don't feel the characters have ever been treated seriously on film. Josephine has almost become a cliche." Despite the heavy competition, Forbes was not ready to give up: "How it will resolve itself I don't know, but I don't want to make it a race."[705]

In late 1968, Kubrick submitted a screenplay to MGM, confident of an imminent start in September 1969. Unfortunately, the Hollywood major that had dominated the industry for half-a-century was in trouble.

Robert H. O'Brien, who was president at MGM, had successfully steered the company from the brink of bankruptcy with a series of profitable ventures: *Doctor Zhivago* (1965) and *The Dirty Dozen* (1967). He had persuaded the jittery stockholders to believe in the expensive ongoing production of *2001*. He was the breed of executive a filmmaker like Kubrick needed; backing the talent and ensuring the budget. Unfortunately, the money was running out and threatening to silence the studio's iconic lion's roar.

During 1968, Las Vegas businessman Kirk Kerkorian had been busily buying up stock in the company before taking control the following year. It quickly became apparent that Kerkorian just wanted to use the MGM name — and asset strip the studio's historic artefacts to fund luxury hotels on the Nevada desert strip. Out went O'Brien and in came the ruthless TV executive James Aubrey, dubbed "The Smiling Cobra" who was tasked with turning the studio's fortunes around from a $35 million loss in the fiscal year of 1969.[706]

By the time Kubrick submitted his screenplay, MGM under James Aubrey declined to take it further, as part of an economy drive with several other productions being cancelled (David Lean's *Ryan's Daughter*, then in the midst of a snail-paced year-long schedule only narrowly avoided the chop). It was rumoured that the imminent start of production on *Waterloo*, and the inevitable competition, was also a factor in the decision. Having already spent $420,000 ($3 million in 2020) the studio had only agreed to finance the pre-production, which meant a layoff for Kubrick's small army of researchers and students. Another attempt in early 1969 to set up a deal with United Artists eventually fell apart, as they too were struggling under the weight of debt. The discovered script draft above was completed in September (just as the *Waterloo* shoot was ending) when the project's future was still uncertain.

With two studios passing company with Kubrick, a white knight came to the rescue in the shape of John Calley, head of Warner Bros., who was from a similar mould to former MGM boss Robert H. O'Brien; an enlightened executive keen to nurture talent, who one wag described as the "blue in the toilet bowl."[707] He offered Kubrick a sweetheart three-picture deal, with Warner Bros. supplying the funds that would allow the director to make what he wanted — the way he wanted. And a guaranteed "final cut," all the rights would revert to Kubrick after seven years. It was an almost unprecedented arrangement in Hollywood history.

Interestingly, *Napoleon* was not chosen as his first production for Warner Bros. One suspects that the studio, who, although in better shape than their rivals (helped by the success of *Woodstock*), balked at such a high budget/risk production. At the time, the studio had another similar, if more modest, project set to go.

It was Bryan Forbes' *Napoleon and Josephine* with Ian Bannen as the Corsican, but it appears the race to the cameras was over before it had begun, as the British director recalled ruefully: "I slaved over writing it for three years, but then Warner Brothers junked it because Stanley Kubrick was going to make a film on the same subject, although he never did."[708]

In 1969, Forbes' own career took a different turn as he was appointed managing director of EMI Studios at Elstree. "I had complete autonomy up to a million pounds…anything over a million pounds I had to go to the main board. The most expensive film I made was *The Go-Between* (1971), and that was 680,000 pounds." Winning the Grand Prix at 1971's Cannes Film Festival, Joseph Losey's masterpiece was just one of several other instant well-loved British classics: *The Railway Children* (1970), *The Tales of Beatrix Potter* (1971) that Forbes oversaw during his three-year tenure at the studio. "Everybody thought I had a lot of power, but I lacked power in the one area it really mattered in the film industry and that is distribution. The creative people are always at the mercy of the distributors."[709]

Ultimately, EMI's financial woes would see Forbes resign in 1971. Described as a "Renaissance man, with an ability to take risks and engage a multitude of skills,"[710] before his death in 2013, Forbes would explore many creative avenues, including as a novelist. Although it seems he never revisited Château de Malmaison and its nineteenth-century ghosts. While his project would not have had the broad expanse of Kubrick, one can surmise that Forbes would have delivered an intelligent, emotionally subtle piece, perhaps tinged with a sense of melancholia, and the fragility of the human soul that imbued much of his best work.

As a curious footnote to these smaller and less epic projects, Dino, about to plunge in to his own epic within weeks, had also announced an identically titled project to Forbes, but with no other details surviving, this can easily be dismissed as a "spoiler."[711] There was even talk of a *third* project, again with the same title, this time a bizarre Leslie Bricusse *(Doctor Dolittle)* musical starring Anthony Newley and Barbra Streisand![712] The story, with — "A love story" — added to the title, eventually made it to the small screen in a mini-series starring Armand Assante and Jacqueline Bisset in 1987.

Despite cancelling Forbes film, it appears Warner Bros. were reluctant to proceed with their star director's epic, and wanted a logistically modest, but still artistically ambitious project for their first joint venture. Christiane Kubrick, speaking years later, recalled his initial disappointment: "After feeling very down for about two weeks, he hit on *Traumnovelle (A Dream Novel*, a 1926 novella by the Austrian writer Arthur Schnitzler)...but he didn't know how to do it. He wasn't happy..." Abandoning for now what would eventually become his final film, *Eyes Wide Shut* (1999), he happened upon Anthony Burgess's dystopian novel *A Clockwork Orange* "and fell in love with it."[713] Announced in February 1970, it would be the fastest and cheapest production the director would subsequently ever make. Cameras turned at several British locations in October 1970 — the same month as *Waterloo*'s world premiere.

Seven months later, having seen the Dino film, Kubrick wrote a brief note to Felix Markham, describing it as "silly," but without any further comment. While he considered its existence would make their project harder to achieve, he was confident that eventually they would be able to do it, as he mentions discussing making a deal.

Strangely, only a day or two later, *Variety* reported that according to John Calley of Warner Bros., Kubrick intended to make *Traumnovelle* as his next production.[714] The Markham letter makes no reference to this eminent change of direction, and potentially another furlough for the Oxford Don. Nothing more is heard about the dream story, but with *A Clockwork Orange* only weeks from release, he returned to *Napoleon*.

In a memo dated 20 October 1971, he set out his fresh approach with a completely revised screenplay. The below-the-line budget was envisaged at $4 million, with a quarter of that amount allocated for the battle scenes to be filmed in Romania. He noted the above-the-line costs would include a "Napoleon," and also the accumulated debts from the aborted MGM and United Artists planning periods. He was adamant that quality actors rather than stars would be a better and cheaper option; suggesting Patrick Magee, fresh from *A Clockwork Orange*, as an example. The memo ends with action to be taken, which included locations to be scouted, a deal with Romania for their army, and additional writers.

One of those was Anthony Burgess, author of *A Clockwork Orange*, and fired up by the creative possibilities, Kubrick urged him to write a novel (as he had done with Arthur C. Clarke for *2001*) which *could* be the basis for a screenplay. Eagerly, Burgess set to work, but his early treatment, which used Beethoven's *Eroica* symphony as a structure, was considered too experimental, playing fast-and-loose with the facts for the director's taste, not helped by Burgess's dialogue, which Kubrick found unconvincing and weighed down with too much exposition. It highlighted the director's own problem of how to tell a great story which did not trivialise the historical record. He questioned whether this was even possible without profoundly distorting the facts. One senses he recognised the same flaws in his own previous script as he profusely thanked the writer with admiration and respect as a fellow artist. Undaunted by the rejection, the author pressed on and published the *Napoleon Symphony* in 1974, complete with a warm, and ever hopeful, dedication to the director.

How far did *Waterloo*'s fate affect this fresh start for *Napoleon*?

As we have seen, the first attempt to set up the film in 1968/9 was scuppered by the two studios pulling out — all before *Waterloo*'s release. By the time of the '71 memo, the film had been and gone — its failure clear to all. Jan Harlan later stated in his documentary about the director, that the film was ready for filming.[715] While acknowledging it had some merit, Harlan cited its box office failure as the reason for Warner Bros. decision to abort the project. As Harlan would have been privy to the conversations between Kubrick and his studio backer, his verdict must be taken seriously.

Yet, there is no evidence that the project was any further along after the hiatus; Jack Nicholson had passed on playing the lead with no one else in the frame. Harlan's comments, spoken some thirty years later, probably conflate the frustrating four-year saga into a bite-sized interview answer — and perhaps should not be taken too literally. If *Waterloo*'s failure had been an overriding concern, it seems strange that the studio wouldn't have poured cold water on Kubrick's initial enthusiasm as he wrapped up *A Clockwork Orange*.

It would be churlish, though, to suggest that it wasn't considered an issue around the boardroom table in Burbank, Hollywood. It should be remembered that the "crash" that had almost washed away many of the studios in 1970/71, had led to an industry-wide pull back from expensive productions. Arguably, it could be said that this helped contribute to the goldmine of medium-budget instant classics: *The French Connection* (1971), *The Last Picture Show* (1971), *Chinatown* (1974), etc — for which the decade is rightly celebrated as a true golden age of cinema. While there may have been some wariness over a potentially large budget, both sides were very keen to maintain a good business relationship, and Warner Bros. may have been willing to wait and see what their star director planned to do.[716]

So, if we subtract Bondarchuk's film from the equation, the question remains: why didn't Kubrick make his movie after 1972? Around New Year 1972 *Variety* announced that Kubrick "shifts back in time"[717] for an untitled Napoleon project with no further details, or subsequently thereof. According to Julian Senior, a long-time friend and executive at Warner Bros., Kubrick never officially submitted a new screenplay to the studio for serious consideration.[718] It was later suggested that the studio finally "nixed" the project because, according to an unnamed executive, they were unable to gauge its feasibility without "a kind of finite sense of what Kubrick would do with the material."[719]

By late 1972, Kubrick had fallen in love with another project which had echoes of *Napoleon*; an adaptation of William Makespeace Thackeray's nineteenth-century novel — *Barry Lyndon* (1975).[720] It would consume the next three years and see a $3 million budget balloon to $11 million. Famous for its use of candlelight, Kubrick utilised NASA lenses to capture the natural look of period paintings. Greeted with consternation on its first release; its slow, haunting pace and style has subsequently weathered well. It is now considered one of the director's finest works.

It appears he never *seriously* considered returning to the Napoleon material for the rest of his career. Kubrick scholar Filippo Ulivieri has written a well-researched paper looking at the filmmaker's many unrealised projects, which gives a fascinating and illuminating insight into his preoccupations and tastes, with war subjects particularly prominent.[721] Despite his sweetheart deal with Warner Bros., who would consider any project he submitted, it is not hard to see what really constrained this artist. In a very rare interview, given to the widely respected British critic Barry

Norman, the filmmaker was asked why he had made so few films: "You must have a million ideas." Kubrick's answer, which will resonant with every storyteller since time immemorial, gets to the crux of problem: "No, no, ideas are a trap! You can't make a film based on an idea — you must have a story."[722]

One wonders whether the enormous effort poured into research had become an end in itself and perhaps deep down he never had a grip on the story. For a filmmaker who prided himself on preparation, perhaps being unable to answer profound artistic and philosophical questions within himself would have negated all the rest of the effort.

Even if he had found the story he wanted to tell, Jan Harlan believed Kubrick felt compromised, that he "could not do justice to his vision,"[723] without a much longer running-time and budget. It has been suggested he considered a twelve-hour TV series starring Al Pacino, although Julian Senior thinks this was only a throwaway comment in an interview.[724]

By the time of his death aged 70 in 1999, the era of high-end TV series was just over the horizon, with the explosion of CGI that may have helped realise the spectacular battle sequences Kubrick so dearly yearned to stage.

In the subsequent two decades there have been many announcements of resurrecting the project, most notably from his friend Steven Spielberg. Regardless of the talent of any eventual filmmakers, it could not be described as a Kubrick film. One wonders whether the spirit of the Master would cast too heavy a shadow on any such enterprise.

Perhaps the nearest we can get to this unmade would-be-masterpiece is the voluminous research by Kubrick's assistants, which once occupied two full rooms of his Hertfordshire home. This is now available for all to see as part of the Stanley Kubrick Archive at the University of the Arts in London.

For many cineastes, when compared to *Waterloo*, Kubrick's *Napoleon* is by default the better film — unmade or not. What can be said with certainty is it would have been an iconic cultural event that would have dwarfed all others. The irony being, had his film been made, the former (and Bryan Forbes version too) may have sat as a lesser but still valid companion piece retelling one of the most extraordinary epochs in history.

Rod Steiger as Napoleon, broken and defeated, slumps in his coach on his way into exile. The actor would struggle to get such meaty parts for the remainder of his career. AUTHOR'S COLLECTION

CHAPTER 22

"*The Memory Of Your Greatness...*"

"*Waterloo* was an adventure that gave me great satisfaction." Dino De Laurentiis said reflecting years later on his immense production for which he had marshalled one of the largest budgets to date: a cool $26,160,006.[725]

> There was no way I could lose money on the production, because I had passed on the gross costs to the Russians, who had taken their own territory in return. In the USSR the film was a success: Bondarchuk was a mythical figure in that part of the world.

Pondering the reasons for not attaining box office gold, he concluded it was the lack of star power: "I'm sure that with Burton and O'Toole we would have cleaned up everywhere, even in the places where we didn't do as well." With a hint of "spin" but not backed up by the numbers in North America, as we have seen, he believed the film did:

> Excellent business in all the English-speaking territories, since they were the ones who won the battle (at least that's how I see it). And since Napoleon lost, the film did horribly in all the French-speaking territories. All of which demonstrates once again that the public likes to side with a winner.[726]

His daughter Veronica does not remember his reaction at the time, but recalling his motto — *Andare sempre avanti*: Ever onward, he was never downhearted for long:

> My father, he was upset for one day and then he moved on to the next movie. He always did that. He was the kind of guy that

when his movie came out, we would go with him to the movie to check how the audience was reacting. Then we would go out and he would wait for the box office, and if the movie wasn't doing well — he moved on. You've got to do that otherwise you will go crazy!

Even before the film opened, Dino's life and career had been forced to change gear. His dream of running his own studio was over: "Building Dinocittà was the only mistake I've made in my life," he admitted later: "That facility was enormous and the general expenses were sky high…If I had built it in New York, it would have been fantastic: Rome is no longer the right city for these things. But that's where I built it."[727]

A change of government in Italy had meant that the Andreotti Law (see Chapter Three) which had been so beneficial to big international film productions in Italy had been replaced by the Corona Law. This stipulated much stricter terms to qualify for tax benefits. Aimed at ensuring the "purity" of national Italian film, the policy was self-defeating as Italy was no longer viable for large-scale production, and consequently the money and talent went elsewhere.

Dino felt the winds of change. He and his empire were viewed with suspicion by the Rome politicians; it was time to sell up Dinocittà and leave his homeland. "Just think about it, in his 50s he left Italy where he was the number one producer." Veronica remembered how her father reinvented himself in America:

> He left because they changed the laws in Italy and the state wouldn't finance movies to Italians that did co-production with other countries, which was stupid! I know that he left because of that law, and he became a huge producer in America. So, I mean to do that, you've got to invent yourself, have the desire and the passion that burns so strong inside of you, that you would do anything to get it, and he did everything he could to get those movies going. He did.

Dino would set up shop in Hollywood, eventually opening another, more modest production complex in Wilmington, North Carolina called DEG Studios; eventually this too he was forced to sell. Over the next four decades, he would enjoy varying degrees of success with amongst others: *The Valachi Papers* (1972), *Death Wish* (1974), *Three Days of the*

Condor (1975), *Mandingo* (1975), *Blue Velvet* (1986), *Bound* (1996) and *Hannibal* (2001).

To some, a Dino movie was synonymous with a certain kind of brash, camp, colourful cinematic "minestrone." *King Kong* (1976), *Flash Gordon* (1980), and *Dune* (1984), good examples of some being maligned on initial release that have aged *dis*gracefully to become much loved cult classics (*Flash* being a particular favourite of the author). Perhaps less successful, but quite notorious: *The Drum* (1976), *Hurricane* (1979) and *Tai-Pan* (1986). He continued to make more highbrow films, including Ingmar Bergman's *The Serpent's Egg* (1977), and often with hefty budgets with top directors: Milos Forman on *Ragtime* (1981) and Roger Donaldson (originally David Lean) on *The Bounty* (1984); neither were commercially successful despite some good critical notices.

By the 1980s Dino rarely went to sets and instead delegated. One of those entrusted with multi-million-dollar projects was his daughter Raffaella, then only in her twenties.

> I wanted to be a production designer. I studied architecture, and I pursued that career for a little bit — quite a bit, actually. But then I was a much better organiser of people than I was a production designer…I mean, I would have been a mediocre one. I was much better at doing production than I was doing sets. On movies, I am a nightmare for production designers, because I know more about it than they ever think a producer should know.

To counter any accusations of nepotism, Raffaella, who barely ten years before had hitchhiked into Russia, had first to prove herself by starting at the bottom as the proverbial "tea-girl." She was tasked with scrubbing studio sets clean overnight, before cutting her teeth, producing smaller projects. Having proved her ability to his satisfaction, Dino handed the reins of two of his biggest post-*Waterloo* movies: *Conan The Barbarian* (1981) and *Dune* (1984) to Raffaella, under his aegis — it was the start of a four-decade career.

> I think experience is very important because if you don't love it, you know, you can't really do it. I learned that all from him you know, but sometimes you learn more from the mistakes, from the things not to do than the things to do…Things have also changed so much in movie-making. It's so much easier today to

make movies. So almost anything that happens today on a movie set, I've seen before. I'm still waiting for something to *happen!*

She would spread her wings and become an independent in her own right, while Dino would continue to produce films until he died in 2010, aged ninety-one. "My father used to do those movies because that's what he liked," said Veronica, summing up her father's passion: "He always said (and I agree with him) that movies are about emotion. It's about giving an emotion to the audience of some kind, and I think he did succeed in that."

In 1969, Veronica, aged just 19, standing amid the ballroom set with all eyes watching how the daughter of Silvana Mangano would fare, had high hopes that this would be the start of an exciting career.

> I was supposed to be Juliet, in *Romeo and Juliet* for Zeffirelli. My English wasn't perfect enough to play that part, but my father really pushed me and sent me to acting school to coach my voice, then my mother didn't want me to. They had an argument and I let it go.

Her role in *Waterloo* would be her last — for quarter of a century. "The reality was that I did not (act) because my mother did not want me to and I was very young, and I even thought I really wanted to do it; I wasn't strong enough to say, you know what? I'm going to do it, anyway."

Instead, she found herself in the world of fashion, and launched the Design House Veronica De Laurentiis (VDL studio), with which she enjoyed great success over 15 years.

Yet, there was always a half-buried first love that continued to nag away at her.

The year 1994 would prove to be the pivot of her life. She not only married film producer Ivan Kavalsky, "my angel and the love of my life," but also enrolled in an intensive two-year acting course. Graduating, she has appeared in *Red Dragon* (2002) directed by Brett Ratner, and landed a starring role in Lucio Fiorentino's *Pandemia* (2012). As well as TV shows like HBO's *Entourage*, she appeared in an award-winning short, *While You Were Waiting*. She has also guest-starred on her daughter Giada's popular cookery series, Food Network's *Giada at Home*.

With her candid and compelling autobiography *Rivoglio La Mia Vita* (*Reclaiming Your Life*) published in 2006, now in its 4th edition, she has spoken publicly about violence and the need for healing. She hopes her story will be a voice for women who have no voice.

In 2011 she founded a non-profit organisation, *Association Veronica De Laurentiis*,[728] whose mission is to assist, educate and give a second chance to all victims of violence, abuse and stalking. With the similar tenacity and determination attributed to her father, she is a passionate advocate of one of modern society's most pressing issues:

> After a deep and successful analysis and inner journey, today Veronica is ready to share her vision of the modern woman: the meaning of living a full life, feeling satisfied in our experience as a woman, mother, companion, and leading woman in society.

Sergei Bondarchuk never topped the greatness of *War and Peace*. Whether it was a realisation that he would not develop an international directing career, he joined the Communist Party in 1970 and became a leading figure in Soviet film industry politics. The following year he was elected Chairman of the Union of Filmmakers, a bureaucratic post which quickly made him an unpopular figure amongst his colleagues.

Notwithstanding the failure of their joint venture, he and Dino planned to work again together on a story about the American journalist John Reed in the Russian Revolution, based on his book *Ten Days That Shook the World*. Warren Beatty was keen to star and discussed the project with Bondarchuk; the two didn't gel, and the project stalled. Both would pursue their own versions independently.[729]

Bondarchuk didn't direct another film until 1975 with *They Fought for Their Country / Oni srazhalis za rodinu*. Its arch-propaganda title hides a well-directed and down-to-earth story of Red Army "grunts" in World War Two, in which the title reads more ironic than deferential. It is a film that demands to be better known and regarded. Certainly, as a war movie, it is one of the best of the genre in *any* language.[730]

It is interesting to compare it with *Waterloo*, because it brilliantly illuminates the psychology of men in battle as they prepare to defend a bridgehead, against the advancing German tanks. These are no Soviet automatons dying for Uncle Joe Stalin. These are ordinary men — and they are frightened. One intimate shot follows a soldier's hands as he stands shaking in a dugout, nervously fingering his uniform and shuffling his feet. Bondarchuk also co-starred with his old sparring partner from *War and Peace*, Vyacheslav Tikhonov, this time playing a gentle, mild-mannered middle-aged soldier who suffers shell shock, mentally disintegrating before our eyes. Bondarchuk plays his mate, who is horribly wounded. A teenage girl medic tries to pull his shattered body to a dressing station where follows a lengthy sequence as the soldier writhes in pain. Interspersed with the constant artillery bombardment, Bondarchuk shows surreal images of nature and a windmill consumed by fire to heighten the horror and insanity of conflict.

The director had commented that his war service "still leaves a wound in the soul,"[731] and one wonders if his choice of war subjects for his previous four projects were a heart-felt attempt to expunge an inner pain? At one point, his character voices sentiments that could not have been too far from Bondarchuk's own views on war: "Death is not your dear aunt. She's a formidable bitch feared by communists and non-communists, and all other common people."[732]

He followed this with a lyrical film based on an Anton Chekhov story, *The Steppe* (1977), about a country boy's journey to school in the city, set just before the 1917 Revolution. Considering Bondarchuk's own country roots, it is easy to see his attraction to the material. It was to have been his next film following *War and Peace*, as he sought a change of artistic tempo. With its lack of the epic spectacle, it suggested an intriguing development in his career.

The 1980s would see him making stolid propaganda epics which are devoid of nuance: *Mexico in Flames* (1982) and *Ten Days That Shook the World* (1983). These were the resurrected John Reed project detailing the American journalist's involvement in two pivotal revolutions. With a polyglot cast, including Franco Nero and Ursula Andress, they may have had the scale of his former work but little of the poetry. His once potential collaborator, Warren Beatty, produced, directed and starred in his own version — *Reds* (1982) which fared much better both critically, and commercially.

By 1986, as a fresh wind was blowing in the USSR with Mikhail Gorbachev's *perestroika* (restructuring), Bondarchuk was seen by the younger generation as an old guard conservative and dramatically voted out from his Union chairmanship. His daughter, Natalya, was at the tumultuous meeting to witness his overthrow. "I sat in the hall, holding hands (with a friend). People were shouting and stamping their feet about their imaginary freedom, preventing anyone being heard. My father was not even chosen as a delegate." Only one filmmaker came to his defence, Nikita Mikhalkov, best known for *Burnt by the Sun* (1994): "who spoke from the rostrum, saying that if Bondarchuk had made only two films — *War and Peace* and *They Fought for Their Country*, then he would have knelt before him. Then they hit Mikhalkov. My father was very upset by the onslaught of the so-called 'new wave' in the cinema."[733]

In 1992, despite this rejection in his own country, he would make one last film. Costing $45 million, raised from various European sources, *Tikhiy Don / And Quiet Runs The Don* was based on the Nobel Prize-winning novel by Mikhail Sholokhov, considered one of the most influential novels about the Russian Revolution. It starred a very English Rupert Everett as a Cossack, supported by Delphine Forest and F. Murray Abraham.

Daniele Nannuzzi, who had become a highly regarded cameraman in his own right, photographed it. He fondly remembers working with the director who had mellowed in the intervening twenty years:

> He was more human, like a grandfather, you know. He gave me a lot of freedom to do everything I want. In the morning he told me the story of the scene. Then he asked me to prepare lighting as I wanted, and then he goes. I prepared three cameras. I gave him a Russian movie with very long takes but with the possibility to cut, thanks to using two cameras. I had a fantastic rapport and connection with him.

With filming finished, an incomplete version was screened at the 1993 Cannes Festival and promptly vanished. It fell victim to a complex legal dispute which prevented any further work and resulted in the film being locked away in a bank vault. This legal wrangle was not untangled until 2006, when the film was finally edited by Daniele and Bondarchuk's son, Fedor, as a mini-series for Russian TV. "It's my masterpiece." said Daniele of his career high; "for me, it's like a *Gone with the Wind*. It was a colossal film for me."

In 1994, the author in the pre-internet age found the address of the venerable director who was then living quietly in an apartment in Moscow. Knowing Bondarchuk was not an English speaker, the author found a Russian speaker to help draft a letter with various questions about his career. The letter was duly sent. Many weeks went by and no reply. Driving back from work one evening, the author heard the news on the radio: "The Russian film director, Sergei Bondarchuk, best known for *War and Peace* and *Waterloo,* has died in Moscow. He was 74."

Bondarchuk's hero and inspiration, Leo Tolstoy, would be portrayed on the screen in *The Last Station* (2009), earning an Academy Award nomination for Christopher Plummer. Aged 82, he would become the oldest person to win the coveted award the following year for *Beginners* (2010) playing a late blooming gay man. Holding his Oscar aloft, he quipped: "You're only two years older than me, darling, where have you been all of my life?"[734]

The Academy may have been slow to acknowledge Plummer's huge contribution to Stage and Screen, but he was still working into his 90s; the elder statesman of his thespian generation. He has shown great versatility across his career, whether a Shakespeare-quoting Klingon in *Star Trek VI: The Undiscovered Country* (1991), a foil for Peter Sellers in probably the series' best, *The Return of the Pink Panther* (1975), an eccentric professor in *Hector and the Search for Happiness* (2014) or as Mike Wallace in Michael Mann's powerful *The Insider* (1999), and a star turn as Sherlock Holmes; Plummer avoided being typecast.

He was always a dependable actor both in front and behind the screen. In 2017, when controversial allegations about actor Kevin Spacey came to light, the director of his latest film, *All the Money in the World*, Ridley Scott, took swift action to reshoot all his twenty-two scenes, barely weeks before release. With just a fortnight's notice, Plummer, just shy of 90, agreed to abandon his holiday and step in for the hectic nine-day shoot which cost $10 million. Playing the billionaire J. Paul Getty was yet another portrait to add to Plummer's gallery of patricians and "great men," for which his natural poise and confidence made him a perfect choice.

He would reprise Wellington in a TV series *Witness to Yesterday* (1974) to add to a veritable parade of the famous, including: Franklin D. Roosevelt, Archduke Ferdinand, Caesar, Kaiser Wilhelm II, Rudyard Kipling and Herod Antipas amongst many others.

One great man he regretted playing, or more precisely a wizard, was for Peter Jackson, himself reputedly a fan of *Waterloo*, who sought him for the pivotal role of Gandalf in his *Lord of the Rings* trilogy. After seeing Ian McKellen in the part, Plummer joked: "I hate the son of a b****!" He conceded that he doubted he would have brought enough warmth to the role, as he may have been too "little cold and imperious."

In 2008, he published his memoirs, *In Spite Of Myself*, full of amusing and often insightful anecdotes of his long, eventful career, which suggested another avenue for his talent. Perhaps with the wisdom of age, he was able to look at himself with a candid honesty, warts and all.

But it was acting that remained his biggest love, and even after seven decades he had no desire to retire, feeling sorry for those that do: "It means they haven't loved what they do in life. Nothing could be more marvellous than traveling the world and being paid to do that, I mean, that's extraordinary."[735]

In 2021, Christopher Plummer passed away quietly in his Connecticut home, with Elaine, his wife of fifty-one years, by his side. The deluge of tributes that covered social media following his death, if sometimes unfairly overemphasising his musical *bete noir*, suitably reflected his position as a true acting great. Few put it better than Lou Pitt, his friend and manager of 46 years: "He was a national treasure who deeply relished his Canadian roots…Through his art and humanity, he touched all of our hearts and his legendary life will endure for all generations to come…an extraordinary man who deeply loved and respected his profession."[736]

Plummer had played King Herod in one of the biggest cultural events of the 1970s — Franco Zeffirelli's famous TV mini-series, *Jesus of Nazareth* (1977), which reunited him with cameraman Armando Nannuzzi. The complex shoot presented opportunities for Daniele to strike out from being his father's assistant. Given his own crew, he filmed and directed many sequences which not only had to match his father's work but also the collaborating British cameraman, David Watkin. After completing the editing, Zeffirelli paid him a warm compliment: "You know, Daniele, your stuff — it's like pork. We don't throw out anything."

He was also grateful to Daniele for saving the highly charged emotional scene of an emaciated Robert Powell as Jesus is lowered from the cross.

> When I see the body come down, I go with my zoom lens very slowly on his face. I see the rain on his eye. His eye was still. And I think, *how is it possible not to blink?* That's when Franco said: "Cut!" And the doctor made one injection and a heart massage because Robert was almost dead.

As the exhausted actor recuperated, it was clear there could be no second take. Unfortunately, a wandering extra had obscured the main camera angle at the crucial moment. Luckily, Daniele's shot saved the day.

It was on another war film, *El Alamein: The Line of Fire* (2002), in which Daniele's photography was particularly praised; winning three awards, and nominated for a fourth.[737] He purposely filmed in summer when "the sun is terrible, always on top; bad light." He deployed reflectors to bounce a cold, blue light onto the actors faces, and dyed their costumes in tea, all to give the images a harsh and unforgiving look to supplement the brutal story. "And the light was war. I like special effects made in camera."

In more recent years, with much of the artistry of cinematography being subsumed by the mantra of digital's "fix it in post," Daniele has tired of movies, but found fresh artistic inspiration in the world of opera lighting. "I don't want to be like Gloria Swanson, when she said: 'the movies now are too small for me.' But it's true, they don't need us anymore. They like to shoot without light, without anything; just cannibalise the cinematography. I think every movie is the same. Now I work on the stage."

The man who had ordered Robert Powell's crucifixion, Pontius Pilate, was played by none other than Rod Steiger. While many actors, including fine ones, can be loosely lumped together in types, Steiger was an absolute one off. He invariably upstaged all in his films with a level of intensity seldom seen before or since.

He would follow *Waterloo* with a memorable comedic performance for Sergio Leone in *A Fistful of Dynamite* (1971). Five years later, he realised a long-cherished dream of playing the irascible 1930s comedian in *W. C. Fields and Me* (1975), which was critically mauled. He played another historic despot, Benito Mussolini — twice; *The Last 4 Days of Mussolini* (1975) and *Lion of the Desert* (1980).

For the rest of his career, he would be largely relegated to cameos, in which the power and authenticity of his performance often stole the show. His appearance as Father Delaney in *The Amityville Horror* (1979) briefly raises this schlock horror film to another level. His "big" performances often found him accused of overacting, something he denied in suitably grandiose terms, saying; he was "trying to take the medium of acting to as far as I can go, and that why I sometimes go over the edge."

Few directors fully appreciated Steiger's talent, and it is a shame he somewhat faded from view. When Ron Howard asked him to attend an audition for a cameo for his upcoming Tom Cruise Irish epic, *Far and Away* (1992), Steiger was insulted at the prospect of a further humiliation; the director wanted it videotaped. These tapes often formed a scurrilous after-dinner amusement on the Bel-Air circuit in Tinseltown. Passing up Ron Howard's offer, Steiger commented: "That's Hollywood for you. That's what it's like to be kicked when you're down."

Missing out on portraying *Patton*, he riffed the role in a great comic turn as the mad General in Tim Burton's *Mars Attacks!* (1996). No audition was required this time. As Steiger stepped into the office for an informal chat, Burton welcomed him with suitable homage: "*Maestro!*"[738]

His marriage to Claire Bloom was dissolved in mid-1969, and he would go on to remarry three more times. As he grew older, he struggled with not only obesity, but bouts of depression which became more pronounced following a triple heart bypass operation in 1976. Using his celebrity status, he joined Rosalyn Carter, wife of the 39th US President, in a campaign to erase the stigma attached to fellow depression sufferers. He was vocal in maintaining that it is not a mental disease but caused by a chemical imbalance. In one of his last interviews, he commented: "Pain must never be a source of shame. It's a part of life, it's part of humanity."[739]

Rod Steiger passed away aged 77 in 2005.

The warm friendship he forged with Philippe Forquet during the filming continued: "Rod and I kept in touch, we often went to his house in Malibu, he came to the apartment I rented on Sunset, we went to restaurants and had drinks in night places, it always was fun, Rod was a really good friend."

Forquet did not see the finished film until it opened in America, and went to the screening with high hopes.

> I was happy having done several most interesting scenes from an actor's viewpoint. When the movie was released, I was in Los Angeles, so I went to the theater, but these scenes weren't in the movie I saw on the screen. So, the scenes I was most proud about were missing in the *Waterloo* version I saw in L.A. Which ended up, I'm sure, on the cutting-room floor.

Despite his disappointment at the finished product, the making of it had been a positive experience. "When I think about it, working on that film was quite exciting. Working in such an important movie with all these interesting people, Russian director, Technicians, Actors — the lot, was quite an experience, and I was really happy about it."

Becoming a titled aristocrat Viscount de Dorne upon the death of his father, he left acting to manage the family estate in French city of San Quentin, until his death in 2020.

"The filming of *Waterloo* is one of the greatest experiences of my life." For seventeen-year-old Peter Davies, his time on the hot, dusty plains of the Ukraine cast a long shadow. "You know, it's not something that I speak with people much about. My mum would talk about it. If I was down in the dumps, she'd say: 'But you were in *Waterloo!* — And you were so young then.' — 'Yes, Mum, and what the heck happened?'"

Thanks to the energy of his scotch drinking agent Jimmy Fraser, Peter was sent to many auditions but found himself just one of many young, struggling actors. A highlight was playing alongside Timothy West in a two-hander play based on Oscar Wilde's essay, *The Critic As Artist*. Moving to America, he found some theatre work, and even played a British Butler in a TV soap opera.

By his own admission, Peter's life post-*Waterloo* has been chequered. In the early 70s he landed a job with RCA Records, this involved accompanying various recording artists on their promotional trips to Europe. "It was a heady two years and I left my position at the request of one of the artists to become his manager. 'Yes', I told Iggy Pop, and embarked on another path for which I had neither experience or qualifications. But we achieved many things and I am proud of my association with this iconic figure, and deeply thrilled to watch from afar as he is having some of his best years now in his seventies."

Unfortunately, the downside of the music industry, namely drink and drugs, found a willing victim in Peter, for which he paid a heavy price — losing his wife and son. "I dived into self-destruction until I hit bottom. It's a clumsy and probably hackneyed analogy but when you finally hit bottom, you can touch it with your feet and if you're very lucky, like me, start to push yourself back."

Relocating to Cincinnati, and thanks to the help and support of his son's grandmother, Peter was able to slowly rebuild his life, working in restaurants and even doing a little theatre, whilst most importantly reconnecting as a father. Acquiring as much education that he could, he forged a successful career as a general manager at one of New England's most distinguished private clubs, Wianno Club on Cape Cod. As a recognition of his reputation in the industry he was elected a national director of the Club Managers Association of America.

With a new wife, Shelley, and budding family at his side, he was content that he had succeeded in getting his life back on track. "And then, one evening in September, I came home to tell my family that I had lost my job. I had lived in fear of this moment, and it has taken six years to get back on track." Now settled in Dayton, Ohio, he counts his blessings: "I have Shelly and our children and I most certainly have a north star, the One who is there for us all." Celebrating his 70th birthday, he reflected on his teenage self, half-a-century before: "You know, just to me, it has somewhat defined my life. It's not that I'm going around living on the laurels — "Oh yeah, I was a star of *Waterloo*" — no one knows, no one cares, but it was a huge thing because it was an extraordinary adventure for anyone, especially a teenager."

Even as Richard Heffer left Russia in October 1969, he knew he had survived a unique experience:

> As I sat in a slow Russian troop-train travelling west to Budapest, surrounded by hundreds of conscripts busy attempting to smuggle illicit drink and foreign cigarettes, I realised that never again would this style of filming recur. Despite the heat, the living conditions, the long days of waiting, the frantic activity on a smoke-filled battlefield, with the constant danger from explosions, runaway horses, and the ever-present possibility of being overrun by cavalry or galloping artillery, I survived, as had the Officer I played.

Surviving Waterloo became the title of a lecture he gave at Bath's Jane Austen Festival detailing the travails of the shoot. Perhaps more than any other involved, the filming experience has gently echoed throughout his life. Having studied the memoirs of his character Mercer to prepare for filming, he maintained an abiding interest in the Artilleryman. Along with Robert Pocock, an expert on the Waterloo campaign, who led the restoration of the famous captain's grave, the two travelled in Mercer's footsteps across the Belgian countryside. From Bruges to Waterloo, using his picturesque memoir as a guide, visiting the soldier's various pit stops at several chateaux along the way, before pinpointing the actual sites of his renowned G Troop RHA on that bloody day upon the battlefield itself. The two enjoyed debating the accuracy of the film, as well as latest interpretations of the battle.

Following *Waterloo*, Richard exchanged the world of film for the theatre; Bristol Old Vic, London West End, and new plays at the Orange Tree and Tricycle theatres, and international work for the British Council. In the early 1970s he became familiar to TV audiences locked up in *Colditz* (1972), and a variety of work in TV, Film and Theatre before retiring to Cambridge in 2005 to care for his mother.

But, after surveying his career "though greatly interesting, nothing quite matched the extraordinary experiences of filming *Waterloo* in 1960s Ukraine." If the older and more experienced actors were a little blasé, for the younger members it was unforgettable. "Now, fifty years later, there are very few of us alive to recall these amazing months. However, I have discovered a forgotten diary and unearthed many on-set photographs now in safe-keeping; witnesses to the last days of the Epic Film."

Richard was in no doubt to whom the glory is due: "My admiration for Sergei Bondarchuk has only increased over the years; despite having no English, he was able to explain through interpreters clearly his plans and thoughts with all performers, as I so well recall. An actor himself of great note, he always listened to his performers and respected their input. A charming man, carrying a huge responsibility."

And what of the thousands of soldiers who toiled for months under the Ukrainian sun obeying orders of an "obsessive madman?" One story will have to stand in for them all. Mykola Kholodnyak, who had charged riding his faithful Bunchuk in not only *Waterloo* but *The Flight*, had been one of the very last to leave the Uzhgorod location in 1969. He would appear in another twenty-two historical films with the 11th Separate Cavalry Regiment. Years later, he could identify himself in just one: *Kochuyushchiy Front* (1971) by the Sverdlovsk Film Studio, directed by Baras Khalzanov. "We were costumed in Red Army uniforms — the enemy, White Guards are advancing, and we are retreating. They told me not to look at the movie camera, but to lower our heads, as if exhausted, and walk past the camera. I walked, hanging my head, and I was taken in close-up."

After two years, he completed his military service in this most unusual, archaic part of the immense Soviet army. When, after demobilisation, he returned to his native Radekhiv and reported to the military registration office, the major took one quizzical look at the young man and shouted: "What are you wearing on your boots?" Mykola, answered: "Spurs, I am a cavalryman. "What spurs, what cavalry?" exclaimed the incredulous major, "Rockets are flying!"

Back in civvy street, Mykola worked at a local dairy before putting down roots when he married Jevgeniya in July 1972. With the birth of his son, Oleg, the young family moved to Chervonograd, north of Lviv in Western Ukraine. With a daughter Natalia born in 1980, the family enjoyed the comparative peace of the crumbling Soviet system's final years.

In 1989, the fall of the Berlin Wall may have brought about the demise of the USSR, but it also heralded a period of uncertainly almost as brutal as Stalin's Five-Year-Plans. The unfettered free-market economy unleashed a great deal of hardship for the have-nots. Mykola, remembered the early 1990s as a period of substantial challenge: "My salary was not paid for 6-7 months, but I still worked. These were hard times for all people in Ukraine."

His old regiment, the 11th Separate, did not survive The Cold War. The Russian film industry, at least for a time, lost its ambition — and capital. The need for mass cavalry charges was out of place in the new era of freedom, as modern filmmakers found more relevance in contemporary stories amid Russia's painful social transformation. In 2006, the rump of the unit was incorporated into the Presidential Cavalry Escort Battalion, Kremlin Regiment, and is regularly deployed on ceremonial occasions in Moscow.

In 2016, Ukraine joined the European Union, which it hopes in time will greatly improve the country's economic prospects as it integrates with the western side of the continent. While his daughter Natalia moved to the USA and has a family with Oleksandr Dolotko in Iowa, Mykola now retired, stills works as an electrician at the Chervonogradvodokanal Municipal Enterprise. "It is difficult to live on a retirement payment in Ukraine, therefore I have to keep working until now. However, I am happy to observe the life and development of my children and granddaughter Elina."

Having lived through half a turbulent century, Mykola, looks back fondly on his youthful cavalry days, and is always happy to regale any and all, with tales of life in the saddle upon a sturdy steed, tinkling spurs on his boots, tin sword drawn and a cardboard hat upon his head, charging pell-mell into the smoke of movie magic.

Veronica De Laurentiis was immensely proud of her father's mammoth five-year production, and her final words can equally apply to the producer, the director, and the epoch-making character himself.

> I thought the movie was beautiful. I really liked it; it's just that the subject is so sad. It's the defeat of a man, but it also tells you what sort of man he was…He did what he did. And production wise — it was incredible. He made the movie look like a million *(sic)* dollars.

Perhaps Steiger summed it up best: "We did not make a movie for history buffs; we were telling the story of a man."[740]

Sergei Bondarchuk (centre) with Vyacheslav Tikhonov (left) in the underrated war film, They Fought for Their Country *(1975).* IVO BLOM & PAUL VAN YPEREN COLLECTION

Dino De Laurentiis with his daughter Raffaella, at the premiere of their production of Dune *(1984).* © RAFFAELLA DE LAURENTIIS

Richard Heffer touring the Waterloo battlefield in the footsteps of his character, Mercer. © ROBERT POCOCK

As the guns fall silent, Wellington surveys the stricken field. The film leaves one in no doubt there are no victors in war. AUTHOR'S COLLECTION

CHAPTER 23

"A field of glory is never a pretty sight." The Conclusion.

"It would be very sad if all that was shown consisted of various kinds of attacks and counter-attacks with nothing further than this back-drop... nothing looked into deeper."[741] These bold, assertive words were Sergei Bondarchuk's aspiration for his unofficial follow up to *War and Peace*.

Did he succeed?

"It was an incredible undertaking, and it's too bad that the movie kind of didn't work, because it's such a great story," was how Raffaella De Laurentiis summed up her father's epic, "It's just the rest, the character work, it didn't quite work. Basically, it's like saying today, a movie had great visual effects, but it didn't quite work emotionally. I think that's the same problem…normally it's always the script!"

It is hard to disagree with this statement. It is customary in a book such as this for the author to ascribe superlatives and make bold justifications for their subject. As already related in the introduction, the author fell in love with this film as a ten-year-old boy, and it has been a love affair longer than any other in his life. Now with the head of an adult, as we draw to the end, it is time to assess and conclude with sober judgement.

Waterloo is an anomaly. Considering the Herculean effort and colossal amount of money it cost, that it even *exists* in the first place is confounding. In the twenty-first century, Hollywood primarily spends the equivalent dollars on almost *guaranteed* crowd pleasers; CGI-laden Action-adventure fare which often follows a proven commercial trend.

Looking back to 1970/1, it is hard to see which coat tails *Waterloo* was designed to latch onto. It obviously belongs to the Historical Epic genre, but this cycle, after a series of hefty failures, had largely run out of steam five years before its release. Instead, it appeared as part of a wave of enormous budgeted roadshow attractions, predominantly Musicals, by which Hollywood hoped would lure back a waning audience that appeared to crave more intimate, realistic fare.

Some historical films *had* enjoyed success during the 1960s, but in most cases their modest budgets were recoupable, or their failure survivable. Subjects with a strong romantic narrative fared better than those offering just solid action. The string of World War Two epics were the exception; made only a quarter of a century after the conflict, one can easily understand their popularity and relevance. These stories set in a "good war" became more important as America was perceived at home, and abroad, to be mired in the "bad war" of Vietnam. Even so, "good war" films like *Patton*, and the tragic-comic *Kelly's Heroes*, had a weary, cynical feel that seemed to capture the troubled times. War, in all its forms, was out of fashion as the 1960s counterculture moved into the next decade. For the average cinema goer, the question of into which category to file the Napoleonic Wars, elicited little more than a disinterested shrug.

History becomes History not just because it *happened* but because the best bits stick out as high-stakes drama. The reason big events still resonate long after their political or social importance has evaporated is because these moments say something about the human condition — how ordinary people (and by that, all of us) deal with extraordinary times. The 1815 battle was the culmination of one of the shortest military campaigns in all history — four days that ended with a decisive climax. Had the battle happened in Shakespeare's lifetime, there is little doubt he would eagerly have penned a narrative around it, and perhaps played fast-and-loose with the facts!

The problem that historical films have for many is the "history." Unlike most other genres where fiction rules, an audience needs only to appreciate the milieu, or at least find a latch to understand the drama being presented. This could also be said for Westerns, which are also period stories, but as the tropes and conventions have already been hot-wired into popular culture the world over for 150 years, almost any audience can understand an "Oater." This is also partially true of other historical periods which have soaked into the popular imagination; for example, the Ancient World. The conventions and even clichés allow storytellers to circumnavigate the need to explain to the audience, say, the geo-political landscape of the Roman Empire / Ancient Egypt, etc., which would otherwise tax even the most learned Oxbridge professor.

Perhaps this is because ancient society and politics were so different from our own, it may as well be science-fiction; requiring merely a few choice lines of narration before we plunge into togas, orgies and crucifixions. As story settings approach our own time, we discern contemporary similarities, for which, paradoxically, those minute differences require more explanation. This is less of a problem with stories about everyday folk, à la Jane Austin, but *critical* when dealing with the titans; the movers and shakers of history. Put simply, the power structures within which those larger-than-life personalities acted *must* be explained for the story to be comprehended. This presents a daunting challenge to an audience — evoking perhaps unpleasant memories of homework projects, school trips to dusty museums, or rain-soaked outdoor pageants.

Without an even basic appreciation of the twenty years preceding Waterloo, it is almost impossible to see why anything in *Waterloo* is relevant. By the same token, at the close, we are denied a brief what-happened-next, which might have helped retrospective understanding. To a casual viewer (which would have been the bulk of the audience), the story of Waterloo is like a shard of time in which we glimpse events of huge significance enacted by people of great renown. It is top-down history which few human beings ever get to experience first-hand.

Yet, for many, including this author, the responsibilities and stresses that must have weighed on the "stars" of history is compelling. In much the same way as we enjoy nerve-tingling horror or tales of derring-do, the appeal is surely — "better you than I" — as we sit riveted, watching how other humans battle to survive, deploying their skills as they are pushed to the edge of physical and mental endurance.

The story of Waterloo is high drama on steroids.

"In the beginning was the Word…" For all its visual splash and dash, like any movie, the script is the bedrock, and *Waterloo's* is made from brittle stuff. Considering all the dramatic ingredients of the subject allied with almost half a decade of preparation, it is difficult to fathom *why* the script is as weak as it is. Without being able to compare other drafts, it's impossible to say when the problem arose. Several screenplays of other epics of the era — *Cleopatra, The Longest Day, Mutiny on the Bounty* and *Lawrence of Arabia* — all have one thing in common: they are almost always, for good or ill, longer and meatier than the finished film. They all attempt to dig deep into the characters and events portrayed. While sometimes straying into verbosity, it's easier to nip and tuck excess than fan a fire from a tiny spark.

Perhaps the biggest flaw with the script is not ascribing powerful motivations to the principal characters. Why are they compelled to throw the lives of thousands into the mincer? Both men are masters on the battlefield, and like two sporting pros, they must compete to settle the question: Who is best? In the script, like a chess game, there is more emphasis on each move and countermove, but little on the very real human consequences.

Where a script is underwritten, it is incumbent on the actors to lift the material. Happily, for the finished film, some effort was spent during production to help create three-dimensional characters. The leads, Steiger and Plummer, had the clout and the confidence to adapt their dialogue, and did so for the better, to inject some humanity into these military greats.

The film, for all its spectacle, is really about one man, an extraordinary figure who for good or ill bestrode Europe like few others. To encapsulate the vast intellect and vaulting ego of this diminutive man is a tall order. The problem is well summed up by historian David Chandler: "Napoleon is not to be judged solely as a commander, or as a national leader, or even as a man."[742] The historian also liked to borrow, and adapt, a phrase from Clarendon's famous assessment of another controversial figure — Cromwell, to epitomise the Corsican as "a great, bad man."[743]

Rod Steiger's presence dominates, enabling him to more than hold his own against the tumultuous smoke-filled background. His performance does not ask us to *like* Napoleon but to see him as a flawed, almost haunted and hollowed out man. It must be accepted that, to use a popular British expression, Steiger is like "Marmite" — you either Love him or Hate him, no half-measures. For some contemporary reviewers, he was "terrible" — "just awful", etc. We all speak as we find. The author firmly believes the actor delivers an extraordinarily powerful and brave turn with hints of self-pity and even self-loathing, while also displaying the pathos of a man caught in a hell of his own making, all wrung from a unique performer who was fighting his own demons of depression. He makes you believe this man bestrode Europe for a decade. There have been many screen "Napoleons" but Steiger's must be one of the most memorable, if idiosyncratic. Some Historians, like Professor Charles J. Esdaile, find his portrayal close to the mark:

> Steiger captured the French ruler's mercurial nature and personal magnetism, not to mention the dynamism of which he was still capable in 1815 (though Bondarchuk chose above all to emphasise the increasing physical infirmities).[744]

This "Marmite" Napoleon is often the hinge on whether or not, you enjoy *Waterloo*.

Christopher Plummer was better received critically, and works as an effective foil to Steiger's eruptions of passion and angst. He gives a credible portrait of the Iron Duke, even if too "Byronic" for some; but again, like Steiger, he is suitably commanding, with a hint of the flint and steel beneath the courtesy and charm. On the page, the line: *"Time for the Heavy Cavalry, I think,"* could suggest a brain of muddle and confusion, but Plummer gives it that British clipped and haughty politeness that leaves no doubt as to the word of supreme authority.

It cannot be denied that the script does little with the legion of other characters and wastes many opportunities for drama. Any screenwriter worth his or her salt, would see a ballroom setting as dramatic manna from heaven. Despite the money spent on the set, we see a parade of characters, but most are mere animated dolls, as they are given almost nothing to chew on. A series of pithy vignettes could have easily set up the relationships, while giving a sense of the tensions and challenges of the impending conflict.

The possibilities that a room full of handsome young men and beautiful ladies present is just too obvious. Richard Heffer noted his ballroom partner was given a name — Lady Webster; Wellington's mistress. The dramatic options of a young captain dancing with the lover of his commander-in-chief are endless, yet nothing is made of this. One brief moment with Veronica De Laurentiis' walk-on as De Lancey's fresh-faced bride suggests what could have been created. In the script, her character of Magdalene has but one line, turning to her husband played by Ian Ogilvy, and using his character's first name: *"Willy?"* This grew into a touching scene between husband and wife, forced to part so soon after the first flush of marriage. It is a sketch, and no more, but anchors the human dimension simply and directly. Over all, one wishes Becky Sharp, that feisty and irreverent fictional heroine of *Vanity Fair*, could have been allowed to stray from Thackeray's memorable depiction of the same ballroom, and ruffle some feathers amongst Craig's characters.

Once the dancing is over, we are plunged with a quick march into battle. The myriad of warriors are given little opportunity for us to invest in them, with little or no progression, and crucially who even *survived* the carnage. Of these, Private O'Connor, played by Donal Donnelly, enjoys the most screen time, but in both the film and the script, we last see him in one of the smoke-shrouded infantry squares. We know from Richard

Heffer's diary that the Irish "grunt" was given a "death" — that was cut. It is an elementary scripting mistake not to pay-off your characters once you have asked the audience to invest in them.

If the characters are short-changed, this is not a charge that can be aimed at the panoramic canvas of history and battle framed in Panavision. It is for this that the film is justifiably celebrated, as the thousands of Russian soldiers shoulder their guns and take up positions amid the smoke-shrouded battlefield. We are quickly seduced by the visual symphony that unfurls before our eyes; individual characters become just tiny pieces of the colourful, if ghastly, mosaic. It is great cinema, but how close is it to what a mud-covered, tired and hungry soldier might have witnessed in 1815?

The dreaded high, and strict, bar of "accuracy" has sunk many an epic. I will now come out of my corner and say *Waterloo*, within the bounds of Hollywood cinema, does an excellent job in this department. Of course, there are a litany of "mistakes," as we have seen over the past few pages, but I still contend the film gets more right than wrong. It *broadly* sticks to the general outline of the campaign as detailed in Chapter Two, and where it wanders off the strict highway of "facts," it telescopes and compresses for the needs of drama.

Overall, the physical detail of the sets, particularly Mario Garbuglia's reconstruction of the field, and those legions of costumes are, again, *broadly* correct. Historian Steven Dwan who compiled a fascinating list in the appendix, as a fan of the film himself, concludes: "Overall it's a great film and whilst I found more errors than accuracies, it in no way detracts from the overall impact it delivers." The movie's magnificent survey of a dramatic, epoch-marking event is awe-inspiring — and the simple reason many of you are reading this book.

If questions of accuracy are binary, that cannot be said for interpretation, and for *all* historical films, this is a minefield. The original aim of Dino De Laurentiis was to tell the story of the battle as neutrally as possible. Hiring an Irish writer in H.A.L. Craig was perhaps an attempt to steer away from an undiluted Anglo-centric point-of-view, but still keep a British sensibility. The early attachment of leading French playwright Jean Anouilh was again an attempt to balance the telling, but the finished film overly emphasises British characters over their opponents, except for the Emperor himself.

That being said, critics back in 1970, and some historians now, level the accusation that the film perpetuates the Napoleonic myth. Among them Professor Esdaile, who has written extensively about the era:

Bondarchuk conveys a "pocket battleship" version of the Napoleonic legend that is, alas, all too plausible. Thus, we see Napoleon as a man of the Revolution, a Napoleon beloved by the people, a Napoleon facing the unrelenting hostility of the *Ancien Régime*, a Napoleon desperate for peace, and finally a Napoleon prisoner of destiny (as he always claimed) whose fate lay with forces beyond his control.[745]

It is true the film does not deconstruct or challenge this view of Napoleon. Rather than deliberately perpetuating the myth, I believe the filmmakers simply followed the popular cultural perception of the time to connect with a general audience. Also, it is worth considering, the contrary concept of flipping-on-its-head revisionism so beloved by modern TV executives was barely considered in mainstream 1960s cinema.

But in this "Post-Truth" world of the twenty-first century, historical films like *Waterloo* have taken on a new relevance. Fifty years after the film's release, the battle has become talismanic, as Britain once again struggles with its relationship to her nearest neighbours. Already, during the tortured divorce process with the European Union begun in 2016, the battle has been held up as a marker of Britain's "innate greatness." Who actually won the battle — The British? The German allies? Or the Prussians? — is still hotly debated. In my humble opinion, I believe the evidence points overwhelmingly to a *joint* effort by all concerned. To justify one faction over another is both fatuous and insulting to all who fought and died.

It is a pity that the filmmakers didn't choose to costume more of Wellington's army in the colours of his European allies, which the script describes as: *"his bouillabaisse of English, Scots, Dutch, Irish, Belgians and Brunswickers."* The visual effect would have been far more effective and accurate than a handful of throwaway lines. It would have reinforced the fact for a modern audience that the battle was not just a British victory alone, but Pan-European. Surely the lesson to take from the savage encounter is one of co-operation between nations against a common foe. At the time of writing, the world is gripped by the Covid-19 pandemic, with consequences yet unclear, but full of foreboding; surely, no better time than to heed lessons from history.

Waterloo was one of the very last, true epics in the grand manner; where what you see on screen was largely created for real. Since 1970 there have only been a handful of historical epics which come close to matching

Waterloo for sheer logistics and ambition; *A Bridge Too Far* (1977), *Zulu Dawn* (1979) and *Apocalypse Now!* (1979). Ted Turner's TV epic *Gettysburg* (1992) offered similar vistas of thousands of real extras (actually highly motivated re-enactors) in a creditable reconstruction of the pivotal Civil War encounter, followed ten years later by *Gods and Generals* (2002). Both are probably the very last epics to be shot largely for real.

With CGI coming to dominate cinema for the past twenty-five years, seeming to offer the ability to replicate reality and fantasy to an extraordinary degree, why is it that so often this phenomenal work fails to emotionally engage? Perhaps the author is jaded, but seeing virtual cameras move around action through gravity defying moves in worlds clearly born in a computer, elicits more of a yawn before a whoop. Many modern filmmakers are now aware of this, and it is interesting how some will creatively restrict themselves to techniques that mirror closely doing it in the real world, or utilise older, practical effects techniques with their inherent limitations. This is highly admirable and often works very effectively.

Fifty years on, it is unarguably the "realness" of *Waterloo* that most excites. The film has amassed over two million views of one of its YouTube incarnations — a Fan Edit, using some stills from deleted scenes, which still garners many, mainly positive, comments every day.[746] Most extol the virtues of the film; the sheer expanse and expense which could not be replicated convincingly with CGI. It shouldn't matter *how* images are created, but in an increasingly synthetic world, it seems we more and more appreciate the sheer hard work of doing things for "real."

It is all those faceless thousands of people and horses toiling upon a sun-baked plain in the Ukraine that this book intends to celebrate. There is something noble and gloriously insane about the entire enterprise. So much effort was spent, by so many people, to create a fleeting experience that only exists on a strip of film.

Throughout this book's research, my admiration for the energy and drive of Dino De Laurentiis has grown enormously; his sheer tenacity in just setting up the project is massively to his credit. Once green-lit, the care and craftsmanship displayed by the technical departments from Mario Garbuglia's extraordinary production design, along with his team of art directors, to the costumes both military and civilian by Ugo Pericoli and Maria De Matteis, all impress hugely. Once the pre-production was done, the output of these craft departments could not have looked as effective as it does without Armando Nannuzzi and his camera team, capturing so many breath-taking images. The star-laden cast does the best they can with such a wafer-thin screenplay amid the blazing heat and smoke of make-believe warfare. Although one wishes some editing decisions could have allowed more characters to not only breathe — but exist! One cannot fault the pace of the editing or the masterful sonic soundscape created by the Pinewood team.

Of course, Sergei Bondarchuk orchestrates all the "various kinds of attacks and counter-attacks" with great skill and imagination, but to echo Raffaella's words above, artistically the film "didn't quite work." To re-ascend the dizzy heights of *War and Peace* was always going to be a tall order. With Tolstoy as his road map in his previous work, the director's imagination and creativity patently soared. In his follow-up, he appeared less sure-footed and perhaps even timid. While an artist shouldn't be expected to reuse the same techniques on another work, it seems a shame he didn't inject some of that *War and Peace* texture of subjective camerawork onto the *Waterloo* battlefield (some of this "style" infuses his subsequent war film, *They Fought For Their Country*). Bondarchuk's camera is often aloof; offering a god-like tableaux, rather than up-close-and-personal viscerality. We do, however, see his often-stated affinity for nature, which recurs in much of his work. Deploying rain, a storm, and even a hurricane to remind us who really has the power in the World — Mother Nature. The "tussle" he said he had with the producers over this last elemental "prop" gives some hint into the compromises he was often forced to make.

Bondarchuk was serving two very different masters — Capitalist Hollywood and Communist Moscow, with Dino as the breakwater. He stated the producer gave him a great deal of freedom, but one senses that there must have been tensions between the two very different economic philosophies. The Hollywood investment, which would have required the largest possible audience engagement, must have resulted in pressure to "dumb down" and simplify, which would have been anathema to a man who had filmed seven hours of Tolstoy. These conflicting viewpoints, one suspects, reared their heads during the editing process, where much of the freedom the director enjoyed during filming met the cold steel of the film splicer. His off-the-record reference to the Hollywood executives as "gangsters" probably says it all.

For half-a-century, a persistent rumour has abounded of the existence of a longer cut. As we have seen, this does not exist, but in the many hours of discarded material, it is believed, lies a lost masterpiece. I do not believe this to be the case. The film's inherent flaws were already baked into the under-developed screenplay. It has been suggested (by Dino himself), that because the script was in English that the Russian-speaking Bondarchuk could not understand it. This is patently absurd. Not only does he share the on-screen writing credits, but all directors will have an intimate knowledge of the material they are working with. That said, he was caught amid the vagaries of culture; as we have seen he was often perplexed by the Anglo-Saxon mindset. Inevitably, in this most multi-national of productions, the barriers of language, even with the best translators, must have added some "fog-of-war" and compelled him to trust to the "improvements" offered by others. The creation of later on-set vignettes points to a sincere attempt to humanise the drama.

But the lack of gripping emotional engagement is the most significant, unadorned weakness of the film. Most epics which attempt to tell an overreaching story suffer from this because of the inevitable reduced screen time for characters. Yet at the end of, say, *Zulu* or *A Bridge Too Far*, we equally feel the same sense of relief and fatigue that the grimy, bloodstained soldiers exhibit on screen. As we have seen, *Waterloo* gives us little idea of who had actually survived, and instead offers an image of total devastation, again from a remote god-like vantage point.

How far an audience will engage is totally subjective, and it is impossible to second guess what Bondarchuk's inner thoughts and intentions were, and how far he believed he had got us to care about his human shadows on-screen. All artists endeavour to do the best they can, but like all of us, are prisoners to their innate flaws and prejudices. It is possible that the sheer size of the production, in both an aesthetic and logistical sense, may have dulled his sensitivity. Perhaps the material was too close to his previous work, which by then had consumed a decade of his life. It is easy to see why he intended to make a diversion with Chekhov, an intimate chamber piece, which may have reset his creative instincts.

Bondarchuk approached the film with a sincere desire to retell a great historical event, simply and directly. It is possible that in this honest attempt at neutrality he edged away from the subjectivity and poetry engendered by Tolstoy's intense prose. Even if he never fully "looked into deeper" some fundamental questions of war and power, we must applaud his extraordinary achievement in visualising so effectively, almost as close to being there, one of history's greatest battles.

Finally, we the audience, are left engaging with just three elements — Napoleon, his nemesis Wellington, and the battle itself, which, of course, is the real star. The actual fighting is a grizzly waltz of death and destruction, in which we are invited to revel, safe and sound from harm. Bondarchuk stressed he wanted to display an anti-war sentiment in *Waterloo*. Yet as we have seen from the critics' reaction, the film's extraordinary visual beauty and spectacle mitigates against that.

Perhaps the director was cleverer than he was credited with; suggesting perhaps, that there is something about war, however repellent and repulsive, that draws the human psyche time and time again. Before the industrial slaughter of the twentieth-century warfare was "Politics by other means,"[747] a necessary evil for nations flexing their muscles, and a rite of passage for young men — a chance to prove themselves, earn glory and even the hand of a fair maiden.

There is something noble and moving about this at the same time as being morally contradictory. Perhaps that was exactly the point Bondarchuk was making; this ambivalence suggesting the duality of man. Stanley Kubrick's Vietnam drama *Full Metal Jacket* (1986) delineates this very well when Joker, the lead US Marine character, is chastised by a general for having "Born to Kill" written on his helmet alongside the Peace symbol. *"It's the Jungian thing,"* the soldier replies. Carl Gustav Jung, Swiss psychiatrist and founder of analytical psychology, wrote in 1933: "Every good quality has its bad side, and nothing that is good can come into the world without directly producing a corresponding evil. This is a painful fact."[748]

The devastation depicted at the film's end, under the steely grey moonlight, leaves the audience in no doubt about the true cost and waste of war. As an exhausted Napoleon heaves himself into his coach, Steiger's haggard, broken visage hints at the character's realisation that this Man of Destiny must now face the consequences of his hubris; condemned to be tied to a rock and suffer the torment of guilt and failure. It should be noted that the real Napoleon wrote self-aggrandising memoirs that sought to blame others and took no personal responsibility for the defeat. While even an egotistical actor (such as some unfairly describe Steiger) could suggest empathy latent in Napoleon, we are reminded that in the real world, it is the lack of this very trait which is so often the trademark of those who would control and direct our lives; small cliques who think nothing of economic or military ruin of the many, as long as it serves the lust, greed and ambition of a few.

It is very fashionable to trivialise popular cinema, which ostensibly sets out to merely entertain. Since the dawn of the moving image, its power, for good or ill, has been an undeniable force across society and culture. This has never been so apparent than with the popular conceptions of the historical past, has largely created by cinema. While legions of history books continue to be written on all manner of subjects, and seemingly refute

Spanish philosopher George Santayana's famous aphorism, "Those who cannot remember the past are condemned to repeat it,"[749] it is the moving image that will always trump the very best writing. Historical movies, which due to their often-high cost, must appeal to the largest potential audience, have mostly been written off for dumbing down, perpetuating myths, or just plain distorting the facts by almost any critic one cares to mention. But not by all.

The novelist and occasional screenwriter, George Macdonald Fraser, who successfully played fast and loose with history to embody that most notorious of heroes — *Flashman*, in meticulously researched period romps, gave historical movies a thumbs up. In his book *The Hollywood History of the World*, he believed the medium had done a great service: "What is overlooked is the astonishing amount of history Hollywood has got right, and the immense unacknowledged debt which we owe to the commercial cinema as an illumination of the story of mankind."

After surveying a few thousand years of celluloid depicted history, he singled out *Waterloo* as: "…quite the best battle film ever made, both as motion picture and as a piece of history…For once it is possible to understand what is happening, and why it mattered." In his final analysis of the film's impressive reconstruction, he judged: "It is a ghastly film, as a depiction of war; it is also a very honest one, and a credit to all who made it."[750]

I hope you, the reader, have enjoyed our journey through seven months of 1969; from Dinocittà with its dripping candle wax, to the opulent splendour of Caserta, before bedding down with bedbugs and poor food in Uzhgorod, and then to the hot, dusty plain of "battle." The previous pages offer just a glimpse of the sheer hard work it took to capture history on film. It is that accumulated effort by so many people that this book aims to celebrate.

Hopefully, now inspired to watch this film again, you will appreciate even more the extraordinary effort of all concerned. Even if the final product didn't quite fulfil the makers' artistic aspirations, it is undeniably a great *movie* that can still wow and entertain after half a century.

Let us leave the last word to Sergei Fedorovich Bondarchuk, with his heartfelt sentiment, for which the film, if flawed, will ever remain relevant:

> For me a film about War is a film against War. The idea of War must arouse strong feelings in Man, must spark off his involvement in the problems to be overcome…he must join the ranks in the struggle for peace, in the struggle to avoid War.[751]

"A field of glory is never a pretty sight." The remains of Mario Garbuglia's plastic army strewn over the Ukrainian countryside. FORTEPAN/ ALEXANDER BOJAR

APPENDIX

Things They Got Right, Things They Got Wrong.
by Stephen Dwan

Here is a summary in the order that they appear in the film:

Fontainebleau.
   WRONG: The first abdication — the film's opening scene. Marshal Soult (Ivo Garrani) is shown present in error — Soult was still in the south of France facing Wellington's invasion from Spain, where he was outmanoeuvred at Toulouse on 10 April 1814, and forced into a wise strategic withdrawal. Napoleon's confrontation with the Marshals (Ney, Lefebvre, Macdonald and Moncey) took place between 4-6 April (not 20 April as shown on the film's caption) and he signed his draft abdication on the 6, ratifying it by signing the Treaty of Fontainebleau on the 13th. It's a great scene and (other than Soult's attendance and the condensing of timeline) delivers the facts pretty well.
   RIGHT: Marshal Marmont *did* surrender his corps — but only because he had placed himself in a bad position that invited defeat. It was seen by Napoleon as losing his last "bargaining chip" which made unconditional abdication inevitable. The Marshals were trying to avoid civil war, and Paris had already fallen.
   The farewell to the Guard at Fontainebleau Palace on 20 April, is also correct in essence, and delivers the emotions between soldiers and emperor at the moment of parting company. The speech is edited for cinema expediency, of course, but the version does it justice. Whilst Napoleon is shown approaching the *porte-aigle,* it was the commander of the 1st Grenadiers, Maréchal de camp Petit, who took hold of the eagle and presented it to Napoleon who embraced him, and then kissed the standard.

The Tuileries — King Louis XVIII.

WRONG: The caption shown at the start of the scene where the messenger brings the King the news of Napoleon's return, says "1st March," whereas Louis did not learn of this until 5th March.

RIGHT: Ney was ordered south to confront Napoleon and reached Besancon on 10th March — he did make the famous promise about the iron cage.

Grenoble.

WRONG: Marshal Ney was not at the pass of Laffrey as depicted, when the 5th de Ligne abandoned the Bourbons to join their returned Emperor — This episode took place on 7th March, and Ney did not join Napoleon until the 17th, further north at Auxerre. The scene also shows Foot Artillery and Carabiniers, who were not present either (the Carabiniers are shown in their full-dress white uniform, but went on campaign wearing the light blue "undress" tunic).

The terrain is also wrong — the single battalion of the 5th de Ligne had their left flank on the lake — the scene in the film depicts a pass flanked by higher ground. Again, it's just cinematic licence in play by condensing events — so it's hard to criticise.

Also, in Grenoble town square, the proclamation read out by the soldiers placed around the town square is invented, but sums up the words used to galvanise the mood of the people.

RIGHT: Napoleon was dismounted and approached the 5th de Ligne alone at Laffrey. He also gave orders for his Grenadiers to reverse arms and halt. He then addressed the 5th de Ligne using the words ascribed to him in the script.

The Tuileries — Napoleon.

WRONG: The assembly of generals and dignitaries appears to be on the 19th or 20th March — Marshal Soult is made Chief of Staff — an event that happened later. Also, the film could have done more to show Soult as being unpopular with the army (some officers would not salute him).

The urgent news Soult delivers to a bathing Napoleon that Wellington and Blucher have separated is only partially correct. Since the allied armies had been in the Low Countries even before Napoleon's return, they had maintained themselves in widely dispersed cantonments between Brussels and the French border. This presented Napoleon with a very obvious plan for a strike at Charleroi — i.e., to come between them.

RIGHT: Napoleon was carried up the palace steps by an enthusiastic crowd. It captures the delirious mood very well.

Brussels — The Duchess of Richmond's ball.
WRONG: The ball is shown in a lavish hall, bedecked with chandeliers and expensive furnishings — it was actually held in a large room adjoining the house the Richmond's occupied — previously used to store carriages and tidied up for the event.

General von Muffling is seen interrupting the ball, covered in mud and bearing a verbal message reporting the French invasion. Wellington himself claims that he was first informed of the French incursions over dinner, which started at 3 pm, by the Prince of Orange in person. He responded by issuing concentration orders around 5-6 pm, before the severity and outcome of the crossing of the Sambre and defence of Charleroi were known. Muffling then heard from Prussian General Ziethen, without knowing the outcome of the fighting, and went to inform Wellington around 6 pm. His duty was to be as close to the British commander as possible acting as the conduit for messengers, and not as the film suggests, riding the muddy roads between the two commanders.

At the ball, just after midnight, a British officer, Henry Webster, arrived to deliver a report to the Prince of Orange from his Chief of Staff, General Constant Rebeque, from Braine le Comte, issued timed 10.30 pm, which showed just how far and in what direction the French had pushed up towards Quatre Bras.

More intimately, there was no love affair between the soon to die Lord Hay and Lady Sarah Lennox — this was invented. But there *could* have been a relationship between Hay and her sister (Georgy). The scene does however encapsulate those elements of Regency society that had moved to Brussels. So, it probably represents several likely romantic liaisons.

RIGHT: The Gordon Highlanders provided pipers and dancers for the guests' entertainment. Although their commander Gordon is a fictional character, the Duchess (née Lady Charlotte Gordon) was closely associated with the regiment which her father had originally raised in 1794. Therefore, her reference to "uncle Gordon" allowing her to pick "such big ones" to perform at her ball, is partially correct. The scene portrays very well the fact that many of the senior Anglo-Allied officers attended.

Charleroi.
WRONG: French foot soldiers fording the Sambre at Charleroi — the water reaches the top of their gaiters in the shot, yet the minimum draft of

the river is 6'9". Too many flags — e.g., the Guard infantry are shown with a score (at least) of *porte-aigle*s — yet only two were carried on campaign by the whole 12 infantry regiments present, one for Grenadiers and one for Chasseurs.

Tail End of battles at Ligny and Quatre Bras.

WRONG: The film telescopes the inactivity of the 17 June into the evening of the 16th, and suggests the two battles Ligny and Quatre Bras took place the night before Waterloo, rather than two days. Ney did not arrive in person to tell Napoleon that Wellington was retreating — he learnt this only the following day at about 11:00 am. Napoleon wasted the morning of the 17th and effectively lost the campaign himself. Ney, however, should have attacked Wellington again on the 17th after the stalemate at Quatre-Bras. The scene at least drives home the fact that the chance had been missed and Wellington was now "free to choose his ground."

Blucher is shown with his troops receiving their adulation during their retreat at dusk. He was in fact badly bruised and in Wavre by 6:00 am on the 17 June.

RIGHT: Wellington's army is shown retreating during a downpour where he speaks of the Prussian's defeat. The rain had started earlier on the 17th, but a deluge is referred to at around 6:00 pm so the timing is right — the Duke had learnt of his allies' defeat at 10:00 am that morning.

Marshal Ney presents a captured British flag to Napoleon at Ligny — technically wrong, but the French captured one colour of the 69th Regiment at Quatre-Bras (this is visible on the flag Ney throws to the ground), and at least two at Waterloo (which were later recovered during the French retreat).

The night of 17 June.

RIGHT: Wellington had seen the Mont St. Jean position the year before. He had intentionally surveyed it then for its suitability as a defensive position. Wellington had read about Marlborough extensively, and his great military predecessor had already identified the position more than a hundred years earlier, during the war of the Spanish succession when he faced a French army very close to the 1815 field. After his decision to attack was overruled by his Dutch allies, the opportunity for the first battle of Waterloo was lost. Marlborough's descendent, Winston Churchill, discussed the similarities of the two encounters in his magisterial biography.

Napoleon makes irritated reference to the slow marching of Grouchy's detached 30,000 men — this is correct, the right wing of the army had halted at 6:00 pm at Gembloux when the storm broke — just a few miles from their starting point on the blooded Ligny battlefield on the 17th.

Wellington receives a guarantee that the Prussians will support him. It is highly unlikely, as depicted, that he would have known anything about Grouchy as a potential threat to his plans. This is an understandable dramatic inclusion to ramp up the tension.

Napoleon may have been sick the night before — thanks to a combination of having pushed himself hard since the early hours of the 15th June, and a recurring stomach problem. He was out of shape by 1815, and was unaccustomed to such rigours since his abdication and exile.

The morning of the 18 June 1815.
WRONG: British troops are shown as having bivouacked on the forward slope in the valley east of La Haye Sainte — instead they slept and were positioned on the reverse slope. While red coats are shown in La Haye Sainte — it was actually defended by green-clad Hanoverians of the King's German Legion, who had spent the night before there.

There is no evidence I have found to suggest the British spent part of the morning cheering or singing about their commander.

RIGHT: Napoleon inspected his army that morning (but did not gallop along on his horse — not in his physical condition at the time) to the cheers of his men. There is no record of Mercer asking permission to try a shot (Mercer wore a moustache in 1815 — while Richard Heffer, who played him, does not). The battle started at about 11:20-11:35 am with an advance on Hougoumont.

Opening shots of both positions and of Hougoumont.
WRONG: When we see the initial panning shot of Wellington's position, there are too many troops shown (most of these were the plastic dummies) on the crest or forward slopes — the vast majority were on the reverse slopes of the ridge — and there was no cavalry visible. We also see only red-coated troops (at least a quarter to a third along those sectors wore blue or green — and those visible troops, van Bylandt's Netherlanders, wore blue).

Hougoumont comes into pan and we see the buildings from the French left flank (Napoleon was back near Rossomme at this time). The ridge the French are on is too high — the buildings were not visible because of the wood, though. Also, the alignment is wrong as we see the gardener's house and storage shed square on from the front — from the position it is viewed; you see it from the south-west corner — the aspect is completely different. It's the same with La Haye Sainte — the French ridge was not as high, and you cannot see La Haye Sainte from this aspect near La Belle Alliance. It's a good effort, though, and the best available in the Ukrainian countryside, so it may be unfair to criticise the good work done to recreate the scenery.

The view of the French troops west of the Brussels Road (Reille's II Corps) shows the many brigades of cavalry belonging to Kellermann's III Cavalry Corps, who were actually much further back, and out of sight.

The troops attacking Hougoumont were initially Light infantry — but regular Line infantry are shown in these opening scenes. There was no Allied cannon positioned outside the garden wall of the chateau — they were much farther back on the ridge. The French would have been wearing greatcoats in a large number of the regiments — this is not shown in the film — only a brief scene where a few hundred in grey coats cross the meadows. The green-clad Nassau troops formed the chateau's initial garrison with the British Guards outside — this is not shown at all.

The walls are shown to be blown up by shells, whereas cannon was sparingly used but created no breaches. A French howitzer placed near the wood breached the south gate, but this was quickly repaired and barricaded. We also see the French using scaling ladders, which they did not have. There is no scene showing the 1st Légère and their forced entry at the north gate. Nor several other well-known occurrences at Hougoumont (a missed opportunity, to be frank).

RIGHT: The woods to the south of Hougoumont is shown a fairly sparsely planted, which is how it was.

The French infantry attack — 1:30 pm

WRONG: the 27th (Inniskilling) Regiment of Foot are shown in the front rank awaiting the approaching French (Donal Donnelly's Corporal O'Connor and Oleg Vidov's Tomlinson). Their brigade was resting further back beside the Mont St. Jean farm, having just arrived after a forced march. The soldiers are seen receiving an issue of gin (like the Navy; the army were mostly given rum although local spirits would have been substituted), but worse still the liquid is poured into white enamelled tin mugs of the kind issued to British soldiers during the Second World War — at Waterloo, many soldiers just put the issue of spirit into their water canteens.

We then have Wellington saying to Picton: *"Bylandt's Brigade has broken..."* but we now know thanks to recent research, that these Netherlanders had been pulled back behind the chemin de Ohain before contact was made — except for the 7th Belgian Line Battalion, that stood and exchanged fire with the leading regiment of Quiot's Division.

We do not see the exchange of musketry between d'Erlon's corps (again too many flags and parade uniforms) and Picton's division, but do see the British advance when Picton falls, and hundreds of Gordon Highlanders (92nd Foot) descending the forward slope in a massive 20 deep column.

This is followed by the Scots Greys charge, which ignores the rest of the Union /Household Brigades. The Greys charge at full pelt like a steeplechase (whereas they would have trotted at most) wearing full-dress uniforms, uncovered bearskins, no moustaches and with their guidon (flag) flying. The British cavalry did not take their standards on campaign, and the imagery of the scene tries to capture Lady Butler's famous painting (which she painted in the 1880s from real life — they charged her at the easel — when her husband commanded the regiment's Victorian descendants).

To counter-attack, Napoleon launches Polish Lancers from his right flank (there were only about 100 Poles, and they were just east of La Belle Alliance). In reality it was a brigade of plain green uniformed Line Lancers. This is one error that has received massive attention, and the Polish Guard Lancers were probably used in the scene because they look so good!

The Ponsonby death scene error is also well known — he was not killed like his father had been, by seven French Lancers who caught him in a pit — Ponsonby's father died of natural causes, while the general himself was captured by a French lancer. He surrendered, but when 4 or 5 of his men saw him, they charged to his rescue. A French lancer killed both him and his ADC before turning on the five approaching Greys, dropping three of them before the others made off.

It's a tough to praise d'Erlon's attack scene — it does not come near to representing the event at all — only the massed columns (which were battalion lines, one behind the other) give an idea of scale. Incredibly, there is no scene showing the simultaneous attack on La Haye Sainte at all. Rockets were launched at this time — we don't see that — but we see explosions of a twentieth-century nature, apparently fuel being ignited; similar to Napalm.

RIGHT: The British cavalry charged the guns and temporarily disable about 15 of them. Napoleon's lancer counter-attack came from the

east — but also from the south when two of the Cuirassier brigades joined in. Picton falls dead at about the time and spot where he actually fell.

La Haye Sainte — 3:00 pm.
WRONG: It seems to be about 3:00 pm because Napoleon gives Ney a direct order to capture La Haye Sainte — which is correct, but it follows him becoming aware of the Prussian menace on his right — which happened much earlier.

He is then taken sick and retires for at least an hour (because the cavalry charges are underway when he returns), I have not found mention of him actually retiring from the battlefield with La Bedoyere to rest in a windmill. Maybe it is just the storyline attempting to illustrate his inactivity during the battle (after drafting the initial orders for the day, he let Ney manage most of the attacks on the ridges and only intervened at certain times during the battle — e.g., Plancenoit, the Guard's attack and the cavalry counter-charges against the Union and Household Brigades). Other than mentioning the farmhouse, nothing is shown of what was a key contest during the day.

The French Cavalry Charges — 4:00 to 5:30 pm.
WRONG: Wellington pulls back his army by 100 paces and Ney mistakes it for a withdrawal. In essence, correct, but Wellington had been adjusting positions of troops all afternoon and most of the moves were concealed because they happened on the reverse slope. What Ney actually appears to have seen was 2,000 French prisoners captured from d'Erlon's corps being escorted back to Brussels. This and numerous wounded and empty ammunition carts (the slowly approaching Prussians had also seen this from their positions on Napoleon's right flank).

A British officer calls out: *"the 27th will take position behind the Gordons"* — but whilst the 27th had by now moved up to the crossroads, they were ahead of all other battalions in this sector standing in square and vulnerable to artillery (hence their very high casualties that day — 64%) — The Gordons were a few hundred yards to their left, and lying down on the reverse slope.

We then see Ney call on General Milhaud to charge with him and catch the Allies retreating. Ney initially ordered a single brigade for the job, but meeting resistance from the divisional commander, he ordered the whole of the 3rd Cavalry Corps to advance instead.

The charge is shown conducted in lines (it was conducted by squadron fronted columns) and a mixture of cavalrymen are included. The

Carabiniers are shown even though they were not committed until subsequent charges — as are the Guard Lancers and even the 5th Hussars (who were with Grouchy at Wavre at this time). The effect is good, though, and the aerial shots of squares were visually stunning.

There was, however, no conscientious objector present with the British infantry, and I imagine that was just a salute to the "peace and love" movement of the time.

RIGHT: The cavalry charges mix into an attack being made at Hougoumont, and then the capture of La Haye Sainte. This portrays accurately the fact that fighting at Hougoumont continued throughout the long day, and also gives a time of 6:00 — 6:30 pm — but there are then more Napalm-like explosions for cinematic effect.

The Crisis — *6:30-7:30 pm & La Haye Sainte captured.*

WRONG: An officer tells Wellington that "General Lambert requests reinforcements — at Hougoumont" — Lambert was at the crossroads with his brigade — about a kilometre away.

We see De Lancey severely wounded in the back by a shell fragment or ball. His wound completely exposes muscle and ribs. Whilst the timing is right, and he stood up before falling again, the wound was not visible as a ball had passed very close to his back (Wellington called it a ricochet) in so doing; it separated eight ribs from the spine and punctured a lung (he died a week later).

We see no mention of Napoleon's morale boosting (lie!) announcement to the army that Grouchy had arrived. I can't find evidence of a message sent to Paris (Napoleon says 6:00 pm) where a false claim of victory was made. He certainly would not have said: "*We won the war; we won the war.*" (I seem to recall that was a chant we took up as schoolboys in the UK in the 1960s — its origins stem from the victory in WW2, the memory of which still resided in the nation's psyche, and was passed down to the children. I believe the chant may also have been directed against (West) Germany during the many soccer contests of the period!)

We see La Haye Sainte captured by red-coated soldiers (most of the garrison were wearing green — KGL Light infantry and Nassauers — but there was one company of KGL Line infantry wearing red when the 5th Battalion sent a company there). We see the caption "6:00 pm" but it was about 6:30 pm — the attack by the 13th Légère and the 1st Sappers started at 6:00 pm. These were dressed either in greatcoats or full blue uniforms (tunic and lapels — and trousers) — what we see are Line infantry, even a Guard Grenadier — although, despite reference records state that Line/Light Grenadiers/Carabiniers had given up their bearskin caps by 1815 (some as early as 1812), there is some evidence that some caps were kept.

We see explosions coming off interior walls — which of course would not have happened while French troops were inside. At any rate, the French were famous for having deployed very few guns against the position. We see the wall that skirts the Brussels Road, and French infantry are climbing it. The wall shown is too low as we can see heads and shoulders beyond. But a few men scale it, jumping down inside — the main incursions, though, came through the main gate that the sappers had breached, and the west (barn) gate that was missing its door (used as firewood the night before).

Finally, we see a French flag carried to the chimney stack of the barn roof by a cuirassier. Flags were not placed on captured buildings (although the Nassauers in Hougoumont displayed their battalion flag on the roof of one building for a while). The French carried eagles and these would never be risked in such a way — plus, having an armoured cuirassier perform the duty is just taking it too far (even though the cuirass was only about 10 pounds in weight, it was still too cumbersome for climbing). Showing cavalrymen involved in La Haye Sainte at all seems far-fetched, of course — but cuirassiers did actually join in on the skirmishing around the farmhouse after they were unhorsed — using their carbines and probably with their cuirass discarded.

RIGHT: The overall impression is one of desperation for the Allies as the French laid on the pressure. Napoleon did refuse Ney's request for infantry — because of the Prussian menace that was taking up all his attention. But when he was happy that threat was contained, he prepared the final attack.

The attack of the Guard Infantry — 7:30 pm.
WRONG: the scene seems to infer that the Old Guard were sent in to attack just after the capture of La Haye Sainte — but a full hour was to pass before the Middle Guard and French line troops made the final effort. The advance was made in battalion squares throughout, but we see massive columns advancing with far more eagles held aloft than were present. The Guard are all Grenadiers and wear their full-dress uniform — whereas it is well known they wore a mixture of greatcoats, overalls and tunics.

Wellington announces he is abandoning his left (since the Prussians were arriving, he could free up troops there and draw them to the centre) but he had been doing this for the past hour — not when he saw the

Guard approaching. The Guard is defeated when Maitland's Brigade delivers a series of volleys into their front. But whilst these thousand redcoats were formed in four ranks, it was not as shown in the film — where the clear mistiming of each successive volley would have caused casualties to the ranks in front.

Whilst Maitland's Foot Guards checked the attack of two Chasseur battalions before being chased back themselves by a third, the contest had started a few minutes earlier on their left — where the French Grenadiers (after initial success) were decimated by Belgian artillery and driven back by rallying British infantry under General C Halkett.

The real decisive moment, that is not shown, is where the 1/52nd Foot outflanked the last square of Chasseurs, stopped them with their fire, and gave Maitland the opportunity to rally. The Guard did not rout when they spotted the Prussians swarming the field — the rout was another half hour away. The attack was not delivered by the Guard alone — the whole French army from Hougoumont to Papelotte swept forward, too.

RIGHT: We see Napoleon lead the attack as far as La Haye Sainte (out of shot) before his officers demand he retire to a safer position. We then see Ney unhorsed (the fifth time that day) and he continues on foot. The Foot Guards' volleys portray the destructive fire they were able to deliver, and the French Guardsmen are seen falling in droves.

Ney did try to rally the Guardsmen and did so until the mob swept him back towards their reserves on the valley floor. We do see some French Guard wearing shakos rather than bearskins — a few Middle Guardsmen were short on equipment, having only been raised a couple of months earlier when drafts were taken from the Line regiments to complete their personnel.

The Prussians — 8:00 pm.

WRONG: The messenger arrives to tell Napoleon that the Prussians are in the woods (presumably the Bois de Paris). There is no record of him saying he regretted not burning Berlin (regrettably, that possibly infers he was prone to municipal destruction, and possibly that line found its way into the script because the (Russian) director felt that there was prior "track record" to justify it — i.e., the burning of Moscow in 1812.)

Whereas two of the three Prussian army corps had passed through the Paris Woods earlier that afternoon (between 2-4 pm), Napoleon had been aware that at least one Prussian corps was operating on his right flank, since Lobau's troops and the Young Guard had been fighting to stem their advance since late afternoon.

There is no mention of this fighting in the east that had been going on since 4:30 pm, nor the fighting at Plancenoit that started an hour later. The scene seems to depict the moment the Prussians literally flooded the field from the east, which was mainly with their cavalry driving across the field towards the Brussels-Genappe Road. At this position on the field, Blucher was still at Plancenoit and not at the head of his hussars as the scene depicts.

This scene was originally filmed to depict the battle of Ligny two days earlier — and when Ligny was cut, the scene (which depicts Blucher leading a cavalry charge before being unhorsed in the evening) was restructured to portray the dramatic eruption of Prussians at the crucial moment.

RIGHT: Whilst Blucher's words, "*I'll shoot any man I see with pity in him!*" have no evidence, the use of the line in the screenplay sums up the sanguine "no quarter asked, none given" attitude between French and Prussian. Both at Ligny and Waterloo there are examples of brutality between both sides (the French and British were more "gentlemanly"); wounded and prisoners were not spared when these two foes confronted each other.

The Defeat — the last Square — 9:00 pm.

WRONG: We see La Haye Sainte recaptured at 8:00 pm (the allies retook it, but the French had already left). We again see a flag placed on the bar roof — a British one this time — although they would most likely not have placed a precious King's Colour on the roof. When the Allies made their general advance, Napoleon was in the square of the 1/1st Grenadiers before retreating towards Le Caillou. We see him struggling and being led forcefully away by his officers. The square is then left on a completely silent battlefield where its commander is asked to surrender, to which he replies: "*Merde!*" Then some 16-20 guns fire explosive shells into the formation and wipe it out. The whole scene is fanciful yet impressive. It appears the director wanted to symbolise the French defeat and the stubborn no-compromise Guardsmen, by using the example of the defeat of General Cambronne's 2/1st Chasseurs which took place near La Belle Alliance around this time. Cambronne himself later denied saying any of the well-known words attributed to him ("…the Guard dies, it does not surrender…") and was in fact captured by Oberst William Halkett as he led forward his Hanoverian Landwehr brigade. After the Guards are wiped out, we see an eagle lying discarded among the dead. The French did not lose any of their eagles during the retreat, however.

In the closing scenes on the battlefield, we see disabled British guns on the ridge northeast of La Haye Sainte — but none were wrecked there — although some were abandoned when ammunition ran out. As the dead are being collected and laid in neat lines, we see modern day stretchers in use. The dead were actually carted to mass burial pits — a service forced on the local Belgian peasants, some at bayonet point — over the following 4-5 days. The clearing was so time-consuming and corpses were close to exploding, that after a couple of days, both men and horses were eventually burnt instead. We see scores of horses standing around among the dead — whereas any cavalry mounts wandering stray would be the first thing the soldiers rounded up after a battle.

Napoleon, Soult, Ney and La Bedoyere are seen near the battlefield at night as it rains. There had been rain over the past couple of days, but the night of the 18th was clear with a bright moon. Ney was separate from the others and was being guided out of Belgium by a Grenadier. Napoleon had already lost his carriage and had no time to stop and wait around. Maybe this scene represents his later brief halt on the Quatre Bras battlefield.

RIGHT: The last scene shows the dead who in several places were piled up — it also shows the dead horses of which about 10,000 were killed, and the ghoulish scavengers that came out to loot the corpses after each Napoleonic battle. Wellington is depicted alone at the end with no staff officers because most of them had been killed or wounded.

Overall, it's a great film and whilst I found more errors than accuracies, it in no way detracts from the overall impact it delivers.

APPENDIX

The screenplay.

The following is a précis of H.A.L. Craig's December 1968 draft script with extracts in *italics*. Following standard industry practice, a new character or element is in UPPER CASE. The cast member is listed where identified. {}: denotes scenes all/or part *not* included in the final film. This is a grey-area as several scenes were re-staged differently from the printed page, and/or re-edited. This does not include the majority of cases where the dialogue was changed but the sense stayed the same.

The script opens to the strains of Beethoven's "Eroica" as the picture fades up a series of famous paintings of the Napoleonic era.
FONTAINEBLEAU PALACE: The marshals demand NAPOLEON (Rod Steiger) sign the document of abdication: *"No. I will not consent to be a fallen statue."* Led by NEY (Dan O'Herlihy), the others, SOULT (Ivo Garrani), BERTHIER (Giorgio Sciolette), SAINT-CYR (Filippo Perego), MACDONALD (Giuliano Raffaelli) and OUDINOT (Jean Louis) explain in brief the dire situation France is in. (Soult): *"Four nations, four armies, four fronts against us."* Ney presses the defeated Emperor to sign, who retorts: *"I despise ingratitude as the most foul defeat of the heart."* His defiance is soon neutered with the arrival of LA BEDOYERE (Philippe Forquet), Napoleon's aide, who whispers in his ear some calamitous news. *He crumbles.* The last remaining army has surrendered. Finally accepting defeat, he signs the *scurrilous paper.* He ponders his place of exile: *"Elba? I had better take what it I can get."* To shouts of: *"The Emperor!"* Napoleon stands silently for a long while, then walks out.
A series of quick shots show Napoleon aboard ship to the island of Elba.
PALAIS DES TUILERIES: LOUIS XVIII (Orson Welles*), a big, gouty man, white powdered and smiling, with a huge stomach and great bundles of red velvet protecting his legs.* An elderly courtier DE VITROLLES (Camillo

Angelini-Rota) bursts in exclaiming; *"The monster has escaped from Elba."* Unflappable, Louis orders Marshal Soult to keep charge in Paris and orders Ney, Napoleon's most critical and outspoken Marshal, to *"be the first to confront the werewolf."* The wise King notices the *turmoil of conscience* in Ney, *"I know you have loved this man."* Ney, gritting his teeth, *"I hate him now for the evil he is doing. I will bring Napoleon to Paris in an iron cage."* As Ney and Soult leave, Louis, perhaps no fool, is bemused by a soldier's boast: *"In an iron cage. No one is asking that much."*

ROAD NEAR GRENOBLE: Ney and his troops are drawn up across the road, *they wait in a terrible stiffness and stillness.* Napoleon and his small band of troops make their way forward cautiously. {He orders a small detachment of Lancers to ride up to the waiting soldiers. The waiting troops cross their bayonets in defence causing the horsemen to halt, who after a moment's hesitation then withdraw. It is only a feint.} *Suddenly, Napoleon appears at the bend of the road.* The tension builds as Ney orders his men to aim — both sides are ready to fire at point blank range. Napoleon walks towards them: *"Soldiers of the Fifth. Do you not recognise me?"* An order wraps out: *"Fire!"* There is a terrible silence. A YOUNG SOLDIER (Valery Guryev) *faints.* The tension snaps. *There is an explosion of enthusiasm.* "*Long Live the Emperor!*" *They kiss his hands, embrace him.* Only Ney has yet to make his move: *pale and tense, like a statue...* *"You should not have come back, Sire."* Then Napoleon: *"France and I are the same. Did you think I could stay away from myself?"* He tells him to follow him only to Grenoble, he is still not forgiven or trusted.

GRENOBLE, TOWN HALL: *The* CROWD *is in almost revolutionary fervor* as SERGEANTS read out a proclamation: *"It was the cry of injured honour that brought me back to France."* Napoleon, inside the town hall dictates his message to the European kings: *"Europe has nothing to fear from me. I want peace."* When Ney appears, he chides him, still punishing disloyalty: *"You there, Ney? You haven't emigrated yet?"* Ney is silent, hurt.

Ordering the doors open, he invites Ney to stand upon the balcony before the crowd; *wild, happy faces screaming their joy. Then, suddenly, they give Napoleon silence:* *"I have come back only to make France happy."* The crowd respond with great enthusiasm as Napoleon *hisses coldly through his teeth to Ney.* *"I will never forget your chin at Fontainebleau...forcing me to abdicate."* The frosty conversation continues with Napoleon goading Ney over his wild boast to the King. Ney defends it limply: *"I wanted to hide my true feelings."* The crowd erupts at Napoleon's words: *"The Fat King in Paris has corrupted the honour of Frenchmen. He will be carried from his throne."* The enormity of his second betrayal is not lost on Ney: *"If we do not succeed, I will be shot."* Ever the cynical gambler, Napoleon agrees: *"And I shot with you…if that's any comfort to you."*

PARIS, TUILERIES: The KING quietly leaves his palace at the dead of night. *He flops back on to the cushions with a long, resigned sigh. He is escorted away into exile amid the darkness.*

PARIS, TUILERIES: Twenty-four hours later and a wildly enthusiastic CROWD surrounds Napoleon's COACH as he arrives back in his palace. He is carried up a huge staircase on the shoulders of the crowd. *His eyes are closed. There is a forced, fixed smile on his lips. It is as if they were carrying a man killed by his own triumph.*

Later: He stands in a crowded room of COURTIERS and summons various POLITICIANS, declaring: *"France must have a government tomorrow morning."* He recognises DROUOT (Gianni Garko), *a stooping short-sighted general, but greatest artilleryman of his day,* and congratulates him on his loyalty, a clear barb against those, including Ney, who had deserted him the previous year. Chiding Soult: *"Are you no longer the King's War Minister?"* who shuffles awkwardly before being appointed Chief of Staff.

NAPOLEON'S STUDY: Napoleon paces the room — *the freshest man in this feverish work room prowls among the* SECRETARIES, *dictating several letters simultaneously.* One is to a grieving widow whose son was killed at a military review, another to a Prince insisting on his desire for peace, while another complains about the lack of recruits. Alternating between sentences, Napoleon completes each letter simultaneously. But one secretary waits patiently for his dictation, which Napoleon ignores *if he was afraid to approach his own letter.* Instead, he begins another to the Prince Regent of England, protesting the presence of Wellington's army on the French border. Perhaps to conflate his deep-seated concerns, Napoleon finally begins the last letter which is to his wife, now ensconced with her father, the Emperor of Austria in Vienna — his enemy. He pleads for the return of his son: *"…he is my future. But I had rather he were thrown from the walls of Schonbrunn than brought up a captive Austrian prince."*

TUILERIES: *Napoleon and La Bedoyere, with Ney and Drouot, walk past a series of colonnades.* Napoleon announces that the continental allies have declared war on *him* — not France — therefore making him an outlaw. La Bedoyere tries to flatter him: *"They dignify you, Sire, by making you a nation."* Napoleon muses: *"They have denied me the civilisation of law — any corporal who can get me under the branch of a tree can hang me."* He enquires after any news of his opponents, Wellington and Blucher. Hearing they are waiting around Brussels, he boasts that: *"Wellington's army when it's dead and laid in rows — that will be my peace table."* Before quipping to Drouot: *"I have made a mark in this world, haven't I, Drouot?"*

Later: Napoleon is lying in a bath; Soult arrives to tell him Wellington and Blucher have separated, much to the satisfaction of the bathing Emperor. *"Everything will depend on one battle…as it did at Marengo. But at Marengo I was young…"*

DUCHESS OF RICHMOND'S BALL: *a marvel of colour…we see that braids cannot compete with bosoms.* HIGHLAND SOLDIERS display a traditional Scottish sword dance. Among them is DUNCAN (Roger Green) whose fine legs captivate the watching ladies. The DUCHESS (Virginia McKenna) confides to a cavalry general PONSONBY (Michael Wilding) how she was invited to a parade of Highlanders: *"So I just rode up and down, in and out, and picked my fancy."* Her sixteen-year-old daughter SARAH (Susan Wood) approves: *"Mama, you chose such big ones."* Mother chides daughter as *the suggestion is slightly lewd.* {As the Highlanders leave amid enthusiastic female applause — a girl throws a flower at Duncan. Watching are two *rough* looking SENTRIES, MULHOLLAND (Charles Borromel) and MCKEVITT (Colin Watson)}. The ballroom is soon packed with waltzing couples before the MUSIC FALTERS. *There is a moment's confusion.*

The band plays *"See the Conquering Hero Come."* All eyes turn to the door and the entrance of WELLINGTON (Christopher Plummer), *tall, beaky, handsome. He had the unique ability of combining good manners with the most abrupt command.* Greeting the Duchess warmly: *"In none of my campaigns have I had such a brilliant company."* She replies: *"This season soldiers are the fashion. We ladies just have to follow the drum."*

The two discuss the merits of the British soldier while glancing at Mulholland and Mckevitt; the Duchess eulogising: *"they're the salt of England,"* Wellington disparagingly, replies: *"They're scum, Charlotte…Gin is the spirit of their patriotism."* Wellington emphasises his aloofness, almost coldness, as he expects them to do their duty and die for him. The Duchess doubts Napoleon could inspire men with *just* duty. Wellington disparages his opponent in the most damning terms: *"Napoleon is not a gentleman."* But he does admire him, conceding: *"In a field of battle his hat is worth fifty-thousand men…"* Joining Sarah, her mother admits: *"I'm a little bit of a Bonapartist myself!"* Despite Sarah's horror, this is not challenged, but Wellington believes that *"Bonaparte has cheapened life by bringing back glory into war."* The Duchess wonders: *"And when, my dear Arthur, will you venture into his lair?* {Wellington describes the slow process of amassing armies, but considers there is no immediate threat as Napoleon: *"The night before last he was seen clapping at the opera."*}

NIGHT: On the banks of the Sambre River, Napoleon and Ney flanked with staff officers appear. Napoleon gazes across the moonlit water. *The moment is fateful. The Sambre is more Rubicon than river.* "Cross the river, tomorrow we'll dry our boots in Brussels." The vast French army crosses the water barrier. *The moonlit water gives these huge soldiers an almost supernatural appearance.*

Back at the ball, Wellington watches approvingly as LORD HAY (Peter Davies) dances with Sarah. Her mother shudders with foreboding: *"Don't let young Hay get killed, Arthur."* A marriage is in prospect. The young couple rush over, Sarah beams how her beau has promised to bring back a French helmet: *"...without any blood on it, Mama."* Her mother replies: *(playfully) "And one for me, young man, with the blood."* Wellington challenges Hay on how he will achieve this feat. Hay suggests: *"I thought under the arm, Your Grace."* Gruff General PICTON (Jack Hawkins) takes the young man down a peg or two, telling him when he faces a French Cuirassier: *"You'll be lucky if you bring your life away with you, never mind his helmet."* He and Ponsonby withdraw, declaring: *"I never saw such a set of sprats."* Young Sarah cheekily comments on Picton's lack of refinement in a ballroom, Wellington defends his general's honour: *"But he's very good, Sarah, when he's dancing with the French."* But the young lady wins a schoolgirl victory: *"But one dances with them in a field."*

Wellington and the Duchess join the waltz. {She compliments him on his dancing, observing how he must win his battles: *"You danced the enemy to death."* He replies: *"The whole secret of combat is in the legs; you stand fast or you run fast."* She winces in mock horror: *"The ladies must not hear you. Imagine those unshaven horsemen here — lusting for partners!"*}

A mud-splattered guest arrives in the large shape of Prussian General MUFFLING (John Savident). His dishevelled appearance causes a *mixture of courtesy and exasperation* across the ballroom. *His fat personality makes him slightly comic. But he is too good a soldier to be a figure of fun.* "That gentleman will spoil the dancing," remarks the Duchess. MADELEINE HALL[752] (Veronica De Laurentiis) catches the concern on her husband's face DE LANCEY (Ian Ogilvy). Wellington greets Muffling, who looks uneasily around, then blurts out: *"Napoleon has crossed the border with all his forces."* Wellington, unruffled, asks where. *"At Charleroi,"* Muffling replies. The answer surprises the commander, and he realises: *"He has gone between both our armies. He has humbugged me."*

The news spreads quickly through the ballroom. The Duchess offers to stop the ball. Wellington declines: *"I want no panic."* She instructs the Musicians to strike up *with spirit.* Wellington issues some orders for the army to march, but insists: *"All officers obliged to ladies will finish their dance."* {Turning to SOMERSET (Viktor Murganov), he asks if there is a good map in the house. The Duchess watches the *dancing with a sad smile: "Before tomorrow night, many of my guests will be corpses."*} OFFICERS leave; *some of them are accompanied by frightened, tearful girls.* Including *Sarah in decorous tears on Lord Hay's sleeve.* {The sentry Mulholland, *his eyes twinkling in his Caliban face, whispers across to Mckevitt: "Boney's the boy for bothering a ballroom."*}

In an Anteroom, Wellington, Muffling, De Lancey and UXBRIDGE (Terence Alexander) bend over a map, discussing their options. Wellington cannot deny his adversary has outwitted him attacking via Charleroi: *"In a night's march he has made us piece-meal."* Realising he must not lose the initiative he tells Muffling: *"If Marshal Blucher will stay in Belgium, I, too, will stay — to the last ditch and the last flag."* Muffling seals the fateful deal: *"On that promise, Lord Duke, Blucher would tie his men to trees — if necessary."* Studying the map, Wellington recognises the strategic significance of the crossroads. At *"Quatre Bras!"* says De Lancey. *"He's bound to cover them, Sir."* They will allow him to join with Blucher. With the stage set, Wellington is impressed by his opponent: *"Charleroi? By God, that man does war honour."*

{LIGNY: The French army march past a windmill while Napoleon dozes undisturbed by the music and the cheering men. Some break rank and embrace his WHITE HORSE. MESSENGERS ride up and hand their dispatches to Soult, who bids Drouot to wake him: *"The Prussians are coming, Sire."* Napoleon snaps awake, fully lucid. He orders Ney to: *"keep Wellington entangled at Quatre Bras. He must not help Blucher with a single horse."* Another dispatch arrives, and Soult announces that: *"Blucher is waiting, your Majesty, at Ligny. In line of battle."* This pleases the Emperor: *"Quick! We'll satisfy that old man's thirst."*

{By the evening the battle of Ligny reaches its climax. MARSHAL BLUCHER (Sergei Zakhariadze), *a splendid old warrior of seventy-two, charges sabre in hand, at the head of the* PRUSSIAN CAVALRY: *"Hell, and Sulphur to them! The gates of hell to them!"* He thunders as his cavalry hurtle towards the French. His horse is hit and throws Blucher to the ground where his own cavalry ride over him. He tries to free his legs, now tangled in the reins. FRENCH LANCERS counter-attack, and unseeing, ride past their enemy commander. He uses his sword to cut through the tangled reins. A small party of PRUSSIAN HUSSARS gallop up to free him, including GNEISENAU (Karl Lipanski), his Chief of Staff, who announces the grim news: *"They have broken our centre, sir…I have ordered a retreat."* Blucher, in a daze, is bundled onto a horse and led at an unceremonious run to the cover of some trees. {Blucher is helped off the horse and asks for gin.} Looking at a map, he and Gneisenau debate their next move. The thought of retreat enrages the old warrior: *"Have I come all this way to meet that runt of a Frenchman only to run from him?"* Gneisenau does not trust Wellington and instead wants to retreat to Prussia. Blucher, rubbing gin over his chest, says to desert his allies would bring dishonour. Grabbing his sword, he declares: *"I'm seventy-two and a soldier; this steel is my word. I am too old to break it."* Gneisenau, despite his misgivings, and out of respect for his commander, says he has ordered the retreat to Wavre — which will allow them to aid Wellington: *"But God help us if he does not stand."* {This pleases Blucher, who enacts a regular ritual, declaring: *"I am the only man alive who can kiss his own head,"* before kissing Gneisenau's forehead: *"This is my head. You are the brains of the army."* Gneisenau replies: *"You, Prince Blucher, are its heart."*}

Later, in the gloom and rain, the beaten but orderly Prussian army trudge through the night. The appearance of Blucher on his horse, pipe in hand, quickly raises spirits.

On the stricken field of Ligny, Napoleon surveys the aftermath: *"A field of glory is never a pretty sight."* Then, a little cynically to Drouot: *"But still sixteen thousand Prussian corpses: Slap that news on the wall of Paris."* Ney gallops up to the annoyance of Napoleon, who demands to know where is Wellington's army. Ney insists that it is retreating. *"Why are you not following?"* Napoleon blasts back: *"Marshal, you are ruining France, if Wellington can choose where he goes, the campaign that I have won, you, Ney, will have lost."*

With Ney dismissed, Napoleon consults the maps with his trusted aide, La Bedoyere. Goaded into action, as he summons two of his leading commanders, GROUCHY (Charles Millot) and GERARD (Vladimir Druzhnikov) *There is hostility between them.* Napoleon issues the fatal order to divide his army, trusting them with a third of his force to pursue Blucher's Prussians. *"He must not reach Wellington."* Grouchy points out, *"There are ten different roads and directions Blucher might go."* Sensing an opportunity, Gerard retorts with a sneer, *"Blucher is not a scatter of birds, Marshal Grouchy, we will find him on one road."* Napoleon *senses the hostility between the two men — a hostility that was to lose him Waterloo.* He says significantly, *"Blucher must feel your swords in his back!"* As they leave to carry out their orders, Napoleon returns to his maps, behind him lie *the* DEAD *of Ligny.*

WATERLOO, ROAD: In the rain, Wellington and De Lancey watch the army take up positions on the Waterloo Ridge: "*Old Blucher's had a damned good licking and has rolled back eighteen miles. So, we must go too.*" The weary SOLDIERS file past with hardly a glance at their commander; amongst them is O'CONNOR (Donal Donnelly) of the 27th (Inniskilling) Regiment of Foot: "*Boney has kicked the Prussians in the arse, but it's us who's doing the running.*" This amuses Wellington: "*A retreating army is hardly ever in love with its commander.*" De Lancey is confident that after a few shots from the enemy, "*they'll be themselves again.*" {Wellington dryly replies: "*Napoleon Bonaparte is a wonderful tonic to us all.*"}

The HIGHLANDERS, led by BAGPIPERS, march past in *a thrust of great exhilaration that completely kills the impression of retreat.* To the tune of MACPHERSON'S LAMENT, the men sing, amongst them is Duncan. In the middle rides their commander GORDON *beaming with pleasure.* He joins Wellington, who congratulates "*the cut of your men.*" Gordon is proud of them: "*Damned forward fellows with the bayonet… Wellington. Meat an' eggs from the cradle up… Some of 'em might call me something more than Colonel, eh.*" As Gordon re-joins his men, Wellington looks at the dark sky: "*It'll be a hard day tomorrow.*"

WELLINGTON'S ARMY *taking position on the ridge of Waterloo.*

"*His whole army is there,*" says Napoleon, joined by La Bedoyere, Soult and Ney as they survey the opposite positions filling with soldiers. Ordering the army to "rest," Napoleon adds: "*When your enemy is making a mistake it is a bad policy to interrupt him.*"

While the allied army takes position behind them, Picton voices his concern to Wellington: "*It's unsound.*" He is concerned that the army has its back to the woods. Wellington tells him he saw this very ground a year before, and: "*I've kept it in my pocket for a day like tomorrow.*" Picton worries the woods will be if a death trap if they are pushed back. Wellington is adamant: "*There's no undergrowth in that wood. The whole army can slip through it, like rain through a grate.*"

Napoleon abruptly concludes about his opponent: "*He is ignorant even of Caesar's basic principles — standing there with the trees in the small of his back.*" He suspects his enemy may retreat, and cautions any provocation, {before asking the name of the field. "*It's called Waterloo, Sire,*" replies Soult, *consulting a map.*}

Later: Napoleon and BERTRAND (Boris Molchanov) stand in the rain looking over *the long line of Allied Fires. There is a heavy clap of thunder. {A flash of lightning lights up Napoleon's face: "We are in accord."*

{French soldiers huddle under makeshift cover, some have *constructed clever racks of branches to keep clear of the mud.* A GUNNER *sleeps on the barrel of his cannon.*

{Under a crude tent, camp follower MARIA (Irina Skobtseva) is sleeping in the arms of the Grenadier, CHACTAS (Gennadi Yudin). Nearby, on sentry duty, is SAURET (Andrea Checchi), a fifty-year-old veteran. Like a father, he watches over two DRUMMER BOYS sleeping beside their drums. One BOY (Vladimir Levchenko) wakes up shivering, and Sauret shows: "*The old trick of Russia… The Cossack fires, they'd be all around…and us, we'd be icicles. Warm up, boy." The boy warms his hands energetically.*}

{Back on the allied positions, MERCER (Richard Heffer) *sits under an umbrella, smoking a cigar.*}

FARMYARD: O'Connor finds a pig *rooting against a wattle fence… "Poor crathur, you're nosing yourself into the pot."* {To the cry of *"Thief!"* he dashes off with his plunder.

{NO-MAN'S-LAND: O'Connor stumbles and loses his pig in the darkness, scrabbling after the runaway he comes face-to-face with — Sauret — holding the escaped plunder! The two face off before Sauret returns it. In exchange, O'Connor offers him tobacco *with some by-play of exaggerated courtesy. Suddenly O'Connor runs at Sauret, who snaps into a position of defence.* The Irishman turns his face in profile, and with a wink says, *"So that tomorrow…if ye see me."*

{ALLIED RIDGE: By a fire sit GREEN and COLSON (Vaclovas Bledis), *they have constructed clever racks of branches to keep clear of the mud.* Nearby lies TOMLINSON (Oleg Vidov) *staring up into the rain.*} The Irish INNI-SKILLINS regiment is busy digging emplacements for cannons. O'Connor, his knap-sack squirming, surreptitiously joins his mates, including PATSY (Félix Eynas). Wellington and De Lancey appear, causing the soldiers to work furiously: *"My old friends, the Inniskillins. I hang and flog more of them than I do the rest of the army put together."* He notices something moving in O'Connor's knapsack, and orders him to open it: *"You know the punishment for plundering?"* O'Connor has to think fast: *"Stoppage of gin, Sir."* Wellington thunders back: *"Damn you, it is death."* Opening his pack, *he jumps back in mock horror,* as the pig is revealed: *"I knew something quare was scratching me back."* Wellington questions him on how he *"acquired this plunder?"* Thinking quickly, O'Connor cooks up a story of how, *"This little pig has lost her way and I'm carrying her home to her relations."* The absurdity moves Wellington to laughter: *"He knows how to defend a hopeless position."*

{Sitting in the rain, Artillery Captains Mercer and RAMSAY (Willoughby Gray) are eating soup. They discuss the slaughter that is sure to happen the next day. Mercer estimates that: *"forty thousand of us are sure to die tomorrow."* A third Officer NORMYLE (Pauls Butkēvičs), *testing the thickness* — *lifts out and pours back a spoon of soup.* An annoyed Ramsey tells him to eat up, as *"it might well be your last supper."*}

LE CAILLOU: Napoleon, in his temporary HQ, peers out of the window at Wellington's army. He is baffled: *"Why is he standing there? Why has he lost his caution? Is there something in his reasoning I do not understand?"*

WELLINGTON'S HQ: Wellington discusses his options: *"If Blucher can outrun Grouchy, and give me the help of even one Corps — then, I will try a battle tomorrow."*

(INTERCUT the two locations)

Napoleon demands to know why Grouchy's men: *"only do six miles when I do ten."* Soult suggests it is: *"the state of the roads."*

Wellington: *"The mud here will help us. They must slither up to us. But the mud on the roads will slow Blucher and that could beat us."*

Napoleon: *"The roads are the same for everyone. Grouchy must walk faster."* He wonders why the allied army is standing to fight; Drouot suggests that they are counting on the Prussians. Napoleon scoffs at this suggestion: *"Blucher is an old hussar and an abuse of nature — he has four legs. But Blucher cannot fly."*

Muffling plunges into Wellington's HQ. He announces the vital news of Blucher's retreat with Grouchy trudging behind. Muffling assures him: *"You may fight your battle, Lord Duke."* Wellington asks Muffling to return to Blucher this night, and begs him: *"to come to Waterloo by one o'clock."* Picton is elated, they have set a trap. Wellington is more cautious, if Grouchy turns and catches the Prussians on the march: *"Then it will only be a matter of counting Prussian dead and our dead."* Uxbridge wonders: *"dare we rely on Blucher?"* Aware of the high stakes, Wellington replies, *"We have to rely on him…and he on us."*

LE CAILLOU: Napoleon is in pain. His generals including Ney voice concern and suggest calling Doctor Larrey. {Handed the battle orders, he quips: *"There was a time, the night before a battle, when my anteroom was as busy as the stomach of the horse of Troy."*} He dismisses all the men and consents to see the doctor. Alone, he muses: *"My body is a mess. Only my hands are still good."* He looks out of the window of his HQ. It is still raining.

He sighs, expressing his agitation as he falls asleep on his bed. Soon, the rain stops just as the early rays of sun appear.

DAWN. In both armies *thousands of filthy, unshaven, hungry, soaked men rumble like a distant stormy sea. Horsemen are cooking their breakfast at fires.*

ALLIED POSITIONS: {*Rows of sleeping soldiers resting their heads on their packs, wrapped up in rain-soaked blankets.*} MERCER *shaves and puts on a clean shirt.*

{WELLINGTON'S HQ: Wellington calmly shaves.}

{LE CAILLOU: Napoleon too splashes water over his face.} *Fresh and merry,* he joins his generals for breakfast. Announcing his intention to attack at 9 a.m., he is advised that the ground is still too muddy, and therefore useless for moving cannons. A distant church bell is heard from the village of Plancenoit; La Bedoyere says the priest won't give up his Sunday Mass. Napoleon, his mind wandering, muses: "*He won't have much of a congregation.*" All wait for his next words, before he *suddenly throws down his serviette and stands up.*

Later: With their breakfast left half-finished, Napoleon and the generals pour over maps. Drouot enters and says they must delay the attack: "*The ground is too soft.*" Napoleon as ever is impatient: "*If I had waited four hours, I'd have lost Austerlitz!*" Ney scoffs at Wellington being able to resist "*with his bouillabaisse*" motley force. Drouot reiterates his concern at moving the cannon: "*If Wellington were on the move then I'd say: go now! But he's sitting, Sire, with the mud in his favor.*" Napoleon is persuaded to wait — but on *his* terms: "*Before they die, I'll dazzle them…We must dine tonight in Brussels.*"

WATERLOO: To cries of "*The Emperor!*" The French army takes up position, lines of infantry followed by Kellerman's Cuirassiers.

Wellington and his staff of *Golden Boys* watch the spectacle with a mixture of awe and determination. (Picton) "*No man alive has ever seen so foolish a performance.*" Lord Hay watches nervously, his DALMATIAN HOUND beside him. Wellington calms his young ADC: "*Music and flags. Quite beautiful, Hay. You are lucky to see such a wonder in your first battle.*" The French army continues to march into position, MEN, HORSES, CANNON *come up the road as far as the eye can see.* {(De Lancey) "*He has filled his stage — seventy-thousand men.*" The scale of the impending slaughter is not lost on the commander: "*The slaughter will be deep, I'm afraid.*"}

Napoleon appears on horseback *amidst enthusiastic shouts:* "*The Emperor!*" Despite his horse slithering in the mud, he is jubilant.

The excitement is contagious as Lord Hay shouts, "*There. Near the road, Your Grace. His white horse. The monster.*" Wellington regards his opponent with slight amusement: *"So there is the great thief of Europe himself."* Mercer, his cannons primed and ready, rides up and offers to fire at the "monster," but is given short shrift by Wellington: *"Certainly not. Commanders of armies have something better to do than shoot at each other."*

Napoleon continues to bask in the euphoria of his army, to shouts of *"The Emperor!"* The allied soldiers take up a refrain of their own in *a perverse admiration… Then the first verses of the good-natured satirical song…* "Boney was a warrior, John Francois…"

With both armies in full song, Wellington reflects: *"Quite brotherly business — isn't it, De Lancey — killing?"* When De Lancey suggests shutting them up, but seeing the strategic value, Wellington replies: *"Anything that distracts or wastes time this morning we must indulge."* Overcoming his natural dislike of cheering, Wellington asks De Lancey to *"kindly announce me."* His subordinate obliges and exhorts the army with: *"Three cheers for the Duke!"* As his army dutifully obeys, Wellington rides past with *an amused gleam in his eyes.*

Napoleon, with his tour complete, dismounts, *his feet sink into the mud.* Handed the battle orders, he quips *"…six pages would be too long for the Siege of Troy."* Surveying the allied line, he surmises that Wellington: *"fears for his right. Very well, we'll begin by teasing him there…I'll know the length of this English aristocrat in the first hour."*

A tremendous silence reigns over the battlefield.

WELLINGTON'S TREE: Wellington and his staff are gathered around a solitary tree on the ridge that will be his impromptu HQ for most of the battle. They engage in a British sporting ritual as a tray of cherry brandy is handed around for a toast: *"Gentlemen — today's fox."*

{A group of newly arrived ALLIED SOLDIERS are amazed and frightened by the impending battle; they include Colson who, *in the silence, whistles through his teeth.*}

Napoleon stands up and turns suddenly to his right: "Here we begin our attack."

Wellington watching, now senses: *"They appear to be ready to start."* Glancing at his watch, De Lancey notes it is: *"Eleven thirty-five."*

The sky is full of flying specks. But for a moment, the day seems darkened by the terrible almost slow-moving projectiles — the cannon balls of Waterloo…

The allied Ridge is hit by cannon fire, causing substantial damage. A RIDERLESS HORSE *runs wildly along the ridge.*

HOUGOUMONT: French infantry moves against the fortified farm complex of Hougoumont.

Watching by Wellington's tree, De Lancey believes Napoleon *"intends to turn us on the right."* Wellington is unperturbed: *"What the Master intends and what he seems to intend will be as different as hare from hound."* De Lancey suggests a switch of troops to counter the threat, but the Duke snaps back, irritated: *"I do not intend to run around like a wet hen. Besides, there'll be plenty of time today to throw living men in after dead ones."*

HOUGOUMONT: The French attack through the woods. Breaking through, they come up against the farm's stone wall, studded with loopholes and firing muskets. A young DRUMMER is shot in the face by gunfire. He is just one of many French soldiers who are hit as they attempt to storm the formidable defences. {The *Cantiniere*, Maria, appears and along with others tend to the wounded. She cradles one SOLDIER by giving him brandy.}

The French charge Hougoumont again; THE WALL EXPLODES WITH FIRE. GENERAL BAUDIN (Attilio Severini) is hit. {A huge Sapper LEGROS (Armando Bottin) runs to the wall and flings a grappling hook over, making a foot hold.} Soon, more take hold and in moments men climb up onto the wall over corpses as *a ladder of dead flesh*. The FIRST MAN *to charge up dies and becomes himself the top rung of this grotesque machine of assault.* {Burning branches are deployed and flung into the farm buildings. Inside, a small, private chapel is on fire, its wooden crucifix licked by the flames.} *Hougoumont is burning.*

Napoleon surveys the battle through his telescope, and observes Wellington has not fallen for his ruse: *"He has not moved a man."* He now orders his heavy guns against the *right* of Wellington's army — Picton's division. Soult scribbles the orders. {Napoleon is unhappy with their deployment, and orders more guns for the cannonade. Seeing them move, he declares: *"There go twenty-four beautiful girls."*}

The French cannon firing pulverises Picton's men. *The roars of the cannon merge into a single, prolonged thunderclap.* Wellington joins Picton, who wears *civilian clothes, and puffing at a pipe*, and observes, *"It seems he's swinging his weight to you, Picton."*

{A BATTERY OF HORSE ARTILLERY gallops across the valley floor. It is an impressive sight,} as Picton says admiringly: *"I never saw guns going so smartly."* Wellington concurs: *"He can use a hundred cannon with the lightness of a pistol."*

{Napoleon orders Ney to attack and *"to put glory into the afternoon."* As Ney rides off, *his red hair shining in the sun...'A hundred times that man has given me his life, now he gives it again."*}

The RIGHT WING of the French Army, resembling *creeping monsters*, moves down the slope into the shallow valley. *The* FRENCH ARTILLERY *fire over their heads*. {Leading the marching men is RATA, an old drummer "boy" who makes a song and dance as he skips and prances *along the line of drums, tapping on each in turn*. Ney rides ahead *as if he were asleep*. While the men shout: "*The Emperor.*"}

Standing on the opposite ridge, Wellington and Picton watch the advance, calmly discussing tactics. "*They can win this battle at a walk,*" observes Picton. Wellington says the counter-attack is all a question of timing. {Picton agrees — hoping he has set his watch correctly. This causes a nervous laugh from his staff officers. Wellington cuts the mirth: "*When you're in the presence of so many brave men, who are about to cut each other's throats, it is best not to be amused.*"}

The French continue their advance: *Dark sinister, overwhelming.*

Wellington comes to a decision, and orders Lord Gordon to move his men to the ridge crest, "*Alone. You'll face them all.*" Picton points out they will be overwhelmed. Wellington disagrees as, "*That would cost them their momentum.*" Gordon nonchalantly agrees that "*every lad of mine will want to go.*" Wellington appreciates his quality: "*You are my arm's length, Gordon.*"

Preceded by Bagpipers playing THE FLOWERS OF THE FOREST, Gordon's Highlanders take position on the crest of the ridge. *They are noble — but in numbers, less than three hundred; they seem sacrificial.*

{Napoleon and Soult watch them with respect: "*Such men are fortresses, only machines can reduce them.*"} Hearing the Pipes, Napoleon fancies he is Caesar in the woods of Germany: "*Has Wellington only these Amazons to offer me?*"

The FRENCH COLUMNS continue advancing up the slope to shouts of "*The Emperor.*"

Waiting behind the Allied lines is Ponsonby's cavalry 1200 horses strong. These include the SCOTS GREYS who move splendidly into line around their colours (flags).

The French are advancing ever closer up the Allied ridge.

{*Two English Batteries swing their fire against the French columns. Supported by the deadly fire of the 95th and of Bylandt's battalions scatter the French formation.*}

Uxbridge has joined Ponsonby, who offers him a hit of snuff. With a sneeze Uxbridge finds it, "*A savage snuff, Ponsonby.*" Despite the sound of the French drawing nearer, Ponsonby reminisces about his father. The old man had got the snuff from "*A Jew in Alexandria had the blend…*" Sneezing, Uxbridge questions its "*blend!*" Ponsonby relates how his father was killed by the French; when caught by Lancers in a muddy field, his horse *"just gave up…had my father like a tiger in a pit."* The irony being, Ponsonby's father had four hundred better mounts on his country estate.

Wellington rides along the ridge.

The French infantry has almost reached their objective. *The screen is filled with their power and menace of annihilation.*

Lying in wait behind a hedge is the FRONT RANK *of* PICTON'S DIVISION. *They do not know what is over the hill. N.C.O. are going along the line pouring gin into nervous cups.* O'Connor quips: *"Isn't it nice of a busy man like the King of England to think of us 'ejuts' now."* His mate MACMAHON (Valentin Koval) wonders how many are on their way, while nervously fingering rosary beads: *"It's like the whole of bloody hell is coming up out of the ground."* This makes O'Connor shudder: *"Nothing scares me like being next to a friend of the Almighty."*

The leading French column is only fifty yards from the top of the Ridge.

{Watching closely is Wellington, *who suddenly takes off his hat and holds it over his head towards the French.*}

Ponsonby sees the signal and orders his Scots Greys to charge. From a walk, a trot, and then a gallop — the Greys surge forward *like centaurs in their magnificence* — *men with the chests of horses.* With his TRUMPETER blowing the charge by his side, Ponsonby leads his men forward. *The* TROOPERS *encourage their horses by name:* "Go Rattler," "Up, Up, Up, Foxhunter," "Go, Beauty, Go." {*They gallop through the* GORDON HIGHLANDERS; *some break ranks and, catching hold of the stirrups of the* SCOTS GREYS, *are propelled into Battle.* "Scotland forever".}

The Scots Greys crash into the French left flank. *Horses and infantry stagger together in a state of weird and frightening concussion.*

{A French HUSSAR MARBOT (Sergio Testori) appears. *A corridor opens up in the chaos of the battle…*Marbot *gallops forward like a whirlwind.* Mercer and Normyle watch the rider come closer. Wellington and De Lancey both speculate: *"A deserter? A traitor?"* Marbot gallops angrily straight towards Wellington and shouts, *"The Emperor!"* Then leaving a stunned Wellington, he turns around and gallops back towards the French lines.

{*The huge French columns burst apart as* Ponsonby's cavalry strike. FROM THE AIR, *the destruction of the columns resembles ice breaking.*} Allied infantry follows up behind. The Allied Artillery fire at the French third column. {These men take the hedges and *for a few moments the French are in possession of the Allied Ridge.*}

Picton beats his horse as he orders his men to counter-attack; *"roaring with a voice of twenty trumpets."* A musket ball hits him in the forehead. As he falls, his men spring up and fire into the French, throwing them into confusion.

{*The exultant* SCOTS GREYS *gather in the valley. The field is theirs.* Ponsonby is satisfied for the day: *"Wipe your blades, boys, you have killed enough."*}

The French guns open up again. *In the wildness of victory, the* SCOTS GREYS *react like a mob. They surge forward out of control* towards the firing guns. Ponsonby *orders his Trumpeter to sound the recall. To no avail, the men do not hear as they hurtle to destruction.*

"You're killing yourselves," Ponsonby cries. *"They'll cut you off."*

Napoleon stands with KELLERMAN (Lev Polyakov) watching the charge, who observes: *"They are the noblest Cavalry in Europe and the worst led."* Napoleon orders Jacquinot's Lancers to counter-attack them.

Wellington and Uxbridge, realising the charge has gone too far, order the recall. *The* TRUMPETER *is red-faced and frightened. His eyes bulge in the exertion of blowing.* The call is ignored; Wellington makes the boy desist: *"Stop that useless noise. You'll hurt yourself."*

In the valley, the French LANCERS advance from the right *interposing themselves between the* SCOTS GREYS *and the Allied Heights… They sting forward the heads of their lances… They hit, slash, pierce with their lances, scattering the* SCOTS GREYS.

Ponsonby and his Trumpeter are cut off from their men and are pursued by seven French LANCERS. Ponsonby's horse struggles in the mud. With the Lancers closing, he hands his snuff-box and watch to the Trumpeter, with instructions to give the keepsakes to his son. The Trumpeter obeys and makes his escape just as the Lancers kill Ponsonby. Three Lancers give chase to the Trumpeter, killing him also, leaving the keepsakes lost in the mud.

The FRENCH CANNONADE *begins again with an even greater intensity.*

Some miles away is *The* ARMY OF GROUCHY, *30,000 strong*, the faint sound of cannons in the distance. {*stretched full length on the grass is the extraordinary figure of Commandant* RUMIGUS (Pietro Ceccarelli), *a veteran with one arm and many wounds.*} Grouchy, standing in a garden with a plate of strawberries, is joined by Gerard. *"By God, Sir, the cannons are calling us. March to the sound of the guns. A third of the army is with us. Our duty…"* Grouchy cuts him dead and says his *"orders were precise… to keep my sword in Blucher's back."* He puts down the strawberries and mounts his horse as Gerard continues to press the strategic point: *"if we march for the field, we must cut Blucher off.*" Grouchy is adamant, he is following orders: "*If the Emperor wanted me there, he would not have sent me here.*" The distant booming of cannons continues.

Back at Waterloo, through his telescope Napoleon spots distant movement on the Heights of St. Lambert. *Suddenly his face takes on a suspicious, rather intrigued look:* "*The shadow the clouds have thrown across that hill.*" Soult trains his telescope: "*It is a herd of cattle.*" Drouot concurs with Napoleon: "*His Majesty is right — the shadow of a cloud; it is moving.*" La Bedoyere's younger eyes are sharper: "*I see…five or six thousand men, in marching columns.*" Soult can make out horses, he suggests its Grouchy. All eyes are trained on the DISTANT HILL *with its dark spreading shape and glints of light.*

Wellington and his officers are also scanning the horizon. De Lancey suggests: "*It could be Grouchy's blue.*" Uxbridge fears: "*Grouchy has come across.*" Wellington, ever the optimist: "*Damn it, it could be Prussian black.*" He asks Lord Hay to determine the colour: "*Your eyes are young.*" The sixteen-year-old boy almost blubbers over his inadequacy. "*I think it's b…b…b…*"

Napoleon is now convinced it is the Prussians as he *shuts his telescope with a snap:* "*But they are only a shadow on a hill. They are not yet real.*" Ney rides up and before scanning the Prussians, Napoleon insists they forget them and concentrate on destroying Wellington. The key, he says, is the La Haye Sainte farmhouse: "*That's his throat. Cut it.*" Unable to contain his worry, he cries: "*But where is Grouchy?*" He is convulsed in pain and doubles up. Surgeon LARREY (Yan Yanakiyev) pleads with him to lie down and rest. {He scoffs: "*Going to bed, with men dying and my name rattling in them, it is indecent!*"}

La Bedoyere leads Napoleon away on his horse. He is distraught and babbles how after Austerlitz he had six more years, but it's now been ten. He ponders whether he is too old to gamble. Noticing the sun dimming behind clouds, he questions what men will say of him. La Bedoyere is adamant: "*They will say you extended the limits of glory.*" *Ironically,* Napoleon replies: "*That thought, at least, my son can safely inherit.*"

{The battlefield is strewn with the detritus of war. Riderless horses run free across the valley. The guns have stopped. There is a silence across the field.

{Normyle, his face black with powder, is leaning on a cannon, while looking over the field.

{Picton's body is carried away along with CAPTAIN TAYLOR (Georgi Rybakov) carrying the general's top hat and sword.}

On the French ridge, two batteries of 12 pounders are deployed, ready to fire. French Cavalry line up behind the guns. First line, *the* CUIRASSIERS — *their helmets and breastplates gleaming.* Then the LANCERS OF THE GUARD — *The gaiety of their fluttering lance-flags contrasts with the stillness of the* CUIRASSIERS. *Lastly, the* HUSSARS *of the Guard, splendid in their bearskin shakos and fur-trimmed pelisses.*

Wellington, who has been watching through his telescope, is baffled as to why cavalry is concentrating while the infantry does not move: "*I can't imagine what he means to do.*" He glances in the direction of the anticipated Prussian advance.

The French Artillery opens fire.

The Allied ridge is battered by cannon fire. An ammunition depot is hit and explodes with a terrific force. Wellington's Tree is ripped by a shot, causing much confusion amongst the Staff officers. Wellington orders Lord Hay to ride with instructions for General Alten to retire his men a hundred paces from the withering cannon fire. Hay, along with his dog, starts out on the perilous journey. Wellington now issues a general order: "*The army will retire a hundred paces.*" His Staff officers ride off to issue instructions, leaving the commander alone by the flaming tree. The Inniskillins trudge past, in their midst is O'Connor, who points out to his commander-in-chief: "*It's a bad policy, Sur, to stand under a tree in a thunderstorm. It attracts the bolts, Sur.*" Wellington takes the "*impudent advice*" and rides away through shot and shell. *The* ALLIED ARMY *retires under fire...In a few moments, the ridge is empty.*

Ney is elated at the prospect of imminent victory: "*Wellington is retreating.*" He orders a great cavalry charge with thousands of horsemen. *The jingle of harness, the muffled sound of men in their saddles, the striking of hooves, the breathing of the animals, fill the theatre.* CUIRASSIERS with LANCERS and HUSSARS gallop forward as the TRUMPETER blows the "GALLOP".

{Mercer and Normyle wait by their loaded cannons, *which are pointed at an angle of 30 degrees to the ridge.* Wellington and De Lancey ride up and instruct them to fire till the last minute before seeking shelter in the nearest infantry square. De Lancey notices the *curious angle of Mercer's guns.* Mercer explains there is a bad hollow in front of them: "*worse than a pit. They must go around it.*"}

The FRENCH CAVALRY — *their flags streaming, trumpets sounding, swords held high, lances slanting.* Through the smoke, the cavalry led by Ney are astonished to see *the Allied Army not in flight but standing to meet him.* He notices the hollow way just in time. But not: *The* FIRST RANK OF CUIRASSIERS. *From the gallop, the front horses rear up to the terrible stand-still of their hind legs. But it is too late.* The horsemen are pushed into the pit by the throng behind them.

Mercer's guns fire *to add murder to accident in the* HOLLOW WAY. Before his crew is swamped by the rest of the French cavalry, he and his men make for the nearest square.

Ney leads his men to attack the Allied army, now grouped in thirteen squares. *The* CUIRASSIERS *hurl themselves against the English with sabres between their teeth and pistols in their hands...They leap against the human walls...Bayonets pierce the sides of the horses.*

Ney is unhorsed but quickly finds another...*he is black with gunpowder...yelling like a mad man: "Forward! Again!"*

As French Lancers ride towards the 27th Regiment's square, COLBORNE (Jeffry Wickham) orders his men to: *"Shoot at the horses. Pile up the horses."*

Napoleon, pale and tense, now returned to his vantage point is horrified by Ney's attack and yells: *"The mad man: He's making doubt of what was certain."* {Hoping to right the situation, he orders infantry to attack before messaging Ney to remember: *"the farmhouse."*}

The CAVALRY *scatter chaotically in front of the* SQUARES. *It is no longer a battle, but darkness, a whirlwind of souls...a storm of flashing bayonets.*

In Gordon's square of Highlanders, a Piper continues playing to lift morale as the casualties are piled up in the centre.

Cuirassiers try to breach the square of the 27th (Inniskilling) with carbine fire. O'Connor is one of the defenders firing back. One of his mates, Tomlinson, breaks ranks: *"Leave me alone, can't ye."* Standing amid the swirling cavalry, he ignores all pleas to return. *He shakes his fist between both armies and shouts: "Why do men who have never seen each other do so much harm to each other?"* There is a momentary pause, before Tomlinson throws his gun away and *disappears from sight among the horses — this odd, conscientious objector to the Battle of Waterloo.*

The sky darkens with a storm. *The sounds of shot merge into a single thunderclap...A powerful wind scatters and blows back men and horses.*

Napoleon holds himself against the wind as he turns down a request for more infantry.

Wellington, under his tree and buttressed by the gale, as he too rejects a request for reinforcements. {He turns and notices a square of soldiers lying down, and orders them to get up. As smoke clears, he sees they are *literally lying dead in square.* He murmurs quietly: *"It cannot be done."*

{A few men are gathered around the flag of another square.}

Wellington confides to De Lancey as they ride along the ridge: *"Everyone is going by turns. If he takes the farm house, my centre is broken."* A shell explodes and severely wounds De Lancey. Wellington allows a moment of emotion: *"Mrs. De Lancey will have to be told."*

Lord Hay *decides to do some soldiering* and exhorts the men to hold and fight: *"Remember England, men…the sports of England…the grouse in August."* A SOLDIER quips: *"The bastard wants us hung as poachers."* Hay is hit and thrown dead from his horse. His dog whimpers over his body as Wellington looks on.

Napoleon, *struggling against the pressure of the wind,* dictates to FLA-HAUT (Rostislav Yankovskiy) to write to Paris: *"The war is mine."*

The crucial farm of LA HAYE SAINTE that lies at the centre of Wellington's line — is captured by the French.

The news brings consternation to the allies. (Colbourne): *"We can't hold them."* It is the moment of truth for Wellington, who is fully aware of their predicament: *"It appears, Uxbridge, that I have lost the battle. Give me night, or give me Blucher: At least I will die in the place I myself have chosen."*

The storm subsides, clouds allow through the rays of the setting sun. Napoleon, bathing in the glow, is calm. {A mortally wounded OFFICER (Aleksandr Parkhomenko) rides up and informs him of the farmhouse's capture. Expressing concern at the man's fatal condition, the Officer replies: *"No. I am killed, and I have died for you."* And then promptly expires at Napoleon's feet. Ney rides up, his blood up: *"They are so bled, Sire, their necks are down."*} Napoleon considers it is time for the *coup de grace* and orders the advance of the Guard towards Brussels.

The French cannons roar along the whole front. Napoleon leads his Old Guard forward, six thousand strong, declaring: *"Let all who love me, follow me."* With Ney and CAMBRONNE (Evgeni Samoilov) on either side and a band of 24 musicians playing *"*LA GRENADIERE.*"* {*The* DRUM MAJOR (Valentins Skulme) *throws his stick in the air and as it goes up, shouts* "*The Emperor."* His shout is echoed by an army. Amongst them is Sauret, who shouts the hallowed words.}

Wellington stands in a field of beans while watching the advance, determined to stand and fight after abandoning his position on the left. *"If we make ourselves as tight as stone, and if Blucher comes, we may still do something. I want what remains of us here…"* He orders Uxbridge to: *"put every gun to them…every gun."* Gordon rides up and offers some beans to Wellington, who, trying to keep his cool, replies curtly: *"If there is one thing in the world about which I know positively nothing, it is agriculture."* Gordon shrugs and finishes munching his beans as the cannon fire intensifies.

A line of young FRENCH DRUMMERS *beat on their drums strongly: rum, dum, rum, dum, rum dum…A roar is heard behind them:* 'THE EMPEROR!' Napoleon with Ney, La Bedoyere and Cambronne, ride behind the Drummers.

Allied Artillery fire into the advancing Old Guard's column.

{Napoleon *speaks almost in soliloquy.* "It would take me another twenty years and all my sixty battles to create their like again. Their love is my strength. Yet every battle, every year, I march them off the earth."} La Bedoyere and Ney swing their horses in front of Napoleon to shield him from the fire. Cambronne forces him to retire: *"Sire, if you stay exposed to this gunfire any longer, I shall order your own Guard to nail you up in a box."* With a laugh, he allows his horse to be turned: {*"There is spirit in them still."*}

With Ney at their head {he exhorts his men: "March on, march on. These few yards will give us Europe!"}, The Old Guard, *magnificent but transfigured — expressionless, not quite human,* march on into the intensifying cannon fire. {They reach the gun batteries and, with *bayonets fixed, throw themselves on the batteries. Some are taken, some are destroyed.*}

A wounded OFFICER (Orso Maria Guerrini) gallops up and announces grimly to Napoleon: *"The Prussians are in the woods."* Napoleon cannot believe his ears, and demands: *"Where is Grouchy?"* All turn *toward the sudden sound of* GUNFIRE *in the east.* La Bedoyere is sure they are Grouchy's guns. Napoleon is not convinced; *he is grave and still.* "I made one mistake in my life I should have burned Berlin."

The Prussians debouch from the woods. Led by Blucher, *his leg is bandaged and cocked up in a crude splint:* "Raise high the black flags, children. No pity. No prisoners. I'll shoot any man I see with pity in him." Immediately, *huge* BLACK FLAGS *rise like hideous birds above the massed Prussian troops.*

Napoleon raves before his Staff: *"The Prussians have come too late."* He issues orders to deploy the reserves against the Prussian advance: *"I have never yet been beaten upon the field of battle."* Except, as he says at Marengo, when the battle was lost at five o'clock but won back by seven: *"The day is still mine."*

{The Old Guard *are in absolute possession of the Allied forward slope.* Cambronne shouts triumphantly: "It was a rear-guard. They have run." Linking arms, some Officers stride forward singing: "*La Victoire est a nous.*" The song is taken up in full chorus as soldiers hoist their busbies on their bayonets.}

Wellington shouts to MAITLAND (Vasili Plaksin): *"Up, Guards, and at 'em." Like jack-in-boxes,* Maitland's regiment stand up and take aim, *their vivid red, their precision, the* ENGLISH SOLDIERS *create the greatest visual shock of the Battle.* Maitland orders them to fire.

The FRENCH COLUMN *is suddenly stopped — as if it had struck an invisible wall.* {Sauret spits defiance.} Ney is in front and exhorts the Guard to advance. Another volley causes turmoil in their ranks. Ney is unhorsed, but undaunted: *"Up to them, Must I fight alone?"* Laughing *like a lunatic,* he gathers some men and continues to advance.

{HIGHLANDERS take up position on the *left flank of the column. Every man, a projectile.*}

The Prussian advance — over on the East — a wide, powerful flood.

THE GUARD BEGINS TO BREAK. *In a moment it becomes a helpless mob.* Ney tries desperately to stem the tide: *"Stay with me and see how a Marshal of France can die."* He grabs a fleeing CORPORAL (Ivan Milanov), who yells the stark fact into his face: *"The Guard has broken."* Ney is *a collapsed man.*

Further back, Napoleon cannot believe his ears: *"Broken? The Guard is granite."* {He turns away, putting his hands over his ears. "Do not tell me... lies."}

The Prussian CAVALRY *charges a flank of the French.*

Wellington on the ridge, raises his hat *three times in the manner of a huntsman laying on his dogs. The* ARMY *floods over the ridge and spreads down the forward slope.* Excited, Wellington exclaims: *"Damn me, Uxbridge, if I ever saw thirty-thousand men run a race before."* He and Uxbridge join in "the race."

The defeated French army is in chaos, with thousands in full rout. But their cannons continue to roar. *"They can still sting out of their arses,"* says Gordon. Ordering Uxbridge to charge the guns, Wellington turns to his subordinate who says *in an almost normal voice, "I've lost my leg, by God."* Wellington replies with equal aplomb, *"By God, so you have." The situation is completely deadpan.*

Napoleon and Cambronne try to stop the tide of fleeing men, exhorting them all to stand. Some including Sauret and Chactus obey, and a SQUARE *begins to take shape — resolute, silent and final.* {Inside the makeshift formation Napoleon continues to rant: *"Grouchy will come."*}

As the allied troops gather around for the kill, Colborne suggests an end to the killing. {Wellington is more sanguine: *"We're doing our duty, which cannot stop even at murder."* He hopes the Emperor will *"have the sense to be killed with his men."*

{Inside the Square, Napoleon refuses to countenance defeat: *"I am not rehearsed in surrender."* The allied artillery hits the square with devastating results. Napoleon is on the brink of a mental collapse as he babbles:

"*Twenty years gone in an afternoon.*" Cambronne insists he must leave: "*Your enemies must not have your body.*"} Forcing the issue, Drouot takes the bridle of Napoleon's horse and leads him from the Square. As he leaves, he says ruefully: "*Am I the only one condemned to live?*"

The Square continues its slow retreat, stumbling over the bodies of their fallen comrades. *In the slanting sun these silent men wearing dark skin hats look more and more spectral.* ALLIED CAVALRY forms a circle around them, masking a ring of lethal cannons. A truce is offered as Colbourne carries a white flag, calling on the remnants of the Guard to surrender. Cambronne, *his face gathers into an expression of contempt:* "*Merde!*" *A column of smoke collects in the sky above the Square. A red evening sun finds colours in the smoke.*

{The PRUSSIANS reach La Belle Alliance. *The road sounds with their boots.* Colbourne's men wearily rest around their flags; they become animated and begin shouting: "*Blucher, Blucher.*"

{Blucher meets Wellington amid the ruins of La Belle Alliance to a chorus of cheers. They exchange simple compliments: "*It was hard bargaining, Blucher, all day. Without you it could not have been done.*" Blucher replies, "*You have made history for your England today.*" Wellington ponders the significance. "*I can't say how history will regard it — as a battle we won or he lost.*" Blucher is itching to chase the quarry by the moonlight: "*Stamp them until your boots split. Test the pulse of every corpse with your bayonet.*" This shocks Wellington, who asks for quarter for the enemy, before taking leave of Blucher.

{A party of PRUSSIAN LANCERS gallop back up to Blucher with a TROPHY *on a* LANCE HEAD. *It is Napoleon's* HAT. Blucher snatches it: "*Where is the head?*" The Lancer (Vladimir Udalov) replies that they found it in a ditch. Blucher, his blood up: "*Find him and hang him on the first tree.*" With a great shout "*Forward!*" he disappears into the night.}

Wellington rides alone across the dead moonlit battlefield, followed by Somerset and PERCY (Vasiliy Livanov) *at a discreet distance. He rides in profound distress… Gasping and crying from the wounded (The agony of 40,000 men). Here and there figures move among the dead. Fallen horses writhe in agony.* {A SOLDIER *struggles to his feet, staggers a few paces and falls*}.

He reaches the remnants of Camborne's square of the Old Guard. There lies Rata by his drum, also *Sauret and Chactas. As he moves, he looks down on the dead, as if he were paying them the honour of a review.*

SCAVENGERS pick through the mountains of dead and dying. Percy fires a pistol to disperse them, the *last shot, at Waterloo, reverberates around the field.* Wellington rides through his dead, played out in rows: "*I hope to

God I've fought my last battle. I have lost some of my dearest friends today."
CLOSE ON *Wellington's face: It is streaming with tears.*

Napoleon stands by a fire, tears down his cheeks. *There is a heavy silence.* A YOUNG OFFICER pleads with him to leave. {In a daze, Napoleon stabs at the fire with a stick. THE MUSIC — BEETHOVEN — EXPLODES... *Sparks flash in his eyes; the smoke of the fire now reveals, now hides his face.* He snaps out of it, and asks *(vaguely)*, "Grouchy?"}

Ney arrives, and urges him to leave, before dragging him to his coach. Napoleon babbles incoherently about concentrating his forces in between asking for a map. He *slumps on the seat of his coach with a deep sigh...He puts his hand to his heart.* {Ney remarks: "You are a little pale." Napoleon comments: "*I have lost an Empire and an army of seventy-thousand men...I am a little pale.*" He asks Ney if they will hang him: "*Or will they be satisfied with shooting me?*"...} Ney's voice is gentle but formal, an epitaph: "They will chain you like Prometheus to a rock, where the memory of your own greatness will gnaw you."

The coach...drives away disappearing into darkness.
THE END.

Acknowledgments

"All the business of war, and indeed all the business of life, is to endeavour to find out what you don't know by what you do; that's what I called guessing what was at the other side of the hill."[753] This quote by Wellington himself is particularly apt for a narrative about his most famous battle. Through contemporary articles and recently recorded memories of those who took part in this enormous production, I have made judicious use of educated guess to see what *was* on at the other side of that hill.

Firstly, I must thank several people who gave generously of their time. The star of the show has to be actor Richard Heffer, who from my very first email has replied promptly and concisely to a barrage of questions. "You lucky man! I have just discovered my Waterloo Diary! Unseen for 50 years…Extraordinary…" Without doubt, the most significant artefact in the research was Richard's diary, which had lain unread for fifty years. This has given an invaluable insight into life on set, and living in the dusty town of Uzhgorod, which played host for the unit.

My heartfelt thanks go to the following who gave generously of their time: A three-hour chat via FaceTime with Peter Davies who recalled how daunting it was being a teenager on such a mammoth project. Sisters Veronica and Raffaella De Laurentiis gave fascinating insights into their dynamic father, and their own teenage experiences. Daniele Nannuzzi, who assisted his father, supplied fascinating stories of the many challenges faced by the camera team; also, Heinz Feldhaus, whose job it was to keep them rolling and supplied many wonderful photographs. Philippe Forquet de Dorne, who shone a light upon working with Rod Steiger and the friendship that developed, sadly passed away before he could send more memories. Siobhan S. Craig for valuable insights into her screenwriter father H. A. L Craig. Joan Borsten Vidov for kindly allowing me to make use of material from her documentary about her late husband, Oleg Vidov, as well as extracts from his autobiography, as well as her interview with the venerable actress, Irina Skobtseva. Roger Green, who kindly allowed me to quote from his memoir. Retired Major Nigel Oxley, the commanding officer of the Gordon Highlanders, and his wife Easter, who shared very detailed memories of their time in Rome. Abi Collins, for casting a professional eye over the cavalry charges and giving her verdict on the equine treatment.

Standing in the background were thousands of soldiers of the Soviet army. Most of these are nameless faces amid the smoke and dust of the action. Luckily, a few memoirs have come to light to illuminate the story of some of these men. A chance find of an article in a Ukrainian newspaper led to Mykola Kholodnyak who was many of the cavalrymen. Lots of thanks to the staff at Volyn.com for putting me in touch, and also to Mykola's daughter Nataliya, and son-in-law Oleksandr Dolotko in Iowa, who helped to make a tri-continent Skype interview work with live translations. Thanks to Saida Jaste for her article with another cavalryman, Aslan Khablauk. Also, Kovács Elemér for kind permission to quote from his interview with one of the soldiers, Tibor Tompa. Hearing the story of these men and women, now is their sixties and seventies, has been the most rewarding aspect of the project.

Historian Gareth Glover who viewed the film with me and commented on the variations from the facts, also for allowing me to reproduce maps from his book *Waterloo: Myth and Reality*. He has helped enormously with the history of the battle and corrected my mistakes. Robert Pocock, who is an authority on Captain Mercer, the character Richard Heffer played, added many interesting historical insights and also helped correct my many mistakes. Also, fellow Historian Steve Dwan for compiling a detailed analysis of what they got right and wrong.

Barbara Corsi for her insights into *The Red Tent*, and Stefano Pisu for sending me his excellent book on Italian/Russian co-productions. Johanna Aleksanyan and Producer Evgeni Balamutenko at Art Pictures Studio in Moscow for an enjoyed day filming an interview for a film about Sergei Bondarchuk, *Battle* (2021), and subsequent assistance on many fronts. Fedor Bondarchuk for kindly giving permission to quote from his father's book. Rob McGibbon for some insights into Bryan Forbes and his unmade Napoleonic project. The British Entertainment History Project for permission to quote from their archival interviews with Virginia McKenna, Bryan Forbes and Gordon K. McCallum. Detailed information about Pinewood Studios sound mixing was supplied by Graham V. Hartstone, John Hayward and Stephen Pickard, also thanks to James

McCabe for pointing me towards them. Alan Jones for some insights into the film editing process; you've earnt a pint for that!

Bert Innes, a Research Volunteer at The Gordon Highlanders Museum, and for their kind permission to quote from D.M. Napier's *Life of a Regiment — The History of the Gordon Highlanders*. Alice Crossland's book *Wellington's Dearest Georgy* helped to add some historical flavour to the Ballroom chapter. Ron Poulter and Richard Green for their information and artwork from Bermans costume house (now Angels), who helped to clothed the vast army. Romolo Sormani of the venerable Italian props company, E. Rancati, for digging into the archives and finding some fascinating designs made for the film. Mark Fleischer for kind, allowing me to quote from his father, Richard's very entertaining and perceptive memoir. John Lind, for permission to quote from his three-hour interview with Bondarchuk in 1970, and offering corrections and suggestions. Denise J. Youngblood for permission to quote from her excellent book on *War and Peace,* and Curtis Tsui of the Criterion Collection for permission to use professor Youngblood's comments from their superb extras for their *War and Peace* Blu-ray. Alessandra Levantesi Kezich for kindly allowing me to quote from her excellent biography of Dino De Laurentiis. Jenna McCormick of American Cinema Editors for permission to use Richard C. Meyer's article on the Post-Production process. Dale Bell for quoting from his book about the *Woodstock* film, and interesting overview of the counterculture. Kevin Brownlow for information on his famous *Napoleon* restoration, as well as insights, along with Andrew Mollo, into their work on *Charge Of The Light Brigade*. Craig Lysy of Moviemusic.uk and Jim Paterson of Mfiles for permission to use their quotes of Nino Rota, also John Mansell of Movie Music International (Mmi). for his review of Nino Rota's music for the film. Sheldon Hall for information on box office and TV ratings. Filippo Ulivieri for his overview of Kubrick's unrealised projects. Bob Thorogood and Irthlingborough Historical Society for permission to reproduce rare stills from the 1913 epic made in their town.

Also, and in no particular order: Gayane Ambartsumian at Mosfilm, Nail Bainazarov, Ronnie Bell, Oscar Beuselinck, James Blames, Ivo Blom, Alexander Bojar, Ruth Case-Green, Luca Cianchetta, Joe Crosswicks, Maria Dalakian, Charles. J. Esdaile, Beatrice Forquet De Dorne, Hester Hargett-Aupetit, Tracey Hunt, Hans Kemna, Aslan Khablauk, Matthew Kennedy, Sue Malden, Ruth Marsh, Linda Morand Phillips, Mike Munn, Liam O'Herlihy, Georgina Orgill, Emma and Ian Ogilvy, Dan Parish, Lou Pitt, Rashit Sharafutdinov, Otto Snel, Shahid Shantyz, Igor Starchenko, Paul Stevens, Elena Tafuni, Paul van Yperen, Ed Wacek and Dave Worrall, and the many others who I apologise if I have forgotten. A special mention for Casper Röhrig who during the very early days of the internet shared with me his accumulated info and stills: where are you now?

By far the most frustrating part of this project has been determining copyright for a variety of sources. Strenuous effort has gone into tracking and trying to contact people and organisations, and unfortunately it has not been possible in several instances. Please politely contact the publisher with any issues.

Ben Ohmart at BearManor for saying "yes" to the project, and Stone Wallace for his painstaking proof-reading and encouragement. Brian Pearce of Red Jacket Press for the excellent layout and cover.

Closer to home, huge appreciation to a great friend and screenwriting collaborator, Stephen Graham, for help, advice and encouragement as always.

And last but not least to my family: Sam, three dogs and a cat and of course, my darling wife, Claire, for all the immense support, patience and love.

Abergavenny, 2021.

Bibliography

INTERVIEWS AND CORRESPONDENCE WITH THE AUTHOR:

Bell, Dale, 2021.
Joan Borsten Vidov, 2020.
Kevin Brownlow, 2021.
Abbi Collins, 2019.
Siobhan S. Craig, 2021.
Peter Davies, 2019.
Steve Dwan, 2020.
Heinz Feldhaus, 2019.
Mark Fleischer, 2020.
Philippe Forquet De Dorne, 2019.
Gareth Glover, 2019.
Roger Green, 2021.
Graham V. Hartstone, 2020.
John Hayward, 2020.
Richard Heffer, 2019-21.
Alan Jones, 2021.

Raffaella De Laurentiis, 2020.
Veronica De Laurentiis, 2019.
Mykola Kholodnyak, 2020.
John Lind, 2020.
Rob McGibbon, 2020.
Daniele Nannuzzi, 2020.
Emma Ogilvy, 2020.
Ian Ogilvy, 2019.
Major (retired) Nigel Oxley
    and Easter Oxley, 2020.
Stephen Pickard, 2021.
Robert Pocock, 2020.
Ron Poulter, 2020.
Paul Stevens, 2020.
Denise J. Youngblood, 2020.

ARTICLES

Andrews, Nigel, *Waterloo*, *Monthly Film Bulletin*, December 1970.

Ark Easier For Noah To Build, *The Deseret News*, 02 February 1965.

Baroncelli, Jean de, *Waterloo de Serguei Bondartchouk*, *Le Monde*, 31 October 1970.

Baynazarov, Nail, *A soldier from Bashkiria helped Bondarchuk's continuation of War and Peace*. ProUfu.ru, 26 February 2017.

Bilbow, Marjorie, *Waterloo Today's Cinema*, 30 October 1970.

Bombal, Matias, *Rod Steiger Interview*, MAB Archives, October 2000.

Bondarchuk, Natalya, *Newspaper Trud*, 30 September 2005. https://www.trud.ruarticle30-09-2005/94416_natalja_bondarchuk_na_semkax_vojny_i_mira_otets_pe.html

Capote, Truman, *The Duke in His Domain*, *The New Yorker* magazine, 09 November 1957.

Champlin, Charles, *Los Angeles Times*, 03 April 1971.

Clarke, Graham, *Waterloo*, *Kinematograph Weekly*, 31 October 1970.

Coe, Richard L., *Napoleon Brando Not Quite Vintage, The Washington Post,* 26 November 1954.

Corsi, Barbara, *Italian Film Producers and The Challenge of Soviet Coproductions: Franco Cristaldi and The Case of The RED TENT,* Historical Journal of Film, Radio and Television, 2020, 40:1, 84-107. doi.org10.1080/01439685.2020.1715598

Crist, Judith, *War and Peace — The Greatest, New York Magazine,* 13 May 1968.

Daily Variety, 04 October 1965.

Daily Variety, 08 February 1966.

Daily Variety, 08 March 1967.

Daily Variety, 12 August 1968.

Daily Variety, 23 October 1968.

Daily Variety, 19 March 1969.

Daily Variety, 04 November 1969.

Daily Variety, 05 November 1969.

Day, Felicity, *Before Waterloo what happened at the Duchess of Richmond's ball?* historyextra.com/period/georgian/before-waterloo-what-happened-at-duchess-richmond-ball-belgravia-duke-wellington.

The Manchester Guardian, 25 July 1957.

Ebert, Roger, *Interview with Rod Steiger,* 04 April 1971.

Ebert, Roger, *War and Peace, Chicago Sun-Times,* 22 June 1969.

Ebert, Roger, *Waterloo, Chicago Sun-Times,* 08 April 1971.

Edelstein, David, *Plummer's Peak, New York Magazine,* 27 May 2011.

Elemèr, Kovács, https://www.karpatinfo.net/hetilap/2016/info_201635.pdf

Elley, Derek, *Versatility, Films and Filming,* April 1976.

Esdaile, Charles. J, *Waterloo — A Critical Review,* University of Liverpool. https://h-france.net/fffh/the-buzz/waterloo-1970/

Film Facts, 1971.

Gillett, John, *Sight and Sound,* v39 n3, Summer 1970.

Greenspun, Roger, *A Battle fought Strictly for the Camera, The New York Times,* 01 April 1971.

Guerin, Ann, *Rod Steiger's Napoleon: A Self-Defeated Man, Show Magazine,* May 1971.

Hastings, Chris, *Kubrick's Napoleonic odyssey goes online, The Daily Telegraph,* 05 May 2002.

Hollywood Reporter, 25 September 1967.

Iskusstvo kino 9, 1965.

Israel, Andy, *Waterloo Marks End of Epic Movies, Stanford Daily,* 02 April 1971.

Jaste, Saida, https://www.liveinternet.ru/users/letayushaya_na_barse/post245557116/

L'Express, 23 September 1968.

Le Monde, 07 November 1970.

Lewis, Simon, Focus on: Waterloo, *Cinema Retro* Magazine, Issue 16, vol 44, 2020.

LIFE, 11 June 1965.

Lind, John, *Sergei Bondarchuk: The Road to Waterloo, Focus on Film,* October 1970.

Los Angeles Times, 22 August 1968.

Los Angeles Times, 01 September 1968.

Los Angeles Times, 10 July 2002.

Mahoney, John C., *Waterloo a $25 million still-life*, Los Angeles Free Press, 02 April 1971.

Malcom, Derek, *Cromwell knocked about a bit, The Guardian*, 16 July 1970.

Mastroianni, Tony, *Russians join Battle of Waterloo — Napoleon still loses*, Cleveland Press, 02 April 1971.

Maume, Patrick, *Craig, Harry (Henry Armitage Llewellyn, H.A.L.). Dictionary of Irish Biography*. Cambridge, United Kingdom: Cambridge University Press, 2015. (http://dib.cambridge.org/viewReadPage.do?articleId=a9777)

Meyer, Richard C., *The Second Battle of Waterloo, The Cinemeditor*, Winter 1970/71.

Mollo, John, *Making of the Charge (1), Military Illustrated Magazine*, Issue No. 42, November 1991.

Motion Picture Exhibitor, 10 February 1971.

Mousinac, Léon, *Panoramique du cinéma*, Au Sans Pareil, Paris, 1929.

The Washington Post, 26 November 1954.

Norman, Barry, *Radio Times*, June 1996.

Nothing 'coulda been' about Steiger, The Sydney Morning Herald, 11 July 2002.

Novak, Ralph, *Who's Working for Producer Dino De Laurentiis?* 26 January 1976.

Raymond, Nick, *Steiger's Napoleon, Photoplay*, January 1970.

Rich, *Waterloo, Variety*, 27 October 1970.

Sedgwick, J., Pokorny, M., *The Film Business in the United States and Britain during the 1930s, The Economic History Review, New Series*, Vol. 58, No. 01 Feb 2005, pp.79-112.

Schickel, Richard, *Two Pros in a Super Sleeper, Life*, 28 July 1967.

Sery, Patrick, *Je ferai peut-être un film sur Stalin, Josephe, Magazine de Cinéma Plastique*, November 1970.

Sloane, Leonard, *Aubrey Named M-G-M President, The New York Times*, 22 October 1969.

Souhami, Gerard, *Waterloo, Le Monde*, 29 October 1970.

Soviet Estonia, 28 May 1972. news.technotronic.org/ensv/1972/05/28.

Sullivan, Chris, *Never Meet Your Hero. Unless it's Rod Steiger, Sabotage Times*, 20 November 2011.

The Cork Examiner, 22 June 1962.

The Daily Telegraph, 27 October 1970.

The Daily Telegraph, 02 June 2009.

The Deseret News, April 1971, news.google.co.uk/newspapers?nid=AulkAQHnToC&dat=19710304&b_mode=2&hl=en

The New York Times, 25 January 1935.

The New York Times, 12 August 1956.

The New York Times, 16 May 1968.

The Stanford Daily, 02 April 1971.

The Sydney Morning Herald, 11 July 2002.

The Times, 28 October 1970.

Time, 08 December 1967.

Time, 03 May 1968.

Tveritneva, Svetlana and Lisova, Alla, https://www.volyn.com.ua/news/125014-shche-v-dalekomu-1970-mu-z-radianskoi-armii-nadislav-dodomu-tryzuby. 04 June 2019.

Ulivieri, Filippo, *Waiting for a miracle: a survey of Stanley Kubrick's unrealized projects,* https://cinergie.unibo.it/article/view/7349

Variety, 23 January 1929.

Variety, 03 December 1936.

Variety, 21 June 1966.

Variety, 28 September 1966.

Variety, 14 February 1968.

Variety, 27 March 1968.

Variety, 19 August 1969.

Variety, 28 January 1970.

Variety, January 1971.

Variety, 12 May 1971.

Variety, 02 May 1973.

Variety, 25 March 1975.

Variety, 15 July 2002.

Wallace, Randall, *What Makes a Film an Epic, DGA Magazine,* September 2003.

Waterloo and how they made a film of the famous battle of 1815, Photoplay, December 1970.

Waymark, P, *Richard Burton top draw in British cinemas, The Times,* 30 December 1971.

Webster, John, *The Making of An Epic, Film Review* 1971-72, W. H. Allen, 1971.

Weekly Variety, 09 April 1969.

Weekly Variety, 25 June 1969.

Weekly Variety, 02 July 1969.

Weekly Variety, 06 August 1969.

BOOKS

Barzman, Norma, *The Red and the Blacklist: The Intimate Memoir of a Hollywood Expatriate,* Friction Books, 2005.

Baxter, John, *King Vidor,* Simon & Schuster, Inc Monarch Film Studies, 1976.

Bell, Dale, Woodstock: *An Inside Look at the Movie That Shook Up the World and Defined a Generation,* Moving Mantra, 2012.

Belton, John, *Widescreen Cinema,* Harvard University Press, 1992.

Biskind, Peter, *Easy Riders, Raging Bulls: How the Sex-drugs-and Rock 'n' Roll Generation Changed Hollywood,* Simon & Schuster, 1998.

Bloom, Claire, *Leaving A Doll's House,* Virago, 2013.

Bluhdorn, Charles, *The Gulf + Western Story,* Newcomen Publication, 1973.

Bondarchuk, Natalya, *Edinstvennye dni,* Astrel, 2009.

Bondarchuk, Sergei, *Desire for a Miracle (Zhelanie chuda),* Molodaia gvardiia, 1981.

Brownlow, Kevin, *Napoleon,* BFI 2004.

Carlson, Marvin, *Reference Guide to World Literature*, St. James Press, 1996.

Carr, R.E., R.M. Hayes, *Wide Screen Movies: A History and Filmography of Wide Gauge Filmmaking*, McFarland, 1988.

Ciment, Michel, *Kubrick: The Definitive Edition*, Faber & Faber, 2003.

Douglas, Kirk, *The Ragman's Son,* Simon and Schuster, 1988.

Dunne, John Gregory, *The Studio*, New York: Farrar, Straus and Giroux, 1968.

Durgnat, Raymond and Simmon, Scott. *King Vidor American*. University of California Press, Berkeley, 1988.

Dye, Phillip, *Lost Cleopatra: A Tale of Ancient Hollywood,* Bearmanor Media, 2020.

Emmet, Robert, *John Huston: Interviews (Conversations with Filmmakers)*, University Press of Mississippi, 2001.

Evans, Mike, *Woodstock: Three Days That Rocked the World*, Sterling; Anniversary edition (2019).

Fleischer, Richard, *Just Tell Me When To Cry: A Memoir*, Carroll & Graf Pub, 1993.

Gazzara, Ben, *In the Moment: My Life as an Actor*, Carroll & Graf, 2004.

Gelmis, Joseph, *The Film Director as Superstar*, Doubleday, 1968.

Green, Roger, *Shaken and Stirred,* Green Days Publishing, 2020.

Guillermin, Mary, *John Guillermin: The Man, The Myth, The Movies*, Precocity Press, 2020.

Haines, Richard W., *Technicolor Movies: The History of Dye Transfer Printing*. McFarland, 1993.

Hall, S. and Neale, S., Epics, *spectacles, and blockbusters: a Hollywood history*, Wayne State University Press, Michigan, 2010.

Happé, L. Bernard, *Basic Motion Picture Technology*, Focal Press, 1975.

Herman, Jan, *A Talent for Trouble: The Life of Hollywood's Most Acclaimed Director, William Wyler,* G.P. Putnam's Sons, 1995.

Heston, Charlton, *In the Arena: An Autobiography*, Simon & Schuster, 1995.

Hughes, Howard, *Aim for the Heart*. London, I.B. Tauris, 2009.

Huston, John, *An Open Book,* Da Capo Press, 1994.

Hutchinson, Tom, *Rod Steiger: Memoirs of a Friendship*, Fromm International 1998. Jung, Carl, *Modern Man in Search of a Soul*, New York: Harvest, 1933.

Kaminsky, Stuart M., *John Huston: Maker of Magic*, Houghton Mifflin Co, 1978.

Kennedy, Matthew, *Roadshow! The Fall of Film Musicals In The 1960s*, Oxford University Press, 2014.

Kezich, T., Levantesi, A., *Dino: The Life and Films of Dino De Laurentiis*, Feltrinelli, 2001.

MacDonald Fraser, George, The *Hollywood History of the World*, Michael Joseph Ltd., 1988.

Maltin, Leonard, *Hooked on Hollywood: Discoveries from a Lifetime of Film Fandom,* Paladin Communications, 2018.

Mast, Gerald, A *Short History of the Movies*, Bobbs-Merrill Co, 1981.

Meyers, Jeffrey, *John Huston: courage and art,* New York, Crown Archetype, 2011.

Munn, Mike, *The Stories Behind The Scenes Of The Great Film Epics*, Illustrated Publications, 1982.

Munn, Michael, *Clint Eastwood: Hollywood's Loner*. London, Robson Books, 1992.

Norris, Stephen M., *Tolstoy's Comrades: Sergei Bondarchuk and the origins of Brezhnev culture*, Northwestern University Press, 2013.

O'Faolain, Nuala, *Are you somebody*, 1996.

Ogilvy, Ian, Once *A Saint: An Actor's Memoir*, Constable, 2016.

Osgerby, Bill, *Biker: Truth and Myth: How the Original Cowboy of the Road Became the Easy Rider of the Silver Screen*, Globe Pequot, 2005.

Pirie, D., *Anatomy of the Movies*, Macmillan Pub Co, 1984.

Pisu, Stefano, *La cortina di celluloide. Il cinema italo-sovietico nella guerra fredda*, Mimesis, 2019.

Plummer Christopher, *In Spite of Myself*, JR Books, 2010.

Reed, Rex, *Big Screen, Little Screen*, Macmillan, 1972.

Searles, Baird, *Epic! History on the Big Screen*, Abrams, 1990.

Sedgwick, J., Pokorny, M., *The Film Business in the United States and Britain during the 1930s*, The Economic History Review, New Series, Vol. 58, No. 01 Feb 2005.

Silverman, S., *The Fox that got away: the last days of the Zanuck dynasty at Twentieth Century-Fox*, L. Stuart, 1988.

Smith, Frederick E., *Waterloo*, Pan Books, 1970.

Stevens, George Jr, Conversations *with the Great Moviemakers of Hollywood's Golden Age*, New York, Alfred A. Knopf, 2006.

Tanner, Michael, *Troubled Epic: On Location with Ryan's Daughter*, The Collins Press, 2007.

The Stanley Kubrick Archives, Taschen, 2005.

Tolstoy, Leo, *War and Peace*, 1869.

Wanger, Walter and Hyams, J., *My Life With Cleopatra*, 1963, Republished by Vintage Books in 2013.

War and Peace, Souvenir brochure by Harold Stern, National Publishers, Inc, 1968.

Waterloo, Souvenir brochure designed by Leonard Reeves, Sackville Publishing, 1970.

Young, F.A., Petzold, *The work of the Motion Picture Cameraman*, Focal Press, 1971.

Youngblood, Denise J., *Bondarchuk's War and Peace*, University Press of Kansas, 2014.

DOCUMENTS

De Biase, Div. VII, Rome, *Certificate of nationality*, Rome, 08/10/1970.

Dino De Laurentiis cinema to Matteo Matteotti, Minister of Touris. *Waterloo / Qualification of "product for children,"* Rome, 18/11/1970.

Final balance sheet Waterloo.

Intesa Sanpaolo Historical Archive, Italian Commercial Bank, Minutes of Committees of Management, De Laurentiis Dino Cinematografica SpA, 204, 6/10/1969.

Mosfilm-Dino De Laurentiis cinematographic S.p.A co-production Agreement, Moscow, 17/5/1968, p. 1.

(All of the above: Archivio Centrale dello Stato, Rome/ Ministero del Turismo e dello Spettacolo/ Direzione Generale dello Spettacolo/ Cinema, /Coproduzioni/ 419, *Waterloo*)

Waterloo, publicity notes, 1969/70.

ORAL HISTORY

Forbes, Bryan, interviewed by Roy Fowler for The *British Entertainment History Project* in 1984. https://historyproject.org.uk/interview/bryan-forbes

McCallum, Gordon, interviewed by Alan Lawson for The *British Entertainment History Project* in 1988. https://historyproject.org.uk/interview/gordon-mccallum

McKenna, Virginia, interviewed by Joyce Robinson for The *British Entertainment History Project* in 2002. https://historyproject.org.uk/interview/virginia-mckenna

Steiger, Rod, speaking at the National Film Theatre in London, January 1971. Transcript.

OTHER MEDIA

Dustin Hoffman discusses the Laurence Olivier story, youtube.com/watch?v=Ss7F8BCrNz0.

Later with Bob Costas, NBC, 06 July 1992.

Oleg (2020), Films by Jove.

Roger Green–*James Bond 007–Screen Test*, https://youtu.be/5jNMHX11ZLE

Stanley Kubrick: A Life in Pictures, Warner Bros. 2001.

They Fought For Their Country, https://www.youtube.com/watch?v=xfUlR_nuBb4.

War and Peace, Blu-ray Special Features, Criterion Collection, 2019.

War and Peace, Ruscico, DVD, 2000.

Waterloo–1970–Fan Cut In Full Hd, https://www.youtube.com/watch?v=ZSaGPIpb830.

Waterloo, Imprint No. 5, Blu-ray, 2020.

Waterloo, Special Edition, Mediumrare Entertainment, Blu-Ray, 2021.

Ватерлоо. Серия, https://youtu.be/jjJEQC8T9tQ.

THE REAL HISTORY

Anglesey, Lord, *A History of British Cavalry: Volume 4, 1899-1913*, Pen and Sword, 1993.

Anton, J., *Retrospect of a Military Life*, 1841.

Chandler, David G., *Napoleon*, Weidenfeld, 1973.

Chandler, David G., *The Campaigns of Napoleon: The Mind and Method of History's Greatest Soldier*, Weidenfeld and Nicolson, 1967.

Charms of Melody, No.72. 1805-6, Dublin.

Clay, Matthew, *A Narrative of the Battles of Quatre Bras and Waterloo; With the Defence of Hougoumont*, edited by Gareth Glover, Huntingdon, 2006.

Clausewitz, Carl von, *On War*, 1832.

Cotton, E., *A voice from Waterloo. A history of the battle, on 18 June 1815*, London, 1848.

Crossland, Alice Marie, *Wellington's Dearest Georgy,* Uniform Press, 2017.

De Lancey, Magdalene, *A Week in Waterloo, Lady De Lancey's Narrative*, John Murray, 1906.

Dunn-Pattison, R. P., *Napoleon's Marshals*, Methuen & Co., 1909.

Forbes, Archibald, *Camps, Quarters, and Casual Places*, 1896.

Esdaile, Charles, *Napoleon's Wars: An International History,* Penguin Books, 2009.

Fraser, Sir William, *Words on Wellington — The Duke — Waterloo — The Ball*, 1889.

Glover, Gareth, *Mercer's Troop at Waterloo*. https://www.waterlooassociation.org.uk/Mercer's%20Troop%20at%20Waterloo.pdf.

Glover, Gareth, *Waterloo Archive* vol.VI, Barnsley, 2014.

Glover, Gareth, *Waterloo: Myth and Reality*, Pen and Sword, 2014.

Gronow, Rees Howell, *Reminiscences of Captain Gronow*, 1861.

J. Gurwood, ed., *The dispatches of Field Marshal the Duke of Wellington, KG, during the various campaigns...from 1799 to 1818* (13 vols., new edition, London, 1837–9).

Hibbert, Christopher, *Wellington — A Personal History*, Harper Collins, 1997.

Hooper, George, *Waterloo, the downfall of the first Napoleon* G. Bell & Sons Ltd., 1862.

Howarth David J., *A Near Run Thing: The Day of Waterloo*, Harper Collins, 1968.

Hugo, Victor, *Les Miserables*, 1862.

Kincaid, Captain Sir John, *Adventures in the Rifle Brigade*, 1830.

Kircheisen, F.M., *Napoleon*, Harcourt, 1932.

Markham, Felix, *Napoleon*, New American Library, 1963.

Martin, Jacques-François, *Souvenirs of an ex-officer, 1812-1815*, Paris 1867.

Mackenzie Macbride, ed., *With Napoleon at Waterloo and other Unpublished Documents of the Waterloo and Peninsular Campaigns*, Philadelphia: J.B. Lippincott Co., 1911.

Mercer, Cavalié, *Journal of the Waterloo campaign, kept throughout the campaign of 1815,* W. Blackwood 1870.

Muir, Rory, *Tactics and the Experience of Battle in the Age of Napoleon,* Yale University Press, 1996.

Napier, D.M., *Life of a Regiment — The History of the Gordon Highlanders*, Volume VIII 1787-1994, Mainstream Publishing, 2010/16.

Napier, George, *Passages In The Early Military Life*, 1884.

Roberts, Andrew, *Waterloo: Napoleon's Last Gamble* HarperCollins, 2005.

Spencer and Waterloo: the letters of Spencer Madan, 1814-16.

Swinton, Blanche, *A sketch of the life of Georgiana, Lady de Ros: with some reminiscences of her family and friends, including the Duke of Wellington,* (1893)

The Croker Papers (1885) vol. 3.

Tolstoy, Leo, *War and Peace,* 1868.

Uffindell, Andrew, *On The Fields Of Glory: The Battlefields of the 1815 Campaign*, Greenhill Books, 2002.

WEBPAGES

http://www.bafta.org/learning/a-tribute-to-bryan-forbes,171,BA.html

https://www.bbc.com/culture/story/20190808-was-napoleon-the-greatest-film-never-made.

https://www.bbc.com/news/entertainment-arts-55954950

https://www.bbfc.co.uk/releases/waterloo-1970-5

Cavalry in Mass, Report on Russian cavalry organization and operations in World War II, from the Intelligence Bulletin, May 1946. http://www.lonesentry.com/articles/cavalry/

https://catalog.afi.com/Catalog/MovieDetailsPrintView/2249

https://www.cbsnews.com/news/cbs-news-poll-u-s-involvement-in-vietnam/

https://cinemaretro.com/index.php?/archives/10659-REVIEW-THE-CHAIRMAN-1969-STARRING-GREGORY-PECK;-TWILIGHT-TIME-BLU-RAY-SPECIAL-EDITION.html

https://www.dailymail.co.uk/femail/article-1255821/Are-Christopher-Plummers-vile-tantrums-arrogance-blame-fact-hes-won-Oscar.html

https://www.denofgeek.com/movies/flash-gordon-john-walsh-interview/

https://edition.cnn.com/2021/02/06/opinions/christopher-plummer-sound-of-music-thomas/index.html?fbclid=IwAR3imxPIpCnZ3Hx34_7hTxRZgn7wMVtwZM2-i3XJwtWPsiyS4-j3X2Fql5k

https://en.wikipedia.org/wiki/Italian_lira

https://en.wikipedia.org/wiki/John_Savident?wprov=sfti1

https://en.wikipedia.org/wiki/Thomas_Picton

https://en.wikipedia.org/wiki/The_Bell_(magazine)

https://en.wikipedia.org/wiki/Willoughby_Gray?wprov=sfti1

https://www.everythingzoomer.com/arts-entertainment/2019/05/28/ode-boom-ultimate-camp-film/

https://www.facebook.com/TheManSharonTateAlmostMarried/posts/read-philippes-story-here/122957118352970/

http://www.fernergalleries.co.nz/default,1990.sm

https://www.goodwood.com/globalassets/venues/downloads/goodwood-dancing-into-battle.pdf

https://www.heyuguys.com/a-clockwork-evening-with-malcolm-mcdowell-christiane-kubrick-and-jan-harlan/

http://imh.org/exhibits/online/breeds-of-the-world/europe/orlov-trotter/

https://www.irishtimes.com/opinion/wellington-won-battle-of-waterloo-200-years-ago-but-irish-rejected-his-legacy-1.2254416

https://jonman492000.wordpress.com/2014/11/02/waterloo/

https://jonman492000.wordpress.com/2018/06/09/fellini-satyricon/

https://lareviewofbooks.org/article/dueling-revolutions-abel-gances-napoleon/

https://www.lettersofnote.com/2013/02/i-dont-know-how-to- write-this-letter.html

moviemusicuk.us/2016/05/01/nino-rota-fathers-of-film-music-par

https://www.mfiles.co.uk/composers/Nino-Rota.htm

https://retrospectra.ru/mirovye-zvezdy-v-sovetskom-kino/

https://www.robmcgibbon.com/legendary-director-bryan-forbes-2/

https://www.salon.com/2000/10/04/napoleon/

https://www.sbs.com.au/movies/article/2010/01/04/kubrick-never-met-his-waterloo

https://www.slantmagazine.com/film/interview-christopher-plummer-on-the-exception-and-career-as-an-actor/

https://www.telegraph.co.uk/news/worldnews/northamerica/usa/1393654/Kubricks-Napoleonic-odyssey-goes-online.html

https://www.theguardian.com/media/2009/jun/03/terence-alexander-obituary#_=_

https://www.theguardian.com/news/2002/jul/10/guardianobituaries.filmnews1

https://www.theguardian.com/stage/2010/jan/07/donal-donnelly-obituary.

https://www.vice.com/en_uk/article/nndadq/stanley-kubricks-napoleon-a-lot-of-work-very-little-actual-movie

https://www.worldwideboxoffice.com/

nymag.com/arts/books/features/62378/

screenvoicesarchive6304.wordpress.com/2005/04/10/robert-rietty/

superman.fandom.com/wiki/Superman: The_Movie

theminiaturespage.com/boards/msg.mv?id=366305.

telegraf.com.ua/kultura/kino/557232

tv.avclub.com/christopher-plummer-on-the-greatest-piece-of-direction-1798241203

http://veronicadelaurentiisonlus.com/

whc.unesco.org/uploads/nominations/549rev.pdf

https://www.warhistoryonline.com/instant-articles/filming-of-the-bridge.html

UNPUBLISHED

Borsten Vidov, Joan, *Happiness Belongs to the Risk Takers: The Oleg Vidov Story.*

Heffer, Richard, diary 1969.

McKernan, Luke, *The Battle of Waterloo or, Why Can't We Film Such a Thing If We Won the War in the First Place?* Talk given at the National Film Theatre, 30 March 1996.

Starchenko, Igor, *The abyss of sclerosis,* unpublished memoir.

Endnotes

1. Letter to John Croker (08 August 1815), as quoted in *The History of England from the Accession of James II* (1848) by Thomas Babington Macaulay, Volume I Chapter 5; and in *The Waterloo Letters* (1891) edited by H. T. Sibome.

2. Quoted in an article by Charles N. Wheeler, *Chicago Tribune*, 26 May 1916.

3. *Jackals* (2012) PF Bristol. https://www.amazon.co.uk/Jackals-Pete-Townsend/dp/B071G9YT4Z

4. *Cinema Retro,* issue 44, vol. 16, cinemaretro.com

5. *The Croker Papers (*1885) vol. 3 ch. 28.

6. Hutchinson, Tom, *Rod Steiger: Memoirs of a Friendship*, Fromm International 1998.

7. https://en.wikipedia.org/wiki/Italian_lira

8. This recreation of the first day on the battle set is based on two articles: Guerin, Ann, *Rod Steiger's Napoleon: A Self-Defeated Man, Show Magazine*, May 1971 and *Photoplay* January 1970, also 16mm behind-the-scenes footage.

9. Sery, Patrick, *Je ferai peut-être un film sur Stalin, Josephe, Magazine de Cinéma Plastique*, 29 October 1970.

10. Fleischer, Richard, *Just Tell Me When To Cry: A Memoir,* Carroll & Graf Pub, 1993.

11. Bondarchuk, Sergei, *Desire for a Miracle (Zhelanie chuda),* Molodaia gvardiia, 1981.

12. *Ibid.*

13. All extracts from the *Waterloo* December 1968 draft screenplay by H.A.L. Craig are in italics.

14. *Daily Variety*, 05 November 1969.

15. Bondarchuk.

16. Daniele Nannuzzi to author, 2020. All subsequent quotes by him are from the same source.

17. Heinz Feldhaus to author, 2020. All subsequent quotes by him are from the same source.

18. Mykola Kholodnyak to author, 2020. All subsequent quotes by him are from the same source, unless otherwise stated.

19. Tibor Tompa interviewed by Elemèr Kovàrcs, https://www.karpatinfo.net/hetilap/2016/info_201635. All subsequent quotes by him are from the same source.

20. Kholodnyak.

21. Peter Davies to author, 2019. All subsequent quotes by him are from the same source.

22. This "slate-number" is described in Raymond, Nick, *Steiger's Napoleon*, *Photoplay*, January 1970. What is curious is that although the scene number correlates with the script, it almost certainly would not have been written on the clapperboard. The procedure on this film, usual in many European productions, was to number consecutively from the very first shot, cross-referenced with the screenplay. It suggests this article was *not* written first-hand, but constructed from publicity material. Behind-the-scenes footage shows a lady with the clapper-board, but it is not possible to identify the "slate number."

23. *Waterloo and how they made a film of the famous battle of 1815*, *Photoplay*, December 1970.

24. Wallace, Randall, *What Makes a Film an Epic*, *DGA Magazine*, September 2003.

25. Mast, Gerald, *A Short History of the Movies*, Bobbs-Merrill Co, 1981.

26. Bartlett, Randolph, *Photoplay*, 1918.

27. He is credited with shooting the first feature-film in Hollywood in 1914 with *The Squaw Man*, before then only shorts had been filmed in the area.

28. The film, along with almost all of the Theda Bara's output is considered lost. The tale is well told in in Dye, Phillip, *Lost Cleopatra: A Tale of Ancient Hollywood*, Bearmanor Media, 2020.

29. Charlton Heston speaking at the National Film Theatre, London, 1969.

30. The others being *Titanic* (1997) and *The Lord of the Rings: The Return of the King* (2003).

31. See the producer's own account; Wanger, Walter and Hyams, J., *My Life with Cleopatra* by 1963, Republished by Vintage Books in 2013.

32. Comparison figures are calculated for 2020 for rest of chapter. https://www.usinflationcalculator.com/

33. Thanks to a sale to TV and other re-releases, the film did make a profit. But at the time it was judged to have been a failure. This figure includes the full cost of prints and advertising. Quoted in Hall, S. and Neale, S., *Epics, spectacles, and blockbusters: a Hollywood history*, Wayne State University Press, Michigan, 2010.

34. *Variety*, January 1971.

35. *Variety*, February 14, 1968 (advertisement).

36. Osgerby, Bill, *Biker: Truth and Myth: How the Original Cowboy of the Road Became the Easy Rider of the Silver Screen*, Globe Pequot. 2005.

37. https://www.worldwideboxoffice.com/

38. A.H. Howe, the leading film investment banker at Bank of America, wrote in Journal of The Producers Guild of America in 1971. Quoted in Pirie, D., *Anatomy of the Movies*, Macmillan Pub Co, 1984.

39. Quoted in Hall, Neale.

40. Pirie.

41. *Variety*, 28 September 1966.

42. Dunne, John Gregory, *The Studio*, New York: Farrar, Straus and Giroux, 1968.

43. *Variety*, 02 May 1973.

44. This chapter is made up of a multitude of sources. See the bibliography.

45. See Bernard Cornwall's *Sharpe* series of novels.

46. Mercer, Cavalié, *Journal of the Waterloo campaign, kept throughout the campaign of 1815*, W. Blackwood 1870.

47. Napier, George, *Passages In The Early Military Life*, 1884. (Original emphasis.)

48. The painter Adam writing in 1809, quoted in Kircheisen, F.M. *Napoleon*, Harcourt, Brace, 1932.

49. While they generally proved to be stalwarts on the battlefield, Wellington was often exasperated at the conduct of his troops after the guns fell silent. Writing following his victory at the Battle of Vitoria in 1813, he said: "We have in the service the scum of the earth as common soldiers…and of late years we have been doing everything in our power, both by law and by publications, to relax the discipline by which alone such men can be kept in order. The officers of the lower ranks will not perform the duty required from them for the purpose of keeping their soldiers in order; and it is next to impossible to punish any officer for neglects of this description. As to the non-commissioned officers, as I have repeatedly stated, they are as bad as the men, and too near them, in point of pay and situation, by the regulations of late years, for us to expect them to do anything to keep the men in order. It is really a disgrace to have anything to say to such men as some of our soldiers are." Wellington to Henry, Third Earl Bathurst, from Huarte in Spain, on 2 July 1813. J. Gurwood, ed., *The dispatches of Field Marshal the Duke of Wellington, KG, during the various campaigns…from 1799 to 1818* (13 vols., new edition, London, 1837–9).

50. Sir George Lapent. *The Private Journal of Judge-Advocate Lapent: Attached to the Head-Quarters of Lord Wellington during the Peninsula War*, 3rd edition 1854.

51. *Memoirs of Baron Lejeune*, London 1897.

52. Quoted in Muir, Rory, *Tactics and the Experience of Battle in the Age of Napoleon*, Yale University Press 1996.

53. Kincaid, Captain Sir John, *Adventures in the Rifle Brigade*, 1830.

54. Mercer.

55. Dunn-Pattison, R. P., *Napoleon's Marshals*, Methuen & Co. 1909.

56. Clay, Matthew, *A Narrative of the Battles of Quatre Bras and Waterloo; With the Defence of Hougoumont*, edited by Gareth Glover, Huntingdon, 2006.

57. Mackenzie Macbride, ed., *With Napoleon at Waterloo and other Unpublished Documents of the Waterloo and Peninsular Campaigns,* Philadelphia: J.B. Lippincott Co., 1911.

58. Martin, Jacques-François, *Souvenirs of an ex-officer, 1812-1815*, Paris 1867. Quoted in Glover, Gareth, *Waterloo: Myth and Reality*, Pen and Sword, 2014.

59. Anton, J., *Retrospect of a Military Life*, 1841.

60. Clay, Glover, p.26

61. Mercer.

62. Mercer disobeyed the order. The square he and his battery were protecting consisted of very young and inexperienced Brunswickers. Mercer feared they would flee and to steady them, he decided to "Stick to his guns" and created havoc against the French cavalry.

63. Gronow, *Reminiscences of Captain Gronow*, 1861.

64. Glover, Gareth, *Waterloo Archive* vol.VI, Barnsley 2014.

65. Gronow.

66. Cotton, E., *A voice from Waterloo. A history of the battle, on 18 June 1815*, London, 1848.

67. Dunn-Pattison.

68. Hooper, George, *Waterloo, the downfall of the first Napoleon* G. Bell & Sons Ltd. 1862.

69. First Capt. Ross, commander of the HMS Northumberland, quoted in Kircheisen, F.M.

70. Dunn-Pattison.

71. *The 28th Regiment at Quatre Bras* (1875), painted by Elizabeth Thompson.

72. *Life* Magazine, 11 June 1965.

73. Kezich, T., Levantesi, A., *Dino: The Life and Films of Dino De Laurentiis*, Feltrinelli, 2001.

74. Veronica De Laurentiis to author, 2019. All subsequent quotes by her are from the same source.

75. Fleischer, Richard, *Just Tell Me When To Cry: A Memoir*, Carroll & Graf Pub, 1993.

76. Kennedy, Matthew, *Roadshow! The Fall of Film Musicals In The 1960s*, Oxford University Press, 2014.

77. Fleischer. "Funny that Richard Fleischer wrote Dino's eyes were black, because they were actually green!" Raffaella De Laurentiis to author 2020.

78. *Ibid.*

79. Raffaella De Laurentiis to author 2020. All subsequent quotes by her are from the same source.

80. Kezich/Levantesi.

81. Corsi, Barbara, *Italian Film Producers and The Challenge of Soviet Coproductions: Franco Cristaldi and The Case of The* RED TENT, Historical Journal of Film, Radio and Television, 2020, 40:1, 84-107. doi.org10.1080/01439 685.2020.1715598

82. Kezich/Levantesi.

83. Douglas, Kirk, *The Ragman's Son*, Simon and Schuster, 1988.

84. It was never released in the format as its popularity had waned by the time of the film's release. As filming required using two interlocked cameras, the 2-D version simply involved using the output of one of them.

85. Kezich/Levantesi.

86. Durgnat, Raymond and Simmon, Scott. *King Vidor, American*. University of California Press, Berkeley, 1988.

87. *The New York Times*, 12 August 1956.

88. Baxter, John, *King Vidor*, Simon & Schuster, Inc Monarch Film Studies, 1976.

89. Kezich/Levantesi.

90. Fleischer.

91. Kezich/Levantesi.

92. Barzman, Norma, *The Red and the Blacklist: The Intimate Memoir of a Hollywood Expatriate*, Friction Books 2005.

93. Richard Fleischer prepped *Night Runners of Bengal* for Bronston, and later recalled in his memoir how the production designers planned numerous exquisite sets, most of which the camera would not see. The film was never made.

94. Fleischer.

95. Mark Fleischer to author, 2020.

96. Kezich/Levantesi.

97. *Ibid.*

98. *Ibid.*

99. *Ibid.*

100. Novak Ralph, *Who's Working for Producer Dino De Laurentiis?* 26 January 1976.

101. Kezich/Levantesi.

102. Silverman, S., *The Fox that got away: the last days of the Zanuck dynasty at Twentieth Century-Fox*, L. Stuart, 1988.

103. Kezich/Levantesi.

104. *Daily Variety*, 04 October 1965.

105. Stevens, George Jr. *Conversations with the Great Moviemakers of Hollywood's Golden Age*, New York. Alfred A. Knopf, 2006.

106. Later he returned to the USA, where he spent the rest of his life.

107. Huston, John, *An Open Book*, Da Capo Press, 1994.

108. Emmet, Robert, *John Huston: Interviews (Conversations with Filmmakers)*, University Press of Mississippi, 2001.

109. Huston.

110. *Ark Easier For Noah To Build*, *The Deseret News*. 02 February 1965.

111. Huston.

112. Silverman, S.

113. Meyers, Jeffrey, *John Huston: courage and art*, New York, Crown Archetype, 2011.

114. Reed, Rex. *Big Screen, Little Screen*, Macmillan, 1971.

115. *Daily Variety*, 08 February 1966.

116. Heston, Charlton, *In the Arena: An Autobiography*, Simon & Schuster, 1995.

117. Richard Heffer to author 2019. All subsequent quotes by him are from voluminous correspondence between 2019-21. The exception are his 1969 diary entries.

118. *Variety*, 21 June 1966.

119. *Daily Variety*, 08 March 1967.

120. *Hollywood Reporter*, 25 September 1967.

121. https://www.youtube.com/watch?v=g1abpPHb1Hc

122. Huston.

123. Kezich/Levantesi.

124. *Variety*, 27 March 1968.

125. Kezich/Levantesi.

126. Corsi.

127. *Ibid.*

128. *Ibid.*

129. *Mosfilm-Dino De Laurentiis cinematographic S.p.A co-production Agreement*, Moscow, 17/5/1968, p. 1.

130. *Waterloo*, publicity notes, 1969/70.

131. Sergei Bondarchuk was paid ITL100 million, approx. $150,000. *Final balance sheet Waterloo*.

132. De Biase, Div. VII, Rome, *Certificate of nationality*, Rome, 8/10/1970, p. 1.

133. Pisu, Stefano, *La cortina di celluloide. Il cinema italo-sovietico nella guerra fredda*, Mimesis, 2019.

134. Both these applications were attempted *after* the film was completed.

135. Bluhdorn, Charles, *The Gulf + Western Story*, Newcomen Publication, 1973.

136. *Time,* 08 December 1967.

137. *Weekly Variety,* 02 July 1969.

138. *Variety,* 26 August 1968.

139. *Variety,* 28 January 1970.

140. There had been five silent versions produced before the 1917 Revolution.

141. Lind, John *Sergei Bondarchuk: The Road to Waterloo, Focus on Film,* October 1970.

142. Bondarchuk, Natalya, *Newspaper Trud,* 30 September 2005.

143. *Dustin Hoffman discusses the Laurence Olivier story,* youtube.com/watch?v=Ss7F8BCrNz0.

144. Bondarchuk.

145. Sergei Khaniutin, quoted in Youngblood, Denise J., *Bondarchuk's War and Peace,* University Press of Kansas, 2014.

146. Lind.

147. Youngblood, Denise J., *Bondarchuk's War and Peace,* University Press of Kansas, 2014.

148. Youngblood, Denise J., Blu-ray feature, *War and Peace,* Criterion Collection, 2019.

149. Norris, Stephen M., *Tolstoy's Comrades: Sergei Bondarchuk and the origins of Brezhnev culture,* Northwestern University Press, 2013.

150. Youngblood, Criterion, 2019.

151. At the time *Cleopatra* (1963) cost in the region of $44 million, and when adjusted to inflation, it still stands as one of the most expensive films ever made ($370m in 2020). *War and Peace's* budget has been estimated at anywhere from $9 million to $100 million. As so many of the resources, like the Soviet military, would have been "free" to the filmmakers, it is impossible to get an exact figure. More recent research suggests it was around $10 million, which seems much more plausible given its particular economic environment.

152. These figures come from the souvenir book produced for the American dubbed Kressel version of film. There is a great deal of hyperbole in this book, and so "facts" should be accepted with caution. But the point is, even if you halve them, it still constitutes a colossal effort.

153. Sovscope 70 was identical to the American 70mm formats (Todd-AO, Super Panavision 70 etc), except that the Russians used a 70mm negative while the Americans used 65mm in the camera. The difference in film width did not affect the frame size which was identical. The American systems introduced in the 1950s had been adapted from the first introduction of widescreen photography in 1930 which had used 65mm as a negative format.

154. Lind.

155. *Radio Times,* Christmas 1977. A brief introduction (probably derived from publicity production notes) to the first UK TV showing of the film; when the author first saw it aged eleven!

156. Bondarchuk.

157. *War and Peace,* souvenir brochure by Harold Stern, National Publishers, Inc 1968.

158. Youngblood, Criterion, 2019.

159. This behind-the-scenes footage is featured in a Blu-ray extra on *War and Peace,* Criterion Collection, 2019.

160. In 2019 the planned UK release of the Criterion Collection's *War and Peace* Blu-ray was pulled while on pre-order because the BBFC declined to classify it due to the horse falls.

161. Bondarchuk.

162. Bondarchuk, Natalya, *Edinstvennye dni,* Astrel, 2009.

163. Zoltan Fabri's *Twenty Hours / Husz ora* (1965)

164. Natalya Bondarchuk, who starred in Andrei Tarkovsky's *Solaris* (1972), was Sergei's daughter from his first marriage to actress Inna Makarova, which ended in divorce.

165. Bondarchuk, Natalya, *Newspaper Trud,* 30 September 2005.

166. telegraf.com.ua/kultura/kino/557232

167. Gillett, John, *Sight and Sound,* v39 n3, Summer 1970.

168. See, *War and Peace,* Blu-ray, Criterion Collection, 2019.

169. *War and Peace,* souvenir brochure.

170. Youngblood, Criterion, 2019.

171. Aleksei Romanov, Head of Goskino.

172. Wikipedia notes three citations for this.

173. This assertion is attributed to Natalia Tendora, a film writer, but according to Denise J. Youngblood in her book, Tendora gives no actual reason.

174. Daneliia, Georgii, *Iskusstvo kino 9,* 1965.

175. It is still not clear what was the original running time, but most sources suggest it was around 433 minutes (one suggests 460) for the domestic version with the export version being slightly trimmed. Many of the film elements did not survive (including the 70mm negative) the upheavals of the early 1990s which saw the dismemberment of the USSR.

176. Ebert, Roger, *War and Peace, Chicago Sun-Times,* 22 June 1969.

177. *Time,* 03 May 1968.

178. Crist, Judith, *War and Peace — The Greatest, New York Magazine,* 13 May 1968.

179. The author remembers periodic screenings in London, and watched the 35mm version in Cardiff in the early 1990s.

180. According to the BBFC website: *Submitted run time 511m 7s Approved footage 46000 feet classified 30/12/68.* One of these figures has to be wrong. As no Russian source mentions this running time we must conclude that the time is wrong. The footage count for 70mm equals 410 minutes, which is in line with the documented Export Version. To confuse matters, London Continental Films Ltd are listed as the distributor, the company behind the Kressel 360 minutes version which would have been 32,444 feet for 35mm, and 40,320 feet for 70mm. The 2019 restoration version is 422 minutes.

181. At time of writing, a 4K DCP of the restoration has been shown theatrically in the US and Europe.

182. Tolstoy, Leo, *War and Peace,* Book Ten: 1812, Chapter 38. Published 1869. Translation by Louise and Aylmer Maude.

183. Traudl Junge was Hitler's secretary. She described her working relationship in the documentary film — *Blind Spot: Hitler's Secretary* (2002). Her story was superbly dramatised in *Downfall / Der Untergang,* 2004.

184. Tolstoy, Leo, *War and Peace,* First Epilogue: 1813–20, Part 16. Chapter 16. Published 1869. Translation by Louise and Aylmer Maude.

185. Youngblood, Criterion, 2019.

186. https://www.slantmagazine.com/film/review-war-and-peace-is-an-epic-film-of-epic-cinematic-gestures/

187. Bondarchuk.

188. *Soviet Estonia*, 28 May 1972. news.technotronic.org/ensv/1972/05/28. Bondarchuk would realise this project ten years later, see Chapter Twenty-Two.

189. There is a story that when Saveleva arrived back in Russia, the authorities boarded the plane and "confiscated" the statuette. Professor Youngblood is unconvinced: "this sounds like Cold War propaganda to me. The Soviets were extremely proud of garnering the Oscar for the film; it doesn't ring true." Denise J. Youngblood to author, 2019.

190. *Soviet Estonia*, 28 May 1972

191. Lind.

192. Anglesey, Lord, *A History of British Cavalry: Volume 4, 1899-1913*, Pen and Sword 1993.

193. Quoted in *The Battle of Waterloo: or, Why Can't We Film Such a Thing If We Won the War in the First Place?* by Luke McKernan, Talk given at the National Film Theatre, 30 March 1996.

194. Mousinac, Léon, *Panoramique du cinéma*, Au Sans Pareil, Paris, 1929.

195. Quoted in https://lareviewofbooks.org/article/dueling-revolutions-abel-gances-napoleon/

196. *Variety*, 23 January 1929.

197. Brownlow, Kevin, *Napoleon*, BFI 2004.

198. This was released on a Blu-ray three-disc set from the BFI in 2017.

199. Kevin Brownlow to author, 2021.

200. Legend suggests 100,000 soldiers took part, but it is evident from the film there are significantly less than this. It is possible large numbers rotated during filming, but it seems highly unlikely it was anything near the above figure. What can be said, is that most of those men would have much preferred this assignment to the alternatives on the bloody Eastern Front.

201. *Variety*, 03 December 1936.

202. *The New York Times*, 25 January 1935.

203. Sedgwick, J., Pokorny, M., *The Film Business in the United States and Britain during the 1930s*, *The Economic History Review*, New Series, Vol. 58, No. 01 Feb 2005, pp. 79 — 112.

204. *Napoleon Brando Not Quite Vintage*, *The Washington Post*, 26 November 1954.

205. *Death of Sacha Guitry: Playwright, actor, and wit. The Manchester Guardian*, 25 July 1957.

206. The late 1960s would see a number of Napoleonic subjects announced, including Bryan Forbes's *Napoleon and Josephine*, and a certain Stanley Kubrick planned his own Napoleon project (see Chapter Twenty-One). Two rather lack-lustre films did get made, and then promptly vanished; *The Adventures of Gerard* (1970) (written by H.A.L. Craig) and *The Eagle in the Cage* (1972).

207. ITL75,933,540. *Final balance sheet Waterloo*.

208. *The Cork Examiner*, 22 June 1962.

209. https://en.wikipedia.org/wiki/The_Bell_(magazine)

210. Maume, Patrick, *Craig, Harry (Henry Armitage Llewellyn, H.A.L.)*. Dictionary of Irish Biography. (ed.) James McGuire, James Quinn. Cambridge University Press, 2015. (http://dib.cambridge.org/viewReadPage.do?articleId=a9777)

211. O'Faolain, Nuala, *Are you somebody?*, 1996.

212. Siobhan S. Craig to author, 2021.

213. Jean Anouilh in Carlson, Marvin, *Reference Guide to World Literature*, St. James Press, 1996.

214. ITL13,008,155. *Final balance sheet Waterloo.*

215. He was paid ITL6,760,458, ($11,000) half of what Anouilh got paid. *Final balance sheet Waterloo.*

216. *Hollywood Reporter,* Jun 28, 1965.

217. ITL18,658,281. *Final balance sheet Waterloo.*

218. He received ITL1,839,200. ($3000). *Ibid.*

219. Craig.

220. Howarth, David J., *A Near Run Thing: The Day of Waterloo,* HarperCollins 1968.

221. Smith, Frederick E., *Waterloo,* Pan Books 1970.

222. *Waterloo,* publicity notes, 1969/70.

223. *The Communist Manifesto* by Karl Marx and Friedrich Engels, 1848.

224. Guerin, Ann, *Rod Steiger's NAPOLEON: A Self-Defeated Man, Show Magazine,* May 1971.

225. Haden-Guest, Anthony, *How Moscow And Hollywood Met at Waterloo, The Sunday Telegraph,* 05 December 1969.

226. As is so often the case this phrase is attributors to many, but it does neatly sum up the continual tension, particularly in Hollywood cinema, between art and commerce. See: http://listserv.linguistlist.org/pipermail/ads-l/2012-January/115893.html

227. It has been suggested he never actually said this, but instead the line was said of him by the Irish Nationalist politician, Daniel O'Connell. It is fairly clear that the Duke was embarrassed by his Irish roots, and perhaps his sentiments are most clearly understood from one of his letters: "They are disaffected to the British Government; they don't feel the benefits of their situation; attempts to render it better either do not reach their minds, or they are represented to them as additional injuries; and in fact we have no strength here but our army. Surely it is incumbent upon us to adopt every means which can secure the position and add to the strength of our army." See, https://www.irishtimes.com/opinion/wellington-won-battle-of-waterloo-200-years-ago-but-irish-rejected-his-legacy-1.2254416

228. Haden-Guest.

229. *The New York Times,* May 1968.

230. Gareth Glover to author 2019.

231. https://www.theguardian.com/news/2002/jul/10/guardianobituaries.filmnews1.

232. Quoted in *Nothing 'coulda been' about Steiger, The Sydney Morning Herald,* July 11, 2002, from an unnamed interview with the actor in 1976.

233. Hutchinson, Tom, *Rod Steiger, Memoirs of a Friendship,* Fromm International 1998.

234. Sullivan, Chris, *Never Meet Your Hero. Unless it's Rod Steiger, Sabotage Times,* 20 November 2011.

235. Steiger speaking in 1991. Quoted in *Los Angeles Times,* 10 July 2002.

236. Quoted in *Nothing 'coulda been' about Steiger, The Sydney Morning Herald,* July 11, 2002, from an unnamed interview with the actor.

237. Capote, Truman, *The Duke in His Domain, The New Yorker* magazine, 09 Nov 1957.

238. *Later with Bob Costas,* NBC, 06 July 1992.

239. *Los Angeles Times,* 10 July 2002.

240. Schickel, Richard, *Two Pros in a Super Sleeper, Life,* 28 July 1967.

241. https://www.theguardian.com/news/2002/jul/10/guardianobituaries.filmnews1

242. Hutchinson.

243. Herman, Jan, *A Talent for Trouble: The Life of Hollywood's Most Acclaimed Director, William Wyler*. G.P. Putnam's Sons. 1995. P.449

244. Guerin.

245. Sir John Abbott, (1821–1893). A member of the Conservative Party, he served as the third prime minister of Canada from 1891-2.

246. Between 1939-46 the pair starred in a series of fourteen films based on Sir Arthur Conan Doyle famous detective stories, including a number with a contemporary setting often fighting Nazis.

247. Edelstein, David, *Plummer's Peak, New York Magazine*, 27 May, 2011.

248. Davis, Victor, *Are Christopher Plummer's vile tantrums and arrogance to blame for fact he's never won an Oscar?*, *The Daily Mail*, 06 March 2010, https://www.dailymail.co.uk/femail/article-1255821/Are-Christopher-Plummers-vile-tantrums-arrogance-blame-fact-hes-won-Oscar.html.

249. Edelstein.

250. *Ibid.*

251. Ultimately, his voice would be "ghosted" by Bill Lee.

252. http://cinemagumbo.squarespace.com/journal/2011/12/13/december-13.html

253. https://tv.avclub.com/christopher-plummer-on-the-greatest-piece-of-direction-1798241203

254. Davis, Victor. This is according to show business writer Victor Davis. It should be noted that he and the actor had come to blows during a press junket in 1974, and his words should be seen through this lens.

255. Plummer, Christopher, *In Spite of Myself*, JR Books, 2010.

256. https://www.slantmagazine.com/film/interview-christopher-plummer-on-the-exception-and-career-as-an-actor/

257. tv.avclub.com/christopher-plummer-on-the-greatest-piece-of-direction-1798241203.

258. Ogilvy, Ian, *Once A Saint: An Actor's Memoir*, Constable 2016.

259. Rupert Davies, *Your Dictionary*. LoveToKnow. biography.yourdictionary.com/rupert-davies.

260. *The Daily Telegraph*, 02 June 2009.

261. Richard Heffer to author.

262. https://www.theguardian.com/stage/2010/jan/07/donal-donnelly-obituary.

263. Peter Davies to author, 2019. All subsequent quotes by him are from the same source.

264. Fleischer

265. Quoted from an unsourced 1971 interview with the actor. This is taken from various interviews the actor gave during the 1970s while making short-lived American TV series, *The Young Rebels*. https://www.facebook.com/TheManSharonTateAlmostMarried/posts/read-philippes-story-here/122957118352970/

266. Philippe Forquet de Dorne to author 2019. All following quotes by him are from this source, unless otherwise stated.

267. ITL223,537,397. *Final balance sheet Waterloo.*

268. ITL250,629,922. *Ibid.*

269. https://cinemaretro.com/index.php?/archives/10659-REVIEW-THE-CHAIRMAN-1969-STARRING-GREGORY-PECK;-TWILIGHT-TIME-BLU-RAY-SPECIAL-EDITION.html

270. Tanner, Michael, *Troubled Epic: On Location with Ryan's Daughter*, The Collins Press, 2007.

271. Hughes, Howard, *Aim for the Heart*. London, I.B. Tauris, 2009/Munn, Michael, *Clint Eastwood: Hollywood's Loner*. London, Robson Books, 1992.

272. https://www.everythingzoomer.com/arts-entertainment/2019/05/28/ode-boom-ultimate-camp-film/

273. *The Chairman* (1969): $5 million, *Boom* (1968): $10 million, *Paint Your Wagon* (1969): $20 million, *Ryan's Daughter* (1970): $14 million. The first three flopped badly, while the fourth made $30 million in North America alone.

274. The film has been restored and released on home video in US and UK.

275. Gazzara, Ben, *In the Moment: My Life as an Actor*, Carroll & Graf, 2004.

276. https://www.warhistoryonline.com/instant-articles/filming-of-the-bridge.html

277. According to the director's biography, some of the "leading" stars "saved their own skins" by requisitioning their own transport leaving the rest, including children, to fend for themselves. All did reach Austria safely. See: Guillermin, Mary, *John Guillermin: The Man, The Myth, The Movies*, Precocity Press, 2020. Production resumed at Lake Albano, near Castel Gandolfo in Italy. The surrounding mountains were considered a good match for the original location, here they built one end of the bridge complete with a replica tower. As a fan of this under-rated war film, the author has watched it many times but has not been able to see the "join" between the two locations; a testament to great filmmaking skills. For a summary see: https://catalog.afi.com/Catalog/MovieDetailsPrintView/22490

278. *Los Angeles Times*, 01 September 1968.

279. *Daily Variety*, 12 August 1968.

280. *Los Angeles Times*, 22 August 1968. The second unit under William Kronick was allowed back into the country to film, "critical footage of a simulated battle and crossing of the bridge by U.S. troops", according to *Daily Variety* (23 October 1968). The confiscated military equipment was all returned to the Austrian army.

281. *Waterloo*, publicity notes, 1969/70.

282. The author remembers seeing a decayed musket prop for sale on the internet in the 2010s.

283. https://www.erancati.com/eng/

284. Heffer, 1969. He along with many of the officer characters who appeared in the ballroom scene had two different costumes. For the battle, they were dressed in a striped-down campaign style. During the actual campaign some attendees of the ball had no time to change, and so rode to war in their finery.

285. Andrew Mollo to author, 2021.

286. Mollo, John, *Making of the Charge (1), Military Illustrated Past & Present Magazine,* Issue No. 42, November 1991.

287. Andrew Mollo to author, 2021.

288. Kevin Brownlow to author, 2021.

289. Ron Poulter to author, 2020. All subsequent quotes by him are from this source.

290. Heffer, 07/03/69.

291. Heffer, 11/03/69.

292. Dowager Lady De Ros 1889, p.40.

293. These were the Mitchell BNC studio camera.

294. Daniele Nannuzzi to author, 2020. All subsequent quotes by him are from the same source.

295. *Ryan's Daughter* (1970) and *The Last Valley* (1971) were the last to be shot on 65mm for over a decade.

296. Stanley Kubrick's use of the zoom lens in *Barry Lyndon* (1975) being one of the most creative examples.

297. https://www.monroeandmain.com/blog/fashion-tips/wear-figure-flattering-empire-waist-style/

298. According to her children's tutor Spencer Madan.

299. Heffer, 14/03/69.

300. McKenna, Virginia, interviewed by Joyce Robinson in 2002 for The British Entertainment History Project. https://historyproject.org.uk/interview/virginia-mckenna

301. https://www.bornfree.org.uk/animals

302. McKenna, Virginia. The British Entertainment History Project.

303. Davies.

304. Heffer, 13/03/69.

305. Mary, Sarah, Georgiana, Jane, Louisa, Charlotte and Sophia and ranged in age from 23 to just 5. The four eldest were described by Spencer Madan, their tutor "…(they) are the most good-humoured unaffected girls I ever met with, exceedingly highbred but without an atom of pride."

306. Swinton, Blanche, *A sketch of the life of Georgiana, Lady de Ros: with some reminiscences of her family and friends, including the Duke of Wellington*, (1893) p.137, quoted in Crossland, Alice Marie, *Wellington's Dearest Georgy*, Uniform Press, 2017.

307. Lady Georgiana Lennox to Lady Georgina Bathurst, Brussels 22 June 1815, quoted in Crossland.

308. Heffer, 24/03/69.

309. Heffer, 25/03/69.

310. Letter from Lady Louisa Tighe, 13 January 1889, *The History of the Gordon Highlanders*, vol.1 p.349, quoted in Crossland.

311. Napier, D.M., *Life of a Regiment — The History of the Gordon Highlanders*, Volume VIII 1787-1994, Mainstream Publishing 2010/16.

312. Major (retired) Nigel Oxley to author 2020. All quotes by him are from this source, unless otherwise stated.

313. Easter Oxley to author, 2020. All quotes by her are from this source.

314. Green, Roger, *Shaken and Stirred*, Green Days Publishing 2020.

315. Heffer, 12/03/69.

316. Heffer, 14/03/69.

317. Heffer, 21/03/69.

318. Heffer, 18/03/69.

319. Heffer, 21/03/69.

320. Heffer, 22/03/69.

321. https://en.wikipedia.org/wiki/Willoughby_Gray?wprov=sfti1

322. Heffer, 09/09/69.

323. Plummer.

324. Craig. He is the portly soldier on the left-hand side of the screen who opens and closes the door behind Wellington and his generals.

325. Heffer, 14/03/69

326. Willoughby Gray; related a similar version of this story to Anthony Haden-Guest but without Plummer, and less amusing! He said it was *he* that corrected the director's misunderstanding about the phrase.

327. *Weekly Variety*, 09 April 1969.

328. Heffer, 24/03/69.

329. Heffer, 20/03/69.

330. Forbes, Archibald, *Camps, Quarters, and Casual Places*, 1896, quotes Captain Bowles account, citing from the *Letters of the First Earl of Malmesbury*.

331. https://en.wikipedia.org/wiki/John_Savident?wprov=sfti1.

332. Quoted in Glover, Gareth, *Waterloo: Myth and Reality*, Pen and Sword 2014.

333. The letter was written by Caroline Capel, although she was not at the ball, she knew many of the guests. *The Capel Letters: Being the Correspondence of Lady Caroline Capel and Her Daughters with the Dowager Countess of Uxbridge from Brussels and Switzerland* 1814-1817, quoted in Crossland.

334. Lady Jane Lennox, quoted in Crossland.

335. Ogilvy.

336. De Lancey, Magdalene, *A Week in Waterloo, Lady De Lancey's Narrative*, John Murray 1906.

337. http://www.fernergalleries.co.nz/default,1990.sm

338. Heffer, 16/03/69.

339. Napier, D.M.

340. *Ibid.*

341. *Ibid.*

342. Heffer, 26/03/69.

343. whc.unesco.org/uploads/nominations/549rev.pdf.

344. Haden-Guest.

345. Bondarchuk.

346. Plummer.

347. Haden-Guest.

348. Rod Steiger speaking at the National Film Theatre in London, January 1971.

349. *Waterloo*, publicity notes, 1969/70.

350. Bondarchuk.

351. Guerin.

352. Bondarchuk.

353. Rod Steiger speaking at the National Film Theatre in London, 1971.

354. Quoted in Rod Steiger Obituary, *The Telegraph*, July 10, 2002.

355. https://retrospectra.ru/mirovye-zvezdy-v-sovetskom-kino/

356. Ogilvy.

357. Bondarchuk.

358. Guerin.

359. Haden-Guest.

360. Hutchinson.

361. *Ibid.*

362. Bloom, Claire, *Leaving A Doll's House*, Virago 2013.

363. Ebert, Roger, *Interview with Rod Steiger*, 04 April 1971.

364. Hutchinson.

365. Ebert.

366. Hutchinson.

367. Heffer, 1969.

368. Ogilvy.

369. Forquet de Dorne.

370. Intourist contract, Mosca, 10/12/1968.

371. Ogilvy.

372. Green.

373. Heffer, 28/08/69.

374. Ebert.

375. Nannuzzi.

376. Heffer, 23/07/69.

377. https://www.tripadvisor.co.uk/ShowTopic-g294473-i3662-k6638348-Waterloofilm_1970_where_were_the_battle_scenes_filmed-Ukraine.html

378. Jaste, Saida, https://www.liveinternet.ru/users/letayushaya_na_barse/post245557116/

379. De Laurentiis, R.

380. Ogilvy.

381. Guerin.

382. It is *just* visible at the extreme edge of frame as Napoleon finishes his review of his army and prepares to dismount into the mud. Also, in one extreme long shot of Hougoumont under fire, with a row of red coated infantry in foreground, it is visible to the left of the farm complex for a few frames before being obscured by smoke.

383. Raymond, Nick, *Steiger's Napoleon*, *Photoplay*, January 1970.

384. Gleb, Ivan. http://telegraf.com.ua/kultura/kino/557232-50-let-nazad-na-zakarpate-snimali-voynu-i-mir-i-vaterloo.html

385. Elemèr, Kovács, https://www.karpatinfo.net/hetilap/2016/info_201635.pdf

386. Bondarchuk.

387. Jaste.

388. Denise J. Youngblood to author 2020.

389. This footage now held by the Russian Film Archive can be seen on *The Making of Waterloo*, produced by the present author for the 2021 UK Blu-ray release of the film, released by Mediumrare Entertainment.

390. Baynazarov, Nail, *A soldier from Bashkiria helped Bondarchuk's continuation of War and Peace*. ProUfu.ru, 26 February 2017.

391. The company had just introduced their reflex model: Panavision PSR-200, which was used on *Catch-22* (1970), filming in Mexico during 1969. Only 29 units were ever built, and it is probable that there were none available in Europe via Samuelson at the time.

392. Elemèr, Kovács.

393. Starchenko, Igor, *The abyss of sclerosis*, unpublished memoir.

394. Lind.

395. Nannuzzi.

396. Tveritneva, Svetlana and Lisova, Alla, https://www.volyn.com.ua/news/125014-shche-v-dalekomu-1970-mu-z-radianskoi-armii-nadislav-dodomu-tryzuby. 04 June 2019.

397. Jaste.

398. On HD copies of the film, if you look very carefully, it is possible to see these plastic figures — just.

399. *They Fought for Their Country / Oni srazhalis za rodinu* (1975). See Chapter Twenty-Two.

400. Historian Gareth Glover believes this drummer boy was the survivor of a *later* attack, which hitherto has been hidden from the records.

401. Quoted in Roberts, Andrew, *Waterloo: Napoleon's Last Gamble*, HarperCollins, 2005.

402. He would eventually marry an English woman and move to Romford in the UK, where he ran a gym. He died in 1989.

403. *Waterloo*, publicity notes, 1969/70.

404. Haden-Guest.

405. Ebert.

406. See, *The Making of Waterloo*, Mediumrare Entertainment. Produced by the present author for the 2021 UK Blu-ray release of the film.

407. Haden-Guest.

408. *Weekly Variety*, July 02, 1969.

409. Haden-Guest.

410. Kezich/Levantesi.

411. *Ibid.*

412. Quoted from an unsourced interview with the actor. See: https://www.facebook.com/TheManSharonTateAlmostMarried/posts/read-philippes-story-here/122957118352970/

413. Ogilvy.

414. *Daily Variety*, 05 November 1969.

415. Bondarchuk.

416. Ogilvy.

417. Guerin.

418. Raymond.

419. Ebert.

420. Gillett, John, *Sight and Sound*, v39 n3 Summer 1970.

421. Ebert.

422. *Variety*, 06 June 1969.

423. *Weekly Variety*, 25 June 1969.

424. *Weekly Variety*, 06 August, 1969.

425. The whereabouts of the finished 13-minute film is still a mystery.

426. This stills format yields a much bigger negative than the standard movie 70mm systems, and was often used for billboard advertising images.

427. Heffer, 20/07/69.

428. Heffer, 21/07/69.

429. Heffer, 28/07/69.

430. Heffer, 27/07/69.

431. Heffer, 23/07/69.

432. Some historians doubt the veracity of his memoirs, but their powerful and atmospheric descriptions could only come from an eye-witness. According to historian Gareth Glover, the memoir is full of exaggerations of his losses and overstating his role in the battle. Mercer believed he had not received the attention and recognition he deserved. He spent the rest of his life complaining vociferously, that he was not given later command of the Royal Artillery. See Glover, Gareth, *Mercer's Troop at Waterloo*. https://www.waterlooassociation.org.uk/Mercer's%20Troop%20at%20Waterloo.pdf.

433. Heffer, 23/07/69.

434. Haden-Guest.

435. Heffer, 24/07/69.

436. Heffer, 25/07/69.

437. Heffer, 28/07/69.

438. The glass of Christopher Plummer's telescope appears to have been painted matt black to prevent it reflecting the movie lights.

439. *Waterloo*, publicity notes, 1969/70.

440. Heffer, 28/07/69.

441. Heffer, 29/07/69.

442. Heffer, 30/07/69.

443. Starchenko.

444. Heffer, 30/07/69.

445. *Daily Variety*, 05 November 1969.

446. Nannuzzi.

447. Starchenko.

448. Heffer, 31/07/69.

449. Colonel Colbourne commanded the 52nd Light regiment. But in the script, it suggests he commands the 27th (Inniskilling) Regiment of Foot — O'Connor's regiment. In reality, this regiment was not involved in the French cavalry attacks.

450. In the battle, Mercer and his men stayed with their guns and never retreated back to the squares. See, Note 62.

451. Heffer, 05/08/69.

452. Ogilvy.

453. Heffer, 05/08/69.

454. Heffer, 06/08/69.

455. *Escape by Night* (1960), directed by Roberto Rossellini.

456. Joan Borsten Vidov to author, 2020.

457. Veljko Bulajić in conversation with Joan Borsten Vidov, 2019.

458. Borsten Vidov, Joan, *Happiness Belongs to the Risk Takers: The Oleg Vidov Story*.

459. It has to be one of the most butchered films of the era. It has appeared on home video in many guises, running anywhere from 100-150 minutes but rarely its full 175.

460. Irina Skobtseva in conversation with Joan Borsten Vidov, 2019.

461. Heffer, 06/09/69.

462. Heffer, 07/09/69.

463. Borsten Vidov.

464. Joan Borsten Vidov to author, 2020.

465. Borsten Vidov.

466. Borsten Vidov to author, 2020.

467. Heffer, 08/08/69.

468. Heffer, 08/08/69.

469. He is spelled Rams*e*y in the script and credits, but was probably meant to be Captain Norman Rams*a*y, who commanded H battery RHA.

470. Heffer, 08/08/69.

471. Quoted from an unsourced interview with the actor in 1971 and collated by Joe Crosswicks for a Facebook Page. In the brief correspondence the present author had with the actor before his death, he only touched briefly on this painful episode but intended to expand on in subsequent emails. His words here emphasis the veracity and honesty of his grief. See:https://www.facebook.com/TheManSharonTateAlmostMarried/posts/read-philippes-story-here/122957118352970/

472. Christopher Jones speaking in 1996, quoted in Tanner, Michael, *Troubled Epic: On Location with Ryan's Daughter*, The Collins Press, 2007.

473. Heffer, 12/08/69.

474. Heffer, 11/08/69.

475. Heffer, 13/08/69.

476. Heffer, 19/08/69.

477. Unlike his fellow artillerymen characters of Mercer and Ramsay, Normyle appears to be completely fictional. But as Ramsay's first name was Norman, one wonders if something got lost in translation along the line.

478. Heffer, 12/09/1969.

479. Hans Kemna to author, 2021.

480. Heffer, 19/08/69.

481. Heffer, 22/08/69.

482. Heffer, 25/08/69.

483. Mercer.

484. Heffer, 25/08/69.

485. *Variety*, 19 August 1969.

486. Heffer, 25/08/69.

487. Heffer, 31/08/69.

488. Maltin, Leonard, *Hooked on Hollywood: Discoveries from a Lifetime of Film Fandom*, Paladin Communications, 2018.

489. Searles, Baird, *Epic!: History on the Big Screen*, Abrams 1990.

490. Ogilvy.

491. Heffer, 2019.

492. Starchenko.

493. *Les Misérables* by Victor Hugo. Book One: Chapter IX — The Unexpected 1862.

494. Heffer, 04/08/1969.

495. https://www.volyn.com.ua/news/125014-shche-v-dalekomu-1970-mu-z-radianskoi-armii-na-dislav-dodomu-tryzuby.

496. Heffer, 04/08/1969.

497. Abbi Collins to author 2019.

498. Munn, Mike, *The Stories Behind The Scenes Of The Great Film Epics*, Illustrated Publications, 1982.

499. *Daily Variety*, Nov 01, 1972. *A Gunfight* (1971), starring Kirk Douglas also drew equal condemnation from the AHA.

500. Heffer, 2019.

501. Roger Green to author, 2021.

502. Heffer, 1969.

503. Green.

504. Heffer, 01/08/69.

505. Heffer, 2019.

506. Heffer, 23/07/69.

507. Heffer, 06/08/69.

508. Green.

509. Heffer, 16/08/69.

510. Heffer, 31/07/69.

511. Heffer, 07/08/69.

512. Heffer, 09/08/69.

513. Heffer, 01/08/69.

514. Heffer, 03/08/69.

515. Feldhaus.

516. Heffer, 29/07/69.

517. Heffer, 04/08/69.

518. Heffer, 26/07/69.

519. Heffer, 14/08/69.

520. *The Name of the Game*, season 2, episode 1, *Lady on the Rocks* (1969).

521. Heffer, 16/08/69.

522. Heffer, 17/08/69.

523. Emma Ogilvy to author, 2020.

524. Heffer, 19/08/69.

525. Heffer, 20/08/69.

526. Heffer, 21/08/69.

527. Heffer, 24/08/69.

528. Heffer, 18/08/69.

529. Heffer, 27/08/69.

530. Heffer, 10/09/69.

531. Heffer, 13/09/69.

532. Davies.

533. Heffer, 14/09/69.

534. Heffer, 26/08/69.

535. Heffer, 01/09/69.

536. Heffer, 06/09/69.

537. Green.

538. Heffer, 10/08/69.

539. Heffer, 18/09/69.

540. Heffer, 05/09/69.

541. He died in 1979 following a fall down stairs during an epileptic seizure.

542. The name was not officially recognised until 1877, when the regiment was retitled as 2nd Dragoons (Royal Scots Greys).

543. It is said Lady Butler prepared for her painting by having the regiment charge at her to get a sense of the effect. It must have been a truly exhilarating, if frightening experience for both her, and the later film crew.

544. Napier, D.M.

545. Heffer, 03/09/69.

546. https://en.wikipedia.org/wiki/Thomas_Picton

547. He was arrested following his governorship of the island. Picton was charged on a number of instances of cruelty to slaves, but principally for approving the illegal torture of a 14-year-old girl. Although convicted, this was over-turned later upon appeal. In 2020, in the wake of the slave trader Henry Colston's statue being torn down in Bristol, one of Picton's descendants lobbied for his ancestor's statue in Cardiff City Hall be removed.

548. Heffer, 05/09/69.

549. Heffer, 08/09/69.

550. Ian Ogilvy to author 2019.

551. Heffer, 08/09/69.

552. Heffer, 09/09/69.

553. Heffer, 10/09/69.

554. *Recollections of Samuel Rogers*, Henry Manners Chichester, 1886.

555. Heffer, 10/09/1969.

556. Fraser, Sir William, *Words on Wellington — The Duke — Waterloo — The Ball*, 1889.

557. For a full list, see: https://www.theguardian.com/media/2009/jun/03/terence-alexander-obituary#_=_

558. Heffer, 11/09/69.

559. Roger Green to author, 2021.

560. Roger Green–*James Bond 007–Screen Test*, https://youtu.be/5jNMHX11ZLE

561. Roger Green to author, 2021.

562. Davies.

563. Heffer, 12/09/69.

564. Conan Doyle, Arthur, *Through The Magic Door* (1907).

565. Directed by Jerzy Skolimowski, *The Adventures of Gerard* was released in early 1970, and quickly sunk at the box office. Despite a fine cast led by Peter McEnery, with Jack Hawkins, Claudia Cardinale, Eli Wallach as Napoleon and John Neville as Wellington, it fails to capture the zest of the source material, seemingly lost between an Anglo-Saxon and Polish comedic sensibility.

566. Heffer, 15/09/69.

567. According to Steven Dwan: The Iron Duke — did not earn this nickname until after the Napoleonic Wars — it came about because of his immovable opposition to reform — which largely led to his government's loss of power. In the early 1830s at his house in London (Apsley House) he suffered broken windows from angry protestors — when it happened a second time, he had iron shutters fitted over the windows — it seems this could be where the nickname arose. But the first instance of it appearing in the press was in 1842 when he was still stirring opposition to the Whig government's policies.

568. Plummer.

569. Heffer, 16/09/69.

570. Heffer, 17/09/69.

571. Heffer, 19/09/69.

572. Heffer, 13/08/69.

573. Heffer, 19/09/69.

574. quoted in Uffindell, Andrew, *On the Fields Of Glory: The Battlefields of the 1815 Campaign*, Greenhill Books, 2002.

575. Heffer, 20/09/69.

576. Heffer, 21/09/69.

577. Heffer, 22/09/69.

578. Heffer, 24/09/69.

579. Heffer, 25/09/69.

580. Heffer, 26/09/1969.

581. John Walsh interviewed by Kirsten Howard in 2020. https://www.denofgeek.com/movies/flash-gordon-john-walsh-interview/

582. Kezich/ Levantesi.

583. Heffer, 28/09/1969.

584. Heffer, 29/09/1969.

585. Joan Borsten Vidov to author, 2020.

586. Heffer, 29/09/1969.

587. Heffer, 30/09/1969.

588. Heffer, 01/10/1969.

589. Heffer, 02/10/1969.

590. Starchenko.

591. Webster.

592. https://www.volyn.com.ua/news/125014-shche-v-dalekomu-1970-mu-z-radianskoi-armii-nadislav-dodomu-tryzub

593. Starchenko.

594. The remains of the set are visible on Google Earth. 48°32'54.6" N 22°27'53.0"E.

595. His co-editor was John C. Howard.

596. *The Second Battle of Waterloo* by Richard C. Meyer, *The Cinemeditor,* Winter 1970/71. All quotes in this chapter, unless otherwise noted, are taken from this source.

597. screenvoicesarchive6304.wordpress.com/2005/04/10/robert-rietty/

598. *Ibid.*

599. Alan Jones to author, 2021. Alan worked as an assistant editor on a number of films during this time, notably *Deliverance* (1972), before cutting *The Pink Panther Strikes Again* (1976).

600. Alan Jones to author, 2021.

601. The documentary *Woodstock* (1970), being edited at the same time, used these techniques to great effect.

602. Elley, Derek, *Versatility, Films and Filming,* April 1976.

603. *Charms of Melody*, No.72. 1805-6, Dublin.

604. Elley.

605. John Mansell. jonman492000.wordpress.com/2018/06/09/fellini-satyricon/

606. Craig Lysy. moviemusicuk.us/2016/05/01/nino-rota-fathers-of-film-music-part-15/

607. Jim Paterson, https://www.mfiles.co.uk/composers/Nino-Rota.htm

608. See, and hear, *Nino Rota Film Scores*, conducted by Gianluigi Gelmetti, CD, EMI, 1993.

609. John Mansell. https://jonman492000.wordpress.com/2014/11/02/waterloo/. *Waterloo* (OST), Legend, 1995.

610. Graham V. Hartstone to author, 2020. All subsequent quotes by him are from this source.

611. Stephen Pickard to author, 2021. All subsequent quotes by him are from this source.

612. *Variety*, 30 March 1970.

613. McCallum, Gordon, interviewed by Alan Lawson for *The British Entertainment History Project* in 1988. https://historyproject.org.uk/interview/gordon-mccallum. All subsequent quotes by him are from this source.

614. John Hayward to author, 2020. All subsequent quotes by him are from this source.

615. A simpler 3-Track system had also been introduced with the short-lived 3-D craze of the early 1950s, and quickly disappeared. A very cheap alternative called Perspecta lasted for ten years but bore no relation to the impact of the 4-track/6-track discreet mixes.

616. At Pinewood Studios during this time, the standard format for mixing stereo was 4-track (left, centre, right and mono surround). As no British facilities were able to mix full Discrete 6-track stereo as required for the 70mm prints, Technicolor London created an ersatz 6-track spread (left, left centre, centre, right centre, right and mono surround), which used the left and right audio channels of the 4-track to fill in and create a wider spread.

617. Kezich/ Levantesi.

618. John Lind to author, 2020. When his article for *Focus on Film, Sergei Bondarchuk: The Road to Waterloo*, was published in October 1970, it appears the director took issue with it. "He flew into a rage after reading my published article because of something I had written that inferred he was critical of the USSR. I became *persona non grata* for a while." This may have been a case of "lost in translation," as the article is a very detailed, and balanced, over view of the director's career, without any apparent political slant.

619. https://www.bbfc.co.uk/releases/waterloo-1970-5. This UK version was only passed after two sections, with a total of 28 seconds of horse falls were deleted. The longest available version on video actually runs 133'42," which includes 50" of music over black after the end credits. This is the version released across the rest of Europe in 1970. Some sources list the running-time between 132-4 minutes but the confusion may be due to this last vestige of the roadshow experience — the exit music at the end. Had it been released a few years earlier it would probably have also have played with an overture and ent'racte like *Lawrence of Arabia*, et all. There is no evidence that *Waterloo* was ever presented in this manner.

620. Hutchinson.

621. Kevich/Levantesi.

622. Souhami, Gerard, *Waterloo*, *Le Monde*, 29 October 1970.

623. Baroncelli, Jean de, *Waterloo de Serguei Bondartchouk*, *Le Monde*, 31 October 1970.

624. Sery, Patrick, *Je ferai peut-être un film sur Stalin, Josephe, Magazine de Cinéma Plastique*, November 1970.

625. *Le Monde*, 07 November 1970.

626. Gibbs, Patrick, *The Daily Telegraph*, 27 October 1970.

627. *The Times*, 28 October 1970.

628. *Le Monde*, 07 November 1970

629. Rich, *Waterloo*, *Variety*, 26 October 1970.

630. Andrews, Nigel, *Waterloo*, *Monthly Film Bulletin,* December 1970.

631. Rich.

632. Clarke, Graham, *Waterloo*, *Kinematograph Weekly*, 31 October 1970.

633. Bilbow, Marjorie, *Waterloo, Today's Cinema*, 29 October 1970.

634. Clarke.

635. Waymark, P, *Richard Burton top draw in British cinemas*, *The Times*, 30 Dec 1971.

636. These figures appeared in *Kine Weekly* 1971.

637. West End engagements: Odeon Leicester Square 26/10/70-02/12/70, Metropole 03/12/70-02/06/71, Columbia 17/06/71-29/09/71, Odeon Kensington 30/09/71-06/10/71. These figures appeared in *Kine Weekly* 1971.

638. Sometimes termed the "Reithian Principles," this continues to be the BBC's mission as propounded by Lord Reith, the first Director-General of the BBC. https://publications.parliament.uk/pa/ld201516/ldselect/ldcomuni/96/9606.htm

639. *Blue Peter*, BBC TV, 08 March 1971.

640. First broadcast in 1958, it has run continuously ever since with over 5000 episodes and 40 presenters. As of 2021 it is now the longest-running children's TV show in the world. In the mid 1980s, one of the author's first jobs was working for a London-based film company that edited many of the film inserts for not only this, but other popular BBC programmes of the era, including *The Val Doonican Music Show*, and the now infamous, *Jim'll Fix It*.

641. They would be screen on New Year's Eve and New Year's Day respectively, when the author saw them both for the first time.

642. With just three channels on offer at the time in the UK, TV viewing during the festive period was the major activity before the advent VCRs and computer games.

643. Greenspun, Roger, *A Battle fought Strictly for the Camera*, *The New York Times,* 01 April 1971.

644. Kernan, Michael, *The Washington Post*, 01 April 1971.

645. Zimmerman, Paul, *Newsweek,* 02 April 1971.

646. Greenspun.

647. Mahoney, John C., *Waterloo a $25 million still-life*, *Los Angeles Free Press*, 02 April 1971.

648. Champlin, Charles, *Los Angeles Times*, 03 April 1971.

649. Mastroianni, Tony, *Russians join Battle of Waterloo — Napoleon still loses*, *Cleveland Press*, 02 April 1971.

650. Israel, Andy, *Waterloo Marks End of Epic Movies*, *Stanford Daily*, 02 April 1971.

651. Mahoney.

652. Ebert, Roger, *Waterloo, Chicago Sun-Times*, 08 April 1971.

653. Greenspun.

654. Israel.

655. Mahoney.

656. The story of these musical behemoths is well told in Kennedy, Matthew, *Roadshow! The Fall of Film Musicals In The 1960s*, Oxford University Press, 2014.

657. Kennedy.

658. By the 1980s, it was not usual for the negative budget to be exceed two and a half times with the additional costs of release prints and advertising. In 1971, these costs were less as fewer prints were made and less options available for advertising.

659. Israel.

660. *Variety*, 15 July 2002.

661. *The Deseret News*. news.google.com/newspapers?nid=Aul-kAQHnToC

662. Although it opened strongly at The Criterion in New York with a "hefty" take of $25,436 in its second week before tumbling to $1,775 by week four. *Variety*, 16 /23 April 1971.

663. *Variety*, 12 May 1971.

664. WorldwideBoxoffice.com.

665. Pirie.

666. Coupled with a very strong income from its Japanese release, it is believed the film passed the break-even figure of $37 million by the end of 1970. Silverman, S., *The Fox that got away: the last days of the Zanuck dynasty at Twentieth Century-Fox*, L. Stuart, 1988.

667. *Ball scores in Viet War*, *Stanford Daily*, 02 April 1971.

668. Cartoon drawn by Joel Beck, *Stanford Daily*, 02 April 1971.

669. *Woodstock* (1970) Warner Bros.

670. A young Martin Scorsese was one of the team of editors, headed by his future long-term collaborator Thelma Schoonmaker. Their extraordinary work received an Academy Award nomination for Best Editing and Best Sound respectively. For the extraordinary story of this landmark film, see: Bell, Dale, *Woodstock: An Inside Look at the Movie That Shook Up the World and Defined a Generation*, Moving Mantra, 2012.

671. https://www.the-numbers.com/movie/Woodstock#tab=summary. These figures also include the later re-release of the Director's Cut in 1994, although the vast majority of its earnings would be in 1970/1. Some sources even mention a figure of $50 million by 1980. With just a $600,000 budget, suffice to say it made a great deal of money.

672. Bell, Dale. *Woodstock: An Inside Look at the Movie That Shook Up the World and Defined a Generation*, Moving Mantra, 2012.

673. https://www.cbsnews.com/news/cbs-news-poll-u-s-involvement-in-vietnam/

674. theminiaturespage.com/boards/msg.mv?id=366305.

675. Steve Dwan to author 2020.

676. Paul Stevens to author 2020.

677. These prints were very rare at the time, they cost three or four times more than the regular 35mm prints and could only play in a handful of cinemas in any territory. This would change in the 1980s with runs of 100 70mm prints not uncommon. The cost was not only the extra size of film, but also the addition of magnetic stripes for the soundtracks and then recording in real time. Apparently, the mass print run of this format badly dented the profit margin of the successful initial release of *Alien* (1979) see, Pirie. The increased use of the format was due to the outstanding sound quality, nullified almost overnight with the introduction of digital stereo formats in the early 1990s.

678. superman.fandom.com/wiki/Superman: The_Movie

679. Upon its release in December 2019, it suffered a mauling from critics who were particularly scathing of some of the CGI fur. The director hastily had the offending fur redone as well as some sound tweaks, before updating the DCP versions via satellite downloads to cinemas. The improvements failed to save the film from becoming a major flop.

680. Jaste.

681. *Daily Variety,* 04 November 1969.

682. *Motion Picture Exhibitor,* 10 February 1971 *Film Facts* 1971.

683. Malcom, Derek, *Cromwell knocked about a bit, The Guardian,* 16 July 1970.

684. Guerin. This exact figure lies between the stated European and US running-times, which suggests her "source" was not fully cognisant of the facts.

685. Vladimir Dostal, President of Mosfilm Studios to author, 28 May 1993.

686. Mosfilm to author, 2019.

687. Ватерлоо. Серия, https://youtu.be/jjJEQC8T9tQ.

688. *First Light* (2010) BBC TV.

689. James Blames writing in 2020 on the Facebook group — *The Stanley Kubrick Appreciation Society.*

690. *L'Express,* 23 September 1968.

691. Gelmis, Joseph, *The Film Director as Superstar,* Doubleday 1968.

692. Chandler, David G., *The Campaigns of Napoleon: The Mind and Method of History's Greatest Soldier,* Weidenfeld and Nicolson, 1967. The present author met Chandler in 1980 who described his historical advising work on the BBC adaptation of *War and Peace,* and various conversations with Kubrick who still at the time harboured a desire to make his epic film. Apparently, he continued to pick the historian's brains over numerous aspects of Napoleonic minutiae.

693. Hastings, Chris, *Kubrick's Napoleonic odyssey goes online, The Daily Telegraph,* 05 May 2002.

694. https://www.vice.com/en_uk/article/nndadq/stanley-kubricks-napoleon-a-lot-of-work-very-little-actual-movie

695. https://www.bbc.com/culture/story/20190808-was-napoleon-the-greatest-film-never-made.

696. Gelmis.

697. *Ibid.*

698. The actor would later portray him three times: *Napoleon and Love* (TV Series in 1974), *Time Bandits* (1981) and *The Emperor's New Clothes* (2001).

699. Hastings.

700. nymag.com/arts/books/features/62378/

701. *Ibid.*

702. Gelmis.

703. *Daily Variety,* 19 March 1969.

704. Rob McGibbon to author, 2020.

705. *Daily Variety,* 19 March 1969.

706. Sloane, Leonard, *Aubrey Named M-G-M President: Kerkorian Moves in as Bronfman and Forces Lose Out. The New York Times.* 22 October, 1969.

707. Biskind, Peter, *Easy Riders, Raging Bulls: How the Sex-drugs-and Rock 'n' Roll Generation Changed Hollywood*, Simon & Schuster 1998.

708. https://www.robmcgibbon.com/legendary-director-bryan-forbes-2/

709. Forbes, Bryan, interviewed by Roy Fowler for The British Entertainment History Project in 1984. https://historyproject.org.uk/interview/bryan-forbes

710. http://www.bafta.org/learning/a-tribute-to-bryan-forbes,171,BA.html

711. This is mentioned in a few editions of *Variety* in early 1969, then completely disappears. The absence of any details suggests it was merely a ruse to throw the competition.

712. This may have just been a prospective Broadway production. In any case, it never happened.

713. https://www.heyuguys.com/a-clockwork-evening-with-malcolm-mcdowell-christiane-kubrick-and-jan-harlan/

714. *Variety*, 21 April 1971.

715. *Stanley Kubrick: A Life in Picture* (2001), Warner Bros.

716. Kubrick famously pulled *A Clockwork Orange* from UK cinemas due to media concerns over copycat violence, supposedly inspired by the film. Despite enjoying great box office success at the time, the studio was fully aligned with this decision. He continued to purge rogue UK screenings up and till his death.

717. *Variety*, 30 December 1971.

718. https://www.salon.com/2000/10/04/napoleon/

719. *Variety*, 25 March 1975.

720. The author's more famous *Vanity Fair*, set around the battle of Waterloo, was briefly considered by the director.

721. Ulivieri, Filippo, *Waiting for a miracle: a survey of Stanley Kubrick's unrealized projects*, https://cinergie.unibo.it/article/view/7349

722. Norman, Barry, *Radio Times*, June 1996.

723. https://www.bbc.com/culture/story/20190808-was-napoleon-the-greatest-film-never-made.

724. Ciment, Michel, *Kubrick: The Definitive Edition*, Faber & Faber, 2003.

725. ITL 17,004,004,411. With Mosfilm covering approximately half, Dino's expenditure amounted to $12,313,852 (ITL 8,004,004,411), divided as follows: $10,680,961 (ITL 6,942,624,890) for technical and artistic contributions; $1,542,831 (ITL 1,002,840,210) fees to Mosfilm; finally, $105,445 (ITL 68,539,311) for Intourist, to cover hotel costs etc. *Final balance sheet Waterloo*.

726. Kezich/ Levantesi.

727. *Ibid.*

728. http://veronicadelaurentiisonlus.com/

729. After wrapping up *Cromwell* (1970), its director Ken Hughes also announced he planned to film John Reed's book. Inability to raise finance killed the project.

730. It is freely available on Mosfilm's YouTube channel, with English subtitles. https://www.youtube.com/watch?v=xfUlR_nuBb4.

731. Bondarchuk.

732. *They Fought for Their Country / Oni srazhalis za rodinu* (1975). Screen-play by Sergei Bondarchuk and Mikhail Sholokhov.

733. Bondarchuk, Natalya, *Newspaper Trud,* 30 September 2005

734. Christopher Plummer. *imdb.com.*

735. https://edition.cnn.com/2021/02/06/opinions/christopher-plummer-sound-of-music-thomas/index.html?fbclid=IwAR3imxPIpCnZ3Hx34_7hTxRZgn7wMVtwZM2-i3XJwtWPsiyS4-j3X2Fql5k

736. https://www.bbc.com/news/entertainment-arts-55954950

737. Winner of Best Cinematography: David di Donatello Awards 2003, Busto Arsizio Film Festival 2003, Golden Globes, Italy 2003, and nominated: Italian National Syndicate of Film Journalists 2003.

738. Hutchinson.

739. Bombal, Matias, *Rod Steiger Interview, MAB Archives,* October 2000.

740. Guerin.

741. Lind.

742. Chandler, David G., *Napoleon,* Weidenfeld, 1973.

743. Writing in 1667, Edward Hyde, 1st Earl of Clarendon, who was a supporter of King Charles I, described Cromwell as "a brave bad man."

744. Esdaile, Charles. J, *Waterloo — A Critical Review,* University of Liverpool. https://h-france.net/fffh/the-buzz/waterloo-1970/

745. *Ibid.*

746. *Waterloo-1970–Fan Cut In Full HD,* https://www.youtube.com/watch?v=ZSaGPIpb830

747. Clausewitz, Carl von, *On War,* 1832.

748. Jung, Carl, *Modern Man in Search of a Soul,* New York: Harvest, 1933.

749. George Santayana, *The Life of Reason,* 1905.

750. MacDonald Fraser, George, *The Hollywood History of the World,* Michael Joseph Ltd, 1988.

751. Lind.

752. This is the spelling in the script, rather than the correct "Magdalene."

753. *The Croker Papers* (1885) vol. 3, Ch. 28.

About The Author

Born in 1966, SIMON LEWIS is a TV editor, video journalist, writer and filmmaker. In 2012 he achieved a life-time ambition to make his own feature film, *Jackals*. He admits to being a self-confessed movie nerd, with a deep love of most genres of twentieth-century cinema. As an avid reader of history since childhood, these twin interests have fuelled his love of the epic genre, and in particular the "biggies" of the 1950s and 60s. This is his first book. He is married and lives with his family in Abergavenny, Wales.

Index

11th Separate Cavalry Regiment, 107, **119**, 242, **250**, 318, 348, 353, 483, 484, 516, 517
16mm, 300, 390, 469, 585
1900 (1976), 471
2001: A Space Odyssey (1968), 41, 124, 480, 491, 492, 493, 495, 496, 499
21 Century Theater, 466
35mm, 37, 38, 113, 183, 263, 429, 449, 469, 480, 481, 608
3-D, 36, 37, 74, 638
55 Days at Peking (1963), 39, 448
633 Squadron, 137
65mm, 590, 596
70mm, 38, 85, 105, 110, 112, 113, **118**, 184, 301, 447, 453, 461, 480, 481, 482, 491, 493, 590, 591, 600, 606, 608
A Bridge Too Far (1977), 471, 528, 530
A Clockwork Orange (1971), 198, **490**, 498, 499, 500, 610
A Fistful of Dollars (1964), 326
A Gunfight (1971), 602
A Man for All Seasons, 129
A Man for All Seasons (1965), 39
A Town Like Alice (1956), 185
Abussi, Mario, 10, 272
Academy Awards, 116, 149, 161, 446, 509
Across the Bridge (1957), 147
Actors Studio, 146, 158, 292
Adamson, Joy and George, 185
Adventures of Gerard, The (1970), 130, 399
African Queen, The (1951), 83
Agfacolor, 125
Agony And The Ecstasy, The (1965), 85
Airfix, 14, 462
Al Capone (1959), 147
Alabino, 243
Alamo, The (1960), 39, 414, 480

Albonico, Isabella, 9, 194, 195
Alexander, Terence, 9, 155, 165, **173**, 370, 391, 394, 395, 398, 552
Alien (1979), 608
All the Money in the World (2017), 510
Altman, Robert, 332
Altobelli, Rudy, 329
Amann (1899), 121
Ambrosi, Guglielmo "Memo", 10, 272, 413
American Humane Society, 347, 354
Amici, Vanio, 433
Amityville Horror, The (1979), 512
An Age of Kings (TV series), 332
An Elephant Called Slowly (1969), 187
Anderson, Gerry, 155
Anderson, Lindsay, 156
Andrei Rublev (1966), 111
Andreotti Law, 81, 91, 504
Andress, Ursula, 508
Andrews, Julie, 40, 152
Angels One Five (1952), 154
Angry Silence, The (1960), 495
ANICA (Associazione Nazionale Industrie Cinematografiche & Affini), 73, 74, 89
Anouilh, Jean, 87, 131, 132, 133, 151, 526
Anthony, Peggy, 129
Antigone (play), 131
Anzio (1968), 85, 93, 130
Apocalypse Now! (1979), 528
Arliss, George, 126
Armstrong, Neil, 302
Arnhem, 75
Arnold, Elliott, 133, 134
Around the World In Eighty Days (1955), 38
Arriflex, 184, 263
Asphalt Jungle, The (1950), 83
Attenborough, Richard, 495

Aubrey, James, 496
Auschwitz, 236
Austerlitz (1960), 87, 128, 215
Austerlitz, Battle of, 49, 104, 128
Avincola, Alfonso, 10, 301
Badajoz, 50
Baez, Joan, 469
BAFTA (British Academy Film Awards), 430, 463
Balaclava, 347
Balaclava, Battle of, 166, 168
Ball, George, 468
Ballad of a Soldier (1959), 103
Bara, Theda, **32**, 37, 586
Barabbas (1961), 77, 78, 79, 83, 93, 158
Barbarella (1968), 85, 160
Barry Lyndon (1975), 471, 500, 596
Barry, John, 186
Battle of Algiers, The (1965), 88
Battle of Britain (1969), 40, 152, 198, 462, 487
Battle of Neretva (1969), 94, 157, 216, 323
Battle of San Pietro, The (1945), 87
Battle of the Bulge (1965), 40
Battle of Waterloo, The (1913), 121, 122, **142**
Battleship Potemkin (1926), 122
Bau, Gordon, 149
BBC, 13, 14, 114, 129, 156, 157, 181, 191, 313, 332, 462, 463, 472, 607, 639
BBFC (British Board of Film Classification), 113, 453, 471, 472, 590, 591
Beatty, Warren, 507, 508
Beauharnais, Eugène de, 51
Beauharnais, Josephine, 184, 231, 232, 494, 496
Becket, 151
Becket (1964), 131
Beethoven, Ludwig Van, 106, 123, 499
Beginners (2010), 509
Belgium, 23, 50, 52, 53, 54, 163, 165, 232, 266, 406, 420, 546, 552
Belmondo, Jean-Paul, 494
Ben-Hur (1959), 14, 38, 80, 82, 85, 163, 465
Ben-Hur: A Tale of the Christ (1925), 36, 37, 346
Berardini, Giuseppe, 10, **283**
Berger, Helmut, 206
Bergerac (TV series), 156
Bergman, Ingmar, 505
Berlin, 259, 516, 544, 567
Bermans, 164, 168, 169, **176**, 480, 573
Best, George, 369
Bible... In the Beginning, The (1965), 82, 83, 84, 85, **97**, 133, 139

Big Parade, The (1925), 75
Birth of a Nation (1915), 35
Bitter Rice / Riz Amer (1949), 73
Black Narcissus (1946), 76
Blakely, Colin, 156
Bledis, Vaclovas, 9, 555
Blondell, Joan, 346
Bloom, Claire, 149, 230, 231, 512
Blucher, Marshal Gebhard, 51, 52, 53, 54, 55, 60, 64, 125, 198, 405, 406, 409, 537, 545
Blue Max, The (1965), 480
Blue Peter (TV), 462
Blue Velvet (1986), 505
Bluhdorn, Charles, 92, 93, 289, 465, 466, 467
Boccacio 70 (1962), 442
Bogart, Humphrey, 82
Bolognini, Mauro, 487
Bolt, Robert, 129
Bonaparte, Emperor Napoleon, 24, 25, 26, 45, 48, 49, 50, 51, 52, 53, 54, 55, 56, 57, 58, 59, 60, 62, 63, 64, 65, 71, 92, 104, 105, 114, 116, 121, 122, 123, 125, 126, 128, 132, 134, 138, 150, 158, 159, 184, 190, 193, 198, 213, 214, 215, 223, 224, 225, 226, 227, 229, 231, 232, 245, 255, 274, 287, 291, 292, 294, 295, 296, 298, 299, 315, 330, 336, 337, 395, 406, 415, 435, 436, 458, 459, 460, 461, 464, 491, 492, 494, 495, 503, 524, 527, 530, 531, 534, 535, 536, 537, 538, 540, 541, 542, 543, 544, 545, 546
Bonaparte, General Jerome, 57
Bond, James, 40, 81, 216, 301, 397, 448
Bondarchuk, Elena, 414
Bondarchuk, Fedor, 414, 509, 572
Bondarchuk, Natalya, 508, 591
Bondarchuk, Sergei, 10, 17, **22**, 23, 24, 25, 26, 27, 28, 29, 89, 91, 95, **98**, 100, 101, 102, 103, 104, 105, 106, 107, 108, 109, 110, 111, 112, 113, 114, 115, 116, **117**, **118**, 128, 132, 133, 138, 139, **144**, 156, 157, 158, 160, 167, 168, 169, **174**, **175**, 184, 187, 189, 190, 193, 196, 197, 200, 204, **210**, 214, 216, 217, 218, **220**, 224, 225, 227, 228, 229, **233**, 238, 241, 242, 245, 256, 258, 260, 261, 262, 264, 266, 267, 268, 269, 270, 272, 274, **282**, **284**, 288, 290, 296, 299, 300, **304**, 312, 314, 315, 316, 322, 323, 327, 328, 337, 385, 386, 393, 394, 395, 406, 407, 409, 410, 412, 413, 414, 416, 418, **422**, **426**, 431, 437, 439, 441, 450, 451, 457, 458, 459, 464, 465, 483, 484, 485, 486, 495, 500, 503, 507, 508, 509, 516, **518**, 521, 524, 527, 529, 530, 531, 532, 573, 589, 592, 606

Bonicelli, Vittorio, 10, 133
Bonnie And Clyde (1967), 41
Boom (1968), 160, 595
Born Free (1966), 185
Borodino, Battle of, 51, 76, 108, 109, 110, 111, 114, 116, 224, 267, 369
Borromel, Charles, 9, 201, 326, 436, 550
Borsten Vidov, Joan, **174**, 322, 326, 415, 571
Borzelli, Paolo, 10, 185
Boston Strangler, The (1967), 440
Bottin, Armando, 9, 271, 559
Bound (1986), 505
Bounty, The (1984), 505
Boyer, Charles, 125
Bradbury, Ray, 149
Brando, Marlon, 87, 89, 100, 127, 129, 130, 146, 147
Brezhnev, Leonid, 161, 325
Bricusse, Leslie, 498
Bridge at Remagen (1969), 161, 467
Bridge on the River Kwai (1957), 154, 441
Brief Season (1969), 329
Brine, Adrian, 332
Broken Arrow (1950), 134
Bronston, Samuel, 79, 151, 447, 448, 588
Brownlow, Kevin, 14, 124, 167, 495, 573
Bruce, Nigel, 151
Brussels, 23, 332
Brynner, Yul, 77, 323
Bulajić, Veljko, 94, 323
Buñuel, Luis, 158
Burgess, Anthony, 498, 499
Burnt by the Sun (1994), 508
Burton, Richard, 39, 85, 87, 131, 134, 145, 160, 503
Burton, Tim, 512
Butch Cassidy and the Sundance Kid (1969), 430
Butkēvičs, Pauls, 9, 332, 482, 556
Buzina, Nadezhda, 10, 256
Bylandt, General, 58, 538, 540
Cabiria (1914), 34
Caillou, 292, 545
Calley, John, 497, 498
Cambronne, General, 64, 69, 245, 460, 545
Camerini, Mario, 74
Camille 2000 (1969), 158, 329
Cannes Film Festival, 111, 322, 413, 497
Canutt, Yakima, 347
Captain Blood (1935), 346
Captain Corelli's Mandolin (2002), 213
Cardiff, Jack, 76

Cardinale, Claudia, 90, 604
Carlile, Tom, 10, 300, 301
Carter, Rosalyn, 513
Carve Her Name with Pride (1959), 185
Caserta, 10, **212**, 214, 215, **222**, 223, 415, 486, 532
Cat Ballou (1965), 148
Catch 22 (1970), 93, 466, 467, 599
Cats (2019), 481
Ceccarelli, Pietro, 10, 562
Celi, Adolfo, 434
Cellini, Benvenuto, 129
Centro Sperimentale di Cinematografia, 72
Chairman, The (1969), 159, 595
Chandler, David, 492, 524, 609
Chaplin, Charlie, 83
Charge of the Light Brigade, The (1936), 346, 347
Charge of the Light Brigade, The (1968), 40, 87, 166, 167, 168
Charleroi, 535, 536, 551, 552
Charterhouse of Parma, The (TV series), 486
Château de Fontainebleau, 127, 215, 534
Château de Malmaison, 127, 232, 496, 497
Checchi, Andrea, 9, 158, 290, 411, 412, 413, 414, 415, **424**, 555
Chekhov, Anton, 116, 370, 508, 530
Chemodurov, Anatoli, 10, 270, 316, 331, 395
Chen, Iolanda, 105, 270
Chinatown (1974),,, 500
Chop, 235, 237, 303
Churchill, Winston, 126, 537
Cinecittà, 36, 80
CinemaScope, 38, 127, 469
Cinerama, 37, 38, 41, **43**, 124, 447, 466, 491
Citizen Kane (1941), 159, 494
Ciudad Rodrigo, 50
Clausewitz, Carl Von, 406
Clay, Private, 57, 60
Cleopatra (1917), **32**, 37
Cleopatra (1963), 14, 39, 41, 80, 163, 523, 590
Closely Watched Trains / Ostre sledované vlaky (1966), 161
Coghill, Nevill, 86
Colditz (TV series), 515
Collins, Abbi, 352, 353, 572
Columbia Pictures, 39, 93, 261, 289, 353, 390, 433, 466, 480, 484
Conan Doyle, Arthur, 130, 398, 594
Conan The Barbarian (1981), 505
Condemned of Altona, The (1962), 442
Conformist, The (1970), 463
Connery, Sean, 90, 397

Conquest (1937), 125
Coppola, Francis Ford, 467
Corona Law, 91, 504
Corsi, Barbara, 90
Costas, Bob, 147
Costner, Kevin, 481
Country Joe McDonald, 469
Courtneys of Curzon Street, The (1947), 154
Covid-19, 493, 527
Craig, H.A.L. (Harry), 10, 17, 85, 87, 128, 129, 130, 131, 132, 133, 134, 136, 137, 139, 196, 201, 202, 298, 336, 350, 399, 407, 460, 494, 524, 525, 526, 547, 585, 592
Craig, Siobhan S., 129, 130, 131, 196, 571
Cranes are Flying, The (1957), 103
Crawford, Michael, 157
Crist, Judith, 112
Cristaldi, Franco, 89, 90
Cristiani, Nino, 10, **221, 281, 283**
Cromwell (1970), 39, 94, 168, 466, 467, 485, 610
Cromwell, Oliver, 524, 611
Crowd, The (1928), 75
Cruel Sea, The (1953), 154
Cruise, Tom, 512
Curtiz, Michael, 346, 347
Czechoslovakia, 28, 90, 160, 161, 162, 235, 236, 242, 300, 366, 368
D'Amico, Elvira, 10, **283**, 313, 432
D'Andria, Emilio, 10, 215
d'Erlon, General, 54, 58, 60, 267, 540
Damned, The (1969), 183
Dances with Wolves : The Special Edition (1991), 481
Danger : Diabolik (1968), 85
Danger Man (TV series), 155
Dante, Joe, 429
Darling Lili (1970), 41, 93, 466, 467
Davies, Peter, 9, 157, **173**, 182, 187, 188, 189, 194, 196, 197, 202, 203, 206, 207, **208**, 218, 230, 237, 238, 239, 256, 259, 272, 273, 311, 312, 313, 319, 336, **343**, 348, 361, 362, 364, 365, 366, 370, 371, 391, 397, 398, 446, 458, 513, 514, 551, 571
Davies, Rupert, 9, 155, 156, 172, 309, **338**, 361, 370, 371, 392
Davis, Carl, 124
Davle, 161
de Gaulle, Charles, 123
de Havilland, Olivia, 185
De Lancey, Sir William, 156, 200, 201, 392, 393, 542

De Laurentiis, Alfredo, 10, 241, 242, 291, 365, 369
De Laurentiis, Dino, 10, 17, 23, 28, **70**, 71, 72, 73, 74, 75, 76, 77, 78, 79, 80, 81, 82, 83, 84, 85, 87, 88, 89, 90, 91, 93, 94, 95, 99, 105, 116, 126, 128, 130, 133, 138, **144**, 156, 158, 160, 162, 163, 168, 169, 181, 182, 189, 190, 192, 214, 238, 240, 241, 245, 263, 288, 289, 290, 291, 300, 325, 329, 412, 413, 430, 433, 435, 441, 443, 451, 457, 458, 460, 463, 482, 487, 495, 498, 503, 504, 505, 506, 507, **518**, 521, 526, 528, 529, 610
De Laurentiis, Giada, 506
De Laurentiis, Luigi, 81, 88, 89, 240, 300
De Laurentiis, Raffaella, 72, 78, 89, 95, 240, 241, 246, 505, **518**, 521, 529, 571
De Laurentiis, Veronica, 9, 71, 72, 80, 81, 82, 83, 169, **178**, 188, 189, 197, 199, 200, **208, 210**, 238, 241, 288, 291, 393, 457, 503, 504, 506, 507, 517, 525, 551
De Matteis, Maria, 10, 184, 463, 528
De Mille, Cecil B., 36
De Nobili, Lila, 167
De Rossi, Alberto, 10, 196, 197, **285**
De Sica, Vittorio, 133, 442
Dead Calm (1989), 159
Dearden, Basil, 155
Death Wish (1974), 504
DEG Studios, 504
Del Toppo, Federico, **283**
Deliverance (1972), 605
Desirée (1954), 127
Destiny of a Man (1959), 102, 103, 104, 270
Diamonds Are Forever (1971), 397, 446
Dieudonné, Albert, 122, **141**
Dimension-150, 85, 184
Dinocittà, 24, 81, 83, 85, 87, 90, 136, 138, 156, 168, **171, 178**, 181, **208**, 213, 289, 292, **379**, 413, 430, 440, 504, 532
Dirty Dozen, The (1967), 496
Doctor Dolittle (1967), 159, 462, 465, 498
Doctor Faustus (1967), 85
Doctor Zhivago (1965), 40, 166, 496
Dolby Stereo, 452, 453
Donaldson, Roger, 505
Donat, Robert, 126
Donnelly, Donal, 9, 156, 157, 268, 302, 320, 321, 322, 328, 333, 334, 366, 367, 369, 370, 371, 396, 400, **401**, 411, 412, 479, 480, 525, 539, 554
Dosne, Andrea, **212**

Dostal, Vladimir, 10, 24, 27, 29, 261, 264, **285**, 451, 486
Douglas, Kirk, 74, 602
Dracula (1930), 483
Drum, The (1976), 505
Druzhnikov, Vladimir, 9, 158, **175**, 553
Dubček, Alexander, 160, 162
Duel in the Sun (1946), 75
Dune (1984), 240, 505, **518**
Dwan, Steven, 16, 479, 526
E. Pompei, 163
E. Rancati, 164, **179**, 292, 573
Eady Levy, 81
Eastmancolor, 106, 183
Eastwood, Clint, 86, 92, 159, 326
Easy Rider (1969), 41, 465, 470, 494
Ebert, Roger, 112, 231, 287, 299, 465
EEC (European Economic Community), 91
Egyptian, The (1954), 154
Eisenstein, Sergei, 99, 101, 122
El Alamein - The Line of Fire (2002), 511
El Cid (1961), 38, 79
Elba, 19, 52, 134, 190, 213, 214, 223, 231, 294
Elizabeth II, 129, 457, 458, 480, 481
Elkins, Hillard, 230, 231
Emergency—Ward 10 (TV series), 155
EMI Studios, 497
Emperor's New Clothes, The (2001), 609
Entourage (TV), 506
Eon Productions, 397
Equine influenza, 348
Escape by Night (1960), 102, 601
Esdaile, Charles J., 524, 526
Evans, Robert, 92, 93, 289, 465, 466
Eyes Wide Shut (1999), 498
Eynas, Félix, 10, 555
Fabri, Zoltan, 591
Fall of The Roman Empire, The (1964), 39, 79, 151
Fantasia, Franco, 9, 348
Far and Away (1992), 512
Faust (1926), 125
Fedotova, Natalia Vasilievna, 325
Feldhaus, Heinz, 10, 219, 241, 257, 261, 263, 272, 283, 299, 302, 319, 351, 419, 571
Feldhaus, Miku, 241
Fellini, Federico, 70, 73, 79, 81, 183, 227, 326, 412, 442
Ferrer, Mel, **96**, 443
Fetwin, Tony, 492
Fiddler on the Roof (1971), 446
Fielding, Fenella, 152

Finch, Peter, 90, 185
Fiorentino, Lucio, 506
Fistful of Dynamite (1971), 512
Flash Gordon (1980), 412, 505
Fleischer, Richard, 71, 72, 75, 77, 78, 79, 94, 158, 159, 588
Flight, The / Beg (1970), 420, 484, 516
Flynn, Errol, 185, 346, 347
Foley, 444
Fonda, Henry, 75, 76, 77, **96**
Fonda, Jane, 116
Forbes, Bryan, 495, 496, 497, 498, 501, 572, 592
Forman, Milos, 505
Forquet de Dorne, Philippe, 9, 157, 158, **174**, 216, 239, 291, 292, 293, 294, 297, 298, 302, **305**, 328, 345, 349, 432, 477, 486, 513, 547, 571
Fountainhead, The (1949), 75
Fraulein Doktor (1969), 130
Frazier, Jimmy, 206
Frederick the Great, 406
French Connection, The (1971), 500
Friedland, Battle of, 49
Fry, Christopher, 83
Full Metal Jacket (1986), 531
G. Rocchetti, 163
Gagarin, Yuri, 244
Gance, Abel, 87, 122, 123, 124, 128, 167, 215, 495
Garbo, Greta, 125
Garbuglia, Mario, 10, 160, 161, 163, 215, 269, **278**, 290, 413, 463, 526, 528, **533**
Garden of the Finzi-Continis, The (1970), 133, 463
Garko, Gianni, 9, 158, 549
Garrani, Ivo, 9, 158, 262, 297, 547
Gazzara, Ben, 161, 366
Gebuhr, Otto, 125
Gélin, Daniel, 127
Gerard, General, 60
Gerasimov, Sergei, 101, 109
Géricault, Théodore, 165
Gettysburg (1992), 528
Giada at Home (TV), 506
Gielgud, John, 168
Giovannoni, Ferdinando, 10, 163
Girl I Left Behind Me, The, 441
Gissa Khaneshevich Mezuzhok, 243
Gladiator (2000), 471
Gleb, Ivan, 257
Gneisenau, General, 9, 406, 407
Go-Between, The (1971), 497
God's Little Acre (1957), 429
Godard, Jean-Luc, 127

Godfather, The (1972), 467
Gods and Generals (2002), 528
Goebbels, Josef, 125
Goldfinger (1964), 216
Goldwyn, Sam, 139
Gorbachev, Mikhail, 261, 508
Goskino (Soviet film distributor), 111
Graduate, The (1967), 41
Grand Prix (1966), 440
Grande Armée, La, 50, 51
Gray, Willoughby 'Willo', 9, 10, 195, 196, 227, 255, 256, **284**, 288, 291, 313, 316, 328, 330, 331, 365, 367, 368, 370, **373**, 388, 394, 395, 399, 416, **426**, 436, 460, 556, 597
Great Escape, The (1964), 155
Great Patriotic War, 267
Great Race, The (1965), 40
Great War, The (TV series), 440
Greatest Story Ever Told (1965), 39
Green, Roger, 9, 191, 239, 302, 361, 362, 363, 371, 396, 397, 398, 436, 550, 572
Gremlins (1984), 429
Griffith, D. W., 35, 122, 124
Grouchy, Marshal, 26, **31**, 54, 55, 60, 63, 64, 65, 135, 298, 538, 542
Grune, Karl, 125
Guadalcanal, Battle of, 146
Guerrini, Orso Maria, 9, 567
Guidi, Guidarino, 214
Guillermin, John, 162
Guinness, Alec, 151, 494
Guitry, Sacha, 127, 128, 215
Gulf + Western, 92, 288
Guns of Navarone, The (1961), 40, 434
Haden-Guest, Anthony, 217, 223, 227, 301, 597
Hall, Drum Major "Nobby", **180**, 191
Hall, Magdalene, 9, 200, 393
Hall, Peter, 230
Hall, Sheldon, 472, 573
Hallelujah Trail, The (1964), 40
Hannibal (2001), 505
Harlan, Jan, 492, 494, 499, 501
Harlan, Veit, 125
Harris, Julie, 151
Harrison, Rex, 85, 159
Harrison, Richard, 326
Hartstone, Graham V., 10, 444, 448, 572
Hawaiians, The (1966), 84
Hawkins, Jack, 9, 154, 155, **173**, 181, 195, 237, 239, 264, **277**, 302, 311, 334, 335, 366, 367, 368, 369, 371, 372, 385, 389, 434, 435, 551, 604

Hawks, Howard, 154
Hayward, John, 10, 447, 448, 450, 451, 572
HCUC (House Committee on Un-American Activities), 83
Heaven's Gate (1980), 467
Hector and the Search for Happiness (2014), 510
Heffer, Richard, 9, 85, 156, 164, 166, 181, 188, 192, 193, 194, 197, 202, 206, 207, **211**, 238, 239, 302, **308**, 309, 310, 311, 313, 314, 315, 320, 321, 324, 327, 328, 329, 330, 331, 332, 333, 336, 337, 351, 353, 361, 362, 364, 365, 366, 367, 368, 369, 370, 372, 385, 387, 388, 389, 390, 392, 393, 395, 397, 398, 399, **401**, 405, 406, 407, 410, 411, 413, 414, 416, **426**, 429, 432, 439, 480, 482, 485, 515, 516, **519**, 525, 526, 538, 555, 571
Hello Dolly! (1969), 41, 465
Hemmings, David, 168, 494
Hendrix, Jimi, 469
Henry V, 150
Hepburn, Audrey, 75, 76, **96**, 99, 443, 494
Heston, Charlton, 38, 85
Hitchcock, Alfred, 154, 494
Hitler, Adolf, 114, 125, 126, 236, 259, 395, 435, 591
Hoffman, Dustin, 100, 590
Hollywood, 28, 35, 36, 37, 40, 41, 42, 73, 74, 78, 81, 82, 91, 92, 93, 99, 102, 115, 125, 126, 131, 146, 154, 158, 159, 183, 197, 237, 261, 263, 288, 289, 346, 347, 366, 418, 430, 432, 465, 470, 478, 483, 491, 496, 497, 500, 504, 512, 521, 522, 526, 529, 532, 586
Hollywood (TV series), 14
Holm, Ian, 494
Hot Rod Rumble (1957), 429
Hougoumont, 57, 60, 255, 270, 271, 274, **275**, 479, 538, 539, 542, 543, 598
Howard, Ron, 512
Howard, Trevor, 168, 405
Howarth, David J., 136, 137
Hughes, Ken, 485, 610
Hugo, Victor, 122, 349, 351
Hunt, George P., 66
Hurn, David, 301
Hurricane (1979), 505
Huston, Anjelica, 83
Huston, John, 82, 83, 84, 85, 87, 88, **97**, 102, 129, 134, 136, 138, 495
I-Feel-Like-I'm-Fixin'-To-Die Rag (song), 469
Illustrated Man, The (1969), 149, 230
In the French Style (1962), 157

In The Heat Of The Night (1967), 148
Insider, The (1999), 510
Intolerance (1916), 35
Intourist, 237
Irthlingborough, 121
It Happened Here (1964), 167
It's A Mad, Mad, Mad, Mad World (1964), 40
Ivan's Childhood (1962), 103, 111
Ivanhoe (TV series), 155
J'Accuse (1919), 122, 123
Jackson, Peter, 510
Jean-François de Nantes, 333
Jena, Battle of, 49, 125, 406
Jesus of Nazareth (TV series), 511
Jewison, Norman, 148
Joe 90 (TV series), 155
Joe and the Gladiator (TV series), 332
Johns, Glynis, 152
Johnson, Grady, 10, 300, 301
Jones, Christopher, 159, 329, 330, 601
Josephs, Wilfred, 10, 440, 441
Jung, Carl Gustav, 531
Junge, Traudl, 591
Jürgens, Curt, 323
Kalatozov, Mikhail, 90
Kavalsky, Ivan, 506
Kazan, Elia, 146, 151
Kelly's Heroes (1970), 467, 522
Kemna, Hans, 332
Kemp, Jeremy, 206
Kerkorian, Kirk, 496
Kerr, Joe, Pipe Major, 190, 205
Key Largo (1948), 82
KGB, 239
Khablauk, Aslan, 243, 244, 245, **250**, 269, **373**, 483, 484, 572
Khalzanov, Baras, 516
Khartoum (1966), 40, 301
Kholodnyak, Mykola, 244, **250**, 260, 261, 267, 271, 314, 318, 351, 353, 363, 408, 418, 420, 477, 478, 484, 516, 517, 572
Khrushchev, Nikita, 99
King and I, 38, 77
King and I (1956), 38
King Kong (1976), 162, 505
King of Kings (1927), 36
Kingdom of Heaven (2005), 471
Kings of the Sun (1963), 134
Kinnear, Roy, 152
Kirby, John, **338**
Knack...and how to get it, The (1965), 157

Kochuyushchiy Front (1971), 516
Kolberg (1945), 125
Konchalovskiy, Andrey, 450
Koscina, Sylva, 323
Koster, Henry, 127
Koval, Valentin, 9, 561
Kramer, Stanley, 40
Kravchenko, Galina, 106
Kremlin Letter, The (1970), 87, 138
Kressel, Lee, 112, 113, 590, 591
Kronick, William, 595
Kruger, Hardy, 90, 323
Ktorov, Anatoli, 106
Kubrick, Christiane, 494, 498
Kubrick, Stanley, 18, 41, 198, 269, 272, 470, **490**, 491, 492, 493, 494, 495, 496, 497, 498, 499, 500, 501, 531, 592, 596, 609, 610
Kurosawa, Akira, 94
Kutuzov, Field Marshal, 51, 105, 106
L. Daffini, 163, 164, 227
La Bedoyere, General, 158, 291, 292, 297, 298, 302, 477, 541
La Belle Alliance, 56, 64, 255, 273, **276**, 293, 330, 336, **374**, 409, 539, 540, 545
La Haye Sainte, 56, 62, 63, 255, 273, **276**, 327, 330, 331, 335, **344**, **381**, 399, 411, 538, 539, 540, 541, 542, 543, 544, 545, 546
La Roue (1923), 122
La Strada (1954), **70**, 73, 442
Lancaster, Burt, 366
Land of The Pharaohs (1955), 154
Last 4 Days of Mussolini, The (1975), 512
Last of the Mohicans (1992), 266
Last Picture Show, The (1971), 500
Last Valley, The (1971), 467, 596
Lawrence of Arabia (1962), 14, 38, 39, 129, 145, 154, 467, 480, 523, 606
Lazenby, George, 397
Le Mesurier, Colin, 449
League of Gentlemen, The (1960), 155
Lean, David, 14, 39, 40, 129, 154, 159, 329, 452, 466, 494, 496, 505
Legros, 9, 271
Leighton, Margaret, 155, 367
Leipzig, Battle of, 45, 51, 398
Lennox, Jane, 199
Lennox, Lady Georgiana 'Georgy', 181, 188, 199, 536, 596
Lennox, Lady Louisa, 189
Lennox, Lady Sarah, 187, 188, 199, 536, 596
Leone, Sergio, 326, 512

Leopard, The (1963), 442
Les Miserables, 349, 351
Lester, Richard, 157
Levchenko, Vladimir, 9, **425**, 555
Ligny, Battle of, 54, 60, 132, 288, 406, 407, 436, 477, 478, 537, 538, 545
Likhacheva, Tatiana, 113
Likhachov, Vladimir, 10, 108, 110, 264, 265, 266, 301, 391
Lili Marlene, 333
Lincoln, Abraham, 121
Lind, John, 103, 106, 451, 573
Lion of the Desert (1980), 130, 512
Lipanski, Karl, 9, 407, 553
Lock Up Your Daughters (1969), 152
Lollobrigida, Gina, 207
Lom, Herbert, **96**, 126
London, 45, 113, 129, 156, 157, 164, 167, 168, 181, 184, 186, 188, 201, 263, 302, 310, 388, 416, 417, 433, 444, 446, 453, 457, 458, 465, 480, 491, 501, 515, 606
Longest Day, The (1962), 40, 168, 468, 523
Lord of the Rings, The: The Return of the King (2003), 586
Losey, Joseph, 497
Louis XVIII, King, 52, 159, 215, 294, 535
Love Story (1970), 466, 467
Loved One, The (1965), 147
L-Shaped Room, The (1962), 495
Luchinsky, General Alexander, 10, 259, 300, 316
Ludwig (1973), 471
Lumet, Sidney, 147, 151
Macbeth (1948), 158
Macdonald Fraser, George, 532
Macdonnell, Colonel, 57, 60, 271
Magee, Patrick, 499
Maigret (TV series), 155, 156, 361, 371
Maitland, General, 64, 188, 330, 544
Maltese Falcon, The (1941), 82
Manchon, Béatrice, 329
Mancini, Silvano, 10, **283**
Mandingo (1975), 80, 505
Mangano, Silvana, 73, 74, 77, 200, 290, 291, 506
Mann, Anthony, 151, 429
Mann, Michael, 510
Mansell, John, 443
Manson, Charles, 328
Marathon Man (1976), 100
Marbot, Colonel, 398
Marketa Lazarova (1967), 161
Markham, Felix, 492, 498

Marlborough, Duke of, 537
Marmont, Marshal, 534
Mars Attacks! (1996), 512
Marsh, Edward O., 134
Marshall, General George C., 87
Marvin, Lee, 148, 159
Marx, Karl, 138
Marx, Samuel, 133
MASH (1970), 467
Mason, James, 151
Master and Commander: The Far Side of the World (2003), 266, 471
Matteotti, Matteo, 91
Mayuzumi, Toshiro, 85
McCallum, Gordon "Mac", 10, 446, 447, 448, 449, 450, 452, 485
McCarthy, Senator Joseph, 102
McKellen, Sir Ian, 157, 510
McKenna, Virginia, 9, 185, 186, **210**, 550
Meltzer, Newton E., 300, 390
Men in War (1957), 429
Menzel, Jirí, 160
Mercer, Cavalié, 47, 55, 61, 156, 310, 336, 337, 398, 515, **519**, 538, 572, 587, 600, 601
Message, The (1977), 130
Messalina vs. the Son of Hercules (1963), 201, 326
Method, The, 25, 100, 127, 145, 158, 224, 230, 292, 461
Metropolis (1927), 125
Metzger, Radley, 158
Mexico in Flames (1982), 508
Meyer, Richard C., 10, 429, 430, 431, 432, 434, 435, 436, 437, 438, 445, 446, 451, 452, 478, 482, 484, 485
MGM, 36, 38, 125, 470, 491, 492, 496, 499
Mikhajlova, Yelena, 10, 430
Mikhalkov, Nikita, 508
Milanov, Ivan, 9, 568
Millot, Charles, 9, 157, **175**, 446, 553
Misfits, The (1962), 83
Mitchell BNC studio camera, 194, 263, 595
Mitchell, Peter, 10, 301, 410, 411
Mitchum, Robert, 159
Molchanov, Boris, 9, 555
Mollo, Andrew, 167
Mollo, John, 166, 167
Molly Maguires, The (1970), 93, 466
Mondy, Pierre, 128
Monroe, Marilyn, 83
Montand, Yves, 127
Monty Python (TV series), 394

Moonraker (1979), 448
Morand, Linda, 158, 329
Moreau, Jeanne, 77
Morecambe & Wise Show, The (TV series), 13, 155, 463
Moscow, 51, 89, 105, 106, 108, 110, 116, 224, 238, 261, 301, 310, 348, 353, 363, 370, 385, 386, 405, 478, 485, 509, 529, 544, 572
Moscow International Film Festival, 110
Mosfilm, 10, 24, 28, 42, 90, 91, 99, 100, 104, 105, 113, 115, 138, 162, 238, 243, 300, 370, 478, 482, 485, 486, 610
Motion Picture Association of America, The (MPAA), 40
Muffling, Karl Freiherr von, 198, 199, 536
Muggleston, Kenneth, 10, 215
Mukachevo, 370, 371, 408
Munn, Mike, 353
Murat, Marshal, 214
Murch, Walter, 429
Murganov, Viktor, 10, 552
Mussolini, Benito, 72, 123, 130, 163, 512
Mutiny on the Bounty (1962), 38, 523
Mỹ Lai massacre, 468
Myra Breckinridge (1970), 467
Nannuzzi, Armando, 10, 24, 25, **171**, 182, 183, 184, 203, 262, 264, **282**, **283**, 290, 299, **307**, 317, **341**, 411, 418, **422**, 463, 511, 528
Nannuzzi, Daniele, 10, 182, 193, 194, 213, 214, 228, 229, 238, 258, 261, 262, 263, 268, 272, **281**, **283**, **285**, 289, 290, 312, 317, 331, 349, 351, 354, 386, 387, 408, 412, 417, 419, 509, 511, 512, 571
Napalm, 265, 540, 542
Naples, 72, 214, 223
Napoléon (1955), 127, 215
Napoleon (Kubrick), 18, 470, 491, 497, 498, 499, 500, 501
Napoleon and Josephine, 495, 497
Napoleon and Love (TV Series), 609
Napoleon Symphony, 499
Napoléon vu par Abel Gance (1927), 37, 122, 128, **141**, 167, 495
Nathan, Simon, 301
Naumov, Vladimir, 484
Neagle, Anna, 154
Nelson, Lord Horatio, 48, 126, 214
Nero, Franco, 323, 508
Newley, Anthony, 498
Newman, Nanette, 496

Ney, Marshal Michel, 26, 50, 51, 52, 54, 55, 60, 61, 62, 63, 64, 65, 158, 288, 294, 295, 296, 315, 317, 349, 534, 535, 537, 541, 543, 544, 546
Nicholas and Alexandra (1971), 471
Nicholson, Jack, 494, 499
Night of The Generals, The (1966), 446
Nights of Cabiria (1957), 73, 442
Nino Lembo, 163
Niven, David, 151, 346
Nizhny Solotvyn, 23, 163, 246, 306
Noah's Ark (1927), 346
Norman, Barry, 501
Northwest Passage (1940), 75
Novak, Ralph, 81
O'Faolain, Nuala, 129, 130
O'Brien, Robert H, 496, 497
O'Connell, Daniel, 593
O'Herlihy, Dan, 9, 26, **31**, 158, **175**, 213, 216, 217, 221, 287, 288, 294, 295, 296, 302, **306**, 317, 318, **375**, **380**, 410, 411, 446, 547
O'Herlihy, Elsie, 241, **306**
O'Toole, Peter, 85, 87, 129, 131, 145, 154, 197, 494, 503
Odd Man Out (1947), 158
Odyssey (Homer), 74, 133
Oedipus the King (1968), 219
Ogilvy, Diane, 237, **281**, **338**, 365, 370
Ogilvy, Emma, 237, 238, 320, **360**, 367
Ogilvy, Ian, 9, 156, 200, 203, **208**, **210**, **211**, 237, 238, 241, 246, 320, **338**, 349, 362, 367, 368, 390, 392, 393, 398, **428**, 525, 551
Oklahoma! (1955), 38, 147
Olivier, Laurence, 100, 126, 405, 494
On a Clear Day You Can See Forever (1970), 93, 466
On the Waterfront (1954), 146
Once Upon a Time... In Hollywood (2019), 330
Operation Bagration, 259
Operation Danube, 161, 242
Ordinary Man, The (1956), 413
Oriolo Romano, **144**, 213, **221**, 415, **424**
Orlando, Orazio, 9, 288, 314
Orlov Trotter, 243, 244, 260, 353
Oslikovsky, General Nikolay, 10, 259, 260, **284**, 300, 316, 353
Otello (1955), 102, **117**, 413
Ovchinnikov, Vyacheslav, 111, 441
Oxley, Captain Nigel, 190, 191, 192, 197, 204, 205, 206, 572
Oxley, Easter, 190, 191, 197, 205, **209**, 572
Oxley, Nigel, **209**

Paint Your Wagon (1969), 41, 92, 93, 160, 465, 466, 493, 595
Palace de Tuileries, 215, 415
Panavision, 10, 164, 167, 183, 257, 261, 263, 317, 461, 471, 526, 599
Pandemia (2012), 506
Papelotte, 57, 63, 544
Paramount Pictures, 85, 92, 131, 145, 207, 261, 288, 289, 300, 390, 433, 465, 466, 467
Paris, 48, 49, 51, 65, 123, 157, 184, 214, 215, 232, 294, 406, 458, 459, 491, 496, 534, 542
Parkhomenko, Aleksandr, 10, **455**, 566
Parrish, Robert, 157
Patton (1970), 463, 466, 467, 512, 522
Paul VI, Pope, 205
Pawnbroker, The (1964), 147, 150, 223, 232
Pearl Harbor, 41, 42, 94, 467
Peck, Gregory, 159, 434
Peckinpah, Sam, 439
Pellegrin, Raymond, 127
Peplum, 74, 86, 201, 271
Perestroika, 508
Pericoli, Ugo, 10, 165, 166, **176**, 256, 463, 487, 528
Perspecta, 606
Pétain, Marshal, 131
Peter Davies, 202
Petersen, Wolfgang, 471
Petritsky, Anatoli, 107
Phillips, Siân, 145
Piccadilly Incident (1946), 154
Pickard, Stephen, 10, 445, 446, 449, 572
Picton, General, 58, 154, 389, 540, 541, 604
Pimple's Battle of Waterloo (1913), 122
Pinewood Studios, 39, 444, 445, 446, 447, 450, 452, 485, 529, 572, 606
Pink Panther, 127
Pink Panther Strikes Again, The (1976), 605
Plaksin, Vasili, 9, 567
Plancenoit, 62, 63, 64, 292, 541, 545, 557
Plummer, Christopher, 9, **12**, 150, 151, 153, 159, 171, **173**, 181, 192, 193, 195, 196, 199, 203, 204, **210**, 219, 225, 226, 238, **277**, 287, 299, 300, 301, **304**, 310, 319, 320, 336, 337, **338**, 365, 366, 385, 391, 393, 394, 395, 397, 400, 409, 410, 419, 445, 446, 460, 461, 464, 509, 510, 511, 524, 525, 550, 597, 600
Plummer, Elaine, 152, 241, **338**, 368, **401**, 511
Pocock, Robert, 471, 515, 572
Poitier, Sidney, 148
Polanski, Roman, 158, 328, 329

Poldark (2015), 352
Polyakov, Lev, **280**, 562
Polyvision, 124, **141**
Ponsonby, General William, 58, 60, 154, 386, 388, 540
Pontecorvo, Gillo, 88, 89
Ponti, Carlo, 73
Pontius Pilate (1961), 201
Popova, Anna, 10, 27, 262
Poulter, Ron, 168, **178**, **476**, 480, 481, 482, 573
Prague, 161
Prague Spring, The, 17, 28, 160, 161, 460
Pravo, Patty, 245
Price, Vincent, 156
Production Code, The, 41
Pudovkin, Vsevolod, 99, 101
Quatermass II (TV series), 155
Quatre Bras, Battle of, 54, 55, 132, 288, 336, 396, 536, 537, 546
Quayle, Anthony, 151
Quinn, Anthony, 77, 130
Quo Vadis (1951), 36, 75, 80
Quo Vadis? (1913), 34
Ragtime (1981), 505
Railway Children, The (1970), 497
Rampling, Charlotte, 494
Rathbone, Basil, 151
Ratner, Brett, 506
Reade, Jr, Walter, 112
Red Dragon (2002), 506
Red Heat (1988), 327
Red Shoes (1950), 76
Red Tent, The (1971), 90, 138, 162
Redell, Harry, 301
Redford, Robert, 327
Redgrave, Vanessa, 168
Reds (1982), 508
Reed, Carol, 85, 158
Reed, John, 507, 508, 610
Reed, Oliver, 156
Reeves, Michael, 156
Reflections in a Golden Eye (1967), 87
Reform School Girl (1957), 429
Resnais, Alain, 127
Return of the Pink Panther, The (1975), 510
Return of the Saint (TV Series), 156
Rhys, Paul, 332
Richardson, Tony, 166
Richmond, Duchess of, 54, 181, 184, 185, 189, 536
Rietty, Robert, 154, 433, 434, 435, 446, 478

Ring of Bright Water (1969), 187
roadshow, 639
Roadshow, 14, 17, **32**, 37, 38, 39, 40, 41, 42, **43**, 91, 111, 112, 132, 151, 184, 453, 461, 466, 469, 479, 480, 484, 485, 491, 522, 606
Robbie, Margot, 330
Robinson Crusoe (1954), 158
Roccastrado, 77
Romanov, Aleksi, 111
Rome, 10, 17, 34, 36, 39, 72, 74, 77, 80, 90, 116, 130, 151, 156, 158, 163, 164, 165, 168, 169, 181, 190, 191, 204, 205, 206, 207, 213, 291, 292, 310, 329, 385, 396, 397, 429, 430, 433, 441, 442, 444, 452, 484, 487, 504, 572
Romeo and Juliet (1968), 442, 506
Ronald, Paul, 10, **283**, 301
Rorke's Drift, Battle of, 333
Rossellini, Roberto, 102, 601
Rota, Nino, 10, 441, 442, 443, 444, 446, 451, 458
Roth, Tim, 332
Rothwell, Talbot, 133
Rotunno, Giuseppe, 183
Royal Hunt of the Sun, 159
Royal Hunt of the Sun (1969), 153
Rule, Janice, 366
Run of The Arrow (1957), 147
Ruski Komarovtsi, 242
Russell, Ken, 156
Ryan's Daughter (1970), 159, 329, 446, 452, 466, 496, 595, 596
Rybakov, Georgi, 9, 563
Saida Jaste, 484
Saint Helena, 65, 215
Saint, Eve Marie, 100, 146
Salt Lake City, 466
Saltzman, Harry, 40
Samoilov, Evgeni, 9, **69**, 158, 227, 245, 566
Samson And Delilah (1949), 36
Satyricon (1969), 442
Savchenko, Igor, 101
Saveleva, Lyudmila, 106, 112, 116, **118**, 420, 484
Savident, John, 9, 198, 199, **211**, 297, 551
Scala, Domenico, **355**
Schell, Maria, 127
Schickel, Richard, 149
Schoonmaker, Thelma, 608
Schulberg, Budd, 146
Scipione l'africano (1937), 163
Scorsese, Martin, 608
Scott, George C., 150
Scott, Ridley, 471, 510

Séance on a Wet Afternoon (1964), 495
Selfish Giant, The (2013), 352
Sellers, Peter, 85, 127, 149, 510
Senior, Julian, 500, 501
Sergeant, The (1968), 149
Serpent's Egg, The (1977), 505
Severini, Attilio, 9, 559
Shaffer, Peter, 153
Sharafutdinov, Rashit, 263
Shatner, William, 151
Shaw, Robert, 153
Shelenkov, Aleksander, 105, 270
Sherlock Holmes, 151
Sholokhov, Mikhail, 509, 610
Sienkiewicz, Henryk, 36
Sign of the Cross (1933), 36
Simmons, Jean, 127
Skobtseva, Irina, 9, 102, 112, **117**, **118**, 225, 324, 413, 415, 416, **424**, 436, 457, 555, 572
Skolimowski, Jerzy, 604
Skulme, Valentins, 9, 566
Slater, William, 10, 157, **172**, 188, 191, 313
Smallest Show on Earth, The (1957), 185
Smith, Frederick E., 137, 301, 462
Smoktunovskiy, Innokentiy, 450
Söderbaum, Kristina, 125
Solaris (1972), 591
Soldati, Mario, 76
Solomon and Sheba (1959), 75
Soult, Marshal, 50, 262, 297, 534, 535
Sound of Music, The (1965), 40, 152, 159
South Pacific (1958), 38
Soyuzmultfilm Studio, 327
Spacey, Kevin, 510
Spartacus (1960), 38, 269
Spiegel, Sam, 446
Spielberg, Steven, 501
Spring in Park Lane (1948), 154
Squaw Man, The (1914), 586
Stage Fright (1950), 154
Stage Struck (1958), 151
Stalag Luft III, 155, 361
Stalin, Joseph, 99, 101, 106, 259, 260, 261, 507
Stanford University, 468, 469
Stanislavsky, Konstantin, 100
Star Trek VI: The Undiscovered Country (1991), 510
Star Wars (1977), 462, 471
Star! (1968), 465
Starchenko, Igor, 242, 265, 318, 349, 417, 419
Stark, Ray, 74
Steadicam, 107, 409

Steiger, Anna, 149, 230, 232
Steiger, Rod, 9, **12**, 18, 25, 26, 28, 29, **31**, 100, 112, 130, 133, 145, 146, 147, 148, 149, 150, 159, 163, **170**, **174**, 181, 213, **221**, **222**, 223, 224, 225, 226, 227, 228, 229, 230, 231, 232, **233**, 237, 238, 240, 257, 267, 270, 274, **280**, **285**, **286**, 287, 289, 291, 292, 293, 294, 295, 296, 297, 298, 299, 300, 301, 303, **304**, **305**, **306**, 314, 335, 337, 368, 411, 415, 431, 436, 446, 451, 457, 458, 459, 461, 464, 485, **502**, 512, 513, 517, 524, 525, 531, 547, 571
Steppe, The (1977), 116, 508
Stevens, Jr., George, 82
Stone, Norman, 112
Strasberg, Lee, 146
Streisand, Barbra, 498
Stroheim, Erich Von, 127
Strzhelchik, Vladislav, 114
Super-8, 66
Superman: The Movie (1978), 446, 471, 481
Surin, Vladimir, 90, 91, 162, 300
Swimmer, The (1968), 366
Tai-Pan (1986), 505
Talbott, Strobe, 301
Tales of Beatrix Potter, The (1971), 497
Talleyrand, Count, 127
Tamba, Tetsurō, 434
Taming of the Shrew, The (1967), 156, 442
Tarantino, Quentin, 330
Taras Shevchenko (1951), 101, 260, 484
Tarkovsky, Andrei, 103, 111, 591
Tate, Sharon, 158, 329, 330
Taylor, Elizabeth, 39, 85, 86, 87, 155, 160, 367
Technicolor, 10, 30, 36, 76, 429, 453, 481, 606
Technirama, 77
Ten Commandments, The (1923), 36
Ten Commandments, The (1956), 36
Ten Days That Shook the World, 507
Ten Days That Shook the World (1983), 508
Testori, Sergio, 9, 399, 561
That Hamilton Woman (1941), 126
The Adventures of Gerard (1970), 592, 604
The Eagle in the Cage (1972), 592
The Iron Duke (1935), 126
The Last Station (2009), 509
The Nile, Battle of, 214
The Patriot (2000), 266
The Who, 469
They Fought for Their Country / Oni srazhalis za rodinu (1975), 415, 507, 508, **518**, 529, 599, 610

This Is Cinerama (1952), 37
Three Days of the Condor (1975), 505
Three Into Two Won't Go (1969), 230
Thunderball (1965), 434
THX-1138 (1971), 467
Tikhonov, Vyacheslav, 107, 507, **518**
Time Bandits (1981), 609
Titanic (1997), 586
Tito, Josip Broz, 94, 323, 325, 493
Todd-AO, 105, 447, 590
Tolentino, Battle of, 215
Tolstoy, Leo, 74, 75, 76, 77, 104, 105, 106, 108, 112, 114, 115, 224, 266, 267, 299, 509, 529, 530
Tompa, Tibor, 257, 264, 265, 572
Tonti, Aldo, 77, 183
Tora! Tora! Tora! (1970), 41, 94, 466, 468
Torriero, Umberto, **279**
Trafalgar, Battle of, 126, 127
Traumnovelle, 498
Travers, Bill, 185
Treasure of the Sierra Madre (1948), 83
Triumph of the Will (1936), 470
Troy (2004), 471
True Grit (1970), 466
Truffaut, François, 127, 326
Tulard, Jean, 495
Tushingham, Rita, 157
Twentieth Century-Fox, 40, 82, 84, 150, 158, 159
Twenty Hours / Husz ora (1965), 591
Udalov, Vladimir, 9, 409, **423**, 450, 569
Ukraine, 23, 28, 155, 160, 163, 231, **234**, 235, 236, 244, 293, 310, 314, **379**, 420, 513, 515, 516, 517, 528, 637
Ulysses (1954), 74
Uncle Vanya (1970), 450
Under Capricorn (1949), 154
Undersea Girl (1957), 429
UNESCO, 215
United Artists, 497, 499
Unrepeatable Spring (1957), 413
Ustinov, Peter, 75
Uxbridge, Henry Paget, Lord, 55, 58, 61, 155, 165, 394
Uzhgorod, 10, 24, 160, 161, 162, 231, 235, 236, 237, 241, 242, 245, **248**, 272, 273, 291, 300, 302, 303, 309, **360**, 361, 362, 363, 364, 365, 366, 368, 369, 370, 385, 417, 420, 484, 532, 571
Valachi Papers, The (1972), 504
Vanel, Charles, 125

Vanity Fair, 525, 610
Varda, Agnès, 127
Vidor, King, 75, 76, 104, 105
Vidov, Oleg, 9, 157, **174**, 268, 322, 323, 324, 325, 326, 327, 328, 362, 364, 370, 371, **401**, 415, 539, 555
Vienna, 52, 231, 326
Vietnam War, 15, 29, 40, 88, 237, 468, 469, 470, 522
Vikings, The (1958), 77
Vincent & Theo (1999), 332
Visconti, Luchino, 183, 206, 442
Vistavision, 76
Visual Projects Ltd, 300
Vitoria, Battle of, 51, 587
Vltava River, 161
Voice of America, 302
W. C. Fields and Me (1975), 512
Waddingtons, 462, **475**
Wadleigh, Michael, 469, 470
Walewska, Marie, 125
Wallach, Eli, 100, 604
War and Peace (1956), 74, 77, 80, 85, **96**, 99, 126
War and Peace (1968), 17, 24, 89, 95, 103, 104, 111, 113, 115, 116, **118**, **119**, 128, 160, 165, 167, 183, 189, 218, 224, 243, 258, 260, 261, 263, 264, 270, 299, 323, 414, 420, 439, 441, 443, 459, 465, 482, 484, 486, 495, 507, 508, 509, 521, 529, 590
War and Peace (Tolstoy), 75, 609
Warner Brothers, 346, 347, 497, 500
Waterloo (1929), 125
Waterloo (1970), 13, 14, 15, 16, 17, 18, **22**, **68**, 73, 82, 84, 86, 88, 89, 93, 94, **97**, 100, 116, 128, 130, 131, 151, 154, 155, 157, 159, 160, 162, 168, 169, **178**, 183, 204, 216, 219, 230, 236, 247, 261, 266, 267, 272, 296, 323, 325, 329, 345, 347, 352, 353, 361, 414, 415, 430, 432, 434, 440, 441, 443, 447, 448, 450, 453, 460, 463, 464, 465, 466, 467, 468, 469, 470, 477, 478, 481, 482, 484, 485, 486, 487, 491, 492, 493, 494, 495, 496, 497, 498, 499, 501, 503, 505, 506, 507, 509, 510, 512, 513, 514, 515, 516, 521, 523, 526, 527, 528, 529, 530, 532, 571, 606
Waterloo, Battle of, 47, 63, 66, 71, 86, 116, 126, 133, 138, 190, 195, 200, 232, 256, 322, 333, 336, 351, 352, 396, 398, 399, 418, 439, 458, 466, 492, 515, 523, 537, 539, 545, 610
Waterloo, Belgium, 47, 55, 60, 64, 515, **519**
Watkin, David, 167, 511

Watson, Colin. *See* Webster-Watson, Colin
Wavre, 54, 55, 57, 60, 537, 542
Wayne, John, 414, 466
Webster-Watson, Colin, 9, 201, 202, **211**, 550
Weimer Cinema, 125
Weir, Peter, 471
Welch, Raquel, 467
Welles, Orson, 9, 14, 127, 128, 157, 158, 159, **212**, 215, 216, 217, 218, 219, **220**, 323, 415, 547
Wellington, Arthur Wellesley, 1st Duke of, 11, 16, 18, 47, 49, 50, 51, 52, 53, 54, 55, 56, 57, 58, 60, 61, 62, 63, 64, 65, 71, 132, 138, 165, 166, 182, 194, 196, 197, 199, 200, 202, 246, 255, 270, 271, 315, 330, 334, 336, 389, 390, 392, 394, 396, 400, 409, 460, 462, 525, 527, 530, 534, 535, 536, 537, 538, 541, 542, 571, 587
Werba, Hank, 93, 94
Weston, Charles, 121
Westrex, 448
Whisperers, The (1967), 495
Whistle Down the Wind (1961), 495
Wickham, Claire, 241
Wickham, Jeffry, 9, 192, **211**, 321, 367, 368, **373**, **401**, 410, 565
Wiggins, Les, 10, 444, 450
Wild Bunch, The (1969), 439
Wild Orchid (1990), 327
Wilding, Michael, 9, 154, **172**, 310, 321, 334, 366, 367, 368, 385, 386, 387, 388, **402**, 550
Williams, Bransby, 150
Williams, Richard, 167
Wind And The Lion, The (1975), 471
Winner, Michael, 206
Winning (1968), 430
Wise, Robert, 152
Witchfinder General (1968), 156
Witness to Yesterday (1974), 510
Wolper, David L., 162
Women in Love (1969), 156
Wood, Charles, 168
Wood, Susan, 9, 187, 188, **208**, 550
Woodstock (1970), 469, 470, 497, 605
World War One, 51, 121, 123, 125, 235
World War Two, 40, 195, 259, 333, 458, 522, 539
Wuthering Heights (2011), 352
Yanakiyev, Yan, 9, 563
York, Michael, 332
York, Susannah, 152
You Only Live Twice (1967), 434
Young Guard, The (1948), 101
Young Mr. Pitt, The (1942), 126

Young Rebels, The (TV series), 594
Young Winston (1972), 471
Youngblood, Denise J., 103, 104, 108, 111, 115, 261, 573
Yudin, Gennadi, 9, 414, 415, **424**, **425**, 555
Yutkevich, Sergei, 102, 413
Z Cars (TV series), 332
Zabriskie Point (1970), 467
Zakhariadze, Sergei, 9, **404**, 405, 406, 407, 409, 410, **421**, **422**, **423**, 437, 552
Zakhava, Boris, 106

Zanuck, Darryl F., 40, 42, 82
Zanuck, Richard, 40
Zeffirelli, Franco, 156, 207, 442, 506, 511
Zigzag of Success (1969), 414
Zulu (1964), 13, 40, 154, 333, 463, 530
Zulu Dawn (1979), 528

Printed in Dunstable, United Kingdom